SAGE was founded in 1965 by Sara Miller McCune to support the dissemination of usable knowledge by publishing innovative and high-quality research and teaching content. Today, we publish over 900 journals, including those of more than 400 learned societies, more than 800 new books per year, and a growing range of library products including archives, data, case studies, reports, and video. SAGE remains majority-owned by our founder, and after Sara's lifetime will become owned by a charitable trust that secures our continued independence.

Los Angeles | London | New Delhi | Singapore | Washington DC | Melbourne

Issues and Challenges of Development

Issues and Challenges of Development

An Introduction

B. K. Pattanaik

Professor, School of Extension and Development Studies,
Indira Gandhi National Open University (IGNOU),
New Delhi

SAGE | TEXTS

Los Angeles | London | New Delhi
Singapore | Washington DC | Melbourne

First published in 2017 by

SAGE | TEXTS

SAGE Publications India Pvt Ltd
B1/I-1 Mohan Cooperative Industrial Area
Mathura Road, New Delhi 110 044, India
www.sagepub.in

SAGE Publications Inc
2455 Teller Road
Thousand Oaks, California 91320, USA

SAGE Publications Ltd
1 Oliver's Yard, 55 City Road
London EC1Y 1SP, United Kingdom

SAGE Publications Asia-Pacific Pte Ltd
3 Church Street
#10-04 Samsung Hub
Singapore 049483

Published by Vivek Mehra for SAGE Publications India Pvt. Ltd, typeset in 10/12 pts Stone Serif by Zaza Eunice, Hosur, Tamil Nadu, India and printed at Sai Print-o-Pack, New Delhi.

Library of Congress Cataloging-in-Publication Data Available

ISBN: 978-93-860-6218-5 (PB)

SAGE Team: Amit Kumar, Indrani Dutta, Vandana Gupta, Kumar Indra and Ritu Chopra

Dedicated to Lord Sankat Mochan

BRIEF CONTENTS

DETAILED CONTENTS

LIST OF ABBREVIATIONS

ADB	Asian Development Bank
ADP	Area Development Programme
ARWSP	Accelerated Rural Water Supply Programme
AUWSP	Accelerated Urban Water Supply Programme
BMF	Biomass Fuel
BNP	Bharat Nirman Programme
BPL	Below Poverty Line
BPO	Business Process Outsourcing
BRGF	Backward Region Grant Fund
CADP	Command Area Development Programme
CIP	Competitive Industrial Performance
CPI	Consumer Price Index
CPR	Common Property Resources
CRRID	Centre for Research in Rural and Industrial Development
CSR	Corporate Social Responsibility
CVOs	Civil Society Organizations
DADP	Desert Area Development Programme
DPAP	Drought Prone Area Development Programme
DPC	District Planning Committee
DUGYY	Deendayal Upadhyaya Gram Jyoti Yojana
DWCRA	Development of Women and Children in Rural Areas
EAS	Employment Assurance Scheme
EDI	Educational Development Index
FAO	Food and Agriculture Organization
FDI	Foreign Direct Investment
FP	Flagship Programme
FWP	Food for Work Programme
GDP	Gross Domestic Product
GER	Gross Enrolment Ratio
HADP	Hill Areas Development Programme
HCI	Head Count Index
HDI	Human Development Index
HPI	Human Poverty Index
HYV	High Yielding Variety
IAY	Indira Awas Yojana
ICDS	Integrated Child Development Scheme
ICT	Information and Communication Technology

ICT-BPO	Information and Communication Technology-Business Process Outsourcing
IDP	Integrated Development Programme
IDSMT	Integrated Development of Small and Medium Towns
IFAD	International Fund for Agriculture Development
IFOAM	International Federation of Organic Agriculture Movements
IGI	Income Gap Index
IGNDPS	Indira Gandhi National Disabled Pension Scheme
IGNOU	Indira Gandhi National Open University
IGNWPS	Indira Gandhi National Widow Pension Scheme
ILO	International Labour Organization
IMF	International Monetary Fund
IPRs	Intellectual Property Rights
ISIC	International Standard Industrial Classification
ISRO	Indian Space Research Organization
JNNURM	Jawaharlal Nehru National Urban Renewal Mission
JRY	Jawahar Rozgar Yojana
MCH	Maternal and Child Health
MDGs	Millennium Development Goals
MDM	Mid-day Meal
MFALDA	Marginal Farmers' and Agricultural Labourers' Development Agency
MGNREGA	Mahatma Gandhi National Rural Employment Guarantee Act
MSP	Minimum Support Price
NBA	Narmada Bachao Andolan
NCEA	National Classification of Economic Activities
NCERT	National Council of Educational Research and Training
NEA	National Environment Agency
NGOs	Non-Government Organizations
NIHFW	National Institute of Health and Family Welfare
NOAPS	National Old Age Pension Scheme
NPK	Nitrogen Phosphorus-Potassium
NREP	National Rural Employment Programme
NRHM	National Rural Health Mission
NSAP	National Social Assistance Programme
NSDP	National Slum Development Programme
NSSO	National Sample Survey Organization
NUEPA	National University of Educational Planning and Administration
OBCs	Other Backward Classes
OCD	Obsessive Compulsive Disorder
ODL	Open and Distance Learning
OECD	Organization for Economic Co-operation and Development
OSH	Occupational Safety and Health
PAFC	Punjab Agro Foodgrain Corporation
PBF	Programa Bolsa Familia
PBSM	Plano Brasil Sem Miséria
PHCs	Primary Health Centres
PMGSY	Pradhan Mantri Gram Sadak Yojana

PMIUPEP	Prime Minister Integrated Urban Poverty Eradication Programme
PPF	Productive Possibilities Frontier
PPP	Public–Private Partnership
PRIs	Panchayati Raj Institutions
PURA	Provision of Urban Amenities in Rural Areas
PVOs	Private Voluntary Organisations
RAI	Rural Access Index
RCH	Reproductive and Child Health
RGGVY	Rajiv Gandhi Grameen Vidutkaran Yojana
RGNDWM	Rajiv Gandhi National Drinking Water Mission
RTC	Record of Rights, Tenancy and Cultivation
SBM	Swatch Bharat Mission
SC	Scheduled Castes
SCM	Smart Cities Mission
SDGs	Sustainable Development Goals
SEP	Self-Employment Programme
SFDA	Small Farmers' Development Agency
SGPC	Shiromani Gurudwara Prabandhak Committees
SGRY	Sampoorna Grameen Rozgar Yojana
SGSY	Swarnajyanti Gram Swarozgar Yojana
SHGs	Self-Help Groups
SI	Sen Index
SIEZ	Special Industrial Economic Zone
SPSRD	Software Package for Sustainable Rural Development
SSA	Sarva Shiksha Abhiyan
SSPD	Shelter and Sanitation for Pavement Dwellers
ST	Scheduled Tribe
STEP	Support for Training and Employment Programme
TFR	Total Fertility Rate
TKS	Traditional Knowledge System
TRYSEM	Training of Rural Youth for Self-Employment
TSC	Total Sanitation Campaign
TVEs	Township and Village Enterprises
UCC	Union Carbide Corporation
UIP	Universal Immunization Programme
ULBs	Urban Local Bodies
UNEP	United Nations Environment Programme
UNFF	United Nations Forum on Forest
UNWTO	UN World Tourism Organization
UR	Unemployment Rate
VDP	Village Development Plan
VIC	village information centre
WEP	Wage Employment Programme
WFP	World Food Programme
WPI	Wholesale Price Index
WTTC	World Tourism and Travel Council

PREFACE

'Development' is one of the most versatile concepts. While it is one of the most widely used terms, it is also, perhaps, the one that has been least precisely defined, and often mistakenly considered to be synonymous with economic growth. Development has various dimensions and indicators; therefore, its measurement varies from one country to the other as well as from one subject to the other. Some of the well-known indicators of development are literacy rates, maternal and infant mortality rates, access to basic needs such as housing, drinking water, sanitation, communication, energy for cooking and lighting, and so on. When related to these indicators, as well as the rest, the issues and challenges of development, especially in developing countries, are found to be numerous. Economic issues, such as poverty, income inequality, unemployment and inflation, are posing insurmountable challenges to these economies and are deeply affecting the quality of life of the people in these countries. The resource deficiency has affected the effective and adequate provisioning of infrastructure, energy and technology for enhancing the efficiency and productivity of the primary, secondary and tertiary sectors.

Integration of developing countries into the globalization process since 1990s has engendered economic disparities and posed challenges to inclusive and sustainable development. The urge for higher economic growth at the cost of environment has substantially affected the livelihood of indigenous people living in the forest and hilly areas. The marginalization of the socio-economically backward sections of the population, women and disabled because of the attached stereotypes has put a question mark on the inclusive and participatory development model of developing countries. Issues of promoting faster rural and sustainable urban development and bridging the rural–urban development divide are ongoing challenges that developing countries are facing for the last few decades. Sundry factors are responsible for the underdevelopment of developing countries; to name a few are low capital formation, poor infrastructure development, lack of innovation and deficiency of technology. Identification of other socio-economic, political and cultural factors hindering development through the conduction of systematic development studies and researches would be helpful in the formulation of appropriate policy measures and strategies. It would also help in the effective implementation of development programmes and projects.

In this book, an attempt is being made to discuss the important issues and challenges of development, particularly from the perspective of developing countries.

Chapter 1 is an introduction, which defines the concept of 'development' and delineates its broad objectives. As 'development' is a versatile and challenging concept, it is very difficult to define it precisely and delineate its objectives accurately to universal satisfaction. Besides, this chapter also gives a brief description about scope of development. Further, a comprehensive analysis of various factors responsible for the development of developing countries has been penned at the end of the chapter.

Chapter 2 is on Basic Needs and Poverty. Basic livelihood issues and challenges with many of the poverty-stricken people in developing countries are food, clothing, housing, sanitation, safe drinking water, energy for cooking and lighting, roads for commuting to nearest cities to have access to markets and other services, care institutions for education and health and for employment. Besides basic needs, this chapter has also covered one of the outstanding basic economic issues and challenges, i.e. poverty, which developing countries have been facing since their independence from the colonial rule.

Chapter 3 is on Education, Health and Human Development. This chapter broadly covers two important social development issues: health and development, and education and development. It also gives a description of human development. The two other important social development issues and challenges which the developed as well as developing countries are facing in the social sphere, which is ultimately leading to inequality in development, are gender and development and the critical issue of marginalization, social exclusion and development inequality.

Chapter 4 is on Population and Development. Population growth is one of the factors responsible for the underdevelopment of developing countries. This chapter discusses the role of population in development, various components of population issues, population and development theories and challenges of population for sustainable development.

Chapter 5 is on Income Inequality, Unemployment and Inflation. In this chapter, an endeavour is being made to define these three important concepts posing challenges to the sustainable development of at least developing countries. While dealing with inflation, an attempt has been made to explain the relationship between inflation and economic inequality and challenges that these three critical issues are posing to holistic development in at least developing countries.

Chapter 6 is on Agriculture Sector and Development. Agriculture plays an important role in provisioning livelihood to the people in developing countries; therefore, it is pivotal to the development of developing countries. However, decline in the contribution of agriculture to the GDP in India and also in many other developing countries is a cause for concern for the achievement of higher economic growth and development of these nations. In this chapter, a description of various aspects such as the role of agriculture in development, critical issues in agriculture development and challenges of agriculture development have been mainly dealt with.

Chapter 7 is on Industry Sector and Development. Industry has played a critical role in the development of the developed countries of Europe and America as well as many of the developed countries of Asia like Japan, South Korea and Singapore. More recently, the manufacturing sector has played a key role in China's development. Developing countries have to strengthen and improve the performance of the industrial sector in order to achieve a sustainable growth rate. This chapter gives an account of various aspects associated with industry such as the role of industry in growth and development, and various issues and challenges industrial sector is facing in developing countries.

Chapter 8, which is on Service Sector and Development, describes the role of the service sector in economic growth and development. It also discusses types of various service sectors and their role in economic growth and development. The issues and challenges pertaining to the service sector have also been highlighted in this chapter.

Chapter 9 is on Infrastructure, Energy, Technology and Development. This chapter comprehensively deals with various issues and challenges associated with these three important ingredients of development. It also analyses the role of infrastructure, energy and technology in the process of development.

Chapter 10 deals with Rural Development. At the outset, it defines the concept of rural development as given by various exponents and its features. As rural development is central to the development of developing countries, this chapter analyses various issues and challenges faced by the rural sector in the context of developing countries. This chapter also describes the concept of smart village and its various features. The provision of urban facilities in rural areas also constitutes an important component of this chapter.

Chapter 11 is on Urban Development. Urbanization is an increasingly important development issue in both developed and developing countries. However, in developing countries, faulty urbanization has created sundry problems. In this chapter on urban development, various aspects such as features of urbanization, various challenges of urbanization and smart cities have been discussed.

Chapter 12 deals with Globalization and Development Disparities. This chapter broadly describes what globalization is and its impact on economic growth and development, particularly of developing countries. The second vital component of this chapter is development disparities. In this section, various aspects related to disparities, such as types of disparities, groups of population subject to disparities particularly in India and challenges of disparities and how to overcome disparities in developing countries, have been discussed.

Chapter 13 is on Environment and Sustainable Development. Since environment plays an important role in development, the role of environment and how environmental degradation and climate change affect development are discussed in this chapter. Environment and sustainable development are interconnected. Various factors influencing sustainable development and various challenges of sustainable development are also discussed in this chapter.

Chapter 14 deals with Marginalization, Women Empowerment and Inclusive Development. These are important issues and challenges before developing countries. Marginalization has pushed many socially disadvantaged sections of the society to the nadir of development. Therefore, inclusive development is sine qua non for assuring social justice to the poor and excluded groups in almost all the countries, particularly developing countries. This chapter describes the meaning and types of marginalization and why inclusive development is important for holistic development.

Chapter 15 on Good Governance and Ethical Approach to Development gives an account of various attributes of good governance and the role of good governance in development. It tries to enlist the scope of development philanthropy to deal with the development process of developing countries.

In the context of developing countries, certain issues and challenges are common. These common issues have been largely covered in this book. It will not only be helpful to the students of development studies but to the students of other disciplines also, i.e. economics, public administration, sociology, sustainable development, management and so on. It will also be useful for the development practitioners, NGOs, civil society organizations, development activists, researchers, policymakers, administrators, elected representatives of local self-government institutions and opinion leaders engaged in various development projects, programmes and activities.

I take this opportunity to thank all my colleagues and friends. The comments and suggestions received from the reviewers have been of great help. My sincerest gratitude to Dr Jenia Mukherjee, Institute of Development Studies, Kolkata, and Dr Kavita Baliyan, Giri Institute of Development Studies, Lucknow.

I am also thankful to SAGE Publications for accepting my manuscript for publication, particularly Amit, Indrani and Vandana for their valuable suggestions at various stages of the publication process of this book. Last but not the least, I underscore the invisible blessings of my late father (a primary school teacher) which have always been a support in disguise to undertake any assignment and complete it with full dedication. The indiscernible *ashirvaad* (blessings) of Lord Sankat Mochan was an omnipresent powerful force always felt during the writing of this book. I dedicate this book to his *Charankamal* (feet equivalent to the flower of lotus).

ABOUT THE AUTHOR

B. K. Pattanaik is currently a professor at the School of Extension and Development Studies in the Indira Gandhi National Open University (IGNOU), New Delhi. He is the editor of the *Political Economy Journal of India*. He is also on the editorial board of the *Journal of Economics and Development Studies*, American Research Institute for Policy Development, New York; *Asian the Journal of Social Sciences and Humanities*, Oyama, Japan, and the *European Journal of Education Studies*, Bucharest, Romania. Professor Pattanaik holds master's degree in economics, MA in human resource management and PhD in economics. He has more than 25 years of research and teaching experience to his credit in various national-level organizations, e.g. National Council of Educational Research and Training (NCERT), New Delhi; National Institute of Health and Family Welfare (NIHFW), New Delhi; and Centre for Research in Rural and Industrial Development (CRRID), an ICSSR Centre, Chandigarh. He has worked with and completed 26 projects sponsored by various international agencies such as the World Bank, USAID, the Ford Foundation, UNICEF, the European Commission, UNFPA, the Bill & Melinda Gates Foundation as well as projects sponsored by various government departments such as the Department of Panchayati Raj, Rural Development, Health and Family Welfare, Water and Sanitation, Agriculture and Planning Commission of Government of India. He has also completed projects and studies sponsored by various departments of state governments of Punjab, Haryana and Himachal Pradesh in different areas of development such as drinking water and sanitation, border areas, migrant labour, contract farming, studies on scheduled castes and scheduled tribes, health and family welfare, panchayati raj, education, rural development and decentralized planning, women and child welfare and preparation of district development plans.

So far Professor Pattanaik has authored three books, co-authored four books and edited one book. He has more than 130 publications (research papers, articles, editorial column and book reviews) in various national and international journals. He has also been guiding PhD students in different areas of development studies, and six candidates have already been awarded PhD Degrees. He has been instrumental in designing MA programme in development studies and PG diploma programme in urban planning and development. He has visited countries such as USA, China, Spain and Finland and attended international seminars, conferences and study tours. He has conducted an international conference on diaspora and development at IGNOU in which more than 100 participants from 25 different countries participated. Professor Pattanaik has been awarded the Distinguished Leadership Award in 1999 by the American Biographical Institute, USA, and the International Man of the Millennium by the International Biographical Centre, Cambridge, London.

1 Development: An Overview

The ultimate purpose of development is to provide increasing opportunities to all people for a better life to bring about a more equitable distribution of income and wealth for promoting both social justice and efficiency of production, to raise substantially, the level of employment, to achieve a greater degree of income security, to expand and to improve facilities for education, health, nutrition, housing, and social welfare and to safe guard the environment.

—The United Nations Generally Assembly Resolution (1970)

The challenge of development, in the broadest sense, is to improve the quality of life.

—The World Development Report (1991)

The concept 'development' has become an important subject of study and a vital issue for debate and discussion in the developed as well as developing countries after the Second World War. Countries that got independence from the colonial rule after the Second World War were reeling under various maladies of underdevelopment, e.g. poverty, illiteracy, mortality, morbidity, insanitation, poor access to safe drinking water, unsafe housing and lack of electricity and road communication. It was because of their maladies that these nations were largely branded as 'underdeveloped', 'less developed', 'developing' and 'Third World' nations by their counterparts—the developed nations of the West. Since then, everybody—be it parliamentarians, legislatures, economists, political scientists, sociologists, developmental activists or even the common men in the political economy of developing countries—has been frequently using the term 'development'. Politicians are more frequently using the term during their election campaigns in order to win the election and common men are uttering the term with a hope that the development measures to be taken by the government will improve their quality of living.

The sordid condition of development in many developing countries of Asia, Africa and Latin America has attracted the attention of the developed countries to conduct studies and invest resources for the development of the underdeveloped countries. Many developed nations are also investing their resources for the development of developing countries through bilateral and multilateral agencies, e.g. World Bank, UNDP, WHO, UNESCO, JICA, CIDA and so on. Even after a lot of endeavours put in by the developed countries, the multilateral and bilateral organizations and developing countries themselves, the condition of underdevelopment is enduring in many developing countries of the world. This divulges the elasticity and complexity of the term 'development' and the incessant search of appropriate processes and strategies to achieve it. Shanmugaratnam has rightly remarked, 'Put simply, it is the failure of what is generally regarded as "the development processes" to change the conditions of large numbers of people for the better that compels us to ponder the meaning of development' (Shanmugaratnam 2001).

It is not a flight of fancy, but truly, the term 'development' considered to be very simple in common parlance is, however, one of the complex concepts from the perspectives of developing countries to be defined comprehensively and precisely to universal satisfaction. Castigation of one political party by the other during the election campaign for several decades through questions such as 'what development you have done during your tenure' and highlighting people's unhappiness with the performance of the government clearly led us to conclude that 'development' is one of the most bewildering terms and a relatively ceaseless process, at least in developing countries. Unlike economic growth, it is very difficult to concretely measure achievements made in development. Even if a government takes a lot of development policy measures, all of them are not found to be translated into practice because of poor development governance. There are a lot of gaps between the development policies and practice. Because the dimensions, variables and indicators of development are multiple and the level of achievement with regard to different indicators varies across the countries, it is very difficult to define the concept of 'development' to universal satisfaction and measure it with precision. To quote the Brandt Commission (1980), '[D]evelopment never will be and never can be defined to universal satisfaction.' It can be rightly remarked that development, like beauty, lies in the eyes of the beholder and there is too much exclusivity attached to it. Therefore, it can be stated that 'development is what development means'. For an impoverished person, development may mean fulfilment of basic human needs such as food, clothing and shelter; for a rich person, it may mean availability of a better quality of life facilities such as 24-hour electricity, good market complexes, quality education and health care institutions, good quality roads and so on; and for a developing nation, it may mean abolition of poverty, unemployment and inequalities, provision of good quality infrastructure, good governance with zero corruption and so on. World Bank in its write-up 'What is Development?' has rightly envisaged that 'different countries have different priorities in their development policies. But to compare their development levels you would first have to make of your mind about what development really means to you, what it is supposed to achieve.'[1]

Despite the complexity of the definition of development, the multiplicity of its dimensions and its relativities, it is one of the spiciest and the most debated concepts for the politicians, economists, sociologists, development scientists and more recently journalists of both developed and developing countries. It is not a flight of fancy, but delicately, the term 'development' has remained a popular contemporary issue and challenge in national as well as international spheres because of the persistence of underdevelopment conditions in the countries of Asia, Latin America, Africa and the Caribbean. Myrdal (1968) has rightly viewed that 'development' means improvement of the host of undesirable conditions in social systems that have perpetuated a state of underdevelopment.

After reading this chapter, you will be able to:

1. Define development
2. Delineate the aim and objectives of development
3. Explain the role and scope of development
4. Describe various factors influencing development

If we dissect the word 'development', it leads to two terms, i.e. 'develop' and 'ment'. The dictionary meaning of the term 'develop' is 'to grow' or 'to move to a more advanced state'. On the other hand, the meaning of the term 'ment' is 'the process' or 'the action'. Thus, etymologically, development implies to the processes and actions that promote growth (economic) and take a nation to a more advanced state (in social, political, cultural and human terms). According to Myrdal (1968), development is the upward movement of the whole social system by providing better living conditions, namely adequate food, better housing, improved facilities for health, education and training, and the general improvement of cultural facilities, which are all desirable. Todaro (1977) described development as a multidimensional process involving changes in structures, attitudes and institutions, as well as the acceleration of economic growth, the reductions of inequality and the eradication of absolute poverty. According to Preet and Hartrick (2009), development means making a better life for everyone. Development incorporates the diverse and broad aspirations of what might be called a 'good life' in all its economic, social and political dimensions (Cypher and Dietz 2009).

AIM AND OBJECTIVES OF DEVELOPMENT

Development is a versatile concept and its basic aim is to raise the standard of living and the quality of life of the people through various interventions in different dimensions, such as economic, social, political, human, cultural and so on, through the balanced contribution of all the sectors and effective engagement of all the actors in the process. The important objectives of 'development' are to reduce poverty, inequality, unemployment, illiteracy, ill-health and insanitation; to provide each individual and his or her family members with sustainable access to basic needs, such as healthy housing, safe drinking water, sanitation, primary education and primary health care services; and to make safe energy for cooking and surface and telecommunication facilities available to all. Countries that fail to provide all these basic amenities to its people irrespective of the caste, class, ethnicity, religion and gender are basically categorized as underdeveloped.

Development projects and programmes should adopt appropriate participatory processes and strategies so that development becomes 'of the people, by the people and for the people'—in other words, development of all through the participation of all (*sab ka saath, sab ka vikas*). The intention is to achieve holistic, inclusive and sustainable development in a secular, democratic and participatory way.

ROLE AND SCOPE OF DEVELOPMENT

Dimensions of Development

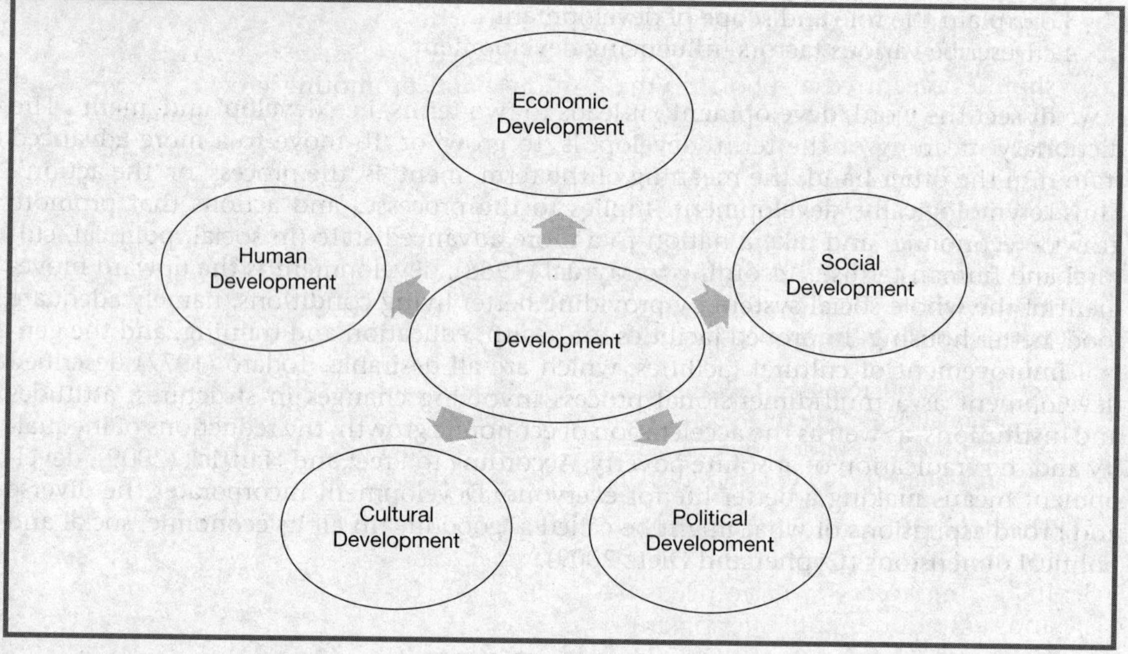

Source: Author.

The role and scope of development are as follows:

1. Increasing the economic growth rate and the per capita income through structural transformation and the modernization of agriculture, industry and service sectors. Higher growth rate can be achieved by making investments in infrastructure, energy and technology. These are critical ingredients for the development of these three sectors and enablers of the enhancement of their contribution to the gross domestic product (GDP). The trickle-down effect of the GDP in developing countries is helpful for the amelioration of the socio-economic conditions of the poor. Higher growth rate is desirable in developing countries if its benefits trickle down to the poor. However, if its benefits are accumulated among the rich, it is detrimental to development with social justice. In other words, benefits of growth should be pro-poor. According to the trickle-down theory (Todaro 1997), economic growth is favourable because economic gains from growth are transmitted to the poor through various means, such as favourable labour market conditions and improved service provisions by the government (e.g. health, schooling, infrastructure etc.). The International Monetary Fund (IMF) advocates policies derived from an economic philosophy of strict adherence to market-oriented programmes coupled with an inherent belief that a 'trickle down' of benefits will occur.[2]

2. Reducing poverty, unemployment and income inequalities in the economy through the implementation of various poverty eradication programmes. Such programmes need to provide sustainable employment and income-generating opportunities to the impoverished. Any rise in the income of the have-nots will curtail the income disparities between the haves and have-nots. Thus, policies should be centred at boosting the economy and promoting growth to improve living conditions of the people, eventually reducing poverty and improving the living conditions of the poor (Parel 2014). Besides, economic social and political disparities have to be synchronized through policy and programme measures. The key aim is to promote the well-being of the impoverished and raise their standard of living. For growth to be beneficial to the poor, it must be associated with the creation of new jobs, thereby providing opportunities to the poor and aiding them in moving out of the agriculture sector (McKay and Sumner 2008). According to Melamed, Hartwig and Grant (2011),

    > [T]he key determinants of the relationship between growth, poverty reduction and inequality are whether economic growth generates new jobs, the quality of these jobs, whether poor people are able to take up new opportunities, and whether jobs are stable enough to last in the face of economic shocks.

    The benefits acquired through higher economic growth need to be spent for raising the employment, income and well-being of the poor.
3. Increasing access to basic needs, i.e. food, clothing, shelter, safe drinking water and sanitation for all, and making the right to basic needs a fundamental right. It is the duty of the state to consider basic needs as public good, and the government has to take responsibility to deliver them as essential items for human survival. Besides the public sector, the benevolent private and corporate sectors, through corporate social responsibilities, have to make provision of these services to the impoverished by adopting villages and urban slums nearer to their vicinity. Jawaharlal Nehru once said,

    > [P]olitical and economic theories and doctrines are important as they are presumably based on knowledge and experience. But if they are to be worthwhile, they have to satisfy basic human needs. It is pathetic that these basic human needs are not satisfied in India and in many other countries.

    Boasting to have achieved high economic growth rate without making provision of adequate access to basic needs for all is socio-economically futile.
4. Removing illiteracy and increasing the level of primary, secondary and tertiary education. One of the developmental duties of developing countries is to make primary education universal and tertiary education available to all at affordable prices. Not only should primary education be made a fundamental right but also ensuring that children belonging to each and every family receive primary education should be a fundamental duty of the citizens as well as of the government. The provision of adequate classrooms, educational aids, e-education facilities, play grounds, toilets, safe drinking water and nutritious mid-day meal; the appointment of trained teachers; curtailment of teacher and student absenteeism; reduction in student dropout rates and so on will go a long way to democratize basic and primary education in developing countries. Vocational and skill education

need to be an essential component of the school education system. It should be area specific, so that the students are educated and self-employed locally. The open and distance education systems must be strengthened in order to democratize secondary and tertiary education. Other cost-effective education systems intended to reach the unreached should be explored for the massification of education at all levels. Education is the king pin of development. Schavan (1998) observed that education will help the people to understand the ills of their society, develop a vision of a better world based on a conception of social justice and religious tolerance, improve human rights, tackle poverty and reduce the spate of corruption in society.

5. Making primary health care accessible to all at the doorstep free of cost and making tertiary/referral health care facilities available at a reasonable distance at affordable prices. The objective is to check infant and maternal mortality rate, curtail the declining sex ratio and also to effectively control communicable and non-communicable diseases and morbidities of all kinds in all societies and across all communities and sexes. The health transition—referring to the transformation of a society with high morbidity and mortality rates into one in which people standardly live long, disease-free lives—has to be the central feature of significant social progress (Dreze and Sen 1995). The World Health Assembly in its historic Alma Atta Declaration, 1978, advocated that the main social target for countries should be that all citizens of the world attain a level of health that will permit them to lead a socially and economically productive life.
6. Reducing hunger and malnutrition and ensuring at least two square meals in a day to each and every family living below the poverty line. To launch various innovative schemes relating to hunger and malnutrition for the prevention of hunger deaths and the control of nutritional anaemia among children and women. A malnourished woman will give birth to feeble children, who in future will become malnourished parents. A sub-committee on Nutrition 2000 of World Food Programme has noted that if the special nutritional needs of women and children are not met, then physical and psychological insults to individuals become a drag on the development potential of entire households for multiple generations. Hunger and hunger-related deaths are a curse on the society. 'Food Security for All' is a desirable strategy for the abolition of food poverty and hunger from developing countries.
7. Providing infrastructure facilities such as roads, renewable and non-renewable energy, telecommunication facilities, irrigation facilities and so on is sine qua non for improvement in the living conditions of the people. The provision of irrigation facilities for raising agricultural productivity, construction of rural markets for the growth of the service sector in rural areas and, further, the establishment of rural industrial corridors and development for the generation of sustainable employment and income in rural areas will go a long way in checking rural to urban migration and synchronizing the rural–urban divide. It will be helpful for the removal of rural poverty and distress from developing countries. Development economists have considered physical infrastructure to be a precondition for industrialization and economic development, where physical infrastructure, in general, consists of two parts: economicinfrastructure such as telecommunications, roads, irrigation and

electricity, and social infrastructure such as water supply, sewage system, hospitals and school facilities (Murphy, Shleifer and Vishny 1989).

8. Enhancing social networking among the different strata of society by the way of increased and improved access to social infrastructure and social capital. The construction of village panchayat houses, youth clubs, *mahila mandals* (women groups), cooperative societies, farmers' clubs and so on will strengthen social networking. The cultural dimension must also be taken into consideration while the formulation of strategies of social networking in culturally sensitive tribal and rural areas. As a measure, the village-level organizations have to be encouraged to promote cultural-specific foods, dance, local theatre, song, art, handicrafts and other home-used items which will enable impoverished families to eke out a sustainable income and livelihood. Mahrey (2004) emphasized,

   > [W]e need strong social institutions, strong families, and strong communities to thrive in a demanding global environment. We have to invest in people as a top priority, so that they feel secure and are able and willing to participate in our society and to face the challenges arising from constant change.

9. Empowering women, disabled and other marginalized sections. Removal of social and economic discrimination on the basis of gender, disability, caste and ethnicity is sine qua non for an inclusive society. The motto is to promote inclusive development and involve all in the process of development. All should be given opportunity and be made capable to contribute as per their ability. A welfare society is judged by how effectively and accountably it deals with the three groups of population at their time of needs: those who are in the dawn of life, its young; those in the twilight of life, the elderly; and those in their shadows of life, the disabled (Pattanaik 2000). The empowerment of marginalized is essential for the achievement of sustainable development goals in developing countries.
10. Controlling population size and unwanted fertility among all irrespective of caste, class and religion and especially among the poor and vulnerable, those who are living below the poverty line, as lager family size reduces the per capita income and would dampen the socio-economic and human development of the family, society and the nation. The objective is to attain optimum population concomitant to economic growth and development. The endurance of poverty, unemployment and inequality in developing countries is largely due to population growth which will also have negative effects on environment and sustainable development. In a speech delivered at Geneva in 1983, JRD Tata while highlighting the urgency of population situation said that of the main causes of poverty, ill-health and misery which blight the life of billions of people on earth, excessive population growth is the dominant one, and that of all the problems and tasks facing humanity, none is more urgent and has greater priority than that of reducing the birth rate as a first step towards saving the present and future generations from disaster (Tata 2004). The ICPD (1994) has encoded that 'population related goals and policies are integral parts of cultural, economic and social development, the principal aim of which is to improve the quality of life of all people.'

11. Promoting happiness and well-being of all. The effective implementation of land reform measures, sharing of resources and distribution of resources for bringing social justice are the needs of the hour. The principle should be 'giving more to those who have less and extracting more from those who have more'. In other words, extracting more from the rich through taxation and distributing more to the poor through public expenditure on development programmes and schemes. Franklin D. Roosevelt once said, '[T]he test of our progress is not whether we add more to the abundance of those who have much; it is whether we provide enough for those who have too little'. The Gandhian principle is, '[W]orld has kept enough for human needs not for human greed.' Good governance and prevention of corruption at all levels will bring happiness, i.e. *achhe din* (good days), in developing countries reeling under mal-governance.
12. Striving to achieve sustainable development by maintaining functional balance between environment, economy and society. Society and the individual should not impose atrocities on the environment for meeting their gluttonous present needs by putting the fate of the future generations in danger and darkness. The economy should not formulate such policies and undertake those actions that can damage environment and jeopardize the peace and well-being of the future generations. The world is more sustainable when both present and future are more secure. UNICEF desires that sustainable development must balance the scales of equity on all fronts to break cycles of poverty and ensure that the children of today and tomorrow are able to have and inherit a livable, safe world.[3]
13. Providing sustainable livelihood to all irrespective of the place of living such as urban and rural areas, hilly and plain areas and tribal and non-tribal areas; reducing regional disparities by launching special development programmes for the backward regions. Inclusive and sustainable development can only be possible when the regional, sub-regional and grass-roots level disparities are controlled through policy and programme measures. Trends in regional disparities have been a major issue in regional science for many decades and the knowledge of ways to overcome such disparities has great importance in regional policy-making.[4] According to Rao (2010), inter- and intrastate disparities in development have not only persisted but have even increased in certain cases in the post-reform period in India, especially where backward regions do not have necessary political clout in decision-making regarding public investment and where the provision of jobs has led to regional tensions and persistent demand for carving out separate states consisting of backward areas. Uttarakhand, Jharkhand, Chhattisgarh and Telangana are some of the recent examples. The World Bank in its World Development Report has noted that, paradoxically, in a world which is rapidly globalizing, one of the most important determinants of well-being is still where a person is born: in which community, in what province within the country and whether in a city or the countryside within that province (World Development Report 2009).
14. Empowering and energizing the sectors, i.e. primary, secondary and tertiary, effectively by following judicious balanced and unbalanced approaches to play a

proactive role in dealing with various issues and challenges of development. It is seen that the contribution of the agriculture sector to the GDP in most of the transitional developing economies is reducing. Less emphasis on the agriculture sector will have a detrimental effect on the future generations, who may face hunger and food scarcity most probably in developing countries. On the other hand, the industry and service sectors need to be promoted for ensuring employment to the youth and are crucial for sustainable development. The development must facilitate structural changes and shifting of workforce across the sectors based on the knowledge, skill and dexterities of the workforce.

15. Empowering all the actors of development, i.e. public sector, private and corporate sectors, international organizations, NGOs, CSOs and local self-government institutions, either individually or in partnership, so that they effectively contribute towards the holistic development of the economy. The public private partnership should not give rise to crony capitalism leading to corruption through middlemen. The scams that have taken place in India in the past several years show that they happened because of the strategic nexus between politicians, bureaucrats and corporate houses. The NGOs have to selflessly work for the social, economic, human and cultural development of the society.
16. Providing social security measures to the people working in the informal sector, and also to the aged, widowers and disabled, is a fundamental duty of the government. Across the world, the size of aging population is on the rise. Like in the Western countries, old age homes have to be built both in rural and urban areas of developing countries for the well-being of the aged and destitute people. The corporate sector under corporate social responsibility can be engaged to carry out this benevolent measure. The role of NGOs and private voluntary organizations (PVOs) will go a long way in setting up of old age homes in rural as well as urban areas. The old age pension scheme has to be effectively implemented with the help of local self-government institutions at the grass-roots level. In India, direct transfer of benefits through opening of bank accounts and AADHAAR cards, if implemented religiously, will go a long way in wiping out corruption and providing social security and all other benefits to the poor.
17. Development governance is sine qua non for developing countries, where a large percentage of money earmarked for the various development projects are plundered by the middlemen, bureaucratic functionaries and politicians. Good governance and removal of corruption from the bureaucratic, political, social and economic sphere is an immediate and contemporary concern of developing countries. The UNDP Human Development Report has aptly envisaged that each element of governance is both a means and goal of development, and lends insight into how development efforts are succeeding (or not succeeding) in securing choices of the people of a nation. There is strong evidence that governance matters significantly in accelerating development and in reducing poverty in developing countries (Khan 2006). The key components of governance, i.e. political governance, economic governance, social governance and bureaucratic governance, have to be made effective through suitable policy and administrative reform measures.

The Five Pillars of Development

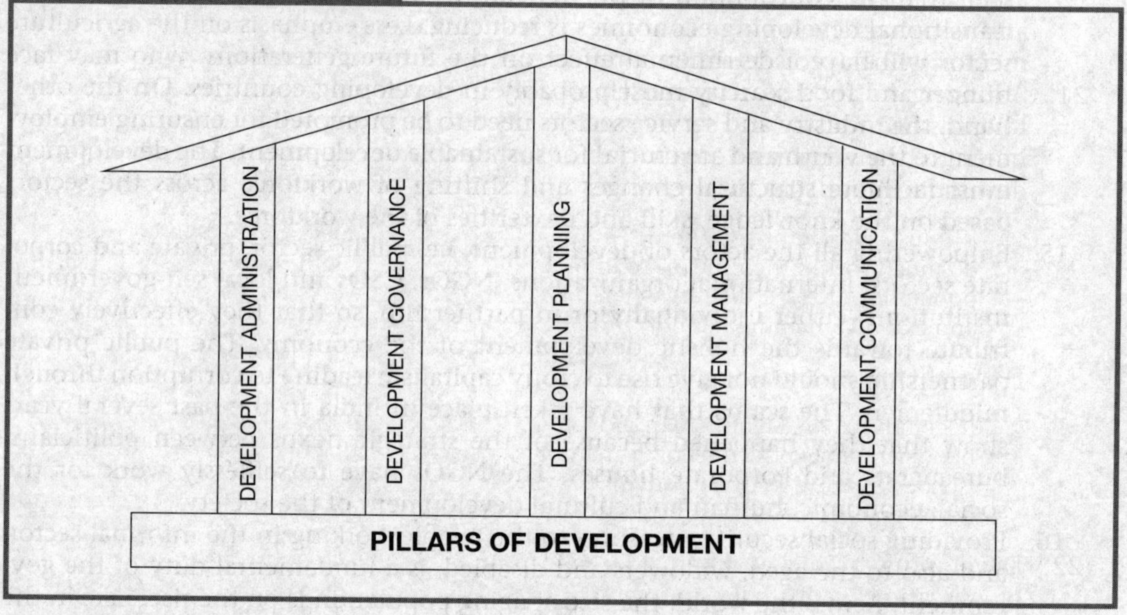

Source: Author.

18. Strengthening development administration and building up its capacity from time to time so that various issues and challenges of development can be effectively and efficiently faced. The honest and proactive role of bureaucracy is one of the factors behind the development of the countries such as Japan and South Korea. Bhambri (1980) was of the opinion that bureaucracy plays a decisive role in nation-building in modern societies and that the success or failure of various programmes of socio-economic development depends on its performance and capacity.
19. Development management must be one of the integral parts of the development actions and practices. Government, NGOs and PVOs involved and engaged in the management of development projects and programmes have to aptly apply a systematic approach to development project management and should possess critical understanding of various components and dimensions of development management in order to deal effectively and efficiently with various development issues and challenges at all levels. Brinkerhoff and Coston (1999) were of the view that the term development management has widened its scope and is no longer restricted to the public sector; for instance, a development manager can be an NGO staffer, members of the community groups and business people as well as civil servants (quoted in Saifullah 2001).
20. Developing countries facing the challenges of financial, physical and human resource deficiencies have to adopt development planning at least at the grass-roots level for the judicious and effective utilization of various resources. To Marcellus (2009), development planning comprehensively involves predetermining a nation's visions, missions, policies and programmes in all facets of life such as social, human, political, environmental, technological factors and so on and the means of

achieving them. The planning also needs to cover other four essential aspects such as appraisal, monitoring, evaluation and impact assessment so that accountability and responsibility are fixed for the delay in the completion of planned development activities, projects and programmes and wastage of resources at various levels.

21. Adhering to an ethical approach to development so that the rich contribute towards the well-being of the poor. In other words, development philanthropy needs to be an inherent component of the development process and strategies in developing countries. In the words of JRD Tata,

    > [I]ndustrial enterprise, whether in the private or the public sector, can and could do much within their means to improve the conditions of life of the surrounding population, relieve distress where it exists, help find work for the unemployed and extend a helping hand to those who need it.

    He further advocated,

    > [L]et industry be established in the countryside 'adopt' the villages in their neighborhood; let some of the time of its managers, its engineers, doctors and skilled specialists be spared to help and advise the people of the villages and to supervise new developments undertaken by cooperative effort between them and the company.[5]

22. Developing countries, where a large number of people are illiterate and the level of education is low, have to formulate a well-planned development communication strategy in various sectors. It is required for the effective implementation of various projects and programmes. The aim of development communication is to provide development education on various sectoral activities, programmes, projects and their objectives, possible beneficiaries and other modus operandi to the people through effective non-formal and extension education methods. It will be helpful to the beneficiaries to effectively participate in the implementation process of the development projects, programmes, schemes and activities. The ultimate goal of 'development communication' is to raise the quality of life of populations, including increasing income and well-being, eradicating social injustice, promoting land reform and freedom of speech and establishing community centres for leisure and entertainment (Melkote 1991). The success and failure of most development projects are often determined by two crucial factors, i.e. communication and people's involvement (Fraser and Restrepo Estrada 1998).
23. Strengthening development education, research and training so that continuous feedback is available to the planners, policy-makers and executives to design and formulate appropriate development programmes and projects. It will also be helpful in the formulation of appropriate development strategies at the national, state and grass-roots levels. The universities and the centre for development studies established by the public and private sectors must undertake fundamental and concurrent research on development issues and challenges.
24. Judicious application of theoretical principles advocated by the classical, neoclassical, developmentalist and heterodox social scientists in the concurrent development approaches and strategies is essential in order to increase economic growth and development. In other words, the importance of development theories and paradigms cannot be belittled in the formulation of development approaches and strategies in developing countries.

ISSUES AND CHALLENGES OF DEVELOPMENT

Identification of various issues and challenges of development is an arduous task. However, it is a fact that developing countries have been confronting various issues and challenges for centuries. They are struggling to achieve holistic development and making endeavours to ensure good quality of life to its population. Moreover, most of them are under tremendous pressure to tackle various issues and challenges of development in order to make their development process inclusive and sustainable. The issues and challenges, which most of developing countries and even some developed countries are facing, can be broadly categorized as (a) fundamental issues and challenges, (b) economic development issues and challenges, (c) sectoral issues and challenges, (d) social and human development issues and challenges, (e) emerging issues and challenges and (f) concurrent issues and challenges.

FUNDAMENTAL ISSUES AND CHALLENGES OF DEVELOPMENT

One of the fundamental objectives of development is to raise the quality of life of its population. The minimum quality of life depends on the access to basic needs. It is observed that majority of population in developing countries are deprived of access to basic needs such as food, clothing and shelter. They also lack access to other basic amenities, i.e. safe drinking water, sanitation and energy for cooking and lighting. All these variables of basic needs constitute important determinants of the poverty measurement index in many developing countries. The basic needs approach has formed an integral part of the socio-economic and human development agenda of developing countries from the beginning and many international organizations and particularly the International Labour Organization (ILO) has still been using the concept actively in their work. Besides basic needs, poverty, existing in various relative forms in both developed and developing countries, is one of the fundamental challenges that has existed for centuries. It has to be curtailed and removed from the earth at the earliest. As long as there is poverty, there will be underdevelopment. Poverty acts as insulin to underdevelopment. The Austrian Development Cooperation has viewed that the reduction of poverty is one of the greatest challenges of our times.[6] The third most important issue which poses fundamental challenge to the development of developing countries is population growth. Unbridled population growth in many of developing countries is a vital source of augmentation of poverty, unemployment and inequality. Households with a large family size and low income are found to have poor access to basic needs and other household amenities. Moreover, population growth in developing countries is also posing surmountable challenges to environment and sustainable development. UNFPA has recognized that population dynamics have a significant influence on sustainable development and efforts to promote sustainable development that do not address population dynamics will continue to fail.[7]

ECONOMIC ISSUES AND CHALLENGES OF DEVELOPMENT

The important economic issues and challenges which developing countries are facing for centuries are income inequality, unemployment and inflation. Because of high population growth rate in developing countries, the percentage of adult population in the total population is high in these countries as compared to the developed countries. The number of people aspiring for jobs and employment is increasing in a geometric proportion, while the availability of employment opportunities is growing in an arithmetic proportion, leading to unemployment, disguised unemployment and underemployment in developing countries. The governments in developing countries are under tremendous pressure to provide employment to its burgeoning youth. There is unbridled growth of informal employment in developing countries both in rural and urban areas. The life in the informal sector is dull, dump and monotonous. The wage rate is low and there is no provision of job and social security. The economic dualisms, e.g. formal and informal sectors, agricultural and industrial sectors, rural and urban sectors and so on, are stimulating factors that increase income inequality across the sectors. The poor are the drawers of the water and hewers of the wood and are still struggling to eke out a minimum level of living. In contrast, the rich eat from silver spoons, stay in palatial buildings, use flashy cars and possess all household gadgets required for comfort and luxury.

The economic disparities between the rich and poor have further increased with the continuous price rise (inflation) of the basic necessary food items, i.e. rice, wheat, dal (pulses), oil and other grocery items, and of staple vegetables such as potatoes, onions and tomatoes. These have also shaken the backbone of the poor people living below the poverty line and of those who are at the border line of the above poverty line (APL) families in developing countries. Most of developing countries have not been successful enough to provide basic necessities to their population at affordable prices, thereby leading to miseries like hunger and malnutrition. Todaro and Smith (2012) see economic development in terms of the reduction or elimination of poverty, inequality and unemployment within the context of a growing economy.

Sectoral Issues and Challenges of Development

Every economy comprises three sectors, i.e. primary, secondary and tertiary sectors. The primary sector largely refers to agriculture and its allied activities such as poultry, fishery, diary and piggery. The secondary sector broadly comprises industrial and manufacturing activities. The tertiary sector refers to all other activities which do not fall under the primary and the secondary sectors. The tertiary sector is otherwise known as the service sector which comprises education, health, banking, insurance, information technology and tourism to name a few fields among many. The development activities largely revolve around these three key sectors. The GDP, which is an indicator of economic development, depends on the contribution of these three sectors. The contribution of the service sector to the GDP in the developed countries is quite high as compared to developing countries. In many developing countries, agriculture is the mainstay of majority of its population, although its contribution to the GDP is declining. In a few developing countries, the contribution of the service sector to the GDP is on the rise per se India.

The Africa Human Development Report, 2012, has envisaged that 'increased agricultural productivity would end the ravages of hunger and malnutrition and will nurture capabilities and conditions for human development.' The challenge before developing countries is to raise the contribution of the agriculture sector to the GDP as the food habits and lifestyle of the people living in the countryside of developing countries has not adequately changed and modernized as it has happened in the Western countries. Therefore, developing countries cannot afford to neglect the agriculture sector. However, modernization of agriculture and structural changes are the need of the hour for developing countries to achieve higher growth rate. For the development of developing countries, the transfer of manpower from the primary to the secondary and tertiary sectors is vital for economic and social changes and development in these countries. The structuralists were of the view that as the process of economic development proceeds, the share of the agricultural sector in national income and employment—which was typically high in the early stages of development—will begin to decline and that of the non-agricultural sectors will experience a rise (Joshi 2008).

Social and Human Development Issues and Challenges

Social and human development are important dimensions of development. The economic development depends on the social and human development. A nation cannot achieve higher economic growth rate and holistic development if large number of its population is illiterate, unskilled, morbid and systematically discriminated in the social sphere and labour market. Social discrimination on the basis of caste, class, ethnicity and gender is one of the important factors contributing to the prevalence of economic disparities in developing countries. Systematic marginalization of some group of population in all spheres such as economic, political and cultural is an inherent social feature of many developing countries. Therefore, any discussion on development will be considered as incomplete if it fails to assign importance to social and human development issues and challenges.

The two key determinants of social and human development are education and health. The level of education and health status has to be improved in developing countries. It is not a flight of fancy, but delicately, the contribution of educated, skilled and healthy population to economic growth and development is higher as compared to their counterpart illiterate, morbid and unskilled population. UNDP (1990) stated that '[H]uman development is a process of enlarging the people's choices. The most critical of these wide-ranging choices are to live a long and healthy life, to be educated and to have access to resources needed for a decent standard living.' Therefore, the state, civil society and market can create opportunities for social action and for expanding human capabilities (Sen 1999). Cohen (1994) noted that human resources development and utilization are regarded as the means to meet basic human needs and to contribute to overall development by reducing fertility; by transmitting cultural, religious, political and technological values and by preserving national identity, cohesiveness and stability.

Emerging Issues and Challenges of Development

A wide range of issues have been emerging in the context of developing countries in order to pull them from the spectre of underdevelopment and drive them towards the pageantry of development. The vital inputs that can accelerate the pace of development in the underdeveloped countries are infrastructure, energy and technology. Developing countries have poor infrastructure facilities that not only prevent the public sector investment in various sectors but also do not cajole the private sector investments and FDIs in these countries. The infrastructure facilities such as housing, water and sanitation, roads, irrigation, dams, telecommunications, electricity and other renewable sources of energy and market complexes are essential elements of development. Estache (2006) from the World Bank study has rightly remarked that infrastructure seems to be returning to the agenda of the development of economists. He was of the view that growth is constrained by infrastructure bottlenecks in several developing countries and proposed that the poorest countries need to spend 9% of their GDP on the operation, maintenance and expansion of infrastructure.

Sustainable and affordable energy for all purposes including household purposes is an arduous challenge, and energy production and pricing politics are very popular in many developing countries. Third, undeveloped countries are featured with poor technological advancement. The application of traditional technology in the agriculture sector and the poor technological advancement in the industrial and the service sectors is affecting their economic growth and development. Bannon and Roodman (2004) were of the view that rich countries arguably make their single greatest contribution to long-run development in poor countries by creating new technologies, as both producers and consumers and people in developing countries benefit from technological advancement. They suggested that government investment in new technologies can enhance life throughout the world.

The other two vital issues that effectively emerged in developing countries, particularly after they joined in the globalization process, are inclusive and sustainable development. The rising disparities between the poor and the rich, skilled and unskilled workforce and among the various regions of a nation-state and finally among the different sections of population across the caste, class, ethnicity and gender are a concern for developing countries. Inclusive development advocates that any systematic exclusion and discrimination of a certain group of population in the social, human, political, cultural and economic development processes is a gross violation of human rights and is detrimental to social justice and inclusive development. However, despite several affirmative measures formulated and implemented by various countries, exclusion exists egregiously more particularly in developing countries impeding a participatory development process in these countries. Besides inclusive development, sustainable development has become an emerging concern for developing countries. The international organizations as well as the developed nations of the West are putting tremendous pressure on developing countries to maintain a balance between the society, economy and ecology to save mother earth and ensure its people have sustainable livelihood in the present and also by securing a safe and sustainable livelihood for the future generations.

In the Rio+20 Outcome Document (2012), UNIDO has envisaged that

> we recognize that people are at the centre of sustainable development and in this regard, we strive for a world which is just equitable and inclusive and we commit to work together to promote sustained and inclusive economic growth, social development, environmental protection and thereby to benefit all.

Concurrent Issues and Challenges of Development

Many issues concurrently coexist for centuries with the birth of developing countries mostly after the Second World War. These issues and challenges in developing countries are consistently disturbing the minds of the planners and policy-makers. The two prominent among them are the issues and challenges with regard to the rural and urban development.

A gigantic size of populations in developing countries resides in the countryside. The rural areas of developing countries are devoid of basic infrastructural facilities. They are also technologically poor. On the contrary, the urban areas are endowed with better infrastructure and technology facilities. The socio-economic and digital divide is visible between these two sectors, which is critically called as development dichotomy. People residing in rural and urban slum areas are facing many challenges concerning to the quality of life such as housing, water, sanitation, electricity, communication, employment, technological facilities, education, health care, and so on. The challenges are to make these provisions available and accessible to these populations at affordable prices. Despite the formulation and implementation of several policies and programmes, the socio-economic development issues relating to rural and urban slum areas will remain concurrent challenges for developing countries even for several decades and may continue throughout the 21st century and beyond. The unbridled population growth and rural–urban migration if not checked will foil the development endeavours of the government for the upliftment of the quality of living of the people residing in both rural and urban areas in developing countries.

Also from the perspectives of European countries, Ulied and others (2009/10) have advocated that it is needless to say that the debate on urban and rural concepts and urban–rural relationships provides particularly relevant insights to analyse spatial development policies.[8] The rural–urban dualism, digital divide and development disparities have been a contemporary challenge before the developed as well as developing countries for decades. However, after globalization this divide has elongated and is posing surmountable challenges before developing countries.

Good governance is a contemporary felt need of developing countries. Governance issues such as corruption, lack of accountability, transparency, redtapism, dishonesty and violation of the rule of law because of political and bureaucratic interferences are a few among many governance challenges that developing countries are facing. Half of the developmental problems in developing countries are associated with mal-governance. It is not only influencing but also retarding their economic growth and development. Good governance is essential for the achievement of various goals of inclusive and sustainable development. Adherence to the principles of good governance at all levels, i.e. at the political and bureaucratic levels and by NGOs and civil society organizations involved in the implementation of development projects and programmes at the grass-roots level, is a formidable challenge before developing countries. IMF considers that 'good governance is important for countries at all stages of development' and identifies 'promoting good governance in all its aspects, including ensuring the rule of law, improving efficiency and accountability of the public sector and tackling corruption' as an essential element of a framework within which economies can prosper.[9]

Most importantly, it is felt that the governments of developing countries cannot solve the problems of their vast population with limited resources at their disposal and therefore consider development philanthropy to play a role in the eradication of poverty and achievement of sustainable development goals. Under development philanthropy, the rich have to sacrifice a portion of their wealth for the well-being and improvement of the quality of life of the poor. Besides, the rich nations have to sponsor the development of the poor nations. This is otherwise known as benevolent capitalism or creative capitalism or large-hearted capitalism. To energize a feeling of philanthropic atmosphere in the corporate and business sectors in this neo-liberal world is a contemporary challenge before developing countries. Therefore, development philanthropy has to play a key role in dealing with various development issues and challenges in developing countries. The UNDP has also realized the importance of philanthropy in international development. UNDP has advocated that '[p]hilanthropy, no matter where it originates, is driven by the imperative to meet human needs, alleviate suffering, and tackle the systemic challenges that prevent human development and progress.'[10]

FACTORS INFLUENCING DEVELOPMENT

Before triggering off any discussion on the issues and challenges of development, it is pertinent to note various factors which essentially influence 'development'. A few important factors which influence development particularly in developing countries are discussed further.

Economic Growth: For the developing and transitional economies, higher growth rate is very much essential for the acceleration of multidimensional development. The trickle-down effect of higher economic growth rate will be helpful in the eradication of poverty and inequality. Economic growth is a quantitative aspect measured in terms of GDP, GNP and per capita income. However, development is a multidimensional quantitative and qualitative concept and covers many indicators such as poverty, employment rate, literacy rate, mortality rate, morbidity rate and so on. The gains from higher economic growth rate will be utilized in the development of education, health, poverty alleviation, employment generation and provisioning of basic needs. For developing countries, the achievement of higher development without higher growth rate is very difficult. Higgins (1990) states, 'It is conceptually possible for an economy to grow without developing, however, development without growth is a little harder to imagine.' OECD has recognized that economic growth is the most powerful instrument for reducing poverty and improving the quality of life in developing countries. Both cross-country research and country case studies provide overwhelming evidence that rapid and sustained growth is critical to making faster progress towards millennium development goals (MDGs).[11]

Structural Changes: Developmentalists after conducting several studies in developing countries were of the view that structural changes are essential for the development of the underdeveloped countries. In order to achieve higher economic growth and development in all spheres, developing countries have to internalize structural changes. They have to develop strategies and implement actions for the transfer of surplus manpower from the primary sector to the secondary and tertiary sectors. It will reduce rural disguised unemployment and promote effective utilization of manpower employed in the agriculture sector of rural areas and raise their per capita income and standard of living. Margaret McMillan and Dani Rodrik were of the view that 'the countries that manage to pull themselves out of poverty and get richer are those that are able to diversify away from agriculture and other traditional products. As labour and other resources move from agriculture to modern economic activities, the overall productivity rises and incomes expand. The speed with which this structural transformation takes place is the key factor that differentiates successful countries from unsuccessful ones.'[12]

Infrastructure Development: Infrastructure is the prime ingredient of development. It is required for the effective and efficient functioning of all sectors, i.e. primary, secondary and tertiary sector activities. The construction of infrastructure such as road, rail, ports and so on by the governments of developing countries will trigger off private investment and attract FDIs in various sectors. It will also enhance the efficiency of the personnel engaged in various sectors. One of responsible factors for the development of the developed countries is quality infrastructure, which is lacking in developing countries. Therefore, for the acceleration of development and in order to effectively engage the private sector and FDIs in development activities, the possession of good quality infrastructure is sine qua non. Infrastructure adds efficiency to financial and human capital. As infrastructure is the social overhead capital, it has to be created by the government of developing countries for enhancing the efficiency of the public sector and for attracting private investment. UNESCAP has recognized that the provision of adequate infrastructure, along with macroeconomic stability and a long-term development strategy, is one of the necessary conditions for sustainable economic and social development.[13]

Technology and Innovation: Technology and technological innovations are the powerful drivers and prolific energizers of economic growth and development. Technology is required for the enhancement of productivity as well as for the saving of time and resources and removal of poverty from the earth. Almost all the capitalist economies have tested the benefit of technology in achieving higher economic growth rate during the initial phases of their development endeavour. It has been proved that the application of technology in the farmers' fields in the Green Revolution belt of India during the 1970s has enhanced food grain productivity in these regions. It has also been instrumental in managing the hunger and food poverty in the dry land parts of India. Many countries of Asia, i.e. Japan, South Korea, Singapore, Taiwan and Hong Kong, have achieved higher socio-economic development through the application of technology in the various sectors of their economies. Therefore, technology is a strong influencing factor of development. According to UNDP (2001), the 20th-century countries' unprecedented gains in advancing human development and the eradication of poverty came largely from technological breakthroughs. The developing nations have to create more innovative entrepreneurs who can use technology in the process of production. They have to invest in research and development for maintaining the circular flow of innovation and make innovation a continuous process. They require more job creators than job seekers. Innovation is the kingpin of development.

Modernity: It is a vital necessity for the multidimensional development of developing countries. The prevalence of traditional believes and values in developing countries is obstructing their socio-economic development process. Modernization advocates acceptance and application of modern and Western ideas into all the sectors of development. Modernization, mechanization and Westernization go hand in hand and the Asian countries that have adopted the Western modernization model have achieved higher economic and social development. Singapore is one of the illustrious examples where the adoption of modernization has enabled the country to achieve higher growth rate and holistic development in all fronts. The heart of modernization theory is the idea that economic growth can be stimulated in any country by following a USA/European model (Phil Green 2008). It was well said that economic development is indeed difficult (although not completely impossible) where a country is ruled by a landed aristocracy with deeply embedded feudal attitudes, strongly opposed to industrialization, mass education and technological change (Higgins 1990).

Urbanization: It is one of the important parameters of development. Urbanization promotes industrialization and leads to the growth of the service sector in the economy. In the highly urbanized Western economies, the contribution of the service sector to the GDP is very high as compared to developing countries. There is a robust relationship between urbanization and per capita income: nearly all countries become at least 50% urbanized before reaching the middle-income status, and all high-income countries are 70–80% urbanized (Vaidya 2009). In the developing economies where urbanization is taking place at a faster pace, the contribution of urban areas to the GDP is on the rise as compared to rural areas. Urbanization brings technological innovations, provides better infrastructural facilities and attracts investors to invest, thus providing higher employment and higher income and leading to a better quality of life of the people living in urban areas. The status of various development indicators, i.e. literacy rate, per capita income, life expectancy rate, infant mortality rate, maternal mortality rate and so on are better in urban areas as compared to rural areas. The IMF and World Bank have recognized that urbanization has been a major force behind poverty reduction and progress towards other MDGs. With over 80% of global goods and services produced in cities with relatively higher levels of urbanization, such as China and many other from East Asia and Latin America, have played a major role in lowering extreme poverty (Table 1.1).[14]

Good Governance: Development governance is an essential element for the development of developing countries. Because of the wider size of the public sector, corruption takes place largely at the bureaucratic and political levels. Corruption at the bureaucratic

Table 1.1 *US Foundation Centre Data Showing Contributions towards MDGs*

Foundation Giving for Programmes Related to the Millennium Development Goals, 2011			
Millennium Development Goals	**Amount ($)**	**No. of Grants**	**No. of Fdns.**
Goal 1: Eradicate extreme poverty & hunger	770,761,183	1,663	318
Goal 2: Achieve universal primary education	42,756,909	294	80
Goal 3: Promote gender equality & empower women	223,768,315	312	56
Goal 4: Reduce child mortality	456,276,756	337	54
Goal 5: Improve maternal health	211,008,135	215	38
Goal 6: Combat HIV/AIDS, malaria & other diseases	1,572,823,543	426	48
Goal 7: Ensure environmental sustainability	534,927,086	1,747	224
Goal 8: Develop a global partnership for development	278,124,929	363	109

Source: http://www.undp.org/content/dam/undp/documents/partners/civil_society/UNDP-CSO-philanthropy.pdf (accessed 28 May 2016).

and political levels has hindered development in developing countries. The resources earmarked for the development activities are observed to be siphoned off by the middlemen being patronized by the bureaucrats and politicians. Therefore, money which is allocated to be spent for the well-being of the poor is found to be plundered for the luxuries and comfort of the dishonest bureaucratic functionaries, middlemen and politicians operating at various levels. A lack of accountability can lead to poor implementation and feeble achievement of the objectives of development projects and programmes. Faulty identification of the development beneficiaries has led to leakages in many programmes. Moreover, crony capitalism, i.e. the nexus between the corporate sector, politicians and bureaucrats, has led to massive corruption in various deals. Therefore, the role of good governance cannot be ignored in the development process of developing countries. Governance intends to make institutions and rules more effective and efficient, in order to achieve equity, transparency, participation, responsiveness, accountability and the rule of law (United Nations 2012). For instance, in India, development indicators such as education, health, sanitation, housing and poverty status are better in southern Indian states as compared to other states, one of the reasons being a good governance environment in these states.

Public–Private Partnership (PPP): The liberalization process started during the 1990s has augmented the role of the private sector in the development process of developing countries. The failure of the private sector to meet the welfare needs of the people and limitations of the state to honestly solve all developmental challenges has resulted into a partnership between the public and private sectors to effectively fulfil the development aspirations of the people. The state-guided capitalism of Japan is an illustrious development model in the world. Neither the public sector nor the private sector would be in silo able to deal with all the problems of development. Therefore, effective public–private partnership with clear-cut demarcation of duties and responsibilities of both the partners will hasten the process of development. The aim should be to raise productivity and income, generate employment and provide social security so that welfare is promoted and the GDP is augmented. The African Development Bank[15] has recognized that the PPP has emerged over the last decade as one of the best ways to foster development, fuelled by insufficient investment growing pressures on government budgets and a general concern about service provision by state enterprises and agencies. The strategy should be to leave those activities to the private sector where they can better perform and make partnership in those activities where both public and private sectors can jointly perform better. The PPP is seen in infrastructure, energy, power, telecommunication, transport, housing, water and sanitation. The PPP model must be based on the comparative advantage principle. Two illustrious examples of market and government partnership are Japan's 'Guided Capitalism' under Emperor Meiji (1886–1912) and reliance on state initiatives for large investment in infrastructure and China's 'Market Socialism' where the economic system combines state ownership of the means of production with the use of market to allocate resources (Nafziger 2006).

Women Empowerment: Women constitute nearly 50% of the total population of the world. However, despite their near demographic equality, their potential and participation in the process of economic growth and development has not been adequately harnessed by many countries. The gender stereotype attached to women has restricted their participation in many sectoral activities of development. However, it is not a flight of fancy but a fact that everything remaining constant, households with employed women will have a better standard of living than their counterparts with unemployed and dependent women. One of the reasons of the high social and human development index of the Scandinavian countries as compared to other countries of Asia and Africa is the higher economic, social and political participation of women. Empowerment of women for development means making them capable and supporting, encouraging and giving them the opportunity to take part in the process of development and contribute towards the economic growth and development of the nation-state. For instance, in India, the contribution of women towards the GDP and multidimensional development of Kerala is higher than that of the women of other states such as Chhattisgarh, Jharkhand and Bihar. Women and men are the two sides of the coin of development, and therefore, both the sides of the coin will not glitter to its fullest strength if one side is kept dark and dull. Equal participation of women in all development spheres and in all kinds of development projects, programmes and activities and in all sectors will hasten the pace of development. OECD has recognized that increasing the role of women in the economy is part of the solution to the financial and economic crises and is critical for economic resilience and growth.[16]

Skilled Manpower: A skilled labour force is vital to the economic growth and development process of any nation. The developed countries have realized the role of skilled manpower in their economic development process much ahead of developing countries. The productivity growth of the industrial and service sectors depends on the availability, employability and efficiency of the skilled workforce. The globalization process that has brought technology in its wave has reinforced the requirement of the skilled labour force in the transitional economies. Skilled labour force is *sine qua non* for the acceleration of economic growth and development, particularly in developing countries. It is an important driver to address poverty reduction by improving employability, productivity and helping sustainable enterprise development and inclusive growth.[17] Moreover, ILO (2010) has recognized that 'ultimately, each country's prosperity depends on how many of its people are in work and how productive they are, which in turn rests on the skills they have and how effectively those skills are used. Skills are a foundation of decent work.' Number of people matters and so does their training and experience; however, a well-developed entrepreneurial class, motivated and trained to organize resources for efficient production, is often missing in poor countries.[18] The National Skill Development Mission of India aims at creating skilled workforce in the country (a list is given in a box on page 22).

International Economic Relationship: The globalization process triggered off since the 1990s has hastened the economic relationship between the developed and developing countries. The inflow of FDIs from the developed countries to developing countries, outsourcing of activities mainly in the IT sector from the developed countries to developing countries and remittances have promoted investment in various sectors, particularly in the service sectors of developing countries. The relationship has led to the transfer of technology, innovation and ideas. The construction of beautiful houses in the rural areas of Punjab and Kerala by NRIs through the investment of remittances has made living in the countryside of these states very pleasant. The contribution of Indian, Chinese and African diasporas to socio-economic development at the household level has been widely

Skill India

Objectives of 'Skill India'

'SKILL INDIA'—A multi-skill development programme launched with the objectives of job creation and entrepreneurship for all socio-economic classes. It intends to establish an international equivalent standard of the Indian framework on skill development. Its objective is to create workforce mobility and enhance youth employability.

Features of 'Skill India'

1. The emphasis is to skill the youth in such a way that they get employment and also improve entrepreneurship.
2. It provides training, support and guidance for all occupations that were of traditional type such as carpenters, cobblers, welders, blacksmiths, masons, nurses, tailors, weavers and so on.
3. More emphasis will be given to new areas such as real estate, construction, transportation, textile, gem industry, jewellery designing, banking, tourism and various other sectors, where skill development is inadequate or nil.
4. The training programmes would be on the lines of the international level so that the youth of our country can meet not only the domestic demands but also of other countries such as the USA, Japan, China, Germany, Russia and those in west Asia.
5. Another remarkable feature of the 'Skill India' programme would be to create a hallmark called 'Rural India Skill', so as to standardize and certify the training process.
6. Tailor-made, need-based programmes would be initiated for specific age groups which can be like language and communication skills, life and positive thinking skills, personality development skills, management skills, behavioural skills, and job and employability skills.
7. The course methodology of 'Skill India' would be innovative, which would include games, group discussions, brainstorming sessions, practical experiences, case studies and so on.

Source: See https://www.linkedin.com/pulse/skill-india-program-objectives-features-advantages-dr-subodh-kulkarni (accessed on 14 June 2016).

acknowledged in various studies conducted on diasporas and development. Developing countries having better economic relationship in terms of trade and investment with other countries are found to be developing faster as compared to closed economies and economies having limited economic relationship with other countries, particularly the developed countries. A report by OECD (1998) states that more open and outward-oriented economies consistently outperform countries with restrictive trade and (foreign) investment regimes. Fischer (2000) was of the view that integration into the world economy is the best way for countries to grow.

Proactive NGOs and Civil Society Organizations: The NGOs and PVOs are the third force of development and are vital actors in the development process of both developed and developing countries in recent years. To Bratton (1989), NGOs are significant bolsters of the civil society by virtue of their participatory and democratic approach. In both industrialized and developing countries, there is a growing body of experiences, which attests the positive roles that non-profit organizations play in development (Clark 1991). However, it is an irony that in developing countries, where they have to become more service-oriented, many of them are seen to be profit-oriented and a few of them have been opened with the mala fide intention of embezzling the funding money by establishing a nexus with the bureaucracy and politicians. In fact, many of them are being opened with the patronage of politicians and retired bureaucrats. Despite the disadvantages, the role of NGOs and CSOs in the implementation of education and health projects, programmes and other developmental activities is widely acknowledged. It is observed that NGOs are involved in many development sectors such as health, education, sanitation, safe drinking water, child and women development, women empowerment, old age care, disabled care, watershed management, vocational education and allied activities of agriculture such as bee keeping, mushroom cultivation training, flowery culture, awareness generation, capacity building, action research and so on.

In India, the role of NGOs and CSOs in the social development sector, particularly health, education and women empowerment in the southern Indian states, is more visible and widely acknowledged. Besides, in India, religious institutions are also playing an important role in the social development sector; one of the illustrious examples is Shri Balaji Trust, Andhra Pradesh, which has opened a large number of health and educational institutions. In Punjab, Shiromani Gurudwara Prabandhak Committee (SGPC) is an important social capital of the state and is playing an important role in the development of education, health care and other human welfare activities. Mersland et al. have opined that faith-based organizations are not only involved in development efforts but also are common in other industries, especially in the health care, retirement/nursing home and education industries.[19] The NGOs and CSOs have to be effectively involved in the process of development as the government functionaries with functional constraints cannot effectively reach the unreachable.

Local Self-government Institutions: Decentralization of economic and political powers to the hierarchically lower institutions and its impact on development, more particularly at the grass-roots level, is a buzz word in many democratic countries of the world. The democratic decentralization approach believes that development must start from below and must not be imposed from above. Local self-government institutions, being closer to the people, can better understand peoples' problems and help in the formulation of appropriate strategies for the effective implementation of development projects and programmes. Haque (1977) argued that decentralization is a way of increasing the effectiveness of development programmes by making them more relevant and responsive to local needs and conditions, allowing greater flexibility in their implementation, thus making the state more participatory, more acceptable and more effective and efficient.

Local self-government institutions worldwide are found to be involved in the implementation of several development programmes, projects and activities at the grass-roots level. In India, urban local bodies, local self-governments for urban areas, have been constitutionally assigned (74th constitutional amendment) developmental duties and responsibilities on 18 subjects to be implemented at the municipal corporation, municipal council and nagar panchayat levels, while the three-tier panchayati raj institutions (PRIs) such as zilla parishads, block samitis and village panchayats have been constitutionally assigned (73rd constitutional amendment) developmental duties and responsibilities on 29 subjects to be performed at the grass-roots level. The PRIs are observed to be involved in the implementation of many developmental activities such as the construction of various types of infrastructure, e.g. roads, houses, school buildings, building of the health centres, toilets, construction of drinking water projects, construction of water conservation projects, panchayat building and so on, identification of BPL families, identification of the beneficiaries for social security schemes, overseeing mid-day meal scheme, distribution of books and scholarships to the students belonging to the disadvantaged communities and so on along with government functionaries at the grass-roots level. It is observed that rural development is faster in those states where PRIs are proactive and committed to their duties and responsibilities. One of the factors responsible for the success of the rural–urban continuum in Kerala is the committed and empowered village panchayats in the state. The Maharashtra Development Report (Planning Commission 2007) has recognized that 'Maharashtra's better performance in the field of primary education is mainly due to the effective role of PRIs. Besides, the PRIs have succeeded in bringing qualitative changes in the rural society in terms of stimulating popular participation.'

Peoples' Attitude to Development: Last but not the least, the attitude of the people of a nation-state is a fundamental force behind development. It is well said that if a horse is not thirsty, any amount of dragging it to the water will not make it drink. If the people of a state are not laborious and hardworking and are not enthusiastic to move out of poverty and from the spectre of underdevelopment, then any endeavour by the state will not be able to successfully pull them out of underdevelopment. For instance, if you compare the various development indicators of Orissa and Andhra Pradesh, two costal region states, during the 1970s, both the states had more or less the same percentage of population below the poverty line. Now, Andhra Pradesh has moved far ahead of Orissa in terms of poverty and various development indicators. At the international level too, Japan gives an illustrious example where the strong determination and hard work of Japanese have made them one of the most developed nations of the world. For instance, nobody can wake up a person who knowingly pretends to be sleeping. Gunnar Myrdal's famous quotation, 'a country is poor because it is poor' is befitting to the people's attitude towards development in the underdeveloped countries. United Nations has therefore urged that it is important to make people realize their strength and potential to solve their problems and to improve their lifestyle by increasing their income.[20] Motivated and hardworking human resources are a potent force for sustainable development.

SUMMARY

Development is a commonly used word in developing countries. For the common man, it is a simple word, but for a nation, it is the most complex concept. It can neither be defined nor achieved to universal satisfaction. Development aims at ensuring better quality of life to the citizens of a nation by raising the per capita income and literacy rate; reducing mortality, morbidity and malnutrition; reducing the percentage of people living below the poverty line, income inequality and unemployment; restricting inflation and provisioning increased access to healthy housing, sanitation, safe drinking water and energy. In fact, 'development' is a continuous process. It is an evergreen terminology. It is a relative concept which has given rise to many relative terminologies such as 'more developed', 'less developed', 'underdeveloped' and 'developing', making its meaning and measurement more cumbersome and argumentative. It is not a flight of fancy, but delicately the term 'development' has germinated the concepts of the 'First World, 'Second World' and 'Third World'.

The issues and challenges of development before developing countries are many. With scanty resources at disposal, developing countries are finding it difficult to attain various developmental goals. The issues and challenges determine the determinants of the factors influencing the development of developing countries. The factors determining failure at the developmental front are many; to name a prominent few among many are infrastructure deficiency, poor application of technology in various sectors of development, malgovernance and so on. Development will remain a debated and spicy concept in developing countries in the 21st century, because of its interface with the globalization.

Keywords: public–private partnership, underdevelopment, disparities, quality of life, standard of living, inclusive development, sustainable development, infrastructure, technology, social capital, urban local bodies, panchayati raj institution, human development, good governance, innovation, rural development, urban development.

REVIEW QUESTIONS

1. Discuss the objectives and scope of development.
2. Explain three important issues and challenges of development.
3. What are the emerging issues and challenges of development? Explain environment and sustainable development as an emerging challenge of development.
4. Developing countries are deficient infrastructure and innovation. Explain.
5. Narrate four important factors that are influencing development.
6. Discuss the influence of NGOs and local self-government institutions on development.
7. Write short notes on the following:
   (i) Role of infrastructure in development.
   (ii) Local self-government institutions.
   (iii) International economic relationship and development.
   (iv) Public–private partnership.
   (v) Innovation in development.
   (vi) Structural change.

NOTES

1. See 'What Is Development?' Available at: http://www.worldbank.org/depweb/beyond/beyondco/beg_01.pdf (accessed on 31 May 2016).
2. See https://www.lindenwood.edu/jigs/docs/volume2Issue2/essays/1–20.pdf (accessed on 12 June 2016).
3. See http://www.unicef.org/post2015/files/SD_children_FINAL.pdf (accessed on 24 May 2016).
4. See http://www.unece.org/fileadmin/DAM/hlm/archive/Conference/10th_Bratislava/Response%20Papers/Topic%202/4_polycentricity%20versus%20regional%20disparities%20paper%20UNECE%20KSEM.pdf (accessed on 24 May 2016).
5. JRD Tata's views were quoted from his letters in the book edited by Mambro, (2004).
6. See http://www.entwicklung.at/uploads/media/PD_Poverty_reduction_Dec2009_01.pdf (accessed on 12 June 2016).
7. See http://www.unfpa.org/publications/population-matters-sustainable-development (accessed on 12 June 2016).
8. See http://81.47.175.201/urban_rural/220710_URBAN… (accessed on 8 May 2016).
9. See http://www.imf.org/external/pubs/ft/exrp/govern/govindex.htm. (accessed on 8 May 2016).
10. See http://www.oecd.org/derec/unitedkingdom/40700982.pdf (accessed on 12 June 2016).
11. See https://www.wto.org/english/res_e/booksp_e/glob_soc_sus_e_chap2_e.pdf (accessed on 13 June 2016).
12. See http://www.unescap.org/resources/infrastructure-development-key-economic-growth-and-regional-economic-cooperation (accessed on 13 June 2016).
13. See http://www.undp.org/content/dam/undp/documents/partners/civil_society/UNDP-CSO-philanthropy.pdf (accessed on 28 May 2016).
14. See http://www.worldbank.org/en/news/press-release/2013/04/17/developing-countries-need-to-harness-urbanization-to-achieve-mdgs-imf-world-bank-report (accessed on 31 May 2106).
15. See http://allafrica.com/stories/201411050286.html (accessed on 12 April 2016).
16. See https://www.oecd.org/dac/gender-development/47561694.pdf (accessed on 10 May 2016).
17. See http://wps.prenhall.com/wps/media/objects/1310/1341624/Chapter36W.pdf (accessed on 13 June 2016).
18. See https://www.google.co.in/url?url=https://www.rug.nl/research/globalisation-studiesgroningen/research/conferencesandseminars/conferences/eumicrofinconf2011/papers/13.mersland-despallier-supphellen.format.doc&rct=j&frm=1&q=&esrc=s&sa=U&ved=0ahUKEwjl9t3nraTNAhXLnpQKHYHxD-3kQFgg0MAQ&usg=AFQjCNGKCkZrkcJ-dskOxMuInLWS6O40Wg (accessed on 13 June 2016).
19. See http://niti.gov.in/mgov_file/skill%20Development%20and 20%Productivity20%of20the%20Workforce (accessed on 8 May 2016).
20. See http://www.un.org/esa/socdev/publications/FullSurveyEmpowerment.pdf (accessed on 10 May 2016).

BIBLIOGRAPHY

Bannon, A., and D. Roodman. 'Technology and Commitment to Development Index', 2004. Available at: http://www.cgdev.org/doc/CDI/technology_200… (accessed on 8 May 2016).

Bhambri, C. P. 'Bureaucracy in India: Challenges of the Eighties.' *The Indian Journal of Public Administration*, 26, no. 3 (July–September 1980): 520.

Brandt Commission. *North-South: A Programme of Survival*, p. 48. London: Pan Books,1980.

Bratton, M. 'The Politics of Government–NGO Relations in Africa.' *World Development*, 17, no. 4 (1989): 569–87.

Clark, J. *Democratizing Development: The Role of Voluntary Organizations*. West Hartford, CT: Kumarian Press, 1991.

Cohen, S. I. *Human Resource Development and Utilization*. Aldershot: Avebury Publishers, 1994.

Cypher, J. M., and J. L. Dietz. *The Process of Economic Development*. London and New York: Routledge, 2009.

Estache, A. 'Infrastructure: A Survey of Recent and Upcoming Issues.' The World Bank, 2006. Available at: http://siteresources.worldbank.org/INTDECABCT… (accessed on 8 May 2016).

Fischer, S. 'Lunch Address.' Given at the Conference on Promoting Dialogue: Global Challenges and Global Institutes, Washington American University, 2000.

Fraser, C., and S. Restrrepo-Estrada. *Communicating for Development Human Change for Survival*. London and New York: IB Tauris Publishers, 1998.

Green, P. 'Are Development Theories of the 1950s, 1960s and 1970s Still Relevant Today? Discuss With Reference to Modernization Theory.' 2008. Available at: http://philmgreen.files.wordpress.com/2010/08 (accessed on 31 January 2014).

Haque, S. 'Local Governance in Developing Nations: Re-examining the Question of Accountability.' *Regional Development Dialogue*, 18, no. 2 (Autumn, 1977): IV–XXIII.

Higgins, B. *Economic Development Problems, Principles and Policies*. New Delhi: Universal Book Stall, 1990.

ILO. 'A Skilled Workforce for Strong, Sustainable and Balanced Growth.' AG 20 Training Strategy, ILO, Geneva, 2010.

Joshi, S. *Growth and Structure of Tertiary Sector in Developing Economies*. New Delhi: Academic Foundation, 2008.

Khan, M. H. 'Governance and Anti-Corruption Reforms in Developing Countries Policies, Evidence and Ways Forward.' G-24 Discussion Paper Series, United Nations Conference on Trade and Development, 42, November 2006.

Mahrey, S. 'Opportunities for All New Zealanders.' Ministry of Social Development, 2004. Available at: www.arc.govt.nz/......./social%20development%20theme%20paper.pdf (accessed on 29 November 2013).

Mambro, A. *JRD Tata Letter*. New Delhi: Rupa Publications, 2004.

Marcellus, I. O. 'Development Planning in Nigeria: Reflections on the National Economic Empowerment and Development Strategy (NEEDS) 2003–2007.' *Journal of Social Science*, 20, no. 3 (2009): 197–210.

McKay, A., and A. Sumner. *Economic growth, inequality and poverty reduction: does pro-poor growth matter?* (Issue 03). Institute for Development Studies, 2008. Available at: http://www.ids.ac.uk/F124720E-5056-8171-7B233B5D99E0CB4A (17 May 2012); http://dirp4.pids.gov.ph/webportal/CDN/PUBLICATIONS/pidsdps1402.pdf (accessed on 11 May 2016).

Melamed, C., R. Hartwig, and U. Grant,. 'Background Note.' In *Jobs, Growth And Poverty: What Do We Know, What Don't We Know, What Should We Know?* Overseas Development Institute, 2011. Available at: http://www.odi.org.uk/resources/details.asp?id=5752andtitle=jobs-growthpoverty-employment (accessed on 17 May 2012); http://dirp4.pids.gov.ph/webportal/CDN/PUBLICATIONS/pidsdps1402.pdf (accessed on 11 May 2016).

Melkote, S. R. *Communication for Development in the Third World, Theory and Practice*. New Delhi: SAGE, 1991.

Murphy, K., A. Shleifer, and R. W. Vishny. 'Industrialization and Big Push.' *Journal of Political Economy* 97, no. 5 (1989): 1003–1026.

Myrdal, G. *Asian Drama*. New York: Pantheon, 1968.

Nagziger, E. W. *Economic Development*. New York: Cambridge Press, 2006.

OECD. *Open Market Matter: The Benefits of Trade & Investment Liberalization*. Paris: OECD, 1998.

Parel, D. K. C. 'Growth and Redistribution: Is There "Trickle Down" Effect in Philippines?' Discussion Paper Series no. 2014–02, 2014. Available at: http://dirp4.pids.gov.ph/webportal/CDN/PUBLICATIONS/pidsdps1402.pdf (accessed on 11 May 2016).

Pattanaik, B. 'Better Deal for disabled.' *Yojana*, March 2000.

Planning Commission. 'Maharashtra Development Report.' Government of India, Academic Foundation, New Delhi, 2007.

Preet, R., and E. Hartrick., *Theories of Development Contents, Arguments, Alternatives.*, New York: The Guilford Press, 2009.

Rao, H. *Regional Disparities, Smaller States and Statehood for Telangana*. New Delhi: Academic Foundation, 2012.

Saifullah, A. K. M. 'NGOs Capacity in Development Management, Experience from Bangladesh.' Acta Universities Tamperesis, 848, Tampere University Press, Tampere, Finland, 2001. Available at: http://tampub.uta.fi/bitstream/handle/10024/67161/9 (accessed on 19 October 2013).

Schavan, A. 'The Educational Outlook in Germany: The Volkshochschulen as Partners.' *Adult Education and Development* 67 (1998). Available at: http://www.iiz-dvv.de/index.php?article_id=184 (accessed on 29 November 2013).

Sen, A. *Development as Freedom*. London: Oxford University Press, 1999.

Shanmugaratnam, N. 2001 'On the Meaning of Development: An Exploration of the Capability Approach', *Forum for Development Studies* 2: 263–88.

Tata, J. R. D. *J R D Tata Key Note*. New Delhi: Rupa Publications, 2004.

Todaro, M. P. *Economic Development*. Boston: Addison-Wesley, 1997.

———. *Economics for a Developing World*. London: Longman, 1977.

Todaro, M. P., and S. C. Smith. *Economic Development*. Third Edition. New Delhi: Dorling Kindersley (India) Private Ltd., 2012.

UNDP. 'Human Development Report.' United Nations Development Programme, Oxford University Press, Oxford, 2001.

United Nations. 'United System Task Team on the Post-2015, UN Development Agenda: Governance and Development.' United Nations. Available at: http://www.un.org/millennuimgoals/pdf/Think%20Pi (accessed on 13 October 2013).

Vaidya, C. 'Urban Issues, Reforms and Way Forward in India.' Working Paper No. 4/2009-DEA, Department of Economic Affairs, Ministry of Finance, Government of India, 2009. Available at: http://finmin.nic.in/workingpaper/urbanissues_reforms.pdf (accessed on 10 May 2016).

World Bank. 'World Development Report 1991.' World Bank, Oxford University Press, 1991.

———. 'World Development Report 2009'. Spatial Disparities and Development Policy, 2009. Available at: http://siteresources.worldbank.org/INTWDR2009/Resources/outline.pdf (accessed on 29 November 2013).

2 Basic Needs and Poverty

Concern with the condition of the poor, and expression such as 'basic needs' have existed for thousands of years.

—Overseas Development Institute (1978)

A higher level of basic needs satisfaction appears to lead to higher growth rate in future.

—Hicks (1979)

Even many decades after the end of the colonial rule, a large number of people living in the less developed and developing countries of the South Asia, Africa, Latin America and Caribbean nations are largely deprived of the basic needs. Basic needs are critically linked to survival issues like malnutrition, hunger, morbidities and mortalities. It is not a flight of fancy; the basic needs are the critical minimum welfare measures which a nation has to ensure to its population to enable them to lead a healthy life. Adequate access to basic needs contributes to the growth and development of the family, society and the nation. These are primary determinants of well-being and are capability enablers. Fulfilment of basic needs of its entire population is one of the fundamental duties of a nation. The International Labour Organization (ILO 1976), while defining development, insists on incorporating the basic needs strategy in the development plans for developing countries. First, a plan should include the minimum requirements of a family for private consumption: adequate food, shelter, clothing and the necessary household equipment such as furniture. Second, it would include essential services provided by and for the community such as safe drinking water, sanitation, public transport and health and education facilities. All development initiatives must begin with the endeavour of fulfilling the basic needs and elementary aspirations of the people. These include the provisions for (a) food, clothing and shelter—the most important basic needs; (b) water, electricity and communication—more important basic needs and (c) elementary education, primary health care and sanitation—important basic needs. Besides, the country must try to remove poverty and income inequalities existing in all their forms and dimensions.

In developing countries, poverty is commonly being seen as the deprivation and lack of access to basic minimum needs of a household. In other words, poverty-stricken households are those which lack capability to afford to fulfil their basic needs, because of which they suffer from malnutrition, become vulnerable to hunger death, remain illiterate and succumb to various kinds of morbidities, mortalities and various socioeconomic hardships. Poverty and basic needs are in some way or other synonymous and are deeply and positively interrelated.

After reading this chapter, you will be able to:

1. Explain the various components of basic minimum needs and various issues and challenges associated with this problem.
2. Define poverty and describe various dimensions, causes and remedies of poverty.
3. Discuss various issues and challenges of poverty.

SECTION I: BASIC NEEDS

One of the important goals of development is to empower people to earn and have access to basic needs for themselves and for their family members. In the less-developed countries, a large number of impoverished people are lacking basic requirements of life because of various reasons related to availability, accessibility and affordability. Deprivation of basic needs means denial of fundamental rights to an individual. The universally recognized basic needs of life—critical to the sustainable living—are food, clothing, shelter, safe drinking water, sanitation, energy for cooking and lighting, and road and surface connectivity for the access to the nearest city or town for the fulfilment of other exigencies, particularly access to education and health care and exploring the possibility of employment avenues. These basic requirements of life can be broadly categorized into four types as discussed next.

FOOD, CLOTHING AND SHELTER

Food is the primary need of life, and human survival is impossible without it. Food provides energy, and nutrition gives strength and vitality to life and also enhances human being's mental and physical capabilities. In other words, food is the fuel for survival of life, while nutrition is the lubricant for better life functioning. Food and nutritional security must be the key component of the basic needs policy and programme formulations in the political economy of developing countries.

The World Food Summit of 1996 defined that the food security exists 'when all people at all times have access to sufficient, safe, nutritious food to maintain a healthy and active life.' According to Maxwell and Wiebe (1998), a complete definition of food security needs to incorporate three dimensions of access to food: (a) sufficient food to meet every individual's needs, (b) individuals must have the ability to generate sufficient food without sacrificing their endowments and (c) societies must be able to protect individuals from shocks, i.e. loss of jobs, disasters, financial crisis and so on. However, even today, some countries still equate food security with food self-sufficiency, even though widespread evidence demonstrates that hunger can exist with abundant food supplies at regional, national and international levels (Stringer 2000). Empirical evidence demonstrated that while availability of food supplies is important, access to food by individuals is the greater constraint (Dreze and Sen 1989; Ravallion 1987; Sen 1981). Despite the overall success in food production at the global level and in every region except Africa, access to food and the lack of essential nutrients remain serious problems (Stringer 2000).

One of the illustrious example is the Kalahandi district of Odisha, India, which was experiencing hunger deaths for several years despite having sound food grain productivity in the district. This was happening largely because of income poverty and faulty targeting and leakages in the public distribution system. Many a times, distribution and accessibility rather than production and availability are critical factors behind food poverty and food insecurity. Poverty, large family size, lower production of food grain in dry land areas, poor employment opportunities, lower wage rate and income, lack of access to agricultural land, high food prices and ineffective public distribution system are a few among many responsible factors that have deprived many impoverished families their right to food. It is remarked that the availability and accessibility to food are affected by population growth, demographic trends, economic development, government policies, income levels, health, nutrition, gender, environmental degradation, natural disasters, refugees, migration, diseases and concentration of resource ownership (Stringer 2000). The low agricultural growth rate has led to rise in the prices of food grain such as rice, wheat, millet, *bazra* (pearl millet) and so on. Besides, because of the poor productivity of cash crops such as pulses and oil seeds, and allied products such as milk, fish, eggs and so on, many impoverished families were denied regular access to two square meals a day and other basic nutrition requirements. The serving of poor-quality food in the mid-day meal programmes in the schools and *anganwadi* (courtyard shelter) centres of India can be considered as basic needs anomalies or basic needs frauds, which is affecting the physical and mental growth of the children. The Food and Agriculture Organization (FAO) of the United Nations estimated that nearly 870 million out of the 7.1 billion people in the world, or one in eight, were suffering from chronic under nourishment in 2010–12. Almost all the hungry people—852 million—live in developing countries, representing 15% of the total population of developing countries (FAO 2012).

Next to food, many people lack purchasing power even to have bare minimum quantity of clothes to cover their body. It is quite humiliating that women in many impoverished families, belonging to tribal and rural areas of many less-developed nation states, manage with a couple of pieces of cloth to cover their bodies, and many of them even cover their bodies with a single piece of cloth. Lack of proper clothing deprives many children to attend school in spite of free primary education. Many impoverished families are found to manage with hand me down clothes donated by middle- and upper-class families. Proper clothing is also an obstruction for women to move out of the house and search for decent jobs. Want of clothing in general and lack of warm clothes during winters have led to many deaths among homeless and footpath dwellers. Lack of proper clothing is also an influencing factor for poor social mobility and social networking. Some studies have also revealed that the impoverished even in developed countries lack essential clothing, and about 5.5 million adults go without essential clothing in the United Kingdom (PSE 2013).

House/shelter is a basic human requirement for leading a safe, healthy and sustainable life. It is the duty and responsibility of a nation to provide healthy housing facilities to its citizens. Healthy houses are those houses which are well lit and ventilated, have space for cooking and bathing with toilet facilities and are of proper size, and the houses should not be too congested and be kept neat and clean in a hygienic condition. Moreover, it must have separate living arrangement for cattle, away from the residential compound.

Table 2.1 *Overcrowded Dwelling in Selected Countries*

Countries	**Household Living in Overcrowded Dwellings (%)**
Cambodia (2005)	35
Hungary (2001)	2
India (2001)	77
Romania (2002)	20
Senegal (2002)	72
United States (2005)	0

Source: World Bank, World Development Indicators, 2011.

In developing countries, particularly in Sub-Saharan Africa and South Asia, a large part of population living in rural areas does not have healthy houses. Besides in rural areas, the houses of impoverished families are made of mud, thatch and other low-quality materials, which are vulnerable to disaster, i.e. flood, cyclone and hailstorms. Many of them are single-room accommodations without kitchen, bathroom and proper ventilation. The overcrowded dwellings, a room shared by two or more persons, are high in percentage in developing countries of South Asia and Sub-Saharan Africa. In urban areas, many homeless poor migrant people, particularly the casual labourers, are found to be staying in temporary accommodations, overcrowded slums and make-shift sheds near railway stations, construction sites and filthy unoccupied spaces near sewerages and *nala*s (drains). According to UN-HABITAT (2010), more than 30% of world's population is either living in poor housing conditions in slums or homeless. The percentage share of urban people who live in poor housing conditions in Sub-Saharan Africa is about 61%, followed by South Asia (35%) and South Eastern Asia (31%; see Table 2.1).

The most disadvantaged are the low-income families: they are the agricultural labourers, casual labourers, people working in the informal sector, petty self-employed workers and impoverished women-headed households, who, because of lack of houses, are dwelling in informal shelters vulnerable to disasters. In many of Africa's cities and towns, less than 10% of the population lives in formal sector housing (Struyk and Gidding 2009). Adequate housing is a necessity for social and human well-being. It provides protection from bad weather, a place to nurture families, an asylum for good health and provisions study environment for children. It provides an enabling environment for the overall development of the family members, particularly children and antenatal and postnatal women. Lack of housing has deprived many children belonging to urban slums and other rural impoverished families their right to basic and primary schooling. Housing for all is the biggest challenge before the nation states of the Third-World countries. Even in a few developed countries, many families are deprived of adequate housing. Almost 18 million people, and roughly 14 million in the United Kingdom, cannot afford adequate housing conditions and one or more essential household goods respectively (PSE 2013). Healthy housing also seeks provisions for minimum household amenities such as utensils for cooking, bed and mattresses to sleep, water for drinking and bathing and toilet facilities for sanitary defecation.

DRINKING WATER AND SANITATION

Unsafe water and poor sanitation cause an estimated 80% of all diseases in the developing world (United Nations 2000). Access to safe drinking water and sanitation facilities influences the human health and quality of life. It checks mortality and morbidity, especially among children and pregnant and lactating women who are more vulnerable to infectious diseases arising out of unsafe drinking water and insanitation. In developing countries of Africa and Asia, many impoverished households are utterly devoid of these two basic needs. They have poor access to good-quality tap water and water-ensured sanitary latrines for defecations. The *Merlin Water, Sanitation and Hygiene Guide 2012* has envisaged that

> [a]lmost 900 million people still lack access to safe drinking water and 2.6 billion people still lack access to basic sanitation. Diarrhoeal disease takes the lives of 1.8 million people each year—most of them are children under five—with millions more left permanently debilitated. Over 40 billion work hours are lost in Africa due to the need to fetch drinking water.

WHO and UNICEF (2006) have stated that safe drinking water, sanitation and hygiene are fundamental to health, survival, growth and development; however, these basic necessities are still a luxury for many of the world's poor people.

Disparities in access to these two basic needs are distinctly observed between developed and developing countries, urban and rural areas and rich and impoverished households. Many rural and tribal people living in hills and deserts in South Asian countries are defecating in the open places and drawing water from the uncovered wells and open streams and using them for drinking and cooking purposes. It is a shame for a nation when its women, who are supposed to be most protected, defecate in open places even during day time. The incidences of kidnapping, molestation and rape are reported in the newspapers. These incidences take place while women are away from their houses for drawing water from a distance and defecting in open place in the dark. Nearly 653 million rural dwellers lack improved sources of drinking water (UNICEF and WHO 2012). The unprotected sources of drinking water include water drawn from dug wells, unprotected springs, water delivered by cart or tanker and water collected directly from rivers, lakes, ponds, irrigation channels and other surface sources (UNICEF and WHO 2012). Many impoverished families cannot afford even the low-cost toilets; and even if constructed through government schemes, many toilets in rural and urban slum areas are found in dilapidated conditions, not in hygienic condition or not even functioning. A good number of these toilets in rural areas are used for dumping cow dung cakes and paddy husk for cattle. Moreover, cleaning of toilets because of lack of piped water connectivity to the toilets is a fundamental problem, particularly in rural areas. It was even observed that in a few household, toilets are being constructed adjacent to the hand pumps which are contaminating the drinking water sources. It is ironic that every year, unsafe water, coupled with the lack of basic sanitation, kills at least 1.6 million children under the age of five years—more than eight times the number of people died in the Asian Tsunami of 2004 (WHO and UNICEF 2006) (Table 2.2).

As far as sanitation is concerned, globally 63% of the population use improved sanitation facilities, and still 15% of the population practise open defecation defined as defecation in fields, forests, bushes, bodies of water or other open spaces (UNICEF and WHO 2012). Most of the countries with low sanitation coverage are in Sub-Saharan Africa (see Table 2.3).

Table 2.2 *Improved Drinking Water Sources in Developed and Developing Regions, 2010*

Region	Coverage (%)
Oceania	54
Sub-Saharan Africa	61
Southeast Asia	88
Southern Asia	90
Northern Africa	92
Latin America and the Caribbean	94
Developing Regions	86
Developed Regions	99
World	89

Source: UNICEF and WHO (2012).

Table 2.3 *Improved Sanitation Facilities by Region, 2010*

Region	Use of Improved Sanitation Facilities (%)
Sub-Saharan Africa	30
Southern Asia	41
Oceania	55
Southeast Asia	69
Latin America and the Caribbean	80
Developing Regions	56
Developed Regions	95
World	63

Source: UNICEF and WHO (2012).

Ban Ki-moon (2010) has righty remarked that 'more people die from unsafe water than from all forms of violence, including war. These deaths are an [affront] to our common humanity, and undermine the efforts of many countries to achieve their development potential.' Use of unsafe drinking water and insanitation causes many types of diseases and morbidities, such as malaria, cholera, dysentery, hepatitis A, leptospirosis, typhoid, guinea worm disease, dengue, worm infection and so on, among the impoverished who are struggling for their livelihood both in rural as well as in urban areas. The worst victims of unsafe drinking water and unhygienic sanitation are the children and women belonging to impoverished families of urban slums and rural areas; they silently suffer, struggle and die.

ENERGY FOR COOKING AND LIGHTING

Safe and low-cost energy for cooking and lighting is a basic requirement for healthy living. Energy services are required for cooking, lights for reading and refrigeration to store medicines, vegetables and cooked food items. Besides, energy is required for transportation to promote rural–urban connectivity, for agricultural modernization through the use of mechanical implements and for industrialization. The effective functioning of service sectors, such as health, education, banking, insurance, electronic and information system and so on, also requires electricity and other forms of energy. All are essential for the growth and development of an economy. Use of traditional sources of energy for cooking such as firewood, paddy husk and cow dunk cake in rural areas and some part of the urban areas of developing countries has resulted in many health problems such as asthma, eye infection, tuberculosis and so on, particularly among women. Biomass fuel (BMF), which refers to burned plant or animal material, wood, charcoal, dung and crop residues, accounts for more than a half of domestic energy in most of developing countries, and for as much as 95% in lower income countries (Smith, Mehta and Maeusezahl-Feuz 2004). Around 2.4 billion people rely on BMF as their main source of domestic energy for cooking, heating and lighting (Smith et al. 2004). Energy usage in developing countries is associated with high levels of indoor air pollution, resulting in an increase in the incidence of respiratory infections, including pneumonia, tuberculosis, chronic obstructive pulmonary disease and asthma. Other effects of pollution are women giving birth to low-weight babies, premature deliveries, abortions, cataracts, cardiovascular diseases and all-cause mortality and morbidity in adults, women and children.

According to IEA (2004) report, the number of deaths from this kind of indoor air pollution is currently more each year than the number of deaths from malaria or tuberculosis. The report also estimates that by 2030, the number of premature deaths from household air pollution will be more than the number of deaths from HIV/AIDS, malaria or tuberculosis. The experts in the area are emphasizing upon alternative sources of energy such as solar energy and wind energy and *gobar* gas (bio gas produced from cattle dung) energy in rural areas. Besides, it is also suggested to use solar energy and energy generated from urban waste to supplement the energy requirement and easing out energy crisis, particularly for cooking and lighting in the urban areas. The development of a nation in a globalized world is judged in terms of its building up infrastructure to generate power and possession of energy for basic needs of cooking and lighting. Low-cost and safe energy is also required for the prevention of environmental pollution and sustainable development. World Energy Outlook focuses on two key dimensions—access to electricity and access to clean cooking facilities—as important indicators of energy development of nation states. Numerous studies have shown that access to energy services is positively linked to human development and that access to electricity is particularly important (World Energy Outlook 2012). Lack of access to clean and affordable energy is a major obstacle to economic growth and development.

It is estimated that out of 1.5 billion people who do not have access to electricity, 585 million are living in Sub-Saharan Africa and 404 million in India (Relich 2011) (Table 2.4).

> From an economic standpoint, energy poverty is a serious hindrance to growth of households and countries as a whole cannot develop economically if a significant portion of the population is living in energy poverty. Time that could be spent working must be spent gathering fuel for cooking and heating. This task usually falls on women, preventing them from pursuing economic opportunities like starting their own business. (Relich 2011)

Energy and development are intimately interconnected. The availability of energy accelerates agricultural and industrial development activities, and it also enhances the efficacy

Table 2.4 *Access to Electricity, 2009*

Country	Population (%)
Afghanistan	15.6
Bahrain	99.4
Brazil	98.3
Botswana	45.4
China	99.4
Ethiopia	17
India	66.3
Kenya	16.1
Romania	98.7
Singapore	100
Trinidad and Tobago	99
Zambia	18.8

Source: World Bank, World Development Indicators, 2011.

of the service sectors. In recent years, the success of e-Governance in rural areas depends on the availability of electricity and power connections. Creation of infrastructure for the construction of energy generation projects, such as thermal plants, hydroelectricity projects and so on, is a critical challenge before the resources crunch developing countries. Besides, conservation and judicious use of energy and curtailment of wastage are also challenges faced by these nations.

ROAD FOR TRANSPORT AND SURFACE COMMUNICATION

Provision of road connectivity network to rural and far-flung areas can reduce travelling time and enhance accessible opportunities for emergency care, delivery of services and access to higher education institutions largely situated in the cities and towns. Lack of fair-weather roads, particularly in rural areas, creates sundry problems for countryside people. It deprives many girl children of access to educational institutions situated far away from their village. It has prevented the movement of many critical patients to avail referral health care services largely available in towns and cities. A lot of infant and maternal deaths occurring in the rural areas could have been prevented, had there been good road connectivity between rural and urban areas. It is also one of the main reasons of low level of education among the rural youth in developing countries. Many man days are lost since people belonging to far-flung areas sit idle because of the poor road connectivity and transport facilities. It becomes difficult for them to walk to the distant places for jobs.

Benefits of increased road connectivity are as follows:

1. Increased accessibility to schools, colleges and health centres.
2. Accessibility to public safety services, i.e. police, fire, ambulance and so on.
3. Accessibility to national highways and regional street systems.

4. In rural areas, it helps in active walking during nights.
5. It helps in the growth of agriculture, industry and service sector.
6. It strengthens cultural institutions such as marriages, folk dances and dramas and other kinds of inter- and intra-village cultural activities, mostly undertaken during night hours.
7. Indirectly, it helps in poverty reduction by providing the rural youth better access to employment opportunities available in urban areas.
8. Better road and rail connectivity creates more day workers, who would go to the workplace in the morning and come back home in the evening.
9. It promotes rural–urban import and export of goods and services.
10. It promotes private sector investment in rural areas.

African Infrastructure Country Diagnostic (AICD 2009) noted that feeder roads are proposed as a potential way to take people out of poverty in rural areas. A study conducted in Sub-Saharan Africa found that the agricultural productivity is highly correlated with road connectivity and proximity to urban markets, and reducing transport costs and travel time to these areas would expand the feasible market size for these regions (Dorosh et al. 2010). The road connectivity is particularly essential for all-round development of rural areas. It is a key component of rural development; it promotes access to economic and social services, thereby generating increased agricultural productivity, non-agricultural employment as well as non-agricultural productivity, which in turn expands rural growth opportunities and real income through which poverty can be reduced (Mahapatra and Chandrasekhar 2009). The Rural Access Index (RAI) developed by the World Bank measures the number of rural people who live within two kilometres (typically equivalent to a walk of 20–25 minutes) of an all-season road as a proportion of the total rural population (Table 2.5). An 'all-season' road is a road that is motorable all year round by the prevailing means of rural transport. RAI is poor for Sub-Saharan African countries, followed by Middle East and North Africa where 30% and 34% of rural population, respectively, have

Table 2.5 *Rural Access Index of Selected Countries*

Country	RAI (%)
Angola	42 (2003)
Guinea	22 (2004)
Uganda	27 (2003)
Germany	89 (2003)
Netherlands	100 (1999)
India	61 (2001)
Nepal	17 (2003)
Afghanistan	22 (2003)
China	97 (2003)

Source: World Bank; http://databank.worldbank.org/data/download/catalog/rai-updated-model-basedscores5-20070305.xls (accessed date 17 November 2016).
Note: Figures in parentheses show years.

Figure 2.1 *Basic Needs Flag*

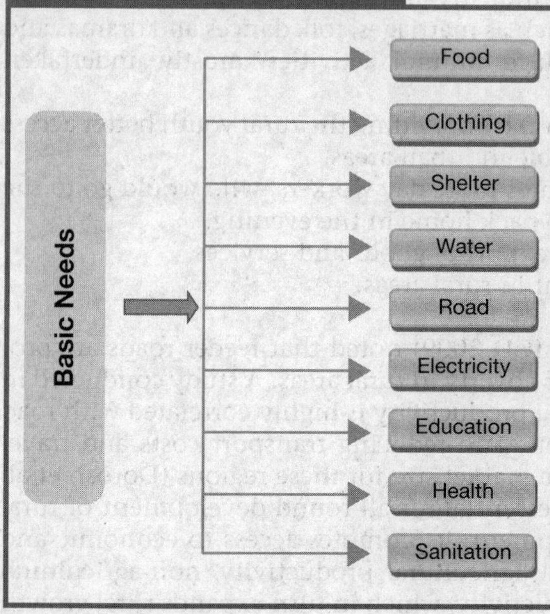

Source: Author.

access to nearest all-weather roads in terms of walking times (Roberts, Shyam and Rastogi 2006). In a nutshell, road connectivity will also enhance people-to-people contact and promote social, political, economic and cultural connectivity between rural and urban areas, and thus will hasten the process of modernization and globalization. The good road connectivity may be one of the concomitants of higher growth and economic development in China. The 'rural–urban continuum' through good road connectivity between rural and urban areas in Kerala is one of the vital factors of Kerala's high social development indicators such as high literacy rate and low maternal and infant mortality rates. One of the factors that have promoted modernization of agriculture in Punjab and Haryana in India is good rural road connectivity.

Needs such as *roti*, *kapda* and *makan* (food, clothing and shelter), *bijli, sadak* and *pani* (electricity, road and water) and *shiksha, swasthya* and *safai* (education, health and sanitation) are the nine basic needs or the needs for survival and well-being of an individual. The fair and sustainable access to all these needs will enable him or her to lead a decent livelihood. However, in many developing countries, a large number of people are devoid of these facilities and therefore their quality of life has been deeply affected. Basic needs are the fundamental needs, and therefore it is the fundamental right of an individual to have all of these. The basic needs flag given in Figure 2.1 suggests that the nine basic needs have to be important components of the flagship programme of a developing country.

SECTION II: POVERTY

Poverty, like beauty, lies in the eye of the beholder.

—Mollie Orshansky (1965)

Poverty is generally characterized by the inability of individuals, households or entire communities, to command sufficient resources to satisfy their basic needs.

—Woodlard and Klasen (2005)

Poverty is a manifold phenomenon and the world has never been free from poverty.

—Silungwe (1999)

The most popular term used in developing countries and the most common parameter used by the developed countries of the West for the categorization of countries as less developed is 'poverty'. Poverty is one of the unique and universally important features of an underdeveloped country. However, poverty of different degrees prevails both in developed as well as the underdeveloped countries. But, the problem of poverty is more vexing and perplexing in the underdeveloped countries than the developed countries. It can be rightly remarked that poverty is a universal phenomenon and the whole world is suffering from this problem in different degrees.

Like development, poverty is also a multidimensional concept, and its meaning and interpretation varies across the nation, and even from one individual to the other. Although it is the most frequently used term in the economics and social sciences literature, yet it is the most difficult term and has never been defined in a universally acceptable form. Non-inclusion and over inclusion in the below poverty line (BPL) family list are the common complaints of many households in the rural areas of developing countries. The provinces within a nation are seen to be fighting to include more percentage of households in the BPL list by conducting their own poverty line surveys to get additional grant from the national government. Fighting to be in the poverty is another bizarre dimension of poverty in the underdeveloped countries. Poverty fraud is also being frequently reported in the newspapers. Besides this, definitional problem, poverty syndrome is also vexed with the measurement problem. It is customarily observed that a definition given by one exponent is countered by the other and the measurement formulated by one individual or agency is being criticized by the other. There is less agreement about the measurement and definition of poverty at least in developing countries both at the macro and micro levels, although a nation fixes its own criteria of poverty measurement. The most common demarcation of the poverty line is that a household is said to be in poverty if it is incapable to fulfil the basic needs of life. In other words, a household is said to be in poverty if its earning is insufficient to meet the basic needs of the family.

To Rector (2011), the word 'poverty' suggests destitution—an inability to provide yourself or your family with reasonable shelter, nutrition, food and clothing. Joseph and Sumption (1979) viewed that 'a family is poor if it cannot afford to eat.' For some researchers, 'poverty' is a state of being unable to meet 'basic needs', which refers to physical (food, health care, education, shelter and so on) and non-physical (participation, identity and so on) requirements of a meaningful life (Streeten 1979). Ojha (1970) and Reutlingen and Selowsky (1976) defined the poor as a portion of the population that is unable to meet basic nutritional needs. Alcock (1997) has rightly pointed out that it is the issue of definition that lies at the heart of the task of understanding poverty. Different countries and even different provinces within the countries use different indicators for the measurement of poverty. It is remarked that poverty is a multidimensional phenomenon and is less amenable to simple solutions (Haughton and Khandker 2009). As per Chilosi (2010), we live in a very unequal world phased by poverty. The definition of poverty is nicely synthesized by the World Bank (2000) as 'poverty is pronounced deprivation in well-being.' The National Human Development Report 2001 of Government of India envisaged that 'poverty is a state of deprivation. In absolute terms, it reflects the inability of an individual to satisfy certain basic minimum needs for a sustained, healthy and a reasonably productive living' (Planning Commission of India 2002).

Poverty is 'helplessness' and 'destitution', and the worst happens when it pushes an individual to hunger death, destitution and begging. Therefore, Yunus (2006) said, 'poverty deserves only to be in the museums, where small children can see it in the future and be shocked how we allowed such an inhuman condition to exist for so many people for so long.' The capabilities to overcome poverty are ensured through access to physical and financial resources such as sustainable income from occupations, sustainable income from land and sustainable earning from the self-employment. UNDP (1998) termed it as constrained choices and unfulfilled capabilities, and to the World Bank (1990), it is the inability to attain a minimum standard of living. The South African Participatory Poverty Assessment envisaged that poverty was perceived to be when individuals and households were (a) alienated from the community; (b) facing food insecurity; (c) living in crowded homes; (d) using basic forms of energy; (e) having lack of adequately paid, secured jobs and (f) facing fragmentation of family. Politics in the name of poverty is popular in developing countries.[1] A household or a person is said to be in poverty, if it is incapable of affording the basic necessities of life such as (a) food, clothing and shelter, (b) safe drinking water and sanitation, (c) rudimentary requirements of primary health care and elementary education, (d) basic forms of energy for cooking and lighting and (e) a certain amount of basic household amenities such as bed, mattresses, utensils and other accessories of minimum sustainable living. It is very well remarked that many politicians, bureaucratic functionaries, NGO activists and so on have become rich in the name of poverty by implementing various poverty-eradication programmes and projects and launching campaign against poverty; however, poverty has not been eradicated from the earth. In other words, poverty is a curse as well as a blessing in disguise for some others in developing countries reeling under mal-governance.

MEASUREMENT OF POVERTY

Like defining poverty, the measurement of poverty is also an arduous task. The measurement of poverty is important for the reason that it helps us to know the answers to many questions on poverty such as

1. Who are the people in poverty?
2. Why are they below the poverty line?
3. What are the reasons of poverty?
4. What are the indicators to be used for the measurement of poverty?
5. How will it be removed?

It will provide input to the government and also to the various national and international organizations trying to formulate policies and programmes for the alleviation of poverty. It is well viewed that the way poverty is conceived and measured is important for framing policies to overcome it (Espindola and Nieves Rico 2010). Haughton and Khandker (2009) suggest four reasons to measure poverty:

1. To keep poor people on the agenda.
2. To be able to identify poor people, and so to be able to target appropriate incentives.

3. To monitor and evaluate project and policy interventions geared to poor people.
4. To evaluate the effectiveness of institutions whose goal is to help poor people.

Measures to control poverty could be initiated only when the people living below the poverty line are effectively identified and the factors responsible for poverty are effectively compiled. Different countries use 'poverty line' as a device for the measurement of poverty. The definition of 'poverty line' developed by Rowntree in 1901 was based on the income necessary to support a person at the subsistence level of food, shelter, clothing and other necessities. To Haughton and Khandker (2009), poverty line is a level of consumption (or income) needed for a household to escape poverty. The poverty line is defined typically as the minimum income level required for purchasing the socially determined essentials for living (Blackwood and Lynch 1994). Customarily, the poverty line is a hump or a landmark between the poor and non-poor, which a poor has to cross in order to become a non-poor. The measurement of poverty and fixation of poverty line from time to time are quite pertinent for developing countries. They will enable the governments of these countries to initiate appropriate measures to tackle poverty. Poverty is a versatile and dynamic concept; therefore, the measurement of poverty is not a one-time affair but a continuous process. The thermometer used to measure poverty has to be put into the mouth of a country, and the fever of poverty has to be checked and appropriate corrective measures have to be initiated by the country. Poverty has several dimensions and manifold indicators, and therefore measurement of poverty is the most controversial affair and a highly debatable topic at least in developing countries. Planning Commission of India had constituted several expert groups/task forces from time to time to review the methodology of measurement of poverty. These, to name a few, include Task Force under the chairmanship of Y. K. Alagh in 1977, the Expert Groups under the chairmanship of D. T. Lakdawala in 1989 and Suresh D. Tendulkar in 2005. According to Sen (1976), poverty measurement involves two problems: the identification of the poor and the aggregation of information about the poor.

Some of the commonly used methods of measurement of poverty are discussed below:

Head Count Index (HCI): It is the easiest and the most popular method of measurement of poverty. The poverty head count, which is popularly known as the head count ratio, measures the percentage of population that falls below the poverty line out of the total population in a country, a state, a province or an area for which the poverty is being calculated. As per Haughton and Khandker (2009), it measures the proportion of the population that is poor. The formula used for the calculation of HCI is

$$HCI = M/N,$$

where M = number of people living below the poverty line and N = total population.

Some of the lacunas of head count index are (i) it does not take into account the intensity of poverty. As poverty is a relative concept, using this method, it would not be possible to identify the severely affected people and moderately affected people by poverty; (ii) it does not indicate the extent of immersion of the poor; (iii) one of the important shortcomings of the HCI is that it implies that the income distribution of the poor population is homogeneous, which is not so. As population below the poverty line varies across and within the caste, gender and ethnic groups, cognizance of heterogeneity is essential in any formula used in the measurement of poverty; (iv) Finally, the HCI is unsatisfactory in that it violates the transfer principles, of which Dalton was of opinion that transfer from a richer to a poorer person should improve the measures of welfare (Blackwood and Lynch 1994; Haughton and Khandker 2009).

Income Gap Index (IGI): It is the aggregate short fall of average income of all the poor from the specified poverty line (Sen 1979). In other words, the income gap method measures the difference of the mean income of poor from the poverty line, and this difference or gap is called 'income gap'. According to Blackwood and Lynch (1994), the average income shortfall (I) measures the amount of money it would take to raise the income of the average poor person up to the poverty line. The formula used in the calculation of IGI is as follows:

$$\text{IGI} = \frac{\sum_{i-1}^{M} (z_{i-y_i})}{\text{Mz}},$$

where Mz = number of people living below the poverty line, Z_i = poverty line income and y_i = mean income of the poor.

The Sen Index (SI): Amartya Sen (1976) gave an index which takes into consideration the combined effects of the number of poor, the depth of their poverty and distribution of poverty within the group. In other words, it reflects the number of poor, the extent of their immersion and the distribution of income among the poor (Blackwood and Lynch 1994). SI takes the HCI, IGI and Gini coefficient into consideration in the calculation of poverty. The formula used in the calculation of SI is as follows:

$$\text{SI} = \text{H} \times [\text{I} + (1 - \text{I}) \times \text{G}]$$

where H = Head Count Ratio, G = Gini Coefficient and I = Income Gap Index.

SI of poverty is an increasing function of the head count ratio, the income shortfall as well as the Gini coefficient.

The other measures of poverty developed and propagated by the World Bank and UNDP are as follows:

1. **World Bank Global Poverty Measures:** The World Bank measures poverty in terms of expenditure of a dollar ($) in a day. The World Development Indictor, annually published by the World Bank, has interpreted poverty line in terms of one dollar a day and two dollars a day. As dollar is one of the international key currencies, measuring poverty in terms of dollar seems like an acceptable international standard of measuring poverty in various countries of the world.
2. **UNDP's Human Poverty Index (HPI):** HPI was developed by UNDP in 1997 (Human Development Report 1997) to promote human development rather than economic development focused on poverty. HPI is a composite index using three main indicators: (a) a short life, i.e. the percentage of people expected to die before the age of 40 years; (b) lack of basic education, i.e. percentage of adults in the country who are illiterate and (c) lack of access to public and private resources. The third indicator is made up by the simple average of three basic variables, i.e. the percentage of

population with access to health services, percentage of population with access to safe drinking water and the percentage of malnourished children under five.

Measurement of poverty and formulation of an appropriate and acceptable poverty line to the universal satisfaction, particularly in developing countries where poverty is more of a relative concept, are not easy tasks. However, developing countries have to measure poverty and draw a poverty line, and they must try to pull more and more number of poor living below the poverty line out of the poverty through the implementation of suitable poverty eradication programmes. It must not be a one-time affair but a continuous process. The path of measurement of poverty may be filled up with many contradictions; however, its measurement is critically essential to promote human well-being. Woolard and Leibbrandt (2006), from the experience of African countries, said that a poverty line will always be an imperfect construct, but for purposes of analysis, one frequently has to draw the line somewhere in order to go forward in understanding the nature of poverty (quoted in Ingrid Woolard 2002).

APPROACHES TO MEASUREMENTS OF POVERTY

Poverty is a multidimensional concept. Therefore, there is a need for multiple approaches to deal with the measurement of poverty. Ruggeri et al. (2003) provided different approaches to poverty measurement: Those are: (a) the monetary approach, (b) the capability approach, (c) the social exclusion approach and (d) the participatory approach.

The Monetary Approach: This is the most frequently used approach to measure the poverty. Here, the poverty is defined as the monetary income falling short of for an individual to attain a minimal standard of living. An individual with income falling below the poverty line is considered to be poor.

The Capability Approach: This approach was pioneered by Dr Amartya Sen, who considers that the income is only valuable in so far as it increases the capabilities of individuals, thereby permitting him/her to function in society. In capabilities approach, poverty is considered to be a deprivation in well-being. To Sen(1976), 'capabilities that a person has, that is, the substantive freedoms he or she enjoys to lead the kind of life he or she values.' Furthermore, to Sen (1981), capability is what people can 'do' and 'be', and this is what determines their living standards. Capabilities of earning income and having food, getting treatment and nutrition, sending child for education and living with less anxieties and vulnerability are the signs of a quality life (Mamun and Miah 2005).

The Social Exclusion Approach: It believes in the philosophy that poverty occurs among certain group of people who are unable to participate fully in the society in which they live. Because of social exclusion, the income capabilities or other characteristics of the poor become unacceptably distant from the other strata of population in the society. The social exclusion approach treats poverty as a social construct and has characteristics of groups rather than individuals. The exclusion of a certain group of population, e.g. SCs in India, in the labour market is one of the most powerful reasons for higher poverty among these groups of people.

The Participatory Approach: It takes into account the views regarding the poverty of the people who are in poverty. Here, people themselves decide what it means to be poor. People themselves, or through their representatives, determine the magnitude of poverty, and also jointly implement poverty eradication programmes which give preferential advantage to socio-economically backward and excluded sections of the society. The South African Participatory Poverty Assessment (1997) is an illustrious example of the participatory poverty measurement approach. The participatory approach to poverty is an appropriate way to deal with the poverty as the percentage of population living with poverty varies from one community to that of the other. Easterlin (2001) argued that people in industrialized countries are not happier, even after the considerable economic growth overtime.

DIMENSIONS OF POVERTY

Poverty, particularly in developing countries, has several dimensions, which are discussed as follows.

Income Dimension of Poverty: That is lack of adequate and subsistent income to fulfil basic needs. The income of an individual depends on the type of employment and the amount of wage rate. Therefore, the self-employed and daily-wage casual labours suffer more from income poverty as compared to their counterparts employed in the organized public and private sectors. Income poverty is more prevalent in the informal sector than the formal sector of the developing economies. Besides, in the rural areas, the poverty is more acute among the landless labourers as compared to the middle- and large-scale farmers both in dry land as well as in irrigated areas. The landless farm labourer possessing livestock such as mulching cows and buffalos are observed to be comparatively better off than the landless daily wage earners in terms of per capita income and poverty.

Hunger Dimension of Poverty: It includes living with food insecurity and the risk of dying of hunger. The landless people living in the dry land areas and the deserts face more hunger poverty than those living in the irrigated areas. For instance, in India, percentage of people suffering from hunger is more in the eastern part of India such as Bihar, West Bengal, Orissa, Chhattisgarh and Jharkhand as compared to the western Indian states such as Punjab and Haryana. Even the status of hunger varies across the district of a state, e.g. people living in the Kalahandi district of Odisha are more prone to hunger as compared to the residents of Puri district.

Nutrition Dimension of Poverty: It includes the risk of being malnourished and having access to the food lacking required micronutrients. Nutritional dimension is vital for the development of human resources of any country. The malnourished children are not only burden on their family but also on the society and the nation. Malnourishment among the adults affects the productivity of a nation, and thus influences economic growth rate and development. The FAO of the United Nations estimates that about 795 million people of the 7.3 billion people in the world, or one in nine, were suffering from chronic undernutrition in 2014–16, and almost 780 million of them live in developing countries. Poverty and malnutrition go hand in hand and constitute a vicious circle. The Rio Group has envisaged that 'adequate nutrition is one of the most basic human needs and it is therefore a central element in the construction of absolute poverty lines' (quoted in Woolard 2002).

Basic Needs Dimension of Poverty: Lack of access to healthy shelter, minimum clothing, safe drinking water, sanitation, primary health care services and elementary education depicts a condition of minimum needs poverty. In recent years, poverty line is determined in many countries on the basis of their people's access to basic minimum needs. African countries also used (Tanzania) basic needs poverty line for the identification of BPL families. The basic needs poverty line, developed by Samoa, includes food and non-food basic needs, and the non-food basic needs includes expenditure for housing/ shelter, essential transport and communications, school fees and other education-related costs, medical expenses and clothing (UNDP 2010).

Gender and Ethnicity Dimension of Poverty: The percentage of population living below the poverty line varies across the gender and various ethnic groups of people. Worldwide poverty is higher in the case of women-headed households, and percentage of women living in poverty is higher than men. According to UN Women, 'women bear a disproportionate burden of the world's poverty. According to some estimate, women represent 70% of the world's poor.'(See Note 1.) In a stratified society like India, percentage of SC and ST population living below the poverty line is higher as compared to the general caste population. Besides, poverty also varies across the various sub-caste groups among the SC and ST population. According to a World Bank sponsored study in India, on the HCI, poverty among the STs, SCs and Other groups of population in 2004–05 is 43.8%, 37.9% and 22.7% respectively.[2]

Human Poverty Dimension: Human dimension of poverty was emphasized by the UNDP in 1997. Human beings are the most important resources of a country, and the human capital is the supreme capital among all. The National Human Development Report 2001 brought out by the National Planning Commission (2002) had developed HPI which measures the state of the deprivation in the society. HPI had considered three types of deprivation with multiple indicators:

Health Deprivation. This deprivation includes life expectancy below 40, proportion of population without access to basic medical services, proportion of deliveries not receiving medical attention and proportion of children not immunized.

Education Deprivation. It includes illiteracy rate and children in the school-going age group not enrolled in schools.

Economic Deprivation. It comprises proportion of population living below the poverty line, proportion of population without access to sanitation, proportion of population living in *kutcha* houses (houses made of mud bricks, wood, hay stack and so on), proportion of population without access to safe drinking water and proportion of population without electricity.

Human poverty dimension is more relevant for developing countries where the deprivation of basic needs is very high in percentage as compared to developed countries.

The World Bank (2000) provided a powerful description of poverty which reflects various dimensions of poverty in the following words:

> Poverty is hunger. Poverty is lack of shelter. Poverty is being sick and not being able to see a doctor. Poverty is not being able to go to school and knowing how to read. Poverty is not having a job, is fear for the future, living one day at a time. Poverty is losing a child to illness brought about by unclean water. Poverty is powerlessness, lack of representation and freedom.

CAUSES OF POVERTY

The entire world is caught up with the universal problem of 'poverty'. Despite multi-prone attacks on poverty, it continues to exist in both the developed and developing world, more egregiously in the developing world. The quality of life of the people in developing countries is being deeply influenced by poverty. The causes of the poverty are many; however, some of the important causes of poverty in developing countries are over population, large family size, unequal distribution of agricultural land in rural areas, lower agricultural productivity, inequality in distribution of income and wealth, lower wage rate, casualization of work, informal economy, market imperfection, price rise and unemployment, to name a few. A few important causes of poverty are discussed below.

1. In rural areas, the poverty-stricken households are mainly the landless households irrespective of whichever caste and community group they belong to. Agriculture and land cultivation is the primary source of livelihood of the people belonging to rural areas of Asian and African countries. Green Revolution has reduced poverty in Punjab and Haryana, and it is the main factor responsible for lower poverty rate in in these two states. Moreover, development of agriculture has seen to be producing tickle down effect on the rural poverty, e.g. in Punjab and Haryana, many landless families sustainably manage their livelihood by working in the farming fields of large- and medium-scale farmers. Concentration of land in the hands of a few and poor implementation of land reform measures are causes of rural poverty in developing countries. Effective implementation of land reform measures in Kerala and redistribution of land in Himachal Pradesh have reduced poverty in these two states of India. Because of lack of irrigation facilities, higher percentage of land under black soil and many other supporting factors, people belonging to Eastern region of India are poorer compared to the Northern region of India.
2. The socio-religious factors such as law of inheritance, caste system, tradition and customs, restriction on women workforce participation and so on are also responsible factors of poverty in rural areas in many developing countries. For instance, as per traditions and customs, Brahmins in many states in India do not cultivate the land, even if they possess land, which affects their income. Similarly, women in many caste groups of Indian states are not allowed to move out of the home and village, and in case of many religiously orthodox families, they are under the veils

which restrict their workforce participation. Poor workforce participation of women is a responsible factor for rural poverty in many countries. In a macro context, ethnicity and geographical positioning of the nation states are also the causes of poverty. In India, poverty is more pervasive in its eastern part than the northern part, and it is more, in percentage, among the SCs and STs. The American Community Survey (2011) demonstrates a strong correlation between racial breakdowns and poverty, with Americans of colour living in statistically significantly higher levels of poverty than Whites or Asian–Americans.

3. Individual characteristics such as level of education, skill, intelligence, attitude to work, health and prejudices influence poverty. The poverty is found to be less in percentage among the people who possess skill, education and higher aptitude as compared to their unskilled and illiterate counterparts. Education in general and skill education in particular either formal or informal have a negative correlation with poverty of the household.
4. The dependency syndrome is a bizarre cause of poverty, and it is observed that in developing countries even the well-to-do adults are dependent on the pension of their retired parents. The high dependency ratio pushes a family into the vicious circle of poverty. In the case of women, who constitute nearly 50% of the population, except a few, a gigantic percentage is mostly dependent on the husband's income in developing countries. Gender deprivation is an important cause of poverty in developing countries.
5. A gigantic percentage of population in developing countries is dependent on agriculture, which is not modernized. The disguised unemployment is a sincere feature of agriculture in developing countries. The contribution of disguised unemployed to the family income is zero. However, the agriculture in these countries is subject to natural vagaries, i.e. flood, draught, cyclone and so on, which ramshackle their economic backbone and put them into the whirlwind of poverty. The continuous natural disasters and crop failures are seen to have pushed many small- and medium-scale farmers into the basket of poverty in many dry land and rain-fed areas. Farmers committing suicide, reported in the print and electronic media, is an illustrious example of agriculture-related poverty in India.
6. The poor structural transformation is one of the important causes of poverty in developing countries. The industrialization in many developing countries is very slow because of poor capital formation. At the same time, the service sector, because of labour intensive technological approach, is not being able to create more jobs in the market. Thus, the tortoise pace of industrial development and snail-pace scope of service sector job opportunities are not supportive factors of poverty reduction in developing countries.
7. People who are migrating from rural to urban areas to escape rural poverty are caught in urban poverty syndrome. A large percentage of them are working in the urban informal sector at lower wage and in unpredictable working conditions and are living in slums. Besides, many of them are found to be informally employed in the urban formal sector with lower wage rate, and are in contractual employment. They are roped in bizarre urban poverty. Urban informal sector is a vital cause of urban poverty.

8. The poverty eradication measures taken up by the governments of developing countries are in piecemeal and found to be less effective in providing a sustainable livelihood to the poor. They merely fulfil the consumption need of the poor and are totally incapable to enhance their saving and investment potential, which can only ensure them a sustainable livelihood.
9. The populist economic measures such as giving dearness allowances to the public sector employees on the basis of the price index. On the contrary, a vast majority working in the informal sector is deprived of such benefits. The income gap between the formal and informal sector workers put the onus of inflation on the informal sector workers. Unemployment, less employment, low wage rate and the scourge of inflation ramshackle the backbone of impoverished in developing countries. This elongates the inequality and makes the poverty more pervasive. The job dichotomy is the main cause of endurance of poverty in developing countries.
10. Informal economy in developing countries, which is characterized by exploitation of labour, no rule and regulation for wage rate, lower wage rate, no job security and so on, is a responsible factor for the endurance of poverty in both rural and urban areas of developing countries. In rural areas, informal workers are employed in agriculture and in urban areas informal workers are employed in construction work, as daily wagers in offices, self-employed in petty business activities such as vendors, hawkers, beetle shop owners, roadside food sellers, rickshaw pullers, petty tailors and so on. These workers are found either moderately or severely under poverty.
11. Last but not the least, poor governance is one of the main reasons of endurance of poverty in developing countries, despite many endeavours. Poverty persists, because of corruption and faulty targeting and leakages of the benefits aimed at uplifting the status of poor. Majority of the poor do not receive the benefits targeted towards them. This is rather grasped by the middlemen, i.e. corrupt contractors, businessmen, bureaucratic apparatus, politicians and so on.

In a nutshell, the political economy of a developing country does not sincerely want to end poverty, rather it likes to live in with it because it benefits the elites and has created a layer of crony capitalists in the country. For the vote bank politics also, politicians want to keep it alive in developing countries. They require poor to woo in the electioneering campaign. It is the politics of poverty that has endured poverty in developing countries.

MEASURES FOR THE ERADICATION OF POVERTY

The measures to arrest poverty in these countries would be many but a few noted among them are:

1. Government in developing countries with vexing poverty in the rural areas should honestly implement land reform measures and distribute land above

the ceiling of landholding to the poor and the landless. It was found that the access to even a small amount of land provides an important safety net, a source of self-employment and an alternative insurance to the economic contingencies of life (Dasgupta and Ray 1987; Deininger and Binswanger 1999). In Republic of Korea, land reforms did not only redistribute land to significantly reduce inequalities in landownership but also served as a powerful social policy, lessening poverty and increasing the educational level of the rural population (Kwon and Yi 2008). The distribution of land to the landless in Himachal Pradesh through government measures has resulted in reducing poverty in the state. On the other hand, the success of land reform measures, particularly the consolidation of land holding in the green revolution of belt of the Northern Indian state of Punjab, has not only enhanced agricultural productivity but also reduced poverty in the rural areas. The effective implementation of land reform measures in Kerala is another illustrious example, where land reform measures are considered to be one of the factors for the reduction of rural poverty. Ravallion and Chen (2007) provide evidence of important role of agricultural development in explaining poverty reduction in China while Hanmer and Nashchold (2000), through their empirical study, found that higher rates of agricultural labour productivity relation to the modern sector productivity are associated with lower poverty headcounts in Sub-Saharan Africa and South Asia.

2. Government needs to emphasize on inclusive agriculture for the reduction of rural poverty. Besides, it has to promote allied sector activities such as fisheries, poultry, dairy, horticulture, sericulture and so on in the dry land and hilly areas and among small and marginal farmers. In other words, holistic agricultural development is a sustainable way of dealing with the problem of poverty reduction in rural areas of the underdeveloped countries. Dairy, piggery, poultry, and horticulture and floriculture activities have been found to be providing sustainable income to many poverty-stricken households in rural areas. In Punjab and Haryana, dairy sector is seen to be providing sustainable income to the rural households and landless households and is providing support to the slow agricultural growth rate of these economies. Not the green revolution, but the holistic rainbow revolution can effectively deal with household poverty in developing countries.
3. Effective implementation of 'food for work' programme and cash transfer policy can effectively deal with poverty. In this case, the daily-wage earners in the rural areas are paid in terms of food as well in cash for working for the construction of schools, wells, roads, dispensaries and other useful rural infrastructure development. Effective implementation of these programmes through Village Development Committees and ward committees in the urban areas and electronic transfer of money directly to the account will keep a check on the corruption being done by the middleman. The concurrent monitoring of poverty eradication schemes will help keeping a check on governance deficiency-related poverty in developing countries.

China's Poverty Eradication Programme

The three important poverty alleviation programmes of China among others are:

1. *Subsidized loan for poor people.* These loans were given on project-to-project basis and are being implemented by the county or township-oriented enterprises. It is pertinent to mention here that these loans were not given directly to the beneficiaries.
2. *Launching food-for-work programme.* The scheme focused on the construction of infrastructure such as building of roads, drinking water scheme and irrigation projects.
3. *Agriculture tax reform/agriculture subsidies.* Under this the measure 'tax-for-fees' was introduced. Under this system, a unified agricultural tax replaced various fees based on the size of the cultivable land. The new Agriculture Policy of 2004 introduced agriculture subsidies by which farmers would receive direct payment for high-quality grains and soybeans and subsidies for the purchase of machinery.

Lauding the successful implementation of poverty eradication programme of China, the World Bank Group President said that China has lifted 600 million people out of poverty in the last 30 years.

Source: http://www.gerhard-k-heilig.com/pdf/Poverty_5.pdf (accessed on 15 June 2016).

Brazil's Poverty Eradication Programme

The two important programmes which successfully reduced poverty in Brazil are:

1. *Plano Brasil Sem Miséria (PBSM; Brazil without Extreme Poverty).* The programme aimed at a strategy to eradicate extreme poverty by 2014, targeting 15 million extremely poor Brazilian. PBSM had three main commitments: (a) to raise per capita household income of the target population; (b) to expand access to public goods and services and (c) to provide access to job and income opportunities through productive inclusion initiatives. This programme seeks to hone skills and expand opportunities for people living in extreme poverty by improving cash-transfer policies such as Programa Bolsa Familia (PBF; Family Allowance Programme), increasing access to social protection services and improving their quality and implementing productive inclusion initiatives aimed at different vulnerable groups such as informal urban workers, family farmers, collectors of recyclable material, homeless people, traditional communities and indigenous people.

> 2. *Programa Bolsa Familia*. It is a conditional cash transfer programme through which parents receive a fixed monthly stipend in exchange of sending their children to schools and complying with different health check-ups. This programme in its decade of implementation has managed to reduce poverty by half in Brazil (from 9.7% to 4.3%).
>
> Source: IPC-IG (2013).

4. The programme like 'employment guarantee' scheme for the poverty-stricken households with sustainable minimum wage rate will help the poor to overcome poverty. Many studies have found that the effective implementation of Mahatma Gandhi National Rural Employment Guarantee Act (MGNREGA) in India has enhanced household income, raised women's workforce participation and wage rate, and provided employment opportunities to the socio-economically backward sections of rural population to overcome household poverty.
5. Promotion of self-employment programmes to the unemployed youth and women through entrepreneurship and skill-development programmes will reduce poverty. It is universally clear that no government in developing countries can provide income-based regular employment to its population in the public sector, and therefore effective self-employment programme will enhance household income and enable them to fight against household poverty.
6. Governments in developing countries should strengthen non-farm employment programmes through opening up small-scale and cottage industries in rural areas. Rural industrialization in general and opening up small-scale and cottage industries in particular is a viable measure to overcome poverty in the countryside. China's rural industrialization through compulsory foreign direct investment (FDI) flow for rural industrialization is one of the factors for lower poverty in rural China. Governments of developing countries need to encourage entrepreneurs to invest in rural areas. Moreover, government itself, through financial investments, should initiate rural industrial corridors and further encourage the private sector and individual entrepreneurs to start activities in these corridors. Active rural industrial sector is required for the removal of rural poverty and unemployment.
7. There is a need to strengthening the public distribution system of food grains. The initiation of conditional cash-transfer programme to low-income families is a better option. Desired food stamp programme for the impoverished people living below the poverty line can be launched. Strengthening of pubic distribution in many states of India has enabled these states to overcome poverty. Kerala is one of the illustrious examples and even in recent years, streamlining of public distribution system in the hunger prone Kalahandi district of Odisha has successfully reduced the hunger deaths.
8. To strengthen the rule of law for effective implementation of poverty eradication programmes, there is a need for increased accountability and reduction of corruption at the grass-roots level. The poverty eradication programmes have failed to ameliorate the economic condition of the poor because of faulty implementation

and corruption at various levels. Strict implementation of the rule of law and rigorous punishment for the guilty middlemen and good governance will be helpful to eradicate poverty from the rural as well as urban areas.

9. To provide skill education and entrepreneurship training to youth and women and provide them with concessional credit facilities to start business, so that they do not rely on the government for employment. In other words, there is a need for creation of more job providers than job seekers. It is generally observed that the skilled self-employed people earn more than the unskilled wage earners. For instance, skilled and semi-skilled plumbers, carpenters, masons and others earn more than the contractual public sector unskilled workers. Poverty among the semi-skilled and skilled workers is lesser as compared to unskilled daily-wage earners.
10. To enhance employability of women and paying them salary and wages at par with their male counterparts. Household poverty will be better tackled only when both male and female in the poverty-stricken households become the earners. Everything remaining constant, families with single income earner will have less per capita income and more likely to be vulnerable to poverty in the long run. Special employment drive for women belonging to BPL families will arrest poverty among them. Promotion of women workforce participation in rural industrial sector has reduced poverty in rural China. The effective functioning of the women self-help groups (SHGs) in Bangladesh, also in many states of India, have reduced poverty in the family having members of SHGs than their counterparts without a membership of SHGs.
11. The labour reform is also an instrument to reduce poverty. It is required to strictly implement minimum wage rate for labour, and provide leisure and other benefits to the workers in the workplace. According to Lustig and McLeod (1997), minimum wages and poverty are inversely related, i.e. an increase in real minimum wages is accompanied by a fall in poverty; however, one cannot conclude that a rise in minimum wage is the most effective way to reduce poverty. The wage rate which falls below the sustainable level amidst continuous inflation would ultimately affect real income and could not solve the problem of poverty, at least, in developing countries. Daly and Cobb (1990) were of the view that

    > Labour is not just commodity like any other, to be priced by supply and demand. The price of other commodities can approach or become zero if necessary to clear the market. The wage of labour cannot fall below a subsistence minimum, which may be defined biologically in poor countries or by custom and social standards in wealthy countries.

12. To ensure effective implementation of social security measures, i.e. old age pension, widow pension, disability allowances and so on. Make the social benefits more inclusive and broad based. According to Barrientos (2010), the broader developmental role of social protection in developing countries involves three main functions: (a) to help protect basic levels of consumption among those in poverty or in danger of falling into poverty; (b) to facilitate investment in human and other productive assets which alone can provide escape routes from persistent and

intergenerational poverty and (c) to strengthen the agency of those in poverty so that they can overcome their predicament.

13. Ensure subsidized minimum need facilities such as housing, sanitation, drinking water facilities to the poor and impoverished. These facilities are the capabilities enablers to fight against poverty. The Minimum Needs Programme of India and China's provisioning of basic needs under the poverty eradication programme are illustrious examples of provisions to fight against poverty.
14. Poverty is pervasive in the rural areas and among the large size poor families. Effective implementation of rural development programmes and control of population will go a long way to eradicate poverty from rural areas. Population and poverty are interlinked. Poverty is more pervasive in developing countries because of high fertility. It endures despite poverty eradication measures because the poverty-stricken households are having large family size, and any kind of public support may fall short of meeting their basic requirements. Families with more dependent population, i.e. more number of children and aged, will be more prone to poverty.
15. The effective industrialization and proliferation of employment opportunities in the secondary and service sector will be helpful to pragmatically deal with the problem of poverty in developing economies. More dependence on the agriculture sector for livelihood and employment can create a vicious circle of low productivity and poverty. It is believed that industrialization can break this vicious circle by raising incomes to levels that raise saving and investment rates high enough to produce self-sustained growth (Kaldor 1966; Lewis 1954).
16. The proactive role of private and corporate sector cannot be ruled out in poverty reduction in developing countries. After the liberalization and globalization, private sector in many developing countries are creating a lot of employment; however, these are found to be grasped by the elite middle-class population. Pro-poor private sector will go a long way to reduce poverty in developing countries. According to Pfeffermann (2001), 'in almost all developing countries including China, private enterprises are the main source of new jobs' and 'countries with poor investment environments and lower level of private investment tend to experience mediocre-growth, hence more enduring poverty.'
17. Last but not the least, the political and bureaucratic will to fight against corruption will go a long way to reduce poverty in developing countries. Moreover, a holistic and multi-pronged attack is *sine qua non* in developing countries which are vexed with sundry problems ranging from resources crunch to corruption. Hayami and Godo (2005) proposed that an effective poverty reduction strategy would consists of (a) making production systems as labour intensive as possible for increasing labour employment and income; (b) increasing government expenditure on training and education to enhance the capacity of the poor to participate in the economy and (c) providing social safety nets for those who cannot be productive.

Poverty is a vexing and multidimensional problem, and therefore, there is no single magical solution to eradicate poverty. It must be attacked from different angles, i.e. economic, social, cultural, human and political and also at individual attitude levels.

ISSUES AND CHALLENGES OF POVERTY

Poverty is a surmountable issue in developing countries and most of these nations are struggling to eradicate poverty from their landscape. According to a recent statistics of United Nations, of the world's 6 billion people, 2.8 billion, almost half, live on less than $2 a day and 1.2 billion, one-fifth, live on less than $1 per day.[3] Poverty still poses a surmountable challenge to Sub-Saharan Africa and South Asia and it varies within the regions across the countries, and within country from one province to the other and from one community to the other community. As per the World Bank (2013) statistics, 69.9% and 66.7% of population are living below the poverty line at $2 day purchasing power parity in Sub-Saharan Africa and South Asia respectively (Table 2.6).

The worst challenge of poverty is hunger and malnutrition and deaths associated with these maladies. This happens in two situations: one, where there is a lack of availability of food grains, and second, when the people lack capability or affordability to buy despite the availability, this results in 'hunger' leading to human deaths. Hunger is a situation, where an individual is in need of food to sustain body for physical movement, functioning and being fit for activities, but does not get it. Hunger is defined as a condition in which people lack the basic food intake to provide them with the energy and nutrients for fully productive lives (Hunger Task Force 2003). The facts about hunger around the world run as stated in Table 2.7.

1. In the world, 1.02 billion people do not have enough to eat—more than the populations of the Unites States of America, Canada and the European Union.
2. About 25,000 people die of hunger or hunger-related causes every day.
3. In developing world alone, about 907 million people are hungry.
4. The number of undernourished people in the developing world is 820 million.
5. Worldwide hunger and malnutrition are still the number one risks to health.
6. More than 60% of chronically hungry people are women.
7. About 65% of hungry people live in seven countries, i.e. India, China, The Democratic Republic of Congo, Bangladesh, Indonesia, Pakistan and Ethiopia (Minchew 2010).

Table 2.6 *Status of Poverty in Various Regions of the World, 2010*

Region	$1.25 a Day Poverty (%)	Population (in Million)
East Asia & Pacific	16.8	1,884
Latin America and the Caribbean	8.2	550
South Asia	40.4	1,476
Sub-Saharan Africa	50.9	763
Total Developing Countries	28.8	4,673
Europe & Central Asia	0.04	473
Middle East & North Africa	0.04	305
Total		5,451

Source: http://www.worldhunger.org/articles/Learn/old/world%20hunger%20facts%202002_2012 version.htm (accessed on 19 December 2016).

Table 2.7 *Status of Hungry People in Various Regions of the World, 2010*

Region/Countries	Hungry People (in Millions)
Developed Countries	19
Near East/North Africa	37
Latin America and the Caribbean	53
Sub-Saharan African	239
Asia and the Pacific	578

Source: FAO (2010).

The hunger arises due to three factors: (a) neglecting agriculture relevant to very poor people by governments and international agencies; (b) the current worldwide economic crisis and (c) the significant increase in food prices in the past years which has been devastating for those with only a few dollars a day to spend (FAO, IFAD and WFP 2002). In developing countries, a host of factors are responsible for hunger, and important among them are low production of food grain, lack of proper distribution system, inflation in food prices, lack of purchasing power among the impoverished, large family size and landlessness, natural calamities, lack of infrastructure for raising food productivity and lower wage rate and scanty employment opportunities in rural areas. Poverty is the principal cause of hunger, and hunger is an outcome of dire poverty.

Vital fallout of poverty is malnutrition, which is causing deaths among the children and women in developing countries. According to Asian Development Bank (2001), 'malnutrition has long been recognized as a consequence of poverty. It is widely accepted that higher rates of malnutrition will be found areas with chronic widespread poverty.' UNICEF figure depicts that, one of every five children in Latin America or a total of more than 32 million children were living in extreme poverty in 2007 (UNICEF 2010). The State of World's Children 2005 affirms that 'children living in poverty experience deprivation of the material, spiritual and emotional resources needed to survive, develop and thrive, living them unable to enjoy their rights, achieve their full potential or participate as full and equal members of society' (UNICEF 2005). Besides malnutrition in children, malnutrition among women particularly the pregnant women has resulted in premature deliveries, giving birth to low birth weight babies and miscarriages. It is observed that the maternal morbidities relating to malnutrition is high among the women belonging to the poverty-stricken households in the South Asian countries. Malnutrition among the adults reduces their work capabilities, thus affecting the productivity which ultimately resulted in low income. If this situation continues for long then their families are in the danger of being trapped in the vicious circle of poverty.

Poverty has an adverse impact on access to basic needs like food, clothing and shelter. The poverty-stricken households in developing countries of Asia, Sub-Saharan Africa and Latin America are found to be residing in the low-quality houses. These houses are devoid of adequate rooms, proper ventilation and bathing and sanitation facilities. Because of lack of purchasing power, they are forced to manage with a bare minimum quantity of low-quality clothes. World Summit for Social Development, Copenhagen 1995, noted absolute poverty as a condition characterized by severe deprivation of basic human needs, including food, safe drinking water, sanitation, health, shelter, education and information. The basic minimum needs, i.e. food, clothing and shelter, are required for survival of human being. However, other essential human needs such as healthy housing, safe drinking water, sanitation and energy for cooking enhances human capabilities and enables them to increase their vigour and strength to remain healthy and earn for their families. It will contribute towards the economic growth and development of the nation.

Poverty affects the social development status of the household, as the poverty-stricken households are less capable to afford quality health care and education of their children. Higher is the rate of poverty of the household, lower is the health and education status. According to WHO, poverty creates ill-health because it forces people to live in environments that make them sick, without decent shelter, clean water or adequate sanitation.[4] In the poor developing countries of the world, diseases of poverty are dominated by malnutrition, diarrhoea, measles, respiratory infections and tuberculosis (Azubuike 2007). Poverty also affects the education of the impoverished families. Many of them are even unable to send their children to schools because of lack of school uniform and incapability to afford other bare minimum necessities for pursuing study, i.e. text books, pen, pencils, note books and so on.

Besides, even if admitted, children belonging to the poverty-stricken households drop out in the middle of their schooling because they are required to support their families. In the extreme poverty situation, it is the girl child who is at the edge to be dropped out from the school first. Household poverty and women education are positively correlated, and the poverty-stricken families are less likely to send their girl children to the school as compared to the families above poverty line. Children from low-income families often start schooling behind their peers who come from more affluent families, and the incidence, depth, duration and timing of poverty all influence a child's educational attainment (Ferguson 2007). Furthermore, children of poverty, in addition to the obvious problems they face, have very little access to reading material; they have fewer books in the home, inferior public libraries, inferior school libraries and inferior classroom libraries (Duke 2000; Neuman and Celano 2001). Poverty and the related disadvantages not only affect children's enrolment, attendance rate and dropout rates but also their academic achievement in terms of pass out rate, securing of higher academic grade and other educational outcomes.

Another stupendous challenge before the nation state is to mitigate and lessen the impact of poverty on children and elderly. Even in the economically developed countries of North America and Europe, children from poor families have been shown to have higher rates of asthma, increased risk of lead poisoning, high rates of lower respiratory tract infections, higher risk of physical abuse and neglect, poorer cognitive development, higher rates of conduct and behaviour disorders, high risk of drug abuse and are more likely to suffer the adverse consequences of low birth weight and have higher risks of obesity then children from the richer strata of society (Aber, Bennett and Conley 1997; Wood 2003). A report has noted that more than one in five of all US children live in poverty, and that percentage is substantially higher for some subgroups of the population (Coley and Baker 2013). A household in poverty is first to reduce its expenditure on the nutrition and education of the children. In many poverty-stricken families, children are forced to be engaged in the household and child-labour activities to repay family debts and earn to meet the day-to-day expenses of their families. Poverty has direct impact on the well-being of children in the poverty-stricken families.

Unlike children in poverty, the people in the old age both in developed and developing countries are in poverty. The condition of elderly poverty is widely observed in developing countries. Most of the impoverished elderly living in the rural areas of developing countries have inadequate old-age pension facility. Even if it is there, is too meagre to meet the old-age requirements, i.e. food, clothing, nutrition, medicine and so on. In case their children abandon them, their condition becomes precarious. Poverty found to have forced many of the elderly resorting to begging and putting up in the poorly maintained old age homes. Alcock (1997) asserted that old age is one of the three periods in the life cycle when there is an increased risk of poverty. According to Lloyd-Sherlock (2000), reduced capacity for income generation and growing risk of serious illness are likely to increase vulnerability of elders to fall into poverty, regardless of their original economic status. Putting children and elderly people in work is still prevalent in many poverty-stricken families of South Asian countries. In the households headed by poverty-ridden widows, old women are found to be engaged as the daily wage labours, domestic workers and in other menial activities to feed their children, provide them proper clothing, spend on their health care, and give them education and perform their marriages.

Women in general and women-headed households (widow/separated) are disproportionately affected by poverty both in developed as well as developing countries. According to United Nations (1996), six out of ten of the world's poorest people are women. The Platform for Action adopted at the Fourth World Conference on Women in Beijing in September, 1995, has noted that 'more than one billion people in the world today, the great majority of whom are women, live in unacceptable conditions of poverty, mostly in developing countries' (United Nations 1996). Poverty among women is high because most of them are engaged in household activities, a meagre percentage of them are owners of landed property, and their workforce participation in paid work is less. Moreover, they also get lower wage rate as compared to the male workforce. During disasters, women-headed households are more prone to be affected by poverty than male-headed households. Therefore, gender poverty is an issue as well as a challenge before the developing nations to overcome. One of the studies in the United States of America has shown that the female-headed households are disproportionately poor due to lower wages paid to women, few hours work in the households with one adult earner and few hours available to work due to care giving responsibilities (Rynell, 2008).

Besides women, people belonging to the socially backward communities and groups are also disproportionately affected by poverty. In India, poverty is more pervasive among the SCs and STs than the other Caste groups, particularly those residing in the countryside. Similarly, the percentages of population living below the poverty line in rural areas are higher than those living in urban areas. A report of the ETS Centre for Research on Human Capital and Education has noted that in the United States, percentage of poverty is substantially higher for some subgroups of the population (Coley and Baker 2013).

Poverty Situation in the United States of America

In 2011, 46.2 million Americans were in poverty, according to the official poverty rate. This represents 15% of the population, broken out as follows:

- 30.9 Million White, i.e. 12.8%
- 19.2 Million Non-Hispanic White, i.e. 9.8%
- 13.2 Million Hispanic (any race), i.e. 25.3%
- 10.9 Million Black, i.e. 27.6%
- 2 Million Asian, i.e. 12.3%

Source: Coley and Baker (2013).

SUMMARY

Provisions of basic needs and putting up endeavour to eradicate poverty are the fundamental duties and responsibilities of a nation. The developmental initiatives of developing countries must begin with the provision of basic needs to its people and relent when the poverty is totally eradicated. A country cannot claim to be developed if majority of its population is devoid of basic needs and is in severe poverty. However, many of the Asian, African and Latin American developing countries are still struggling to provide basic minimum needs to its people. These basic needs are not being sustainably met by many households in developing countries, largely because of poverty, inequality and unemployment. These three maladies, i.e. poverty, inequality and unemployment, are the primary factors responsible for the prevalence of hunger, malnutrition, homelessness, insanitation, illiteracy and ill health in developing countries. Poverty anywhere is a curse on the entire humanity. The United Nations document 'We the Peoples' has rightly envisaged that 'we are all impoverished if the poor are denied opportunity to make a living.' The World Bank has advocated that overcoming poverty is not just a matter of getting economic policies right, it is also about promoting social development, which empowers people by creating more inclusive, cohesive, resilient, and accountable institutions and societies.[5]

Keywords: basic needs, poverty, Sen's index, income poverty, head count ratio, rural access index, malnutrition.

REVIEW QUESTIONS

1. What is basic need? Explain important components of basic needs of developing countries.
2. Energy is an essential need of households and a basic determinant of development. Explain.
3. Why is communication and connectivity important for the development of developing countries? Explain.
4. What is poverty? Explain various methods of measurement of poverty.
5. What are the various causes of poverty? Explain how developing countries can overcome them.
6. Explain how safe drinking water and sanitation are important basic needs for the quality of life.
7. What are the different dimensions of poverty? Why is economic dimension of poverty more important than any other dimensions?
8. Write short notes on the following:
   (i) Head count ratio
   (ii) Basic needs paradigm
   (iii) Energy development nexus
   (iv) Sanitation and development
   (v) Sen's poverty index
   (vi) Rural Access Index
   (vii) Healthy housing

Pfeffermann, G. 'Poverty Re-education in Developing Country: The Role of Private Enterprises.' *Finance & Development, Quarterly magazine of the IMF* 38, no. 2 (2001): 42–45.

Planning Commission of India. 'National Human Development Report–2001.' Planning Commission of India, Government of India, 2002.

PSE. 'Impoverishment of the UK.' Economic and Social Research Council Grant RES-060-25-0052. 2013. Available at: http://www.poverty.ac.uk/system/files/attachments/The_Impoverishment_of_the_UK_PSE_UK_first_results_summary_report_March_28.pdf (accessed on 29 December 2013).

Ravallion, M. *Markets and Famines*. Oxford: Oxford University Press, 1987.

Ravallion, M., and S. Chen. 'Measuring Pro-poor Growth.' Policy Research Working Paper No. 2666, World Bank, Washington, DC, 2007.

Rector, R. 'A Poor Definition of Poverty.' 2011. Available at: www.heritage.org/research/commentary/2011/07/a-poor-definition-of-poverty (accessed on 25 September 2016).

Relich, N. 'Solving the Energy Poverty Problem.' 2011. Available at: http://leadenergy.org/2011/02/solving-the-energy-po (accessed on 18 February 2014).

Rentlinger, S., and M. Selowsky. *Malnutrition and Poverty*. Baltimore: John Hopkins Press, 1976.

Roberts, P., K. C. Shyam, and C. Rastogi. *Rural Access Index: A Key Development Indicator*. Washington DC: The World Bank, 2006.

Rynell, A. 'Causes of Poverty: Findings from Recent Research.' The Heartland Alliance Mid-America Institute of Poverty, 2008. Available at: http://www.woodsfund.org/site/files/735/69201/26070 (accessed on 5 November 2013).

Sen, A. 'Poverty: An Ordinal Approach to Measurement.' *Econometrica* 44, no. 2 (1976): 219–31.

———. 'Issues in the Measurement of Poverty.' *Scandinavian Journal of Economics* 81, no. 2 (1979): 285–307.

———. *Poverty and Famines: An Essay on Entitlement and Deprivation*. Oxford: Clarendon Press, 1981.

———. 'Poor, Relatively Speaking.' *Oxford Economic Papers* 35, (1983): 135–69.

Silungwe, S. M. 'Facing Poverty and Impoverishment: The Challenges and Some Churches' Response in South Africa.' A proposal for a Dissertation, Department of Rehabilitation Studies, University of Cape Town, South Africa, 1999.

Smith, K. R., S. Mehta, and M. Maeusezahl-Feuz. 'Indoor Air Pollution from Solid Fuel Use.' In *Comparative Quantification of Health Risks: Global and Regional Burden of Disease Attributable to Selected Major Risk Factors* edited by M. Fzzatti, A. D. Lopez, A. Rodgers, and C. J. L. Murray, 1435–93. Geneva: World Health Organization, 2004.

Streeten, Paul P. 'From growth to basic needs', *Finance and Development* 16, no. 3 (1979b): 28–31.

Stringer, R. 'Food Security in Developing Countries Policy.' Discussion Paper No. 0011, Centre for International Economic Studies, University of Adelaide, Australia, 2000.

Struyk, R., and S. Gidding. 'The Challenge of an Urban World: An Opportunity for US Foreign Assistance.' International Housing Coalition (IHC), Housing for All, Washington, 2009.

UNDP. *Human Development Report 1997*. New York: Oxford University Press.

———. *Progress against Poverty in Africa*. New York: UNDP, 1998.

———. SAMOA A Report on the estimation of basic needs poverty lines and the incidence and characteristics of hardship and poverty, Government of SAMOA Bureau of Statistics and UNDP Pacific Centre, 2010.

UN-HABITAT. 'State of World's Cities 2010–11.' Press Release, United Nations Human Settlement Programme, UN Habitat, Nairobi, 2010.

UNICEF, and WHO. 'Progress on Drinking Water and Sanitation, 2012 Update.' UNICEF and World Health Organization, 2012. Available at https://www.unicef.org/media/files/JMPreport2012.pdf (accessed on 25 November 2016).

———. 'The State of the World's Children 2005: Childhood Under Threat.' New York, December 2005.

———. 'Child Poverty: A Priority Challenge.' *Challenge* 10 (May 2010).

United Nations. *The Beijing Platform for Action*. New York: United Nations, 1996.

———. '56th Commission Human Rights, Item 7: The Right to Development.' United Nations, Geneva, 2000.

WHO, and UNICEF. 'Meeting the MDG Drinking Water and Sanitation Target.' The Urban and Rural Challenge of the Decade World Health Organization and United Nations Children's Fund, Geneva and New York, 2006.

Wood, D. 'Effect of Child and Family Poverty on Child Health in the United States.' *Pediatrics* 112 (2003): 707–11.

Woodlard, I., and S. Klasen. 'Determinants of Income Mobility and Household Poverty Dynamics in South Africa.' *Journal of Development Studies* 41, no. 5 (2005): 865–97.

World Bank. 'World Development Report 1990.' World Bank, Washington DC, 1990.

———. 'World Development Report 2013.' UN, Hunger and Word Poverty Sources, United Nations World Food Programme, Oxford UNice, 2013. Available at: www.poverty.com (accessed on 23 May 2013).

———. 'Entering the 21st Century (World Development Report 1999–2000).' World Bank, Washington DC, 2000.

Woolard, Ingrid. 'Poverty and Inequality in South Africa.' Working Paper Prepared for DFID, July 2002. Available at: http://www.sarpn.org/documents/e0000006/Poverty_Inequality_SA.pdf (accessed on 10 November 2015).

World Energy Outlook. 2012. Available at: http://www.worldenergyoutlook.org/resources/energydevelopment/mea... (accessed on 12 November 2013).

Yunus, M. 'The Nobel Peace Prize Laureate 2006.' Osolo, The Fipel Foundation, Stockholm, Sweden, 2006.

3 Education, Health and Human Development

A good education confers great indirect benefits on the ordinary workman. It stimulates his mental activity; it fosters in him a habit of more inquisitiveness; it makes him more intelligent; more ready; more trustworthy in his work; it raises the tone of his life in working hours and out of working hours, it is thus an important means towards production of material wealth.

—Marshall (1961)

Social development is one of the vital dimensions of development. It is one of the most critical and vital sectors required to be strengthened in developing countries for the abetment of economic growth and development. It is immensely important to fight against the multiple challenges of development in developing countries. Social development is a much wider concept and covers a lot of social issues such as education, health, marginalization, social exclusion, role of women and youth in the society, social networking and the social capital. All these are critical not only to the social development but also for the holistic development, taking into consideration all other dimensions of development such as economic, human, political, cultural and so on. Carlson (1999) was of the view that effective, efficient and equitable social performance of governments and societies is a necessary public policy ingredient for making a fundamental transition in the structure of society. The social backwardness, particularly in the areas of education and health, is one the important responsible factors of poverty, inequality and unemployment in developing countries. It is generally perceived that socially backward people and community groups are also economically backward, and are subject to low human development, political exclusion and cultural segregation.

The social developments that emphasize on the improvement of education and health status—raising literacy and adult literacy rate and reduction in mortality and morbidity—are essential for the enhancement of economic growth and development of a nation. Mukherjee and Banerjee (2009) were of the view that education and health are considered to be two vital sectors that can play a crucial role in determining the level of social development. Economic development of a nation depends on its educated, skilled and healthy manpower ensured through high-quality education and health care institutions and an efficient and effective education and health care delivery system. Therefore, social performance in education, health and social security has to be made sufficient and sustainable over the long term for countries to prepare their citizens for today and for the future (Carlson 1999).

After reading this chapter, you will be able to:

1. Explain the role of education in development, and various issues and challenges relating to development of education particularly in developing countries.
2. Describe the role of health in development, various components of health care development and issues and challenges associated with health care development of a nation particularly the developing nations.
3. Analyse the importance of human development, its components and measurements and various issues associated with human development.

SECTION I: EDUCATION AND DEVELOPMENT

Education is the backbone of any society. The human resources are considered as the supreme to all other resources, i.e. financial, physical and technological, because effective functioning of these resources depends on the efficiency of the human resources. Therefore, human resources development is critical to the enhancement of economic growth and development of developing countries. Education is one of the critical elements not only of human development but also of the socio-economic development. The role of education in development has been recognized ever since the days of Plato, who considered that education is indispensable to the economic health of good society.[1] Adam Smith in his illustrious book *The Wealth of Nations* identified human capital as skills, dexterity (physical, intellectual and psychological) and judgment essential for economic growth and development. It is believed since long that it is the human resources that ultimately determine the character and pace of economic and social development of a nation. Alfred Marshall (1961) affirmed that 'the most valuable of all capital is that invested in human beings.' Educational institutions are the creators of 'human resources' and are considered as the industry's energizing human capital formation. Early and continued investment in education seemed to be the crucial element in creating a satisfactory threshold level of human capital accumulation, which is critical for economic growth (Adams 2002). Coulombe, Tremblay and Marchand (2004) found that a country which achieves literacy scores 1% higher than the average will have an approximately 2% higher labour productivity and GDP than those countries which have lower test scores while using both quality and quantity of schooling to test the relationship between education and economic growth. According to Krueger and Lindahl (2000), each additional year of schooling appears to raise earnings by about 10% in the United States, although that rate of return to education varies overtime as well as across countries. The rapid development of South Korea was attributed to its focus on human development through increased access to and the improved quality of education (Lee 1977).

United Nations (2013) has defined human resources development as empowering people by fostering the contributory capacities that they can bring to the improvement of their own quality of life and that of their families, communities, enterprises and societies. The human capital emphasizes on the skills and attributes embodied in an individual and assumes that they can be enhanced through education, training and capacity building. Human capital formation is considered as a means of production into which additional investment can yield additional output. The resources allocated to the augmentation of human capital—whether 'financed' by an individual, a family, a firm or a government—are therefore viewed as investments (Mincer 1989). It has been remarked that

> [i]n the knowledge age, nothing counts more for economic success than the educational qualifications of the workforce... A country with a high percentage of tertiary education graduates is generally credited with greater innovative potential and a higher ability to move into high value added sectors of the economy, than a country featuring a lower share of graduates. (The Lisbon Council 2006)

Therefore, any expenditure on education needs to be considered as productive investment for the future development. No doubt, higher expenditure on education in general and the skill education in particular of their children pinches parents in their middle age, yet its outcome in the long run, particularly during their old age, is sweet and relaxing when the children are well settled. Rather being dependent on their old-age pension, they can rely on their children.

Two important theories relating to education and development are (a) Human Capital Theory and (b) Screening Theory. The Human Capital theory which was developed during 1950s in the United States and Europe considers human being as an important capital for a nation. The exponents of the theory were of the view that the human capital is equally important like that of physical and financial capital. It considers expenditure by a family on the education of its family members, especially children and adults, as an investment on human capital formation. The expenditure by the government of a nation state on education has to be considered as future investment. It enhances an individual's productivity capacity and increases productivity and economic growth of the nation respectively. Education is an enabler and capability builder, and therefore government as well as the family need to investment on education. The whole society gains out of the education. The research finding shows that in developing countries, the rate of return on investment in education was higher compared to the rate of return on other physical capital. Therefore, the proponents of human capital theory proposed that the government in both developed and developing countries need to investment on education.

On the other hand, Screening Theory believes that education is necessary but it is not a sufficient condition to enhance productivity of an individual. It considers that the educational qualifications such as degrees and diplomas are mainly used as screening mechanism by the institutions and industries while providing employment to the individual. However, the actual fruit of education to individual's output and productivity begins when they are put into the job, or in other words, in real work situation. According to their argument, specific skills required for a profession are gainfully acquired when somebody is on the job, rather than at school and educational institutions. Therefore, it is very difficult to predict the future performance and productivity of an individual on the basis of the educational qualifications. It is seen that in developing countries, because of lack of employment opportunities, the mechanical and chemical engineers are found to be working as clerks in the bank and insurance companies. Engineering education has little relevance in banking–clerical job. This is happening because of engineering degree boom. This is one among many examples where acquired degrees have least functional values in the job conditions. The proponents of screening theory were of the opinion that much of education in developing countries is irrelevant, and considered as 'degree boom'. Both the human capital theory and screening theory have their advantages and disadvantages.

However, they are important propositions as far as the role of education to development is concerned.

ROLE OF EDUCATION IN DEVELOPMENT

Education—formal, informal and non-formal—and the community and extension education programmes help to raise the national productivity and economic growth rate. It also promotes social, economic, political and human development of a nation. Education imparted to the farmers, either through farmers' training school or through extension education, raises agricultural productivity. Similarly, educated and skilled manpower employed in the industry and service sectors of a nation contributes towards national productivity and economic growth rate. If we take an example, it was the extension education and farmers' field training which enabled the farmers of Punjab to effectively implement Green Revolution during the late 1960s and early 1970s, even when the literacy rate of Punjab was less than 25%. Therefore, education is a powerful tool of development of agriculture, industry and services sector. Estimates by Chen and Feng (2000) suggest that the stock of higher-educated population has had a statistically significant, positive and robust relationship with economic growth across provinces of China in the 1980s and 1990s. Lim (1996) noted that education contributes to economic growth in six ways.

1. It improves generally the quality of the labour force by imparting skills and work knowledge.
2. It increases labour mobility, and therefore promotes the division of labour.
3. It enables new information to be absorbed faster, and unfamiliar inputs and new processes applied more effectively.
4. It improves management skills, which leads to a more efficient allocation of resources.
5. It removes many of the social and institutional barriers to economic growth.
6. It encourages entrepreneurship by promoting individual responsibility, organizational ability, risk-taking in moderation and planning over the long-term.

Educated, skilled and trained manpower make proper and effective use of all capitals, physical as well as financial. Physical capital like land and machinery, financial capital and other physical inputs are essential but not sufficient conditions to raise productivity unless these are handled by trained and skilled manpower. Other things remaining constant, two farmers given the same amount of physical capital but endowed with different level of knowledge and skill would operate in two different production functions and would likely to have two different levels of productivity. Japan is an illustrious example where the knowledgeable and skilled farmers have been crucial in raising their farm productivity, although the quality of land is not so good. One of the World Bank (1998) studies found that enrolment in primary education in 1960s enabled the countries like Hong Kong, Thailand, Singapore and South Korea to raise their economic growth by more than 50%. Lin (2004) found that higher education played a strong role in Taiwan's economic growth, i.e. 1% rise in higher education lead to 0.35% of rise in industrial output and 0.15% rise in agricultural output. Muktdair-Al-Mukit (2012) from his study in Bangladesh found that 1% increase in education expenditure will increase GDP per capita

Table 3.1 *Total Predicted Growth of Selected Countries*

Countries	**Predicted Growth (%)**
Hong Kong	86
Indonesia	79
Japan	58
South Korea	67
Malaysia	73
Taiwan	69
Singapore	75
Thailand	87

Source: Cypher and Dietz (2009).

by about 0.34% in the long run. Lim (1996) argued that the rapid growth of the Japanese and South Korean economies probably owed much to the mass literacy and numeracy achieved early in the process (Table 3.1).

The education in general and extension education in particular was instrumental in the successful implementation of green revolution and raising productivity by the farmers of Punjab, Haryana and Western Uttar Pradesh of India since 1970s, which was instrumental in tackling the problem of hunger in the country. It has been an established fact that investment in education and human capital formation are essential for economic growth and reduction of economic inequalities and poverty. Generally, the higher the level of education in general and vocational education in particular, the lesser will be the incidence of poverty. The vocational education impacts knowledge and skills which is supportive in earning a higher wages. Thus, it reduces the wage rate differential and income gap between the rich and poor.

Education has a direct effect on the various other social development indicators, i.e. health, women empowerment and upliftment of disadvantaged section of society. People with higher level of education are likely to live longer, experience better health outcomes and practice health-promoting behaviours such as refraining from smoking and obtaining timely health care check-ups and screening (Ross and Wu 1995). A National Health Interview Survey in the United States of America has revealed that more educated people are less likely to die or suffer from health problems, i.e. heart conditions, stroke, hypertension, high cholesterol, diabetes and asthma, primarily because they exercise more, smoke and drink less and use seat belts and preventive medicines more often (Cutler and Lleras-Muney 2006). One body of literature contends that education causes better health as it improves the technology of the health production function (Grossman [1972] 2000). Succinctly, the positive association between education and health is widely reported and accepted by health economists (Adams 2002). In the development discourse, it is found that higher the level of education of women in a society lower is the fertility rate.

Education is a powerful instrument of democratization and a great equalizer. It acts as a deterrent against social taboos, beliefs and values, and leads to social capital formation and modernization. Education can promote social networking in the society between the socially powerful and socially laggard, between the genders and across all sections of the society, irrespective of their caste, class, gender and ethnicity. Education is not only the most important means of empowering women with the knowledge, skills and self-confidence but also a great enabler, necessary for women to participate fully in the development process. It is education which can promote effective participatory development at the grass-roots level. Women's education is strongly associated with desirable social outcomes such as increased health and education status. It is well said that if you educate a man you educate an individual, but if you educate a woman you educate a family, a society and promote education status of the nation. Besides, education of the women and the socially disadvantaged sections of the society is also important for promoting social equity, doing away with marginalization and promoting development.

In most of the societies, education is widely seen as one of the fundamental instruments for creating equal opportunities. B. R. Ambedkar (1997), the architect of the Indian constitution and one of the prominent Dalit leaders, said,

> Coming as I do from the lowest order of the Hindu society. I know what the value of education is. The problem of raising the lower order is deemed to be economic. This is a great mistake. The problem of raising the lower order is not to feed them, and to make them serve the higher order, as is the ancient ideal of this country. The problem of lower order is to remove from them that inferiority complex, which has stunted their growth and made them slaves to others, to create in them the consciousness of the significance of their lives for themselves and for the country, of which they have been cruelly robbed by the existing social order. Nothing can achieve this except the spread of higher education. This in my opinion is the panacea of our social trouble.

However, in many developing and some developed countries, a persistent problem of unequal access to quality education exists, leading to both social and economic backwardness of the deprived sections. Sustained long-term inclusive growth calls for governments to ensure all segments of the population have equitable access to quality education. The early modernization theorists argued that education weakens traditional and ascriptive attachments based on characteristics such as gender, hereditary positive, ethnicity or religion in favour of achievement and merit (Levy 1966). Vocational and skill education among the differently abled person can enhance their chances of wage employment, and it can also empower them to undertake self-employment activities.

Educated people build up a strong democratic society, which is an essential requisite for socio-economic equality and development. Lipset (1959), in his classical work on modernization theory, argued that education promotes democratization. A higher level of education promotes popular participation, which in turn increases the potential for successful democracy (Dahlin 2005). Huntington (1991) argued that education was a key contributor to the 'Third Wave of Democratization' in the 1970s and 1980s. A strong correlation between education and political interest and participation and voting is documented among individuals in wealthy countries (Verba and Nie 1972; Wolfinger and Rosenstone 1980). It is generally seen that the less educated people are more gullible to allurement by the political parties to vote in their favour by accepting money and other kickbacks. Vote buying is more prevalent among the poor and less educated (Stokes 2005). Basu and King (2001) in a study in Bangladesh found out that educated women are three times more likely to participate in political meetings and speak up during the proceedings.

Education is a great harbinger of peace and stability. Education makes individuals considerate and enhances their ability to develop positive attitude towards solving contentious issues. In order to sensitize children and youth on peace education, governments of various countries have tried to integrate peace curriculum at various levels of education and in different subjects, either through independent or integrated way. Lack of education among the tribal population is one of the important factors for growing Naxalism in the tribal areas of Odisha, Jharkhand and Chhattisgarh. In South Asian countries that have lower adult literacy rate and gross enrolment ratio, education is one of the durable solutions to reduce tension among the community and among different countries in the region. According to UNESCO (2011) report, an increased primary school enrolment, from 77% to universal provision, reduced the likelihood of civil war by nearly 50%. Thyne (2006) found that an increased male enrolment from 30% to 81% in secondary schools seemed to reduce the probability of civil war by 67%. Evidences show that educational inequalities significantly heightened the risk of conflict (Fasih 2008). UNICEF (2000) believes that the pupils need to learn the skills of negotiation, problem solving, critical thinking and communications that enable them to resolve conflicts without resorting to violence. High-quality education systems can help prevent civil unrest and encourage conflict resolution, tolerance and reconciliation (Rose and Greeley 2006). UNESCO (1995) was of the view that higher-education institutions can contribute in many ways to education for peace, human rights and democracy by inculcating the curriculum of knowledge, values and skills relating to peace, human rights and justice. The higher education and research programme on peace education and conduction of seminars and conferences on peace and conflict would promote proper international understanding on contentious issues which promotes conflict between the countries.

Education is critical to the formulation of a knowledge society. Education in general, and tertiary and technical education in particular, is a fundamental capital to accelerate the process of growth and development in a knowledge society. In the globalized world, knowledge revolution marks a fundamental shift in human development. The pace of knowledge generation and adoption is so rapid in the world today that learning is no longer confined to formative years of youth but has become a lifelong process. Knowledge society is a fundamental requisite for development, as innovation and development have always been based on the creative and imaginative capacity of the human mind. Knowledge contributes to development in several ways: It makes an individual more productive, understanding and useful; helps in the development of scientific research, innovation and technological advancement; acts as a catalyst for social change and economic development; and promotes peace, social integrity and harmony. All of these are essential foundations of holistic development. Without adequate knowledge, all the other essential inputs—land, infrastructure, factories, capital, technology, administrative and social organization—cannot yield full result (Jacobs and Asokan 2003).

INDICATORS OF EDUCATION STATUS DEVELOPMENT

A few important indicators of educational development are discussed further.

1. One of the rudimentary determinants of education development status in a society is the literacy rate; however, nowadays the education development of a nation is measured in terms of adult literacy rate and its status on GER. The principal aim of the simple literacy and functional literacy is to empower a person in

Table 3.2 *Gross School Enrolment Ratio of a Few Countries*

Countries	Primary	Secondary	Tertiary
Bangladesh	114 (2011)	54 (2012)	13 (2012)
China	126 (2013)	92 (2013)	30 (2013)
India	114 (2012)	71 (2012)	25 (2013)
Pakistan	92 (2013)	38 (2013)	10 (2013)
Finland	100 (2013)	144 (2013)	92 (2013)
USA	98 (2013)	94 (2013)	89 (2013)

Source: World Development Indicators, World Bank 2015.
Note: Figures in parentheses show year.

three R's—reading, writing and arithmetic. According to UNESCO (2002), a person is functionally literate, if he or she is able to engage in all those activities in which literacy is required for effective functioning to continue to use reading, writing and calculation for own and the community's development (Table 3.2).

Although the world has achieved youth literacy rate (15–24 yr.) of 90%, the literacy rate in Sub-Saharan Africa and South Asia is still 72% and 79% respectively. Economically poor and less developed nations are poorly performing in education front and vice versa. However, in this globalized world, meaning of 'literacy' must go beyond the conventional way of defining it in terms of literacy and numeracy to include in it the life-skill, vocational and livelihood education. In many countries, prior learning and education acquired through informal system are being given credit for assessment in the issuance of certificate to the learner. According to Szirmai (2005), fundamental education is not limited to literacy alone; it also includes vocational skills, domestic skills, knowledge of hygiene, knowledge of the principles of science, artistic skills, an understanding of one's environment and the development of personnel skills and moral traits.

2. Expenditure on education directly affects the educational development of a nation, such as opening of new educational institutions, provision of educational infrastructure, appointment of teachers, training of teachers, provision of audio–visual materials and soft and hard infrastructure. According to Dahlin (2005), investment in education is very beneficial to the society, both at the micro as well as at the macro level, and affects the system both directly and indirectly. Besides educational development, expenditure on education also influences overall economic growth and development of a nation as educated and trained manpower have more productivity capability than their counterparts who are illiterate and lack skill education.

A study in Bangladesh has shown that public spending on education has a positive and significant impact on economic growth in the long run—a 1% increase in public expenditure in education contributes 0.34% increase in GDP per capita in the long run (Dewan 2012). Similarly, Kamara, Bousri and Nyende (2007) observed that public expenditure on education is positively correlated with economic growth in African countries. According to Musila and Belassi (2004), a 1% increase in average educational expenditure per worker led to about 0.04%

Table 3.3 *Government Expenditure on Education*

Countries	Expenditure (% of GDP)
Bhutan	5.6 (2013)
Brazil	6.3 (2012)
Finland	7.2 (2012)
India	3.9 (2012)
Pakistan	2.5 (2013)
United Kingdom	5.8 (2011)
United States	5.2 (2011)

Source: World Development Indicators, World Bank 2013.
Note: Figures in parentheses show year.

increase in output in the short-run and 0.6% output in the long-run. In his study on the impact of education expenditure on the economic growth of India, Tamang (2011) found that a 1% increase in physical capital per labour will lead to 0.28% increase in GDP per labour, and a 1% increase in government expenditure on education per labour will lead to 0.11% increase in GDP per labour. Education as an investment secures returns in the form of skilled manpower that is geared to the needs of development, both for accelerating economic development and for improving the quality of the society (Yogish 2006). Expenditure on education has a positive impact on the socio-economic development of developing countries (Table 3.3).

3. Educational technology is a vital indicator of educational development in the globalized world. E-classroom has become a popular teaching–learning method in this globalized world. The online learning and e-learning with the use of Internet and educating through MOOC (Massive Online Open Courses) are gaining popularity even in developing countries. Application of educational technology would enhance the productive capacity of the educational institutions. The Information and Communication Technology (ICT) can empower teachers and learners by facilitating communication and interaction, offering new modes of delivery and the overall transformation of teaching–learning pedagogy. Countries that have introduced ICT in education have done substantial advancement in the field of education and have gained substantially in economic terms. Countries that fail to recognize and act according to the trends in new content and new methodologies in education and training may find it very hard to compete in the global economy (Christensen 1997; Delannoy 2000). Jhurree (2005) suggests that technology in education offers following benefits to the educational community and the society:
   (i) It enhances learning environment for learners.
   (ii) It is a powerful tool to supplement teacher's instruction in the classroom.
   (iii) It is an administrative tool for teachers and administrators.
   (iv) It increases access to education and inclusive education in the school.
   (v) It is a communication platform.
   (vi) It is a passport to employment and to gaining competitive edge in the global economy.

Ironically, school and college going children and adults of developing countries, particularly from rural areas, are devoid of facilities of educational technology. As a result, these nations as a whole are unable to reap the benefits of educational technology. The digital divide between the rural and urban areas create educational disparities between both these set ups. It can be rightly said that educational development in the global world is conditioned and enriched by technological advancement.

4. Proper educational environment is another vital indicator of educational development. It will augment effective education in the educational institutions. Good environment in the educational institutions, i.e. availability of neat and clean classroom, audio–visual aids, toilet and safe drinking water facilities, communication facilities, playgrounds, yoga hall and so on, motivate parents to send their children to the school. This also develops children's affinity towards their school and classroom. Moreover, availability of good quality teachers is a motivational factor for the students to regularly attain classes and be attentive. This directly and indirectly helps to influence the enrolment and dropout rate in an educational institution. According to Korir and Kipkemboi (2014), the school as an institution of learning, which also acts as a second home for learners, has been found to have a strong relationship with students' academic performance, and school environments exert potent influence on students' academic performance. Many schools in developing countries lack minimum required infrastructure and manpower facilities such as minimum number of classrooms, boundary walls and a playground, for the students and minimum number of trained teachers for a functional school.

   The *Global Education Digest 2012* by UNESCO states that in South Asian countries, 13.54 million children are leaving school before completing primary education, and this number is equal to the primary school age population of Sri-Lanka, Iran, Bhutan and one-third of Afghanistan put together. In Sub-Saharan Africa, 42% of pupil leaving school early with one in six leaving before grade 2. Attraction towards private educational institutions by the parents as against public sector institutions in many developing countries is largely because of poor educational environment in the public sector educational institutions. The educational institutions should provide good ambiance to its pupil. Teacher absenteeism and poor teaching–learning environment discourage student's attendance and even lead to rise in dropout rate.

   Besides poor environment and infrastructure, developing countries are also featured with poor pupil–teacher ratio, i.e. most of the public schools in the rural areas in particular do not have required number of teachers as per the number of student enrolled. This demotivates students to attain school and also does not enthuse parents to send their children to schools. This also affects student's achievements.

5. Educational Development Index (EDI) is another important parameter being used to assess the educational development of the nation state. The Education for All Development Index, as envisaged in the Education for All Global Monitoring Report 2012 by UNESCO, is a composite index that provides a snapshot of overall progress of national education systems towards education for all. The components covered in the index were universal primary education, measured by net enrolment ratio; adult literacy, measured by literacy rate of population aged 15 and

Table 3.4 *Education for All Index of a Few Selected Countries, 2010*

Countries	EDI	Rank	Order
Japan	0.997	1	High
Sweden	0.996	2	High
Norway	0.995	3	High
USA	0.982	25	High
Botswana	0.912	80	Medium
Philippines	0.898	84	Medium
Bhutan	0.803	98	Medium
India	0.790	102	Low
Uganda	0.771	104	Low
Pakistan	0.658	113	Low

Source: Education for all Global Monitoring Report 2012, UNESCO.

above; gender parity and equality, measured by gender specific primary and secondary GER and the adult literacy; and the quality of education, measured by survival rate to grade 5 and learning outcomes. On the basis of calculated index, the countries were classified into three categories (Table 3.4).

(i) *The top categories*. Mostly countries of Europe and North America.
(ii) *The middle categories*. Mostly the countries of Arab World, Latin America and the Caribbean.
(iii) *The low categories*. Countries mostly belonging to Sub-Saharan Africa and South and West Asia.

In the index calculated for 120 countries, India ranks 102 in low categories while Japan occupies the first place.

In India, the EDI was calculated for different states of India by the National University of Educational Planning and Administration (NUEPA) by using 23 indicators in three broad categories, i.e. access, infrastructure and teacher. Outcome indicators are given in Table 3.5. The calculated values in Table 3.6 show that Delhi ranks 1, while Jharkhand ranks 35, the lowest among all the states of Indian Union.

6. Ranking of the educational institutions, particularly, the higher-education institutions, in the recent years are considered as an important barometer of the educational development of a nation. Educational institutions belonging to developing countries of Asia, Africa and Latin America do not fall within the rank of 100 educational institutions in the World. In the neoliberal and globalized world, to acquire an international rank by any institution of a country does not only reveal the standard but also gives a pride to the educational development of the nation. World's top 10 universities largely belong to the United States of America. Out of the 10 universities, 8 universities belong to the United States America and only two to the United Kingdom. The National Institute of Ranking Framework in the Indian Ranking 2016 has assigned rank 1 to Indian Institute of Technology Madras in the engineering category, Indian Institute of Management Bangalore in the

Table 3.5 *Indicators Used in Computing EDI in India, 2013–14*

Component	Indicators
Access	Density of schools per 10 sq. km
	Availability of schools per 1,000 child population
	Ratio of primary to upper primary schools/sections
Infrastructure	Percentage of schools with student–classroom ratio: primary>30 and upper primary>35
	Percentage of schools with 1:1 classroom–teacher ratio
	Percentage of schools with drinking water facility
	Percentage of schools with boys toilet
	Percentage of schools without girls toilets
	Percentage of schools required and have ramp
	Percentage of schools with kitchen shed (government and aided schools)
Teacher	Percentage of schools with female teachers (in schools with two and more teachers)
	Percentage of schools with pupil–teacher ratio: primary>30 and upper primary>35
	Percentage of single–teacher schools
	Teachers without professional qualification
Outcome	Average number of instructional days: upper primary
	Average number of instructional days
	Average working hours for teachers
	Percentage of change in enrolment in government schools over the previous year
	Gross enrolment ratio
	Participation of SC children—percentage of SC population (2001 census)—percentage of SC enrolment
	Participation of ST children—percentage of ST population (2001 census)—percentage of ST enrolment
	Participation of Muslim children—percentage of Muslim population (2001 census)—percentage of Muslim enrolment
	Ratio of girls to boys enrolment
	Dropout rate
	Transition rate for primary to upper-primary level

Source: http://schoolreportcards.in/media/m188.html (accessed on 20 May 2016).

Table 3.6 *Rank of Different States in EDI, 2012–13*

Top Five States			Lower Five States		
Rank	**States**	**EDI Score**	**Rank**	**States**	**EDI Score**
1	Lakshadweep	0.712	31	West Bengal	0.527
2	Puducherry	0.696	32	Assam	0.527
3	Tamil Nadu	0.683	33	Goa	0.520
4	Sikkim	0.672	34	Uttar Pradesh	0.508
5	Karnataka	0.661	35	Jharkhand	0.452

Source: http://schoolreportcards.in/media/m188.html (accessed on 20 May 2016).

Table 3.7 *Ranking of National Higher Education System*

Rank	Country	Score
1	United States	100.0
2	Sweden	83.6
3	Canada	82.8
4	Finland	82.0
5	Denmark	81.0
6	Switzerland	80.3
7	Norway	78.0
8	Australia	77.8
9	Netherlands	77.4
10	United Kingdom	76.8
41	Thailand	46.6
42	Iran	45.8
45	Turkey	44.4
48	India	34.4

Source: *Hindustan Times*, New Delhi, Wednesday, May 16, 2012, p. 8.

management category and Indian Institute of Science Bangalore in the university category (National Institute of Ranking Framework 2016) (Tables 3.7 and 3.8).

7. Quality education regulatory bodies are other important indicators of educational development. The effective and qualitative functioning of the education system and institutions in a country necessitate good and effective education regulatory bodies for fixing standard and monitoring of the educational system at various levels. In India, Central Board of Secondary Education (CBSE) regulates the secondary and higher secondary education system at the central and state level. University Grant Commission (UGC), All India Council for Technical Education (AICTE) and Medical Council of India (MCI) are other regulating bodies that regulate the higher education, technical education and medical education system in India. These bodies decide the qualification of teachers, give recognition to

Table 3.8 *World's 10 Most Prestigious Universities, 2016*

Universities	2016 Reputation Rank	Country
Harvard University	1	USA
Massachusetts Institute of Technology	2	USA
Stanford University	3	USA
University of Cambridge	4	UK
University of Oxford	5	UK
University of California, Berkley	6	USA
Princeton University	7	USA
Yale University	8	USA
Columbia University	9	USA
California Institute of Technology	10	USA

Source: https://www.timeshighereducation.com/world-university-rankings/worlds-most-prestigious-universities-world-reputation-rankings-2016-results (accessed on 17 June 2016).

educational programmes, curriculum, infrastructure requirement, staffs and their qualification, pay fixation and perform other related tasks. The function of the professional regulatory bodies is to provide a structure through which competence and commitment can be publicly affirmed and validated.[2] For the accreditation of the educational institutions, various regulatory bodies have also been created. Empowerment of these bodies and formulation of effective rules and regulations for the management of educational institutions are critical indicators of educational development. Developed countries have quality regulatory bodies as compared to the regulatory bodies of developing countries of Asia, Africa and Latin America. It is a fact that good regulation can enhance the higher-education sector's reputation.[3]

ISSUES AND CHALLENGES OF EDUCATIONAL DEVELOPMENT

In developing countries, educational development faces several challenges such as financing, educational disparities, quality of education, poor community participation and so on. A few and important challenges education is facing, particularly in developing countries, are discussed further in this section.

Inclusive Education: Making education system inclusive is a critical challenge before the countries vexed with the problems of socio-economic stratification. Inter- and intra-country as well as inter- and intra-community educational disparities and the gender disparities are widely observed across developing countries and even across various provinces within these countries. The access to educational facilities is distributed unequally (Coombs 1985). Exclusion on the basis of caste, sex, creed and ethnicity in South Asia is a common phenomenon. To Sayed (2009), children from the marginalized ethnicity, religion, tribe or class often experience educational exclusion due to negative social attitudes, sometimes over a long period of history. UNESCO (2012a) said while there has been rapid progress made in expanding access to formal basic education worldwide, significant inequalities between countries persist and national averages in many countries continue to mark striking inequalities in levels of educational attainment and outcomes. Educational disparities are also one of the responsible factors of socio-economic disparities in most of the developing nations. The Education for All Global Monitoring Report 2008 says, 'inclusion means encompassing the marginalized and disadvantaged, whether they be poor, belong to urban and rural slums, ethnic and linguistic minorities or the disabled; all age groups from early childhood education to adults.' The ultimate goal of inclusive education is to end all forms of discrimination and foster social equity.

The impoverished, largely belonging to socially backward section of the society, in general and rural areas in particular in the countries of South Asia and Sub-Saharan Africa are largely deprived of higher education in general and technical higher education in particular. According to UNESCO (2011), the traditional factors of marginalization in education, such as gender and urban–rural residence, continue to combine with income, language, minority status, HIV/AIDS, age (particularly in the case of young adolescent girls) and disability to create 'mutually reinforcing disadvantaged,' particularly so in low-income and conflict-affected countries. The challenge before these countries is to reduce the social exclusion and promote an inclusive society where elementary education is free and higher education is available and accessible to all at an affordable price. Not only 'education for all' but also motivating 'all for education' is a key challenge before the socio-economically backward countries of the world.

Quality of Education: Quality is a big issue, particularly in the higher education system of developing countries. Dakar Framework for Action 2000 affirmed that 'quality was 'at the heart of education'—a fundamental deterrent of enrolment, retention or achievement. Quality set out the desirable characteristic of learner (healthy, motivated students), processes (competent teachers using active pedagogies) content (relevant curricula) and systems (good governance and equitable resource allocation).' The poor quality of teacher, outdated course curriculum, poor-quality teaching–learning materials, lower number of

Table 3.9 *Pupil–Teacher Ratio of a Few Selected Countries*

Countries	Ratio
Bhutan	24 (2012)
Barbados	13 (2012)
Brazil	21 (2013)
China	17 (2013)
India	35 (2011)
Pakistan	43 (2013)
United Kingdom	18 (2012)
United States	14 (2012)

Source: World Development Indicators, World Bank 2015.
Note: Figures in parentheses show year.

teacher to pupil ratio and higher number of pupil to classroom ratio largely affect the quality of education in these countries. According to Ankomah et al. (2005), question regarding quality may be posed about any important aspect of the educational system—infrastructure, school building, administration, leadership, management, teacher training, educational materials, teaching, student achievement. All the elements associated with educational quality are interrelated and a serious defect in one element is likely to have implications for quality in others (Dare 2005). Data on education, given in the world development indicator, suggest that the teacher–pupil ratio in primary schools of South Asian and Sub-Saharan countries is low as compared to the developed countries of Europe and North America (see Table 3.9). Improving educational quality in terms of its difficulty and differentiation index is an important challenge before developing countries.

Vocational and Skill Education: One of the reasons for the prevalence of unemployment and underemployment among the educated youth is the 'degree boom' and poor relevance of these degrees in the job market. The general higher-education degree holders have poor takers in the national and global market. Besides, because of being highly educated, they seem misfit and also consider themselves irrelevant in the rural agriculture sector; therefore, if they do not get any employment, they prefer to remain in disguised unemployed. In order to overcome rural disguised unemployment and urban underemployment, developing countries have to impart relevant and better quality skill and vocational education to the youth. In many developing countries, because of high population growth rate, youth constitutes a sizable proportion of the total population. Imparting proper skill education to them will not only make them useful to the home country but also raise their demand in the international market. Proper accreditation of the vocational institutions and relevant curriculum framework is a challenge before developing countries. Imparting need-based high-quality skill and vocational education is a challenge for developing countries. Skill education has potential to eradicate poverty and inequality, and can release pressure on wage employment. OECD ([Organization for Economic Co-operation and Development] 2008) has remarked that vocational education and training has a key economic function in upskilling and integrating young people into the labour market and in providing high quality technical skills.

Financing of Education: Financing of education is a big challenge before developing countries. Expenditure on education must be treated as future investment. It should be provided as a public good with no price or minimum affordable price so that poorest of the poor can have access to education. However, with the globalization, education at all levels—primary, secondary and tertiary—has become a million dollar business. It has attracted private investment in most of developing countries in recent decades and created disparities. The public investment at the secondary and tertiary sector is shrinking. UNESCO (2002) has calculated that there is a shortfall of 5.6 billion US dollar to meet the external finance requirement to achieve the goal of Education for All by 2015.

The challenge before developing countries is to raise the public expenditure on education for the universalization of primary education and rationalization of the pricing of the private education in the tertiary education system, so that it can be affordable to the poor and middle-class people. One of the other challenges is investment in the skill education at the tertiary education level for enhancing employability of youth. Financing of education must be innovative and flexible. The spending on education must be towards promoting equity and targeted towards the benefit of the most vulnerable and disadvantaged section of the population. The free skill education at the tertiary and even in the primary and secondary schools will enable the youth to earn a sustainable livelihood in future. Higher capitation fee charged by technical education institutions run by the private bodies has debarred many impoverished youth to pursue skill education. Education needs to be subsidized for the socially backward sections of population. Educational loan facilities with lower interest rate are critical to meet the educational expenses particularly for pursuing higher and technical education at home and abroad.

Open and Distance Education: Universalization and massification of secondary and higher education is a big challenge in the developing country. Open and distance education in recent years has become an important means to raise GER in both developed and developing countries. In India, both the secondary and tertiary education is offered in open and distance mode. Certainly, with the limited resources and relatively dense population in developing countries are obstacles for the availability of on-campus education for the whole population; therefore, distance education is relatively a better solution to overcome this problem (Khan, Khan and Al-Abaji 2001). For the developing world, open and distance learning (ODL) is a promising and practical strategy to address the challenge of widening access, thus increasing participation in higher education (Pityana 2009). Distance education reaches a broader students audience and better addresses students' needs, saves money and more importantly uses the principles of modern learning pedagogy (Fitzpatrick 2001). It uses open learning as education patterns, approaches and strategies that permit people to learn with no barriers in respect of time, space, sex, age and previous educational background—no entry qualification, no age limit, no biases against any gender, race, tribe, state of origin, quota system and so on. (Alaezi 2005).

According to Juler (1990), distance education means creating educational communities in which teachers, students and others are linked in discourse wherever they may be, through networks appropriate to their circumstances. Globalization and ICT revolution has further invigorated the pace and use of distance education in the developing world. Zondiros (2008) has remarked that online and distance education can be seen as products and producers of globalization. In the Unites States America, 94% of all colleges and universities are either currently (63%) or planning to be (31%) engaged in distance and distributed learning (Twigg 2001). Enrolment in Indira Gandhi National Open University (IGNOU), the first Central Open University in India, has gone up from a meagre 4,857 in 1987 to 2.6 million in 2011. The open and distance learning system provides opportunities to the impoverished, school and college dropouts and scope of pursuing higher education to the pupil of rural, hilly and other inaccessible areas. It aims at democratization of higher education. Therefore, there is a need for strengthening open and distance education. The quality, cost effective, online and e-distance education system must be evolved which can easily reach to the unreached.

Education for Sustainable Development: Education is one of the best means to promote awareness, knowledge, skill and practices on various important aspects of sustainable development at the school, college and community level. The sustainable development needs to be the part of the educational curriculum both at the school and higher-education level and also in the non-formal and extension education system imparted at the community level. Another dimension of the education for sustainable development is that the education system of the country needs to be such that it will be helpful in providing sustainable livelihood to its people. The United Nations General Assembly, in its 57th meeting in December 2002, declared the decade 2005–14 as the UN Decade of Education for Sustainable Development. The vision of Education of Sustainable Development is of a World[4]:

(i) Where everyone has the opportunity to benefit from quality education and learn the values, behaviour and lifestyles required for a sustainable future and for positive societal transformation;
(ii) It is for everyone, at all stages of life and in all possible learning contexts;
(iii) It engages multiple sectors and stakeholders including media agencies and private sector;
(iv) It utilizes all forms and methods of public awareness raising, education and training to promote broad understanding of sustainable development;
(v) It address, all three pillars of sustainable development i.e. society, environment and economy; and
(vi) It enables all individuals to fully develop the knowledge, perspectives, values and skills necessary to take part in decision to improve the quality of life.

UNESCO (2005a) urges that education should 'encourage changes in behaviour that will create a more sustainable future in terms of environmental integrity, economic viability and a just society for present and future generations.'

One of the vital challenges of education in developing countries is to make sustainable livelihood education a part of the formal and non-formal education system. In other words, provide sustainable livelihood education to the people. Livelihood education which provides knowledge, skills and abilities specifically intended to have a direct transference of an occupation or vocation and activities of daily living.[5] A livelihood comprises the capabilities, assets and activities required for means of living. A livelihood is sustainable which can cope up with and recover from stress and shocks, maintain or enhance its capabilities and assets, and provide sustainable livelihood opportunities for the next generation (Chambers and Conway 1992). In the culturally and religiously oriented societies, the skill and life-skill education are the powerful means to provide sustainable livelihood to its population. The avocation-oriented education, such as hair cutting, welding, washing and stitching of clothes, chanting of mantras, fish processing, for example, performed by the barbers, blacksmiths, washermen and tailors, Brahmins and fishermen mostly in rural areas in India per se, be given in the school and also through non-formal and extension education system so that children belonging to these communities will develop professionalism and earn their livelihood in future. The life-skill education of yoga, physical education, dance, drama, singing, music and so on, both through formal as well as non-formal education system, will go a long way to raise capacity building of the grass-roots people.

Governance in Education: Good governance in education is essential for increasing the efficiency, quality and output of the education system in developing countries. According to Lewis and Pettersson (2009), good governance in education system promotes effective delivery of education services. Also, appropriate standards, incentives, information and accountability, which induce high performance, are critical. Good governance intends to (a) improve the quality of education; (b) enhance efficiency and functioning of the educational system, including educational administration; (c) bring accountability and transparency in the educational administration and in educational institutions; (d) prevent corruption in education system; (e) promote equity and remove discrimination in the access to education at all levels; (f) make teacher and teaching institutions accountable to the students and students should not suffer at any cost for the mal-governance of the educational institution; (g) check wastage, i.e. teacher absenteeism, student absenteeism rate, dropout rate, pass out rate and so on and (h) finally improve the performance of the students, teachers and educational institutions. Good governance in education desires that

(i) state creates conducive, transparent and accountable environment to build the capability of the educational system in totality;
(ii) there should be market to provide affordable high-quality education to all sections of the society under the corporate social responsibility; and
(iii) the civil society should facilitate mobilization of people's participation in educational development.

Nowadays, e-Governance is in vogue to bring transparency, improve efficiency and effectiveness in the education system. It has reduced the cost and corruption in education. The hi-tech classroom and use of Internet, apps, mobile phone massaging, educational television, radio and community radio has made teaching–learning process easier, interesting and cost effective. To Alhomod and Shafi (2012), e-Governance has enabled universities to expand their current geographical reach, interact with perspective students all around the world and establish themselves as global education providers.

Education in Globalized Era: Globalization has become the order of the day. Most of developing countries have become the beneficiaries as well as victims of globalization policies promoted by the West. Education, which is a basic requirement of livelihood, has not been spared from the influence of globalization. According to Bloom (2006), globalization is increasing the pressure on education systems in both rich and poor countries. The migration of technical manpower from the developing to the developed countries and from the one developing country to another has called for changing educational system and strategies of developing countries. Now they are focusing on the generation of technical manpower to meet their own requirements as well as the requirement of various other countries. Globalization has affected education in many ways and few of them are mentioned here.

(i) With globalization, there is an expansion of science and technical education across the globe.
(ii) There is a trend in reduced public expenditure on education and rise of private investment in education particularly on secondary, tertiary and technical education. WTO (1998) has remarked that with the rapid changes in higher education, 'education exists as a private consumption item with a price freely determined by the providing institution.' According to a more powerful version of GATS (General Agreement on Trade in Services), education services will be progressively commercialized, privatized and capitalized.

(iii) There is a growing emphasis on tertiary education with particular focus on skill and vocation education.
(iv) The notion of education is compared internationally, and therefore, there is growing emphasis on quality education.
(v) Explosion in the use of ICT at all level of education.
(vi) Globalization had affected the education policy, planning and investment pattern on education particularly of the developing world.
(vii) With globalization, there is a growing interest among the students from developing countries to pursue higher education in the developed countries and from educationally backward developing countries to educationally more advance developing countries.
(viii) Globalization has elongated the gap of income disparities between the skilled and unskilled educated worker; between those who have received education in rural and urban educational institutions and the educational achievement between the public and private education institutions.
(ix) Developing countries are allowing foreign universities to open their branches in developing countries. It is remarked that higher education institutions have been both the agents and objects of globalization (Scott 1998).
(x) There is mushrooming growth of private universities in developing countries, which are largely offering higher and technical education.

The challenge of education is to meet the exigencies of manpower requirement of various sectors of development, i.e. agriculture, manufacturing and services. The four strategic and long-term questions that privatization, liberalization and globalization poses to the higher education system, particularly in developing countries, are (a) commodification—the use of knowledge as a purchasable and saleable good; (b) alternative providers—the use of e-learning and ICT in education; (c) massification—use of conventional and distance education system for massification of higher education and (d) universalization—universalization of primary, secondary and tertiary education in rural and urban areas and among all section of society irrespective of caste, sex, creed, colour and ethnicity. The challenges of globalization before developing countries having 'demographic dividends' are to universalize primary and secondary education and enhance the quality of higher and technical education, so that it enables their youth to find opportunity in the local as well as global market.

SECTION II: HEALTH AND DEVELOPMENT

Better health is central to human happiness and wellbeing and makes an important contribution to economic progress, as healthy populations live longer, are more productive and save more.

—CWS (2010)

Skilled, healthy and well-educated people are in better position than others to take their lives into their own hands.... They are more valuable to society and better able to help themselves and development of the people means investing in human capabilities, whether in education or health or skills, so that they can work productively and creatively.

—UNDP (1991)

Health is one of the vital social determinants of economic growth and development. Healthy human beings are the economic assets of a nation, who through their health, skill and dexterity help the nation to accelerate the pace of economic growth and development. A morbid person is less capable to work for longer hours, have less productivity and, therefore could earn less as compared to a healthy and active person. Cole and Neumayer (2000) were of the view that health can effect economic growth through its impact on human and physical capital accumulation. Poor health has an adverse effect on productivity, thus it appears to be a key factor in explaining the existence of underdevelopment in many regions throughout the world (Baltagi and Moscone 2010). There exists a strong relationship between health and development, as good health of people enable nation state to achieve higher economic growth and development. According to Szirmai (2005), improving the state of health contributes to the realization of other developmental objectives such as economic development, labour productivity growth, responsiveness to innovation and future orientedness.

The relationship between health and development is a reciprocal one. Improvement in the economic status of the family tends to improve its health status. In the same vein, better health status of the family's income earners contribute to economic development and well-being of the family. Basta et al. (1979) found that in Indonesia, men with anaemia were 20% less productive than men without anaemia. Gallup and Suchs (1998) found a significant negative relationship between the incidence of malaria and economic growth. According to Chambers (1982), illness leads to reduced production in subsistence agriculture. In a historical research, Fosel (1986) claimed that about one-third of economic growth in England in the past 200 years is due to improvements in nutrition and health. Investment in health care makes substantial positive contribution to economic growth and development. Therefore, any expenditure on health care must be considered a productive investment. 'Health is wealth' and healthy population is considered as an asset to a nation, and it contributes towards productivity, economic growth and development.

In developing countries in particular, the health and development relationship forms a vicious circle which supports one another. Poor health leads to loss of stamina, which further results in less hours of work, less productivity and less income. Less income leads to poor consumption which further affects the health, and this vicious circle continues. The poor productivity and low income of the labour force of an economy affect GDP as well as per capita income. Less GDP and low per capita income ultimately reduce economic growth and development. The vicious circle of health and development relationship is shown in Figure 3.1.

Considering the importance of health, the Millennium Development Goals (MDGs) formulated by the United Nations have accepted health as an important component of development. The three important health components of MDGs are (a) reduction in child mortality; (b) improvement in maternal health and (c) combating HIV/AIDS, malaria and other diseases. The health and health related items in the UNDP 2030-Agenda for Sustainable Development Goals are (a) to ensure healthy lives and promote well-being for all at all ages and (b) to ensure availability and sustainable management of water and sanitation for all.

Figure 3.1 *Vicious Circle of Health and Development*

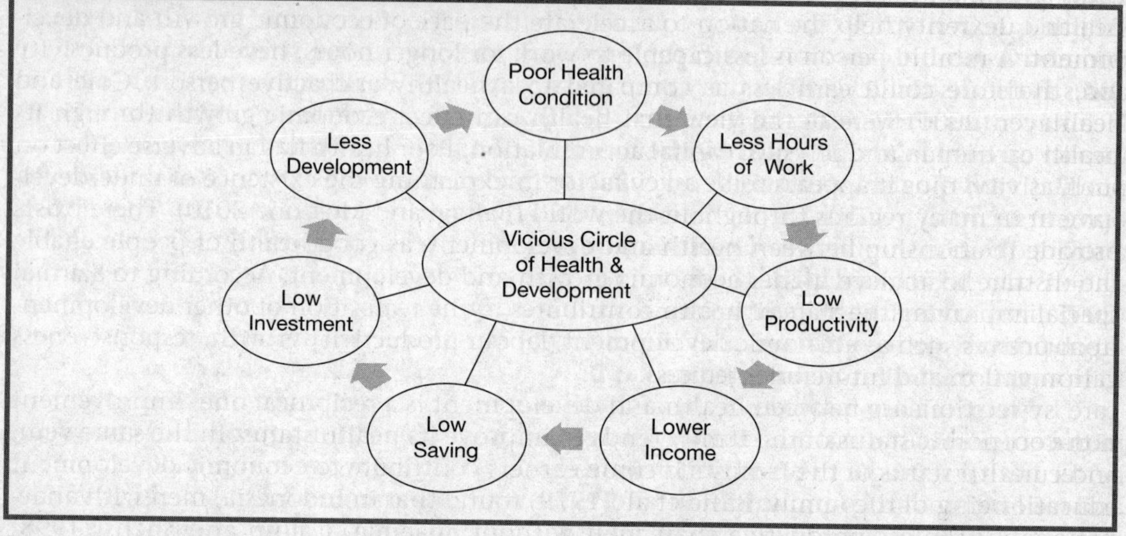

Source: Author.

KEY ELEMENTS OF HEALTH CARE

The key components of health care system can be broadly categorized into three types:

1. Health care services consisting of primary, secondary and tertiary health care.
2. Occupational health care that relates to the health care of individual engaged in various occupations, which has adverse repercussion on health.
3. Mental health care which refers to taking care of the mental health condition of an individual, so that individual's mental condition not only adversely affects his or her capabilities but also the functioning of the family, society and the nation.

As far as primary health care is concerned, WHO advocates that the primary health care should, at a minimum, include

1. education concerning prevailing health problems;
2. promotion of food and proper nutrition;
3. basic sanitation and adequate supply of safe water;
4. maternal and child health care including family planning;
5. immunization against major infectious diseases;
6. prevention and control of locally endemic diseases;
7. appropriate treatment of common diseases and injuries and
8. provision of essential drugs.

Some of the key features of primary health care suggest that it should be essential; scientifically sound and socially acceptable; accessible to individual and community through full participation; it is affordable and cost effective; it encompasses preventive, curative, promotive and rehabilitation services; it is delivered through the existing health structure easily and it takes care of all common health problems of the community. The primary health care system in developing countries is strongly oriented towards preventive and promotive health care along with the provision of curative and referral health care services at the district level. In India, at the grass-roots level, health sub-centres and primary health centres (PHCs) cater to the primary health care needs of the people. The secondary health care is mainly provided by the medical specialists and other health professionals, such as cardiologists, urologists, psychiatrists and dermatologist, who generally do not have first contact with patients. The secondary health care services in India are generally provided by the Community Health Centres situated at the sub-division levels and also by the district hospitals. Lastly, the tertiary health care services are provided by the highly specialized consultative health care institutions, usually for inpatients and on referral from primary or secondary health professionals. These are for advanced medical investigation and treatment mainly situated at provincial (state) and national level. The health care system mainly provides general health care services to cure communicable and non-communicable diseases among all age group of population, preventive, promotive and curative reproductive and child health care services to women and children, health education through communication and extension programme and implements various national health programmes launched by the government from time to time.

Important National Health Programmes Launched by the Government of India

1. National Programme for Prevention and Control of Deafness
2. Universal Immunization Programme
3. National Cancer Control Programme
4. National AIDS Control Programme
5. National Mental Health Programme
6. National Iodine Deficiency Disorder Control Programme
7. National Programme for Control of Blindness
8. National TB Control Programme
9. National Leprosy Eradication Programme
10. National Tobacco Control Programme
11. National Rural Health Mission

Promotion of occupational health is critical to the economic growth and development of a nation. The occupational health aims at the prevention of diseases and maintenance of the highest degree of physical, mental and social well-being of workers in all occupations. According to Alli (2008) of the ILO, occupational safety and health (OSH) is generally defined as the science of the anticipation, recognition, evaluation and control of hazards arising in or from the workplace that could impair the health and well-being of workers, taking into account the possible impact on the surrounding communities and the general environment. Work-related injuries and illness kill an estimated 1.2 million people around the world every year (Lim 2005). In terms of morbidity, 250 million work-related accidents and 160 million work-related illness occur annually (Somavia cited in Lim 2005), and these numbers translate into an annual economic loss of approximately 4% of the world's GDP (ILO 2001). Workers in all types of occupations relating to various sectors of the economy, be it agriculture, industry or service sectors, are subject to occupational specific diseases and health hazards. Workers in the agriculture sector suffer from the use of pesticides and technology-related health hazards, while those are working the industrial sectors are suffering from multiple health hazards that vary from industry to industry. For example, workers in the tobacco industries are subject to diseases like tuberculosis, asthma and cancer, while workers in recent emerging IT sectors are subject to many cardiovascular diseases and eye-related problems. Enhancing productivity at the cost of health of the workers is detrimental to sustainable development. Therefore, economic growth rate in general and industrial growth rate in particular must be critically linked to the health of the working force.

Bhopal Gas Disaster and Dow Chemical: Need for CSR

The disaster at Union Carbide Corporation (UCC) plant at Bhopal released 40 tons of poisonous methyl isocyanate gas from its pesticide plant. The disaster killed more than 15,000 and caused serious harm to even a larger number of people. Till 20 years of the disaster, 25,000 tons of toxic waste remained in premises, which continued to pollute surrounding water bodies. Around 100,000 peopled suffered from 'chronic and debilitating illness'. It had caused blindness, respiratory trouble and gynaecological disorder in the victims. It contaminated the local ground water and wells with mercury at the level of 20,000 units.

Source: S. L. Anand, see https://www.scribd.com/doc/74262559/Bhopal-Gas-Tragedy-Case-Study (accessed on 24 May 2016).

Another important element of health care which affects employment, productivity, economic growth and development is mental health. According to NHS Employer (2008), the term mental ill health covers harmful levels of stress, depression, anxiety, schizophrenia, bipolar disorder (manic depression), psychosis, obsessive compulsive disorder (OCD), and is often associated with drug, alcohol abuse and eating disorder (e.g. anorexia nervosa and bulimia nervosa). The WHO (2003) report on mental health states that 'mental disorders occur in persons of all genders, ages and backgrounds. No group is immune to mental disorder, but the risk is higher among the poor, homeless, the unemployed, persons with low education…' The Mental Health Foundation research has found that 47% of people who had experienced mental distress said that they had experienced discrimination in the workplace; 37% had experienced discrimination when seeking employment; 80 million work days are estimated as being lost each year to stress, depression and anxiety and 10% estimated proportion of GDP lost due to work related issues (NHS Employer 2008).

According to WHO (1995) statistics, about 500 million people in the world are believed to be suffering from neurotic, stress-related and somatoform ailments—psychological problems which present themselves as physical complaints. According to WHO (2001), in recent years, morbidity which is receiving more attention is a mental disorders. Worldwide, 45 million people are affected by schizophrenia, 29 million suffer from dementia and

40 million people suffer from different types of epilepsy (WHO 1997). Some of the effects of mental health problem are (a) mental health affects the physical health as well; (b) people suffering from mental health problem create problem in the family as well as in the work place; (c) mental health affects individual's ability to work, and thus impact output and productivity; (d) mental health has a cause and effect relationship among the youth; (e) persistent mental health problems may lead to indebtedness and household poverty; (f) persistent mental health problem among children will affect educational achievement and mental and physical health of the parents and (g) mental health problem among the aged may lead to their abandonment by the family members particularly by the impoverished families. The health care system at all levels, i.e. primary, secondary and tertiary, must be adequately geared up to meet the various issues and challenges relating to mental health care.

INDICATORS OF HEALTH STATUS DEVELOPMENT

The health care development status of a nation is assessed by looking at its health indicators, i.e. mortality, morbidity, expenditure on health care, availability of trained health care delivery personnel and so on. Certainly the developed nations are far ahead of the developing nations in terms of achievement in different health care development indicators. A few important indicators of health care development are discussed further.

1. The percentage of expenditure on health to the total GDP of a country is one of the key indicators of health development. Health care expenditure customarily constitutes expenditures on the following areas:
   (i) Infrastructure development, i.e. establishment of health care institutions, such as medical colleges, hospitals, dispensaries, training centres, and so on, at various levels.
   (ii) Provision of essential drugs and medicines in the health care institutions.
   (iii) Equipping health care institutions with required medical and paramedical personnel.
   (iv) Expenditure of information, education and communication (IEC) in creating awareness.
   (v) Generating community participation in the delivery of preventive, promotive and curative health care services and practices.

   All of these are essential for health care provisioning aimed at improving the health status of the population. Expenditure on health care by any country must be considered as public good. It must be available and accessible to all sections of the population, especially to those who are poor, staying in rural, hilly and extremely difficult areas. The primary health care services need to be free, and the secondary and tertiary health care must be provided at affordable cost. However, it is seen that the governments of developing countries are spending less percentage of their GDP on health care. As a result, the per capita availability of health care infrastructure and health care personnel is lesser as compared to the developed countries. Physicians available per 100,000 population in the United States and the United Kingdom is 256 and 449 respectively, while in South Asian and

Table 3.10 *Health Expenditure in Selected Developed and Developing Countries*

Country	Out of Pocket Health Expenditure (%)	Percentage of GDP	Per Capita Health Care Expenditure ($)
US	22.7	17.6	8,233
UK	53.1	9.6	3,495
Japan	82.0	9.2	3,958
China	77.2	5.0	219
India	86.0	3.7	51
Sri Lanka	81.9	3.5	82
Nigeria	95.6	5.4	67
Zambia	66.7	6.0	74

Source: World Development Indicators 2012, World Bank.

Sub-Saharan African countries, India and Zambia, the rates are 60 and 12 respectively. This reveals the apathy of the government of developing countries with regard to expenditure on provisioning of health care services. As far as health expenditure is concerned, the United States of America spends 15.2% of its GDP on health, while the percentages are lower in the Asian, African and Latin American countries, and the percentage of expenditure on health by China and India are 5.6% and 4.8% respectively (see Table 3.10). Besides, at the household and individual health care level, also the amount of expenditure on the health and nutritional care influences the health status of the family members as well as that of the individual. Anyanwu and Erhijakpor (2007), using data from 47 African countries between 1999 and 2004, found that health expenditures have a statistically significant effect on infant mortality and under-five mortality.

Baltagi and Moscone (2010) found long economic relationship between health care expenditure and income, using a panel of 20 OECD countries during 1971–2004. On the other hand, Elmi and Sadeghi (2012) found that a significant impact of health spending on economic growth justifies the necessity of governments' intervention aimed by implementing the policies to encourage health spending required to build up a healthier and productive society to support economic growth and development in developing countries.

2. Demographic status of nation state is correlated with the health status of population. However, the health and developmental scientists have not sufficiently addressed this issue in the health and development agenda. The demographic indicators such as population growth rate, fertility, birth and death rate, life expectancy and dependency ratio influence health status of population. Joshi and Schultz (2007) found that reduced fertility produced persistent and significant positive effects on the health, earnings and household assets on women and on the health and earnings of children. The high population growth rate in Sub-Saharan Africa and South Asia influences the health status such as mortality and morbidity rates. Fertility transition in Oman has attributed to the socio-economic development such as increased education of women and empowerment of women, which will increase the age at marriage of females in future, contributing

to the small family size (Kabirn and Rahman 2012). On the contrary, the growing number of aging population in developed countries has enhanced the public health care expenditure in North America and European Countries (Table 3.11).

3. The mortality, i.e. infant mortality, child mortality and maternal mortality, and morbidity particularly happening from major diseases, such as cancer, tuberculosis, lung problems, mental health disorder, heart diseases and others, are the indicators that manifest the health status of population in a country. The infant as well as maternal mortality rates are very high in Sub-Saharan Africa, where, for example, the infant mortality rate of under-five children is 20 times higher than that of the United Kingdom. The maternal mortality ratio of India and Pakistan is 200 and 260 per 100,000 live births respectively; while of the United Kingdom and the United States of America, it is just 12 and 21 respectively (see Table 3.12). This shows the poor health status of the two developing countries of South Asia.
4. Morbidity is more perilous than mortality. It does not only eat away financial resources but also posits a lot of mental stress on the family suffering from

Table 3.11 *Growth Rate, Fertility Rate, Life Expectancy and Dependency Rate in Selected Countries, 2010*

Countries	Annual Growth Rate (%)	Fertility Rate (%)	Life Expectancy at Birth	Population Ages 65 Above
Bangladesh	1.1	2.2	69	5
Nigeria	2.5	5.5	51	3
Zambia	1.6	6.3	48	3
India	1.4	2.6	65	5
China	0.5	1.6	73	8
Japan	–0.1	1.4	83	23
UK	0.7	2.0	80	17
USA	0.8	1.9	79	13

Source: World Development Indicators 2012, World Bank.

Table 3.12 *Mortality Ratio and Under-Five Mortality Rate in Selected Countries, 2010*

Country	Maternal Mortality Ratio Modelled Estimate (per 100,000 Live Births)	Under-Five Mortality Rate (per 1,000 Live Births)
Bangladesh	240	49
Mozambique	490	108
Pakistan	260	74
India	200	63
UK	12	5
USA	21	8

Source: World Development Indicators 2012, World Bank.

Table 3.13 *Prevalence of HIV and Incidence of Tuberculosis per 100,000 People in Some Selected Countries, 2010*

Countries	Prevalence of HIV of the Population Aged 15–49 (%)	Incidence of Tuberculosis
Bangladesh	0.1	225
Botswana	23.7	503
China	0.1*	78
Ethiopia	1.6	269
Japan	0.1	21
India	NA	185
UK	0.3	13
US	0.7	4

Source: World Development Indicators 2012, World Bank.
Notes: * Data for the year 2011.
NA=Not Available.

debilitating illness. In the recent years, HIV/AIDS-related morbidity and mortality in poor Sub-Saharan African countries is astoundingly high. The money which could have been used for other developmental purposes is being used in controlling STD, HIV and AIDS in these countries. Orem et al. (2012) found that malaria morbidity results in a substantive loss in GDP of Uganda, and the high burden of malaria leads to decreased long-term economic growth and works against poverty eradication efforts and socio-economic development of the country. The morbidity relating to lifestyle diseases, such as diabetes, blood pressure, and others, is on the rise in developing countries (Table 3.13).

5. Malnutrition is also one of the main causes of morbidity and mortality in developing countries. It is the direct cause of about 300,000 deaths per year and indirectly responsible for about half of all deaths of young children (Black, Moriss and Bryce 2003). The percentage of population suffering from malnutrition is quite high in Sub-Saharan Africa and South Asia as compared to developed countries. Rentlinger and Selowsky (1976) had remarked that in Asia, the Middle East and Africa, there were shortfall of calories ranging from 135 to 230 per day. To bring the average for these regions up to the standards would require an additional 269,000 million calories daily or approximately 25 million metric tons of food grains annually. Malnutrition causes a lot of health hazards among the children and women in developing countries. Malnutrition in children affects their education. Malnutrition among women affects the child birth, resulting in low birth weight baby, premature delivery, still birth, spontaneous abortion and neonatal death. Malnutrition among adult population affects the labour productivity and ultimately economic growth of the nation. Iron deficiency can cause poor pregnancy outcome among the antenatal women, impair physical and cognitive development among children and can reduce work productivity among adults. Similarly, during pregnancy, malnutrition can lead to still birth,

Table 3.14 *Under-Nourishment around the World, 1990–2012 and 2012–16*

Country	1990–2012 Number (in Millions)	1990–2012 (%)	2014–16 Number (in Millions)	2014–16 (%)
World	1,010.6	18.6	794.6	10.9
Developed Regions	20.0	<5	14.7	<5
Developing Regions	990.7	23.3	779.9	12.9
Africa	181.7	27.6	232.5	20.0
Sub-Saharan Africa	175.7	33.2	220.0	23.2
Asia	741.9	23.6	511.7	12.1
Eastern Asia	295.4	23.2	145.1	9.6
South Eastern Asia	137.5	30.6	60.5	9.6
Southern Asia	291.2	23.9	281.4	15.7
Latin America and Caribbean	66.1	14.7	34.3	5.5
Oceania	1.0	15.7	1.4	14.2

Source: http://www.worldhunger.org/2015-world-hunger-and-poverty-facts-and-statistics/ (accessed on 19 May 2016).

spontaneous abortion, and future congenital abnormality in children, and it can cause impaired cognitive development in children. The malnutrition status of the population is very high in the African and South Asian countries as compared to the countries of other continents of the globe (Table 3.14).

Malnutrition Status in the World

1. There are an estimated of 276 million chronically undernourished people in 2014–16.
2. In Sub-Saharan regions, one in four people remain undernourished.
3. Hunger continues to take its largest tool in South Asia, which includes the countries of India, Pakistan and Bangladesh.
4. Globally, 161 million under-five year children were estimated to be stunted in 2013.
5. Globally, 51 million under-five year children were wasted and 17 million were severely wasted in 2013.
6. In developing countries, every second pregnant woman and about 40% of preschool children are estimated to be anaemic.
7. Anaemia contributes 20% of all maternal deaths.
8. An estimated 250 million preschool children are vitamin A deficient.

Source: http://www.worldhunger.org/2015-world-hunger-and-poverty-facts-and-statistics/ (accessed on 19 May 2016).

Table 3.15 *Immunization: Measles and DTP (Diptheria, Tetanus Toxoids and Pertussis) (% of Children Aged 12–23 Months), 2014*

Countries	DTP	Measles
Afghanistan	75	66
Belgium	99	96
China	99	99
India	83	83
Japan	98	98
Nepal	92	88
Pakistan	73	63
Sri Lanka	99	99
UK	95	93
USA	94	91

Source: World Development Indicators; also see http://data.worldbank.org/indicator#topic-8 (accessed on 24 June 2016).

6. One of the reasons of high maternal and infant mortality rate in developing countries is poor access to and adoption of preventative health care services. Therefore, in developing countries, immunization of children and women against preventable is critical to health development. It is studied that the immunization of children against vaccine preventable diseases has checked infant mortality rate, and immunization of women during antenatal care has reduced maternal mortality rate. During immunization, parents do not only vaccinate their children but also get health education from the medical and health personnel regarding the holistic health care of their children. Similarly, antenatal women also get many health care tips from the medical and health personnel regarding management of nutritional anaemia, physical labour and rest during pregnancy, mental health care and so on. Figures in Table 3.15 show that in the developed countries like United States of America, United Kingdom and Japan, the immunization of children in the age group of 12–23 months have crossed more than 90%, but in the South Asian countries except Sri Lanka and other mentioned countries, the immunization is lower than 90%.

ISSUES AND CHALLENGES OF HEALTH DEVELOPMENT

Health care services are vital social and economic goods. As social goods, it aims at social well-being and human survival. As an economic good, it helps indirectly to enhance productivity and economic growth of the country. Therefore, protection and promotion of health and well-being of individual is supreme to the social and economic development of any nation. The developed countries have rightly acknowledged the importance of health care in national economy; one the illustrious examples is the USA which spends 17.6% of its GDP on health care. However, the issues and challenges faced in the area of health development, particularly by developing countries, are numerous; a few important of them are discussed further in this section.

1. There are disparities in the availability, accessibility and affordability in health care services. The victims of health disparities are (a) racial and ethnic minorities; (b) residents of rural areas, hilly and far flung desert areas; (c) women, children and elderly; and (d) persons with disabilities. The cost of treatment is rising in the tertiary private specialized health care institutions. This rising prices of medical consultancy, drugs and medicines has elongated the disparities between haves and have-nots in terms of accessing curative referral health care services. Health as a public good is available in the government hospitals, health care dispensaries and centres (i.e. sub-centre, PHC and community health centre) run by the government in developing countries. However, functioning of these public sector institutions suffer from poor quality and governance deficiency. Lack of adequate trained health personnel and the cursory visit by the appointed medical and paramedical personnel to the health care centres and their negative attitude to serve in rural and far flung areas with disadvantaged section of population affects the health status of the marginalized sections. The challenge is to make private health care affordable and government health care services accountable and accessible. Special attention has to be given towards the health care of disadvantaged sections of population, those belonging to rural and far flung areas and also to the population staying in the unorganized slums and in the ghettos of the urban areas. A few experts have stressed that it is important to improve drug supply chains, ambulance services, referral systems and clinical capacity at public clinics and to address the financial constraints faced by the socially disadvantaged. This should also be considered how the providers can be engaged with patients in a way that strengthen the therapeutic alliance (Goudge et al. 2009).
2. There has to be a conscious move from the supply-driven to demand-driven community centric approach. Because of the lack of resources, the health care in general and primary health care in particular follow a stereotyped supply driven approach in developing countries. Here, certain kind of services are made available in almost all health care institutions without taking into consideration the area specific needs. However, with globalization and availability of media and Internet facilities, patients have become well informed. Besides, the pattern of diseases has also changed and patients are increasingly becoming stakeholders. These situations call for a demand-driven approach rather than centralized supply-centred approach. With rise in literacy and awareness, health care system has been subject to close scrutiny by the society. The demand-driven or community-centric approach believes in delivery of health care services with the active community participation. Here, the community members are not treated as passive beneficiaries of health care programmes and projects rather the active promoters and contributors to health care programmes and projects. Hori, Ohashi and Suzuki (2005) were of the view that the future health care must take into consideration (a) providing patients with medical information and supporting their decisions; (b) building a structure to provide a more efficient, high quality health care service; and (c) creating an assuring and confronting medical environment for citizens.

3. Changing demographic scenarios according to time and space also pose varied challenges. The rate of population growth effects long-range planning of community health and medical facilities (Perrott and Holland 2005). The developed countries having more and more population in the age group of 60+ are confronting the challenge of providing health care facilities to this critically important age group. On the other hand, developing countries having more percentage of population in the categories of adolescents and adults have to cater to the health care needs of these vulnerable groups. Alteration in age composition, internal migration of racial or industrial groups, changes in population density and urban–rural movement require current adaptation of the health programme to solve the new problems thus created (Perrott and Holland 2005). The low life expectancy in Sub-Saharan African countries, because of many endemic diseases, requires specific attention to curb mortality and morbidity from the least developed countries. Even within a country, the variation in the composition of population across the regions also determines the dynamics of the health care need structure.
4. The success of health care delivery system, particularly in rural areas, relates its effectiveness to coordinate with other related sectors in the effective delivery of various health care services. The health care system in the countryside cannot achieve much success if it works in silos. Numerous previous studies and reports have noted the importance of intersectoral action in improving health equity. Intersectoral action has been identified as a public health practice with potential to allow local public health units to address the social determinants of health and reduce health inequities (Sudbury and District Health Unit 2011). Intersectoral action for health refers to 'actions undertaken by sectors outside the health sector, possibly, but not necessarily, in collaboration with the health sector, on health or health equity outcomes or on the determinants of health or health equity' (PHAC and WHO 2008) (Figure 3.2).
5. Health sector and its functionaries at the grass-roots in developing countries are seen to be working in silos and do not have adequate coordination with health-related sectors, i.e. agriculture, education, women and child development, rural development, public health and so on. This has been considered one of the reasons for which they have not been able to achieve optimum output. De-concentration of burden of promotive health care among the functionaries of the related sectors, rather than its concentration on the functionaries of the health sector alone, is the answer to the effective decentralized health care service delivery at the grass-roots level. In India, the successful implementation of Pulse Polio Immunization programme was possible due to the cooperation of other sector functionaries such as school teachers, village development officers, *anganwadi* workers, SHG members, Mahila Mandal members, Youth club members, members of the Panchayati Raj institutions, and others, and also the support given by the NGOs to the government health sector functionaries at the grass-roots level. This cooperative endeavour has made many states of India polio free. Intersectoral coordination has been among the weakest of strategic inputs that impedes the success of primary health care particularly in developing countries.

One of the important challenges before developing countries where more than 60% of its population are staying in the countryside is to promote effective community participation and active involvement of civil society organizations in the effective formulation, implementation and monitoring of health projects and programmes at the grass-roots level. The community participation is considered important in primary health care development, and it results in positive health outcomes (Preston et al. 2010). Community participation is a process that enables people to become actively and genuinely involved in defining health concerns to them, identify health needs, formulate action plan along with the health care providers and monitor their implementation and give suggestions to the health care service providers to take corrective measures.

> Community participation is a process by which people are enabled to become actively and generally involved in defining the issues of concern to them; in making decisions about factors that affect their lives; in formulating and implementing policies; in planning; developing and delivery services and in taking action to achieve change. A participatory health development process involves relevant partners for health at all levels i.e. home, school, and worksite, local community and country-and that promotes joint decision-making, implementation and accountability. (WHO 2002)

Figure 3.2 *Sectors for Intersectoral Coordination*

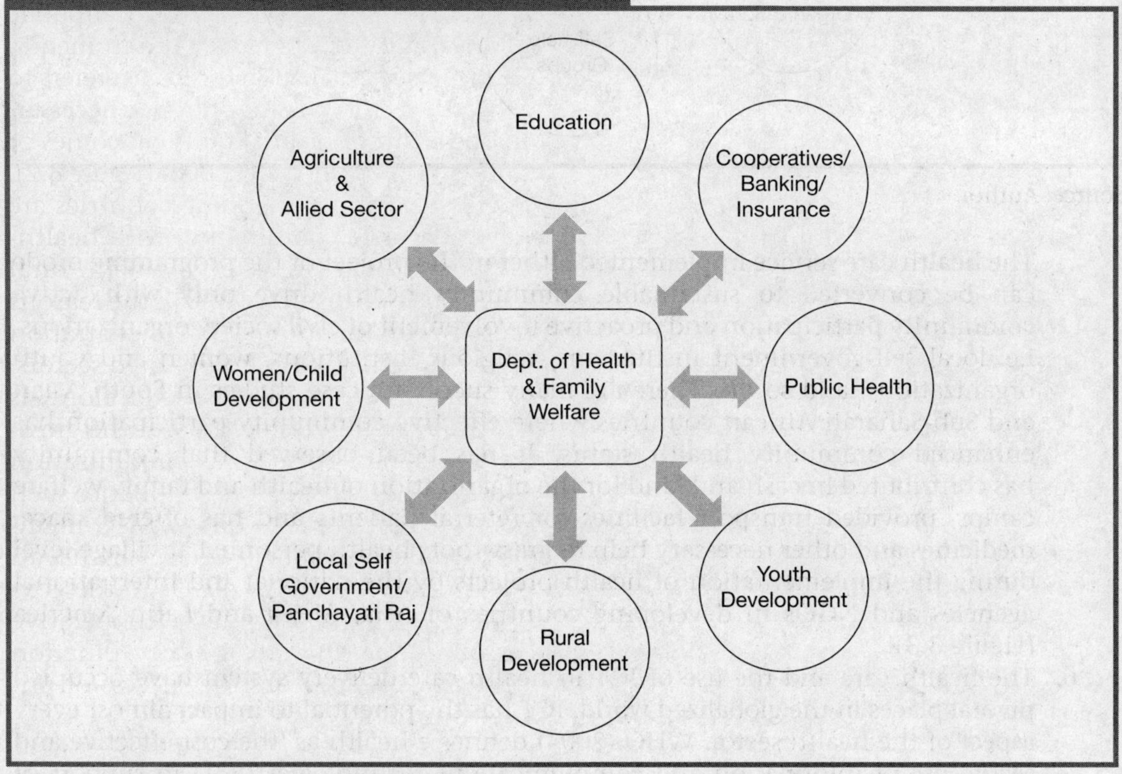

Source: Author.

Figure 3.3 *Actors of Community Participation*

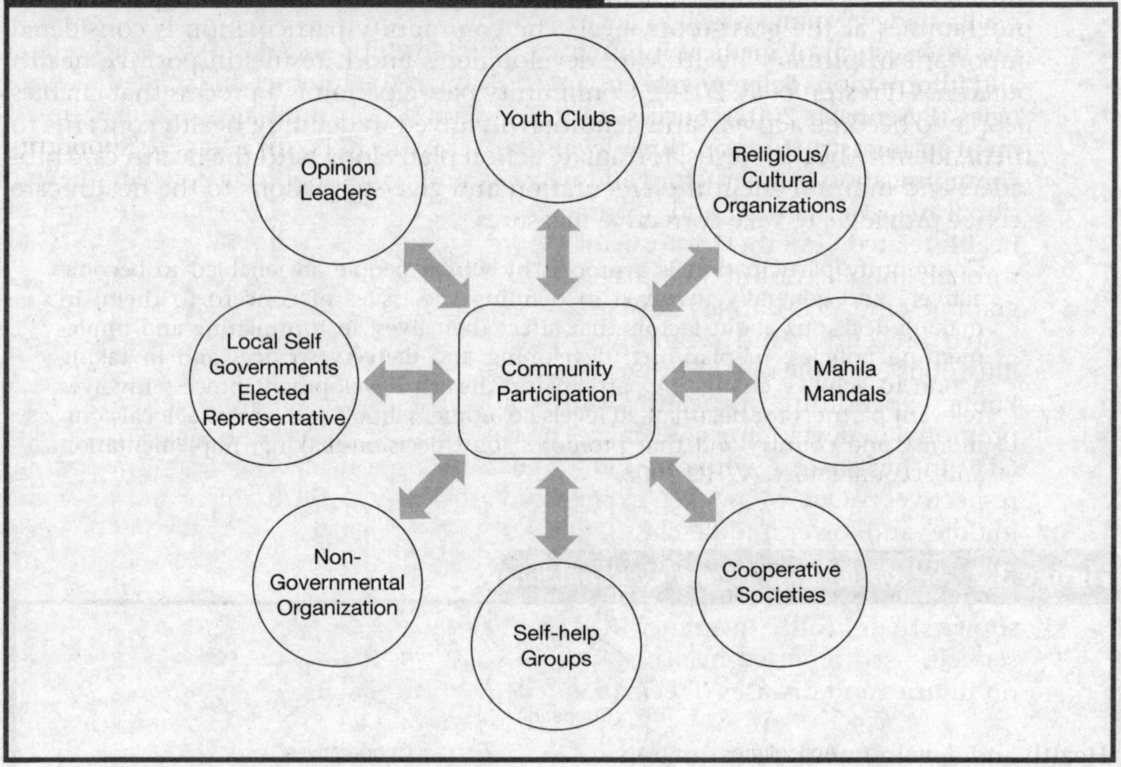

Source: Author.

The health care service implemented either in the project or the programme mode can be converted to sustainable community health drive only with active community participation and proactive involvement of civil society organizations, i.e. local self-government institutions, religious institutions, women and youth organizations, and so on. There are many successful case studies in South Asian and Sub-Saharan African countries where effective community participation has enhanced community health status. It has been observed that community has contributed in cash and kind for the organization of health and family welfare camps, provided transport facilities for referral patients and has offered space, medicines and other necessary help to grass-roots health personnel at village level during the implementation of health projects by the national and international agencies and NGOs in developing countries of Asia, Africa and Latin America (Figure 3.3).

6. The health care and the use of ICT in health care delivery system have occupied pivotal places in the globalized world. ICT has the potential to impact almost every aspect of the health sector. WHO (2004) defines e-health as 'the cost-effective and secure use of information and communications technologies (ICT) in support of health and health related fields, including health care insurance and health

education, knowledge and research.' According to WHO (2004), the integration and assimilation of e-health into the everyday life of health care workers is becoming a reality in developing as well as developed countries. E-health is an emerging field in the intersection of medical informatics, public health and business. With referral and information, delivery gets enhanced through the internet and related technologies (Eysenbach 2001). Successful ICT application in rural areas requires investment in infrastructure on three levels: (a) access to ICTs, (b) access to supporting communication infrastructure and network and (c) a supportive policy framework (Ruxwana, Herselman and Conradie 2010). E-health care broadly comprises health-related Internet information sites, email consultations, consultations through mobile, online pharmacies, virtual clinics, health-related television programmes and so on. It has substantially reduced the cost of consultancy and accelerated preventive and promotive health care practices. The telemedicine is an illustrious example of e-health care.

7. Public expenditure on health security and insurances has not been adequately promoted in developing countries. The United States of America spends 17% of its GDP in health care while in India and China the percentages are 3.7 and 5.0, respectively. Out of pocket expenditure for critical health care pushes many middle- and lower middle-class families into the poverty trap in most of developing countries. Social health insurance schemes are being proposed to meet health care exigencies of the impoverished families in developing countries. Studies have shown that health insurance had substantial effects on the use of physician services—self-reported health status, preventive services and mortality condition on injuries and diseases (Freeman et al. 2008).

Health and development are intimately interconnected, and therefore development of an effective and efficient health care system is critical to the economic growth and development of a nation. The developed countries, where the health status of the population is high as compared to developing countries, have attained higher development in all spheres. It is rightly said, 'health is wealth,' and therefore taking care of the health of the population means a step towards enhancement of the economic wealth of a nation.

SECTION III: HUMAN DEVELOPMENT

Human development is the end, economic growth a means.

—UNDP

In a broader sense the notion of human development incorporates all aspects of individuals' well-being, from their health status to their economic and political freedom.

—World Bank

In the new millennium, any discussion on 'development' will remain incomplete without a discussion on human development. In fact, all other developments, such as economic, social, political and so on, revolve around it. Human development as an important dimension of development has been introduced as early as in the 1960s, but vigorously popularized after 1990s with the publication of Human Development Report by the UNDP. UNDP (2001) has envisaged that human development is much more than just about the rise and fall of national incomes. Human development approach emphasizes on the quality of human capital, their skill, education and health and earning which are critical to human functioning and capabilities. Human development measures need to follow the principle that the human development is of the people for the people by the people, and all the attempts to improve human development need to move around the people as human being and the human capital is the supreme of all other capital. Human being is the key actor of the development. The effective functioning of all other physical and financial capital depends on the knowledge, skill and capabilities of human capital. UNDP launched its first Human Development Report in 1990 and constructed a composite index called Human Development Index (HDI). The three important dimensions of HDI are (a) life expectancy—representing a healthy life; (b) literacy—educational attainment; and (c) per capita income—representing a decent standard of living (see Figure 3.4). HDI measures the average achievement of a country in three basic dimensions of human development, these are as follows (Figure 3.4):

1. A long and healthy life, measured by life expectancy at birth.
2. Knowledge, measured by the adult literacy rate (with two-third weight) and the combined primary, secondary and tertiary GER (with one-third weight).
3. A decent standard of living, measured by GDP per capita.

The formula used in calculation of each dimensions of human development is as follows:

$$\text{Dimension Index} = \frac{\text{Actual Value} - \text{Minimum Value}}{\text{Maximum Value} - \text{Minimum Value}}$$

Figure 3.4 *Key Dimensions of HDI*

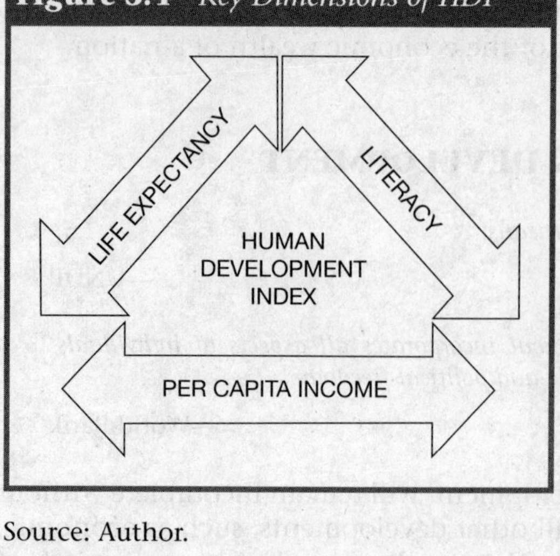

Source: Author.

HDI is a simple average index of all the three dimensions. Human development is vital to inclusive and sustainable development of a nation. Therefore, it is desired that the nation has to emphasize on the upgradation of the status of the three key variables determining HDI of all the population irrespective of caste, class, ethnicity and gender. UNDP (1990), while divulging the components of human development, has emphasized on four basic elements which are as follows (Table 3.16):

Equality: It is defined as equal access to opportunities. It implies the existence of competitive markets and competitors with equal access to productive assets and knowledge.

Table 3.16 *Human Development Index of a Few Selected Countries, 2015*

Country	Value	Rank
Very High Human Development		
Norway	0.944	1
Australia	0.935	2
Switzerland	0.930	3
High Human Development		
Russia	0.798	50
Sri Lanka	0.757	73
China	0.727	90
Medium Human Development		
Botswana	0.698	106
Egypt	0.690	108
India	0.609	130
Low Human Development		
Nepal	0.548	145
Pakistan	0.538	147
Uganda	0.483	1163

Source: https://en.wikipedia.org/wiki/List_of_countries_by_Human_Development_Index (accessed on 22 December 2016).

Productivity: With main contention of economic growth, improved productivity can be achieved through development of human resources and creation of a favourable environment where people can make use of their capabilities optimally.

Sustainability: To accommodate the needs of future generation.

Empowerment: Provision of an adequate social environment in which people participate to achieve a better life. Scandinavian countries rank high in HDI because of their emphasis on equity in access to social capital and social development institutions.

ISSUES AND CHALLENGES OF HUMAN DEVELOPMENT

Broadly speaking, human development of a nation is influenced by a host of factors, i.e. income, poverty, inequality, quality of living, education and health, nutrition and overall good governance. The important issues crucial for raising human development are discussed here.

Income, Employment and Poverty: These are the key factors influencing the key elements of human development such as standard of living, health care and education.

UNDP (1990) observed that the extent to which people can improve their capabilities depends largely on their income and the access they have to basic goods and services. Unequal distribution of income in a society disproportionately affects the access to quality health care and education. In developing countries, there is a wide inter- and intra-regional disparity in terms of peoples' income and access to employment. This also, in turn, affects the health and education status. Southern states of India, i.e. Kerala, Tamil Nadu, Karnataka and Andhra Pradesh, have higher HDI as compared to eastern states such as Orissa, Jharkhand, Bihar, West Bengal and Assam. Higher income, over and above the sustainable income, after meeting the basic needs enables household to spend on other capability-enabling goods and services such as education and health care. In India, the lower education, health and per capita earning of the disadvantaged sections of population, such as SCs and STs, is not only affecting their human development but also influencing the overall HDI of the nation. The provision of sustainable employment and income earning activities can augment HDI of a nation state. There is a positive correlation between per capita income and human development. UNESCO (2005) says, 'it is well established that the distribution of personal income in society is strongly related to the amount of education people have had.'

Sustainable Access to Basic Needs: Some of the common minimum needs for promoting and raising human development indicators, such as literacy, life expectancy and per capita income, are (a) healthy housing, clothing and two square nutritious meal a day; (b) safe drinking water, sanitation and energy for cooking, lighting and reading and (c) education, health and transport communication for access to schools, health centres, nearest town and so on. These are capability-enhancing necessities. Basic needs are fundamental to human development; however, in many developing countries of South Asia and Africa, a large number of households are devoid of these basic needs. The statement of a poor farmer from Sudan runs as 'the rich people are not sick because they can afford good houses, clean water, food and health care necessary to avoid diseases. But living in poverty, how can we afford to avoid diseases' (Sheik 2000). Therefore, one of the fundamental issues and challenges to raise human development is to ensure basic needs to the people.

Education: It is one of the important determinants of HDI. Education is a great enabler which enhances knowledge and skills, and empowers to earn higher income. It also enhances access to quality health care services and helps to raise life expectancy which is one of the indicators of HDI. Countries having higher literacy rate and high GER customarily enjoy higher rank in HDI. According to McNabb and Whitfield (1994), education and training may have an important impact on a person's values, attitudes, norms (socialization effects) on motivation and expectations (psychological effects) and behaviour. Besides, the acquisition of cognitive abilities, the formation of competence and the transfer of information are considered the major link between schooling/training and productivity (Bowman 1980). These factors influence a human being's capabilities as well as willingness to work effectively, and are considered as important elements of human development. The challenge is to ensure free basic and primary education to all, and making higher education accessible to all is the duty and responsibility of the state. Imparting vocational and skill education will enhance employment opportunities and raise the income.

Health: Health is a great wealth of an individual, family and nation. It is a vital determinant of human development. The life expectancy, an indicator used in the calculation of HDI, depends on mortality and morbidity rate status of a country. It is remarked that human development has many goals, one of which is to protect human health in the face of rapid environmental change (Woodward et al. 2000). Quality health care facilities and useful health care related practices enhance life expectancy and reduce morbidity and mortality. Besides raising life expectancy, better health of an individual enables him/her to raise the productivity, per capita income and even mental abilities to pursue education. Inadequate diet contributes to incidences of infectious diseases, learning disabilities, mental retardation, low work capacity and so forth. On the other hand, improved nutrition and health increase school attendance rates and an individual's ability to learn (Griffin and McKinley 1994). Bloom et al. (2004), from their study, have found that health through life expectancy exerts positive and statistically significant effect on economic growth. It suggests that a one-year improvement in the population's life expectancy contributes to a 4% increase in output. Boutayeb (2009), while analyzing the impact of HIV/AIDS on human development in African countries, concluded that the disease is impending development by imposing a steady decline in the key indicators of human development, and hence reversing the social and economic gains the African countries that are striving to attain these.

Health condition is further determined by the nutritional status. Nutrition is a lubricant of human development, and it raises the quality of life and makes individual less prone to diseases and morbidity. FAO considers that

> Nutrition plays a critical role in human resources development since deficiencies in essential nutrients lead to malnutrition, which affects an individual's mental and physical state, resulting in poor health and poor work performance. In addition, a hungry, malnourished child may have mild to serious learning disabilities, resulting in poor school performance; a sick and poorly nourished individual will not respond to quick treatment, could lose many working hours and may continue to drain family and national resources. Thus malnutrition may undermine investments in health, education and other development sectors.[6]

Social Capital: It is one of the most important determinants of human development. The healthy interaction and social networking among the people belonging to different communities lead to participatory learning on many aspects including health and education. Social capital promotes social development which ultimately raises human development. Responsible and accountable social institutions such as civil society organizations, youth clubs, Mahila Mandals and SHGs are found to have augmented social development. Kerala is an illustrious example, where SHGs are playing important role in raising the human development of the state. The society in which people are well educated, healthy and having good amount of per capita income can contribute more towards social development as well as economic growth and development. Strong social capital base of a nation state synchronizes social distance among different communities, and thus will be helpful for inclusive and sustainable human development. Human development and social development are positively correlated, a nation having higher position in HDI will have higher position in Social Development Index as well and vice versa.

Figure 3.5 *Key Factors Influencing HDI*

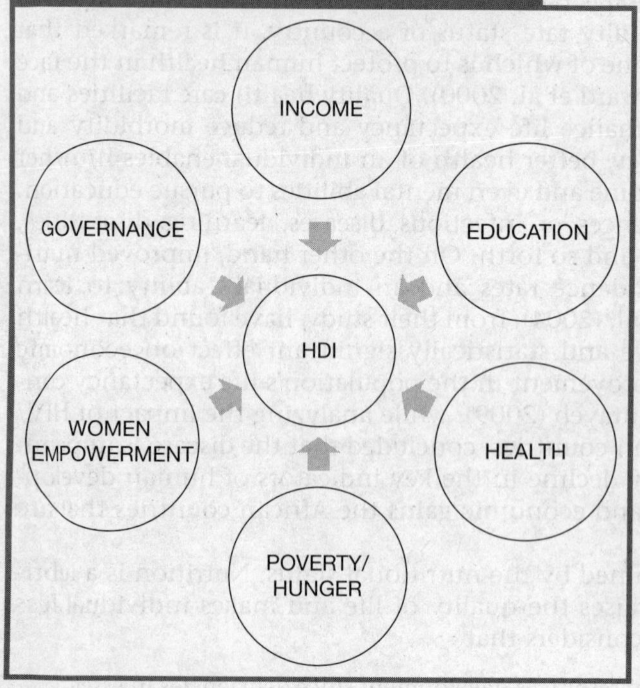

Source: Author.

Empowerment of Women and other Disadvantaged Section: Empowering women and socially disadvantaged section of the society is critical to inclusive and sustainable human development. A society that has educated, skilled and employed women workforce can achieve high rank in HDI as compared to a society where women are uneducated and unemployed. Moreover, better health status of women will have positive impact on the future HDI. Also, social, economic and political empowerment of the disadvantaged sections of the population will go a long way to enable a nation to achieve inclusive and sustainable human development. The perspective of action of the International Conference on Population and Development stresses that the empowerment of women and improvement of their political, economic and health status is both a highly important end in itself and necessary for sustainable human development (UNFPA 2007) (Figure 3.5).

Governance: Good governance is yet another key determinant of human development. Good governance and less corruption lead to effective implementation of poverty eradication programmes and creation of quality education and health care infrastructure. Recruitment of well-qualified trained teachers in the educational institutions and qualified medical and paramedical personnel in the health care institutions will go a long way to help a nation to attain the goal of inclusive and sustainable human development. Kerala, which is the least corrupt state in India, also stands high in literacy rate and high life expectancy rate. Evidence shows that government effectiveness, political stability, controls of corruption and regulatory quality have significant effects on human development (Ahamad and Saleem 2014). According to UNDP, 'good governance and sustainable human development are indivisible.'[7]

Environment: Finally, environment exhorts an important impact on human development. UNDP considers sustainable environment essential for human development. Environmental factors affect health and remain a major cause of sickness and death in many regions, particularly developing regions of the world. Economic development and human development efforts are increasingly constrained by environmental concerns, including degradation of forests and fisheries, lack of fresh water resources and poor human health as a result of air and water pollution (Banister 1998). Therefore, achieving environmental sustainability requires careful balancing of human development activities while maintaining a stable environment that predictably and regularly provides resources and protects people from natural calamities (Melnick et al. 2005).

One of the important challenges before developing countries is to reduce disparities in HDI among the countries and among the provinces and regions in a country. For example, HDI of Kerala and Tamil Nadu is higher than that of Bihar and Chhattisgarh. The regional disparities across the states impact the achievement of national level HDI. In HDI-laggard nation states, the main challenges hindering acceleration of HDI are education, health and women empowerment. Lower literacy rate and GER depress the educational dimension of HDI. High infant mortality and maternal mortality ratios and poor health status of population across the age cohort lead to a higher death rate, reduce life expectancy rate and consequently affect the status of HDI. Poor workforce participation of women and high dependency ratio among the children, aged and even the adults lower the per capita income at all levels, starting from household to the national level. Moreover, in the country like India, concentration of SC and ST population in a state also determines the status of HDI. The lower socio-economic status of these groups of population reduces the status of HDI. Thus, the inclusive and sustainable human development should be paramount goal of human development endeavour.

MEASURES TO PROMOTE HUMAN DEVELOPMENT

A nation state has to make sincere endeavour to upgrade the HDI status at the national as well as international level. Some of the measures to be taken for the improvement of HDI are:

1. Reduce corruption at all levels.
2. Effectively implement poverty reduction and employment generation measures.
3. Reduce social and economic disparities in the society.
4. Build quality education and health infrastructure and produce quality manpower and offer quality services in these institutions.
5. Restrict hunger and malnutrition in the society.
6. Make suitable structural changes in the economy, so that employment and per capita income of the people is raised.
7. Effectively implement women's social, economic, and political empowerment measures.
8. Make the development process more inclusive so that population belonging to the disadvantaged section effectively earns income, becomes educated, remains healthy and contributes towards sustainable development of the nation.
9. Strengthen social capital by promoting social networking across communities.
10. The life expectancy of all need to be improved by reducing mortality, morbidities and effectively handling the communicable and non-communicable diseases in the country.
11. Role of all the actors of development such as public sector, private sector, NGOs, PVOs and opinion leaders be energized towards the promotion of human development of the country.

SUMMARY

Education and health are considered as two vital social needs and important social and human development indicators of a nation. Ironically, illiteracy is high and the level of literacy in developing countries of Asia and Africa are low, and GER is astoundingly low. It is a well-known fact that education is the seed and flower of development and human capital is supreme of all capital. Like education, health status of the population in developing countries is also low as compared to the developed countries. High mortality and morbidity rate along with poor educational status has kept these nations in the lower rung in the ladder of HDI. A society is to be called a socially developed society, where people are educated and healthy and there is no discrimination in the access to education and health care on the basis of caste, class, ethnicity, sex and religion. The challenge before developing countries is to raise their education and health status so that they score high in Social Development Index and HDI. Both social and human developments are vital dimensions of holistic development and are concomitant to the economic development of a nation.

Keywords: literacy rate, educational development index, skill education, education for sustainable development, inclusive education, primary health care, infant mortality rate, maternal mortality rate, communicable and non-communicable diseases, malnutrition, immunization, mental health, occupational health, HIV/AIDS.

REVIEW QUESTIONS

1. Health and development are interconnected. Explain the statement in detail.
2. What is human development? How is it measured? Explain various factors influencing human development.
3. Critically explain human development theories? Explain how they are relevant in the context of developing countries.
4. What is educational development? Explain determinants of educational development.
5. Explain various measurements of health development. How these are important for developing countries?
6. What is primary health care? Explain various components of primary health care.
7. Describe in detail various component of health care development.
8. Maternal Health Care is important for developing countries. Explain various components of maternal health care? What are the factors influencing maternal health care?
9. Write short notes on the following:
   (i) Human Development Index (HDI)
   (ii) Maternal Mortality Rate
   (iii) Infant Mortality Rate
   (iv) Human Capital Theory
   (v) Gross Enrolment Ratio (GER)
   (vi) Intersectoral Coordination in health

(vii) Community participation in health care development
(viii) New Education Policy
(ix) National Health Policy

NOTES

1. Mentioned by S. S. Aboti in an article 'An overview of science of universal educational and relevance of Dr. Parnerkar's thought for detail see http://www.here-noe4u.de/eng/an_overview_of_science (accessed on 24 March 2014).
2. See http://www.ukipg.org.uk/publications/Educ_Position_Statement.pdf (accessed on 15 June 2016).
3. See https://landscape.hesa.ac.uk/wp-content/uploads/2012/01/HEBRG_PRINCIPLES1.pdf (accessed on 15 June 2016).
4. See www.unep.org/training/programmes/undesd.asp (accessed on 5 April 2016).
5. See https://answers.yahoo.com/question/index?qid=20071123211907AABPijx (accessed on 17 June 2016).
6. FAO Corporate Document Repository, 'The role of nutrition in social and economic development'. For detail, see http://www.fao.org/docrep/007/y5343e/5343e04.htm (accessed on 29 November 2013).
7. See ftp://pogar.org/LocalUser/pogarp/other/undp/governance/To-Adel/5-ChapterOne.htm (accessed on 21 May 2016).

BIBLIOGRAPHY

Adams, S. 'Educational Attainment and Health: Evidence from a Sample of Older Adults'. *Educational Economics* 10 (2002): 97–109.

Ahamad, Z., and A. Saleem. 'Impact of Governance on Human Development.' *Pakistan Journal of Commerce and Social Science* 8, no. 3 (2014): 612–28.

Alaezi, C. O. A. *National Open University Plan: Enhancing Higher Education in Nigeria through Open and Distance Learning Delivery System*. Lagos: National Open University of Nigeria, 2005.

Alhomod, S. M., and M. M. Shafi. 'E governance in education: Reasons for introduction and impact', *International Journal of Scientific & Engineering Research* 3, no. 2 (2012): 1–4.

Alli, B. O. *Fundamental Principles of Occupational Health and Safety*. 2nd edition. Geneva: ILO, 2008. Available at: http://www.ilo.org/wcmsp5/groups/public/@dgreports/@dcomm/@publ/documents/publication/wcms_093550.pdf (accessed on 24 May 2016).

Ambedkar, B. R. 'Speech at Bellasis Road.' *Mainstream*, Annual, 1997.

Ankomah, Y., J. Koomson, R. Bosu, and G. K. T. Oduro. 'Implementing Quality Education in Low Income Countries.' Institute for Educational Planning and Administration University of Cape Coast, Ghana, 2005. Available at: http://r4d.dfid.gov.uk/PDF/Outputs/ImpQuality_RPC (accessed on 14 November 2013).

Anyanwu, J. C., and A. E. O. Erhijakpor. 'Health Expenditure and Health Outcomes in Africa.' Economic Research Working Paper No. 91, African Development Bank, Tunis Belvedere, Tunisia, 2007.

Baltagi, B. H., and F. Moscone. 'Health Care Expenditure and Income in the OECD Reconsidered: Evidence from Panel Data.' *Economic Modelling*, 27 (2010): 804–11.

Banister, J. 'Population, Public Health and the Environment in China', *The China Quarterly* 156 (Special Issue: China's Environment) (1998): 986–1015.

Basta, S., K. Soekirman, and N. Scrimshaw. 'Iron Deficiency Anemia and Productivity of Adult Males in Indonesia.' *American Journal of Clinical Nutrition* 32, no. 4 (April 1979): 916–25.

Basu, A., and Elizabeth M. King. 'Does Education Promote Growth and Democracy? Some Evidence from East Asia and Latin America.' Washington DC: World Bank, 2001.

Black, R. E., S. S. Moriss, and J. Bryce. 'Where and Why Are 10 Million Children Dying Every Year?' *Lancet* 361, no. 9376 (2003): 2226–37.

Bloom, D. E. 'Education in a Globalized World.' *World Economics* 7, no. 4 (October–November 2006): 87–109.

Bloom, D. E., D. Canning, and J. Sevilla. 'The Effect of Health on Economic Growth: A Production Function Approach.' *World Development* 32, no. 1 (2004): 1–13.

Boutayeb, A. 'The Impact of HIV/AIDS on Human Development in African Countries.' *BMC Public Health*, 9 (November 2009): S3.

Bowman, M. J. 'Education and Economic Growth: An Overview.' In *Education and Income* edited by T. King, 1–71. Washington DC: World Bank Staff Working Paper No. 402, 1980.

Carlson, B. A. 'Social Dimensions of Economic Development and Productivity: Inequality and Social Performance. An Overview.' In *Social Dimension of Economic Development and Productivity: Inequality and Social Performance, Restructuring and Competitiveness Network, Division of Production, Productivity and Development Series 56* edited by B. Carlson. Santiago, Chile: United Nations Publications, 1999.

Chambers, R. 'Health Agriculture and Rural Poverty: Why Seasons Matter.' *Journal for Development Studies* 18, no. 2 (1982): 217–38.

Chambers, R., and G. Conway. Sustainable Rural Livelihoods: Practical Concepts for the 21st Century, IDS Discussion Paper 296, IDS, Brighton, UK, 1992.

Chen, B., and Y. Feng. 'Determinants of Economic Growth in China: Private Enterprise Education and Openness.' *China Economic Review*, 11, no. 1(2000): 1–15.

Christensen, P. R. 'Educational Technology and Educational Reform: Lessons for South Africa.' Presented at the Proceedings of The Future World International Conference Educating for the 21st Century, Cape Town, 2–4 December 1997.

Coulombe, S., J.-F. Tremblay, and S. Marchand. *Literacy scores, human capital and growth across fourteen OECD countries*. Ottawa: Statistics Canada. Cat. No. 89-552-MIE, no. 11(2004).

Cole, M. A., and E. Neumayer. 'The Impact of Poor Health on Total Factor Productivity.' *Journal of Development Studies*, 42 (2006): 918–38.

Coombs, P. H. *The World Crisis in Education: The View from the Eighties*. New York: Oxford University Press, 1985.

Cutler, David M., and A. Lleras-Muney. Educational and Health: Evaluating Theories and Evidence.' NBER Working Paper no. 12352, National Bureau of Economic Research, 2006. Available at: www.nber.org/papers/w12352 (accessed on 29 September 2016).

CWS. *CWS Christmas Appeal 2010: Week by Week Notice*. CWS, 2010. Available at: http://christmasappeal.org.nz/

Cypher, J. M., and J. L. Dietz. *The Process of Economic Development*. London: Routledge, 2009.

Dahlin, B. G. 'The Impact of Education on Growth: Theory Findings and Policy Implications.' Duke University Working Paper 18, 2005.

Dare, A. L. 'Indicators of Quality.' Paper presented at the National Consultative Workshop on Education Quality Implications in the Low Income Countries, Ghana, 2005.

Delannoy, F. 'Teacher Training or Lifelong Professional Development? Worldwide Trends and Challenges.' *TechKnowLogia* 2, no. 6 (2000): 10–13. Available at: www.techknowlogia.org/ (accessed on 9 August 2004).

Dewan, M. A. M. 'Public Expenditure on Education and Economic Growth: The Case of Bangladesh.' *International Journal of Applied Research in Business Administration and Economics* 1, no. 4 (2012): 16–18.

Elmi, Z. M., and S. Sadeghi. 'Health Care Expenditures and Economic Growth in Developing Countries: Panel Co-Integration and Causality.' *Middle-East Journal of Scientific Research* 12, no. 1 (2012): 88–91.

Eysenbach, G. 'What is E-Health.' *Journal of Medical Internet* 3, no. 2 (April–June 2001): e20.

Fasih, T. *Linking Education Policy to Labour Market Outcomes*. Washington DC: The World Bank, 2008.

Fitzpatrick, R. 'Is Distance Education Better than the Traditional Classroom?' 2001. Available at: http://www.clecrpnt.com/accelepoint/articles/r_fitzpatrick_06001001 (accessed on 31 July).

Fosel, R. W. 'Nutrition and the Decline in Mortality Since 1700: Some Preliminary Findings.' In *Long Term Factor in American Economic Growth* edited by S. L. Engerman and R. E. Gallman, 439–455. NBER, University of Chicago Press, 1986.

Freeman, J. D., S. Kadiyala, J. F. Bell, and D. P. Martin. 'The Causal Effect of Health Insurance on Utilization and Outcomes in Adults: A Systematic Review of US Studies.' *Med Care* 46, no. 10 (October 2008): 1623–32.

Gallup, J., and J. Sachs. 'Development and Poverty in a Global Age: Location, Geography and Economic Development.' *Harvard Institutional Review* 21, no. i1 (1998): 56–61.

Goudge, J., L. Gilson, S. Russell, T. Gumedi and A. Mills. 'Affordability Availability and Acceptability Barriers to Health Care for the Chronically Ill: Longitudinal Case Studies from South Africa.' *BMC Health Service Resources*, 9 (May 2009): 9–75. Available at: http://www.ncbi.nlm.mih.gov/pubmed/19426533 (accessed on 15 November 2013).

Griffin, K., and T. Mckinley. *Implementing a Human Development Strategy*. London: Macmillan, 1994.

Grossman, M. 'The Human Capital Model of the Demand for Health.' In *Handbook of Health Economics* edited by A. T. Culyer and J. P. Newhouse, Chapter 7. Amsterdam: Elsevier, 2000[1972].

Hori, M., M. Ohashi, and S. Suzuki. 'Citizen-centric Approach and Health Care Management Based on the XML Web Services.' *The Electronic Journal of Information Systems Evaluation* 8, no. 3 (2005): 179–86.

Huntington, S. *The Third Wave: Decentralization in the Late Twentieth Century*. Norman and London: University of Oklahoma Press, 1991.

ILO. 'Safe Work.', 2001 Available at: http://www.ilo.org/public/english/protection/safework/management/download/promo.pdf (accessed on 29 September 2016).

Jacobs, G., and Asokan, N. Towards a Knowledge society Final Draft of the Vision 2020 Committee, The Mother's Service Society, Pondicherry, 2003, also see http://planningcommission.nic.in/reports/genrep/bkpap2020/8_bg2020.pdf (accessed on 25 November 2016).

Jhurree, V. 'Technology Integration in Education in Developing Countries: Guidelines to Policy Makers.' *International Education Journal* 6, no. 4 (2005): 467–83.

Joshi, S., and T. P. Schultz. 'Family Planning as an Investment in Development: Evaluation of a Program's Consequences in Matlab, Bangladesh.' IZA Discussion Paper No. 2639, Institute for Study of Labour, 2007.

Juler, M. 'Promoting Interaction: Maintaining Independence: Swallowing the Mixture.' *Open Learning* 5, no. 2 (1990): 24–33.

Kabirn, M., and M. S. Rahman. 'Fertility Transition in Oman and Its Economic Impact.' *Journal of Emerging Trends in Economics and Management Sciences* 3, no. 4 (2012): 308–11.

Kamara, A., L. Bousri, and M. Nyende. 'Growing a Knowledge-Based Economy: Evidence Public Expenditure on Education in Africa.' African Development Bank Economic Research Working Papers No. 88, Tunis, Tunisia, 2007.

Khan, J. A., S. A. Khan, and Reslan H. Al-Abaji. 'Prospects of Distance Education in Developing Countries.' Paper presented at International Conference on Millennium Driven in Training and Continuing Education, University of Bahrain, Bahrain, 24–26 April 2001.

Korir, D. K., and F. Kipkemboi. 'The Impact of School Environment and Peer Influences on Students' Academic Performance in Vihiga County Kenya.' *International Journal of Humanities and Social Sciences* 4, no. 5 (1) (2014): 241–51.

Krueger, A. B., and M. Lindahl. *Education for growth: why and for whom?* NBER, Cambridge, MA, Working paper 7591, 2000.

Lee, J. 'Economic Growth and Human Development, in the Republic of Korea 1945–1992.' United Nations Development Programme, Human Development Office, Occasional Paper 24, 1977.

Levy, M. *Modernization and Structure of Society*. Princeton: Princeton University Press, 1966.

Lewis, M, and G. Pettersson. *Governance in health care delivery: Raising performance*. Policy Research Working Paper 5074. Washington, DC: The World Bank, 2009.

Lim, D. *Explaining Economic Growth: A New Analytical Framework*. Vermont: Edward Elgar Publishing Co, 1996.

Lim, M. K. Health and Economic Impact of Occupational Health Services.' *Scandinavian Journal of Work, Environment and Health*, Supplements, no. 1 (2005): 38–42.

Lin, J. Y., and Z. Liu. 'Fiscal Decentralization and Economic Growth in China.' *Economic Development and Cultural Change* 49, no. 1 (2000): 1–21.

Lin, T. C. 'The Role of Higher Education in Economic Development: An Empirical Study of Taiwan Case.' *Journal of Asian Economics* 15, no. 2 (2004): 355–71.

Lipset, S. M. 'Some Social Requisites of Democracy: Economic Development and Political Legitimacy.' *America Political Science Review* 53 (1959): 69–105.

Marshall, A. *Principles of Economics*. 2 vols. 9th edition with annotations by C. W. Guillebaud. London: MacMillan Publishers, 1961.

McNabb, R., and K. Whitfield. 'The Market for Training: An Overview.' In *Market for Training* edited by R. McNabb and K. Whitfield, 1–18. Aldershot: Avebury Publishers, 1994.

Melnick, D., J. McNeely, Y. K. Navarro, G. Schmidt-Traub, and R. R. Sears. 'Environment and Human Well-Being: A Practical Strategy.' UN Millennium Project, Task Force on Environmental Sustainability, 2005. Available at: http://www.unmilleniumproject.org/documents/Environment-complete-lowres.pdf also, see http://mpra.ub.uni.muenchen.de/17207/1/MPRA_pap (accessed on 29 November 2013).

Mincer, J. 'Human Capital and the Labour Market: A Review of Current Research.' *Education Research* 18, no. 4 (1989): 27–34.

Mukherjee, J., and S. Banerjee. 'Education and Health: Strategic Sequencing in Social Development Contemporary Issues and Ideas in Social Sciences.' 2009. Available at: www.worldwewant2015.org/file/300184/download/325641 (accessed on 28 September 2013).

Muktdair-Al-Mukit, D. 'Public Expenditure on Education and Economic Growth: The Case of Bangladesh.' *International Journal of Applied Research in Business Administration and Economics* 1, no. 4 (2012): 10–18.

Musila, J., and W. Belassi. 'The Impact of Education Expenditures on Economic Growth in Uganda: Evidence from Time Series Data.' *The Journal of Developing Areas* 38, no. 1 (2004): 123–33.

National Institute of Ranking Framework. 'Indian Ranking 2016.' National Institute of Ranking Framework, Department of Education, Ministry of Human Resource Development, Government of India, New Delhi, 2016. Available at: http://mhrd.gov.in/sites/upload_files/mhrd/files/nirf_booklet_FINAL_02_04_16_01--00PM.pdf (accessed on 17 June 2016).

NHS Employer. *Mental Health Employment in the NHS*. Bressenden Place, London, 2008.

OECD. 'Vocational Education and Training in China Strength, Challenges and Policy Options,' 2010. Available at: http://www.oecd.org/education/skills-beyond-sch (accessed on 6 August 2015).

———. 'Teaching, Learning and Assessment for Adults Improving Foundation Skills.' OECD Publishing, 2008. Available at: http://www.oecd.org/edu/ceri/40046822.pdf (accessed on 13 November 2015).

Orem, J. N., J. M. Kirigia, R. Azairwe, I. Kasirye, and O. Walker. 'Impact of Malaria on Gross Domestic Product in Uganda.' *International Achieves of Medicine*, 5 (2012): 12. doi: 10.1186/1755-7682-5-12.

Perrott, G. J., and D. F. Holland. 'Population Trends and Problems of Public Health.' *The Milbank Quarterly* 83, no. 4 (2005): 569–08.

Preston, R., H. Waugh, S. Larkin, and J. Taylor. 'Community Participation in Rural Primary Health Care: Intervention of approach.' *Australian Journal of Primary Health*, 16 (2010): 4–16.

Pityana, N. Barney.'Open and Distance Learning in the Developing Trade : Trends, Progress and Challenges,' Key note speech delivered on the occasion of the M-2009, 23rd ICDE World Conference on Open Learning and Distance education, Flexible Education for All: Open-Global-Innovation, 7–10 June 2009, Masstricht, the Netherlands.

Public Health Agency of Canada (PHAC), and WHO. 'Health Equity through Intersectoral Action: An Analysis of 18 Countries Case Studies 2008.' HP5–67/2008E, 2008. Available at: http://www.who.int/social_determinants/resources/health_equity_isa_2008_en.pdf (accessed on 27 November 2016).

Rentlinger, S., and M. Selowskey.'Malnutrition and Poverty: Magnitude and Policy Options.' World Bank Occasional Paper No. 23, John Hopkins University Press, World Bank Baltimore, 1976.

Rose, P., and M. Greeley. 'Education in Fragile States: Capturing Lesson and Identifying Good Practice.' Paper prepared for the DAC Fragile State Working Group, 2006.

Ross, C. E., and C. Wu. 'The Links Between Education and Health.' *American Sociological Review*, 60 (1995): 719–45.

Ruxwana, N. L., E. M. Herselman, and P. D. Conradie. 2010. 'ICT Application as E-health Solutions in Rural Health Care in the Eastern Cape Province of South Africa.' *Health Information Management* 39, no. 1 (2010): 17–26.

Sayed, Y. 'Overcoming Exclusion in Education.' *State of the World Minorities & Indigenous Peoples*, 2009. Available at: http://www.google.co.in/url?sa=t&rct==j&q==&esrc==s (accessed on 27 March 2014).

Scott, P. Massification, internationalization and globalization, in Peter Scott (ed.), *The Globalization of Higher Education*. Buckingham: The Society for Research into Higher Education/Open University Press, 1998, pp. 108–129.

Sheik, M. R. 'Basic Development Needs Approach in the Eastern Mediterranean Region: From Theory to Practice.' *Mediterranean Health Journal* 6, no. 4 (2000): 766–74.

Stokes, S. C. 'Preserve Accountability: A Formal Model of Machine Politics with Evidence from Argentina.' *American Political Science Review* 99, no. 3 (2006): 315–25.

Sudbury and District Health Unit. '10 Promising Practices to Guide Local Public Health Practice to Reduce Social Inequities in Health: Technical Briefing.' Sudbury, 2011. Available at: http://nccdh.ca/resources/entry/10-promising-practices-guide (accessed on 27 November 2016).

Szirmai, A. *The Dynamics of Socio-Economic Development: An Introduction*. London: Cambridge University Press, 2005.

Tamang, P. 'The Impact of Educational Expenditure on India's Economic Growth.' *Journal of International Academic Research* 11, no. 3 (2011): 14–20.

The Lisbon Council. *European Jobs & Growth Monitor: Indicators for Success in the Knowledge Economy*. Brussels: Allianz Dresdner Economic Research, 2006.

Thyne, C. L. 'ABC's 123's and the Golden Rule: The Pacifying Effect of Education on Civil War, 1980–1999.' *International Studies Quarterly* 50, no. 4 (2006.): 733–34.

Twigg, C. 'Quality Assurance for Whom? Providers and Consumers in Today's Distributed Learning Environment', 2001. Available at: http://www.cnter.rpi.edu/PewSym/mono3.htm (accessed on 22 May 2016).

UNDP. *Human Development Report 1990*. New York: Oxford University Press, 1990.

———. 'Human Development Report.' United Nations Development Programmes, New York, 1991.

———. *Human Development Report 1996*, UNDP, New York, Oxford University Press, 1996.

———. 'Human Development Report 2001.' United Nations Development Programmes, Oxford University Press, Oxford, 2001.

UNESCO. 'Declaration and Integration Framework of Action on Education for Peace, Human Rights and Democracy.' Declaration of the 44th Session of the International Conference on Education Endorsed by the General Conference of UNESCO at its Twentieth Session, Paris, November, 1995.

———. 'The 2002 Global Education for all Monitoring Report: Is the World on Track?' Paris, UNESCO, 2002.

———. 'UN-Decade of Education for Sustainable Development: 2005–2014.' UNESCO-Education for Sustainable Development, 2005a. Available at: http://www.unesco.org/new/en/education/themes/leading-the-international-agenda/education-for-sustainable-development/ (accessed on 27 November 2016).

———. 'UNESCO's EFA Global Monitoring Report 2005.' UNESCO, Paris, 2005b.

———. 'EFA Global Monitoring Report.' UNESCO, Paris, 2011.

———. 'Education and Skills for Inclusive and Sustainable Development Beyond 2015.' UN System Task Team on the Post-2015 UN Development Agenda, UNESCO, Paris, 2012a.

———. 'Thematic Think Piece UNESCO.' UN System Task Team on the Post-2015, UN Development Agenda, Culture a driver and an enabler of sustainable development, UNESCO, 2012b.

UNFPA. Guidelines on Women's Empowerment', 2007. Available at: http://www.un.org/popin/unfpa/taskforce/guide/iatfwemp.gdl.html (accessed on 25 December 2007) also, see http://shodhganga.inflibnet.ac.in:8080/jspui/bitstream/10603/55656/7/07_chapter%201.pdf (accessed on 21 May 2016).

UNICEF. 'The Two Faces of Education in Ethnic Conflict Towards a Peace building Education for Children.' UNICEF, 2000.

United Nations. 'Office for ECOSOC Support and Coordination Human Resources Development,' 2013. Available at: http://www.un.org/en/aboutun/copyright (accessed on 29 September 2016).

Verba, S., and H. H. Nie. *Participation in America: Political Democracy and Social Equality*. New York: Harper and Row, 1972.

WHO. 'Report on Diseases.' World Health Organization, Geneva, 1995.

———. 'World Health Report 1997.' WHO, Geneva, 1997.

———. 'World Health Report 2000.' Mental Health, New Understanding, WHO, Geneva, 2001.

———. 'Community Participation in Local Health and Sustainable Development Approaches and Techniques.' European Sustainable Development and Health Series 4, World Health Organization Regional Office for Europe, 2002.

———. *Investing in Mental Health*. Geneva: World Health Organization, 2003.

———. 'e-Health for Health-Care Delivery: Strategy 2004–2007.' WHO, Geneva, 2004. Available at: www.who.int/eht/en/EHTstrategy 2004-–2007.pdf

Wolfinger, R. E., and S. J. Rosenstone. *Who Votes?* New Haven: Yale University Press, 1980.

Woodward, A., et al. 'Protecting human health in a changing world: The role of social and economic development.' *Bulletin World Health Organization 78*, no. 9 (2000): 1148–1155.

World Bank. *World Development Report*, World Bank, Oxford University Press, New York, 1991.

———. *World Development Report: Knowledge for Development*. New York: Oxford University Press, 1998.

WTO. WTO Secretariat in a document on Education Service in 23rd September in World Conference on Higher Education held in Paris, 1998, for details see http://www.mardias.net/site2010/?page_id=1049 (accessed on 26 November 2016).

Yogish, S. N. 'Education and Economic Development.' *Indian Journal of Social Development* 6, no. 2 (2006): 255–70.

Zondiros, D. 'Online, Distance Education and Globalization: Its Impact on Education Access, Inequality and Exclusions.' EURODL, Technological Education Institute (TEI) of Athens, Hellos, Greece, 2008.

4 Population and Development

The relationship between population growth and economic development has long been thought to be fundamental to understanding of less developed countries.

—Dawson and Tiffin (1998)

The demographic picture is indeed complex and poses some formidable challenges. These challenges are not surmountable, but we cannot deal with them by sticking our heads in the sand.

—Bloom (2011)

Fundamental concerns before developing countries are high population growth and its impact on development. Therefore, any discussion on development, more particularly in developing countries, will remain incomplete if it fails to discuss the impact of population on development. The relationship between the population and development is a classical as well as a contemporary concern, at least in developing countries where the population growth is high. To Hirschman (2004), population and development generally refer to the study of the consequences of population trends on socio-economic development, human welfare and natural resources.

The challenges of development, particularly in developing countries, one way or the other begin with the discussion on population composition and its impact on development issues such as poverty, inequality, unemployment, illiteracy, mortality, morbidity and access to other basic needs and quality of life. Controlling the population growth is always a contemporary challenge for the countries experiencing high population growth rates, as it has an adverse impact on development. Meeting this challenge will be especially important in developing countries considered 'fragile states' wherein booming population would further stress already limited resources (Redding 2007). Skilled, innovative, young and dynamic population is an asset to a nation, as it can hasten the pace of economic growth and development. On the other hand, dull, lethargic, morbid, unskilled and demotivated population is a burden on the economy, as its steady growth will reduce per capita income of the family, affect productivity and economic growth and development. Besides, composition of large percentage of unproductive population in the age group of 0–14 years and above 60 years may also adversely affect the development process of a country to a great extent. Considering young population as an asset and demographic dividend is a hypothetical issue to be critically studied in the context of developing countries.

After reading this chapter, you will be able to:

1. Explain the role of population in development
2. Describe various population theories
3. Discuss various components of population issues
4. Explain various challenges of population growth on development and measures to control population growth

POPULATION AND DEVELOPMENT: THE RELATIONSHIP

It is not a flight of fancy but truly the first thing the developing nations have to do is to control their population, which has an adverse impact on the economic growth and development of these nations. Customarily, everything remaining constant, high population growth retards economic growth and is detrimental to the sustainable development, particularly, in the resources crunch developing countries. However, one of the exponents has remarked that the relationship between population growth and economic development is a complex one and the historical evidence is ambiguous, particularly concerning the cause and effect (Thirwall, 1994). But, there has been a broad consensus that while development institutions, infrastructure, policies, programmes and projects are important factors in shaping the dynamics of economic growth and development, yet population dynamics such as population growth rate, dependency ratio and morbidity and mortality rates also play an important role in determining the pace of economic growth and development.

At the household level, lower fertility has also been found associated with better health and schooling outcomes and lower poverty (Dasgupta, Bongaarts and Cleland 2011). Since the ancient times, statesmen and philosophers have expressed opinion about such issues, as the optimum number of people and the disadvantages of excessive population growth harmed the prospects for development and strong policies to reduce population growth rates were essential preconditions for sustained economic development (National Academy of Science 1971). Easterlin (1967) was of the opinion that 'some theoretical analyses argues that high population growth creates pressures on limited natural resources, reduces private and public capital formation and diverts additions to capital resources to maintaining rather than increasing the stock of capital per worker.' While, Dyson (2010) claims that mortality decline aids economic growth and hence leads to an increase in the standard of living. Evidence from contemporary developing countries tends to show that it is mortality decline that leads to economic growth, as it increases investment in both physical and human capital via increased savings rates and education (Bloom and Canning 2001; Kalemli-Ozcan 2002).

The challenges such as climate change and global warming, fragile and failed states, migration and refugee crisis, food and water insecurity, poverty and inequality, mortality and morbidity, indebtedness, illiteracy, increasing crime rate, unemployment and underemployment and so on are largely consequences of unchecked population growth. From the Indian context, it can be said that the states like Bihar and Uttar Pradesh which have higher fertility rate are lagging behind in all socio-economic development indicators as compared to Southern Indian States of Kerala and Tamil Nadu which have lower fertility rate. Thus, checking unbridled population growth in the 21st century is critical to the development of developing countries which are already overpopulated.

THEORIES OF POPULATION

Any discussion of population and development to begin with has to take into consideration various theories of population. These are important because it will give necessary trigger and understanding on various perspectives of population and development. Various theories propounded at different points of time for studying and establishing the relationship between population and development are the Malthusian theory, pessimistic theories, optimistic theories and the demographic transition theory.

MALTHUSIAN THEORY OF POPULATION

The leading exponent of the pessimistic theory of population and development relationship was T. R. Malthus. It is said that it still provides the starting place for most of the popular discussions on the subject of population change (Robinson 1964). Thus, it can be said that any discussion on population theory begins with the Malthusian theory of population. Since the publication of Malthus's *An Essay on the Principles of Population* in 1798, development economists, demographers, sociologists, social scientists and policymakers of the world have devoted a good deal of effort to address the problem of population growth. Malthus's famous formulation is that population increases in a 'geometric progression' (2, 4, 8,...) while the food production grows at an 'arithmetic progression' (1, 2, 3, 4,...), and he predicted that this would produce adverse effects on the economic growth and development of a nation. He considers population growth a key factor in the whole process of economic development. Therefore, he laid stress on controlling population growth through 'positive' and 'preventive' checks.

The positive checks on population growth are exerted in the form of starvation, diseases and so on, while the preventive checks on population control are in the form of measures like adoption of family planning methods, increasing legal age at marriage and so on. Malthus suggested that when the population growth outpaced the food supply in an economy, the future growth of population must be checked by positive and preventive checks. He strongly believes that if the population growth overtakes the growth of productivity in an economy, then it will have adverse impact on its development.

NEO-MALTHUSIAN THEORY

The Neo-Malthusian demographers Ansely Coale and Edgar Hoover (1958) in their exemplar research work on population growth and economic development in low-income countries argued that declining fertility would lead to rapid economic growth. They put forth their argument by saying that higher fertility will create a very youthful age structure of population and gradually raise the 'dependency ratio'. A reduction in fertility will effect change in the dependency ratio and would allow diversion of economic resources from the care and maintenance of children towards productive economic investment and would raise economic growth rate. They emphasized on controlling population growth rate in the favour of higher economic growth rate.

Optimistic Theory of Population

The main proponents of the optimistic theory of population are Easter Boserup (1965) and Julian Simon (1977). Boserup was an optimist and had a positive outlook towards the effect of population growth on development. Boserup argued that population growth and economic growth create increased demand for resources. By advocating this proposition, he meant that population growth has a direct and positive relationship with economic development. He used the famous quotation 'necessity is the mother of invention' to justify his argument. He contended that with the growth of population, new innovations will take place in the economy. These new innovations, according to his view, could solve the problems caused by overpopulation and create a sustainable world for growing population. Boserup believed that people possess a great resource of knowledge, skill and technological bent of mind. This would be helpful in the innovation of new technologies. With the help of new technologies, food productivity would be enhanced in the economy. Ultimately, this would be helpful to effectively counter unfavourable circumstances and problems created by overpopulation.

Julian Simon (1977), another proponent of the optimistic population theory, argued that each person is a potential possessor of ingenuity and creativity. Societies with large populations would be more likely to develop because they possess a large number of potential scientists, inventors and creative minds. He had a great faith in human resources and human capabilities and considered human beings the most vital asset of economic development. Simon (1996) prominently put forth that 'the ultimate resource is people—skilled, spirited and hopeful people who will exert their wills and imaginations for their own benefits and inevitably they will benefit not only themselves but the rest of us as well.' Therefore, according to his view, high population growth in a country is not a problem but an advantage to exploit the potential of human resources for the benefit and development of the nation.

Demographic Transition Theory

The most recent and one of the scientific theories of population is the demographic transition theory. This theory propounds that as an economy moves from the stage of underdevelopment towards development, the transition also takes place in the population. Similarly, as a nation marches from the state of underdevelopment towards development, the population growth rate also changes from a stage of high birth rate to a stage of low birth rate. According to this theory, there are four stages in population transition which are as follows:

1. **The First Stage: Pre-industrialization Stage.** This is the primitive stage where the traditional agriculture system predominant in the society. This traditional society is governed by the traditional customs, practices and believes beliefs and values. The decision with regard to the number of children a women has to

give birth and the general fertility rate in this society is governed by the traditional and values. Because of non-availability of modern medical care and family planning services both the birth rate as well as death rate is very high. This is the stage of high birth rate and high death rate. The birth rate is high because giving birth to a child is largely considered a gift of god on which a man has no control. Since literacy rate is low among both men and women and astoundingly low among women, women are ignorant about the reproductive and child health care issues and challenges. Because of the poor reproductive health empowerment of women, they resort to pregnancies and give birth to children as per the whim and wishes of the husbands and in-laws. Further, impoverished and illiterate households consider children income earning hands; more the number of children, more are the number of earning hands.

As per the traditional beliefs and values, male children are required in the family to perform the final rituals of the parents. Therefore, the desire to have a male child, in many cases, enhances the fertility rate and birth rate in the family. High death rate occurs because of the lack of availability of modern health care facilities and poor accessibility to quality health care services among the population, especially among the rural population. Thus, high birth rate and high death rate lead to slow growth rate of population in this stage.

2. **The Second Stage: Industrialization Stage.** This is the stage of high birth rate and low death rate. With the advancement of technology, food production increases and the pace of industrialization and urbanization rise. The transition of population from the rural to urban areas and from the agriculture to industrial sector increases their income. With the increase in income, they become capable of feeding and rearing more children. This income capability entices them to have more children. They also become capable of paying for nutritional care of children. Moreover, increase in the availability of food and nutrition products in the market enhances child survival and curtails infant and child mortality rates. This ultimately affects the total fertility rate, which continues to rise. Thus, birth rate and fertility rate are high in this stage. As far as maternal health care is concerned, availability of maternal health care services also ensures women to have safe pregnancy, safe delivery and safe birth. Furthermore, as compared to the birth rate, the death rate also declines because of the availability of modern health care facilities, people's capability to pay for modern health care services and government provisioning of modern health care facilities to control mortality and morbidity among the population. People also become health conscious, and availability of food and nutrition enhances longevity. This stage of high birth and fertility rate and low death rate leads to population explosion. In Western Europe, this stage occurred during the 19th century with the Industrial Revolution. In many of developing countries, few states or regions are experiencing this stage now.
3. **The Third Stage: Post-industrialization Stage.** This is the stage of low birth rate and low death rate, and most of the developed countries of Europe and a few developed countries of Asia are experiencing this stage. As the literacy and level of education increases, people become more conscious to have high standards of living with a small family size. In the rural societies too, people restrict their family size in order to prevent division and fragmentation of land. Besides, the status of

women also increases in the society. With the increase in the status of women in the society, they prefer to engage themselves in income-earning activities rather than be occupied with child bearing, rearing and unpaid household activities. They become more health conscious, prefer to opt for late marriage and have less number of children for the well-being of the children and family. They take most of the decisions regarding their fertility. All these factors lead to low birth rate.

With the availability of maternal and child health care facilities in the health centres, the death rate comes down. Family planning devices are also made readily available in the health centres and even in shops. IEC programmes on family planning are propagated through print and electronic media as well as through individual and group counselling methods. Furthermore, the age at marriage of both male and female population increases. All these factors create an impact on the birth rate and death rate, which become low. Furthermore, the death rate obviously becomes low in the post-industrial society because of the availability of modern health care facilities and social security measures for old age population. In a nutshell, this is the stage of low birth rate and low death rate. The four different phases of demographic transition are given in Figure 4.1.

4. **The Fourth Stage: Globalization Stage.** This is the stage of globalization, where the industrialization and services sector activities are predominant over primary sector activities. Industrialization, modernization and urbanization take place on a massive scale. From the standpoint of population, this stage is popularly called the population stabilization stage. Both males and females become career conscious, job oriented and assign preference to earning and enjoying a good quality of life rather than bearing and rearing of children. In many countries, even fertility rate reduces below the replacement level. This is the stage with very low birth rate and very low death rate. In this stage, the population in the dependency

Figure 4.1 *Four Different Phases of Demographic Transition*

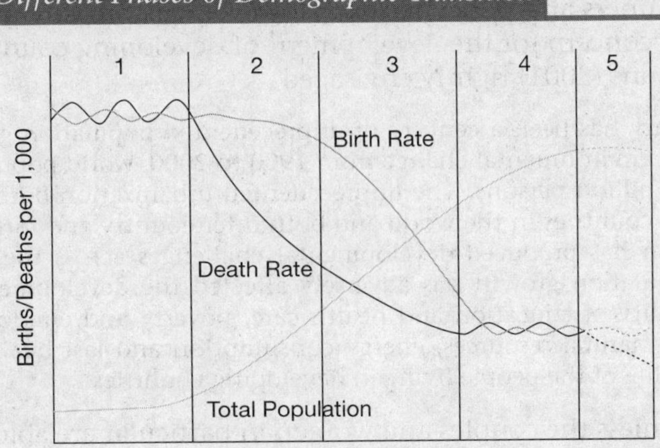

Source: http://www.boundless.com/.../demographic-transition-theory-690-10230/ (accessed on 21 April 2016).

age group, i.e. above 60 years, rises in the demographic pyramid. Most of the European countries and even Japan is experiencing this stage of low population growth rate. Further, this stage features no marriage and less marriage; moreover, contract marriage and even divorce and separation rate are high among the newly married couples. Other features which have an adverse impact on fertility are same-sex marriages which are taking place in many developed countries, and the legal systems of a few countries have approved these marriages. This stage of globalization is the stage of population stabilization; further, even negative growth rate of population has taken place in many developed countries, resulting in a demographic crisis having less percentage of youth population in the total population. If this trend of negative population growth, increasing population in the dependency age group and less percentage of population in the adult age group of the population pyramid continues, it will hasten the process of migration of population from developing countries to the developed countries. This is a major demographic trend that the globalization era is currently experiencing. Continuously having population below the replacement level, many countries are even encouraging the newly married young couples to have children.

Most of developing countries and India too are in between Stage Two and Three. A few states in India, e.g. Kerala and Tamil Nadu, have already moved to Stage Three, having low birth rate and low death rate. However, the two demographically bigger states of Bihar and Uttar Pradesh are still between Stage One and Two, with high birth rate and moderately low death rate. They still have to reduce their infant and maternal mortality rate.

POPULATION SCENARIO

The relationship between population and development, particularly in developing countries, will always remain a dubious debatable topic among the demographers, economists, social scientists, planners and policymakers. However, customarily unabated population growth is a cause of concern for the development of developing countries (Tables 4.1 and 4.2). As United Nations (2001) rightly envisaged,

> [T]wentieth century has been a century of unprecedented population growth, economic development and environmental change from 1900 to 2000, world population grow from 1.6 billion to 6.1 billion persons. The unprecedented urbanization both in developed as well as developed countries in the world and both inter-country and intra-country migration of population has produced developmental challenges across the countries of the world. Rapid population growth has adversely affected the development indicators i.e. quantity and quality of education and health care, poverty and employment situation; environment and natural resources, energy consumption and last but not the least the overall quality of life of the people living in developing countries.

It is a fact that unless the couples and women in particular are able to gain better control over their own reproduction and to achieve their desired fertility, right to take appropriate decision on the size of their family, particularly the small family norm, continuous high fertility and population pressures will not only affect the economic health of their family but it would also make development difficult in developing countries. The UNFPA's

Table 4.1 *World Population Milestones*

Population	Year
1 billion	1804
2 billion	1927 (123 year later)
3 billion	1960 (33 year later)
4 billion	1974 (13 year later)
5 billion	1987 (13 year later)
6 billion	1999 (12 year later)
World Population May Reach	
7 billion	2012 (13 year later)
8 billion	2026 (14 year later)
9 billion	2043 (17 year later)

Source: United Nations (2001).

Table 4.2 *Top Nine Countries in Terms of Population Increase and Top Nine in Terms of Population Decrease from 2000 to 2050: Median Variant*

Country	Population Change During 2000–50 (Millions)
A. Population Increase	
1. India	572
2. Pakistan	162
3. Nigeria	141
4. Democratic Republic of the Congo	127
5. China	118
6. Bangladesh	114
7. United States of America	111
8. Uganda	103
9. Ethiopia	102
B. Population Decrease	
1. Russian Federation	–35
2. Ukraine	–23
3. Japan	–15
4. Italy	–7
5. Poland	–7
6. Romania	–5
7. Germany	–4
8. Belarus	–3
9. Bulgaria	–3

Source: United Nations (2005).

State of World Population 2002 has concluded that (a) population age structures have an impact on development: a high proportion of young dependents holds back economic growth and (b) slower population growth has encouraged overall economic growth in developing countries. However, particularly in developing countries, the various demographic dynamics, i.e. fertility, mortality and dependency ratio will continue to influence the economic growth and socio-economic development of the nation states. It will pose a surmountable challenge to the environment and sustainable development. Principle 8 of the Rio Declaration states that 'to achieve sustainable development and a higher quality of life for all people, States should reduce and eliminate unsustainable patterns of production and consumption and promote appropriate demographic policies.'

The Agenda 21 of the Rio Conference, which covers demographic dynamics and sustainability, states that 'the growth of world population and production combined with unsustainable consumption patterns places increasingly severe stress on the life-supporting capacities of our planet.' The interrelationship between population and development will always remain a hot topic of discussion even in the 21st century development scenario of the less developed countries.

COMPONENTS OF POPULATION AND DEVELOPMENT

The important issues to be taken into consideration while dealing with the population and development issues are discussed below.

POPULATION DYNAMICS

Population dynamics, such as population growth rate, birth rate, death rate, fertility rate, mortality rate, morbidity rate, dependency ratio, sex ratio and so on, certainly have bearing not only on population but also on different dynamics of development.[1] Population growth rate is the prime indicator of population and demographic situation in a country. It indicates the pace of the rise in the population. Customarily, a country calculates its population growth rate in every population census conducted every 10 years. The demographic situation, whether the population growth has increased or decreased, is determined by births, deaths and migrations. The difference between birth rate and death rate of population in a particular period is known as natural increase while difference between in-migration and out-migration is the net migration rate, and the population growth rate is the sum total of natural increase and net migration rate. The birth rate and death rate are the number of births and number of deaths occurred during a given year respectively, divided by the total midyear population for the same year, multiplied by 1,000. However, the important measure of population is the total fertility rate which is the sum total of age-specific fertility rates of women in the age from 15 to 49 years.

The fertility rate in a country's population is affected by several factors such as biological, physiological, religious, educational, economic status, education status of the population, prevalence of beliefs and values regarding population, status of women and availability of reproductive health care services and the population policy of the country. On the other hand, the population dynamics of a country is influenced by the infant and maternal mortality rate. Low infant and maternal mortality rate is largely being observed in the developed countries while these two rates are quite high in developing countries of South Asia and Africa. The infant mortality rate indicates the number of deaths of children below one year of age per thousand live births in a given year. And the maternal mortality rate is the number of female deaths as a result of pregnancy and childbirth-related complications per 100,000 live births in a given year.

Dependency ratio is another important population dynamics, it describes the number of dependent population, i.e. child population below the age of 15 plus elderly population above age of 65 per thousand population in a given year. The rising percentage of elderly population in the European and other developed countries is the cause of concern for their economies. On the other hand, the high percentage of young age population in developing countries is also a cause of concern since these countries need to provide education, health care, employment and other required facilities to this section of population. The sex ratio—the number of female per thousand male in a given year—is another important dynamic of population. The low sex ratio in some of the states of India, such as Punjab, Haryana, Delhi, Himachal Pradesh, and declining sex ratio in other parts of the countries is a cause of concern, and in the future this demographic imbalance will lead to many social problems such as crime against women, rape and molestation, forced marriages, and so on.

Reproductive Health Care

Reproductive health care is one of the important determinants of fertility and population growth. In the words of WHO, reproductive health implies that people are able to have a responsible, satisfying and safe sex life, and that they have the capacity to reproduce and the freedom to decide it, when and how often to do so.[2] Maternal and child health care, family planning services, STDs/HIV/AIDS education and treatment, infertility treatment and adolescent reproductive health education are the core components of reproductive health care. The important aspects covered in the Reproductive Child Health (RCH) care are right age at marriage, antenatal care, natal care and institutional delivery, postnatal care, immunization of children, nutritional care of mother and children, family planning, HIV/AIDS, adolescent health care and infertility care. All these health care services are provided through primary health care services centres, private hospitals and also through NGO-based health care service providers. The basic aim of RCH care services is to prevent infant and maternal mortality rate and check morbidity among women and children. The family planning services, which comprise permanent methods such as vasectomy and tubectomy and other temporary methods such as IUD, condom, oral pills and so on, are mainly aimed at restricting the family size, spacing between the pregnancies and controlling unwanted fertility. However, besides restricting the family size, the reproductive health care intends to control infertility.

STDs and HIV/AIDS are important aspects of reproductive health care in recent years because of the rise in such cases in developing countries among the productive age group of population, particularly in the African countries. Today, the number of people infected with HIV in the world has already reached an estimated 39.4 million with over 95% of them living in the developing world (Chia 2007). The United Nations have expressed that the interactive threats of hunger and HIV/AIDS in parts of the world are leading to complex humanitarian crises, whereby people affected by AIDS are unable to grow food or work for living. Moreover, malnourishments weaken the immune system and strengthen of those with HIV/AIDS, making them succumb more quickly to diseases.[3] The STD and HIV/AIDS is causing loss of life and man hours and adversely affecting the economic development of many African countries. It is remarked that depending on the political environment, good health (low HIV/AIDS prevalence) can contribute directly to economic growth, while poor health (high HIV/AIDS prevalence) and poverty can be mutually reinforcing (Chia 2007).

Population Education

Population education aims at educating people in general and the adults and adolescents in particular regarding various population issues and challenges. UNESCO (1971) defines population education as 'an education programme which provides for a study of the population situation in the family, community, nation and the world, with the purpose of developing in students' rational and responsive attitude and behaviour towards that situation.' The components covered in the population education are population dynamics, age at marriage and responsible parenthood, adolescent reproductive health life cycle, nutritional health care, family planning and small family norms, HIV/AIDS, drug abuse and alcoholism, safe drinking water and sanitation, environmental pollution and its impact on health, girl child education and women empowerment, quality of life and population growth and its impact on development. The population issues and challenges are needed to be integrated into the curriculum at all the levels of education starting from primary education up to tertiary education level. In India, National Council of Educational Research and Training (NCERT) has attempted to integrate population education topics in the school education system.

Population Migration and Diaspora

Migration, both inter- and intra-country migrations are intimately interconnected with development. Although the intra-country migration has helped the nation to gain from the foreign country in terms of remittances, yet the brain drain and migration of skilled population from the developing country to other countries is a loss. The inter-country migration, particularly migration of unskilled population from the rural to urban areas, has created problems in the cities. Besides, rural to rural migration has helped the development of the in-migration state, but created development problems in the out-migration state. The out-migration of people from the rural areas of Bihar and Eastern Uttar Pradesh to rural areas of Punjab and Haryana and working in the agriculture sector, on the one hand, has helped in the agricultural development of in-migrating states, on the other hand, it has created problems for the agricultural development in the out-migrating states.

One of the important challenges of population growth is the migration of population from rural to urban areas through push and pull effect. It has contributed to the explosive growth of cities around the globe and growth of slums in the cities of developing countries. The part of the population, particularly illiterate and unskilled, that has migrated from rural areas to urban areas is seen to be having a lower quality of life and is subject to urban indifference in all fronts, social and economic. Bloom (2011) has remarked that the most painful aspect of the world's future demographic behaviour is likely to be international migration. Migration may become the most important branch of demography in the early decades of the new millennium in a rapidly globalizing world (Samuel and George 2002). Like internal migration, with globalization, international migration and development is a hot topic in demographic dynamics. In 2013, 232 million people or 3.2% of the world's population were international migrants, and the global population of international migrants is growing at about 1.6% per year (United Nations 2013). If the current rate of international migration continues, the number of international migrants worldwide could reach 405 million by 2050 (IOM 2010). International remittances from migrants to their families in low- and middle-income countries are now greater than foreign direct investment and official development assistance (Cecilia 2010). The African Development Bank[4] has noted that China, Korea and India are among the countries which have shown that diaspora contribution can significantly help to transform economies. From the African context, the Bank has noted that 30 million African migrants are living outside their countries and send home about $40 billion on an annual basis.

At the household level, recipients of remittances in Africa were found to have higher level of education, and were more likely to have some form of saving accounts than those who were not receiving money from abroad. The remittances sent by the Indian diaspora working and staying in different parts of world are found to have impact on the development in their own country. The rising socio-economic conditions of the countryside population of Punjab and Kerala are illustrious examples, depicting the impact of population migration and the contribution of Punjabi and Malayali diaspora on the countryside socio-economic development of their states.

In the context of migration and development, the issues and challenges such as in-migration, out-migration, return migration, brain drain and brain gain are the burning topics of discussion and deliberations in developing countries in this globalized era. Furthermore, deciding the optimum number of internal and international migration from the perspective of in-migration and out-migration is a challenge from the population and development perspective.

Population Policy

Many countries in the world and more particularly developing countries have formulated their own population policies. These population policies basically intend to restrict the size of the population to a limit which does not pose any challenge to their economic growth and development. Population policies are customarily defined as purposeful measures aimed at affecting demographic processes, notably fertility, mortality and migration (Demeny 1975). To Schultz (2007), population policies are defined as voluntary programmes which help people control their fertility and expect to improve their lives.

Objectives of the National Population Policy 2000, India

The National Population Policy 2000 was formulated with carefully articulated objectives. The short, medium and long run objectives of the policy are as follows:

1. The immediate objective is to address the unmet needs for contraception, health care infrastructure and health personnel, and to provide integrated service delivery for basic reproductive and child health care.
2. The medium term objective was to bring the total fertility rate (TFR) to replacement levels by 2010, through vigorous implementation of inter-sectoral operational strategies.
3. The long term objective was to achieve a stable population by 2045, at a level consistent with the requirements of sustainable economic growth, social development and environmental protection.

Palpably, the short-, medium- and long-term objectives are intertwined, and failure on short to medium run goals would have serious implication for the long-run objective of population stabilization.

Source: National Population Policy 2000, Ministry of Health and Family Welfare, Government of India, New Delhi.

According to the United Nations World Population Policies 2013, nearly half of the governments in more developed regions had policies to raise their rate of population growth, and only 2% had policies to lower it in 2013. In contrast, nearly half of the governments in less developed regions had policies to lower the rate of population growth, and 10% had policies to raise it. The population policy of China and India intends to control population growth through the use of family planning devices. China's one child family norm (introduced in 1979), which remained in vogue for several years, is a part of their policy for controlling population in the country. Milwertz (1997) wrote that

> In the early 1970s a population policy with the explicit objective of reducing population growth was initiated. The measures implemented to reduce fertility were summed up in the slogan '*wan-xi-shano*' signifying later marriages and child bearing lower interval between children and fewer children. The policy is thus often referred to as the *wan-xi-shano* policy.

India's population policies and the family welfare programmes intend to limit its population growth and human fertility through the use of various family planning methods (Table 4.3).

Health Policy

Health in general and health status of women and children in particular is linked to the fertility rate and population size. The low fertility rate and population growth rate in a country is also featured with lower maternal and infant mortality rate. Generally, in the countries having lower fertility rate and low growth rate of population, the health status of

Table 4.3 *Government Policies on the Rate of Population Growth, 1976–2013 (World)*

Year	Raise	Maintain	Lower	No Intervention	Total
1976	28 (19%)	0	39 (26%)	83 (55%)	150 (100%)
1986	26 (16%)	12 (7%)	53 (32%)	73 (45%)	164 (100%)
1996	25 (13%)	16 (8%)	71 (37%)	81 (42%)	193 (100%)
2005	29 (19%)	32 (16%)	70 (36%)	63 (32%)	199 (100%)
2013	39 (19%)	41 (21%)	73 (37%)	44 (22%)	197 (100%)

Source: United Nations, World Population Policies 2013.

the people is found to be comparatively high, and there are less morbidities and mortalities. One of the illustrious examples is Kerala (India), which has low infant and maternal mortality rate; it also has low fertility rate prevailing below the replacement level. Many nation states have formulated health policies and set various health-related goals to be achieved through stipulated actions delineated in the policy documents. According to WHO,

> Health policy refers to decisions, plans and actions that are undertaken to achieve specific health care goals within a society. An explicit health policy can achieve several things: it defines a vision for the future which in turn helots to establish targets and points of reference for the short and medium terms. It outlines priorities and the expected roles of different groups and it builds consensus and informs people.[5]

The National Health Policy 2000 of the Government of India focuses on the need for enhanced funding and organizational restructuring of the national public health initiatives to facilitate more equitable access to the health facilities, while recently formulated draft, National Health Policy 2015, intends to make health a fundamental right of the citizen. Without a sound health policy and its religious implementation, the population goal cannot be effectively achieved. Developing countries with high population growth rate have to formulate effective health policies and religiously implement them for not only improving the health status of its population but also for controlling its population growth rate and link population with sustainable development.

These are a few vital components of population issues particularly from the perspective of developing countries, where the growing population is posing challenges to its economic growth and development.

POPULATION AND DEVELOPMENT: ISSUES AND CHALLENGES

World population passed 6 billion mark at the end of the 20th century and stands at 6.5 billion in 2005 and is expected to increase by 2.6 billion during the next 45 years, from 6.5 billion to 9.1 billion (United Nations 2005). UNFPA viewed that the countries with the highest poverty levels are generally those that have the most rapid increase in population and the highest fertility levels. On the other hand, countries that have reduced fertility and mortality by investing in universal health care, including reproductive health as well as education and gender equality, have made economic gains. Population growth reflected in terms of higher fertility and large family size, particularly in impoverished families belonging to developing countries, would affect their quality of life. It will affect their access to quality health care, housing, sanitation facilities, education, employment and per capita income. In the Sub-Saharan Africa, the region with the most rapid rate of annual population growth and the lowest level of contraceptive practice appears to have witnessed no progress at all in reducing the level of dire poverty (Merrick 2002). As population growth slows down, countries can invest more in education, health care, job creation and other improvements that help boosting standard of living (Upadhyay and Robey 1999). The high population growth in developing countries with poor resources is a challenge to many socio-economic issues such as education, health, sanitation, housing, poverty and so on.

High fertility and population growth appear to promote the transmission of poverty across the generation (Cincotta and Engelman 1997). Besides poverty, population growth would affect employment situation and lead to more casualization of employment. The rapid growth of informal sector in developing countries is an upshot of high size of population. African Development Bank (2000) has noted that rapid population growth does not only affect the capacity to create jobs and absorb the supply of labour but also leads to tight competition for limited employment opportunities and results in the violation of core labour standards, i.e. the minimum age for employment and child labour, discrimination and so on. Also, the mismatch caused by population growth in labour supply and demand adversely affects the promotion of international labour standards as well as issues of gender equality. Higher population growth in rural areas and their consequent migration to the urban areas for employment have further strengthened the urban informal economy and distrusted the urban labour market. It is characterized by lower wage rate, lack of job and social security and poor quality of life. Population growth and informal employment go hand in hand. Disguised unemployment in rural areas and underemployment in urban areas are mainly caused by high population growth and rural to urban migration.

Poverty, if clubbed with large family size, would affect the health and nutritional status of the children. The malnutrition among the children of large family would affect their physical as well as mental health. Research conducted in many developing countries demonstrates that children in large families tend to be ill-nourished over the long term (Lloyd 1994), which can undermine school performance and hence, future earnings potential (Wolfe and Behrman 1982). At the family level, the capacity to plan the number and timing of childbirths can dramatically affect household economic well-being through improved maternal and child health and more productive use of time, human energy and income (World Bank 1993). Undernourishment among the youth, women and aging population is largely observed in the states having higher population growth rate.

Increase in population in a family will affect the farm size. Larger is the family size, higher is the fragmentation of land holding and smaller will be the size of landholding. In rural areas of Green Revolution belt of India, increase in family size due to higher fertility has caused division of land and pauperization of peasantry, especially among the small, medium and marginal land owners. Besides, in India, due to rapid increase of population, a negative growth trend was noticed in the area under forest, barren and uncultivable land, cultivable waste land, permanent pastoral and grazing lands, miscellaneous trees not included in net shown area, fallow land other than current fallow (Saithal and Bhargava 2007). Population density was a key factor in the conversion of timberland and agricultural land for urban use (Zhang and Nagubadi 2005). The fragmentation of land-holdings because of increase in family size in rural areas of developing countries will create problem for mechanization of agriculture. It will also add to woes of disguised unemployment in agriculture sector, impacting on per capita income.

Excessive population growth in the hilly and forest areas would affect natural resources, affect climate change and adversely affect the environment. In urban areas, it will put pressure on urban infrastructure, i.e. housing, transport, sewerage system, water supply, electricity, energy, schools, hospital and policing. It will add to urban crime, urban pollution and environmental degradation, leading to many fatal diseases and deaths among the urban population. Numerous multi-country studies have professed a strong connection between population growth, deforestation and other forms of land cover changes at the national level (Amelung and Diehl 1992; Rudel and Roper 1997). The poor are more vulnerable to further decline in ecosystem services (Millennium Ecosystem Assessment 2005), as livelihood strategies are significantly more likely to be dependent upon the natural resources (Hope 2002). Slowing the increase in population, especially in the face of rising per capita demand for natural resources, can take pressure off the environment and buy time to improve living standards on a sustainable basis (Green 1992).

Delayed marriage, less marriage and no marriage in European countries, and in the Asian countries like Japan, are indications towards second demographic transition in the developed world. As a result, many socio-economic, psychological and cultural and life style changes have been identified as the driving force behind youth attitude towards delayed entry into the parenthood. Retherford, Oganwa and Matsukura (2001), from their study, have reflected that the Government of Japan is concerned about the trends of later marriages and less marriages, especially because these trends are major contributing causes of Japan's very low fertility, about which government is concerned. One of the reasons discovered by them is the changing nature of women's labour force participation, which is likely to continue to exert upward pressure on age of marriage, as women are more into carrier oriented jobs. This trend found to be transgressing, at least, in the metropolis of developing countries. Staying together as partner without marriage is becoming popular in the metropolitan cities of developing countries. This uncultured and unethical demographic transition is going to posit major social, demographic and cultural challenges to developing countries in the near future.

Another emerging demographic challenge, although minuscule yet profoundly pictured, is gay marriages, as happening in the developed countries. The same-sex marriage is going to affect the demographic scenario in the developed countries. Furthermore, it would also affect the socio-cultural milieu in many other countries, including the developing ones, in the days to come. Some of the countries are legalizing the same-sex marriages, which is going to put pressure on other countries to give recognition to the same-sex marriage in the long run. Moxness (1993), a Norwegian sociologist, has argued that same-sex marriages have been legalized not so much because homosexuality has become more acceptable, but because marriage has become an increasingly empty institution and is no longer seen as a mandatory entrance to adult life, sexual life and parenthood.

The notion of 'demographic dividend' being propounded in the countries like India and China, having large percentage of youth population, is hypothetically considered an opportunity as well as threat to these countries. As an opportunity, if properly skilled, trained, empowered and employed, they will act as great human resource not only for these two countries but also for the world. However, if not properly handled, they are going to be burden on these two countries and would be indulged in crime, drug abuse, alcoholism and extremism which can thwart the growth and development process. While commenting in her article 'The other half of the demographic dividend', Sonalde Desai (2010) advocated that India is unlikely to realize its 'demographic dividend' unless significant strides are made to increase employment opportunities and reduce labour market disadvantages.

SUMMARY

Population and development has always been a contemporary challenge for most of developing countries for centuries. In fact, with limited financial resources, managing a huge population is a herculean task for developing countries of South Asia, Africa and Latin America. The countries that incorporated strong and effective population policies within the broader context of social and economic development policies were able to cash in very profitably on the demographic bonus (Bloom and Canning 2006). Thus, population and development are intimately connected, at least, in developing countries where the fertility rate is high and resources are limited to fulfil the aspirations of the growing population. The high fertility rate among the rural and socio-economically backward section of population is going to add further agonies to their existing low socio-economic conditions such as poverty, illiteracy, mortality, morbidity and so on. Therefore, controlling population, at least, in developing countries is a demographic challenge not only for these nations but also for the international agencies engaged in the population and development issues.

Keywords: dependency ratio, demographic dividend, optimistic theory of population, pessimistic theory of population, population policy, reproductive health, health policy, population education, population dynamics.

REVIEW QUESTIONS

1. Population and development are interrelated, illustrate.
2. Critically discuss various theories of population.
3. Discuss key components of population and development.
4. Population is a boon as well as a bane for development, illustrate.
5. What are the important issues in population and development from the standpoint of developing countries? Explain.
6. Explain various challenges of population and measures to be taken to control population in developing countries.

7. Write short notes on the following:
   (i) Demographic dividend
   (ii) Optimistic theories of population
   (iii) Pessimistic theories of population
   (iv) Reproductive health care
   (v) National Health Policy of India
   (vi) National Population Policy of India 2000

NOTES

1. Crude Birth Rate (CBR) $= \dfrac{\text{Birth in a year}}{\text{Population at mid-year}} \times 1{,}000$

   General Fertility Rate (GFR) $= \dfrac{\text{Birth during year}}{\text{Women 15–49 at mid-year}} \times 1{,}000$

   $\text{ASFR} = \dfrac{\text{Number of live births to women of a specific age group}}{\text{Mid year women population in the same age group}} \times 1{,}000$

   $\text{NRR} = \dfrac{\text{No. of Female Expected to be born to 1,000 Newly Born Girls}}{1{,}000}$

   $\text{CDR} = \dfrac{\text{Deaths in a Year}}{\text{Population at Mid-Year}} \times 1{,}000$

   $\text{IMR} = \dfrac{\text{Number of deaths among infants registered during the year}}{\text{Number of live births in the same year}} \times 1{,}000$

   $\text{MMR} = \dfrac{\text{Number of maternal deaths relating to child bearing}}{\text{Number of live birth}} \times 1{,}000$

   Sex Ratio $= \dfrac{\text{Males}}{\text{Females}} \times 1{,}000$

   Child Dependency Ratio $= \dfrac{\text{Children below age 15}}{\text{Persons 15–64 years of age}} \times 1{,}000$

   Old Age Dependency Ratio $= \dfrac{\text{Persons age 65 years above}}{\text{Persons 15–64 years of age}} \times 1{,}000$

2. See http://www.who.int/topics/reproductive_health/eu (accessed on 21 September 2015).
3. See http://www.unmillenniumproject.org/documents (accessed on 21 September 2015).
4. See 'Role of diaspora in national building: Lessons from fragile and post-conflict countries in Africa'. Available at: http://www.afdb.org/fileadmin/uploads/afdb/Documents/Project-and-Operations/2011%20The%20role%20of%20the%20Diaspora%20in%20Nation%20building%20-%20lessons%20for%20fragile%20and%20post-%20conflict%20countries%20in%20Africa.pdf (accessed on 27 November 2016).
5. See htpp://www.who.int/topics/health_policy/en/ (accessed on 22 September 2015).

BIBLIOGRAPHY

African Development Bank. 2000. *Policy on Population and Strategies for Implementation*. African Development Bank. Also available at: *www.afdb.org/fileadmin/uploads/afdb/Documents/Policy-Documents* (accessed on 23 November 2013).

Amelung, T., and M. Diehl. *Deforestation of Tropical Rain Forests: Economic Causes and Impact on Development*. Tubingen, Germany: JCB Mohr, 1992.

Bloom, D. E. 'Education in a Globalized World.' *World Economics* 7, no. 4 (2006): 87–109.

———. '7 Billion and Counting.' *Science* 33, no. 6042(29 July 2011): 562–69.

Bloom, D. E., and D. Canning. 'The Health and Wealth of Nations.' *Science* 287, no. 5456 (2000): 1207–09.

———. 'Cumulation, Causality, Economic Growth and the Demographic Transition.' In *Population Poverty in Developing World*, edited by N. Birdsall, A. C. Kelley and S. Sinding, pp. 165–200. Oxford: Oxford University Press, 2001.

———. 'Booms, Busts and Echoes: How the Biggest Demographic up heal in History is Affecting Global Development.' *Financial Development*, 43 (2006): 8–13.

Boserup, E. *The Conditions for Agricultural Growth*. Chicago: Aldine Publishing Company, 1965.

Cecilia, T. 'Governance, Migration and Local Development.' *Environment and Urbanization* 22, no. 1 (April 2010): 5–11.

Chia, L. 'Linking health and economic development: HIV/AIDS prevalence as an indicator of economic growth', *Penn McNair Research Journal* 1, no. 1 (2007): 1–15, also see http://repository.upenn.edu/cgi/viewcontent.cgi?article=1004&context=mcnair_scholars (accessed on 27 November 2016).

Cincotta, Richard P., and R. Engelman. *Economics and Rapid Changes: The Influence of Population Growth*. Washington DC: Population Action International, October 1997.

Coale, A., and Edger M. Hoover. *Population Growth and Economic Development in Low Income Countries*. Princeton: Princeton University Press, 1958.

Dasgupta, M., J. Bongaarts, and J. Cleland. 'Population Poverty and Sustainable Development: A Review Evidence.' Policy Research Working Paper No. 5719, The World Bank, Development Research Group, Washington DC, 2011.

Dawson, D. J., and R. Tiffin. 'Is There a Long-run Relationship between Population Growth and Living Standard? The Case of India.' *Journal of Development Studies* 34, no. 5 (1998): 149–56.

Demeny, P. 'Population Policy: The role of national governments', *Population Development Review* 1, no. 1 (1975): 147–61.

Desai, Sonalde. . 'The Other Half of the Demographic Dividend.' *Economic and Political Weekly* 45, no. 40 (2 October 2010): 12–14.

Dyson, T. *Population and Development: The Demographic Transition*. New York: Zed Book, 2010.

Easterlin, R. A. 'Effects of Population Growth on the Economic Development of Developing Countries.' *The Annals of the American Journal Academy of Political & Social Science* 369, no. 1 (1967): 98–108.

Green, C. P. 'The Environment and Population Growth: Decade for Action.' *Population Reports*, Series M, No. 10, p. 31. Baltimore: John Hopkins School of Public Health, Population Information Programme, May 1992.

Hirschman, C. 'Population and Development: What do We Really Know?' Paper Presented at the Conference on 'Development Challenges for the Twenty-First Century' at Cornell University, 1–2 October, 2004. Available at: http://faculty.washington.edu/charles/new%20PUBS/Unpublished%20Papers/U1.pdf (accessed on 18 March 2016).

Hope, R. A. 'Wildlife Harvesting, Conservation and Poverty: The economics of Olive Ridley Egg Exploitation.' *Environmental Conservation* 29, no. 4–5 (2002): 223–36.

IOM. *World Migration Report 2010*. Geneva: International Organization for Migration, 2010.

Kalemli-Ozcan, S. 'Does Mortality Decline Promote Economic Growth?' *Journal of Economic Growth* 7, no. 4 (2002): 411–39.

Lloyd, C. B. 'Investing in the Next Generation: The Implication for High Fertility at the Level of the Family.' Working Paper No. 63, Population Council, New York, 1994.

Merrick, Thomas W. 'Population and Poverty: New Views on an Old Controversy.' *International Family Planning Perspectives* 28, no.1 (2002): 41–45.

Millennium Ecosystem Assessment. *Ecosystem and Human Well-being: Synthesis*. Washington, DC: Island Press, 2005.

Milwertz, C. N. *Accepting Population Control Urban Chinese Women and the One-Child Family Policy*. Cornwall, Great Britain: T J Press, 1997.

Moxness, K. 'Partnerskapsloven-et uttrykk for parforholdets endrede karakler.' (The partnership law: An expression of the changing character of couple) *Lovetann* 3 (1993): 30–31. Available at: http://www.demogr.mpg.de/papaers/working/wp (accessed on 23 September 2015).

National Academy of Science. *Rapid Population Growth: Consequences and Policy Implications*. Vol. 1 & 2. Baltimore: John Hopkins Press, 1971.

Redding, T. M. 'The Population Challenge: Key to Global Survival.' The 21st Century Paper, The Population Institute, Wasington DC, 2007. Available at: https://www.populationinstitute.org/external/fil (accessed on 15 September 2015).

Retherford, R. D., N. Oganwa, R. and Matsukura. 'Late Marriage and Less Marriage in Japan.' *Population and Development Review* 1, no. 1 (2001): 65–102.

Robinson, Warren C. 'The Development of Modern Population Theory.' *The American Journal of Economics and Sociology* 23, no. 4 (1964): 375–92.

Rudel, T., and J. Roper. 'The Paths to Rain Forest Destruction: Cross-national Patterns of Tropical Forest, 1975–90.' *World Development* 25, no. 1 (1997): 53–65.

Saithal, D., and P. K. Bhargava. 'Population Pressure, Agricultural Resources and Environment: Temporal and Spatial Analysis in India.' Paper presented at the PAA Conference, New York, 29–31 March 2007.

Samuel, J., and S. George. 'Globalization, Migration and Development.' *Canadian Studies in Population* 29, no. 1 (2002): 31.

Schultz, T. P. 'Population Policies, Fertility, Women's Human Capital and Child Quality.' Discussion Paper No. 954, Yale University Economic Growth Centre, 2007. Available at: http://papers.ssrn.com/s013/paper.cfm (accessed on 15 October 2015).

Simon, J. *The Economics of Population Growth*. Princeton: Princeton University Press, 1977.

———. *The Ultimate Resource*. Princeton: Princeton University Press, 1996.

Thirlwall, A. P. *Growth and Development*. Basingstoke: Macmillan Press, 1994.

UNESCO. 'Report of Regional Workshop on Population and Family Life Education.' Regional Office for Education in Asia and Pacific, Bangkok, Thailand, 1971.

UNFPA. *State of World Population 2002*. UNFPA, 2002.

United Nations. 'Population, Environment and Development.' The Concise Report, ST/ESA/SERA/202, New York, 2001.

———. 'Population Challenges and Development Goals, Department of Economic and Social Affairs.' Population Division, ST/ESA/SERA/248, UN, New York, 2005.

———. 'Office for ECOSOC Support and Coordination Human Resources Development.' 2013. Available at: http://www.un.org/en/aboutun/copyright (accessed on 19 September 2016)

Upadhyay, U. D., and B. Robey. 'Why Family Planning Matters.' *Population Reports*, Series J, No. 49, p. 31. Baltimore: John Hopkins School of Public Health, Population Information Programme, 1999.

Wolfe, B. and J. Behrman. 'Determinant of Child Mortality, Health and Nutrition in the Developing Country.' *Journal of Development Economics*, 11 (1982): 163–93.

World Bank. *World Development Report 1993: Investing in Health*. New York: Oxford University Press, 1993.

Zhang, D. and R. V. Nagubadi. 'The Influence of Urbanization on Timberland use by Forest Type in the Southern United States.' *Forest Policy and Economics*, 7 (2005): 721–31.

5 Income Inequality, Unemployment and Inflation

High inequality, manifested in large proportion of population having poor health, nutrition, and education is also likely to impact on overall labour productivity and to cause slower economic growth.

—Todaro (1994)

Voters in presidential elections (USA) consider the macroeconomic performance of the economy... two key macroeconomic variables are inflation and unemployment. When voters are concerned about the rate of inflation they pressure politicians to reduce inflation. When they are concerned about unemployment, voters pressure politicians to reduce unemployment.

—Dua and Smyth (1997)

Income inequality, inflation and unemployment are three indomitable contemporary issues influencing the socio-economic development of both developed and developing countries. Income inequality is one of the critical economic paradoxes in both developed and developing countries. Concentration of large quantity of wealth and income in the hands of a handful number of population and a handful of wealth in the hands of a large number of population is a perturbed paradox, vexing the minds of the planners and policymakers in developed as well as developing countries.

The second important development issue discussed in this chapter is unemployment. Unemployment is one of the omnipresent issues in almost all countries of the world. It promotes poverty and inequality. Furthermore, unemployment among youth does not only retard economic development but also leads to social unrest, terrorism and extremism and has enhanced crime and robbery in developing countries. Unemployment exists in various forms, such as underemployment, disguised unemployment, seasonal unemployment, voluntary and involuntary unemployment and so on, in rural and urban areas of developing countries.

The third important development-related aspect which bothers the common men in developing countries the most is inflation. Continuous price rise of the essential goods and services in developing countries has ramshackled the backbone of the poor and the poorest of the poor in these countries. The two false promises customarily given by the political parties during their election campaigns at both national and state levels are 'if come to the power will control inflation and provide employment to the youth.' The 'political price of onion',[1] and defeat of a ruling political party in the hands of the opposition, reminds the political parties how critical inflation of food price is to influence the voter's decision-making to vote in the national as well as provincial elections. Thus, it can be emphatically said that generating employment, controlling inflation and reducing economic inequalities are the three vital economic development issues and challenges before the governments of both developed and developing countries.

After reading this chapter, you will be able to:

1. Define and measure income inequality.
2. Point out various causes and suggest measures to check income inequality.
3. Define unemployment and explain various processes of measuring unemployment.
4. Describe various causes of unemployment.
5. Discuss various measures to control unemployment.
6. Define and describe inflation, its causes, and challenges and issues.

SECTION I: INCOME INEQUALITY

Income inequality has increased in many countries over the last few decades, as the wealthiest individuals have become wealthier while the relative situation of people living in poverty has improved little.

—United Nations (2013)

CONCEPT AND MEANING

Inequality in distribution of income and resources is an age-old problem in both developed and developing countries. Customarily, it is observed that a certain group of population possesses abundant resources, while the others are the drawers of the water and hewers of the woods. During the 18th and 19th centuries, political economists wrote about inequality as a central issue of their time, important as a mechanism of development and for its links with poverty and social harmony (Jolly 2005). To Adam Smith (1776), 'wherever there is great poverty, there is great inequality. For one very rich man there must be at least five hundred poor and the affluence of the few supposes the indigence of the many.' The new political economy literature, on the other hand, links greater inequality to lower future growth paths and considers it an impediment to poverty-reducing growth as the elasticity of poverty with respect to growth found to decline when inequality increases (Nissanke and Thorbecke 2004). Inequality may cause political and economic instability (Kniivila 2007). McKay (2002) was of the view that inequality matters to the development agencies because of several reasons, such as

1. inequality matters for poverty;
2. inequality matters for growth;
3. inequality matters in its own right;
4. inequality is often a significant factor behind crime, social unrest or violent conflict and
5. inequality is likely to be critically important for the attainment of the Millennium Development Goals.

Income poverty and income inequality are the two sides of a coin, which create a vicious circle of impoverishment. To Kovacevic (2010), within the human development framework, 'poverty reflects failure to enhance basic capabilities, while inequality depicts disparities in the capabilities enjoyed by individuals that enable them to do or be what they value in their live.' Income inequalities show the differences in income-earning capabilities between very poor and poor, poor and middle class, middle class and rich, rich and poor, rich and very rich and so on. UNDP's Human Development Report 2001 envisages that 'the world's richest 1% of people receive as much income as the poorest 75%...the income of the world's richest 5% is 114 times that of the poorest 5%.' Inequality is one of the most perplexing problems haunting the minds of the planners and policymakers in developing countries.

During the 1950s and 1960s, there was widespread move towards greater egalitarianism in many developing countries (Kaniivila 2007). The governments, in both the developed and developing countries, introduced several measures, reforms and affirmative actions to reduce economic inequality in their respective countries. The introduction of land reform measures in India after independence is one of the illustrious examples aimed at reducing inequality in access to landholding. Despite a decline, however, inequality remained high in many places because of the persistence of the traditional causes of inequality such as high land concentration, unequal access to education and other public services (Cornia 2005). In Latin America, income inequality increased in many countries in the 1980s and also in the 1990s (Kaniivila 2007). In Thailand, for instance, rapid growth was accompanied by increased income inequality (Sarntisart 2000). While giving example of the United States of America, Colin Gordon said,

> Americans today live in a starkly unequal society. We have in fact, more inequality today in the United States than Americans have experienced at almost any time in the last century. And our gaps in income and wealth now run deeper than the divides in virtually any other democratic and developed economy.[2]

The globalization has elongated inequalities, at least, in developing countries. The rich capitalists, industrialists, businessmen and also corrupt politicians and bureaucracy are largely benefited by the liberalization and globalization processes, while the poor are being found to be left out and their conditions have further pauperized in developing countries.

MEASUREMENT OF INCOME INEQUALITY

Some of the easy and useful methods of measurement of income inequality are (a) range, (b) coefficient of variation and (c) the Gini Coefficient.

Range: This measure divides the difference between highest and lowest incomes by the mean income. The formula is

$$R = \frac{H - L}{\bar{X}},$$

where R is range; H is the highest value or income and L is the lowest value or income.

$$\bar{X} = \text{Mean income}$$

Coefficient of Variation: Coefficient of variation is calculated by dividing a distribution's standard deviation by its mean. The formula is

$$CV = \frac{sd}{\bar{X}},$$

where CV is coefficient of variation; sd is standard deviation and $\bar{X}$ is the mean value.

Figure 5.1 *Inequality Measure*

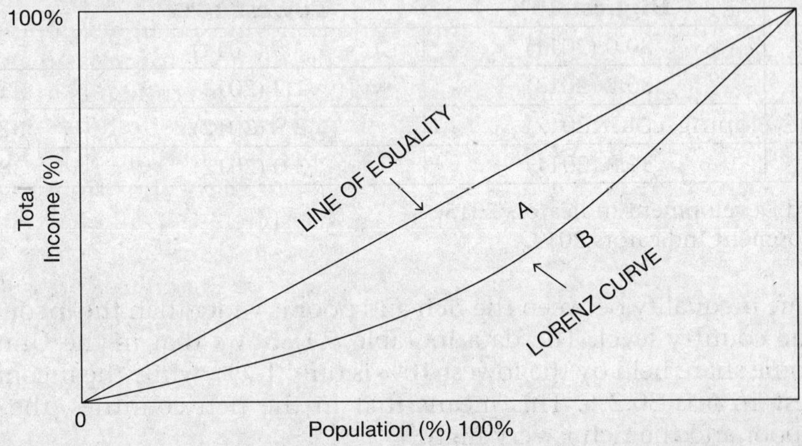

Source: Author.

The Gini Coefficient: The most popular and commonly used measure of income inequality is Gini coefficient. The coefficient varies between 0 and 1; 0 reflects complete equality and 1 indicates complete inequality. The Gini coefficient is calculated with the help of Lorenz curve which provides graphical representation of a nation's income distribution. The Gini coefficient is equal to the area between the line of equality and the Lorenz curve divided by the total (Figure 5.1).

The formula used is

$$\text{Gini Coefficient} = \frac{A}{A+B}.$$

If the income is distributed equally, then the Lorenz curve and the line of equality are merged and the Gini coefficient is zero. Larger the difference between the line of equality and Lorenz curve, higher is the inequality. In other words, higher the value of Gini coefficient, larger is the inequality. According to World Fact Book 2013, the Scandinavian countries with a lower Gini index of 25 represent the case of less inequality, while the Sub-Saharan countries with an index of 50 depict the case of greater inequality of income distribution.

DYNAMICS OF INCOME INEQUALITY

The income inequality exists both in developed and developing countries in different forms. A comparison of Gini index data of the United States of America and Sri Lanka shows that Gini coefficients are 41.1% and 38.6% respectively, which means that income inequality is more pervasive in the developed countries like the United States of America. The data also shows that the Gini coefficient of United Kingdom is 32.6%.

Table 5.1 *Income Inequality Status of a Few Countries*

Country	*Income Share Held by Highest 10%	*Income Share Held by Lowest 10%	**Gini Index
India	30.0 (2011)	3.5 (2011)	—
USA	30.2 (2013)	1.7 (2013)	41.1 (2013)
UK	24.7 (2012)	2.9 (2012)	32.6 (2012)
Sri Lanka	31.8 (2011)	3.0 (2012)	38.6 (2012)

Sources: *World Development Indicators 2015.
**World Development Indicators 2014.

The income inequality between the rich and poor is wider than the income inequality existing at the country level. The data in Table 5.1 shows that in the United States of America, income share held by the lowest 10% is only 1.7%, while the income share held by the highest 10% is 30.2%. This means that in the rich countries, the income gap between the poor and the rich is very high.

Another important dimension of income inequality is the income inequality prevailing between urban and rural areas. Both in developed and developing countries and more particularly in developing countries, there is large income inequality in between the people living in the cities and the people dwelling in the countryside. Li, Sato and Sicular (2013), in a study on the rural–urban income inequality in China, had following findings:

1. China's urban–rural gap has been a central factor underlying national income inequality.
2. The gap contribution to overall inequality was 45% in 2002 and 51% in 2007.
3. The urban–rural income ratio is largest in the Western and Eastern China, 3.85 and 3.44 respectively.

In the same vein, several studies conducted in South Asian countries have also depicted the income inequality between urban and rural areas. There are income differences between the workers engaged in wage and self-employment activities in the rural and urban areas. Even within the urban areas, income of the workers working in the metropolitan cities is comparatively higher than those working in small cities, e.g. the income of informal workers working in Delhi is higher than those working in Patna. Even within the rural areas, income of the informal workers working in the agriculture sector as labourers in Punjab and Haryana is higher than those informal workers working in Bihar and Eastern Uttar Pradesh. One of the studies shows that the migrant workers who have migrated from the rural areas of different states, particularly from Bihar and Eastern Uttar Pradesh to Chandigarh, are earning a significantly higher wage rate than what they were getting in their home place (Pattanaik 2009). This also supports the fact that the workers who are working in the industrial and service sectors, mainly concentrated in the urban areas, are earning more than their counterparts working as wage earners in the agriculture sector of rural areas.

Income Disparities Between Rich and Poor in India

Per Person Monthly Spending (₹)	Rural		Urban	
	Poorest 30%*	Richest 5%	Poorest 30%*	Richest 5%
Milk and Milk Product	58	331	111	422
Egg, Fish and Meat	42	201	66	200
Fresh Fruits	14	118	30	244
Education	20	278	54	908
Medical	43	494	59	659
Durables	17	586	26	1287

Source: NSSO, 2013, *The Times of India*, July 28, 2013, P-1.
Note: * Maximum limit.

According to NSSO 2013 data, the spending and consumption by the richest 5% zoomed up by over 60% between 2000 and 2012 in rural areas, while the poorest 5% saw an increase of just 30%. In urban areas, the richest segment's spending increased by 63%, while the poorest saw an increase of 33%.

Income inequality is quite revealing between organized and unorganized sector workers in almost all developing countries. Sanfey (2010) found that the informal employees earn significantly lesser than those in the formal sector; controlling for a range of other variables, informality plays an increasingly important role in explaining earning inequality in Serbia. On the other hand, Daza and Gamboa (2013), from their study conducted in Colombia, found that formal workers earn between 30% and 60% more, on average, than informal workers.

Income inequality is largely observed across the caste, ethnicity and occupation. Studies in India have shown that the income gap exists between the general caste and SCs and STs, both in rural and urban areas. This is largely because of the caste-based discrimination in the labour market. Even after many affirmative measures, it is seen that many upper-caste Hindu families in India do not prefer to engage some of the SC sub-caste males and females in their houses either as labourers or as household maid servants. Labour market in the informal sector is highly discriminatory, leading to income inequality between the lower and higher castes groups of the population in rural areas. A study conducted by Borooach (2005) revealed that at least one-third of the average income/probability differences between Hindu and SC/ST households were due to 'unequal treatment' of SC/ST attributes (discrimination). Zacharias and Vakulabharanam (2009) found from their study that the groups in India that are generally considered as disadvantaged—known as SCs and STs—have, as one would expect, substantially lower wealth than the forward caste groups while other backward classes (OBCs) and non-Hindus occupy a position in the middle.

The family members who have multiple occupations, such as agriculture, livestock, business and so on, and are also engaged in paid jobs have higher per capita income as compared to those who have single occupation in rural areas. Some studies have also shown that in the agriculturally prosperous villages, the income gap between the landless agricultural labourers and large-scale farmers is very high. In Punjab and Haryana, it is seen that households pursuing both agriculture and dairy farming earn more than ones pursuing either agriculture or dairy farming. The income of the Jat community in rural areas of these two states is astoundingly higher than other communities.

The income inequality also varies across the types of employment and between the skilled and non-skilled workers. On average, across countries, workers on temporary contracts earn 25% lesser than workers on permanent contracts, even if the workers have similar working hours, education, age and gender (OECD 2012a). People who are engaged as regular employees earn higher than the contractual employees. The regular employees are entitled to other benefits, such as dearness allowances, gratuity, leave encashment, leave travel allowances, medical benefits and so on, while contractual employees are devoid of all these benefits.

Last but not the least, gender dimension is one of the important dynamics of income inequality. In developing countries, women are largely found to be engaged either in unpaid household activities or in low-paid jobs. This is one of the important reasons for the gender gap in income inequality, and it also affects the overall income inequality in a country. According to one of the studies of OECD (2015), having more households with women in paid work, especially full-time work, means less income inequality by about 2 Gini points.

CAUSES OF INCOME INEQUALITY

According to the UNDP's Human Development Report 2002, the level of worldwide inequality is 'grotesque', the world's richest 1% of people being reckoned to receive as much income as the poorest 57%, and the combined income of the world's richest 5% being 14 times that of the poorest 5%. The globalization had elongated the intensity of inequality in developing countries. The use of technology and the proliferation of the private sector in the economy have widened the income differences between the skilled and unskilled labour force and also between the rich entrepreneurs and the poor working class. Fruits and benefits of the high economic growth rate in the neoliberalized developing world are being enjoyed by the large entrepreneurs, capitalists, technocrats, businessmen and the salaried middle class in the class III and class IV jobs. The wage earners, petty self-employed people and other landless, small- and medium-scale farmers are the victims of globalization and are earning lesser as compared to the former counterparts. According to OECD, the gap between the incomes of the most highly paid individuals in society and the rest has been increasing markedly over the 30 years since 1980.[3] The various reasons of income inequality are as follows:

1. Unequal distribution of land in rural areas is a vital factor responsible for rural income inequalities. International Monetary Fund (IMF; 2004) from the Cambodia experience has envisaged that Cambodia has a highly unequal distribution of

income caused to the substantial extent by highly unequal land ownership. Incomes of the large- and medium-scale landholders are much higher as compared to the small and marginal farmers. The income gap is wider between the farmers of the Green Revolution belt and the farmers belonging to the dry land areas. The adoption of high-yielding varieties and modern technology into the agriculture by the large-scale landholders has further enhanced their income and profit. On the contrary, the wage rate of the farm casual labourer is very low. There is a huge gap in the income between farmers and farm labourer. Thus, agricultural modernization and inequality in the land distribution are the key reasons of income inequalities in rural areas. While giving the example of Latin America and Caribbean countries, Huber et al. (2005) said that the inequality in landholding and political power is at the centre of the deep historical structural roots of inequality, originating in the colonial order.

2. The disguised unemployment in rural areas and underemployment in the urban informal sectors are other important reasons of income inequality among various groups of population. Disguised unemployment in the agriculture and allied sectors is a vital feature of rural employment. Here, more number of people pretend to be employed in the agriculture sector which actually requires less number for performing the job. This creates income inequalities between the families having disguised unemployed people and families having unemployed people. The open and disguised unemployment in China amounts to about 23%, which has led to the increased income inequality between rural and urban areas.[4] As compared to this, people having regular employment in the organized public and private sectors earn more and have high per capita income.
3. Industrialists and the large- and medium-scale entrepreneurs gain more profit and have higher income as compared to small and marginal entrepreneurs. This income inequality is vividly observed in the secondary sector. The large-scale industrialists use modern technologies to earn a lot of profit. People employed in these industries get better salaries, while their counterparts—small-scale industries with low capital investment and deploying traditional technologies—earn less profit and pay lesser salaries to the employees. Within the industrial sector also, income inequalities have been observed between the skilled and unskilled workforce.
4. Monopoly and oligopolistic forms of market are other responsible factors for income inequality in developing countries where the market is highly imperfect. Ximing et al. (2010) by using the Nation Bureau Statistics of China have found that the wage income in monopoly industries is obviously higher than other industries to a supposedly unreasonable extent. The data shows that the highest annual income in 2000 was 21,342 Yuan in air transport and the lowest was 4,535 Yuan in timber and bamboo logging and transportation. In India as well, income of the auto rickshaw drivers is higher than the hand rickshaw pullers.
5. In the service sector, personnel with technical knowledge and skill earn higher income than those who are unskilled. Besides, income through salaries varies among the employees in the higher, middle and lower level of managerial positions. The income inequality between the managers and ordinary workers is quite large in the service sector. Studies show that the service industry expansion boosted income inequality in South Korea as service firms tended to have lower labour

productivity than manufacturer, and the faster growth in the service industry lifted the Gini coefficient of South Korea from 0.245 in 1992 to 0.295 in 2005.[5]

6. Population growth in developing countries is also one of the important responsible factors for income inequality. The large family size with more number of unproductive population, i.e. children below the age of 14, non-pensionable aged more than 60 years and unemployed youth dependent on family income, reduces the per capita income of the households. According to Boulier (1975), reductions in the levels of fertility and the rates of growth of population may aid in the attainment of more equal distribution of income as well as higher per capita incomes.
7. People with disabilities and women across different groups of population are subject to income inequality. The social disadvantage is also one of the important key factors of income inequality. In India, the income disparity between the SCs and general caste population is very high. Among the SCs, there also exist income differences between the creamy layer of Dalits and socially most backward Dalits (*Maha Dalits*). The income of a gigantic percentage of STs is low as compared to other groups of population. The social stratifications and their poor access to land, labour and job markets are causes of income inequality in the South Asian countries. Moreover, the families headed by the disabled and landless women are largely subject to income disparities.
8. Corruption is also one of the important reasons of income inequality as it creates artificial income inequality among the people employed in the same types of jobs. For instance, a section officer, who takes bribe for appointment and transfer/posting or the one who is in in a lucrative seat, earns more than his/her counterpart who is honest and/or posted in a less lucrative seat. A politician who is corrupt amasses a lot of money than one who is honest. Many theories suggest that political inequality, i.e. the concentration of political power in the hands of a few, is likely to lead to economic inequality as the politically powerful use politics to become richer (Acemoglu et al. 2007). This creates income inequality in the same profession.
9. Knowledge, skill and attitude are other influencing factors of income. Everything remaining constant, an ambitious and hardworking worker will try to earn more as compared to a complacent and lethargic worker. A worker having more knowledge about the job responsibility will get faster promotion and earn more income as compared to the counterpart who is less enterprising, less educated and poorly skilled. There are many examples where many families have come out of poverty and raised their income to a higher level by their hard work. OECD (2012b) has envisaged that technological advances may affect labour income inequality as they can benefit higher skilled workers more than others.
10. Informalization and casualization of employment are important causes of income inequality in developing countries. There exists income inequality between the people working in the informal sector and people working in the formal sector. The informal sector employments are largely temporary, carry lower wage and also do not have other emoluments, i.e. dearness allowances, gratuity, leave encashment and so on, which a formal public sector employee enjoys. Rising wage disparity has the largest impact on the increase of total income inequality (Mitra and Yemtsov 2006). Informalization of employment both in formal and informal sectors is one of the main causes of income inequality in developing countries.

> **World Bank's Report: MGNREGA Is the World's Largest Public Work Programme**
>
> According to the World Bank Group's report 'The State of Social Safety Nets 2015', MGNREGA has been ranked as the world's largest public works programme. Around 182 million beneficiaries (15% of India's population) are provided social security by MGNREGA. The other objectives of the programme are to (a) enhance livelihood security in rural areas; (b) provide guaranteed 100 days employment in a financial year to every household; (c) generate productive assets; (d) protect environment; (e) empower rural women; (f) reduce rural–urban migration; and (g) foster social equity.
>
> Source: http://indiatoday.intoday.in/education/story/mgnrega/1/450310.html (accessed on 20 December 2016).

11. Last but not the least cause of income inequality is globalization. It is remarked that a fundamental challenge posed by the increasing reach of globalization is that global markets are inherently disequalizing—making rising inequality in developing countries more than less likely (Birdsall 2005). Cheng (2007), while citing China's example, noted that

    > Rising income inequality is considered one of the effects of the economic reforms in China. The move from egalitarianism to more market-based income determination has created both winners and losers in China's population. A large income disparity now exists between the urban and rural residents, between different regions and among the urban and rural residents themselves. In recent years, China has had alarmingly high income disparity levels and has become one of the countries with most unequal income distribution in the world.

    According to Foellmi and Oechslin (2010), wealthy entrepreneurs are better off because they can take advantage of new export opportunities that relatively poor business people lose. Globalization and income inequalities in developing countries are interconnected.

MEASURES TO CONTROL INCOME INEQUALITY

Some of the suggested measures to control income inequality are as follows:

1. At the outset, both developed and developing countries have to religiously implement land reform measures to reduce concentration of land in the hands of a few and distribute it among many poor landless households. In developing countries where agriculture plays a predominant role, distribution of land is essential for overcoming income disparities particularly in rural areas. The effect on income through access to land via land reform programmes has been documented in studies conducted in Taiwan, Zimbabwe and Philippines (Hoddinott et al. 2000). To

cite an example from India, Himachal Pradesh, where more than 90% of households have agricultural land, has lower percentage of population below the poverty line as compared to other states having large percentage of landless households. The effective implementation of land reform measures in Kerala is one of the factors for lower poverty in the rural areas of the state. Besides land, access to dairy farming, poultry farming, fishery and other vocational activities, such as carpentry, pottery, blacksmithing, small and cottage industries and so on, would reduce income disparities in rural areas of the developing economies.

2. Implementation of a progressive tax reform needs to cover both income and wealth taxes, so that concentration of excess income accumulated by the rich can be recovered. Later on, this earning can be utilized in the programmes and schemes intended to raise the income of the poor.
3. Effective collection of wealth and income tax is critical to check income inequalities. At the same time, offering tax concession to the lower- and middle-income groups of population would protect their paltry income and thus can reduce the income disparities. Exemption of small, medium and marginal farmers from the wealth tax and imposition of wealth and income tax on the large-scale farmers are the other suggested measures to reduce concentration of wealth in the hands of a few. According to OECD (2012a), progressive tax and transfer systems can reduce income inequality.
4. People's access to financial market will improve their chances to earn more. In rural areas, people's access to financial market is very meagre because of their poor capacity to meet the collateral requirements of the banking and other financial institutions. Bittencourt (2006), while examining the impact of financial development on earning inequality in Brazil in the 1980s and 1990s, found that financial development improved access to credit to the poor, alleviated extreme inequality and consequently improved welfare without distorting economic efficiency. Studies have demonstrated that in the presence of credit market imperfections, inequality enhances segregation across communities, and thus in the presence of local externalities, it generates persistent education and income gaps (Benabou 1996).
5. Various employment-boosting schemes for the unemployed can be launched and attempt be made to raise the income levels of the disguised unemployed and underemployed people. Moreover, more seasonal employment opportunities can be created in the rural sector to enhance the income of the rural people. An increase in employment opportunities, particularly in the organized public and private sectors, will reduce income inequality. In the views of Medgyesi and Toth,[6] in countries where economic growth brings about an increase in the employment rate (or a decrease in unemployment), inequality of earning among those of working age also tends to reduce the proportion of those living in jobless households, thus contributing to a more equitable distribution of employment and labour income among households.
6. Investing in human capital is very important to reduce income inequalities. Imparting vocational skill education to the unskilled and semi-skilled illiterate population will enhance their chances of employability and raise their income. The preferences must be given to the youth belonging to the poorest of the poor families, the socio-economically backward households and households headed by

women. All the developed countries in the world have more percentage of skilled population as compared to developing countries.

7. Keeping a check on black money is a vital element to control the concentration of illegal wealth by dishonest people. It is the need of the hour that a country try to bring back black money deposited in the foreign accounts and utilize it for the well-being and income-raising programmes for the poor. Black marketeers and people indulged in corrupt activities are the income-rich people compared to their counterparts. This creates a layer of crony capitalism mostly in developing countries. The state apparatuses have to take stern actions against the black marketeers, hoarders and other people indulged in corruption.
8. Control of inflation and rationalization of dearness allowances to the public sector employees will indirectly help to curtail the income gap between the rich and the poor. Inflation hits hard the impoverished people, such as wage earners, daily labourers, petty businessmen and self-employed people in the informal sector who are not the beneficiaries of any such concept of dearness allowances on the basis of price index. Continuous inflation by reducing the value of money enhances income inequality between the public sector workers who get inflation-based dearness allowances and others who are deprived of the same.
9. The existence of organized and unorganized sectors and rural and urban sectors is the form of clear-cut dualism and causes of inequality. The size of informal economy, in a way, determines the range of inequality in developing countries. Therefore, there is a need to control, regulate and reduce the size of unorganized sector in developing countries. The income gap between the rural and urban sectors has to be reduced through various measures so that the income inequality between the people staying in rural areas and their counterparts in urban areas is reduced. Aghion and Bolton (1997) were of the view that redistribution of income improves the efficiency of the economy because it enhances equality of opportunity and the trickle-down process from the rich to the poor.
10. Ensuring minimum wage rate to the labour will also reduce the income gap. Workforce engaged in the unregulated market is subject to exploitation. OECD (2012a) has advocated that well-designed labour market policies and institutions can reduce income inequality. Effective implementation of minimum wage rate in the unregulated market will reduce the income gap between the workers in the formal sector and those in the informal sector. Gindling was of the view that raising the minimum wage reduces poverty in most of developing countries, but the impact is modest because the legal minimum wage applies only to a minority of poor workers; in particular, it does not cover workers in the large informal sector.[7]
11. Women constitute nearly 50% of the total population. However, their contribution to the family income is low as a gigantic percentage of women population is engaged in household activities. The income gap is found to be high between the families with employed women and the families where women are dependent on men's income. Provision of employment for women, particularly those of low-income families, will not only enhance the per capita income of these families but also reduce the income inequalities among the families. The evidence suggests that greater gender equity and increasing female economic participation are associated with higher growth, more favourable development outcomes and lower income inequality.[8]

12. In the era of globalization and liberalization, pursuance of pro-poor growth measures and inclusive development strategies will be helpful to curtail income inequality. The reservation of wage and self-employment for the socio-economically disadvantaged section of the society will not only enhance the income of the poor but also synchronize differences between different class and caste groups of the population. In India, under MGNREGA, there has been 33% reservation for guaranteed 100 days of work in a year for women, SCs and STs.
13. In many countries, affirmative constitutional measures have raised the employment status of the socially disadvantaged sections of population. For instance, in India, reservation for the SCs and STs ensured through the Constitution in the government jobs has enabled many families belonging to these communities to raise their employment and income status. Taylor (1991) viewed affirmative action on economic benefits to reduce income inequalities, and reducing income inequalities and increasing opportunities also reduce social strife and the stigmas of inferiority and racial conflict. This affirmative action provides positive opportunities to the traditionally excluded persons.

ISSUES AND CHALLENGES OF INCOME INEQUALITY

The foremost issue and challenge before developing countries is to reduce the income inequality. Income inequality is the main cause of poverty. People who are earning less, particularly the labourers and daily wage earners working in the informal sectors, are incapable of fulfilling their basic needs. The unskilled labourers having poor bargaining power in the labour market are large in supply and are paid less, and in urban areas, they are found to be staying in the slums in precarious conditions having a low quality of living.

Income inequality has promoted the existence of informal economy in developing countries. According to Gutierrez-Romero (2010), in developing countries such as Latin America and the Sub-Saharan Africa, the informal economy is employing over half of the urban labour force. In India, the informal sector accounts for 93% of total employment including agriculture and 82.4% of employment in non-agricultural economic activities, and it accounts for 50% of India's GDP (Kolli and Sen 2009). Inequality is prominently visible in the informal sector where the entrepreneurs and owners earn profits by exploiting the informal workers. The informal economy is not subjected to rules and regulations and even flouts them. There are low wage rate, no service condition and hardly any provisions for old age and health security. There is an empirical evidence of a significant and positive link between the level of income inequality and the share of the informal sector in the economy (Rosser, Rosser and Ahmed 2000). Kristic and Sanfey (2007) viewed that earning inequality is more pronounced in the informal economy relative to the formal economy. Increase in income inequality also tends to be correlated with increase in the share of output produced in the unofficial economy (Rosser et al. 2000). Reducing the inequality in the informal economy is a challenge before developing countries in order to provide a sustainable livelihood to the people dependent on this economy. Winkelried (2005) noted that high inequality leads to a large informal sector, and redistribution towards the middle class decreases the size of the informal sector and increases the capacity of fiscal instruments to reduce informality.

Income inequality also promotes social, human and political inequality in developing countries. Because of lower income among the socially disadvantaged groups, they lag behind the other groups of population in terms of literacy and GER and have higher infant and maternal mortality rate and morbidity rate, and their life expectancy is also low. It has also been observed that the socially backward groups having higher income are closer to the socially forward groups. Reduction in income inequality would overcome the disadvantages of social handicap in the socially stratified developing countries. It is rightly remarked by Room (1990) that individuals suffer social exclusion when they suffer generalized disadvantages in terms of education, training, employment, housing, financial resources and so on. Income inequality is closely associated with political inequality. In recent years, in the democratic countries, contesting an election is a costly affair and a million-dollar proposition, which the poor cannot afford. Therefore, it is seen that the contestants and the winners in the elections of various political parties largely belong to higher income groups and are grossly economically well up. Thus, income inequality and inequality in political empowerment in many cases is closely associated. The greatest challenge before developing countries is not only to overcome the income inequality but also to control its associated effects on social, human and political inequality.

SECTION II: UNEMPLOYMENT

The unemployment is the cankerworm that eats deep into the development of the economy and thus has a lot of negative consequences such as youth restiveness, juvenile delinquency, and high incidence of armed robbery among others.

—Odonwodo and Abdullahi (2009)

Unemployment is one of the contemporary problems in both developed and developing countries. In developing countries, it has given rise to a number of other problems such as poverty, inequality, crime, youth burning and other socio-psychological hostilities among the youth. ILO (2011) has envisaged that a country's prosperity depends on how many people are in work (employed) and how productive they are, which in turn rests on the skills they have and how effectively those skills are used. Employment is a dominant issue of development in developing countries. It is always a key issue in the election campaigns for the parliaments, assemblies and even the local self-government institutions of these countries. Giving false promises of employment during electoral campaigns by the political parties to amass vote is a common practice in developing countries. According to ILO estimates, 60 million young people are searching for work but cannot find any; about 80% of them are in developing countries and economies in transition (United Nations 2000). The massive youth's unemployment in any country is an indication of far more complex problems (Okafor 2011). Citing the example of Nigeria, Ajufo (2013) said that consequence of youth unemployment is exemplified by increasing militancy, violent crimes, kidnapping, restiveness and political instability. The criminal activities such as armed robbery, kidnapping, political thuggery, militancy and other social vices found among the unemployed and jobless youths have contributed greatly to the slow pace development of Nigeria (Adebayo 2013).

Employment, economic growth rate and development are correlated. It is said that the unemployment rate (UR) is the most widely used indicator of the well-being of a labour market and an important measure of the state of an economy (Byrne and Strold 2001). The Millennium Development Goals Report 2011 envisages that while global economic growth is rebounding, the global labour market is seen with stubbornly elevated unemployment and slow employment generation in developing economies, coupled with widespread deficits in decent work in even the fastest-growing developing countries. High economic growth does not necessarily bring in its wave more employment opportunities. The jobless economic growth in developing countries is a cause of concern for the governments of the developing economies. In developed economies, there is a strong link between GDP growth and employment creation; in contrast, in developing economies, changes in informal employment and self-employment dampen the effects of growth cycles on formal employment (UNCTAD 2013).

It is easy to talk of 'unemployment' but very difficult to define, identify and measure it. The conventional classification of an entire population into the categories of employed, unemployed and outside the labour force is one of the most-complicated tasks in any country. In many less-developed countries in comparison with the Western Europe and the United States of America, issues raised by such classifications are even numerous and of greater relevance for the policies (Bruton 1978). In the simplest term, unemployment is defined as the number of people in a country who want to do a job but do not have one. ILO defines unemployed as the number of the economically active people who are without work but are available for and are seeking work, including people who have lost their jobs and those who have voluntarily left work (World Bank 1998). The exponents of developing countries feel that the ILO's definition of unemployment is more applicable to developed countries rather than developing countries, where a large number of arbitrary assumptions are attached to employment. In developing countries, even the underemployed educated people and people engaged in unpaid household productive works, e.g. women and those who are temporarily engaged in jobs, consider themselves unemployed. Therefore, ILO's definition can be loosely applicable to developing countries. According to Fajana (2000), unemployment refers to a situation where people are willing to work and are capable of working but are unable to find suitable paid unemployment.

MEASUREMENT OF UNEMPLOYMENT

Broadly, there are two types of measurement of unemployment, i.e. the generic measurement given by ILO and the country-specific measurement of unemployment developed by individual countries. The labour survey undertaken by the ILO envisaged that to be unemployed, an individual must (a) be aged 16–65 years, (b) have been out of work for 4 weeks, (c) be able to start work in the next 2 weeks, so they must be readily available for work and (d) be available for work for one hour per week, so part-time unemployment is included in the measurement, though these workers are unlikely to claim unemployment benefits.[9]

As far as the country-specific measurement is concerned, the National Sample Survey Organization (NSSO) of India has defined 'work' or 'gainful activity' as the activity pursued for pay, profit or family gain or, in other words, the activity which adds value to the national product. Normally, it is an activity which results in production of goods and services for exchange. However, all activities in the 'agriculture sector' in which a part or whole of the agricultural production is used for own consumption and does not go for sale are also considered gainful.

The survey adopts three different approaches to measure employment and unemployment, which are as follows:

Usual Status Approach: The usual status activity is the activity on which a person has spent relatively longer time of the preceding 365 days prior to the date of survey. The usual status activities are further subdivided into 'principal status activity' and 'subsidiary status activity'. In case of the former, the worker pursues the gainful activity as a principal avocation. While in the case of the latter, a non-worker pursues some gainful activity in a subsidiary capacity for a longer time during the reference period of last 365 days. The principal status workers and subsidiary status workers together constitute 'all workers' according to the usual status classification approach.

Current Weekly Status Approach: Here, a person is considered to be employed if he or she pursues any one or more of the gainful activities for at least one hour on any day of the reference week. However, if a person does not pursue any gainful activity, but has been seeking or available for work, the person is considered as unemployed.

Current Daily Status Approach: Under this approach, all the activities of a person are listed on each day of the preceding week. Here, in this approach, a person is considered working or employed for the entire day if he or she had worked for four hours or more during the day. On the other hand, if the person is not engaged in any work, even for one hour on a day, but is seeking and is available for work for four hours or more, then he or she is considered unemployed for the entire day.[10]

Besides the NSSO, the National Human Development Report 2001 brought out by the Planning Commission of India has used a method in the calculation of workforce participation, i.e.

> Persons in the labour force participation rates is the portion of persons in the age group 15 years and above who are either working (i.e. employed) on the usual principal and subsidiary status or seeking or available for work. A person (15 years and above) considered working or employed, if the person was engaged for a relatively longer time during the preceding year in any one or more work related activities. The activity in which a person spends relatively longer time in the preceding 365 days from the date of survey is considered as the principal status of the person. A person categorized as a non-worker (i.e. unemployed or out of labour force), who pursued some economic activity in subsidiary capacity is called a subsidiary status employed. The principal status workers and subsidiary status workers together constitute all workers as per the usual status classification. (Planning Commission of India 2002)

The unemployment status of the population in a nation is usually calculated by the UR, which is defined as the number of persons unemployed per 1,000 persons in the labour force (employed and unemployed). The formula for UR

$$\text{UR} = \frac{\text{Number of unemployed persons}}{\text{Labour Force}} \times 1{,}000.$$

However, identification and measurement of unemployment is an arduous task in developing countries where there is a large-scale casualization of employment, underemployment and a reserve army of disguised unemployed population in the agricultural sector. Morse (1970) opined that the inadequacy of the concept of unemployment to describe and measure involuntary idleness or more broadly underutilization of labour in developing countries has, of course, been recognized, and the terms 'underemployment' and 'disguised unemployment' have been used to describe the situation of the people who do some work but less than they could or would like to do. In 2010, the percentage of employment to population ratio in developing regions was 62.7%, higher than that of the developed regions, i.e. 54.8% (see Table 5.2). This could be because of more flexibility in defining the employment status in the developing economies.

Different types of unemployment have been observed in developing countries, which are as follows (Table 5.3):

Voluntary Unemployment: It calculates individuals who are not willing or motivated to work at the prevailing wage rate and work condition.

Involuntary Unemployment: It is a situation when an individual is willing to work with the prevailing wage rate and work conditions but does not get work.

Frictional Unemployment: When an individual is out of job or unemployed because of changing job conditions and changing requirement of the job, it is known as the frictional unemployment. This may be happening because of change in technology, shortage of raw materials and other similar conditions.

Structural Unemployment: This arises due to change in the structure of the economy. Change in the structure of the economy from agriculture to industrial sector and also shifting emphasis from industrial to technology-driven service sector necessitate certain kind of job requirement which the currently employed workforce fails to meet and thus becomes unemployed.

Seasonal Unemployment: This is predominantly prevalent in the agriculture sector of the economy. The labour force becomes unemployed during the lean season, and customarily people engaged in agriculture are found to have no work between the planting and harvesting seasons.

Table 5.2 *Employment to Population Ratio in Various Regions (2000, 2009 and 2010)*

Region	2000	2009	2010
Eastern Asia	74	70	70
Southeastern Asia	66	66	66
Southern Asia	57	58	58
Sub-Saharan Africa	63	64	64
Latin America and the Caribbean	58	61	61
Developed Region	55.8	55.4	54.8
Developing Region	63.2	62.7	62.7

Source: Millennium Development Goal Report 2011.

Table 5.3 *Real GDP and Rate of Employment 2009–10 in Various Regions of the World (Annual Average Growth Rate)*

Region	**GDP**	**Employment**
East Asia	8.6	0.4
South Asia	7.5	1.4
Southeast Asia	5.5	2.3
West Asia	5.2	3.6
Sub-Saharan Africa	5.4	2.8
Latin America and the Caribbean	1.7	4.3
Developing Economies	6.4	1.4
Transition Economies	5.4	–0.5
Developed Economies	1.4	–2.4

Source: UNCTAD (2013), 'Employment and Unemployment,' Development and Globalization: Facts and Figures 12, United Nations, New York, see http://dgff.unctad.org/chapter2/2.2.html# (accessed on 30/11/2016).

Disguised Unemployment: This is hidden labour force, particularly prevalent in agriculture sector. In this case, labour force is found to be employed in excess without any substantial work, and although they pretend to be employed, they are actually unemployed.

However, the World Bank shows that although data from developing economies depicts the high employment rate, the vulnerable employment is very high in these countries (see Table 5.4). The vulnerable employment consists of unpaid family workers and own-account workers as a percentage of total employment.

CAUSES OF UNEMPLOYMENT

Unemployment is a universal problem which almost all the countries of the world are suffering to a greater or lesser degree. Many factors are responsible for rising unemployment in developing countries and a few important among them are as follows:

1. The first and foremost reason for existence of high unemployment in developing countries is the population growth. High population growth rate in developing countries is adding more and more unemployed youth population into the already existing large number of unemployed population. Although it is dubious to blame population growth for rising unemployment, its effect cannot be ignored in the capital crunch and resources-poor developing countries. Loku and Deda (2013) were of the view that in both rural and urban areas, unemployment is increasing with the increase in population. Many young people who seek jobs only in the government and public sectors remain voluntarily unemployed for a short period and if do not pursue any job after the expiry of the prescribed age of the government employment, they remain either unemployed, disguised unemployed or underemployed forever. The high percentage of youth population in the total

Table 5.4 *Vulnerable Employment in Various Regions of the World (% Total Employment, 2009)*

Region	Vulnerable Employment (%)
European Union	12
Europe and Central Asia	18
Latin America and the Caribbean	30
Middle East and North Africa	36
OECD Members	15
South Asia	79

Source: World Developing Report, 2013 on job statistical Tables, also see http://data.worldbank.org/topic/labour-and-social-protection (accessed on 25 May 2013).

population, which developing countries are considering as the 'demographic dividend', is a paradox. And, if these adults remain unemployed for a long period, this 'demographic dividend' could be troublesome not only for the family and society but also for the nation. Youth unemployment and unrest will retard economic growth and development of these countries.

2. The increased availability of better health care facilities in developing countries has enhanced the life expectancy and has thus increased the number of potential population who can work but is not getting any work. Moreover, it has added more unproductive old-age population to the total population of the country, and their high social security benefits have constrained many state governments, particularly in India, to create new jobs in the government and public sector institutions. Many Indian state governments are spending a huge percentage of their budget on paying pension to the retired employees. Governments of many provinces in developing countries do not have adequate budget to create additional employment in the public sector. This is also one of the reasons for unemployment.
3. Rise in the public sector employees' salaries because of the implementation of pay commissions in India has compelled both central and state governments to curtail employment. For instance, after the implementation of sixth pay commission report in India, vacancies in the public sector employment have decreased both in state and central government offices. The central as well as state governments are incapable to meet the current pay burden of the government employees. It is also remarked that conventionally, the increase in wage rate through scale effects reduces employment for both low-wage workers and higher wage workers.[11] The increase in retirement age by different state governments and re-employment of the retired employees in India have reduced the scope for further employment. Moreover, use of computers has also reduced the number of clerical jobs in both public and private sectors.
4. Low capital formation and investment in both public and private sectors is an important reason for unemployment. Because of lack of investment climate in developing countries, the private sector as well as investment through FDI is also not increasing. The remittances received by developing countries from the outside

are seen to be largely being used on the consumption head, i.e. construction and purchase of houses, purchase of vehicles, buying high-quality furniture, electronic equipment and other household gadgets, and a meagre percentage is being used as an investment in the industries and service sector to create jobs.

5. Faulty education policies in developing countries are also responsible factors for unemployment. The educational institutions have become more of centres of degree boom. Lack of appropriate skill education and superfluous degree boom have resulted in educated unemployed in these countries. According to Aspiring Minds National Employability Report which is based on a study of more than 150,000 engineering students who graduated in 2015 from over 650 colleges of India, 80% of them are unemployable.[12]
6. Migration of unskilled population from the rural to urban areas has enhanced the urban unemployment and underemployment. People working in the urban informal sector are in sordid job conditions, and with paltry income, they do not consider themselves employed. Roubaud and Torelli (2013) documented the pervasiveness of underemployment in urban labour markets in francophone Africa, which they divide into 'time-related' underemployment, where workers are involuntarily working part time, and defined 'invisible' unemployed as those workers who earn lesser than the minimum wage.
7. Overdependence on the agriculture sector is also a prime reason for unemployment in developing countries. Agriculture sector in these countries is found to be overburdened with disguised unemployment and underemployment. The Rural Labour Enquire (61st Round of National Service Scheme [NSS]) 2004–05 Report (India) on employment and unemployment of rural labour households envisaged that rural unemployment in its perennial underemployment, chronic disguised unemployment and with the increase in population, without corresponding increase in cultivable land, has resulted in underemployment or disguised unemployment which is perennial in nature.[13]
8. The industry sector in developing countries lacks adequate potential for creation of employment. Despite the endeavour of the government, the small and cottage industries in developing countries are not increasing in number. Less number of innovative entrepreneurs in the rural areas is also a vital cause of rural unemployment. UNDP's Industrial Development Report 2013 envisaged that for developing countries—which aim to maintain growth while creating sustainable jobs—manufacturing offers an opportunity not only to rebalance the economy towards higher value-added sectors but also to provide a relatively wide employment base with higher labour productivity.
9. Governments in developing countries have failed to generate adequate self-employment. Lack of marketing facilities for the products of the self-employed entrepreneurs has dissuade many of them not to venture, and many of those who have initiated have even closed down their businesses. Moreover, people in the rural areas lack adequate purchasing power. As a result, products of the rural entrepreneur remain unsold. This is one of the important reasons for non-proliferation of self-employment activities in the rural areas. Rural market is highly imperfect, which affects the functioning of both demand and supply mechanism, causing unemployment.

10. Last but not the least, economic fluctuations occurring in the global scenario have also created fluctuations in the job markets in the private sector of developing countries. The frictional unemployment is the order of the day in the globalization-driven job market. Estimation on the impact of global slowdown on employment in the Indian economy shows that in the year 2008–09, due to negative export growth in sectors such as textiles, gems and jewels, ores and minerals and so on, the total job loss in India was around 1.16 million.[14]

MEASURES TO CURTAIL UNEMPLOYMENT

Some of the suggested measures to control unemployment are as follows:

1. Governments of developing countries have to take policy decisions and plan initiations for the promotion of private investment in industrial and service sectors. Too much dependence on the public sector employment is one of the reasons for rising unemployment in developing countries. Moreover, the attitude of the unemployed youth needs to be changed, and facilities of social and health security measures in the private sector will attract qualified youth towards private sector jobs. In his paper, Dangelmaier (2012) envisaged that for a variety of reasons—especially for the creation and safeguarding of jobs—private sector promotion contributes to achieving qualitative growth in the partner countries, and thus it can be regarded as an engine for employment and qualitative growth.
2. Certain steps such as lowering the age of retirement and fixing the maximum years of service are being taken up by some of the governments in order to absorb more young energetic tech-savvy people in the job market. Here, proper retirement benefits both in the organized and in the unorganized sector will create a positive attitude among the employed people to either retire or take voluntary retirement for the sake of youth unemployment in the country.
3. Governments of developing countries need to attract FDIs for the creation of employment in the perspective sectors of the economy. FDI in the rural industrial sector is sine qua non for the growth of developing countries. Creation of more rural employment will check rural–urban migration and limit the size of urban informal employment. Kumar (1997) remarked that rural industrialization is considered a vehicle for the generation of productive employment and income for the rural poor and a means of productively absorbing a part of the addition to the rural labour.
4. Agriculture and its allied sectors in developing countries have immense potential for enhancing employment. Therefore, mechanization of agriculture and establishment of agro-based food processing industries with strong agriculture and industry nexus will raise employment in both primary and industrial sectors. Agriculture-based service sector activities and self-employment programmes will reduce rural unemployment. Kearney (2014) in his report has envisaged that

   > The food processing industry has significant potential to generate employment (3.1 million people) compared to textiles (2.5 million), apparel (1.8 million) and leather (0.5 million). The industry directly employs more than 16 lakh workers in

factories along with more than 14 lakh workers in the MSME segment. In addition, it has the potential to impact more than 1.2 crore people across its suppliers and supply chain.

5. Governments of developing countries need to enhance employment through public–private partnerships and initiate actions in primary, secondary and tertiary sectors. Strengthening service sector activities either through the corporate sector or through public–private partnership, such as opening up hospitals, schools and colleges, rural information centres, rural tourist spots, banking, insurance and so on, will boost rural employment and check rural–urban migration.
6. It is observed that in developing countries, NGOs are playing an important role in provisioning employment; therefore, a proper mechanism should be formulated for the creation of sustainable employment in the NGO sector.
7. There is a need for a drastic change in the education policies of developing countries. More focus need to be given towards the vocational and skill education at the primary, secondary and tertiary education levels. The linkages of vocational and skill education institutions established by the private, public and public–private partnerships with the primary, secondary and tertiary sector industries will be able to meet the challenges of unemployment effectively. Educational institutions should produce the type of students these industries want and would like to hire. In other words, education system must be demand driven, not one-sided supply driven. Frequent interaction between educational institutions and the industries in the area is required. Emmanuel (2015) from Nigerian perspective viewed that reposition in the area of adequate funding, infrastructure development, human capital development, educational policy restructuring towards skill acquisition, research development and the need to reposition the regulatory body (National Board of Technical Education [NBTE]) among others are necessary to eradicate unemployment from Nigeria. Skill education promotes self-employment and individual entrepreneurship in a country. In India and other South Asian countries as well, many skilled and semi-skilled people, such as plumbers, cobblers, fitters, electricians and so on, are found to have started individual self-employment businesses in the ghettos and unauthorized colonies and rural–urban villages of the cities and earning their livelihood. The 'start-up' programme initiated by the Government of India recently will go a long way to generate self-employment.
8. Various rural and urban employment projects and programmes must be initiated with a focus on employment generation, skill development and viable asset creation. For example, ILO has promoted labour-based appropriate technologies in Cambodia as an effective means to generate employment by improving and maintaining essential rural infrastructure. In doing so, the ILO programme has generated more than 3.3 million working days of rural employment, trained over 300 Cambodian technical personnel, constructed and maintained 550 km of rural roads, rehabilitated 96 km of secondary irrigation canals, cleared and cleaned the environment of Angkor Park and translated and developed technical training materials (ILO 2000).
9. Appropriate financing and loan facilities for the businesses and small and cottage industry sector will help generating more employment. Developing

countries need more entrepreneurs who can create jobs rather than those who are in need of jobs. In other words, the financing policy of the government should be to create more job creators rather than job seekers. It is observed that the microfinancing is playing an important role in generating employment in the rural areas. Yahaya, Osemene and Abdulraheem (2011) from their study in Kenya have found that microfinancing has a significant role to play in the economy, as it helps reducing poverty by providing financial services to the active poor, helps generating employment and also provides small loans to grow small businesses.

10. Last but not the least, local self-governed institutions in the recent years are emerging as important actors of development. They can also play an important role in creating employment at the grass-roots level. One of the illustrious examples is MGNREGA, one of the world's largest employment guarantee scheme, successfully implemented in India by the Panchayati Raj Institutions. The World Bank Group's 'The State of Social Safety Net, 2015' has ranked India's employment guarantee programme MGNREGA as the world's largest public works programme providing social safety net to almost 15% of the country's population.

ISSUES AND CHALLENGES OF UNEMPLOYMENT

Unemployment poses great many challenges to the development of developing countries. Some of the issues and challenges of unemployment are as follows:

1. With the growth of unplanned urbanization and migration of educated and unskilled people from the rural to urban areas, the employment programmes in developing countries are becoming more and more informal and casual. Here, the employment depends on availability of work, and continuation of work depends on the wish of the employer which hardly provides any job security and employment is not legally binding. According to Grant (2012), most urban youth, particularly youth migrants, live in unplanned settlements, often in squalid conditions, and are vulnerable to high levels of unemployment. It is observed that on an average, a casual worker in an urban area remains without work for 10 days in a month. This seriously affects his/her income and economic health of the family. This is a bizarre situation of underemployment in the informal sector, where the worker is available but does not get work. For families with a single wage earner, the situation becomes more precarious. Furthermore, without any social security benefit, the old age of the landless migrant worker becomes vulnerable to destitution. It is rightly remarked that the urban informal sector is linked with the rural sector in that it allows unskilled labourers to escape from rural poverty and underemployment, although it grants them living, working conditions and incomes that are not much better than what they had before moving (Todaro 1997). Casualization of employment is a temporary solution to the problem of unemployment and cannot provide sustainable livelihood to the casual workers. While criticizing the casualization of work in Nigeria, Fapohunda (2012) said that

casualization of labour is against the campaign for full employment. Casualization is detrimental to employees' economic health and has grave consequences on the national economy. Therefore, it is suggested that casualization be seriously checked and, if possible, expunged completely from being practised in the employment system.

2. A gigantic percentage of people in developing countries are found employed in the informal sector. Informal economy is characterized by the miseries of the wage earners and casual workers. According to Heiztz and Vanek (2007), informal employment represents a large share of total employment in many Asian countries and it is, on average, precarious, low-paid and risky. Informal sector contributes to about 55% of Sub-Saharan Africa's GDP and 80% of the labour force (African Development Bank Group 2013). Even though the informal sector is an opportunity for generating reasonable incomes for many people, most informal workers are without secure income, employment benefits and social protection (African Development Bank Group 2013).
3. Existence of underemployment in the semi-urban and urban areas and presence of disguised unemployment in rural areas are causes of concern in developing countries of Asia, Africa and Latin America. Underemployment is a palpable condition of exploitation which creates a lot of frustration among the workers employed in the formal as well as informal sectors in urban areas. On the other hand, disguised unemployment is the main reason of backwardness of rural areas, where the number of people engaged in agriculture sector is over and above what is actually required for the sector. Disguised unemployment, if perpetuates for a longer period in the farming families in agriculture sector of developing countries, will result in frustration among the farming community, fragmentation of landholding, family feud and selling of land among the small and marginal farmers, leading to landlessness and pauperization of the farmer and even to farmers' suicide. To Viner (1964), 'disguised unemployment is a situation in which the removal from a working combination of factors of some units of labour, nothing else of consequence or worth mentioning being changed, will leave the aggregated product of the working combination undiminished and many even increase it.' According to Downes (1998), disguised unemployment represents a serious waste of human resources. The marginal productivity of labour, who are disguisedly or superfluously employed in various sectors in either rural or urban areas, is zero. The disguised unemployed labour force quantity is L_1 and L_2 as depicted in Figure 5.2, as the increase in labour force has not resulted in increase in output. The output remains stagnant at point Q1. Therefore, promotion of allied sector activities, such as poultry, fishery, piggery, horticulture, floriculture and so on, is vital to effectively engage the disguised unemployed workforce in the rural areas.
4. Unemployment would affect per capita income of the households, and thereby could create income inequality in rural as well as urban areas. According to Saunders (2002), unemployment increases the risk of poverty and contributes to inequality, and it also gives rise to a series of debilitating social effects on unemployed people, their families and the communities in which they live. When these three devils, i.e.

Figure 5.2 *Measurement of Disguised Unemployment*

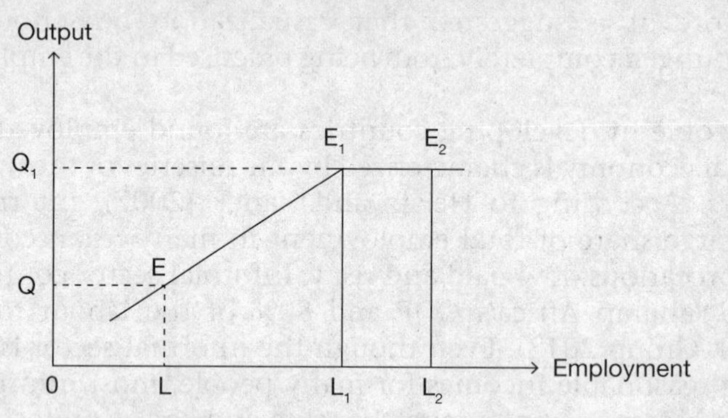

Source: Author.

unemployment, poverty and inequality, are clubbed with inflation, they constitute a gang of four which can create a precarious situation for the poor and downtrodden in developing countries. It can promote family feuds, hunger deaths, suicides, crimes, robberies and all other social evils in the poor countries. Therefore, the ultimate aim of the governments of developing countries is to attain high rate of employment and ensure stability of prices along with sustainable economic growth and development.

5. Unemployment among the youth has caused a lot of social unrest in the resource-poor developing countries. The illiterate and poorly educated youth without any job are found to be engaged in anti-social activities such as robbery, theft, chain snatching and so on. Cities are becoming unsafe for women, and the number of molestation and rape cases committed by the unemployed youth is on rise in the cities. Other problems associated with unemployment are the less marriage and no marriage, and the number of divorces among the newly married couples and even incidences of suicides because of lack of job, forced unemployed, low salary and so on are on rise. Social unrest is one of bizarre gifts of unemployment to the mundane societies. International agencies and experts have warned the developed as well as developing nations that rising unemployment will lead to a greater social unrest in the coming years. Unemployment causes 45,000 suicides in a year worldwide.[15] Unemployment can affect one's mental health, physical health and can cause extensive stress in life. It was found that for every 10% increase in the UR, suicides will also increase by 1.7% and psychiatric hospitalizations will increase by 4.2%.[16]

Unemployment is the most critical economic development problem in developing countries. Political economies of developing countries are relentlessly trying to provide employment to their youth. Nowadays, they are making necessary changes in their education system to make it more employment oriented. Poverty and inequality are bizarre outcomes of unemployment. A person without any land, if remains idle without any alternative sources of employment and earning for a long period, will succumb to poverty. Employment is a fundamental prerequisite for the socio-economic progress of the individual as well as the nation.

SECTION III: INFLATION

Inflation is harmful because it reduces the rate of growth of the natural level of output. Zero inflation would increase the long-run rate of economic growth.

—Dua and Smyth (1997)

Even in its creepiest form inflation robs the needy by decreasing the purchasing power of money. The things that a person or small salary will buy shrink with each creep forward on an inflationary movement. Thus, school teachers, pensioners, and those elder citizens who live upon income from a fixed amount of capital, find themselves poorer and poorer.

—Peterson[17]

One of the most frequently discussed topics and concepts which is hitting hard to the poor as well as the poorest of the poor in both developed and developing countries is inflation. The problem of inflation has been of central concern to American policy-makers since the mid-1960s (Mishkin 1984). Also, inflation management is a significant problem in Sub-Saharan Africa for the past several decades (Canetti and Greene 1991). Inflation has remained the most critical problem in India for the last several decades. Low-income-earning people and the poor—people working in the informal sector, the daily wage earners and self-employed persons in petty income earning activities—suffer the most because of inflation. It is one of the key developmental issues in the national and provincial electoral battles. There are several examples in India where the ruling party was thrown out of power by the people in the general elections because of rise in prices of essential commodities such as onions, potatoes, tomatoes, pulses and so on. Inflation is one of the most powerful development variables in the vote bank politics of developing countries. Development of the underdeveloped sections of the society, particularly in developing countries, and the rate of inflation have a vein–blood relationship. Continuous rise in the prices of goods and services and fall in the purchasing power of money deeply affect the economic condition of the impoverished masses. Also, continuous decline in the real income because of rising prices deeply affects the quality of life of the impoverished people. Therefore, any discussion on the issues and challenges of development in developing countries will remain incomplete if the issues and challenges of inflation are not discussed. Poverty, income inequality, unemployment and inflation are the four interrelated development concepts in developing countries.

Coulborn (1950) opined that inflation is a situation of 'too much money chasing too few goods.' According to Crowther (1940), inflation is 'a state in which the value of money is falling, that is, prices are rising.' To Ackley (1978), 'inflation is a persistent and appreciable rise in the general level or average prices.' Stanford (2008) was of the view that inflation is a 'process whereby the average price level in an economy increasing overtime.' In the opinion of Gupta (2001), 'inflation is a persistent rise in general price level rather than a once-for-all rise in it.' Thus, from all these definitions, it is clear that inflation is a situation where there is a persistent rise in the prices of goods and services and a continuous decline in the value of money. In other words, it is a situation where 'too much of money buys too few of goods and services.' It is a very commonly used term in developing countries where the prices of goods and services are continuously rising and putting the common men in hardship.

MEASUREMENT OF INFLATION

The price index is a customary method of measuring change in prices from one period to another and is used to track the inflation. To define it, 'price index' is a method that measures the cost of purchasing a basket of goods and services at a point of time (current year) relating to the cost of purchasing the similar basket of goods and services during an earlier reference period (last year or base year). The two popular price indices used for tracking the inflation rate are Wholesale Price Index (WPI) and Consumer Price Index (CPI). WPI measures the average price changes of goods and services brought and sold in the wholesale market. The constituents of WPI in India are of three categories: (a) primary articles, largely consisting food items (102 items); (b) fuel and power items (19 items) and (c) manufactured products (555 items). WPI in India is reviewed periodically and the current base is 2004–05. CPI, on the other hand, measures the weighted average of prices paid by a consumer for a specified set of goods and services. Patnaik, Shah and Vronese (2011) were of the view that CPI reflects the consumption bundle of households; thus, it is more relevant than any other measure of inflation. In India, four categories of CPI are estimated for different segments of the population:

1. CPI for industrial labourers,
2. CPI for agricultural labourers,
3. CPI for rural labourers and
4. All-India CPI.

CPI also assigns high weight to primary articles. Subbarao (2010) said,

> In India, we have one wholesale price index and four consumer price indices. There are ongoing efforts at a technical level to reduce the number of consumer price indices, and I believe the technical issues are not insurmountable. But that still will not give us a single representative inflation rate for an emerging market economy with market imperfections, diverse geography and 1.2 billion people.

Brandt and Holz (2006) stated,

> Prices differ across space: from province to province, from rural or urban areas in one province to rural or urban areas in another province and from rural to urban areas within one province. Systematic differences in prices across a range of goods and services in different localities implies regional difference in the cost of living.

A simple formula for the calculation of inflation is as follows:

$$I_n = \frac{P_t - P_{t-1}}{P_{t-1}},$$

where

I_n = Inflation
P_t = Price Index in current year
P_{t-1} = Price Index in previous year

CPI in the United States of America

In the United States of America, CPIs are available for two population groups: a CPI for All Urban Consumers (CPI-U) which covers approximately 87% of the total population and a CPI for Urban Wage Earners and Clerical Workers (CPI-W) which covers 32% of the population. The CPI-U includes expenditures by urban wage earners and clerical workers, professional, managerial and technical workers, the self-employed, short-term workers, the unemployed, retirees and others but not the labour force. The CPI-W covers prices of only those items that are present in the consumption basket of workers with hourly wage earning or clerical jobs. In addition, there are measures of inflation within regions.

Source: Patnaik et al. (2011), also see http://www.nipfp.org.in/media/medialibrary/201... (accessed on 30/03/2016).

CAUSES OF INFLATION

There are many factors which cause inflation in an economy. President Eisenhower's administration, while analyzing inflation in the United States of America during the 1950s, recognized that there are two types of inflation. One is money inflation that is caused by the cheapening of money via deficit spending and printing money, and the other is the inflation arising from cost increases or in his terms, the one 'brought about by the efforts of all people to gain a bigger portion' (Takami 2014). A few important factors causing inflation are as follows:

Demand-pull Factor of Inflation: Here, the demand of goods and services rises more rapidly as compared to the supply or production of goods and services leading to a rise in prices in the economy. The demand-pull factor also takes place because of deficit in financing and printing of money. With the availability of extra money in the market, people are empowered to spend more, and the effective demand in the economy rises. According to Milton Friedman, 'Inflation is always and everywhere a monetary phenomenon.' To Grant and Vidler (2000), demand-pull inflation occurs when aggregate demand exceeds aggregate supply at the current price level. The excess supply of money caused demand-pull inflation in Russia in the 1990s when the Russian government financed its budget deficit by printing rouble (Dwivedi 2010).

Cost-push Inflation: It is a situation where prices of the goods and services rise because of the rise in the cost of production of goods and services in the economy. Cost of production rises because of several factors, such as rising prices of inputs for cost of production, prices of technology used in the production process and the labour cost. If firms incur a higher cost in production process, then they will usually raise the prices of their product to maintain their profit margin. All these factors produce impact on the prices of final goods produced in the economy. For instance, food inflation occurs in the economy because of increase in the cost of fertilizers, electricity and power, fuel, pesticides, and also because of increase in minimum support price and so on. Cost-push inflation is also caused by rise in the labour cost, increase in the rate of interest and raising taxes.

Hoarding and Black Marketing: These two elements also lead to rise in prices. Black marketeers and hoarders create artificial shortage of the supply of goods in the economy leading to inflation. When essential commodities are not made available in the open market and stocks are internationally held back by dealers, it is known as hoarding and its purpose is to create an artificial scarcity in order to push up the prices. Black marketing is the practice of selling hoarded goods secretly at a premium (Fernando 2010). Recently, one of the factors for the rise in the prices of pulses (*Harad daal*; white lentils) in the Indian markets was hoarding. This is mostly observed in the developing country, where the political as well as bureaucratic systems lack will power to control the black marketeers and hoarders.

High Population Growth Rate: Population growth rate is also a cause of inflation in developing countries. The rise in demand for goods and services because of high growth rate of population without adequate growth in output and productivity will lead to inflation in the economy. Juselius and Takats (2015) have found that a larger share of dependent (i.e. young and old) is correlated with high inflation, while a larger share of working age cohorts is correlated with lower inflation.

Income and Wages: The rise in incomes of the employees and wages of the workers are also responsible factors of inflation. In the case of India, government policy to give dearness allowances on the basis of the price index and pay commission implemented in every 10 years produces impacts on inflation in the country. Gowda and Venugopal (2007) were of the opinion that in India, the Union Government appoints pay commission at frequent intervals and these pay commissions are found to be recommending higher salaries and dearness allowances. The state governments, too, appoint pay commissions which also recommend higher salaries and dearness allowances. Both add to the government expenditures which in the absence of proportionate rise in tax revenue enlarge the budget deficits which are patently inflationary.

Import and Export Policies: Import and export policies of goods and services can also affect inflation. Export of goods to other countries without assessing its demand in the home economy leads to rise in prices. Giving Bangladesh's example, Islam (2013) in his empirical study said that Bangladesh being a food importing country, any rise in the food prices in the world market can push up the domestic prices of those commodities. Now the domestic markets of almost all developing countries are interconnected with the international market, and any fluctuation in the international prices affects the domestic prices also. The fluctuation in crude oil prices in India is an illustrious example of impact of import and export on domestic prices.

Globalization: It is yet another determining factor of inflation in the developed as well as developing countries. Globalization helps in lowering inflation in the developed countries which are resorting to cheap import from developing countries. On the contrary, it exerts inflationary pressure on developing countries, those who have higher balance of payment deficit, poor bargaining power and lack of comparative advantage in the international market. Bowen and Mayhew (2008) were of the view that increasing globalization and openness to trade has exerted downward pressure on inflation in developed countries by, e.g. reducing import prices. Kamin, Marazzi and Schindler (2004) found that the increase in the share of the US imports from China had lowered the overall US import price inflation by about 0.8 percentage points per years between 1993 and 2002. Chen, Imbs and Scott (2004) in an investigation of industry-level output prices found that an increase in the economy's openness was responsible for a fall in aggregate manufacturing output price inflation up to 0.14 percentage points per year across European Union countries between 1988 and 2000.

Monetary and Fiscal Policies: Monetary and fiscal policies of an economy are also critical to inflation. Money supply, taxation, excise duties, fiscal expenditure, deficit financing and so on influence the rate of inflation in the economy. Mishkin and Posen (1998) from their study in four countries have found that the inflation targeting monetary policy is appearing to have been successful in increasing the transparency of monetary policy making and in lowering significantly the rate of inflation in countries such as New Zealand, Canada, United Kingdom and Germany.

Other Factors: Use of traditional method of cultivation; lack of irrigation facility; vagaries of monsoon; overdependence of hill, dry land and desert area's people on the fertile plain; and lack of inclusive agriculture lead to low production of food grains, leading to food price inflation. More of continuous climate change and related effects also affect food grain productivity, leading to rise in prices of food grains. A study of the International Food Policy Research Institute shows that global warming may further increase the prices of corn, wheat and rice by at least two-thirds by 2050.[18]

MEASURES TO CONTROL INFLATION

A few important measures needed to be taken for controlling inflation are discussed further.

1. Raising the food grain productivity to control the rise in prices of food grains, pulses and other allied food items. Fixing buyback prices of the essential food items and minimum support prices of the food crops as well as cash crops. Fixing buyback of the agricultural products will encourage the farmers to raise productivity. Moreover, attempts have to be made for controlling the cost of production with the subsidized supply of agricultural inputs to the farmers in developing countries. The labour cost of production can be reduced by transferring labour force from the more populous poor states to the Green Revolution belt. This is to be followed in the case of industrial and service sectors to check cost-push inflation in these sectors also. This will be a step towards checking cost-push inflation. Kaur's (2014) study depicts that the food production is estimated to have a negative (though non-significant) impact on inflation.

2. Public distribution system has to be strengthened, and food grains, pulses and other essential food items have to be provided to the families living below the poverty line at subsidies prices so that they do not fill the pinch of inflation. Kaur's (2014) study depicts that the Public distribution system is estimated to have a negative (though non-significant) impact on inflation. Proper marketing policy and procurement of food grain will also have impact on food prices.
3. Hoarders and black marketeers have to be dealt with firm hands to prevent them from adopting nefarious methods of artificial price rise to earn profit by putting hardship of inflation on the consumers. In India, state governments are empowered to act against hoarders of food items by hoarding in abeyance the removal of restrictions on licensing, stock limits and movement of food articles under the Essential Commodities Act, 1955, and the state governments have to act against them (Kumari 2013).
4. The monetary policy of the country must be carefully formulated to check inflation in the country. A strong monetary policy is sine qua non for dealing with inflation. It should keep control over the money supply in the economy, so that demand-pull or money supply-driven inflation is kept under control.
5. Government of the country should not resort to huge deficit financing which raises money supply in the economy. The taxation policies need to be carefully designed in an economy experiencing inflation, so that it restricts price rise in the country. Better interface between monetary and fiscal policy can also help to control inflation.
6. The populist measures of dearness allowances to the white-collar-job employees of the government and pay commission to the public sector employees may be suitably rationalized, so that they do not enhance inflation in the economy.
7. As non-monetary and non-fiscal measures, in developing countries, population growth has to be checked particularly among the lower strata of the society which faces economic hardships because of inflation.

ISSUES AND CHALLENGES OF INFLATION

Inflation and Poverty

The first and foremost challenge that inflation exerts on the development is poverty. It is generally advocated that mild inflation—3% to 5%—is good for economic growth, while double-digit inflation puts lot of hardship on the common men. Higher inflation may be good for economic growth but is bad for the development. In developing countries with illiteracy, low level of literacy, poverty, unemployment and ill health, the burden of inflation deprives many impoverished families to have access to these services, thus further curtails their opportunity and enhances human poverty. Easterly and Fisher (2001) from their study found that inflation is regarded as more of a problem by the poor than the non-poor, as inflation reduces the relative income of the poor. A study conducted by the Institute for Fiscal Studies (2011) found that inflation hits poorer families much harder than the rich in the United Kingdom. Chaudhury and Chaudhury (2008) found that food price inflation increased poverty in Pakistan. Nepal Living Standard Survey III found that a 10% rise in food prices is likely to increase overall poverty in Nepal by 4 percentage points. It implies that 1% rise in food inflation will push 100,000 additional people into overall poverty and 180,000 additional people into food poverty (Bowen and Mayhew 2008).

Impact of inflation on poverty varies across the sectors and areas. The poverty-stricken people working in the informal sector, in agriculture as landless labourer, engaged in household activities and belonging to rural and urban slum areas would be worst affected if inflation riches double digit. Sugema et al. (2010) from their study in Indonesia have concluded that the rural poor households are more vulnerable to economic shocks, especially inflation. Thus, controlling inflation becomes more challenging before the governments in the countries with high-level poverty. Agenor (1998) found poverty rates to be positively related to inflation in cross-country data.

Inflation and Income Inequality

Inflation will elongate income inequality. With the rise in the rate of inflation, the income gap between the rich and poor, rich and middle class and middle class and poor would enhance. Inflation will relatively have less effect on the real income of the people working in the organized sector and having the facility of dearness allowances. However, the burden of inflation is indomitable on the informal sector workers who are devoid of dearness allowances. Dolmas et al. (1997) from their study found that countries with higher inflation do have higher income inequalities. Cadoso, Barros and Urani (1995) from their study in Brazil found that the deterioration of the income distribution in major Brazilian cities, observed during the 1980s, shows that inflation increases income inequality and has different effects on different education groups. With the globalization era in vogue, the inflation in developing countries is found to have enhanced the gap between the standard of living and income, the ultra rich and rich and the poor and the poorest of the poor. Walsh and Yu (2012) were of the view from the finding of their study that non-food inflation could be strongly correlated with worsening income inequality. Easterly and Fisher (2001) argued that the rich are better able to protect themselves against or benefit from the effects of inflation than the poor.

Inflation and Unemployment

The honeymoon between high rates of unemployment and inflation in developing countries escalates 'miseries' of the poor and the poorest of the poor. The combination of high rates of unemployment and inflation is called 'stagflation'. Stagflation leads to pauperization of the marginalized wage earners who are hard hit by inflation and its effects on the real wage rate. However, the famous Phillips curve (Figure 5.3) shows an inverse relationship between unemployment and inflation. According to Cashell (2004), in a 1958 article that had become a frequently cited reference in the economic literature, economist A. W. Phillips reputed evidence of an inverse relationship between the rate of increase in wages and the rate of unemployment by comparing the rate of increase in wages with URs in Britain between 1861 and 1957. The trade-off between unemployment and inflation depends on the notion of excess of effective demand. Demand in excess of supply will tend to push both wages and prices, so that rising prices tend to be correlated with falling unemployment (Lipsy 1960). Because wage increases are closely correlated with price increases, this relationship was widely interpreted as a trade-off between inflation and

Figure 5.3 *Unemployment and Inflation Relationship*

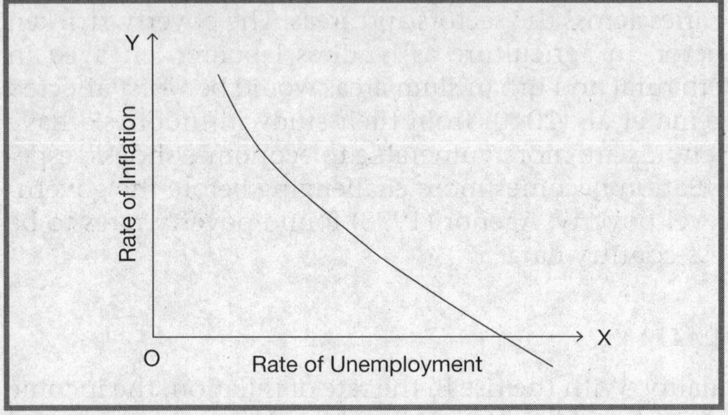

Source: Author.

unemployment (Cashell 2004). This inverse trade-off between inflation and unemployment may be true for the developed countries at that point of time having less number of youth population; however, from the standpoint of developing countries of South Asia and Africa having more number of youth population, this proposition may not hold much ground. Moreover, growing volume of literature on theoretical foundation of the Phillips curve has clearly established that the trade-off between inflation and unemployment is essentially a short-run phenomenon (Kumar and Vashist 2012).

Customarily, if the relationship between rates of unemployment and inflation has to be established, then four hypothetical situations can arise: (a) low rate of unemployment and low rate of inflation; (b) high rate of unemployment and high rate of inflation; (c) low rate of unemployment and high rate of inflation and (d) high rate of unemployment and low rate of inflation. From the above four situations, the second situation of high rate of unemployment and high rate of inflation which most of developing countries are experiencing is a cause of concern for them. This situation is known as 'stagflation', where both the rates of unemployment and inflation are high. This positive trade-off between unemployment and inflation has been occurring in developing countries because of several reasons and a few among the many are as follows:

1. High population growth rate and high percentage of unproductive population in the population pyramid.
2. Fluctuation of food grain productivity in these economies because of several factors, i.e. poor irrigation, use of traditional method of cultivation and impact of climate change, to name a few among many.
3. Inflation-driven dearness allowance to the public sector employees, consequently resulting in overall increase in prices created by the retailers, wholesalers, traders and businessmen.
4. Poor marketing, procurement and distribution of food grains. Inflation created by the hoarders and black marketeers by creating artificial scarcity and lack of policy and political will power to control them.

The relationship between unemployment and inflation is an unpredictable one and varies from country to country, depending on the market situation and the prevailing socio-economic condition. Besides, the market imperfection in developing countries is one of the critical factors that have profound impact on the inflation and its relationship with unemployment. Therefore, in developing countries, it is not as simple that of inverse one as predicted by the Phillips curve. The Phillips curve is more relevant to the developed countries, where the growth rate of population is low and fluctuation in productivity is less. Muhammad et al. (2013) from Nigeria experience commented that unemployment, inflation and wages are termed as continuous and unpleasant situations that describe the endemic nature of a country's economy.

It is not a flight of fancy, but delicately, inflation is anti-poor and results in social injustice. Those who have more get more, and those who have less get less. Both high UR and high inflation rate create unpleasant situation for the country. The economic problem of stagflation may give rise to many social problems, such as robbery, suicide of the impoverished, malnutrition and so on, and it dampens the level of health and education among the impoverished.

Food Price Inflation and Food Security

The rise in the prices of the food grains, pulses and other allied food items, such as fish, egg, milk and milk products, vegetables and so on, is a cause of concern for the poor as well as poorest of the poor in developing countries where hunger and malnutrition are critical issues. It elongates their poverty, enhances malnutrition and is one of the responsible factors for the occurrences of hunger deaths in developing countries. Food security is defined as all people at all times having physical and economic access to sufficient, safe and nutritious food to maintain a healthy and active life (Shrestha and Chaudhary 2012). The food price spikes and volatility are of increasing political, professional and public concern for food security world.[19] FAO has estimated that the 2007–08 price spike increased the number of undernourished people from about 850 million in 2007 to about 1,023 million in 2009. According to FAO (2012), almost 870 million people were chronically undernourished in 2010–12; the number of hungry people in the world remained unacceptably high. Also, Global Assessment Report 2013 has envisaged that Sub-Saharan Africa, Latin America and Asia are at risk of becoming the most food insecure. In the context of monetary policies, the idea of price stability is inflation in the range of 0–2% per year. Recently, the chief economists of IMF suggested that the definition of price stability could be expanded to an annual inflation of up to 8% (Oliver Dell'Ariccia and Mauro 2010). Therefore, a double-digit inflation rate, as it is found happening in many developing countries after globalization, could pose challenge to the economic growth and development of developing countries.

Broadly speaking, food security is a larger issue and has many dimensions. One of the important among them is supply dimension which relates to the enhanced production of food grain in the country, region, state and at the village level. Policy measures relating to land reform, irrigation, use of technology in agriculture, procurement and impact of climate change on food productivity, and so on have to be taken into consideration at the policy as well as programme implementation levels.

The supply dimension can also broadly cover the import and export policy on food grain and, therefore, be called for formulation of a transparent, accountable and rule- and need-based multilateral trade system. Maintenance of food stock and warehouses for the effective procurement of food grain is also a major concern in many developing countries. The fixing of minimum support price for food grain and its impact on the producers and consumers require attention from the perspective of food security.

The second dimension is the demand side of food security which largely covers the quantum of population dependent on food, income of the people to have access to food, food pricing and so on. It is seen that despite the availability of food grain in the free market, the

Table 5.5 *Measures of Food Security in Selected Countries (100% Represents Highest Level)*

Region	Affordability (%)	Availability Measures (%)	Safety and Quality (%)
Botswana	50.9	62.0	46.0
Sri Lanka	42.9	49.2	46.8
Uganda	36.5	42.5	47.2
Pakistan	30.7	37.4	55.5
Bangladesh	31.2	37.6	30.4
Tanzania	19.5	30.3	32.0
Malawi	15.5	36.2	29.7

Source: Economist Intelligence Unit, October 2012, Global Food Security Index. Also see Haynes and Soobramanien (2013).

impoverished lack capacity to pay for them. Table 5.5 clearly reveals that in developing countries, the affordability measure is a larger concern as compared to availability measures.

The third dimension is the management of food security, which includes efficient and effective public distribution system of food grains, transportation and cost management of food grain, logistic management, fair price shop and pricing mechanism taking into the affordability of the poorest of the poor and controlling hoarding and black marketing of food grain in the open market. The most recent food crises have shown that even when there is an adequate food supply, affordable access can be hindered by distribution mechanisms (Haynes and Soobramanien 2013).

The sustainable livelihood to the poor in developing countries cannot be ensured amidst food price inflation, as many studies have revealed that the low-income-earning families spend nearly 60–80% of their total income on food (Ruel et al. 1998). One of the human development measures of the governments of the developing world is to control food price inflation in order to check malnutrition, miseries and hunger among the poorest of the poor for whom food is the only means of survival. Food inflation is an atrocity on the human's right to food.

SUMMARY

Inequality, unemployment and inflation are the vital issues and challenges of development. Income inequalities between the rich and poor, and the low income of the poor, deprive many impoverished households of their access to even basic needs, i.e. housing, two square meals and nutrition, sanitation, drinking water and also to quality health care and education. Reduction of income inequality is a vital factor for the promotion of inclusive and sustainable development in developing countries. Unemployment is one of basic issues of economic development, and providing sustainable employment to their population is a stupendous challenge before the resource-crunch developing countries. Various types of unemployment, such as seasonal unemployment, structural unemployment, frictional unemployment and so on, existing in developing countries need to be strategically dealt with for the attainment of sustainable development. Like economic inequality and unemployment, the continuous price rise, i.e. inflation, is also a development challenge before the developed and developing countries, in particular developing countries, to provide basic minimum needs to the impoverished masses on a sustainable basis.

Keywords: unemployment, seasonal unemployment, disguised unemployment, frictional unemployment, income inequality, stagflation, inflation, Lorenz curve, Gini coefficient, underemployment, Phillips curve, MGNREGA.

REVIEW QUESTIONS

1. What is income inequality? Critically discuss various methods of measurement of income inequality.
2. Discuss various causes of income inequality. Suggest measures to reduce income inequality in developing countries.
3. Why do developing countries have large income inequality? Describe various issues and challenges related to income inequality.
4. Income inequality and unemployment are interrelated. Explain the effects of unemployment on income inequality.
5. Define unemployment. Discuss various methods of measuring unemployment.
6. Critically discuss the causes of unemployment in developing countries. What are the suggested measures to check unemployment?
7. What is unemployment? Discuss various types of unemployment in developing countries with the reasons.
8. What is inflation? Discuss five important causes of inflation.
9. Define inflation. Critically discuss the relationship of inflation with unemployment and economic inequality.
10. Write short notes on the following:
    (i) Phillips curve
    (ii) Disguised unemployment
    (iii) Social inequality
    (iv) Lorenz curve

NOTES

1. The 'Political prices of onions': The defeat of the Bharatiya Janata Party government in the Delhi assembly election in the 1998 was attributed to a large extent to its government's failure to curb the rise in the price of onions. For details, see http://www.thehindu.com/onions/editorial/the-political-price-of-onions/article977100 (accessed on 23 March 2016).
2. The views of Colin Gordon are contained in article 'Growing Apart: A Political History of American Inequality.' For details, see http://www.worldwidehippies.com/growing-apart-a-political-history-of-american-inequality/ (accessed on 2 February 2014).
3. OECD (2011).
4. See handle.dtic.mil/1000.2/ADA416383 (accessed on 7 April 2016).

5. See http://www.china.org.cn/world/Off_the_Wire/2012–12/23/cntent_27493211.htm (accessed on 5 March 2016).
6. Medgyesi, M., and I. G. Toth. 'Economic Growth and Income Inequalities.' See http://www.tarki.hu/adatbank-h/kutjel/pdf/b247.pdf (accessed on 9 November 2013).
7. Gindling, T. H., and IZA World Labour. 'Does Increasing the Minimum Wage Reduce Poverty in Developing Countries?' For details, see http://wol.iza.org/articles/does-increasing-the-minimum-wage-reduce-poverty-in-developing-countries/long (accessed on 28 November 2016).
8. Gonzales C., S. J. Chadra, K. Kochhar, M. Newiak, and T. Zeinullayez. 'Catalyst for Change: Empowering Women and Tackling Income Inequality.' See https://www.imf.org/external/pubs/ft/sdn/2015/sdn1520.pdf (accessed on 5 March 2016).
9. The above definition of ILO is given in Economics Revision. For details, see http://economicsrevision.co.uk/measurign-unemployment (accessed on 21 March 2014).
10. For details, see Pandey, P. N. 'Status of Employment and Unemployment Statistics in India,' Ministry of Statistics & Programme Implementation, New Delhi. Available at: http://e.unescap.org/stat/meet/keyindia/india_current (accessed on 21 March 2014).
11. See 'The Effect of a Minimum-wage Increase on Employment and Family Income.' Available at: https://www.cbo.gov/sites/default/files/113th-congress-2013-2014/reports/44995-MinimumWage_OneColumn.pdf (accessed on 28 November 2016).
12. See http://timesofindia.indiatimes.com/tech/tech-news/Over-80-of-engineering-graduates-in-india (accessed on 5 March 2016).
13. See http://labourbureau.nic.in/RLE%202k%204–5%20chapter%202.htm (accessed on 5 March 2016).
14. See http://wtocentre.iift.ac.in/UNTAD/11.pdf (accessed on 6 May 2016).
15. See http:www.theguardian.com/society/2015/feb/11/unemployment-causes-45000-sucides-a-year-world-wide-finds-study (accessed on 5 March 2016).
16. Mentioned by Holland, K. 'Effect of Unemployment on Health and Mental Health Based on Gender,' Master of Social Work Clinical Research Papers, 38; for details, see http://sophia.stkate.edu/cgi/viewcontent.cgi?article=1038&context=msw_papers (accessed on 30 November 2016).
17. See Peterson, E. E. 'Inflation and Its Control.' Available at: http://ageconsearch.umn.edu/bitstream/17754/1/ar590081.pdf (accessed on 25 March 2016).
18. Quoted from 'Climate Change to Exacerbate Rising Food Prices,' Earth Institute, Columbia University. See http://www.climatechange-foodsecurity.org/uploads/Climate_Change_Food_Prices_11.pdf (accessed on 28 November 2016).
19. Mentioned in the report 'Price Volatility and Food Security: A Report by the High Level Panel of Experts on Food Security and Nutrition July 2011', for details see http://www.fao.org/fileadmin/user_upload/hlpe/hlpe_documents/HLPE-price-volatility-and-food-security-report-July-2011.pdf (accessed on 28 November 2016).

BIBLIOGRAPHY

Acemoglu, D., M. A. Bautista, P. Querubin, and James A. Robinson. 'Economic and Political Inequality in Development: The Case of Cundinamarca, Colombia.' Massachusetts Institute of Technology, Department of Economics, 2007. Available at: http://economics.mit.edu/files/3831 (accessed on 15 March 2014).

Ackley, G. *Macro-Economic Theory and Policy*. New York: Macmillan, 1978.

Adebayo, A. A. 'Youth's Unemployment and Crime in Nigeria: A Nexus and Implications for National Development.' *International Journal of Sociology and Anthropology* 5, no. 8 (2013): 350–57.

African Development Bank Group. 'Recognizing Africa's Informal Sector.' 2013. Available at: http://www.afdb.org/en/blogs/afdb_championing (accessed on 12 November 2013).

Agenor, P. R. 'Stabilization Policies, Poverty and the Labour Market.' Paper, IMF and World Bank, Washington DC, 1998.

Aghion, P., and P. Bolton. 'A Theory of Tickle-down Growth and Development.' *Review of Economic Studies* 64, no. 2 (1997): 151–72.

Ajufo, B. I. 'Challenges of Youth Unemployment in Nigeria: Effective Career Guidance as a Panacea'. *African Research Review* 7, no. 1(2013): 307–21.

Kumar, A. V. *Rural Industrialization in India Aspects of Policy, Technology Employment with Special Reference to Kerala*. New Delhi: MD Publication, 1997.

Benabou, R. 'Equity and Efficiency in Human Capital Investment: The Local Connection.' *Review of Economic Studies* 63, no. 2 (1996): 237–64.

Birdsall, N. 'Rising Inequality in the New Global Economy.' WIDER Angle, 2005.

Bittencourt, Mayer M. F. 'Financial Development and Inequality: Brazil 1985–99.' *Economic Change and Restructuring* 43 (2006): 113–30.

Borooach, V. K. 'Caste, Inequality and Poverty in India.' *Review of Development Economics* 9, no. 3 (2005): 399–414.

Boulier, B. L. 'The Effects of Demographic Variables in Income Distribution.' Discussion Paper 61, Woodrow Wilson School, Princeton, NJ, 1975.

Bowen, A., and K. Mayhew. 'Globalization, Import Prices and Inflation. How Reliable Are the 'Tailwind'?' *Bank of England Quarterly Bulletin* 48, no. 3 (2008): 283–91. Available at: http://www.bankofengland.co.uk/publications/Documents/quarterlybulletin/qb080302.pdf (accessed on 23 March 2016).

Brandt, L., and C. A. Holz. 'Spatial Price Differences in China: Estimates and Implications.' *Economic Development and Cultural Change* (October 2006): 43–56.

Bruton, H. J. 'Unemployment Problems and Policies in Less Developed Countries.' *The American Economic Review* 68, no. 2 (1978): 51–57.

Byrne, P., and E. Strold. 'Defining Unemployment in Developing Countries: The Case of Trinidad and Tobago.' Credit Research Paper, Centre for Research in Economic Development and International Trade, 2001.

Canetti, E., and J. E. Green. 'Money Growth and Exchange Rate Depreciation as Causes of Inflation in African Countries: An Empirical Analysis. IMF Working Paper 91/67, International Monetary Fund, 1991.

Cashell, B. *In‡ation and Unemployment: What Is the Connection?* Federal Publications. Paper 180, 2004.

Cardoso, E. R., Paes de Barros, and A. Urani. 'Inflation and Unemployment as Determinants of Inequality in Brazil: The 1980s.' In *Reform, Recovery and Growth: Latin America and the Middle East*, edited by R. Dornbusch and S. Edwards, 151–76. University of Chicago Press, 1995.

Chaudhary, T. T., and A. A. Chaudhary. 'The Effects of Rising Food and Fuel Costson Poverty in Pakistan'. *The Lahore Journal of Economics*, Special Edition (September 2008): 117–38.

Chen, N., J. Imbs, and A. Scott. 'Competition, Globalization and the Decline of Inflation.' Centre for Economic Policy Research, Discussion Paper No. 6495, October 2004.

Cheng, F. 'Income Disparities in China and Its Policy Implications.' In *Food Policy for Developing Countries: Case Studies* edited by P. Pinstrup-Anderson and F. Cheng, 13. New York, NY: Cornel University Press, 2007. Available at: http://cip.cornell.edu/DPubS?service=UI&version (accessed on 15 March 2014).

Cornia, G. A. 'Policy Reform and Income Distribution.' Paper presented in the DESA Development Forum: Integrating Economic and Social Policies to Achieve the UN Development Agenda, New York, 14–15 March 2005.

Coulborn, W. A. *A Discussion on Money*. London: Longman, 1950.

Crowther, M. *An Outline of Money*. London: Seton Press, 1940.

Dangelmaier, U. 'Private Sector an Engine for Employment and Qualitative Growth.' KFW—Position Paper, July 2012. Available at: https://www.deginvest.de/DEG-Englische-Dokumente/PDFs-Download-Center/Private-sector-as-engine-for-emplyment-and-qualitative-growth.pdf (accessed on 5 March 2016).

Daza, N., and L. F. Gamboa. 'Informal Wage Gaps in Colombia.' ECINEQ 2013–301, ECINE Society for the Study of Economic Inequality, 2013. Available at: http://www.ecineq.org/milano/WP/ECINEQ2013... (accessed on 30 March 2016).

Dolmas, J., G. W. Huffman, and M. A. Wynne 'Inequality, Inflation and Central Bank Independence.' Federal Reserve Bank of Dallas, Research Working Paper 97–05, 1997. Available at: http://www19.iadb.org/intal/intalcdi/PE/2012/11... (accessed on 23 March 2016).

Downes, Andrew S. 'An Economic Analysis of Unemployment in Trinidad and Tobago.' Paper prepared for the presentation at a Seminar on Labour Market: Between Solidarity and Loyalty, Sponsored by Inter-American Development Bank, Montevideo, Uruguay, 1998. Available at: http://citesserx.ist.psu.edu/viewdoc/download?doi=/ (accessed on 12 November 2013).

Dua, P., and D. J. Smyth. 'Public Perceptions of the Relative Seriousness of Inflation and Unemployment in the United States.' *Applied Economic Letters* 4, no. 1 (1997): 49–52.

Dwivedi, D. N. *Macroeconomics: Theory and Practice*. Belmont: Cengage Learning, 2010.

Easterly, W., and S. Fisher. 'Inflation and the Poor.' *Journal of Money, Credit and Banking* 33, no. 2, Part 1 (2001): 160–78.

Emmanuel, O. S. 'Repositioning Technical and Vocational Education Toward Eradicating Unemployment in Nigeria.' *International Journal of Vocational and Technical Education* 7, no. 6 (2015): 54–63.

Fajana, S. *Functioning of the Nigerian Labour Market*. Lagos: Labonfin and Company, 2000.

FAO. *The State of Food Insecurity in the World*. Rome: Food and Agriculture Organization, 2012.

Fapohunda, Tinuke M. 'Employment Casualization and Degradation of Work in Nigeria.' *International Journal of Business and Social Science* 3, no. 9 (2012): 257–67.

Foellmi, R., and M. Oechslin. 'Market Imperfection, Wealth Inequality and the Distribution of Trade Gains.' *Journal of International Economics* xxx (2010): 1–1. Also see http://www.nccr-trade.org/fileadmin/user_upload/nccr-trade.ch/wp6/articleJIE.pdf (accessed on 30 November 2016).

Friedman, M. (1956). 'The Quantity Theory of Money—A Restatement.' In *Studies in the Quantity Theory of Money*, edited by M. Friedman, 1–21. Chicago: University of Chicago Press.

Gowda, K. V., and K. R. Venugopal. 'Salaries Paid by the Indian Companies to Their Personnel.' In *Fiscal and Monetary Reforms in India*, edited by K. R. Venugopal. New Delhi: I K International Publishing House, 2007.

Grant, S., and C. Vidler. *Economics in Context*. Oxford: Heinemann, 2000.

Grant, U. 'Urbanization and the Employment Opportunities of Youth in Developing Countries.' Background Paper prepared for the Education for All Global Monitoring Report, 2012, 2012/ED/EFA/MRT/PI/25, UNESCO, Paris.

Gupta, G. S. *Macro Economic Theories and Applications*. New Delhi: Tata McGraw-Hill, 2001.

Gutierrez-Romero, R. 'The Dynamics of the Informal Economy.' Working Paper Series, CSAEWPS/2010–07, Oxford University, Department of International Development, 2010.

Haynes and Soobramaniem. 'Food Security and Trade Issues for Poor and Small Vulnerable Economies,' *Common Wealth Trade Hot Topics*, no. 97(2013): 4.

Heiztz, J., and J. Vanek. 'Employment, the Informal Sector and Poverty: Data and Analytical Challenges.' For the China India Labour Market, Research Design conference, Cambridge, April 2007. Available at: http://previour.wiego.org/program_areas/gener (accessed on 12 November 2013).

Hoddinott, J., L. Haddad, and S. Mukherjee. *Assets and Rural Poverty*. Working Paper, International Food Policy Research Institute, Washington DC, 2000.

Huber, E., F. Nielsen, J. Pribble, and J. D. Stephens. 'Politics and Inequality in Latin America and the Caribbean.' University of North Carolina, Paper prepared for the Annual Meeting of Research Committee 19, International Sociological Association, Northwestern University, 2005.

ILO. 'Employment Generation Programme Labour-based Technology for Infrastructure Development in Cambodia.' ILO/ASIST-AP and CMB/97/MO2, ILO and the Royal Government of Cambodia, 2000.

———. *A Skilled Workforce for Strong, Sustainable and Balanced Growth*. A G20 Training Strategy, International Labour Organization, Geneva, 2011.

IMF. 'IMF Country Report No.4/331.' IMF, Washington DC, 2004.

———. 'Globalization and Inflation.' In *World Economic Outlook*, Chapter 3. IMF, 2006.

Islam., A. 'Impact of Inflation on Import: An Empirical Study.' *International Journal of Economics, Finance, and Management Sciences* 1, no. 1 (2013): 299–309.

Jolly, R. 'Global Inequality in Historical Perspective.' Wider Angle, World Institute for Development Economics Research No. 2, Helsinki, 2005.

Juselius, M., and E. Takats. 'Can Demography Affect Inflation and Monetary Policy?' BIS Working Paper 485, Monetary and Economic Department, Bank for Information Settlements, 2015. Available at: http://www.bis.org/publ/work485.pdf (accessed on 23 March 2016).

Kamin, S., M. Marazzi, and J. W. Schindler. 'Is China 'Expanding Deflation'?' Board of Governors of the Federal Reserve System, Institute of Finance, Discussion Paper No. 791, 2004. Available at: http://www.bankofengland.co.uk/publications/Documents/quarterlybulletin/qb080302.pdf (accessed on 28 November 2016).

Kaniivila, M. 2007. 'Industrial Development and Economic Growth: Implications for Poverty Reduction and Income Inequality.' Available at: http://www.un.org/esa/sustdev/publications/in (accessed on 7 February 2014).

Kaur, S. 'Food Entitlement, Subsidies and Right to Food in South Asia.' In *Handbook on Food: Demand, Supply, Sustainability and Security,* edited by R. Jha, R. Gaiha, and A. B. Deolalikar, 482–51. UK: Edward Elgar Publishing, 2014.

Kearney, A. T. 'Feeding a Billion People: The Role of the Food Processing Industry.' FCCI, 2014. Available at: http://www.atkearney.in/documents/10192/4408373/Feeding+a+Billion+People.pdf/7b94fe4b-c752-4edb-879e-e5fafdb78ed5 (accessed on 2 March 2016).

Kolli, R., and P. Sen. 'Delhi Group on Informal Sector Contribution and Present Status.' Paper prepared for the Special IARIW-SAIM Conference on Measuring the informal economy in developing countries, Kathmandu, Nepal, 23–26 September 2009.

Kovacevic, M. 'Measurement of Inequality in Human Development: A Review.' Human Development Report Research Paper 2010/35, UNDP, 2010.

Kristic, G., and P. Sanfey. 'Mobility, Poverty and Well-being among the Informally Employed in Bosnia and Herzegovina.' *Economic Systems* 31, no. 3 (2007): 311–35.

Kumar, M., and D. C. Vashist. 'An Empirical Study of Phillips Curve in India.' *International Journal of Economic Research* 3, no. 4(2012): 10–25.

Kumari, R. 'Food Inflation in India: Present Scenario.' *International Journal of Social Sciences and Interdisciplinary Research* 2, no. 2 (February 2013): 49–58.

Li, S., H. Sato, and T. Sicular. 'Introduction-Rising Inequality in China.' In *Rising Inequality in China: Challenges to a Harmonious Society*, edited by S. Li, H. Sato, and T. Sicular. New York, NY: Cambridge University Press, 2013.

Lipsey, R. G. 'The Relation Between Unemployment and the Rate of Change of Money Wages in the United Kingdom, 1862–1957: A Further Analysis', Economica (February 1960): 1–31.

Loku, A., and G. Deda. 'Unemployment Relation of Growth Population.' *International Journal of Research in Social Sciences* 2, no. 2 (2013): 31–38.

McKay, A. 'Defining and Measuring Inequality.' Inequality Briefing, Briefing Paper No. 1 (1 of 3), March, ODI and University of Nottingham, 2002.

Mishkin, F. S. 'The Causes of Inflation.' NBER Working Paper 1453, National Bureau of Economic Research, Cambridge, 1984.

Mishkin, F. S., and A. S. Posen. 'Inflation Targeting: Lessons from Four Countries.' NBER Working Paper 6126, National Bureau of Economic Research, Cambridge, 1998.

Mitra, P., and R. Yemtsov. 'Increasing Inequality in Transition Economies: Is There More to Come?' The World Bank Policy Research Working Paper 4007, World Bank, Washington DC, 2006.

Morse, D. 'Unemployment in Developing Countries.' *Political Science Quarterly* 85, no. 1 (1970): 1–16.

Muhammad, A. B., B. M. Sa'idu, O. J. Nwokobia, and K. M. Yakubu. 'Effect of Unemployment and Inflation on Wages in Nigeria.' *Journal of Emerging Trends in Economics and Management Sciences* 4, no. 2 (2013): 181–88.

Nissanke, M., and E. Thorbecke. 'The Impact of Globalization on the World's Poor Channels and Policy Debate.' WIDER Angle No. 2/2004, World Institute of Development Economics Research, 10–13, 2004.

Odonwodo, C. U., and G. Abdullahi. 'The Imperative of Information and Communication Technology in Reducing Unemployment among Nigerian Graduates.' *International Journal of Creativity and Technical Development* 1, no. 1–3 (2009): 54–65.

OECD. *Divided We Stand: Why Inequality Keeps Rising OECD Publishing*, 2011. Available at: https://positivemoney.org/wp-content/uploads/2013/10/Banking-Finance-and-Income-Inequality.pdf (accessed on 28 November 2016).

———. 'Inequality in Labour Income: What Are Its Drivers and How Can It be Reduced?' OECD Economic Department Policy Notes, No. 8, January 2012a. Available at: http://www.oecd.org/eco/public-finance/49417273.pdf (accessed on 28 November 2016).

———. 'Reducing Income Inequality while Boosting Economic Growth: Can It be Done?' Economic Policy Reforms, 2012b. Available at: https://www.oecd.org/eco/growth/49421421.pdf (accessed on 7 April 2016).

———. 'In It Together: Why Less Inequality Benefits All.' OECD Publishing, Paris, 2015. Available at: http://www.oecd.org/unitedstates/OECD2015-In-It-Together-Highlights-UnitedStates-Embargo-21May11amPArisTime.pdf (accessed on 28 November 2016).

Okafor, E. E. (2011). 'Youth Unemployment and Implication for Stability of Democracy in Nigeria.' *Journal of Sustainable Development Africa* 13, no. 1: 358–73.

Oliver, B. G. Dell'Ariccia, and P. Mauro. 'Rethinking Macroeconomic Policy.' IMF Staff Position Note 10/03, Washington DC, International Monetary Fund, 2010.

Oxford, E. E. 'Youth Unemployment and Implication for Stability of Democracy in Nigeria.' *Journal of Sustainable Development Affair* 13, no. 1 (2011): 358–73.

Patnaik, I., A. Shah, and G. Vronese. 'How Should Inflation be Measured in India?' *Economic and Political Weekly* 47, no. 16 (2011): 55–64.

Pattanaik, B. K. 'Young Migrant Construction Workers in the Unorganized Urban Sector.' *South Asia Research* 29, no. 1 (2009): 19–40.

Planning Commission of India. 'National Human Development Report 2001.' Planning Commission of India. Government of India, 2002.

Room, G. 'Observatory on National Policies to Combat Social Exclusion.' Synthesis Report, University of Bath, 1990. Available at: http://www1.uwindson.ca/criticalsocialwork/social (accessed on 9 November 2013).

Rosser, J. B., M. V. Rosser, and E. Ahmed. 'Income Inequality and the Informal Economies in Transition Economies.' *Journal of Comparative Economics* 28, no. 1 (2000): 156–71.

Roubaud, F., and C. Torelli. 'Employment, Unemployment and Working Conditions in Urban Labour Market Markets of Sub-Saharan Africa: Main Stylized Facts.' In *Urban Labour Market in Sub-Saharan Africa,* edited by P. de Vreyer and F. Roubaud. Washington DC: World Bank, 2013.

Ruel, M. T., J. L. Garrett, S. S. Morris, D. Maxwell, A. Oshaung, P. Engle, P. Menon, A. Slack, and L. Haddad. 'Urban Challenges to Food and Nutrition Security: A Review of Food Security, Health and Care Giving in the Cities.' Food Consumption and Nutrition Division Discussion Paper No. 51, International Food Research Institute, Washington DC, 1998.

Safey, P. 'Earning Inequality and the Informal Economy: Evidence from Serbia.' Working Paper 114, European Bank for Reconstruction and Development, London, 2010. Available at: https://www.researchgate.net/publication/46450155_Earnings_inequality_and_the_informal_economy_Evidence_from_Serbia (accessed on 28 November 2016).

Sarntisart, I. 'Growth, Structural Change, and Inequality: The Experience of Thailand.' WIDER Working Paper 207, WIDER Institute, 2000.

Saunders, P. 'The Direct and Indirect Effects of Unemployment on Poverty and Inequality.' SPRC Discussion Paper No. 118, The Social Policy Research Centre, University of New South Wales, Sydney, Australia, 2002.

Shrestha, M. B., and S. K. Chaudhary. 'The Impact of Food Inflation on Poverty in Nepal.' *NRB Economic Review* 24, no. 2 (2012): 1–24. Available at: http://www.nrb.org.np/ecorev/pdffiles/vol24-2_art1.pdf (accessed on 24 March 2016).

Smith, A. *An Inquiry into the Nature and Causes of the Wealth of Nation*. London: Methuen & Co. Ltd, 1976.

Stanford, J. 'A "How To" Guide: Understanding and Measuring Inflation.' Canadian Centre for Policy Alternatives, 2008. Quoted from the research paper of Z. Abubakar titled 'The value relevance of inflation accounting discourse of quoted petroleum firms in Nigeria'. Available at: http://www.academia.edu/11316890/The_Value_Relevance_of_Inflation_Accounting_Disclosure_of_Quoted_Petroleum_Firms_in_Nigeria (accessed on 28 November 2016).

Subbarao, D. *India and the Global Financial Crisis Transcending from Recovery to Growth, at the Peterson Institute for International Economics, Washington DC* 2010. Available at: http://www.nipfp.org.in/media/medialibrary/2013/04/wp_2011_83.pdf (accessed on 28 November 2016).

Sugema, I., T. Irawan, D. Adipurwanto, A. Holis, and T. Bakhtiar. 'The Impact of Inflation on Rural Poverty in Indonesia: An Econometric Approach.' *International Research Journal of Finance and Economics*, no. 58 (2010): 50–57. Available at: http://s3.amazonaws.com/zanran_storage/www.eurojournals.com/ContentPages/1025686774.pdf (accessed on 30 November 2016).

Takami, N. 'Baffling Inflation: Cost Push Inflation Theories in the Late 1950s United States.' Discussion Paper Series, A, No. 604, Institute of Economic Research, Hitotsubashi University, Tokyo, 2014.

Taylor, B. R. *Affirmative Action at Work Law, Politics and Ethics*. London: University of Pittsburgh Press, 1991.

Thalassinos, E., E. Uguelu, and Y. Muratoglu. 'Income Inequality and Inflation in the EU.' *European Research Studies* 15, no. 1 (2012): 127–40.

Todaro, M. P. *Economic Development*. Singapore: Longman Publication, 1994.

UNCTAD. 'Employment and Unemployment.' Development and Globalization: Facts and Figures, United Nations, New York, 2013. Available at: http://dgff.unctad.org/chapter2/2.2.html# (accessed on 30 November 2016).

United Nations. *56th Commission Human Rights, Item 7: The Right to Development*. United Nations, Geneva, 2000.

———. *Inequality Matters Report of the World Social Situation*. New York: United Nations, 2013.

Viner, J. 'Some Reflections on the Concept of "Disguised Unemployment."' In *Leading Issues in Development Economics*, edited by G. Meier, 14. New York, NY: Oxford University Press, 1964. Available at: http://dyson.cornell.edu/research/researchpdf/sp/197 (accessed on 23 March 2014).

Walsh, J. P., and J. Yu. 'Inflation and Income Inequality: Is Food Inflation Different?' IMF Working Paper WP/12/147, International Monetary Fund, Washington DC, 2012.

Winkelried, D. 'Income Distribution and the Size of the Informal Sector.' St John's College, University of Cambridge, 2005. Available at: http://www.rrojasdatabank.info/inequlity/SSRN-id77 (accessed on 21 March 2014).

World Bank. *World Development Report: Knowledge for Development*. New York, NY: Oxford University Press, 1998.

Ximing, Y., S. Li, and T. Sicular. 'High Incomes in Monopoly Industries: A Discussion.' *Social Sciences in China* 32, no. 2 (2010): 178–96.

Yahaya, K. A., O. F. Osemene, and A. Abdulraheem. 'Effectiveness of Micro-finance Banks in Alleviating Poverty in Kwara State Nigeria.' *Global Journal of Management and Business Research* 11, no. 4 (2011): 13–20.

Zacharias, A., and V. Vakulabharanam. 'Caste and Wealth Inequality in India.' Working Paper 566, University of Hyderabad, 2009. Available at: http://www.levyinstitute.org/pub/wp_566.pdf (accessed on 30 March 2016).

6 Agriculture Sector and Development

Agriculture is important for economic growth in the sense that it guarantees subsistence for society without which growth is not possible.

—Schultz (1964)

Broadly, the sectors in an economy are classified into three types—primary, secondary and tertiary. The primary sector comprises agriculture and allied activities such as fishery, horticulture, poultry, dairy and so on. The secondary sector comprises industry and manufacturing activities, while the tertiary sector covers all other activities which are not covered in primary and secondary sectors, broadly comprising services like banking, insurance, information technology, education, health and so on. The economic growth and development of a nation depends on the contribution of these three sectors to the economy. It is seen that in both developed and developing countries, each sector contributes as per their strength to the economic growth and development of the economy.

In developed countries of North America and Europe, the contribution of service sector to the economic growth is higher as compared to the contribution of agriculture and industry sectors. On the other hand, in the less developed countries of Sub-Saharan Africa, the contribution of agriculture sector to the economic growth and development still holds prime importance. In India, the agriculture which was contributing significantly to economic growth during initial years of development planning has gradually declined. In China, the contribution of industrial or manufacturing sector to GDP is higher as compared to agriculture and even service sector. Thus, the contribution of different sectors to the GDP of a country varies from one country to that of the other. Although after the globalization, the contribution of the service sector to the economic growth is on the rise in both developed and developing countries, agriculture is the primary and one of the key sectors in developing countries where more than 60% of their population are earning their livelihood.

After reading this chapter, you will be able to:

1. Describe the role of agriculture in economic development.
2. Explain various issues in agricultural development.
3. Discuss various challenges of agricultural development.

According to Fisher (1933), economic activities can be classified into three main sectors: (a) primary sector, consisting agriculture; (b) secondary sector, formed by industry and (c) tertiary sector, incorporating all other activities that did not fit in the first two sectors.

During the early phase—the 1940s and 1950s—the contribution of agriculture sector towards economic growth and development both in developed and developing countries was quite high. The history of the world provides overwhelming global evidence that the general economic growth of any nation must be preceded or, at least, accompanied by solid agricultural growth (Rukuni 2006). Agriculture is the lifeblood of developing economies. It provides employment and livelihood to a large percentage of population living in the countryside. Besides, agriculture sector acts as forward and backward linkages to the industrial and service sectors. Therefore, the growth and development of the industrial and service sectors also depend on the growth of the agriculture sector, at least, in developing countries. Hence, economists have explicitly identified strong growth linkages and multiplier effects of agricultural growth to the non-agricultural sectors (Mellor 1998). Meier (1995) argued that agriculture can contribute to the development in following four different ways:

1. By supplying foodstuffs and raw materials to other expanding sectors in the economy.
2. By providing 'investable surplus' of saving and taxes to support investment in other expanding sectors.
3. By selling a 'marketable surplus' for cash, which will raise the demand of the rural population for products of other expanding sectors.
4. By relaxing the foreign exchange constraints, earning foreign exchange through exports or saving foreign exchange through import substitution.

Despite globalization, the agriculture sector has been playing and will continue to play a crucial role in the development of the developing economies. It will continue to provide employment and livelihood to a larger rural population, at least for another one or two decades in developing countries. Schultz said, 'Most of the world's poor people earn their living from agriculture, so if we knew the economics of agriculture we would know much of the economics of being poor' (Schultz quoted in Johnson 2011).

ROLE OF AGRICULTURE IN DEVELOPMENT

Over the period of time, we perceived that the contribution of agriculture towards economic growth is declining. However, its role in provisioning food and nutrition in developing countries is stupendous. Earning from agriculture either as a farmer or a farm labourer empowers them to spend on children's education, health care of the family members and purchase of other essential necessities for the improvement of quality of life, particularly in the rural areas. Therefore, it foretells that the role of agriculture in development is quite livid and calls for strengthening it, at least, in the developing economies. A few important roles of agriculture in development are as follows (Table 6.1):

Main Source of Livelihood for the Rural Population: Agriculture is the main source of livelihood for the farmers and agricultural labourers living in the countryside. It provides basic needs to the impoverished landless agricultural labourers, and it is a determining factor in enabling them to have access to education and health care for their children. Besides, it is a prime source of ensuring luxuries and comforts to the large-scale landholders and agricultural entrepreneurs. The Bill and Melinda Gates Foundation has found that when farmers grow more food and earn more income, they are better able to feed their families, send their children to school and provide for their family's health.[1] Thus, the agriculture sector continues to play a crucial role for development, especially in low-income countries where the sector is large in terms of both aggregate income and total labour force (Dethier and Effenberges 2011). Industrialization and modern economic growth can hardly be successful without healthy developments in the agricultural sector, which is so dominant in the early stage of development (Hayami and Ruttan 1971; Mellor 1998).

Promotes Economic Growth: In the early phase of economic development, agriculture played a pivotal role in contributing significantly to the economic growth. Even now, in many African countries, the contribution of agriculture is higher than that of industrial and service sectors to their GDP. Timmer (1988) argued that agricultural growth become a direct contributor to overall economic growth through greater links with industry, improving the efficiency of product and factor markets and continued mobilization of rural resources. Israr and Khan (2010), in their study, have mentioned that agriculture and livestock are key components of the livelihoods of the rural poor, and nearly 70% of world's poorest people located in rural areas are engaged primarily in subsistence agriculture. Also, an estimated 700 million rural poor in developing countries sustain their livelihood through livestock. In the low-income countries, agriculture contributes one-fourth towards their GDP, while the contribution of this sector to the GDP of the high-income countries is only 1%.

The role of agriculture to economic development and growth is well documented before the pre-liberalization phase of development in most of developing countries. Several traditional roles essential to overall economic growth and development which agriculture plays include (a) providing food and nutritional security to the increasing number of population; (b) supplying raw materials to growing and diversifying domestic industrial sectors, particularly to the food processing and other agro-based industries established both in the public and private sectors; (c) transforming labour from agriculture to the industrial and service sectors as well as from rural to the urban areas; (d) fulfilling the labour requirement of these two upcoming sectors in developing countries and providing feeder manpower support to urban infrastructure development activities; (e) enlarging the size of the market for the domestic industrial sector; (f) providing employment and livelihood for a large percentage of rural population and helping in rural poverty reduction; (g) promoting rural savings and investment through steady income;

Table 6.1 *Contribution of Agriculture to GDP, 2009 (%)*

Countries	Agriculture	Industry	Manufacturing	Services
Low-income Countries	26	24	12	50
Middle-income Countries	10	35	21	55
High-income Countries	1	25	16	74

Source: World Development Report (2011).

(h) promoting rural capital formation through accumulation of domestic saving and investment in agriculture and (i) providing employment to a large number of women. The contribution of agriculture towards economic growth and development is worth noting.

Helps in Poverty Reduction: Accelerated agricultural growth is not only needed to meet growing global demand for food and energy, but it is also seen as the main pathway out of poverty for many poor people and countries (Hazell et al. 2011). Historically, agricultural growth has been the way out of poverty for the developed countries (World Bank 2007). According to the World Development Report 2008, 'GDP growth generated in agriculture…is at least twice as effective in reducing poverty as growth generated by other sectors' (World Bank 2007). Agriculture plays a pivotal role in poverty reduction in general and rural poverty, particularly in developing countries. Income from agriculture, either through selling of agricultural products by the agriculturists and selling of labour by the agricultural labourer, influences the quality as well as subsistent livelihood of the countryside population. Rise in agricultural productivity along with promotion of allied sector activities, such as fisheries, horticulture, dairy, poultry and so on, helps in the reduction of poverty in the rural areas of developing countries. Mellor (2001) argued that it is not economic growth in general that reduces poverty in developing countries but the direct and indirect effects of growth in agriculture. It is estimated by Christiaensen and Demery (2007) that 1% per capita agricultural growth reduces poverty 1.6 times more than the same growth in industry and 3 times more than growth in the service sector. Increased agricultural productivity brings strong indirect benefits for the poor (Byerlee et al. 2005).

Main Source of Employment: Agriculture is the primary source of employment for rural population of developing countries. According to FAO estimates, some 1.3 billion people work in agriculture around the world; 97% of them are in developing countries (Fechter 2012). In Sub-Saharan Africa and South Asia, up to 70% of youth live in rural areas and half of the young labour force works in agriculture. Although, employment in agriculture declined during the decade 1998–2008, it still remains the main source of employment for more than half of the people working in East Asia, Southeast Asia and the Pacific, South Asia and Sub-Saharan Africa.[2] As far as women are concerned, 64.3% women in Sub-Saharan Africa and 64.5% in South Asia are employed in the agriculture (ILO 2009). Due to this high dependency of rural population on the agriculture sector for employment, the sizes of underemployment and disguised unemployment prevalent in agriculture and allied sectors are exceedingly high. Besides, agriculture is the main source of self-employment for the women in developing countries of Africa, Asia and Latin America. A large percentage of employment in agriculture is self-employment having high economic values. In many countries of South Asia and Africa, agriculture is more compassionate to absorb labour force in it as compared to industry and service sectors. Therefore, in the present context, investment-based industry and service-sector-driven economic slowdown as happened in the developed economies of the West, largely, has not produced much impact on the consumption- and agriculture-based developing economies. One of the illustrious examples is India, even during the economic recession of 2014–15, India's economy was found growing at the rate of 7% (Table 6.2).

Table 6.2 *Region-wise Percentage of People Employed in Agriculture*

Region	Agriculture			
	1999	**2007**	**2008**	**2009**
World	40.2	35.4	35.0	35.0
Developed Economies and European Union	5.6	3.9	3.7	3.7
Central and Southeastern Europe (Non-EU) and CIS	27.0	20.0	20.2	20.2
East Asia	47.9	38.9	37.7	36.9
Southeast Asia and the Pacific	49.3	45.0	44.7	44.3
South Asia	59.5	53.5	53.5	53.5
Latin America and the Caribbean	21.5	17.0	16.4	16.3
Middle East	22.1	20.5	19.5	19.1
North Africa	29.2	28.4	28.0	27.8
Sub-Saharan Africa	62.4	59.4	58.9	59.0

Source: ILO, Trends Econometric Models, October 2010.

Plays a Key Role in the Mitigation of Hunger and Malnutrition: The Green Revolution triggered off in developing countries of Asia during the early 1970s was instrumental in controlling hunger in these nations. It is rightly said that agriculture is closely associated in public mind with the Green Revolution which emerged to avoid mass famine and starvation (Ganguly 2006). The Green Revolution supplemented with Rainbow Revolution, i.e. Yellow Revolution in oil seeds, White Revolution in milk production, Blue Revolution in fish production and Golden Revolution in horticulture, has been instrumental in providing food and nutritional security to the population of millions in developing countries. However, the challenge is still stupendous considering the population growth in these countries. Nearly 800 million people in developing countries are already suffering from hunger despite the Green Revolution (Larsen 2007). Agriculture, traditionally as well as culturally, is an important source of livelihood in tribal areas of different countries such as South Asia and Sub-Saharan Africa. In the Green Revolution belt, it is also a source of livelihood for the landless agriculture labour households, which earn their livelihoods by working in the agricultural fields of the large- and medium-scale farmers. According to FAO (2012), agricultural growth involving smallholders, especially women, will be most effective in reducing extreme poverty and hunger when it increases returns to labour and generates employment for the poor. It urged that the economic and agricultural growth rate needs to be 'nutrition-sensitive'. Improved nutritional status and better health could lead to increased productivity, but it is equally plausible that increased productivity leads to higher incomes, thereby improving nutritional and health status (Garcia and Kennedy 1994). Strauss (1986) found that household energy consumption was a positive significant determinant of farm output.

Promotes Rural Saving, Investment and Capital Formation: Income from agriculture was the main source of capital formation during the early 1950s and 1960s as noted by classical economists Adam Smith and David Ricardo. Land and labour are considered important factors of production contributing towards economic growth and development. Besides, in the post-Second World War era, modern development economists mostly agree that the role of agriculture and rural development is absolutely an integral part to the process of nation building and healthy development (Johnston 1970). The surplus income generated by the landlords, agriculturists and corporate sector engaged in agriculture is the main source of capital formation in rural areas. Surplus income from agriculture leads to capital formation in other sectors of the rural economy such as small and cottage industries and investment in rural self-employment. Agriculture and agro industry are linked through their demand for outputs and through their capital stock and new investments (Hazell et al. 2011). Different types of investors operating in agriculture and its value chains, including family and household farmers, large commercial farmers, domestic corporate sector, transnational corporations, sovereign funds, public sectors and donors, have different objectives and roles (Hazell et al. 2011). It will not be out of place to say that most of the capital formation in the primary sector is generated through the agriculture sector itself. Therefore, some academics urged policymakers to treat agriculture like a black box from which resources could be costlessly extracted (Lewis 1954).

Contributes Towards Export and Balance of Payment: In developing countries, agriculture is a predominant economic activity and the export of the economy is mainly agriculture based. Gill (1990) argued that promotion of agricultural exports in India is a possible strategy which can counteract the adverse balance of payment situation and suggested that the export development in agriculture be concentrated of goods like basmati rice, durum wheat and horticultural product. The value addition to agriculture nowadays has enhanced earning from export of primary sector products from developing to developing countries and also from developing to developed countries. However, Ojo (1993) from his study from African countries noted that the growth of agricultural exports and earnings is constrained by low level of production, high level of informal trade, price uncompetitiveness, poor state of infrastructure and protectionism in advanced countries. For countries that have a competitive agricultural sector, the expansion of international trade in agricultural commodities can have a growth-enhancing effect and improve their trade balance (Schutter 2009).

The export growth of agriculture products is higher in developing countries as compared to the developed countries. Figure 6.1 depicts that the export growth in India, Indonesia and Brazil are 21.3, 17.6 and 14.9 respectively, while those of the United States of America and European Union are 9.2 and 10.1 respectively. The agricultural export over the decade in India as shown in Figure 6.2 has tremendously grown from 5 billion dollars in 2001 to nearly 40 billion dollars in 2013. Thus, agriculture plays a key role in the export of goods and services in the developing countries, and its role in India over the past decade is higher as compared to other countries.

Enhances Industrial Development: In the initial phase of industrial development, there would be positive linkage between the agriculture and industrial development. It is known empirically that a large share of manufacturing in the early stages of development is agriculture related (Pryor and Holt 1999). Agriculture has strong direct forward linkages to agriculture processing and backward linkages to input–supply industries (Johnston and Mellor 1961). Agriculture economists cite the example of Japan from the Meiji Revolution

Figure 6.1 *Export Growth in India, Indonesia and Brazil*

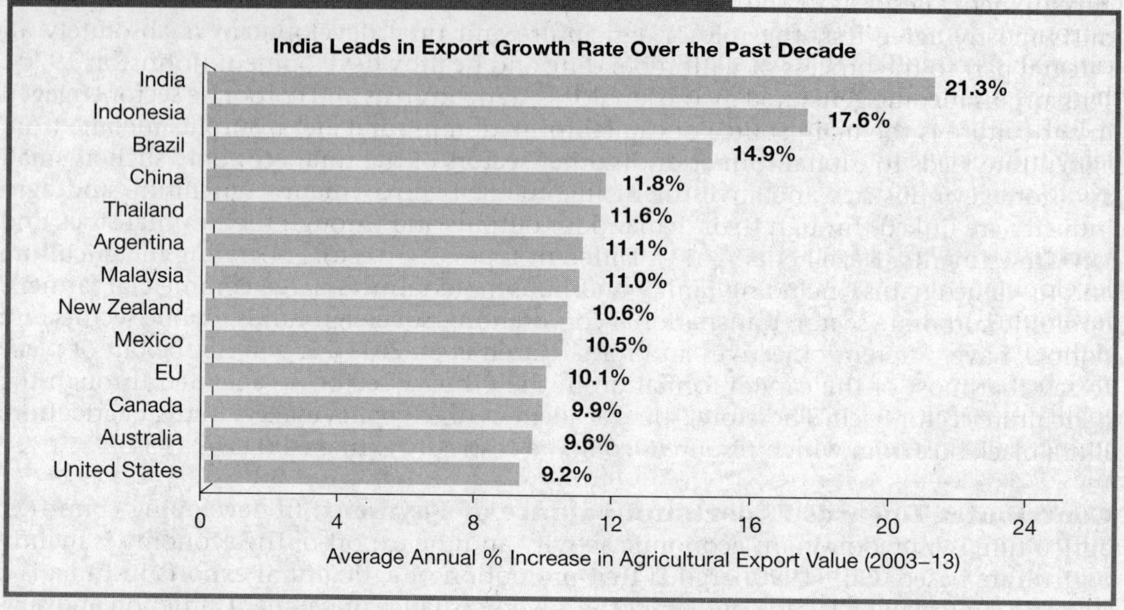

Figure 6.2 *Agricultural Export*

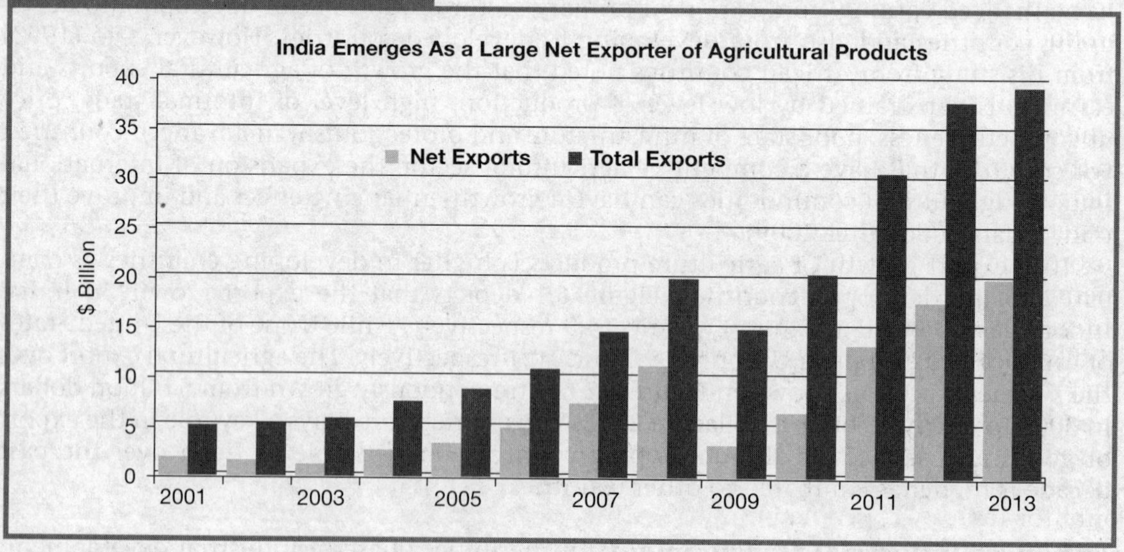

Source: http://www.fas.usda.gov/data/india-s-agricultural-exports-climb-recent-high (accessed on 21 April 2016).

to the First World War, when agriculture and industrial development went forward concurrently. The Brazilian growth process from the early 1930s to the early 1960s has shown a strong relationship between agriculture and industry. Panchamukhi (1990) from empirical analysis remarked that for a large number of developing countries, from 1970 to 1984, there is a significant positive relationship between the growth rate of GDP and the strength of linkage between manufacturing and agriculture. Low productivity in agriculture can delay industrialization, which in turn results in a country's lower per capita income relative to others (Gollin, Parente and Rogerson 2002).

Agriculture Provides Stimulant to Social and Human Development: Agricultural development is a great stimulant to rural social and human development. In rural areas of developing nations, the households possessing cultivable agricultural land and earning higher income from the agriculture, irrespective of caste, religion and creed, are found to have better access to higher level of education, quality health care, and possession of good quality housing and household amenities. Land is the key determinant of social, economic, human and political development status of a household in the agrarian economies of developing countries. International Assessment of Agricultural Knowledge, Science and Technology for Development (IAASTD 2008) has mentioned that the increased agricultural productivity has contributed to improved livelihood for some 2.6 billion people—men, women and children—who rely on farming, livestock production, forestry or fishery. The Africa Human Development Report 2012 has envisaged that 'increased agricultural productivity would end the ravages of hunger and malnutrition and will nurture capabilities and conditions for human development. A well-nourished and empowered population, in turn, is more likely to seek education, participate in society, and expand its productive and human potential.'

Provide Livelihood to Migrant Labour: Agriculture provides livelihood to thousands of rural to rural migrant labourers from the economically laggard states/provinces to the economically developed states in developing countries. In India, it is observed that the rural impoverished people from the economically backward regions of Bihar and Eastern Uttar Pradesh are migrating to work in agriculture sector of Punjab and Haryana in order to earn a better wage rate and ensure a good standard of living to their family members back at home. Punjab, in fact, has been demanding labour for various activities through pull factors from the neighbouring states of Uttar Pradesh, Jammu and Kashmir and Rajasthan for a long time (Sidhu and Rangi 1998). In recent years, it has been observed that the youth in rural areas of Punjab is not motivated enough to work in the agricultural sector as labours, which is why the large- and even medium-scale landholders in the state have been seeking labours from Uttar Pradesh and Bihar during crop sowing and harvesting seasons (Pattanaik 2012). Agriculturally developed states are sources of livelihood not only for their own people but also for the migrants from agriculturally underdeveloped states in many developing countries.

Agricultural Development Promotes Rural Development: Agricultural and rural development in most of developing countries are correlated. Rural development has various dimensions, but it is particularly the development of the agriculture sector which is widely believed to provide the main impetus not only for reducing poverty and hunger but also for ensuring food security for all (Halwart 2005). Approximately 75% of the absolute poor in developing countries live in rural areas, where they depend mostly on agriculture for their livelihood (CIDA 2003). The success of rural development in terms of education, health care, sanitation, drinking water, rural market, road, electricity and telecommunication and so on depends on the development of agriculture. Higher earnings from agriculture through the mechanization and commercialization of agriculture enable the countryside people to have access to all these amenities. In India, people living in agriculturally developed provinces and areas have better access to all these amenities as compared to those living in rural areas of the agriculturally backwards states. Besides, people living in agriculturally developed provinces, such as Punjab and Haryana, are having fewer percentages of people living below the poverty line as compared to their counterparts, i.e. Bihar, Jharkhand, Chhattisgarh and Odisha, where agriculture is still in primitive stage and is not modernized and commercialized. Therefore, it is said that reducing poverty in rural areas and hunger in both rural and urban areas will depend heavily on the sustainable development of agriculture (CIDA 2003). Higher agricultural growth—due to higher agricultural productivity growth—underpinned early development in the Western Europe, Japan and the United States of America and later in China and the Republic of Korea (World Bank 2007).

CHALLENGES OF AGRICULTURAL DEVELOPMENT

Despite agriculture playing an important role in the economic development of developing countries, it is facing a lot of challenges because of which, over the years, the contribution of agriculture to GDP is reducing even in the agriculture-dependent developing countries. A few important challenges that agriculture is facing in developing countries are as follows:

Sustainable Agriculture: In the era of globalization, the concept of sustainable agriculture holds considerable substance. Sustainable agriculture adopts productive, competitive and efficient practices that protect and improve the environment and the ecosystem, without hampering agricultural productivity both at the present and in the future. It helps to improve the socio-economic conditions of local communities and enables them to live a healthy life with dignity by adopting sustainable livelihood practices. United States Congress (1990) suggests that sustainable agriculture means an integrated system of plant and animal production practice having a site-specific application that will, over the long term

- satisfy human food and fibre needs;
- enhance environmental quality and the natural resource base upon which the agricultural economy depends;
- make the most efficient use of non-renewable resources and on-farm resources and integrate, wherever appropriate, natural biological cycles and controls;
- sustain the economic viability of farm operation and
- enhance the quality of life for farmers and society as a whole.

To Shanker (2014), the sustainable agriculture is about growing 'nutritive and protective foods' with the aid of biological 'organic fertilizers' without recourse to agrochemicals. To be environment friendly, sustainable agricultural practices take into account the future productive health of the land and protection of natural resources, i.e. water, air and sunshine. For instance, it has been observed that the excessive use of fertilizers affected the soil health, affecting agricultural productivity. In the same vein, burning crop residue in the farming field has resulted in air pollution and caused asthma, tuberculosis and similar cardiovascular diseases among the people in the Green Revolution belt of Punjab and Haryana (India). The 'sustainable agriculture' enables an economy to meet the current and long-term societal needs for food, fibre and other resources. At the same time, it also maximizes the benefits through the conservation of natural resources and maintenance of ecosystem function.

There has been stagnation in agricultural productivity in the Green Revolution belt of the Indian states such as Punjab and Haryana. Furthermore, the water tables have gone down and in many areas, lands are gradually becoming waterlogged and unfit for cultivation which has put a question mark on the Green Revolution vis-à-vis sustainable agriculture. This has put agriculture at the crossroad in the Green Revolution belt of India, leading to reduction of crop area under food crops, shifting of farmers' interest from farming to non-farming activities and at large reduction in farmer population in the agriculture sector. Stagnation in the agricultural productivity is one of the reasons for migration of Punjab population to foreign countries. Low productivity, stagnation and productivity loss has resulted in farmers' indebtedness and suicide. As Sinha (2009) said, chemical agriculture triggered by widespread use of agrochemicals in the wake of 'Green Revolution' of the 1950s–60s came as a 'mixed-blessing' rather than a 'curse in disguise' for the mankind; it dramatically increased the 'quantity' of the food produced but severely decreased its 'nutritional quality' and also the 'soil fertility' over the years. According to United Nations Environment Programme (UNEP) and WHO, nearly 3 million people suffer from 'acute pesticide poisoning' and some 10,000–20,000 people die every year from it in the developing country (UNEP/GEMS 1992). The US scientists predict that up to 20,000 Americans may die of cancer, each year, due to the low levels of 'residual pesticides' in the chemically grown food (UNEP/GEMS 1992).

Inclusive Agriculture: On one hand, benefits of agricultural development in developing countries are skewed in the favour of large-scale farmers and towards Green Revolution belt. On the other hand, the other small and marginal farmers and landless agricultural labourers and the farmers in the arid and semi-arid areas are largely being neglected and excluded from the mainstream agricultural development. It has been studied that if small landholder farmers had access to the proper tools and resources, such as inputs, financial services and better infrastructure, food production would increase and hunger would be greatly reduced (Buerkle 2012). The focus of inclusive agriculture would largely be on the following elements:

- Promotion of agriculture in the dry land, hilly and sub-mountainous and desert zones.
- Taking care of the concerns and problems faced by the small, marginal and landless agricultural labour and hastening their contribution to agriculture.

- Considering and recognizing the role of women as agriculturists, agricultural entrepreneurs, extension agents and farm labourers.
- Promoting holistic agricultural development by equally emphasizing the role of allied sectors—fruit and vegetable, dairy, fishery and horticulture in agriculture and rural livelihood.
- Promoting access of agricultural land, infrastructure facilities like irrigation and electricity, credit and other input facilities equally to disadvantaged section of rural society.
- Effective implementation of land reform measures and distribution of surplus land among the landless or ensuring land to the tillers.
- Promoting agriculture in the marginalized sections of the society, such as the SCs and STs which are largely landless, must be included in the mainstream of agricultural activities through appropriate land distribution strategy.
- Empowerment of women in agriculture. Land ownership right, women agricultural entrepreneurship, access to credit facilities, equal wage rate as that of male counterparts, equal access to training and extension programme and so on will go a long way to promote inclusive agriculture in the rural areas.

Inclusive agriculture can only promote equity in agriculture sector and would lead to inclusive growth. It is emphasized that the growth to be all inclusive, the agricultural strategy must focus on the famers who are marginal, increasingly female and who find it difficult to access inputs, credits and extension and market to their output.

Organic Agriculture for Healthy Agriculture: Organic farming or organic agriculture is recommended as a means for healthy and sustainable agriculture. The growing need for food in developing countries has given rise to excessive use of chemical fertilizers and pesticides. This has led not only to the reduction of soil health but also caused serious damage to the quality of food grains and given rise to many health hazards. It is advocated that organic agriculture, at its best, promotes sustainable rural development in developing countries and provides a framework for codifying and marketing traditional practices both to produce for grousing local and regional markets and to supply the great demand from developed nation (Candle 2006). The organic farming develops system of farming that sustains and improves soil health and fertility, protects the environment, increases the quality of agricultural product and diminishes health hazards. Organic farming is otherwise being called as healthy farming. The International Federation of Organic Agriculture Movements (IFOAM; 2005) has developed the following principles for organic agriculture:

- *The Principle of Health.* Organic agriculture should sustain and enhance the health of soil, plant, animal and planet as one and indivisible.
- *The Principle of Ecology.* Organic agriculture should be based on living ecological systems and cycles, work with them, emulate and help sustain them.
- *The Principle of Fairness.* Organic agriculture should build on a relationship that ensures fairness with regard to the common environment and life opportunities.
- *The Principle of Care.* Organic agriculture should be managed in a precautionary and responsible manner to predict the health and well-being of current and future generations.

Sinha (2009) had remarked that countries need to embark on a 'Second Green Revolution' and this time by 'organic farming' practices completely giving up the use of agrochemicals. In the United States of America, the top 25% of sustainable agriculture farmers practising 'organic farming' now have better gross margins and better yields than the top 25% of their counterparts still practising chemical agriculture (Sinha 2009).

Gender Role in Agriculture: Women of the Third World countries silently contribute towards agriculture. However, their contribution has not been given due recognition either by the family or the nation. Four of ten agricultural workers in the world are women (UN 1986). Women account for 70% of agricultural workers, 80% of food producers and 100% of those who process basic food stuffs, and they undertake from 60% to 90% of the marketing (Fresco 1998). Although they are contributing significantly, yet they are marginalized in the rural society. Their number as agricultural labour is astoundingly higher as compared to that of agricultural managers such as cultivators and agricultural entrepreneurs. Women cultivators are typically and wrongly characterized as economically inactive, and they play only a supportive role in agriculture as farmers' wives (Samanta 1994). By and large, they have remained invisible workers (Chayal et al. 2010). According to FAO (1990), in many cases in developing countries, women are primarily responsible for weeding, harvesting, transporting, storing, processing and marketing, but they often contribute greatly to ploughing, planting and fertilizer application as well. They are grossly not entrepreneurs and innovators in agriculture.

The obstacles faced by rural women are in terms of limited access to productive resources, i.e. land, credit, inputs transport, extension services, storage and technical assistance, preventing them from adopting new technologies in to agriculture. The role of women needs to be changed, and more number of women should be empowered as entrepreneurs and cultivators. It is also suggested that women cooperatives be formed to enable them to have access to agricultural credit. They are needed to be empowered to participate in seminars and conferences to express and share their views and experiences on agriculture development and related problems. Their voices need to be heard and suggestions offered by them are required to be given due place in the formulation of agriculture policy and programmes. Women should not be treated as passive agents and sympathetic beneficiaries but as active contributors, innovators and policymakers for the agricultural development. Estimates suggest that if women had the same access to productive resources as men, they could increase yields on their farms by 20–30%, lifting 100–150 million out of hunger (FAO 2011).

Public–Private Partnership in Agriculture: The public–private partnership (PPP) is a contractual agreement between a public agency—federal, state or local—and a private sector entity. Through this agreement, skills and assets of each sector—public and private—are shared in delivering a service or a facility for the use of the general public (Kapoor 2007). It is a new institutional innovation to bring in synergy, mobilize resources and generate, validate and transfer technologies (Mruthyunjaya 2007). Under PPP, instead of working separately, the public and private sectors join hands as partners to work together. Each sector operates through a proper demarcation of each other's roles in the implementation of various projects, programmes and activities with an agreed arrangement in different sectors of development which varies from project to project. PPP in agriculture exists in developing countries in the area of contract farming, extension education, technology transfer, provisioning of high yielding variety (HYV) agricultural inputs, agricultural modernization, innovations and research. National Council for Public–Private Partnerships has suggested the following advantages:

- Reduces public capital investment.
- Improves efficiency due to strong profit incentive.
- Private entity is more accountable than government.
- Expedited project completion by grouping multiple responsibilities into a single contract.
- Specialized expertise.
- Relieves government from staffing issues.
- Shares risks and responsibilities.
- Government can still step in when private entities are misbehaving.

However, in order to effectively implement PPP model, the public sector needs to establish proper policies, legal regulators and institutional frameworks. Besides, the other challenge before the government for promoting effective PPP in agriculture is to address the issues like subsidies, incentives, risk management and infrastructure development in agriculture. PPP in agriculture can successfully meet the challenges in agricultural development like production enhancement and post-harvest management, development and dissemination of technology, value chain, employment generation, marketing, human resources development and making farming a viable business proposition.

Rainbow Revolution: The holistic development of agriculture and allied sector activities will be mutually supportive in providing a sustainable livelihood to the rural population in developing countries. Thinking agricultural development in silos without thinking of development of the related allied sector activities—fishery, dairy, horticulture and so on—would not be effective enough to build up sustainable rural development in developing countries. Agriculture and allied sector activities are the two sides of a coin, one without the other is less effective and sustainable. To site an Indian example, the Green Revolution in crops, Yellow Revolution in oil seeds, White Revolution in milk production, Blue Revolution in fish production and Golden Revolution in horticulture constitute a holistic revolution best known as 'Rainbow Revolution'. The Rainbow Revolution advocates a holistic agricultural development, a means to achieve the ends of sustainable rural development. Rainbow Revolution encourages all-round growth in the production of food grains, edible oils, fruits, vegetables and animal and fish products; evergreen revolutions in agriculture through diversified agriculture, precision farming, resource conservation and value addition provide in real sense the required food, nutrition and environmental security. The challenge before the developing nation states is to maintain synergy between agriculture and allied sectors and place emphasis on both the sectors, as a process of inclusive agriculture and sustainable development.

Climate Change and Agriculture: Agriculture is vulnerable to climate change. A higher temperature eventually reduces yields of desirable crops and encourages weed and pest proliferation. Untimely rain, excessive rain and less rain may cause damage to the crops. OECD (2009) has noted that climate change impacts such as droughts, floods, severe weather and sea-level rise are likely to result in food shortages, increase in vector-borne diseases, infrastructure damages and the degradation of natural resources upon which livelihoods are based. Although there will be gains in some crops in some regions of the world, the overall impact of climate change on agriculture is expected to be negative, threatening global food security. Agriculture facilities contribute approximately 20% of the annual increase in anthropogenic greenhouse gas emissions (IPCC 1996), and improved land use applications may work towards the reduction of greenhouse gas emissions (Aydinalp and Cresser 2008). The climate change will not only affect agriculture but also all allied sector activities. The World Bank has envisaged that the climate change will affect agriculture through higher temperatures, greater crop water demands, more variable rainfall and extreme climate events such as heat waves, floods and droughts. It has advocated that farmers are under the great threat from climate change, but they could also play a major role in addressing it. A few findings of an analysis on climate change and agriculture done by IFPRI (2009) are as follows:

- In developing countries, climate changes will cause yield decline for the most important crops. South Asia will be particularly hard hit.
- Climate change will have varying effect on irrigated yields across regions.
- Climate change will result in additional price increase for the most important agricultural crops—rice, wheat, maize and soyabean.
- Calorie availability in 2050 will decline below 200 levels throughout the developing world.

Diversification of Agriculture: Diversification of agriculture is essential to meet people's demand for multiple crops, both food and cash crops. It is also required for the improvement of the soil health. Diversification of agriculture means shifting agricultural land cultivation from single crop to a number of crops. In order to enhance productivity of variety of food crops and cash crops, diversifying agriculture away from the traditional wheat and rice cultivation is the best possible solution. FAO considers agriculture diversification as an important mechanism for economic growth. M. S. Swaminathan was of the view that diversification to high-value enterprises such as vegetables, fruits, other specialty crops, livestock products, fisheries, value-added agricultural products and so on was the new pathway for income growth in agriculture and rural sectors. The diversification of agriculture from rice and wheat production in Punjab to other crops, such as oil seeds, pulses, cereals, vegetables and so on, will not only enhance farmers' income but also improve the soil health and effective management of rural ecosystem.

Contract farming is being used as one of the means to achieve the end of crop diversification (Pattanaik et al. 2008). To Singh (2000), the need for contract farming also arose to bring about crop diversification for improving farm income and employment. The contract farming system is a forward contract agreement between the buyers and the producers in which the producers supply products of a certain type, at a time, at a price, of a certain quality and quantity as agreed upon in the contract. In certain cases, under the contract, buyers also provide HYV seeds, fertilizers and extension services to the producers in order to enable them to enhance the productivity. The contract farming system is in vogue in many parts of India either through private contract or through government contract or through private–public joint contract. It is largely pursued for the promotion and implementation of diversification of agriculture. Government of Punjab, for instance, had engaged different private/corporate sectors, such as Pepsi Foods Limited, Tata Chemical Limited, Mahindra Shubhlabh Services Limited, Rallis India Ltd and few others, for the promotion of different crops, such as Hyola, sunflower, maize, basmati rice, durum wheat, barley and so on, with the active support of the Punjab Agro Industries Corporation. The contract farming which was in vogue in the United States of America since 1940 and 1950 has enabled the country to produce 100% of poultry meat, milk and various vegetables produced under the contract. Contract farming is in operation in many states of India such as Madhya Pradesh, Andhra Pradesh, Haryana and others. Contract farming needs to be pursued for the production of cash crops, such as pulses, oil seeds and vegetables, as the prices of these cash crops are increasing day by day and are essential for the nutritional requirement. Like minimum support price (MSP) for the rice and wheat, the buyback mechanism through the contract farming system needs to be put in place for the cash crops for increasing their productivity.

Contract Farming of Basmati Rice by Pepsi Foods Limited in Punjab

The Pepsi Foods Private Limited was involved in the contract farming of basmati rice in Punjab through the Punjab Agro Foodgrain Corporation (PAFC). Different districts allotted to the company by the PAFC under contract farming are Hoshiarpur, Nawanshahr, Jalandhar, Patiala, Gurdaspur, Muktsar, Sangrur, Amritsar, Ludhiana, Moga, Ferozepur, Fatehgarh Sahib, Kapurthala and Faridkot. The company which had launched contract farming of basmati rice in 14 districts of Punjab successfully enhanced the area from 7,322 acres in 2003–04 to 8,890 in 2005–06 as well as the number of farmers from 1,830 to 2,212 during the same period. The buyback price offered by the company had gone up from ₹1,200 during 2003–04 to ₹1,350 per quintal during 2005–06. However, the procurement of rice by the company had gone up from 3,395 quintals in 2003–04 to 5,649 in 2004–05, but it declined to 3,221 quintal in 2005–06.

The company has supplied HYV seeds of basmati rice to the farmers on payment basis. Another technical service provided by the company to the farmers was the marketing of product. Extension services provided to the farmers included right dose of input, preparation of seedling and plantation, yield improvement, better pest management, harvesting technology and so on. The main motivating factors for the farmers to undertake contract farming are as follows:

- HYV seeds and better seeds.
- Transfer of technology.
- Quality parameter.
- Buyback price.
- Extension education.
- Assure Market.

The finding shows that the contract farming has raised the confidence level of the small and marginal farmers.

Source: Pattanaik et al. (2008).

MEASURES TO AUGMENT AGRICULTURAL DEVELOPMENT

Some of the important measures to be taken for the development of agriculture in developing countries are as follows:

Land Reform Measures: Land reform—the reallocation of rights to establish a more equitable distribution of farmland—can be a powerful strategy for promoting both economic development and environmental quality (Boyce, Rosset and Stanton 2005). Land is a precious household asset in most of the rural areas of developing countries of Asia, Africa and Latin America, where agriculture plays a predominant role in the economy. A recent resentment over Land Acquisition Act brought out by the treasury bench and its opposition by the opposition political parties in the Parliament and farmers' group in different places in India is an illustrious example of people's sensitivity towards land and its ownership. In other words, any land acquisition for the purpose other than that of the agriculture is deeply resisted by the farmers. In agricultural economies, land is the single most important asset (Boyce et al. 2005). However, distribution and access to land is erratic in terms of availability, accessibility and affordability. Land in general and agricultural land in particular are precious and limited, resulting in inequality in accessibility. Land reform measures in India aim at establishing an egalitarian society and eliminating social inequality. Land reform legislations passed in different states of India during the 1950s customarily had the following components:

- Abolition of intermediaries.
- Tenancy reforms to regulate fair rent and provide security to tenants.
- Ceiling on landholding and distribution of surplus land among the landless.
- Consolidation of landholding for the prevention of fragmentation of land.
- Cooperative farming.

Because of poor implementation of land reform measures, particularly the ceiling on landholding, land is concentrated in the hands of a few and many are landless in developing countries. Limited availability of agricultural land has resulted in rising land prices in rural areas, keeping it beyond the reach of the impoverished. Besides, the quality of land also differs from one area to that of the other. It is a determining factor of variation in the agricultural land prices in the rural land market. In addition to this, land right is a critical problem in the forest and tribal areas. Formulation of appropriate land reform measures and their implementation are big issues in developing countries featured with governance deficiencies. The consolidation of landholding in Punjab, Haryana and Western Uttar Pradesh has enabled the farmers of these states to implement modern agricultural technology in the fields. However, because of poor implementation of ceiling of landholding, the number of landless is high in these states. On the other hand, the effective implementation of land reforms, i.e. ceiling on landholding and consolidation of landholding, in Kerala has not only facilitated the redistribution of land among the landless but also empowered the rural households to reorganize their style of living. The structuralist economists argued that backward land tenure systems were at the heart of the lack of development in agriculture (Cypher and Dietz 2004). By expanding land rights to the poor, land reform adds to their wealth and thereby reduces asset poverty (Boyce et al. 2005).

Mechanization of Agriculture: Slow mechanization of agriculture is one of the important factors for poor per capita agricultural productivity in developing countries of Asia, Africa and Latin America. In the developed countries, agriculture is highly mechanized, which has raised the capital output ratio and per capita agricultural productivity. Agricultural mechanization embraces the use of tools, implements and machines for a wide range of farm operations from land preparation to planting, harvesting, on-farm processing, storage and marketing of products (Salu and Takeshima 2010). According to Verma, agricultural mechanization implies the use of various power sources and improved farm tools and equipment, with a view to reduce the drudgery of the human beings and draught animals, enhances the cropping intensity, precision and timelines of efficiency of utilization of various crop inputs and reduces the losses at different stages of crop production.[3]

In the United States of America, the major effort to develop agricultural production technology for the mid-19th century to the early 20th century involved mechanization—first using horses and later using tractors—geared towards cultivating larger area with less labour (Hayami and Godo 2005). In India, the Green Revolution which was introduced during the early 1970s used tractors, harrows and threshers in agriculture as a mechanization strategy. It had resulted in accelerating agricultural growth rate in Green Revolution belt of India, i.e. Punjab, Haryana and Western Uttar Pradesh. Singh and Singh (1972) have found that tractor farms gave higher yields of wheat, paddy and sugarcane and produced a higher overall gross output per hectare than non-tractor farms. The average net return from a tractor owning farm on per hectare basis was reported to be 152% than that of a non-tractor owning farm (Chopra 1974).

Agricultural Inputs: Availability of agricultural inputs, i.e. HYV of seeds, fertilizers and pesticides, to the farmers is vital to enhance agricultural productivity. The use of agricultural inputs is fundamental in modern agriculture for developed countries, and they were a primary ingredient in the Green Revolution that swept through Asia and Latin America during the 1960s and 1970s (Baltzer and Hansen 2011). The rising prices of chemical fertilizers and pesticides have escalated the cost of cultivation particularly in the Green Revolution areas where the lands have become addicted to high dose of fertilizers and pesticides. On the contrary, it has been observed that excess availability of subsidized inputs during the Green Revolution period has resulted in indiscriminate use of agricultural inputs. This, in turn, has led to degradation of land and water, adverse Nitrogen–Phosphorus–Potassium (NPK) ratio in soil, wasteful use of water, soil salinity, water logging, pollution and exorbitant use of electricity and energy. The World Bank (2011) has observed that despite major improvements, agricultural inputs continue to experience problems such as lack of timely availability, poor quality and high price that are even more marked in rural areas. According to Banful (2010), the fertilizer subsidy programmes were proved to be inefficient arising from high administrative costs, government monopolies and political manipulations. Most subsidies tended to benefit relatively well-off and better connected farmers (Baltzer and Hansen 2011). Agricultural input subsidies were a common element in agricultural development in poor rural economies in the 1960s and 1970s and were a common element of successful green revolutions (Dorward, Hazell and Poluton 2007).

Input subsidies are being given to the farmers to keep them motivated towards agriculture for meeting the challenges of food and nutritional security of the rural population in developing countries. However, the input subsidy is a debatable issue in the international arena. It is said that subsidy benefits may be regressive in that they tend to benefit large farmers who can afford subsidized inputs (Dorward et al. 2007). Economizing the use of modern inputs and converting more and more land to the use of traditional/conventional/natural inputs have been suggested by the agriculture experts as a strategy for sustainable agricultural development. Critics of the Green Revolution strategy predicted that the diffusion of HYV would, however, further exacerbate rural poverty and accelerate the tendency towards the concentration of landholdings (Cypher and Dietz 2004). Therefore, balanced use of agricultural inputs is a challenge before the farmers of developing countries having scanty resources to invest in agricultural production process.

Infrastructure and Water Management: Water is the lifeblood of agriculture. Agriculture is the largest user of water in all regions of the world except Europe and North America (FAO 2002). Supply of water to agriculture through irrigation will bring more and more area under cultivation, raise crop yield, provide opportunity for multiple cropping and over and above raise the land prices. According to FAO (2002), high crop yield and multiple cropping are achieved through irrigation. Because of erratic monsoon and impact of climate change, more and more lands are now dependant on irrigation facility. Moreover, traditionally, the dry land areas are mostly rain-fed and suffering from vagaries of monsoon and shocks of drought and flood. The draught dries out the productivity and flood flushes out the agricultural investment. Farmer's suicide occurring in the dry land areas of different states of India is one of the reasons of non-irrigation, less irrigation and monsoon vagaries. Besides, excessive use of ground water has resulted in depletion of water table, which would pose challenge to sustainable agriculture in the years to come. Sprinkle irrigation, rain water harvesting and watershed construction and management are in vogue with government support in developing countries in order to promote, raise and sustain the tempo of agricultural productivity in dry land and rain-fed areas.

Provision of agricultural infrastructure, i.e. good roads, irrigation system, provision of electricity, ware houses and so on, will go a long way to promote agricultural development. FAO has urged that the current and potential roles of rain-fed and irrigated agriculture need to be quantified, taking into account that the probabilities of rainfall, the available irrigation water supplies and their cost, small-scale irrigation including supplementary water for rain-fed agriculture and a variety of water-harvesting and water-spreading techniques have considerable potential and should be developed further.[4]

Agriculture Finance and Credit System: Availability and accessibility of agricultural credit to the farmers are very much essentials in the hour of need. They will help them to purchase technical implements, quality seeds, fertilizers for land upgradation and meeting day to day expenditures on agriculture. Lack of finance is one of the reasons why agricultural productivity in developing countries and Sub-Saharan Africa in particular is very low (Jessop et al. 2012). It is said that rural and agricultural finance innovations have significant potential to improve the livelihoods and food security of the poor (Kloeppinger-Todd and Sharma 2010). The nationalization of commercial banks and opening of cooperative credit societies in India after independence are steps towards making agricultural finance available and accessible to farmers belonging to the rural areas.

However, despite the formal financial credit facilities, farmers in developing countries are largely dependent on the informal financial lending which carries a high rate of interest. Dependency on the money lenders has forced pauperization of peasantry in developing countries. A study conducted in the agriculturally developed state of Punjab has revealed that 65% of farmers are dependent on *aratias* (informal money lenders) for agriculture financing (Pattanaik et al. 2008). Some of the lacunas associated with the formal/public agricultural credit facilities are stringent procedures, delay in sanctioning the loan, collaterals difficulties, bribe to sanction the loan and so on. Repayment problem of loan during crop failure and waiving of loan leading to sickness of some of the formal credit institutions are other problems of agricultural financing system in developing countries. Financial institutions have demonstrated a lack of interest in agriculture finance for four reasons. First, many agricultural households were located in remote parts of the country and were often so widely dispersed that financial institutions found it challenging to provide cost-effective and affordable services. Second, big swaths of the agricultural population were subject to the same weather and climate risks, making it hard for providers of financial services to hedge risks or operate profitable insurance pools. Third, service providers, mainly urban-based, simply did not know enough about the business of agriculture to devise profitable financial products. Fourth, most small agricultural producers in developing countries had little education and little knowledge of how modern banking institutions work (Kloeppinger-Todd and Sharma 2010).

Crop Insurance: Most of the lands in many developing countries are dependent on vagaries of monsoon. Crop failure leading to farmers' suicide occurs every year in many developing countries including India. It has compelled many perspective farmers to leave agricultural profession. Therefore, a comprehensive crop insurance policy is required to compensate the loss occurring due to unforeseen situations and natural calamities. Besides, farmers face a variety of price, yield and resources risks, which make their income unstable from year to year (Hazell et al. 1986). Herbold has mentioned that crop insurance has been successfully implemented in the last decades mostly in industrialized countries.[5] He advocated that to introduce them in developing countries and emerging markets too, a system approach is needed incorporating a PPP between the government, the farmers and the insurance industry. Because of high premium and lack of knowledge, most of the farmers in developing countries are not opting for crop insurance, even if offered. Recently, Government of India in 2016 under the Pradhan Mantri Fasal Bima Yojana (Prime Minister Crop Insurance Scheme) had drastically reduced the premium for the food and oil crops. Under the scheme, a farmer has to pay a uniform premium of only 2% for all *kharif* crops (monsoon crops) and 1.5% of all *rabi* crops (winter crops). The rest of the premium will be borne by the central and state governments equally.

Research and Extension: Research and extension are critical to the development of agriculture. Research and extension play important roles in the enhancement of agricultural productivity. Research generates improved technologies and practices that help to raise crop yields and income, whereas extension provides the mechanism by which those technologies and practices are disseminated for adoption by farmers (Sharma 2003).

Mosher (1966) viewed that agricultural development requires that people should keep on grousing and developing new skills and mastering new knowledge throughout their active carriers. There is a growing debate among the rural sociologist, economists and agricultural scientists that the difference in productivity among farmers is due to information gaps among the farmers. Extension education through systematic approach will enable and empower farmers in enhancing their knowledge, attitude, skill and practices to deal with the changes taking place in the agriculture. Quality research and hands-on extension in the field of agriculture and allied activities will go a long way to energize agriculture and promote sustainable agricultural development.

Agribusiness: Agribusiness holds key to agricultural development in a globalized world. According to FAO, agribusiness denotes the collective business activities that are performed from farm to fork.[6] It covers the supply of agricultural inputs, the production and transformation of agricultural products and their distribution to final consumers. The pillars of agribusiness development include upgrading entire value chains, strengthening finances, stimulating private sector participation, improving infrastructure and facilitating market access (UNIDO).[7] The seven pillars of agribusiness development in Africa identified by UNIDO are as follows:

- Enhancing agricultural productivity.
- Upgrading value chain.
- Exploiting local, regional and international demand.
- Strengthening technological effort and innovation capabilities.
- Promoting effective and innovative financing.
- Stimulating private sector participation.
- Improving infrastructure and energy aspect.

The agribusiness holds key to agriculture, as agriculture is undergoing tremendous amount of metamorphosis in technology and practices. The role of marketing and packaging holds key to the business in this globalized, ICT-driven world. E-agribusiness has been promoted by the government of various countries. One of the objectives of the agribusiness is to commercialize agriculture and ensure sustainable contribution of agriculture to economic growth and development.

SUMMARY

Any discussion on development issues and challenges will remain incomplete if it does not include the issues and challenges faced by three important sectors of development, i.e. agriculture, industry and services, in the process of carrying out development activities in the economy in their respective fields. Declining contribution of agriculture to the GDP in developing countries, while keeping the percentage of workforce engaged in it almost the same, is a cause of concern. Developing countries have to take several measures to enhance the contribution of agriculture to the GDP and take appropriate steps to transfer workforce engaged in agriculture sector to the rural industrial and service sectors in order to raise their per capita income. One of the important challenges of agriculture sector is to enhance agricultural growth rate and raise contribution of agriculture to GDP. Some of the important issues associated with agricultural development are low investment in agriculture, ineffective implementation of land reform measures, application of technology in agriculture, agricultural financing and credit system, poor agricultural infrastructure such as irrigation, energy power to agriculture, marketing and storage, agricultural research, extension and training institutions, to name a few among many. Diversification of agriculture, contract farming through PPP, cooperative farming, inclusive agriculture by empowering women and socio-economically backwards in agricultural entrepreneurship and promoting need-based Green Revolution in dry land, hill and desert areas will enable particularly agriculture-dominated developing countries to provide sustainable livelihood to people dependent on agriculture. In developing countries, being the primary sector, every economic activity at the grass-roots level starts from agriculture, and even the industrial development cannot be effective without agricultural development. Once Jawaharlal Nehru said, 'every thing else can wait but not the agriculture' and 'in India, almost everything begins with agriculture...industry itself depends on the growth of agriculture...out of agriculture grows industry' (Jawaharlal Nehru quoted from Gopal 1984).

Keywords: sustainable agriculture, Blue Revolution, Rainbow Revolution, land reform, contract farming, diversification of agriculture, inclusive agriculture, organic agriculture, climate change, minimum support price, Green Revolution.

REVIEW QUESTIONS

1. Discuss the role of agriculture in development.
2. What is land reform? Critically discuss the role of land reforms in Indian agricultural development.
3. What is Green Revolution? Why is Green Revolution important in the dry land areas of developing countries?
4. What are the critical issues associated with the development of agriculture in developing countries?
5. Contract farming is vital to the diversification of agriculture in India. Illustrate.
6. What is Rainbow Revolution? Discuss its importance in the development of agriculture in developing countries.
7. Why contribution of agriculture to the GDP of developing countries is declining? Discuss various challenges of agricultural development.
8. Write short note on the following:
   (i) Inclusive agriculture
   (ii) Sustainable agriculture
   (iii) Contract farming
   (iv) Cooperative farming
   (v) Organic agriculture
   (vi) Rainbow revolution
   (vii) Climate change and agriculture

NOTES

1. Bill & Melida Gates Foundation 'Agricultural Development Strategy: Overview.' See http://www.gatesfoundation.org/What-We-Do/Global-Development/Agricultural-Development (accessed on 2 April 2014).
2. ILO and FAO Working Together: Youth Employment; for details, see http://www.fao-ilo.org/fao-ilo-youth/en/ (accessed on 2 April 2014).
3. Verma, S. R. 'Impact of Agricultural Mechanization on Production, Productivity, Cropping Intensity, Income Generation and Employment of Labour.' For details, see http://agricoop.nic.in/farm%20much%20pdf/0502 (accessed on 16 December 2013).
4. For FAO observations, see http://www.fao.org/docrep/003/t0800e/t0800e0d.htm (accessed on 27 December 2013).
5. Herbold, J. Focus; for details, see https://www.agriskmanagementforum.org/sites/... (accessed on 25 April 2016).
6. For FAO views on agribusiness, see www.fao.org/ag/ags/agribusiness-development/en/ (accessed on 9 October 2013).
7. For UNIDO's avocations, see www.unido.org/resources/publication/povertyreduction-through-productive-activities/agribusiness-and-rural-entrepreneurship/agribusiness-for-africas-pro (accessed on 9 October 2013).

BIBLIOGRAPHY

Aydinalp, C., and M. S. Cresser. The Effects of Global Climate Change on Agriculture.' *American-Eurasian Journal of Agriculture and Environment Science*, no. (2008): 672–76.

Baltzer, K., and H. Hansen. 'Evaluative Study Agricultural Input Subsidy in Sub-Saharan Africa.' International Development Cooperation, Danida, 2011.

Banful, A. B. 'Old Problems in the New Solutions.' IFPRI Discussion Paper 01002, Washington DC, IFPRI, 2010.

Boyce, J. K., P. Rosset, and E. A. Stanton. 'Land Reform and Sustainable Development.' Working Paper 98, Political Economy Research Institute, University of Massachusetts, Amherst, MA, 2005.

Buerkle, T. Intern Insights: Inclusive Agriculture and Rural Development.' The FAO Washington Blog, FAO in North America, 2012. Available at: http://faowashington.org/intern-insights-inclusive-org (accessed on 26 December 2013).

Byerlee, D., X. Dias, and C. Jackson. 'Agriculture, Rural Development and Pro-poor Growth Country Experiences in the Post Reform Era.' Agriculture and Rural Development Discussion Paper 21, World Bank, Washington DC, 2011.

Canadian International Development Agencies (CIDA). *Promoting Sustainable Rural Development Through Agriculture*. Hull, Canada: CIDA, 2003.

Candle, Angela B. *Our Planet*, The Magazine of the United Nations Environment Programme, UNEP Special (2006): 29. Available at: www.unep.org (accessed on 20 December 2016).

Chayal, K., B. L. Dhaka, and R. L. Suwalka. 'Analysis of Role Performed by Women in Agriculture.' *Humanity and Social Sciences Journal* 5, no. 1 (2010): 68–72.

Chopra, K. 'Tractorization and Changes in Factor Inputs: A Case Study of Punjab.' *Economic and Political Weekly*, (December 1974): A11–A18.

Christiaensen, L. J., and L. Demery. *Down to Earth: Agriculture and Poverty in Africa*. Washington DC: World Bank, 2007.

Cypher, J. M., and J. L. Dietz. *The Process of Economic Development*. London: Rutledge, 2004.

Dethier, J. J., and A. Effenberge. 'Agriculture and Development: A Brief Review of Literature.' Policy Research Working Paper 5553, World Bank Development Economic Research Support Unit, 2011.

Dorward, A., P. Hazell, and C. Poluton. 'Rethinking Agricultural Input Subsidies in Poor Rural Economies.' Discussion Paper 005, Future Agricultures, 2007. Available at: www.future.agriculture.org

FAO. *Women in Agricultural Development*. FAO's Plan of Action, Food and Agricultural Organization, Rome, 1990.

———. *Deficit Irrigation Practices*, Water Report No 22, FAO, Geneva, 2002.

———. *The State of Food and Agriculture: Women in Agriculture, Closing the Gender Gap for Development*. Rome: FAO, 2002.

———. *The State of Food Insecurity in the World*. Rome: FAO, 2012.

Fechter, J. 'Agriculture and Employment, Sector and Policy Division, Agriculture and Natural Resource.' KFW Position Paper, FAO, 2012.

Fisher, A. G. 'Production, Primary, Secondary and Tertiary.' *Economic Record* 15, no. 1 (1993): 24–38.

Fresco, L. O. 'Higher Agricultural Education: An Opportunity in Rural Development for Women, Sustainable Development Department.' Food and Agriculture Organization (FAO) for the United Nation, 1998, 4.

Ganguly, S. 'No Silver Bullet.' *Our Planet,* The Magazine of the United Nations Environment Programme, UNEP Special (2006). Available at: www.unep.org

Garcia, A., and M. Kennedy. 'Assessing the Linkages Between Low Body Mass Index and Morbidity in Adults: Evidence from Four Developing Countries.' *European Journal of Clinical Nutrition* 48, no. 3 (1994): S90–S97.

Gill, K. S. 'Prospects for Agricultural Exports from India.' *Agricultural Situation in India* 45, no. 5 (1990): 273–80.

Gollin, D., S. Parente, and R. Rogerson. 'The Role of Agriculture in Development.' *American Economic Review* 92, no. 2 (2002): 160–64.

Gopal, S. *Jawaharlal Nehru: A Biography*. New Delhi: Oxford University Press, 1984.

Halwart, M. 'Agriculture and Rural Development.' Food and Agriculture Organization, Rome, 2005. Available at: http://www.rural21.com/uploads/media/ELR_aquaculture (accessed on 3 April 2014).

Hayami, Y., and V. Ruttan. *Agricultural Development: An International Perspective*. Baltimore, MD: Johns Hopkins University Press, 1971.

Hayami, Y., and Y. Godo. *Development Economics: From the Poverty to the Wealth of Nations,* 3rd ed. New York, NY: Oxford University Press, 2005.

Hazell P. B., C. Pomereda, and A. Valdes. *Crop Insurance of Agricultural Development: Issue and Experience*. The John Hopkins University Press, 1986.

Hazell, P., S. Syed, M. Zupi, and M. Miyazako. 'Key Issues in Promoting Increased Investments in Agriculture.' Technical Workshops on Policies for Promoting Investment in Agriculture, 12–13 December 2011.

IAASTD. 'Towards Multi-functionality Agriculture for Social, Environmental and Economic Sustainability.' Issues in Brief, International Assessment of Agricultural Knowledge, Science and Technology for Development, Washington DC, 2008.

IFOAM. *Organic Agriculture Principles*. Bonn: International Federation of Organic Agriculture Movements, 2005. Available at: http://www.ifoam.org/about_ifoam/principles/index.htm (accessed in July 2009).

IFPRI. 'Agricultural Adaptation to Climate Change in the Developing World: What Will It Cost?' IFPRI Policy Seminar, Washington, DC, 5 October 2009.

ILO. *Global Employment Trends for Women 2009*. Geneva: International Labour Organization, 2009.

IPCC. 'Climate Change 1995: Impacts, Adaptations and Mitigation of Climate Change: Scientific-Technical Analyses.' Contribution of Working Group II to the Second Assessment Report of the Inter-governmental Panel on Climate Change (IPCC), 1996.

Israr, M., and H. Khan. 'An Analysis of Livelihood Sources in Hilly Areas of Northern Pakistan.' *Sarhad Journal of Agriculture* 26, no. 4 (2010): 665–73.

Jessop, R., B. Diallo, M. Duurasma, A. Mallek, J. Harms, and B. Manen. 'Agence Francaise De Developpment.' 2012. see http://www.afdfr/webdav/shared/PUBLICATION (accessed on 23 October 2013).

Johnson, K. 'Breaking the Persistent Cycles of Ultra-Poverty in Rural Africa.' FSI Stanford, FSE News, 4 May 2011. Available at: http://foodsecurity.stanford.edu/news/2929 (accessed on 26 December 2013).

Johnston, B. 'Agriculture and Structural Transformation in Developing Countries: A Survey Research.' *Journal of Economic Literature,* no. 8 (1970): 101–45.

Johnston, B. G., and J. W. Mellor. 'The Role of Agriculture in Economic Development.' *American Economic Review* 87, no. 2 (1961): 556–93.

Kapoor, R. D. 'PPP: Institutional and Industrial Views.' In *Agricultural Transformation through Public Private Partnership: An Interface,* edited by S. Ayyappan, P. Chandra, and S. K. Tandon, 2–5. New Delhi: Directorate of Information and Publication of Agriculture, Indian Council of Agricultural Research, 2007.

Kloeppinger-Todd, R., and M. Sharma. 'Innovations in Rural and Agriculture Finance Overview.' IFFRI and The World Bank, Focus 18, Brief I, 2020 Vision for Food and Agriculture and the Environment 2010. Available at: http://www.ifpri.org/sites/default/files/publication (accessed in October 2013).

Larsen, A. 'Working Together to End Hunger.' *eJournal USA, US Food AID and Reducing World Hunger* 12, no. 9 (2007): 1–12.

Lewis, W. A. 'Economic Development with Unlimited Supplies of Labour.' *The Manchester School of Economics and Social Studies,* no. 22 (1954): 139–91.

Meier, G. M. *Leading Issues in Economic Development,* 6th ed. London: Oxford University Press, 1995.

Mellor, J. 'Agriculture on the Road to Industrialization.' In *International Agricultural Development,* edited by C. Eicher and J. Staatz. Baltimore, MD: Johns Hopkins University Press, 1998.

Mellor, J. W. 'Faster more Equitable Growth Agriculture, Employment Multiplier and Poverty Reduction.' Research Report, USAID, 2001.

Mosher, A. T. *Getting Agriculture Moving: Essentials for Development and Modernization*. New York, NY: Pager, 1966.

Mruthyunjaya. 'Private–Public Partnership: Problems and Potentials.' In *Agricultural Transformation Through Public Private Partnership: An Interface,* edited by S. Ayyappan, P. Chandra, and S. K. Tandon, 8–19. New Delhi: Directorate of Information and Publication of Agriculture, Indian Council of Agricultural Research, 2007.

NCPPP. 'PPP Fundamentals.' 2010. Available at: http://www.ncppp.org/howpart/pppfundamentals.html (accessed on 25 October 2013).

OECD. *Integrating Climate Change Adaptation into Development Cooperation Policy Guidance*. OECD, 2009.

Ojo, M.O. 'Problems of Monetary Management in Nigeria and Prospects under the Deregulated Financial Environment.' Paper presented at the national conference on financial system and Nigeria economic recovery organized by the Department of Economics, Ahmadu Bello University, Zaria, 1–115, 1993.

Panchamukhi, V. R. 'New Paradigms of Development Some Thoughts.' In *Development Perspectives,* edited by K. S. Ramachandran, 152–160. Noida: Vikas Publishing House Pvt. Ltd, 1990.

Pattanaik, B. K. 'Migrant Labourers in the Urban Informal Sector: A Gender Analysis.' *Indian Journal of Labour Economics* 55, no. 4 (2012): 675–85.

Pattanaik, B. K., K. Singh, S. Singh, and M. M. Singh. *Contract Farming System in Punjab: An Appraisal*. Chandigarh: Centre for Research in Rural and Industrial Development, 2008.

Pryor, S., and T. Holt. 'Agribusiness as an Engine of Growth in Developing Countries.' US Agency for International Development, Washington DC, 1999.

Rukuni, M. 'The Growing Business.' *Our Planet*, The Magazine of the United Nations Environment Programme, UNEP Special (2006): 12–13. Also see http://www.unep.org/PDF/OurPlanet/OurPlanet_WorldBank_web_en.pdf (accessed on 2 December 2016).

Salu, S., and H. Takeshima. 'Agricultural Mechanization and the Smallholder Farmers in Nigeria.' Nigeria Strategy Support Programme, Policy Note No. 22, IFPRI, Nigeria, 2010.

Samanta, R. K. 'The Reap Less Than Show.' *The Hindu* (April 1994): 7, Chennai, India.

Schultz, T. W. *Transforming Traditional Agriculture*. New Haven: Yale University Press, 1964.

Schutter, O. D. 'International Trade in Agriculture and the Right to Food.' Friedrich-Ebert-Stiftung, Occasional Papers, Dialogue on Globalization, Geneva, 2009.

Shanker, Y. 'Production of Bio Pesticide Fertilizer Through Vermicomposting.' *SIRJ-BES* 1, no. 2 (2014): 12–17.

Sharma, R. 'Foreword.' In *Integration of Agricultural Research and Extension,* edited by R. Sharma. Tokyo: Asian Productivity Organization, 2003.

Sidhu, M. S., and P. S. Rangi. 'Out-migration form Rural Bihar: A Case Study.' *Indian Journal of Labour Economics* 41, no. 4 (1998): 583–16.

Singh, R., and B. B. Singh. 'Farm Mechanization in Western Uttar Pradesh: Problems of Farm Mechanization.' Seminar Series-IX, Indian Society of Agricultural Economics, Bombay, February 1972.

Singh, S. 'Contract Farming for Agricultural Diversification in Punjab: A Study of Performance and Problems.' *Indian Journal of Agricultural Economics* 56, no. 3 (2000): 283–94.

Sinha, R. K. 'Concept of Sustainable Agriculture: An Issue of Food Safety and Security for People, Economic Prosperity for the Farmers and Ecological Security for the Nation.' *American–Eurasian Journal of Agricultural and Environmental Sciences* 5, no. S (2009): 1–55.

Strauss, J. 'Does Better Nutrition Raise Farm Productivity?' *Journal of Political Economy* 94, no. 2 (1986): 297–20.

Swaminathan, M. S., ed. *Agriculture Cannot Wait: New Horizons in Indian Agriculture*, 96. New Delhi: Academic Foundation, 2007.

Timmer, C. Peter. 'The Agricultural Transformation.' In *Handbook of Development Economics*, Vol. I, edited by H. Chenery and T. N. Srinivasan, Chapter 8, 276–328. John Hopkins Press, 1988.

UNEP/GEMS. *The Contamination of Food*. UNEP/GEMS Environment Library, No. 5, Nairobi, Kenya, 1992.

United Nations. *World Survey on the Role of Women in Development*, 12. Department of International and Social Affairs, United Nations, 1986.

World Bank. *World Development Report 2008: Agriculture for Development*. New York, NY: Oxford University Press, 2007.

———. *Bangladesh: Priorities for Agriculture and Rural Development*. Washington DC: World Bank, 2011. Also quoted in http://bids.org.bd/uploads/publication/BDS/38/38-1/4_Toward%202021%20Examining%20 Drivers.pdf (accessed on 1 December 2016).

7 Industry Sector and Development

In the twenty-first century manufacturing development remains relevant for poor countries trying to catch up with more advanced economies and to provide increasing standards of living for their populations.

—Naude and Szirmai (2012)

Industrial sector plays an important role in the economic growth, modernization and development of an economy. The contribution of the industrial sector to the development of the developed countries in the initial phase of their development was stupendous. The Industrial Development Report 2013 brought out by UNDP says that to maintain growth in developing countries while creating sustainable jobs, the manufacturing sector offers an opportunity not only to rebalance the economy towards higher value-added sectors but also to provide a relatively wide employment base with higher labour productivity. The industrial development in the Western countries triggered off with their endeavour to promote industrialization through the process which is popularly known as 'Industrial Revolution'. According to Robert Wilde, the term 'Industrial Revolution' was used to describe the period of the 1830s, but modern historians increasingly call this period the 'First Industrial Revolution' characterized by developments in textiles, iron and steam led by Britain, to differentiate it from a 'Second Industrial Revolution' of the 1850s, characterized by steel, electrics and automobiles led by the United States and Germany.[1] Richard H. Tilly (2010) categorized industrialization into three periods:

- Early industrialization from 1830 to 1870.
- Rapid industrialization from 1870 to 1914.
- Slow further industrialization from 1918 to the 1950s.

However, prominently, the three phases of the Industrial Revolution consisted of

1. The first phase (1770s to 1860s) that started with Britain and then spread to other countries in Northern and Western Europe and the United States.
2. The second phase (1870s to 1950s) that brought in Russia, Japan and other parts of Eastern and Southern Europe, Australia and New Zealand.
3. The third phase (1960s to present) that brought in the so-called Asian Tigers (Hong Kong, Singapore, Taiwan and South Korea) and has been tentative development in key economic sectors in Turkey, India, Brazil, Chile and Argentina.[2]

Whatever the reasons, the groundswell of global industrialization, which started in Britain in the 18th century, swept through Europe and the United States of America and reached Japan and Russia by the end of the 19th century, subsided after the 1900s (Pollard 1990). In Asia, China and India experienced some degree of industrialization in the late 19th century, but industrialization only took off after these countries freed themselves from colonial influences and external domination (Naude and Szirmai 2012). The industrialization processes in the Asian countries particularly the Asian giants, i.e. Singapore, Taiwan, South Korea and Hong Kong and a few late comers, i.e. Malaysia, Indonesia, Thailand, and more recently China and India and in a few Latin American countries such as Brazil and Mexico may be termed as the 'Third Industrial Revolution' process in different countries of the world. Economic historians are in agreement that the onset of the Industrial Revolution is the most important event in the history of humanity, since the domestication of animals and plants.[3]

The Industrial Revolution was instrumental in raising the per capita economic growth in capitalist economies. It is a historical and emerging fact that countries with strong and vibrant industrial sectors have showed more economic growth and development.[4] Economists such as Arthur Lewis, Rosenstein Rodan, Ragnar Nurkse, Hirschman and Leibenstein viewed economic development as a growth process that requires the systematic allocation of factors of production from a low productivity, traditional technology, decreasing returns, mostly the primary sector to a high productivity, modern, increasing returns, mostly the industrial sector (Adelman 1999). According to UNIDO (2009), the more advanced economies have more diverse industrial sectors and economies that export more sophisticated products grow faster.

After reading this chapter, you will be able to:

1. Explain the role of industry sector to economic growth and development.
2. Describe industrialization process in Europe and America.
3. Discuss industrialization process in Asia.
4. Narrate various issues and challenges of industrial sector.

According to UN Committee Report (1963),[5] industrialization is a process of economic development in which growing art of the national resources is mobilized to develop technically up-to-date, diversified, domestic economic structure characterized by a dynamic manufacturing sector having and producing means of production and consumer goods and capable of assuming high rate of growth for the economy as whole and of achieving economic and social change. In Asian subcontinent also, countries that resorted to industrial development early have gained in terms of modernization and higher economic growth and development. Therefore, industrialization is an effort in which the underdeveloped countries place a major hope of finding a solution to their problems of poverty, insecurity, overpopulation and ending their newly realized backwardness in the modern economy (Bryce 1960). To UNIDO (2007) 'industrialization is proving a potent force for economic growth in countries of Asia, most recently China and India'.

The role of the manufacturing sector in the Chinese economy is clearly more significant than that of the agriculture and service sectors, whereby the sector contributes the highest to the growth in China (Hussain and Yik 2012). The economic liberalization process that started in developing countries during the 19th century gave more space to the private sector in industrial development, which has enabled them to gradually enhance the contribution of the industrial sector towards the overall economic growth rate in these countries. It is commented that to the majority of people in developing and underdeveloped nations, industrialization, economic growth and modernization are three interchangeable terms which all lead to one ultimate goal: A better way of life (Tsai 1989).

The Industrial sector at the initial phase of development requires infrastructure, which the public sector alone could be able to ensure in developing countries. The infrastructural development by the public sector will attract private investment in the industrial sector. One of the examples is that the Government of Thailand created more than 50 state-owned industries during the 1950s and the 1960s because of the lack of domestic and foreign investment capital and the private sector's weakness in mobilizing resources for expansion (Rondinelli 2006). Government of India also established big industries in the steel sector in the public sector during the 1960s, particularly during the Second Five Year Plan period with the help of Germany and USSR. Private sector intervention in the industrial sector largely came to the picture during the late 1990s with the formulation of the liberalization policy of the governments of the Third World countries, by which the private sector was provided space to play role in the industrial sector.

ROLE OF INDUSTRY SECTOR IN DEVELOPMENT

Industry and manufacturing sectors play a crucial role in multifaceted development of a nation. Particularly, the emergence of a modern manufacturing sector has led to dramatic changes in the structure of the developing economies, and one of this illustrious examples is China. It has led to sustained increase in the growth of labour productivity and economic welfare of the workforce employed in the industrial sector. Even the agriculture-based economies having strong agriculture and industry linkages are found to enjoy more national and per capita income compared to their counterparts having silo thrust on agriculture. According to UNIDO (2009), industrialization is integral to development and scarcely any country has developed without industrialization, and rapidly growing economies tend to have a well-developed manufacturing sector. In China, the manufacturing sector accounts for nearly 35% of the GDP; in South Korea, Malaysia and Indonesia, the share of the manufacturing sector is around 30% of the GDP and even in the Latin American economies such as Argentina and Brazil, the manufacturing sector contributes 24% to the GDP; however, in India this sector contributes only 14% to its GDP (Kumar and SenGupta 2008). Despite the importance of the manufacturing sector to the Indian economy, the sector's exports have had a minimal impact of the global scale, as India's share in world manufacturing exports increased from 0.6% to 1.4% between 2000 and 2009, whereas China tripled its contribution from 3.2% to over 10% in the same period (Mukherjee and Mukherjee, 2012).

Important roles of industrialization in development are discussed as follows:

1. Industrialization enables a nation to achieve a variety of socio-economic objectives such as higher employment rate, poverty eradication, raising standard of living of labours, reduction of economic inequality and greater access to education

Figure 7.1 *Global Manufacturing Competitive Index*

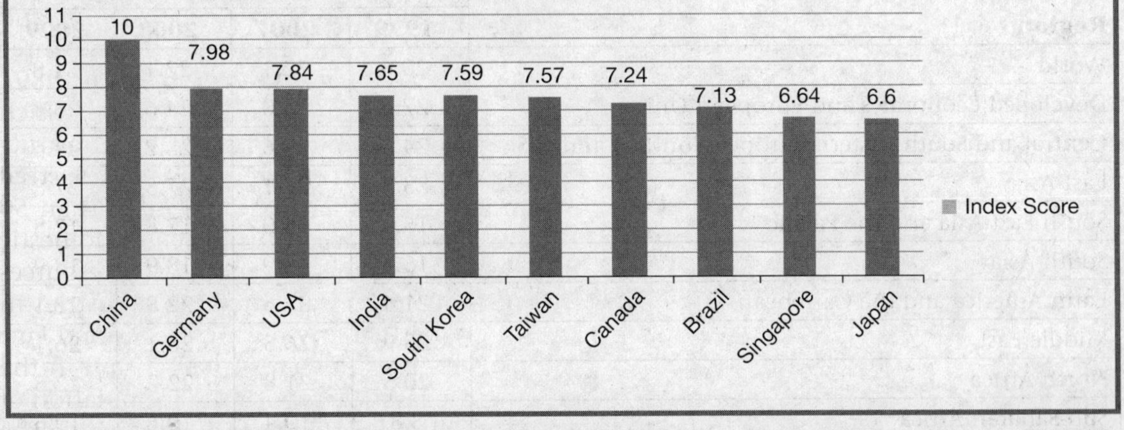

Source: PHD Research Bureau, compiled from Global Manufacturing Competitiveness Index 2012–13.

and health care of the population employed in the industrial sector. A country where the contribution of the manufacturing sector towards the economic growth is high, it enables the nation to achieve better development goals of eradicating poverty in the long run. The illustrious examples are European and American countries which achieved industrial development during 1970s and 1980s. The quality of life of the people living in these countries is far better than the countries which initiated industrialization process late. The UNDP's Industrial Development Report 2013 states that countries need to move from lower to higher technology, from lower value-added to higher value-added and from lower-productivity to higher productivity sectors, industries and activities if they want to develop industrially (Figure 7.1).

2. The industrialization through its positive externalities gives rise to the growth of other service sector activities. The per capita income of the labour deployed in the industrial sector in higher compared to those in primary sector. They are more modernized and urbane than their counterpart in the agriculture sector who are largely rural and traditional. Industrialization creates positive externalities, which leads to opening up self-employment activities, educational and health care institutions near the industrial clusters. United Nations believes that there is a mutually reinforcing relationship between social and industrial development, and industrialization has the potential to promote directly and indirectly a variety of social objectives such as employment creation, poverty eradication, gender equality, labour standards and greater access to education and health care (Table 7.1).[6]
3. Industrialization is a potent instrument of poverty reduction. The labour-intensive rural industrialization and linkages between agriculture and industry through the establishment of agro-based industries will raise income of the rural entrepreneurs. Moreover, establishment of traditional art and craft–based industries and small-scale and cottage industries will reduce poverty in the rural-based Asian and African economies. In China, it has proved to be an important contributor to

Table 7.1 *Region-wise Percentage of People Employed in Industry*

Region	Industry			
	1999	**2007**	**2008**	**2009**
World	20.6	22.1	22.1	21.8
Developed Economies and European Union	27.6	25.0	24.6	23.4
Central and South Eastern Europe (Non-EU) and CIS	24.5	25.6	25.2	24.6
East Asia	23.8	27.1	27.5	27.8
South East Asia and the Pacific	15.9	18.0	17.8	17.8
South Asia	15.4	18.9	18.9	18.9
Latin America and the Caribbean	21.4	22.6	22.8	22.1
Middle East	25.9	26.5	26.1	26.1
North Africa	20.5	21.8	22.2	22.5
Sub-Saharan Africa	8.8	10.4	10.6	10.6

Source: Global Manufacturing Competitiveness Index 2013. See https://www2.deloitte.com/content/dam/Deloitte/global/Documents/Manufacturing/gx_2013%20Global%20Manufacturing%20Competitiveness%20Index_11_15_12.pdf(accessed on 2 December 2016).

poverty reduction and a vast numbers of people have left agriculture to work in factories, as—in the past—did rural population in the now industrialized world (UNIDO 2007). The industrialization in South Korea has enabled the country to achieve remarkable growth with steep reduction of poverty (Kniivila 2007).

4. Industrialization helps in better and effective utilization of raw materials, generates employment for the people and helps in modernization, for instance, opening of the Rourkela Steel Plant during the Second Five Year Plan of India in the mineral and iron ore rich State of Odisha. It effectively utilizes the raw material of the state without incurring much transport cost. It provided employment to the skilled as well as unskilled people and generated a metropolis life style for people. In other words, the plant area has a cosmopolitan life style where people from different states are working, and it has become a ground of hybrid culture.
5. Industrialization ensures a secured and formal source of income to the people. It also enhances skill, thereby unfolds the opportunities for industrial labourers. The wage and income of labourers working in the formal industrial sector is comparatively higher than those engaged in unskilled causal labourer activities in both rural and urban areas. Higher income enhances access to better household basic needs and amenities required for good quality of living. Chenery (1955) was of the opinion that industrialization is the main hope of most poor countries trying to increase their levels of income.
6. Industrialization has brought structural changes in the pattern of foreign trade of developing countries. It has promoted increased export of manufacturing goods, thus acquired enhanced foreign exchange earnings for the industrialized countries. Industrialization in developing countries in particular has promoted south–south export. UNIDO (2009) findings suggest that 'the rapid growth in developing country exports of manufactures was triggered primarily by the very rapid growth

of south-south export.' Asian countries like China, South Korea and Taiwan are illustrious examples of extended markets for their products in both developed and developing countries. However, the failure of the slow-growing middle income countries has been their inability to adapt to rapid change in the global market place (UNIDO 2009). Those who adapt to the globalization have not only enhanced their opportunities in global market but also helped their economies to achieve higher growth rate. Furthermore, the processing of raw materials at home by developing countries has curtailed the import of goods from the foreign markets, thereby reduced expenditure on imports and improved balance of payment situation of the country.

7. Growth of the industrial sector leads to effective supply of inputs, i.e. fertilizers, pesticides, farming tools and so on, to the agricultural sector. Agricultural modernization can be possible only with the help to strong industrialization. Agriculture and industry nexus has promoted economic growth in many countries. A strong and vibrant agriculture sector needs a dynamic industrial sector. Industrialization can bring technological changes in agriculture development. The application of modern technology into the farmers' fields during the Green Revolution was possible only because of the industries manufacturing technology-driven agricultural implements. Thinking of agricultural modernization bereft industries is a remote possibility. The recent revolution of food processing industries in the globalized era is an illustrious example of agriculture–industry nexus. The impact of globalization and changing pattern of food habits in developing countries will bring forth the desire for more agro-based industries in these countries. Industrialization will strengthen the nexus between agriculture and industry in developing countries.
8. Industrialization is an important source of capital formation. Industrialization needs heavy investment; during the early phase of Industrial Revolution in both developed and developing countries, this was materialized through 'forced saving'. More conservative-minded writers had accepted the concept of 'forced savings' at the 'expenses of the working classes' current living standards, but had pointed out that a programme of national industrialization could not be carried out without great hardship of the masses, as heavy investment was a necessary precondition for the rise in income (Court 1953). Eric Hobs stated that industrialization means a relative diversion of income from consumption to investment, i.e. largely from the non-investing classes to the potentially investing ones, from the poor to the rich. He observed that early 19th century economic theory and economic practice stressed the crucial importance of capital accumulation by the capitalists and the maximum diversion of income from the workers to their employers (Hobsbawm 1996).
9. The growing employment in the industrial sector believed to provide impetus to the attainment of MDGs in developing countries. Ross (2008) finds that labour-intensive manufacturing is a key source of wage employment for women. Greater employment opportunities for women would not only increase household per capita income but also enable them to have access to quality education and health care facilities for them and for their children. It will also reduce household poverty and provide sustainable livelihood to poor people engaged as wage earners in the industrial sector. Stable income can only ensure sustainable livelihood, which could be possible through industrial development.

10. Last but not the least, industrialization is a source of social and cultural revolutions in the countries bonded with tradition and customs. It has given a new way of life and a way of livelihood to the people, which is different from agriculture-based rural living. Industrialization has enhanced people's aspiration. It has led to the growth of technical institutions in the developed as well as developing countries, particularly in developing countries. Blumer (1990) has rightly remarked that industrialization is not just a new system of production, like a factory system, but also a variety of social practices and ideas such as system of worker discipline, managerial ideology, spirit of innovativeness, spirit of workers protest, aspiration for a higher standard of living and scheme of rights and privileges. Industrialization has brought modernity to the traditional culture. It has also done value addition to the existing cultural practices. As a result, it has enhanced the productivity of cultural goods and services and has promoted cultural trade.

INDUSTRIALIZATION IN EUROPE AND UNITED STATES OF AMERICA

Industrialization in Europe

The industrialization process in the Western countries was triggered off in the Great Britain during the 1700s. It is interesting to note here that for the proliferation and triggering industrialization in the Great Britain during the 1700s, it was the agriculture sector that created an enabling environment and favourable atmosphere for the Industrial Revolution. In other words, agriculture was the stepping stone for building the pillar of Industrial Revolution in the European countries, starting with the Great Britain. The industrialization was set to motion in the Europe with the establishment of the textile industries. A series of innovations initiatives were undertaken by the Great Britain for the modernization and mechanization of the textile sector. The prominent among them are innovations of new machines, which generated demand for labourers in the economy. The Great Britain took the lead in early-industrialization phase in the Europe because of its advantage of having adequate amount of iron ore and coal resources. It also has very good infrastructure facilities such as rail and road transport system, which was a concomitant to industrial development.

After the 1850s, the industrialization process which was triggered off in the Great Britain was spread to other parts of the Europe such as Belgium, France and Germany. One of the key impacts of the industrialization in the European countries was the migration of people from the villages to urban areas in large numbers. Through this Industrial Revolution, the Great Britain became a highly industrialized nation by 1914. The industrialization resulted in transfer of majority of its population from the rural to urban areas. Therefore, the Great Britain became highly urbanized and majority of its population are now living in urban areas. The advantages of the industrialization to the Europeans were that the government of these industrialized nations subsidized education, sponsored scientific research, oversaw public health and provided social welfare care to those who came and stayed in urban areas. Thus, early industrialization created a base for the systematic urbanization.

One of the important benefits of industrialization is the increase in job opportunities. Creation of power machines and factories provided many new job opportunities. As a result, people from the rural areas travelled to urban industrialized areas for job. Employment in the factories and industries also enabled the industrial workers to acquire skills. Skill development helped them to earn higher wages and salaries, which enhanced their quality of life.

Another important feature of industrialization process in the Europe is that it was spread among different countries through international economic relationships. Import of cotton products by Germany from England enticed the Germans to go for industrialization and development of export market in Europe. Similar changes took place elsewhere in 'Inner Europe' mostly during the same period between 1830 and 1850 in Belgium, France and Switzerland. However, it is pertinent to mention here that the industrial structures in each of these countries developed differently as per their local specific conditions. The intra-European trade between industrialized countries of the European 'periphery' such as Greece, Portugal, Russia or Sweden further injected fresh Industrial Revolution in other countries Europe. Thus it can be said that the industrialization process in Europe was an expansionist endeavour spearhead by the Great Britain. This process enhanced the urbanization in these countries and raised the quality of life of European population. Primarily, the industrialization process of Europe proliferated for their mutual benefits. In other words, it was economic relationship among the European nations as per their comparative advantage which augmented industrialization in Europe.

Industrialization in the United States of America

The Second Industrial Revolution in the world was started in America in early 1800s. It is pertinent to mention here that when Great Britain initiated Industrial Revolution in the early seventies, at that time, America was focusing on the agriculture sector in 1790. The process of industrial development in the United States of America began much later than those of the European countries. However, the quality and quantum of acceleration of the industrialization process in the United States of America was faster than those of the European nations. To cite the example, in 1851, producers from many developed nations gathered at the Crystal Palace in London to display their industrial achievements at the first Great Exhibition. In that exhibition, America's work in the manufacturing sector was the apple of all eyes. This attraction encouraged America to vigorously go for industrialization. As a result, it was not a flight of fancy but delicately by the end of the century, the United States became the World leader in manufacturing. Some of the factors and features that supported the speedy and effective industrialization in the United States of America are discussed below:

- Availability of natural resources and the knowledgeable, skilled and technical manpower was a critical advantage for the effective industrialization in the United States of America.
- Availability of telecommunication and surface transport facilities helped and strengthened the industrial and manufacturing sectors.
- Availability of abundant water supply resources helped to generate hydropower that hastened the process of industrialization.

- Increased capital accumulation for investment in the manufacturing sector.
- Iron and steel was central to the American industry.
- Accelerated technological innovations with emphasis on new inventions and applied science.
- Unprecedented production by the domestic manufacturing sector strengthened American economy and reduced its dependence on import.
- The industrialization in the United States of America was concentrated mostly in Northern part of America.
- One of the unique features of America's industrialization is continuous process manufacturing. This helped mechanization of the manufacturing sector on a continuous basis. The stress was on the processing of yields with uniform quantity of production by the help of minimum human labour.
- One of the positive features of America's industrial development is the standardization of products. Through this process, industries used special purpose machines to produce large quantities of similar or even interchangeable parts. These were assembled to create finished goods.
- Industrialization helped in the mechanization and advancement of agriculture. The advancement in agricultural equipment enhanced agricultural productivity and raised farmers' incomes.
- American industrialization process laid emphasis on the division of labour, specialization and standardization of work. There was a clear job demarcation. Also, the market mechanism was used in the industrial production process.

This second Industrial Revolution started in the United States of America in 1800. In this phase, United States of America surpassed the progress that was achieved by the Great Britain and other European countries. However, industrialization brought out in its wave conflicts, stress and restlessness to the country as was encountered in Britain and in Europe earlier. Table 7.2 shows how manufacturing in the United States of America surpassed that of other European countries during 1928–29. It is not a flight of fancy, but delicately it proved that the Americans are the first learners and progressive innovators.

Table 7.2 *Index of Manufacturing Growth in Five Industrial Countries*

	Manufacturing		
Country	**1913**	**1928–29**	**1937–38**
UK	100	106	139
Germany	100	118	144
France	100	139	119
Sweden	100	143	231
United States	100	172	164

Source: Tilly (2010).

INDUSTRIALIZATION IN THE ASIAN COUNTRIES

Industrialization process in the Asian countries started in the 19th century except Japan where it was triggered off in the mid-1880s. The process of industrial development, as far as Asian Countries is concerned, can be categorized as: (a) at the outset, Japan is the only country in Asia which has achieved status of advanced industrialized countries; (b) the countries such as South Korea, Singapore and Taiwan are in the second tier status in industrialization process (c) while China and India opened their door to industrialization during 19th century are categorized as third tier industrialized nation. In this section, the industrialization process of three countries—Japan, China and India—are discussed.

INDUSTRIALIZATION IN JAPAN

Japan's industrialization process started during mid-1880s. It was triggered off with the creation of a new Ministry of Industry in 1870 by the Japanese Government. The ministry was assigned the responsibility to prepare the road map and policies for operation of industries. The creation of the ministry and its actions pushed the process of industrialization in Japan. As a result of which modern factories were established. It enhanced the industrial productivity in Japan. Furthermore, the Ministry also took initiatives for the establishment of technical education system. These technical institutions offered technical education and training.

During the initial phase of industrialization, Japan gave priority to the export-oriented industries. Japan took a lot of measures and tried to learn from the best practices adopted by the Western countries, i.e. the Unites States of America and European countries in their industrialization process. According to Masayuki Tanimoto (2004), technology transfer from industrialized western countries such as the United Kingdom and France has played foremost roles in directing Japan's early industrialization process. On the other hand, Mark Mauson (1987) mentioned that in the early times, many foreign or multinational farms set up in Japan, and they provided the host country not only advanced technologies but also the way and approach of management, which can be named as knowledge transfer. The speed of industrialization process in Japan started around 1945 and by the year 1970, Japan achieved its goal of being one of the industrialized nations in the world. It became one of the most industrialized nations not only in Asia but also in the world. Japan's model and process of industrialization and Japan's technology and industrial organizations received worldwide attention.

Important features of Japan's industrialization are discussed below:

- At the outset, government played a catalyst role during the early phase of industrialization in Japan, from 1950s to 1960s. The capital investment for the industrialization and in the industrial sector was done by the government. Subsequently the private entrepreneurs came forward and started investment. The tax and expenditure policy of the government during this period was helpful in the enhancement of entrepreneurial incentives. It encouraged savings and corporate investment. According to Sakoh (1984), 'Japan's policy of smalls and balanced budgets has provided a favourable business climate and allowed the private sector to make first claim on investable capital resources.'

- Private sector played a key role during the second phase—the period from 1961 to 1970, the period of rapid industrial expansion in Japan. During this period, the gigantic share of total investments in the industrial sector was done by the private sector. It is said that during the period of most rapid expansion—1961 to 1970—the share of private investment in machinery and equipment amounted to nearly 75% of the total capital formation (Sakoh 1984).
- The state ownership of manufacturing industries was extremely limited in Japan as compared to the European countries. However, government played a proactive role in creating infrastructure such as roads, harbours, airports and hydroelectric projects. The infrastructure created by the government provided favourable climate for the private entrepreneur to invest in the manufacturing sector.
- Some of the industries promoted by the Japan's Industrial Policies are agricultural industries, coal mining industries, petroleum refining and petrochemical industries, shipbuilding industries, computer-related industries and so on.
- Private banking institutions played an important role in provisioning finance to the entrepreneurs and industrialists for proliferating industrialization in Japan. Shortly after the war, Japanese officials, realizing that private banks would be a primary source of ample credit for industrial operations and expansion, decided to maintain an artificially low and stable rate of interest (Sakoh 1984). Free hand given by the government to the private banks enabled them to provide prompt credit facilities to the entrepreneurs to start manufacturing industries.
- Japan's industrialization process provided trade protection to infant industries for their growth. At the very beginning of Japan's industrialization, trade protection played a prominent role in order to provide its fragile industry an opportunity to grow and prosper. According to G. C. Allen (1981a), the main industrial policy for Japan is protectionism, and 'carefully chose industries, in order to present ruinous competition at the infancy stage, and nurse them up to a competition status and then expose them to outside competition.'
- Japan's industrial policy also gave adequate emphasis on the promotion of small- and medium-size industries. The Basic Law for Small- and Medium-sized Industries Act promulgated in 1963 aimed at the modernization and providing strength to these industries to fight against international competition. The Act proposed financial incentives for these industries for their modernization and absorption of new technology.
- One of the outstanding features of Japan's process of industrialization as compared to other Asian countries industrialization process, e.g. China and India, is the role of FDI. It is not a flight of fancy, but truly, FDI has been playing a very insignificant role in the industrialization process of Japan. According to OECD (2002), Japan's inward FDI is extremely low compared to outward FDI. Some other analyst of Japan's industrialization said that FDI did not play a major role in post-war Japan in terms of technology transfer. However, it played an important role to make the market more competitive. It also inspired the local development of technology.
- One of the most important features of Japan's industrialization is the role of R&D in industrial development. Japan invested a lot of resources in the R&D in the

industry sector. According to OECD (2007), Japan owns the highest ratio of researchers to total employment. The R&D expenditure brought out new innovations and pushed up the rapid process of industrialization. According to Peck and Tamura (1976), the expenditures of Japan on R&D focused on improving the quality and lessening the costs of product more successfully.

- Favourable international environment was an added advantage for Japan to exploit to its advantage. For instance, availability of inexpensive raw materials, stable and open world market and availability of foreign technologies are a few among many that enticed Japan to augment the industrial development process. This climate of liberal export and import regime helped even the private firms to import raw material and technologies from the world market and export their industrial product to the world market.
- Congenial domestic climate such as availability of trained and skilled technocrats, managers and disciplined and hardworking labour force have been the key ingredients behind Japan's successful industrialization. They were not only hardworking and disciplined but also had positive attitude towards savings. This saving habit helped the country in capital formation and investment. They save approximately 20% of their income, thereby fuelling future investments in their country's progress (Sakoh 1984).
- By maintaining a small and balanced budget, fairly low and stable interest rates, relatively low rates of taxation, stable prices, brief and mild recessions, minimal defence and social welfare expenditures, the Japanese Government helped provide an exceptionally favourable economic environment for private enterprise (Sakoh 1984).
- Committed, supportive and disciplined bureaucracy helped Japan's industrialization. The bureaucracy provided all possible support to the private entrepreneurs in opening of manufacturing industries. In other words, hassle free bureaucratic environment was the key to success of Japan's industrialization. G. C. Allen (1981) wrote in *The Japanese Economy* that the chief function of the bureaucrats and politicians was to provide a congenial environment for the enterprise of private firms.
- Japanese Government's industrial policies were always influenced by the changing world situation. These were proactive to both internal and external responses. It is well commented that 'guided industrialization' has made Japan one of the most successful industrial countries (Kagami 1995).

Developing countries of Asia, Africa and Latin America have to learn a lot from the Japanese model of industrial development, if they have to successfully develop their industrial sector and augment the contribution of the manufacturing sector for employment generation and raising economic growth and development.

Industrialization in China

China's industrialization process provides an illustrious example of one the most recent and contemporary industrialization processes in the World. China's high economic growth rate was a product of rapid transfer of emphasis from agriculture to manufacturing and export-oriented industry. China initiated industrialization process far behind Japan. China's economic reforms and a shift from agriculture to industrialization process started in the late 1970s and early 1980s. China emphasized on achieving higher growth rate through rapid industrialization, enhanced its manufacturing exports and foreign trade and opened its economy to the world market. According to Dutta (2005), growth was import–export led: technology and know-how have been imported from abroad and adopted to the domestic resources, in particular to the abundant labour force. It is remarked that what China has achieved during the three decades, the same degree of industrialization took two centuries to occur in Europe (Summers 2007).

Some of the important features of industrialization in China are discussed below:

1. China developed industrialization in a planned manner. In the planned economy of China, 'heavy industries' were concentrated in a few locations. On the other hand, small- and medium-scale industries were developed through clustering approach or cluster-based industrialization. It is said that China's rapid industrialization is taking place in 'special cities'. Clustering helped in cost reduction and sharing of technical know-how among the entrepreneurs. It resulted in enhanced productivity and growing profit margin of the entrepreneurs. It is remarked that industrial cluster has been an important subsystem in the Chinese national economic system, the working status of which directly affects healthy development of the Chinese economy (Yingming 2010).
2. Emphasis on rural industrialization is another important feature of China's industrialization process. China laid astounding emphasis on rural industrialization. One of the objectives of rural industrialization is to absorb surplus labour existing in the agriculture sector in order to eradicate rural poverty. Besides, it also aimed at checking rural to urban migration. China's rural enterprises, popularly known as Township and Village Enterprises (TVEs), have contributed a lot to economic growth, generation of employment to the rural masses and structural transformation. TVEs were initiated in 1984. By 1995, TVEs accounted for approximately a quarter of China's GDP, two thirds of the total rural output and more than one third of China's export earnings (Zhang 1999).
3. Industrialization process in China laid emphasis on R&D. It was believed that industrialization is inextricably linked with technological development. Therefore, it considered that technology cannot be improved without input from and investment in R&D. According to OECD (2007), China has increased its expenditure on R&D rapidly.
4. One of the important features of China's industrial development is the role of FDI in the manufacturing sector. FDI inflows dominated in the proliferation of China's manufacturing sector. China introduced several preferential foreign investment policies, which attracted more and more foreign investors to invest in the manufacturing sector in China. FDI inflows brought with them advanced technology and management skills which further stimulated industrial growth rate in China.

> Between 1997 and 2008, the manufacturing sector attracted 62.72% of the total accumulated FDI inflows in China (Chen 2011).

Many Asian countries trying to boost their manufacturing sector and interested to raise contribution of the industrial sector to GDP have to learn a lot from China's rural industrialization strategy.

Industrialization in India

Historically, the industrialization process in India started much before the independence and even before the British rule. The textile industries were the first one to trigger off the process of industrialization in India. The industrialization process initiated before independence laid emphasis on the modernization of textile industries with the use of spindles, looms and spinning mills. Before independence, different types of industries established in India with private initiative were the automobiles, iron and steel. Jamshedji Tata was the pioneer in the field of modern Indian industry in the automobile sector in the private sector. Tata Steel was started in the year 1907.

After independence, the government of India placed emphasis on the industrialization for acceleration of economic growth of the country during the Second Five Year Plan. During the Second Five Year Plan, the industrialization strategy articulated by Mahalanobis placed emphasis on the establishment of heavy industries under the public sector. Besides heavy industries, the government of India has also given adequate emphasis on the establishment of cottage and small-scale industries particularly in rural areas. The Industrial Policy Resolution of 1948 stated that

> Cottage and small scale industries have a very important role in the national economy. Offering as they do scope for individual, village or cooperative enterprise and means for the rehabilitation of displaced person. These industries particularly suits for the better utilization of local resources and for the achievement of the local self-sufficiency in respect of certain types of essential consumer goods like food, cloth and agricultural implements.

From time to time, government of India has come out with industrial policies in order to give a direction to the process of industrialization in the country. The objectives of the industrial policies launched during different periods are to achieve a high growth rate, national self-reliance, reduction of foreign dominance, building up indigenous capacity, encouraging small-scale industries, bringing about balanced regional development, prevention of concentration of economic power, reduction of income inequalities and control of economy by the state. The liberalization, privatization and globalization process started in India during 1990 assigned a private sector a pivotal role in the industrialization process of the country.

India enjoys several advantages to prop up its industrial sector, i.e. (a) country is endowed with rich natural resources such as minerals, iron ore forests and so on which are requisites for smooth industrial development; (b) country is a producer of commercial crops, i.e. sugarcane, raw cotton, jute, tea, tobacco, oilseeds, fruits and so on which can flourish and sustain food processing and manufacturing industries; (c) the country is also

Table 7.3 *Industrialization Thrust in Different Five Year Plans in India*

Five Year Plans	Thrust Areas
1st Five Year Plan (1951–56)	1. Thrust on the large scale industry. 2. Extensive Programme on expansion of village industries, i.e. khadi, coir, village oil, matches, leather, handmade paper, *gur* (jaggery) and *khandsari* (raw white sugar), palm *gur*, woollen blanket and bee keeping.
2nd Five Year Plan (1956–61)	1. Rapid industrialization with particular emphasis on the development of basic and heavy industries. 2. The emphasis was given to the increase in production, expansion of capacity, modernization and re-equipment of important industries and fuller utilization of existing installed capacity.
3rd Five Year Plan (1961–66)	1. Expansion of basic industries like steel, chemicals industries, fuel and power and establish machine building capacity. 2. To improve the productivity of the village and small industries; promote the growth of industries in rural areas and small towns; development of small-scale industries as ancillaries to large industries, and organize artisans; craftsmen on cooperative lines and reduce progressively the role of subsidies, sale rebates and sheltered markets.
4th Five Year Plan (1969–74)	1. Growth in industrial output and capacity without any undue burden on balance of payment deficit. 2. Maximum utilization of already build up industrial capacity. 3. Encourage the emergence of new industries and provide for a flexible approach in the development of industries within the public, private and cooperative sectors.
5th Five Year Plan (1974–79)	1. Promotion of manufacturing sector. 2. Importance was laid to mining and quarrying for production of energy.
6th Five Year Plan (1980–85)	1. Strengthening the infrastructure facilities for industries sector. 2. Enhancement of manufacturing capacities in public and private sector. 3. Correcting regional imbalances in industrial development. 4. Enhancement of efficiency of village and small-scale industries through upgradation of skill and technologies and creation of addition employment opportunities and export promotion.
7th Five Year Plan (1985–90)	1. Restructuring industry, efficient use of capital, improving infrastructural facilities and modernization and upgradation of technology. 2. Concentrate of development of industries with large domestic market and export potential to merge as world leaders in them. 3. To usher in 'sunrise' industries with growth potential and evolve an integrated policy towards self-reliance in strategic fields. 4. To improve the economic and occupational profile of rural and semi-urban and weaker sections of urban communities through promotion of village and small-scale industrial activities.
8th Five Year Plan (1992–97)	1. Quality upgradation and elimination of the weakness in industrialization 2. Increasing role of private sector in industry sector. 3. Establishment of closer linkages between academic institutions, manufactories of equipment, national laboratories by the government.

9th Five Year Plan (1997–2002)	1. Disinvestment in equity at different levels in GAIL, IOC, MTNL and so on. 2. To promote industrialization in backward, hilly, remote and inaccessible areas. 3. A number of initiatives were taken under the new R&D policy for strengthening technological capabilities of the Indian industries.
10th Five Year Plan (2002–07)	1. To provide SSIs (small scale industries) adequate credit/loans, funds for technology upgradation, adequate infrastructure facilities, modern management practice and skill up gradation and marketing assistance. 2. Modernization and technological upgradation, capacity building, PPP, infrastructure and FDI in manufacturing sector are some of the important strategies to augment industrialization in the 10th Five Year Plan.

Source: Quoted from Different Five Year Plan Documents of Government of India, Planning Commission, Government of India.

fairly rich in hydroelectricity, atomic energy and coal lubricant required for acceleration of industries and (d) last but not the least, country has a 'demographic dividend' having a large percentage of youth population who can be skilled and gainfully utilized in the industrial sector. Industry sector is a key sector among the three, which can be seen as intermediary to provide backward and forward linkages to agriculture and service sector.

However, despite the policies and various measures, India has failed to augment its rural industrialization process in the country. Country has not been able to attract much FDIs for its industrial sector, particularly for the purpose of rural industrialization. FDI in the industrial sector is low as compared to China's; as a result, the contribution of industrial sector to the economic growth rate of the country has remained stagnant for the past several years. A World Bank Report 'Doing Business in 2005' has identified following facts about India, that it takes (i) 89 days to start a business in India, compared to 41 days in China; (b) 67 days to register property in India, compared to 32 days in China; (c) 425 days to enforce contracts in India, compared to 241 days in China and (d) 10 years to complete insolvency proceeding in India, compared to 2.4 years in China (World Bank 2005). The National Strategy for Manufacturing has identified some of the challenges which create hurdles in the path of manufacturing sector in India. At the outset, bureaucratic redtapism and hassle in initiating a business in India. The National Manufacturing Policy of India has identified following areas requiring thrust in order to strengthen manufacturing sector: (a) creation of appropriate skill sets; (b) increase in domestic value addition and technological 'depth' in manufacturing; (c) adoption of the best manufacturing practices and production techniques; (d) increasing the scale of operation and delivering on globally acceptable quality levels; (e) attracting FDI in manufacturing sector particularly those of rural entrepreneur; (f) creating appropriate environment, infrastructure and market conditions; (g) ensuring effective coordination between central, state and local levels; (h) enabling small and medium enterprises to achieve competitiveness and (i) creating a standing mechanism for resolving manufacturing policy issues (Table 7.3).

Most recently, government of India has launched 'Make in India' programme in September 2014 to promote manufacturing sector in the countries. It aims at attracting not only FDIs but also foreign investors in India. A gist of the 'Make in India' programme is given in a box on page 212.

Make In India

Aim

The aim of 'Make in India' programme is to make India an attractive destination for manufacturing.

Objectives

1. Wooing investors to set up industries in India, instead of just getting FDI.
2. Encourage multidimensional companies to manufacture their products in India.
3. Providing employment to youth.
4. Empowerment of secondary and tertiary sector and effective utilization of human resources.

Key Strategies

1. **Ease of business:** Make in India is a policy that combines incentives with easy handling of businesses and faster redressal machinery.
2. **Skill and jobs for the youth:** Skill endowment and job creation for youth in 25 key industries. These industries include roads and highways, construction, defence development and automobiles among others.
3. **Making India a manufacturer:** Urging global investors to make India an industrial hub. This includes making India a destination for production of goods and exporting the same to the world over.
4. **Getting away with archaic laws:** Raising FDI caps in a controlled manner and parting with the red tape restrictions in decision-making. Make in India campaign aims at eliminating archaic laws to create business related environment.
5. **100 smart cities:** The investors to become partners in adopting a smart city. This will help to achieve the target of 100 smart cities.
6. **Disinvestment of PSU:** Certain inefficient and loss-incurring PSUs will be disinvested i.e. a certain part of them will be sold off to private players so as to generate revenue and do away with the resource-sucking headaches.

Responses

1. In January 2015, the Spice Group said it would start a mobile phone manufacturing unit in Uttar Pradesh with an investment of ₹500 crore.
2. In February, Samsung said that will manufacture the Samsung Z1 in its plant in Noida.
3. In February 2015, Hitachi said it would increase its employees in India from 10,000 to 13,000 and it would try to increase its revenues from India from ¥100 billion in 2013 to ¥210 billion. It said that an auto-component plant will be set up in Chennai in 2016.

4. In February 2015, Huawei opened a new R&D campus in Bengaluru. It had invested US $170 million to establish the research and development centre.
5. In April 2015, Airbus said that it will manufacture its products in India and invest US $2 billion.
6. FOXCONN has agreed to setup a $5 Billion plant in Maharashtra.
7. POSCO will establish a new steel plant in Maharashtra which is expected to bring an investment of around $2 Billion.

Source: https://www.quora.com/Make-In-India-political-program-What-is-the-Make-in-India-project (accessed on 14 June 2016).

ISSUES AND CHALLENGES OF INDUSTRIAL DEVELOPMENT

Industrialization in developing countries faces a lot of challenges. Some of the important issues and challenges of industrialization are discussed below.

Industrialization, particularly in developing countries, customarily has taken place in or around the urban areas. This has encouraged migration of rural population to the urban area for employment. As industries grow at a faster rate, there will be accelerated migration to urban areas leading to decay in both rural and urban areas, and social tensions will build up, endangering the nation (Krishna 2003). Instead of bringing people from the rural areas to the industrially developed urban areas, the suitable strategy would be to take industries to the rural areas. The challenge before developing countries is to promote balanced industrialization both in urban and rural areas. Japan, during Meiji era (1868–1912), and Taiwan and China, after the World War II, developed rural towns and villages as the production sites of labour-intensive industrial and agricultural commodities (Ho 1982; Ranis and Stewart 1993).

Rural industrial and manufacturing sector entrepreneurship would promote capital formation in rural areas. The de-concentration of industrialization from the centre, i.e. urban areas to the peripheries, to those of rural areas will not only lead to balanced industrialization but also check migration. There is a need for developing rural industrial cluster in the rural areas of developing countries. The clustering of industries in the rural areas of China is an illustrious example of how even with scanty finance industrialization can be effectively promoted. The clustering has several advantages such as dividing an integrated production process into many incremental steps and lower capital entry barriers, thereby enabling more entrepreneurs to participate in nonfarm production, allow inter-farm trade credit, thus reduces need for working capital. It also helps to lower the entry barriers to industries, thereby stimulating competition and enhancing productivity (Long and Zhang 2009). Literature suggests that when firms operate in clusters, it may help them overcome many growth constraints by promoting collective efficiency, facilitating the growth of firms in small steps and making it easier to respond to opportunities and crises (McCormick 1999). By this type of measures, China has achieved in the three decades the same degree of industrialization that took two centuries to occur in Europe (Summers 2007). China's rapid industrialization, despite the lack of a well-developed financial system, seems to defy the conventional thinking on the role of finance in development (Long and Zhang 2009).

Development of rural industrial cluster is a challenge before developing countries in order to promote rural industrialization, particularly growth of small- and medium-scale industries. Acquiring land for the establishment of rural industrial cluster by the government as well as private entrepreneurs is a herculean task for the ruling parties of the governments of developing countries, which is found to be facing a lot of resentment from the opposition in India. Strong opposition to the recent land acquisition bill of the government of India (2015–16) is an illustrious example.

In the resources crunch developing countries, the promotion of small and medium-scale manufacturing activities is the most suitable strategy of industrialization. The small- or medium-scale subsector is now widely recognized by governments, businesses and the academic community as playing a vital role in the development of an economy (Nakizito and Darkoh 2002). One of the pertinent issues before the planners and policy-makers of developing countries is to promote small-scale and cottage industries. It encourages growth of skill labour force in rural areas and provides opportunities to the small and medium entrepreneurs (SMEs) to undertake investment in the secondary sector. Dahlman (2007), while narrating the process of industrialization in Taiwan, wrote

> Unlike Korea, its industrial sector has been made up primarily of small and medium-sized firms, rather than large *Chaebols* with deep pockets to cross subsidized risky ventures. The government developed a supportive technological infrastructure such as technical information services and specialized public research institutes. It also developed special programmes to create technological linkages between foreign firms and small domestic suppliers.

As it has been found out that SMEs are critical to economic development within the South African economy by contributing considerably to the national GNP and private sector employment (Snyman et al. 2013). There is a recent international literature suggesting that when these (SMEs) firms operate in clusters, it may help them overcome many growth constraints by promoting collective efficiency, facilitating the growth of firms in small steps and making it easier to respond to opportunities and crises (McCormick 1999). India's Second Five Year Plan emphasized on the role of small and cottage industries on the following grounds:

1. Generation of employment opportunities.
2. An equal distribution of national income.
3. Mobilization of capital.
4. Mobilization of entrepreneurial skills and
5. Regional dispersal of industries—this is one of the ways to promote inclusive industrial development.

Paul (2004) has stated that rural industrial estates are viable remedies to correct regional imbalances. According to Byrd and Qingsong (1990), rural industrialization has three key components: (a) reducing the difference between factors of production in the countryside and in the cities; (b) rationalizing the division of labour in the urban–rural industrial structure and (c) synchronizing the development of rural industrialization and urbanization. Developing countries can think of giving protection to the SMEs in their initial stage of formation and establishment in order to sustain their activity in the internal as well as external markets. G. C. Allen (1981) maintained that industrial policy for Japan is protectionism and it carefully chose industries to prevent ruinous competition at the infancy stage, nurse them up to a competition status and then expose them to outside competition.

One of the emerging challenges of industrialization is its impact on environment. A host of environmental problems such as air pollution, deforestation, desertification, solid and hazardous waste problems comes forth in the wake of the quest for industrialization. United Nations has noted that as the world has become more industrialized, there have been increasing environmental pressures such as harmful emissions and waste, which have had global, regional or local impacts.[7] These include (a) at the local level, urban air pollution, contamination of soils and rivers and land degradation; (b) regionally, acid rain and waste and coastal zone contamination and (c) globally, climate change, ozone layer depletion, loss of biodiversity, increased movement of hazardous waste and increased land-based marine pollution. Nation states have to take into consideration these impacts while going for industrialization and should not compromise the environmental health in lieu of industrialization. The industrialization programme intended to be launched in the agriculturally fertile land will not only create health hazard among the nearby villages but also create adverse impacts on the future of food security. The climate change and global warming are the products of indiscriminate industrialization.

Industrialization creates many occupational health problems. People working in tobacco factories and even staying nearby areas of these factories are found to be suffering from asthma, tuberculosis and other cardiovascular problems. Children working in the footwear industry are found to be suffering from respiratory problems, lung disease and skin infections through constant exposure to glue and fumes, and are at the risk of nasal cancer, neurotoxicity and adverse physical factors (Tiwari 2005). Various occupational diseases of people working in the rubber industry were found to be gastrointestinal cancer, lung cancer and leukaemia (Peters et. al. 1976). Therefore, adequate insurance coverage and selection of areas for industrial cluster is important, and industrial clusters are required to be established at the outskirt far away from the residential localities. Child labour in the hazardous industries should be strictly prohibited. Liquid waste of industries also contaminates surface as well as ground water of the area, leading to numerous health problems. Industry specific occupational health awareness and training camps along with treatment facility need to be made available by the entrepreneurs for the people working in the industries having high occupational health risk.

Industrialization faces formidable challenge of infrastructure and energy availability. Infrastructure like electricity, coal, road and so on is essential requisites for industrial development. Any attempt to industrialize would end in fiasco if full-fledged infrastructural facilities are not created in those areas (Sundar and Srinivasan 2009). Desai (2007) identified that poor infrastructure facilities in rural segments have been one of the factors holding back rural industrialization in India. However, local power generation based on solar, wind and biomass energies can greatly facilitate rural electrification as a vital supplement for rural-based manufacturers (Hayam 2007). The Special Industrial Economic Zone (SIEZ) can successful in those areas which have advantages of adequate supply of raw materials and have infrastructure facility. UNIDO (2011) has identified that reduction of industrial energy intensified after 1995 were around 30% for high income developing economies and upper-middle income developing economies and around 40% for lower-middle income development economies.

In developing countries, challenge of establishing linkages between agriculture and industry through establishment of agro-based industries in rural areas is enormously acknowledged. In the theory and empirical literature, the interrelationship between agriculture and industry has been discussed in following ways: (a) agriculture supplies inputs like raw cotton, jute, tea, coffee and so on needed by the agro-based industries and (b) on the other hand, industries supply industrial inputs such as fertilizers, pesticides, machinery and so on to the agriculture sector. The experience in Brazil, Chile, Kenya, Mexico, South Africa and Thailand have demonstrated the potential of agro-based small and medium enterprises to generate employment, increase farm and rural non-farm incomes and raise the standard of living of the rural poor (UNIDO 2009). The deteriorating linkages between agriculture and industry have been primarily credited to the deficiency in demand for agricultural products, decline share of agro-based industries coupled with slow employment growth (Bhattacharya and Rao 1986; Chowdhury and Chowdhury 1995; Rangarajan 1982). Kalecki (1976) pointed out the importance of investment and technological advances in agriculture for the rapid development of industry, emphasizing the interrelationship between growth of both agriculture and industry sector for faster development.

Attracting FDI is a challenge before developing countries for faster and sustainable industrial development. FDI plays a key role in industrial development of China. The World Bank (2010) has rightly remarked that China's FDI strategies have taken a more selective approach to attract environmentally sustainable energy efficient and technologically advanced industries. Lall and Urata (2003) said FDI provided foreign exchange, savings needed for industrialization and basic facilities for social development, and there is a link between competitiveness, FDI and domestic technological effort. It is customarily seen that FDIs are largely inclined towards large-scale entrepreneurial industrial activities and lay cursory emphasis on the development of SMEs which are playing crucial role in the industrial development of the developing and transitional economies. FDI in China and Taiwan has promoted SMEs in the rural sector. Ghoshal and Saxena (2012) viewed that in strengthening the indigenous SME sector in a situation of resource scarcity, there is a potential role of FDI in relation to the long-term competitive development and internationalization of the SME sector in transition and developing countries.

Finance is the lifeblood of industrial development, and speedy industrial development is only possible with a strong capital market. According to Rakesh Mohan (2004), cross-country experience suggests that economies that have mature financial systems for allocating fund efficiently among competing uses tend to grow faster. He further emphasized that well-functioning banks, financial institutions and other financial intermediaries such as venture capital funds promote technological innovations and industrial growth by providing risk capital and funds to the entrepreneurs who have the highest probability of developing new products, production processes and competitive production facilities. Inadequate access to credit is a major problem of micro, small and medium entrepreneurs particularly operating in rural areas. Many studies have highlighted the limited access to financial resources available to small enterprises compared to larger organizations and the consequences for their growth and development (Levy 1993). Cook and Nixon (2000) viewed that the role of finance has been a critical element for the development of small- and medium-sized enterprises. Such enterprises usually operate on tight budgets, often financed through owner's own contribution, loans from friends and relatives and a meagre bank credit. Sometimes, they close down their operations due to the shortage of finance, putting livelihood of many industrial workers in peril. Thus, finance in general and particularly for small- and medium-scale industries are critical for industrialization of developing countries. The benefits like tax holidays and soft loan for promotion of small-scale and cottage industries through the initiatives of the women entrepreneur and entrepreneur belonging to disadvantaged section of the society will go a long way to promote inclusive industrial development.

Small- and medium-scale entrepreneurs face a stupendous task of selling their products both in the national and international markets. Performing the marketing functions satisfactorily and successfully in the global context is the major hurdle for SSI and their development (Kumar 2012). Any economic slowdown both nationally and internationally seriously affects their economic health. The adoption and application of marketing concept is one sure way by which small business enterprises can grow and secure places for themselves in the 21st century commerce and industry (Ogechukww et al. 2013). The marketing is one of the problem areas where remedial management development effort should be intensified (CBN 2000). Government and individuals have to join hands and see to the development and appreciation of marketing in all the economies of developing countries (Ewah and Ekeng 2009). Therefore, adequate and timely availability of working capital and marketing avenues for SSI products should be ensured for improving their competitive strength in the domestic and global markets (Antony 2002).

R&D in industry sector is considered one of the important aspects of industrial development. Developing countries need to spend adequate amount of money on research in the industrial sector development. Industrialization is inextricably linked with technological development and technology cannot be improved without input on R&D (Peng 2010). According to OECD (2007), China increased its expenditure on R&D rapidly. In China, R&D expenditure, including capital and manpower, from government and state-owned institutions were accounting for more than 50% (Qi and Zhou 2006).

Proactive and supportive investment climate and bureaucracy are very much essential for the promotion of industrialization. Dollar et al. (2005) found a strong relationship between investment climate, firm performance and economic growth. On the other hand, a study found out that Chinese cities that have created good investment climate in the sense of reducing bureaucracy and corruption and providing appropriate infrastructure and financial services tend to produce more value from given capital and labour, earn higher profits and hence more economic growth (Patunru, McCulloch and Luebke 2009). David et al. (2003) found that a sound investment climate as reflected in low customs clearance times, reliable infrastructure and good financial services attract foreign investment and a good environment for production and trade. In South Korea, a deep sense of corporate loyalty within the bureaucracy inherited from the colonial period made it possible to combine decentralization of administrative decision-making with overall coordination of state intervention helping industrial development of the country (Michell 1984).

The challenge before developing countries is inter- and intra-benchmarking of economy's industrial performance. Developing countries have to benchmark the industrial development of their own country and also various provinces within the country so that they can take plausible measures for the promotion of industrialization in different provinces by assessing their strengths and weakness. It will help the nation to promote industrial competitiveness and achieve balanced industrial development. UNIDO has developed

Table 7.4 *Competitive Industrial Performance (CIP) Index 2009*

Economy	CIP Index	Rank
Singapore	0.642	1
United States of America	0.634	2
Japan	0.628	3
Germany	0.597	4
China	0.557	5
Republic of Korea	0.490	7
Brazil	0.202	44
India	0.206	42
Kenya	0.094	100

Source: UNIDO, 2011.

the competitive industrial performance (CIP) index (see Table 7.4), which assess industrial performance using indicators of an economy's ability to produce and export manufactured goods competitively (UNIDO 2003).

Proactive role of the state has proved to be one of the important factors for industrialization in Asian countries of South Korea, Japan and Singapore. Even the policy of 'guided capitalism' in Japan, where the state played a proactive role in guiding and promoting industrialization in that country is an illustrious example of the role of the state in industrialization. According to Yeoh and Ngee (2007), the success of industrial development in Singapore is attributed to development strategies based on state-led, market-driven intervention, with the government taking a much heavier role in the city-state's economic development than usually observed or considered advisable. However, in the process of gaining an international reputation, corruption-free administration, efficient infrastructure and non-negotiable legal and financial systems are other main selling points. The corruption and redtapism in industrial licensing and financing, lack of state-sponsored industrial culture and special industrial zones and overall effective industrial policy are challenges before the most of developing countries of Asia, Africa and Latin America. Effective industrial policies in the East Asia are characterized by four key features such as flexibility, selectivity, coherence and an emphasis on promotion rather than regulation (Jenkins 1991). Policies in the East Asian newly industrialized countries have been directed towards the promotion rather than the regulation of private enterprises (Myers 1986).

MEASURES TO PROMOTE INDUSTRIAL DEVELOPMENT

Some of the suggested measures for the promotion of industrial development are discussed below:

1. At the outset, governments of developing countries must create infrastructure such as good quality road, hydroelectric projects and thermal plant for generation

of electricity, airports for the import and export of raw materials and finished goods and so on. This will entice the private entrepreneur to invest in building manufacturing industries. Without quality infrastructure, which is also called as social overhead capital, no private investor will come forward for capital investment in the manufacturing sector.

2. A country needs to build good quality educational institutions such as Indian Institutes of Technology (IIT), Industrial Training Institutes (ITIs), Polytechnic institutes and skill-based community colleges for imparting skill education and training. The student and teacher exchange programmes in education and research and training between the industrially backward countries with the industrially developed countries will help in transfer of technical knowledge and techniques from the developed countries to developing countries. For instance, gain of technology and technical knowledge from the industrially advanced Western nations helped Japan to effectively hasten its process of industrialization. The industrial R&D programme must be sufficiently encouraged and be rewarded. Education, training and research are fundamental cornerstones of industrial development.
3. Inclusive industrial development with preference to industrial development in the backward and rural areas and encouragement of industrial entrepreneurship among the disadvantaged sections of society including preference to the women entrepreneur will be helpful for holistic and sustainable industrial development. Women entrepreneurs must be provided with soft loan facilities for the industry 'start-up' programme. The infant entrepreneurs should be provided protection for their growth and development.
4. Proactive political systems, both the ruling and opposition party, must rise above the party line and support and encourage initiatives such as tax rebate to the young entrepreneurs, tax holidays for starting of industries in rural, hilly and desert areas and so on. Besides the political system, the bureaucracy has to be more pragmatic and help the government in the formulation of entrepreneur-friendly industrial policy, economic reforms favourable to industrial development and shun bad governance such as redtapism and corruption.
5. Credit is the fuel for the engine of industrial development. Both the public and private banking systems are required to lend soft loans to the entrepreneurs desiring to invest in the manufacturing sector.
6. Government should attract more and more FDIs in the manufacturing sector. Preference should be given for the promotion of manufacturing industries in the rural areas. Moreover, government has to make convenient policy for tapping of remittances for investments in the manufacturing sector.
7. Industrial corridors, rural industrial cluster must be initiated by the government first, so that the private initiatives must follow. In the federalist structure, the state and the provincial government must divest sufficient amount of budget for the promotion of industrialization based on their local specific conditions. The State should conduct industrial need assessment and invest accordingly. Close coordination and collaboration between the centre and state is *sine qua non* for smooth and sustainable industrial development. Besides, the country need to develop 'ease of doing manufacturing business index,' and industrial development index in order to inject competitive environment among various provinces and states.

8. While promoting industrial development, adequate attention has to be given to the industry's impact on the environment. A clear-cut industrial environment policy has to be formulated and put into practice. The political and bureaucratic pressure should not tamper and violate the law for their personal gains. Many projects initiated by the corporate sector, including those through FDIs, have started and thereafter closed because of non-compliance to environmental clearance, thereby resulting in a loss to industrialists. This will create industrial instability environment, which is not salubrious for the healthy and effective industrialization. A proper project appraisal with social and environmental impact assessment will prevent all such anomalies.
9. The industrial policy must be formulated from time to time and should be flexible and accommodative to the private players. The policy should be such that it produces more job creators and entrepreneurs rather than job seekers. It must respond to the liberalism and take into consideration both domestic and international markets.
10. Formulation of strong international economic relationship on industrial matter by both developing and developed nations is essential for industrial development. Developing countries must not be forced by the developed nations to be in the habit of exporting finished industrial products rather they should try to produce good quality industrial products for the international market. China is an illustrious example.

SUMMARY

The growth and development of a nation depends on the contribution of industrial sector of the economy. A strong and vibrant industrial sector is critical to economic growth. The history of development shows that developed countries of Europe and America were able to achieve high growth rate because of the enhanced contribution of industrial sector to the economic growth during initial years of their march towards development. China is an illustrious example where the contribution of industrial sector has enabled the Chinese economy to maintain their high growth rate for a long period. The other developed countries of Asia such as Japan, South Korea, Taiwan and Singapore have sound industrial base, and industrial development has contributed significantly towards their economic growth and development. A developing country where the industrial sector is not contributing 25% to their GDP has to take appropriate steps and prepare and implement proactive industrial policies for promoting industrialization. A strong industrial sector is a concomitant for sustainable growth of developing countries which are at the nascent stage of industrial development.

Keywords: Asian giants, industrialization, manufacturing, industrial policy, industrial revolution, small and medium entrepreneurs (SMEs).

REVIEW QUESTIONS

1. What is industrialization? Discuss the role of industry sector in economic growth and development of a developing economy.
2. Discuss the process of industrialization in Europe and America.
3. Discuss the process of industrialization in Japan and China and how they are different from India.
4. Discuss the feature and role of industrial policy in the industrialization process of India.
5. Discuss the features of Japan's industrial development. What lessons India has to learn from Japan?
6. What are the critical issues for which the contribution of industrial sector to GDP is low in developing countries?
7. What are the differences in industrialization process of developed economies of Europe and developing countries of Asia?
8. What are the challenges that the industrial sector is facing in developing countries and how they can be overcome?
9. Write short notes on the following:
   (i) Industrial policy
   (ii) Industrialization process in Great Britain
   (iii) Industrialization process in United States of America
   (iv) Industrialization process in Japan
   (v) Industrialization process in China
   (vi) Competitive industrial performance (CIP) index
   (vii) Special Industrial Economic Zone (SIEZ)

NOTES

1. Quoted from 'A Beginner's Guide to the Industrial Revolution'. For details, see http://europeanhistory.about.com/od/theindustrialrevolution/p/OverIndRev.htm (accessed on 7 February 2017).
2. See http://www.princeton.edu/~achaney/Emve/wiki100 (accessed on 26 October 2013).
3. See http://www.princeton.edu/~achaney/Emve/wiki100 (accessed on 26 October 2013).
4. See http://www.cepal.org/dmaah/noticias/paginas/5/2 (accessed on 26 August 2015).
5. The UN Committee for Industrial Development (13–31 May 1963), p. 33, quoted from http://shodhganga.inflibnet.ac.in/bitstream/10603/52875/7/07_chapter%202.pdf (accessed on 4/12/2016).
6. United Nations statement is quoted from the website 'Industry', see http://sustainabledevelopemnt.un.org/index.php?menu=223 (accessed on 12 February 2014).
7. United Nations statement is quoted from the website 'Industry', see http://sustainabledevelopemnt.un.org/index.php?menu=223 (accessed on 12 February 2014).

BIBLIOGRAPHY

Adelman, I. 'The Role of Government in Economic Development.' Working Paper No. 890, Department of Agriculture and Resource Economics and Policy, Division of Agricultural and Natural Resources, University of California, Berkeley, 1999.

Allen, G. C. *A Short Economic History of Modern Japan*. London and Basingstoke: Macmillan, 1981b.

———. *The Japanese Economy*. New York: St. Martin's Press, 1981a.

Antony, V. 'The Prospects and Growth of Small Scale Industries in India: An Overview.' *Southern Economists* 43, no. 6 (2002): 23.

Bhattacharya, B. B., and C. H. H. Rao. 'Agriculture-Industry Inter-relations: Issues of Relative Prices and Growth in the context of Public Investment.' Theme 18, 8th World Economic Congress of the International Economic Association, New Delhi, 1986.

Blumer, H. *Industrialization as an Agent of Social Change: A Critical Analysis*. New York: Aldine de Gruyter, 1990.

Bryce, M. D. *Industrial Development: A Guide for Accelerating Economic Growth*. New York: McGraw Hill, 1960.

Byrd, William A., and Lin Qingsong. 'Development Issues and Policy Choices.' In *China's Rural Industry Structure Development and Reform* edited by He Jiacheng, 112–128. Washington, DC: The World Bank, 1990.

CBN. 'The Changing Structure of the Nigerian Economy and Implications for Development.' Lagos: Realm Communication Ltd., 2000.

Chen, C. *Foreign Direct Investment in China Location Determinants, Investor Differences and Economic Impacts*. Cheltenham: Edward Elgar, 2011.

Chenery, H. B. 'The Role of Industrialization in Development Programmes.' *The American Economic Review* 45, no. 2 (1955): 40–57.

Chowdhury, K., and M. B. Chowdhury. 'Sectoral Linkages and Economic Growth in Asia: Evidence from Granger Causality Test'. *Indian Economic Journal* 42(1995): 59–75.

Cook, P., and F. Nixon. 'Finance and Small and Medium Sized Enterprises Development.' Finance and Development Research Programme Working Paper, Series no. 14, 2000.

Court, W. H. B. *The Rise of the Midland Industries, 1600–1838*. London: Oxford University Press, 1953.

Dahlman, C. 'Technological Globalization and International Competitiveness: Challenges for Developing Countries.' Industrial Development for the 21st Century: Sustainable Development Perspectives, Department of Economic and Social Affairs, United Nations: 29–84, 2007.

Dollar, D. R., M. Hallward-Driemeier, and T. Mengistate. 'Investment Climate and Firm Performance in Developing Economies'. *Economic Development and Cultural Change* 54, no. 1(2005): 1–31.

Dutta, M. 'China's Industrial Revolution: Challenges for a Macroeconomic Agenda'. *Journal of Asian Economics* 15(2005): 1169–1202.

Ewah, O. E., and Alex B. Ekeng. 'Problems and Prospects of Marketing in Developing Economies: The Nigerian Experience.' *International Journal of Business Management* 4, no. 9 (2009): 187–96.

Ghoshal, M., and S. Saxena. 'Role of Foreign Direct Investment in Indian Small Scale Industries.' *International Journal of Management, IT and Engineering* 2, no. 5 (2012): 560–74.

Hayam, Y. 'From the Megalopolis-Centred System to the Rural-Urban Balanced System for the Sustainability of Developing Economies.' Keynote Address at the Science Council of Japan Conference on Sustainability, The Foundation for Advanced Studies in International Development, Tokyo, Japan, 7–8 September 2007.

Ho, Samuel P. S. 'Economic Development and Rural Industry in South Korea and Taiwan.' *World Development* 10, no. 11 (1982): 973–90.

Hobsbawm, E. *The Age of Revolution 1789-1849*. New York: Vintage Books, 1996.

Hussain E., and S.Y. Yik. 'The Contribution of Economic Sectors to Economic Growth: The Cases of China and India.' *Research in Applied Economics* 4, no. 4 (2012): 38–53.

Jenkins, R. 'The political economy of industrialization: A comparison of Latin American and East Asian newly industrializing countries.' *Development and Change* 22 (1991): 197–231.

Kagami, M. 'The Role of Industrial Policy: Japan's Experience.' *Revista de Economia Politica* 15, no. 1 (1995): 119–33. Available at: http://www.rep.org.br/pdf/57–7.pdf (accessed on 7 March 2016).

Kalecki, M. *Essay on Developing Countries*. Sussex: Harvester Press, 1976.

Kniivila, M. 'Industrial Development and Economic Growth: Implications for Poverty Reduction and Income Inequality.' 2007. Available at: http://www.un.org/esa/sustdev/publications/industrial_development/3_1.pdf (accessed on 07 February 2014).

Krishna, K. 'Community Centred Curricula: Need of the Hour.' *Indian Journal of Marketing* 6, no. 1–2: (2003): 12–13.

Kumar, S. N. A. 'A Study of Small Scale Industries: Marketing Strategies', *TRANS Asian Journal of Marketing and Management Research* 1, no. 1 (2012): 12–20.

Kumar, R., and A. SenGupta. 'Towards a Competitive Manufacturing Sector'. In India and the Global Economy, edited by R. Kumar and A. SenGupta, pp. 187–241, 2008. New Delhi: Academic Foundation.

Lall, S., and S. Urata. *Competitiveness, FDI and Technological Activity in East Asia*. Cheltenham, UK: Edward Elgar Publishing, 2003.

Levy, B. 'Obstacles to Developing Indigenous Small and Medium Enterprises: An Empirical Assessment.' *The World Bank Review* 7, no. 1 (1993): 65–83.

Long, C., and X. Zhang. 'Cluster-Based Industrialization in China Financing and Performance.' IFPRI Discussion Paper 00937, International Food Policy Research Institute, Development Strategy and Governance Division, 2009.

Mason, M. 'Foreign Direct Investment and Japanese Economic Development, 1899–1931'. *Business and Economic History* 16(1987): 93–107.

McCormick, D. 'African Enterprise Cluster and Industrialization: Theory and Reality.' *World Development* 9 (1999): 1531–51.

Michell, T. 'Administrative Traditions and Economic Decision-Making in South Korea.' *IDS Bulletin* 15, no. 2 (1984): 32–37.

Mukherjee, S., and S. Mukerjee. 'Overview of India's Export Performance: Trends and Drivers', Working Paper No.363 (2012), Indian Institute of Management, Bangalore.

Nakizito, J., and M. B. K. Darkoh. 'Developing Countries and Incipient Industrialization: A Case Study of Enterprise Clustering and Inter-firm Relations in Small and Medium-scale Manufacturing Industries in Lobatse, Botswana'. *Journal of Social Development in Africa* 17, no. 1(2002): 19–38.

Naude, W., and A. Szirmai. 'The Importance of Manufacturing in Economic Development: Past, Present and Future Perspectives.' Working Paper Series No. 2012–040, Maastricht Economic and Social Research Institute on Innovation and Technology (UNU-MERIT), 2012. Available at: http://www.merit.unu.edu (accessed on 6 February 2014).

OECD. *Foreign Direct Investment for Development Maximising Benefits Minimizing Costs*. Paris: OECD, 2002.

———. 'OECD Review of Innovation Policy.' China, Synthesis Report, Paris, OECD, 2007.

Ogechukww, A. D., J. S. Oboreh, F. Umukora, and A. V. Uche. 'Small and Medium Scale Enterprises (SMES) in Nigeria the Marketing Interface'. *Global Journal of Management and Business Research Marketing* 13, no. 9(2013): 1–13.

Patunru, A. A., N. McCulloch, and C. V. Luebke. 'A Tale of Two Cities: The Political Economy of Local Investment Climate in Solo and Manado, Indonesia.' IDS Working Paper 338, Institute of Development Studies, University of Sussex, 2009.

Paul, V. 'Rural Industrial Estate: A Viable Remedy to Regional Disparities in India.' *Industrial Economist*, fortnightly (29 September 2004): 10.

Peck, M. J., and S. Tamura. 'Technology'. In *Asia's New Giant*, edited by H. Patrick and R. Henry, Washington, D.C. pp. 525–85, 1976.

Peng, S. 'Comparing Industrialization between Japan and China: Why China Chose a Different Way.' Lund University, School of Economics and Management, 2010.

Peters, M. J., R. R. Monson, W. A. Burgess, and L. J. Fire. 'Occupational Disease in the Rubber Industry.' *Environmental Health Perspectives* 17 (1976): 31–34.

Pollard, S. *Typology of Industrialization Processes in the Nineteenth Century*. Switzerland: Harwood Academic Publisher, 1990.

Qi, D. Z. W., and L. Zhou. 'Relations between Technical Innovation and New-Type Industrialization.' (originally written in Chinese) *Science and Technology Management Research*, 11 (2006).

Rakesh, Mohan. 'Finance for Industrial Growth'. *Reserve Bank of India Bulletin*, March 2004, 319–39, see also http://www.rakeshmohan.com/docs/RBIBulletinMarch2004.pdf (accessed on 5 December 2016).

Rangarajan, C. 'Agricultural Growth and Industrial Performance in India.' Research Report 33, International Food Policy Research Institute, October 1982.

Ranis, G., and F. Stewart. 'Rural Non-Agricultural Activities in Development Theories and Application.' *Journal of Development Economics* 40 no. 1 (1993): 75–101.

Rondinelli, D. A. 'Decentralization and Development.' In *International Development Governance*, edited by A. S. Huque and H. Zafarullah, 391–403. New York: Taylor and Francis, 2006.

Sakoh, K. 'Japanese Economic Success: Industrial Policy or Free Market?' *Cato Journal* 4, no. 2 (1984): 521–48. Available at: http://object.cato.org/sites/cato.org/files/serials/... (accessed on 7 March 2016).

Snyman, H. A., D. Kennon, C. S. L. Schutte, and K. Von Leipzing. 'Formulating a Strategic Framework to Promote SME Development.' SIIE25 Proceedings, Stellenbosch, 9–11 July 2013.

Summers, L. 'The Rise of Asia and the Global Economy.' *Research Monitor* Special Issue (2007): 4–5.

Sundar, K., and T. Srinivasan. 'Rural Industrialization: Challenges and Proposition'. *Journal of Social Science* 20, no. 1(2009): 23–29.

Sutcliffe, R. B. *Industry and Underdevelopment*. London: Addison-Wesley, 1971.

Tanimoto, M. 'The Role of Tradition in Japan's Industrialization: A Perspective of Indigenous Development'. *Japanese Studies in Economic and Social History* 2, 2004. Also see http://www.cirje.e.u-tokyo.ac.jp/research/dp/2004/2004cf275.pdf (accessed on 5 December 2016).

Tilly, R. H. 'Industrialization as a Historical Process', 2010. Available at: http://ieg-ego.eu/en/threads/backgrounds/industrialization/richard-h-tilly-industrialization-as-an-historical-process (accessed on 2 December 2016).

Tiwari, R. R. 'Child Labour in Footwear Industry: Possible Occupation Health Hazards.' *Indian Journal of Occupational & Environmental Medicine* 9, no. 1 (2005): 7–9.

Tsai, W. 'Social Changes under the Impacts of Economic Transformation in Taiwan: From Industrialization to Modernization during the Post-World War II Era.' *Studies in Comparative International Development* 24, no. 2 (Summer 1989): 24–41.

UNIDO. 'Industrial Development Report 2003.' United Nations Industrial Development Organization, United Nations Publications, 2003.

———. 'Industrial Development Report 2007.' United Nations Industrial Development Organization, United Nations Publications, 2007.

———. 'Industrial Development Report 2009.' United Nations Industrial Development Organization, United Nations Publications, 2009.

———. 'Industrial Development Report 2011.' United Nations Industrial Development Organization, United Nations Publications, 2011.

World Bank. *Doing Business in 2005, IFC and World Bank*, 2005. Washington DC: Oxford University Press.

———. 'Foreign Direct Investment – The China Story.' The World Bank, 2010. Available at: http://www.worldbank.org/en/news/features/2010/07 (accessed on 29 December 2013).

Yeoh, C., and W. H. P. Ngee. 'State-led Trans-border Industrialization in Asia: A Note on Singapore's Manufacturing Enclaves in Vietnam and China'. *International Review of Business Research* Papers 3, no. 5(2007): 456–71.

Yingming, Z. *Analysis of Industrial Cluster in China*. New York: CRS Press, Taylor & Francis Group, 2010.

Zhang, Z. 'Rural Industrialization in China: From Backward Furnaces to Township and Village Enterprises.' *East Asia: An International Quarterly* 17, no. 3 (1999): 61–87.

8 Service Sector and Development

Historically, service industries have been at the heart of economic growth, stimulating and facilitating production for the market rather than simply for self-sufficiency.

—Riddle (1986)

Productivity and employment growth are highly dependent on the success of service industries and services are strong driver of recent economic growth.

—Tamura et al. (2005)

In the global World, service sector has become the lifeline of economic development of both the developed and developing countries. In most of the developed economies and many of the developing economies, the performance of service sector has outstripped the performance of both agriculture and industry sectors in terms of its contribution to economic growth. In the developing countries in particular, its contribution to employment is significantly higher as compared to agriculture and industrial sectors. However, in many of developing countries, its contribution to GDP is significantly higher as compared to the contribution of primary and secondary sectors; yet its role in provisioning employment is too low. In a nutshell, it is one of the most scintillating sectors in recent times both in developed and developing countries. In other words, it can be emphatically said that the global world is driven by service sector.

Contribution of service sector in the effective functioning of agriculture and industrial sectors is increasing day by day. Many services are key inputs to all or most of the businesses, e.g. infrastructure services such as energy, telecommunications and transportation; financial services, which facilitate transactions and provide access to finance for investment; health and education services, which contribute to a healthy, well-trained workforce; and legal and accountancy services, which are part of the institutional framework required to underpin a healthy market economy (Cali, Ellis and Velde 2008).

Considering its importance in the global scenario, the opening the economy to FDI in service sector has become a heated debate among the economists, politicians and the policy-makers of developing countries of Asia, Africa and Latin America. For example in India, there is lack of consensus among political parties regarding opening up of all sub-sectors of the service sector to FDIs. Many political parties in India have opposed opening up FDIs to retail business sector. There is a little doubt that the service industries will remain in the forefront of economic controversy in the foreseeable future (Lee 1994). Miles and Boden (2000) described services as the 'Cinderella Sector' largely ignored by economists, industrial researchers and students of innovations. They have argued that as the share of services in national economies continues to grow and the linkage between

Table 8.2 *Employment in Service Sector of Selected Countries*

Country	Percentage
Australia	70 (2013)
Belgium	77 (2014)
China	47 (2011)
India	29 (2013)
Japan	69 (2013)
Pakistan	34 (2014)
Sri Lanka	43 (2014)
Singapore	71 (2014)
United Kingdom	79 (2014)

Source: http://data.worldbank.org/indicator/SL.SRV.EMPL.ZS (accessed on 20 May 2016).
Note: Figures in parentheses show year.

women prefer service sector employment. It is pertinent to mention here that service sector has provided employment opportunity to more number of women in both developed and developing countries. The number of women workforce employed in the education, health, hotel, tourism, IT, banking and insurance service sectors is on the increase. Fuchs (1968) was of the view that a significant proportion of the increase in service sector employment is due to the increased labour market participation of women, the effect being driven by both income and especially substitutions effects of the choice between home and market work. According to Ramaswamy and Agrawal (2012), service sector has turned out to be a boon for female workers. Both young and middle-aged female workers increased their share of regular jobs. However, there is greater duality in service sector in terms of informality and wage inequality.

3. Services sector provides stimulant to growth of services in other sectors such as agriculture, industrial sector and also promotes social development. The financial services such as bank and insurance services provide credit facilities for the growth of entrepreneurship in agriculture and industrial sectors. The health service sector provides opportunities to the medical and paramedical persons, such as pharmacists, nurses, auxiliary health workers, physiotherapists, dentistry and so on, job opportunities in government-, private- and NGO-managed organizations. Education service sector is critical to human resources development in almost all sectors. It contributes to t social development in developing countries. Tourism service sector does not only provide employment to skilled, semi-skilled and unskilled personnel but also promotes cultural development of the nation states.
4. Service sector is an enabler and promoter of trade and balance of payment. In globalized world, it is not possible for any country to develop and prosper without a strong and vibrant service sector. Over the period of time, there has been an expansion of the share of commercial services in world export of goods and services. More than 40% of world trade in services is carried on between the major trades—the United States of America, the European Union and Japan (Maurer and Chauvete 2002). Developing countries are still poor performers in world trade in services.

However, the contribution of developing countries in trade services is gradually increasing. Tourism is the biggest export service sector in many low-income developing countries (OECD 2008).

5. Service sector provides both inputs and outputs to the nations to achieve Sustainable Development Goals (SDGs). The public sector laid service sectors i.e. health and education institutions are playing vital role in the achievement of Millennium Development Goals (MDGs) and SDGs of developing countries. Both the goals are aimed at reducing income poverty, hunger and disease and provision of adequate shelter and safe drinking water along with promoting gender equity, health, education and environmental sustainability. Financial services sector helps in poverty reduction, development and improvement of health, education and gender equity, thereby helping the nation to achieve MDGs (Claessens and Feijen 2006). As per UNCDF (2013), financial services for the poor would help a nation to achieve the goal of development in the following ways:
   (i) Microfinance can support entrepreneurship, leading to higher income.
   (ii) Savings, credit and other financial services can empower women and help poor families pay school costs.
   (iii) They enable poor families to respond to health concerns.
   (iv) With the help of financial services, poor families can afford clean water and sanitation technology.
6. Energy is one of the important requisite for technological transformation and an ingredient to usher structural changes in the economy. Energy sector, such as department of electricity, oil and coal, thermal, hydropower and so on, run by the government as well as private sectors employs a large number of population in rural and urban areas. Affordable and clean energy is a prerequisite for sustainable development. Energy crisis has also linkages with the development crisis as well. United Nations (2010) suggests that energy services sector helps to attain development goals in following ways:
   (i) Human and productive development of women in many cases depends on access to energy.
   (ii) In urban areas, access to electricity has been identified as one of the key factors, determining the state of health of children and infants.
   (iii) Energy acts as a prerequisite for overcoming poverty.
7. Tourism is a key service sector of many developed and developing countries. The UN World Tourism Organization (UNWTO) believes that poverty, hunger, gender inequality and environmental degradation can be all alleviated through the sustainable development of tourism. Tourism generates wealth and can play a significant role in the achievement of the development goals such as eradication of poverty, gender equality, environmental sustainability and global partnership for development. UNWTO member countries put emphasis on tourism, especially in terms of its contribution to employment and generating foreign exchange. According to UNWTO, receipts from tourism have more than doubled in the past 15 years to 700 billion US dollars, and tourist arrivals nearly doubled to 800 million in 2005. The World Tourism and Travel Council (WTTC) found that tourism contributes 15% to GDP and 16% to employment in the Caribbean region. Tourism sector employs a large number of semi-skilled and casual workers. The small- and medium-size enterprises involved in the tourism sector provides immense

employment opportunities to women. This helps to raise the household per capita income of a number of families. Ecotourism and rural tourism in recent years have created job opportunities in the semi-urban and rural areas, thus helped in the reduction of poverty, illiteracy and ill health. The ecotourism and religious tourism in the Uttarakhand (India) is a great source of self-employment for many families. Many families are earning their livelihood from this profession in the Himalayan states of Himachal Pradesh and Uttarakhand.

According to OECD (2008), tourism offers labour-intensive and small-scale opportunities compared with other non-agricultural activities, employing semi-skilled and casual workers, small- and medium-sized enterprises and a high proportion of women, and providing opportunities for self-employment. Tourism contributes a large percentage of GDP of the Himalayan region. A large number of people are employed in the hotel and tourism industries in these states. Tour and travel services, tourist guides, travel agents and so on are on the rise nationally as well as internationally after the globalization. Many institutions in various countries are offering courses on travel and tourism. Oversees Development Institute (ODI; 2008) has recognized tourism as the biggest export service sector in many low-income developing countries.

8. ICT services can effectively help the developing nations to achieve development goals by creating economic opportunities and contributing to poverty reduction and managing the process of delivery of basic health and education services at low cost by enhancing coverage in both these social sectors. Evidence suggests that a well-developed ICT sector contributes to faster growth and better economic performance at the firm level because it helps actors in all the related activities to perform efficiently. ICT holds tremendous promise as an enabler of social and economic development. ICT can be increasingly used to deliver e-health care services to patients in remote areas where health care services are neither available nor accessible. ICT is a big concomitant sector to all other sectors such as banking and insurance, education, tourism, wholesale and retail business, transport and communication and so on.
9. Developing countries where the health status is very low, there is immense potential of health service sector to grow. Health sector in the organized and unorganized sector employs a large number of skilled, semi-skilled and unskilled people. Because of the rise in the demand for health care services, the opening of health and medical care education and training institutions is on the rise in developing countries. The immigration of quality health personnel from developing countries to the developed countries has strengthened household economy of many families in a few states of India. One of the illustrious examples is Kerala, where the migration of nursing personnel from Kerala to the gulf countries has enhanced the quality of life of the families in rural areas through remittances. ODI has noted that an efficient and equitable health services sector is not only a development objective per se, but it is also a fundamental driver of growth and poverty reduction at the macro and micro level (Cali et al. 2008). The health care sector as an industry is expanding rapidly in the third world countries because of low health status. The public, private and FDI investment in health sector is on the rise. It comprises hospital services, diagnostic services, diagnostic products, medical

technological services, clinical trial services, clinical research organizations, health and medical training and research organizations and medicine stores.

10. As far as education sector is concerned, ICTs are increasingly being used as a tool to supplement and complement the curricula and teaching–learning pedagogy and have opened new opportunities for skill training. Through education, populations are well-equipped to contribute to and participate in the process of social and economic development. The education–employment link has resulted in numerous governmental initiatives aimed at promoting human capital development. ICT, as the chief economic driver in the present era, is one of the key factors for the rise in service industry (Sapprasert 2007). OECD (2000) shows that services are major users and adopters of new technologies; especially, ICT is seen as the chief enabler of their enormous improvement. It has also further observe that some service sectors such as the health, education, water and sanitation sectors are also directly relevant to achieving social development objectives OECD (2008).
11. People employed in the service sector are having higher per capita income than their counter parts employed in the agriculture sector. Certain sectors of the service sector, i.e. IT, banking and insurances, comparatively pay more salaries to their employees in this globalized era. A study on the OECD economies reveals that, relative to the industrial sector, the service sector is characterized by higher earnings, longer average job tenure and higher job satisfaction (OECD 2001). People engaged in service sectors are financially empowered to afford better quality of life necessities compared to other two sectors.
12. In developing countries, real estate is a booming service sector, which is providing both regular and casual employment to the skilled, semi-skilled and unskilled person in large number. In the transitional economies, largely focusing on infrastructure development, the real estate will be one of the most growing sector days to come. Its contribution to the GDP will be on the rise. Thus, contribution of real estate service sector in the establishment of infrastructure for the agriculture as well as industry sector is noteworthy in both developed and developing countries. In the EU countries, real estate in all its forms accounts for nearly 20% of economic activity and directly employs over four million people.[1] Real estate has forward and backward linkages with more than 250 different sectors; it is the second largest employer generator in India after agriculture.[2] According to the Economic Survey 2014–15, real estate sector constituted 7.8% of India's GDP in 2013–14. Business and society cannot meaningfully function without the real estate services of residential complexes, commercial properties, including provision of offices, shops, factories and many other forms of real estate. Well-designed real estate architectural activities can make a city smart.
13. Business Process Outsourcing (BPO) services in many developing countries are providing employment to large number of people particularly women. BPO, customarily, refers to transaction processing, technical support, email-based support services and so on. The Information technology enabled services-business process outsourcing (ITES-BPO) sector contributed 6.4% of GDP, 14% of India's exports and 10% of all service sector revenues in 2010–11 (Subramanian and Arimohan 2014). ITES-BPO has created an enabling environment for innovation in the service sector. NASSCOM has remarked that this industry has enhanced India's credibility as a

business destination ad put India on the global map.[3] EXIM Bank (2012) has remarked that, in India, within service sector, ITES and the BPO segments have emerged as the anchors of services export growth, and therefore sustaining and developing its competitiveness is important for the economy as a whole.

The contribution of services sector to the economic growth and development is on the rise in both developed and developing countries. Of the late in developing countries, it has been also realized that an effective, efficient and sustainable service sector can provide viable support to the GDP of their economies and promote sustainable development. According to World Bank, service sector requires more human capital as against natural capital, and building up human capital may help global development become more environmentally and socially sustainable.[4] Service sector helps to promote the efficiency of both agriculture and manufacturing sectors through value additions. Value addition to these two sectors, i.e. primary and secondary sectors, through service sector will help to promote sustainable economic development of an economy. The immense contribution of service sector towards economic growth and development in the developed economies of America and Europe foretells the role of service sector in sustainable development.

ISSUES AND CHALLENGES OF SERVICE SECTOR

Service sector over the period of time has produced substantial effect on the development of the developed as well as developing economies. However, this sector still faces a lot of challenges in the developing economies and a few important issues and challenges are discussed below.

The biggest issue and challenge that service sector is facing is the lack of innovation. United Nations (2011) has remarked that

> A well performing service sector is increasingly seen as a key dimension of an effective innovation system. However, innovation policies and strategies relating to the services sector are less developed than those targeting manufacturing. The recognition of the importance of a dynamic services sector has been accompanied by efforts to ensure that the promotion of innovation in services is duly acknowledged in innovation policies.

Lack of dynamism in innovation in service sector makes services obsolete and lethargic. Innovation includes new products, new processes, and new forms of organization, new markets, and new sources of inputs to production (Schumpeter 1939). Innovation is an essential element of service sector in order to make them effective and efficient in the global market. However, its role in the service sector has been underappreciated (Sheehan 2006). The employability of service sector in the developed countries is higher as compared to developing countries because of innovation and persistent endeavour to do better in the job. Therefore, formulation of appropriate education policy with a focus on human resource development will have a significant effect on service-sector innovation as the sector has a high dependence on skilled manpower.

R&D is a fundamental requisite of service sector. Not only science and technology but other service sector industries, like banking, insurance, capital market, communication technology and so on, also require research inputs for the enhancement of effectiveness in their service delivery. Therefore, it is important to secure the supply of the skilled labour, including manual and knowledge-based skills, by keeping the research and education system closely attached to the needs of the service sector (Kuusisto 2008). Kuusisto (2008) while talking in the context of European economy said that R&D and innovation in services are necessary for the growth and prosperity of the European economy.

Service sector, particularly in developing countries, is facing the challenge of quality syndrome. Effective measurement and analysis of service quality is an essential first step in its improvement (Gupta 2012), as the service quality is ultimately evaluated in the minds of the customer (Lehtinen and Lehtinen 1982; Parasuraman, Zeithal and Berry 1988). Service quality depends on the criteria as to how well the service delivered matches to the expectations of the customers. Price of service output depends on the quality of product produced by the service sector. However, the oversupply of services in lieu of earning more and more has reduced the quality of services. Poor quality of health services may not be effective to reduce morbidity and mortality rate. In a similar vein, poor quality of educational services will not improve the employability of the manpower trained by different educational institutions. The importance of quality aspect is growing in service sector. Despite that there are many quality-related success stories of the service sector. India has emerged as the world's leading information and communication technology-business process outsourcing (ICT-BPO) exporter, and Philippines is also a major ICT-BPO hub (Noland 2012). The quality improvement in the service sector will not only promote export but also lead to the migration of skilled manpower, and in return will get remittances back home.

Manpower development is a concern as well as a challenge for the service sector. In the recent years, human resources development in the service industry has started to draw public attention from the perspective of improving productivity and promoting industries that may create new jobs (Fujimoto 2011). Services sector tends to require more human capital than natural capital as required by the agriculture and industrial sectors. With the proliferation of service sector, the demand for skilled manpower has grown considerably. As a result, demand has grown for educated and skilled manpower, thereby promoting countries to invest more in education.

The casualization of employment in the service sector is a cause of concern in developing countries. Employment created in majority of service sector is informal in nature, without any job security and social security. It has excited the youth and at the same time, has created a lot of frustration among many. Wage differences and terms of employment vary between the skilled and unskilled manpower employed in the service sector. Cases of exploitation of women in the service sector industries in developing countries are frequent in the news. OECD (1996 and 1999) has documented that with the growth of service sector, in many countries, the incidence of part-time and temporary work has risen over time. In addition, there has been a decline in job stability in some other countries (OECD 1997). A few countries have also experienced a long-run rise in earning inequality, most notably the United States (OECD 1996).

Performance measurement in the service sector is a challenge. Existence of both quantitative and qualitative aspects makes the assessment of the performance of the service sector difficult. It is comparatively easier to measure the performance of agriculture and manufacturing sectors than that of the service sector. Li and Prescott (2009) have remarked that productivity measurement in services is difficult because it is hard to standardize the inputs and outputs which are highly heterogeneous. On the other hand, Tyagi and Gupta (2008) were of the opinion that the advantages of implementing a performance measurement system in services include the presence of a robust decision support system for managers, timelines of relevant information, improved quality of information for decision-making, more effective and clear communication among various stakeholders and the alignment of goals. However, formulation and implementation of performance index of service sector will not only create competitiveness among the sub-sectors of the service sector but will enable them to implement corrective measures to improve their performances.

Although FDI in the service sector in developing countries is on the rise, attracting FDIs in all sub-sectors of the service sector is an issue in developing countries. Developing countries, because of lack of political will power and consensus among the political parties, have prevented the FDIs inflow to a few service sectors only. For instance, in India, there is lack of consensus among the political parties on FDI in retail business. The most conservative attitude towards FDIs in service sector with a view that it will deeply affect the small businessmen has to overcome through discussion and dialogue. Noland (2012) was of the view that domestic political considerations also reinforce the imperative to strengthen the service sector.

Formulation of well-thought out service sector policy like that of agriculture policy and industrial policy is a big challenge for developing countries. The aim of this policy should be to provide a road map of the service sector and its role in economic growth, employment creation and reduction of poverty and inequality in the country. The issues in front of the service sector policy of a developing country are quality of service, employment potential, export potential and economic growth rate enhancement. As there are many players in the service sectors, i.e. government, semi-government organizations, private and corporate sectors, non-governmental organizations, civil society organizations, and so on, the regulatory mechanism on the functioning of various service sectors is important for raising the quality of service sector, enhancement of growth rate, providing quality services to the economy and raise the quality of life of the people. Nodal (2012) was of the view that government can help laying the foundation for a vibrant service sector through both policy reform and investments in physical infrastructure and human capital. Ironically, in a country like India where service sector is an emerging sector, there is no Ministry of Service Sector either at the centre or at the state level to coordinate the activities and performance data of various sub-sectors of the service sector.

MEASURES TO PROMOTE SERVICE SECTOR

1. It is required to take measures to strengthen service sector for the development of human resources and generation of employment both within and outside the country. Governments of developing countries must allocate resources in their national as well as provincial budgets for the establishment of quality education institutions for the promotion of service sector activities like health and nursing, tourism, IT, insurance, ICT-BPO, postal services and so on. Tamura and others (2005) have remarked that the innovation potential in the service sectors heavily depends on its human capital assets; labour costs of the service sectors could be focused on particularly when governments plan fiscal instruments for fostering innovative activities. For instance, New Zealand has a specific policy to foster innovation across the service sector by strengthening linkages with government research laboratories (Tamura and Others 2005).

2. Government should formulate a national policy on service sector for the development of the service sector in the economy. The role of private and corporate sectors, individual entrepreneurs and the governments must be clearly spelled out. Moreover, it must be an integrated policy for various service sectors such as education, health, insurance, banking, tourism, ICT and so on. The policy paper for India's services sector emphasized on the policy issues to be included such as FDIs, disinvestment, tariff and tax issues, credit and finance, domestic regulation, subsidies and market access issues (Prasad and Sathish 2010). The policy paper also emphasized that immediate and time-bound reforms in the service sector could not only help in attaining India's targeted growth rates but also give a flip to growth and exports of service-led economy.
3. Monetary and fiscal policy supportive environment for the service sector will be helpful to strengthen and improve the performance of the service sector. The liberal interest rate policy and tax concession to the new entrepreneurs entering into the service sector activities will build up their confidence. One of the illustrious examples is the recently declared 'stand up and start up' programme by the government of India, which proposes to provide positive investment environment to the new entrepreneurs.

The Start-up Plan of Government of India

Here are the 19 plans have designed for the start-up programme:

1. Self-certification

Start-ups will adopt self-certification to reduce the regulatory liabilities. The self-certification will apply to laws including payment of gratuity, labour contract, provident fund management, water and air pollution acts.

2. Start-up India hub

An all-India hub will be created as a single contact point for start-up foundations in India, which will help the entrepreneurs to exchange knowledge and access financial aid.

3. Register through app

An online portal, in the shape of a mobile application, will be launched to help start-up founders to easily register. The app is scheduled to be launched on April 1.

4. Patent protection

A fast-track system for patent examination at lower costs is being conceptualised by the central government. The system will promote awareness and adoption of the Intellectual Property Rights (IPRs) by the start-up foundations.

5. ₹10,000 crore fund

The government will develop a fund with an initial corpus of ₹2,500 crore and a total corpus of ₹10,000 crore over four years, to support upcoming start-up enterprises. The Life Insurance Corporation of India will play a major role in developing this corpus. A committee of private professionals selected from the start-up industry will manage the fund.

6. National Credit Guarantee Trust Company
A National Credit Guarantee Trust Company (NCGTC) is being conceptualised with a budget of ₹500 crore per year for the next four years to support the flow of funds to start-ups.

7. No Capital Gains Tax
At present, investments by venture capital funds are exempt from the Capital Gains Tax. The same policy is being implemented on primary-level investments in start-ups.

8. No Income Tax for three years
Start-ups would not pay Income Tax for three years. This policy would revolutionize the pace with which start-ups would grow in the future.

9. Tax exemption for investments of higher value
In case of an investment of higher value than the market price, it will be exempt from paying tax.

10. Building entrepreneurs
Innovation-related study plans for students in over 5 lakh schools. Besides, there will also be an annual incubator grand challenge to develop world class incubators.

11. Atal Innovation Mission
The Atal Innovation Mission will be launched to boost innovation and encourage talented youths.

12. Setting up incubators
A private-public partnership model is being considered for 35 new incubators and 31 innovation centres at national institutes.

13. Research parks
The government plans to set up seven new research parks, including six in the Indian Institute of Technology campuses and one in the Indian Institute of Science campus, with an investment of ₹100 crore each.

14. Entrepreneurship in biotechnology
The government will further establish five new biotech clusters, 50 new bio incubators, 150 technology transfer offices and 20 bio-connect offices in the country.

15. Dedicated programmes in schools
The government will introduce innovation-related programmes for students in over 5 lakh schools.

16. Legal support
A panel of facilitators will provide legal support and assistance in submitting patent applications and other official documents.

17. Rebate
A rebate amount of 80% of the total value will be provided to the entrepreneurs on filing patent applications.

18. Easy rules
Norms of public procurement and rules of trading have been simplified for the start-ups.

19. Faster exit

If a start-up fails, the government will also assist the entrepreneurs to find suitable solutions for their problems. If they fail again, the government will provide an easy way out.

Source: http://indiatoday.intoday.in/education/story/start-up-india-stand-up-india/1/53128.html (accessed on 1 April 2016).

4. Promoting competition in the service sector is also an important factor for strengthening services sector. It will improve the quality of services provided. Service sector, like education, health, baking, insurances, telecommunication, IT, and so on, has improved the quality of services because of competition between the public and private sector and also competition among the private sector entrepreneurs. The OECD Economic Surveys of Japan 2008 has envisaged that accelerating production growth in services requires strengthening competition and making Japan more open to international trade and FDI inflows. Pilat (2005) has envisaged that regulatory reform of markets for transport, communication, finance and certain business services, combined with a reduction in international barriers to trade and investment in services, have opened up services markets that were previously sheltered from competition.
5. As SMEs are the backbone of service sector in most of developing countries, there is a need for strengthening service sector under SMEs. Many developed countries have strengthened the services provided by SMEs in various sectors. Danish action plan for e-commerce took a consultancy and training initiative for e-commerce to 60 SMEs. Japan also supports IT-related SMEs by providing financial support for R&D. In developing countries, the department of SME has to prepare strategies for the training and R&D programme in order to improve the service delivery in the SMEs.
6. Labour market reform is one of the important areas to strengthen the functioning of the service sector in developing countries. Low wage rate and lack of medical and job security especially for those who are working with the individual entrepreneurs in the unorganized sector are matter of concern for the service sector. Implementation of minimum wage and job and social security issues in the service sector will go a long way to promote service sector. It will be helpful to raise the contribution of service sector to the economic growth and development.
7. Clustering and networking are other concerned areas and if these areas are strengthened and created in a systematic manner, they will enhance the efficiency of the services sector. Like the industrial sector corridors, the services sector corridors have to be created at the cluster level. The main benefit of this is that it will foster networking among the various services sector functioning in the cluster. It will lower the cost of innovation, training and R&D. To cite an example, Ireland's policy document 'Opportunities for Ireland's High-Technology Internationally Traded Services Sector to 2007' (ITS 2000) has a key element of its strategy for development of a series of regional infrastructure initiatives or technology hubs known as 'web works' to facilitate networking among companies and encourage mutual learning and information sharing (Martin 2001).

8. The service sector standard setting and establishment of powerful and effective regulatory mechanism will be helpful to improve the quality of services. It would also strengthen the functioning of the services sector. It is very essential in developing countries where the quality of service sector has been questioned many a time. The European Committee for Standardization has developed a work programme for service standards that cover domains related to maintenance, transport, logistic and services, tourism, postal services, facilities management, translation services and funeral services (Tamura et al. 2005). Danish Standards Association has explored ways of adopting ISO 9001 standard to various services industry such as child care, home care, health care, dentistry, social services, hospital care and design (Tamura et al. 2005).
9. More and more FDI inflows to the service sector in developing countries will strengthen service sector in these countries. Besides, Diasporas need to invest their remittances for the proliferation of service sector in their home country. As reciprocation, the country also has to try to create congenial atmosphere for FDI inflow and remittances investment in service sector. The government of India has promoted FDIs in many service sectors such as banking, insurances and even in retail business. The OECD Economic Surveys of Japan 2008 on enhancing the productivity of service sector in Japan has envisaged that accelerating productivity growth in services requires strengthening competition and making Japan more open to international trade and FDI inflow.
10. Political will power across the party line to pass legislative measures on economic reform is very important for the formulation and implementation of liberal policy for the inflow of foreign investment to the service sector. Lack of consensus among various political parties with regard to FDIs in various service sectors has delayed the opening of the economy to FDIs in various sectors. Vij (2003) was of the view that a strong political will is required to attract more FDI inflow in various sector industries.
11. Good governance is an important supporting factor for proliferation of service sector in an economy. Corruption and asking for kickbacks for opening of the business and service sector industries, settlement of tax and other problems have dissuades many to opt for service sector business. Good governance is one of the important reasons for the proliferation of service sector in the developed countries. Many developed countries like United States of America have offered a lot of employment to the migrant population in the service sector.
12. Quality educational and training institutions are vital for the creation of quality manpower for the effective handling of service sector activities. Good quality doctor and nurses are required for health service sector, quality engineers are important for IT sector and well-qualified management personnel are required for the management of hotel and tourism service sector, to name a few among many. Greater emphasis on technology diffusion, to help spread innovative approaches thought the highly fragmented service sector, could also enable advances in productivity (Alic 2001).
13. As over the period to time, role and employment of women in the service sector is on the rise. Therefore, key issues like women safety and security, harassment in the office, provision of proper job conditions, health security, maternity benefit issues

and social security issues from the gender perspective must be taken into consideration by developing countries. Appropriate gender-sensitive social sector development will enhance the contribution of women not only to the service sector but also to the GDP of the countries.

14. There is a need for investment in R&D in service sector. Innovations in service sector must be encouraged like that of the manufacturing sector. As United Nations (2011) has envisaged that a well-performing service sector increasingly requires an effective innovation system.
15. The creation of Department of NRI Affairs and constitution of NRI Commission by the Punjab Government are illustrious examples of proactive role of the State to promote NRI investment and contribution of NRIs to the development of the State. This will woo NRI Punjabis to invest back home. The construction of beautiful houses in the rural areas of Punjab by the Punjabi NRIs staying abroad shows the contribution of NRIs to the socio-economic development of rural Punjab. The similar kind of initiatives need to be taken by other states.

SUMMARY

The role of service sector and the contribution of service sector towards economic growth are rising in developed as well as in developing countries. In the developed countries, a large percentage of population is employed in service sector; however, the employment in the service sector in developing countries is not sanguine. Besides, in advanced economies, the performance of the primary and secondary sectors are directly dependent on the growth of services like banking, insurance, stock market, trade, commerce, tourism and so on. Because of the predominance of informal sector in the developing economies, the employment and livelihood of the people employed in the informal service sector is low as compared to the developed economies. The service sector is also lacking adequate investment and quality manpower. However, service sector has a lot of potential to provide employment and contribute significantly to economic growth rate. An appropriate service sector policy and service sector reform is *sine qua non* for the service sector of developing countries. For the development of service sector, development of agriculture and industry sectors is quite essential; otherwise the service sector will not experience growth in developing countries.

Keywords: Cinderella sector, classification of services, ICT sector, millennium development goals (MDGs), financial services.

REVIEW QUESTIONS

1. What is service sector? Explain the role of service sector in the economic growth and development of the developed as well as developing countries.
2. Classify service sector activities. Discuss which service sector activities are important for the socio-economic development of developing countries.

3. What are the various issues associated with the service sector in developing countries? What steps are required to overcome those issues?
4. What are various challenges faced by the service sector in developing countries? Explain in detail.
5. Write short notes on the following:
   (i) Classification of service sector
   (ii) IT sector as an important service sector in the globalized world
   (iii) Women in the service sector

NOTES

1. See http://www.epra.com/media/Real_estate_in_the_real_economy_-_EPRA_INREV_report_1353577808132.PDF (accessed on 2 April 2016).
2. See http://www.kpmg.com/IN/en/services/Tax/uni... (accessed on 02 April 2016).
3. See http://www.worldbank.org/depweb/beyond/bey... (accessed on 31 March 2016).
4. See http://www.eximbankindia.in/sites/default/files... (accessed on 2 April 2016).

BIBLIOGRAPHY

Alic, J. 'Postindustrial Technology Policy.' *Research Policy* 30 (2001): 873–89.

Ansari, M. I. 'Explaining the Service Sector Growth: An Empirical Study of India, Pakistan and Sri Lanka.' *Journal of Asian Economics* 6, no. 2 (1995): 223–46.

Busari, D. T. 'Service Sector as an Engineer of Growth: A Case of the ECOWAS Sub-Region.' United Nations African Institute for Economic Development and Planning (UNIDEP), Dakar, Senegal, 2007. Available at: www.unidep.org/Release3/conferences/Afea_2007/IDEP-AFEA-07--05.pdf

Cali, M., K. Ellis and D. Willem te Velde. 'The Contribution of Services to Development and the Role of Trade Liberalization and Regulation.' Working Paper 298, Oversees Development Institute, London, 2008.

Chanda, R. *Globalization of Services: India's opportunities and Constraints*. New Delhi: Oxford University Press, 2002.

Claessens, S., and E. Feijen. 'Financial Sector Development and the Millennium Development Goals.' IBRD/World Bank, 2006.

D'Agostino, A., R. Serafin, and M. Ward-Warmedinger. 'Sectoral Explanations of Employment in Europe, The Role of Services.' Working Paper Series No. 625, European Central Bank, Germany, 2006.

EXIM Bank. 'Export of Services and Offshore Outsourcing: An Empirical Investigation in the Indian Context.' Occasional Paper No. 156, 2012. Available at: http://www.eximbankindia.in/sites/default/files... (accessed on 2 April 2016).

Fuchs, V. R. *The Service Economy*. New York and London: Cambodia University Press, 1968.

Fujimoto, M. 'Human Resources Development at Companies in the Service Industries.' *Japan Labour Review* 18, no.1 (2011): 125–49.

Gordan, J., and P. Gupta. 'Understand India's Services Revolution.' Paper Prepared for the IMF-NCAER Conference on A Tale of Two Giants: India's and China's Experience with Reform, New Delhi, 14–16 November 2003.

Griliches, Zvi, ed. *Output Measurement in the Service Sectors, NBER Studies in Income and Wealth*, vol. 56. Chicago: University of Chicago Press, 1992.

Gupta, A. K. 'Growth and Challenges in Service Sector: Literature Review, Classification and Direction for Future Research.' *International Journal of Management & Business Studies* 2, no. 2 (2012): 55–58.

Kuusisto, J. 'R&D in Service-Review and Case Studies.' Paper Submitted for RESI and R&U in Services Working Group, D G Research, European Commission, 1 February 2008.

Lee, C. H. 'The Service Industries.' In *The Economic History of Britain Since 1700, Volume 2: —117–44*, edited by P. Floud and D. McCloskey. Cambridge: Cambridge University Press,1994.

Lehtinen, U., and J. R. Lehtinen. 'Service Quality: A Study of Quality Dimensions.' Working Paper, Service Management Institute, Helsinki, 1982.

Li, X., and D. Prescott. 'Measuring Productivity in Service Sector.' University of Guelph, 2009. Available at: http://cthrc.ca/~/media/Files/CTHRC/Home/research_publications/productivity/Measuring_Productivity_Service_SectorSept_EN.ashx (accessed on 23 May 2016).

Vij, M. *International Financial Management*. New Delhi: Excel Books, 2003.

Martin, T. 'Innovation in Services and the Knowledge Economy the Interface between Policy Makers and Enterprises: A Business Perspective'. *Innovation and Productivity in Services*, pp. 119–33. Paris: OECD, 2001.

Maurer, A., and P. Chauvete. The Magnitude of Flows of Global Trade in Services.' In *World Bank Hand Book: Development, Trade and the WTO*, 235–245. Washington DC: World Bank, 2002.

Miles, L., and M. Boden. 'Introduction: Are Services Special?' In *Services and Knowledge-Based Economy*, edited by M. Boden and I. Miles. London: Continuum, 2000.

National Bureau of Statistics. *China Statistical Year Book*. Beijing, 2005.

Noland, M., D. Park, and G. B. Estrada. *Developing the Services Sector as Engine of Growth for Asia: An Overview*. Peterson Institute for International Economics Working Paper No. 12–18, 2012. Also see https://papers.ssrn.com/sol3/papers.cfm?abstract_id=2159442 (accessed on 3 December 2016).

Nodal, M. 'Asia's Service Sector Imperatives.' Peterson Institute for International Economics, Asian Development Bank, 2012. Available at: http://www.iie.com/publications/opeds/print.cfm?ResearchId=2299&doc=pub (accessed on 31 March 2016).

ODI. *The Contribution of Services to Development: The Role of Regulation and Trade Liberalization*. Project Briefing no. 17, Overseas Development Institute, 2008.

OECD. *Employment Outlook*. Paris: OECD, 1996.

———. *Employment Outlook*. Paris: OECD, 1997.

———. *Employment Outlook*. Paris: OECD, 1999.

———. *Science Technology and Innovation in the New Economy*. Paris: OECD, 2000.

———. 'The Characteristics and Quality of Service Sector Jobs.' In *OECD Employment Outlook*. Paris: OECD, 2001. Available at: http://www.oecd.org/els/emp/2079411.pdf (accessed on 24 October 2015).

———. "Growth in Services" (2005) for detail see http://www.oecd.org/general/34749412.pdf (accessed on 3/12/2016).

———. 'Growth in Services: Fostering Employment, Productivity and Innovation.' Meeting of the OECD Council at Ministerial Level, 2005. Available at: http://www.oecd.org/economy/34749412.pdf (accessed on 31 October 2013).

———. 'Global Forum on International Investment.' The Contribution of Services to Development and the Role of Trade and Liberalization and Regulation, ODI Briefing Note, DFID, UK, 27–28 March 2008.

Parasuraman, A., V. Zeithal, and L. Berry. 'SERVQUAL: A Multi-Item Scale for Measuring Customer Perception of Service Quality.' *Journal of Retailing* 64, no. 1 (1988): 12–40.

Pilat, D. 'Introduction and Synthesis.' In *Enhancing the Performance of the Service Sector*, edited by OECD, 9–27. Paris: OECD, 2005.

Prasad, H. A. C. and R. Sathish. 'Policy for India's Services Sector.' Working Paper No. 1/2010-DEA, Department of Economic Affairs, Ministry of Finance, Government of India, 2010.

Ramaswamy, K. V., and T. Agrawal. 'Service-Led Growth, Employment and Job Quality: A Study of Manufacturing and Service-Sector in Urban India.' Indira Gandhi Institute of Development Research, Mumbai, 2012. Available at: http://www.igidr.ac.in/pdf/publication/WP-2012--007.pdf (accessed on 31 October 2013).

RBI. *Service Industry in India*, 2005. For details see http://shodhganga.inflibnet.ac.in/bitstream/10603/2540/10/10_chapter%204.pdf (accessed on 21 December 2016).

Riddle, D. I. *Service-led Growth: The Role of Service Sector in World Development*. Westport, Connecticut: Praeger, 1986.

Rust, R. T., and T. S. Chung. 'Marketing Models of Service and Relationships.' Working Paper, Robert H. Smith School of Business, University of Maryland, College Park, 2005.

Sapprasert, K. 'The Impact of ICT on the Growth of Service Industries.' Paper provided by Centre for Technology, Innovation and Culture, University of Oslo, 2007.

Schumpeter, J. A. *Business Cycles: A Theoretical, Historical and Statistical Analysis of the Capitalist Process*. New York: McGraw Hill, 1939.

Sheehan, J. 'Understanding Service Sector Innovation.' *Communication of the ACM* 49, no. 7 (July 2006): 43–47.

Subramanian, P. and T. Arimohan. 'Role of Services Sector in Indian Economy.' *International Journal of Innovative Research and Studies* 13, no. 5 (2014): 46–50.

Tamura S., T. Sheehan, C. Martinez and S. Kergroach. 'Promoting Innovation in Service.' In *Enhancing the Performance of the Service Sector*, edited by OECD, 133–79. Paris: OECD, 2005.

Tyagi, R. K., and P. Gupta. *A Complete Balanced Score Card Creating Value Through Sustained Performance Improvement*. New Jersey: Pearson Education, 2008.

UNCDF. *United Nations Capital Development Fund 2013*. Available at: http://www.uncdf.org/sites/default/files/download/global_programmes_spread.pdf (accessed on 3 December 2016).

United Nations. 'International Standard Industrial Classification of All Economic Activities (ISIC).' Department of Economic and Social Affairs, Statistics Division, New York, 2008.

———. 'Preface: Promoting Innovations in the Service Sector.' In *Review of Experience and Policies*. New York, Geneva: United Economic Commission for Europe, 2011.

World Bank. *World Development Indicator*. Washington DC: World Bank, 2013.

9 Infrastructure, Energy, Technology and Development

Structural change is a key driver of rapid growth: countries diversify into new industries; firms learn new things, people moves to new locations.

—World Bank[1]

The structural transformation is the defining characteristic of development process. It is both the cause and effect of economic growth (IFPRI 2012). The developmentalists were of the view that developing countries can fasten their economic growth and development if they inject necessary structural changes into their economy. The structural change could be realized through the investment in infrastructure, technology and energy. This is otherwise called investment in social overhead capital, largely executed by the government. This will be helpful to energize private sector investment in various sectors. It can also attract FDI into the economy in various sectors. Bhattacharya, Romani and Stern (2012) were of the view that many emerging markets and most low-income countries require a major increase in infrastructure investment to alleviate growth constraints, respond to urbanization pressures and meet their crucial goals for inclusive growth, development and sustainability. African Development Bank believes that 'structural transformation' will not be materialized without major investments in infrastructure.[2]

Energy generates power, which enables structural transformation in the industry and service sectors. Energy is the fuel for the vehicle of economic growth and development. Import of energy constitutes gigantic share of import of many developing countries. Almost all the underdeveloped and developing countries are energy deficient. Without availability of cheap and sufficient energy, structural transformation in the industrial and service sectors in developing countries cannot be possible. Improved energy availability contributes in some boarder multiplier ways to economic development (ESMAP 2002). Energy played a crucial role in China's industrial structural change.[3]

Another factor that can accelerate the pace of growth and development in developing economies is the technology. Technological innovation is a key to modernization. Technological advancement will enable nations to achieve higher productivity, economize the use of scarce resources and accelerate economic growth and development. Use of technology across all the sectors, i.e. agriculture, industry and services, not only will enhance their efficiency and raise their productivity but also can open employment opportunities in these sectors. According to Valli and Saccone (2009), an emerging backward economy may benefit from some advantages, such as the adoption of modern technologies coming from more advanced countries and the possibilities of transforming masses of the labour force from low-productivity sector (agriculture and traditional tertiary activities) to sectors with higher productivity (industry and modern services). The technological revolution will promote structural transformation in an economy. It will drag these economies from the traditional agriculture dominated economies to modern manufacturing and service sector-based economies.

Thus, infrastructure, energy and technology are the three important ingredients that play significant role in the economic growth and development of the agriculture, industry and service sectors.

After reading this chapter, you will be able to:

1. Describe the role of infrastructure in the economic growth and development of a nation.
2. Explain the role of energy in the growth and development of various sectors of the economy.
3. Discuss the issues and challenges faced by the infrastructure, energy and technology sectors, particularly in developing countries.

SECTION I: INFRASTRUCTURE AND DEVELOPMENT

Poor infrastructure impedes a nation's economic growth and international competitiveness.

—World Bank (2006)

The link between infrastructure and development is not a once for all affair. It is a continuous process and progress in development has to be preceded, accompanied and followed by progress in infrastructure, if we are to fulfill our declared objectives of a self-accelerating process of economic development.

—V. K. R. V. Rao[4]

Infrastructure is an important capital asset which helps the economy to enhance its efficiency. It boosts productivity and drives the economy towards the path of higher economic growth and development. Poor infrastructure facilities are adversely affecting the efficiency of agriculture, industry and services sectors in many developing countries. As a result, the contribution of these sectors to growth and development is low and not up to its optimum capacity. Infrastructure, although, not sole determinant but an important barometer of development. The developed nations have received rich dividend from their investment on quality infrastructure. ADB (2007) finds that poor infrastructure and lack of investment in infrastructure have constrained growth.

Infrastructure investment is contributing to increase the productivity, and it is expected to contribute to future economic growth in developing countries where infrastructure is still insufficient (Kim 2006). Investment in infrastructure, such as transport (roads, railways, ports and civil aviation), power, irrigation, watersheds, hydroelectric works, scientific research and training, markets and warehousing, communication and informatics, education and health institutions, has strategic importance in the sustainable economic growth and socio-economic development of a nation. These infrastructures are necessary ingredient to provide required vitality to increase the productivity efficiency of various factors of production such as land, labour and capital. Moreover, investment in basic needs infrastructure, such as housing, safe drinking water and sanitation which are poverty reducing infrastructures, strongly influences the quality of life of the people. World Development Report 1994, which focuses on infrastructure, has rightly envisaged that 'the adequacy of infrastructure helps determine one country's success and another's failure in diversifying production, expanding trade, coping with population growth, reducing poverty or improving environmental conditions.'

Broadly, infrastructure refers to all basic inputs into and requirements for the proper functioning of the economy (UN-Habitat 2011). Economic infrastructure, essentially, are transport, energy, information and communications technology, water, sanitation and irrigation. On the other hand, social infrastructure encompasses services such as health, education and recreation (UN-Habitat 2011). According to Ghosh and De (1998), the concept of infrastructure is essentially a follow-up service out of a certain stock of infrastructural facilities created over a length of time. Donald (1974) defined infrastructure as the physical structure and facilities that are developed or acquired by public agencies to enhance governmental function and provide water, power, waste disposal, transportation or similar services to facilitate the achievement of common social and economic objectives. Mody (1997) was of the view that infrastructure can be defined as activities that provide society with the services necessary to conduct daily life and to engage in productive activities. In the opinion of Srinivasu and Rao (2013), infrastructure is the stock of basic facilities and capital equipment needed for the functioning of a country or area. The term usually refers collectively to the road, bridges, rail lines and similar public works that are required for an industrial economy or a proportion of it to function. Hudson et al. (1997) defines infrastructure as combined facilities that provide essential public services of transport and utilities that include water, gas, electricity, energy, telecommunication, waste disposal, sports and recreational facilities.

Bhattacharya (2008) has distinguished between 'hard' and 'soft' infrastructure. The former refers to physical structures or facilities that support the society and economy such as transport (ports, roads and railways); energy (electricity generation, electrical grids and gas and oil pipelines); telecommunication (telephone and internet) and basic utilities (water supply, hospital and health clinics, schools, irrigation etc.). The latter refers to non-tangibles, supporting the development and operation of hard infrastructure such as policy, regulatory mechanisms, systems and procedures, social networks, and transparency and accountability of financing and procurement systems. In a nutshell, infrastructures are the physical assets, such as road, irrigation, electricity, telecommunication network, computer, dams and bridges, railway network, airports, ports, parks, energy such gas and oil pipelines, banking and insurance, school, colleges and universities, hospitals and dispensaries and so on, which are essential and directly as well as indirectly promotes economic growth and development.

Infrastructure is a basic prerequisite for the sustainable and inclusive economic growth and development. Therefore, a country has to invest adequate amount of its resources for building up good quality infrastructure both in rural and urban areas. Some of the characteristics of infrastructure as envisaged by UN-Habitat (2011) are (a) longevity, scale, inflexibility and higher investment costs; (b) essentially public goods, providing in principle, non-exclusive goods accessible to all; (c) fixed investments, bulky and lump sum with long payback periods; (d) having considerable variation in earning power capacity and (e) sensitive to corruption and political shifts.

During the initial phase of their development initiative and planning, the government of a developing country has to make substantial investment on infrastructure. Infrastructure development is a continuous process; therefore, a country has to make a strategic planning for infrastructure development. DFID (2002) has identified various channels through which investment in infrastructure can contribute to sustainable growth, as follows:

1. reducing transaction costs and facilitating trade flows within and across borders;
2. enabling economic actors—individuals, firms, governments—to responds to new types of demand in different places;
3. Lowering the costs of inputs for entrepreneurs of making existing business more profitable;
4. creating employment;
5. enhancing human capital; and
6. improving environmental conditions.

The positive contribution of physical infrastructure to economic growth and development comes through increments in investment, employment, output and income in chain of 'cumulative causation' (Ghosh and De 1998). The investment in infrastructure by the public sector will enhance the private sector investment in the manufacturing sector. Infrastructure development contributes to investment and growth through an increase in productivity and efficiency and acts as a link between resource and factories, people and jobs and products and market (Sahoo and Dash 2008).

ROLE OF INFRASTRUCTURE IN ECONOMIC GROWTH AND DEVELOPMENT

The provision of good quality infrastructure will have profound effect on the quality of life of the people. Good road network between rural and urban areas will enable people to have access to referral health care institutions in the cities, and will be helpful to reduce mortality and morbidity. It will also enable children from rural areas, especially girl children, to pursue higher education in the cities. It can entice the youth to move out of the village for work in the nearby cities and towns for the enhancement of their earning. In India, Kerala is an illustrious example, where the rural–urban continuum with good road connectivity has profound impact on health, education and quality of life of its people. Insufficient infrastructure represents a major cause of loss of quality of life, illness and death (Willoughby 2004). Infrastructure like telephone network and internet connectivity will enhance social networking and will act as social capital energizer. Infrastructure development would act as a great equalizer and help to reduce poverty and social inequality. The Global Competitive Report 2010–11 has noted that the quality and extensiveness of infrastructure networks significantly impact inequality and poverty in a variety of ways. It is remarked that infrastructure plays a crucial role in promoting economic growth, thereby contributes to the reduction of economic disparity, poverty and deprivations in a country (Srinivasan and Rao 2013).

Infrastructure facilities like irrigation canal and deep irrigation, if available to the farmers, will enhance the agricultural productivity and farmers' income and lifestyle.

Breisinger and Diao (2008) have noted that public investment in irrigation and infrastructure supported the introduction of modern technology in agriculture, which changed farmers' saving and investment behaviour—the Green Revolution. Several studies have noted that lack of availability of good quality drinking water to the livestock has a profound effect on milk production in Punjab, Haryana and Western Uttar Pradesh. Availability of infrastructure and agriculture development in developing countries are intimately interconnected.

Infrastructure is vital to the industrial development of a nation. All the developed countries were able to industrialize their nation during 1970s and 1980s because of the availability of better infrastructure facilities such as good roads, ports, airports, railways, electricity, energy and so on. Establishment of industries requires electricity and other energy such as thermal, coal and so on. In Punjab, most of the spinning mills were closed after 2000, one of the reasons being the lack of energy infrastructure facilities. Public investment in infrastructure will lead to private investments in industrial activities. The Infrastructure and Industrial Investment Policy 2012 of Uttar Pradesh has envisaged that 'high-end quality infrastructure facilities are absolutely essential for industrial development. As a result availability of quality infrastructure, industries get established with less capital investment and can function without impediments.'

Good quality of infrastructure would promote trade and business within and across the country; it can attract FDIs. Investment climate surveys repeatedly show that the limited and poor quality of infrastructure facilities act as major impediments to business growth in India (Sahoo and Dash 2008). Asiedu (2002) asserts that good infrastructure is a necessary prerequisite for foreign investors to conduct their operations successfully. Bae (2008) was of the view that in developed countries, infrastructure is not a motivator but an indicator to attract FDI in large emerging economies. On the other hand, the World Trade Report 2004 has envisaged that the infrastructure and related services plays a crucial role in the flow of international trade.

Rural infrastructure provides a good stimulus to the growth of the rural economy (Llanto 2012). Fan and Zhang (2004) show that improved roads lead to the rise of small rural non-farm business, such as food processing and marketing enterprises, electronic repair swifts, transpiration and trade and restaurant services. The literature indicates that rural infrastructure fosters physical connectivity and promotes better integration of rural and agricultural areas with the emerging urban markets. The linkage of the internal market to the national and global trading markets will stimulate economic growth and reduce poverty in these areas. The common saying that with the globalization 'world has become a village,' will come true only when the rural infrastructural facilities are upgraded and the capabilities of the rural economies are enhanced to contribute towards global development.

The areas and people, particularly the tribal people, who are disconnected from the mainstream because of lack of infrastructure facilities sometimes have become victim of extremism. The tribal blocks and villages of Orissa, Chhattisgarh and Jharkhand that lack infrastructure facilities, such as road, electricity, irrigation, telephone connectivity, education and health care institutions, are found to be largely cut off from the mainstream and are vexed with Naxalite problem. People residing in these areas feel neglected and resort to extremism path to assert their demands. Improvement of infrastructure facility in Andhra Pradesh is one of the factors for reduction of Naxalite problem in the state. Infrastructure and tribal development are intimately interconnected. Infrastructure will reduce exclusion and is a powerful instrument of inclusive development.

Investment in infrastructure could narrow down the regional disparities. It will connect various regions and will promote inter- and intra-regional trade within the country. Regions having good basic infrastructure facilities like health, education, transport, communication, water, sanitation, energy, housing and so on will attract more investments especially from the small and marginal entrepreneur to start their production activities (Srinivasan and Rao 2013). Evidences suggest that infrastructure could be a key variable in regional convergence (Llanto 2007). The better allocation of infrastructure investments across regions helps the lagging regions to catch up and increase their growth potential (Mansan and Chatterjee 2003). High-quality infrastructure of East Asian economies is an important factor behind their successful integration into the global economy (Llanto 2012). The Global Competitive Report 2010–11 of world economic forum has envisaged that

> Extensive and efficient infrastructure is critical for ensuring the effective functioning of the economy, as it is an important factor determining the location of economic activity and the kinds of activities or sectors that can develop in a particular economy. Well-developed infrastructure reduces the effect of distance between regions, integrating the national market and connecting it at low cost to markets in other countries and regions.

Infrastructure index values and the position of selected nations from the 144 nations (Table 9.1) clearly show that developing countries belonging to Africa and South Asia have lower calculated values and are in lower position as compared to the European nations and even the 'Asian giants', i.e. Singapore, Honk Kong and Japan. Availability of quality infrastructure has a positive correlation with the development status of the nations. Good quality infrastructure is not only capital asset for a nation but also important physical asset to augment social and human development. The underdeveloped regions are largely characterized by poor infrastructure facility—lack of irrigation hinders the growth and productivity in agriculture sector, lack of electricity and energy forestall industrial growth and lack of infrastructure in health and education would slow down social development.

In a nutshell infrastructure will promote development in the following ways:

1. Infrastructure required for economic development and for raising productivity and growth rate in agriculture and industrial sector are road, railways, airports, electrical power generation, irrigation and so on.
2. The social development such as health and education requires infrastructure like school, hospitals, health centres, training institutions, technical institutions, youth clubs, recreation and so on. The quality infrastructure is critical to the efficient and effective functioning of service sector.
3. Political development depends on soft infrastructures such as good governance, rule of law, strengthening of democratic decentralized institutions, gender participation, inclusion and representation of socially and economically backward sections in the political system, responsible citizenry and so on.
4. Basic infrastructure such as housing, drinking water projects and sanitation raises the quality of life.
5. Infrastructure will raise FDI, enhance foreign trade and boost economic image of the nation in international arena and would promote international economic relationship.

Table 9.1 *Infrastructure Rank of Different Countries in the Global Competitive Index (2012–13)*

Countries	Score	Rank
Bangladesh	2.22	134
China	4.46	48
Denmark	5.74	16
Ethiopia	2.65	119
France	6.28	4
Germany	6.36	3
Hong Kong	6.72	1
India	3.60	84
Japan	5.92	11
Kenya	3.09	103
Malaysia	5.09	32
Nepal	1.81	143
Pakistan	2.73	116
Singapore	6.50	2
Sri Lanka	4.13	62
United Kingdom	6.22	6
Zimbabwe	2.40	128

Source: The Global Competitiveness Report 2012–13 Wans Schwab, World Economic Forum http://www3.weforum.org/docs/WEIGlobalcomp (accessed on 12 February 2015).
Note: Ranks out of 144 economic and scores measured on 1 to 7 scale.

6. Infrastructure will improve the efficiency of the market and raise its contribution to economic growth and development.
7. Infrastructure will improve social networking and trade-off between rural and urban area population and can reduce social exclusion.
8. The cultural development also depends on strengthening soft cultural infrastructure such as cultural values, cultural practices, cultural activities, i.e. song, dance artistic good, etc. These infrastructures in the form of cultural group help them to earn their livelihood. For example film industry has one of the biggest cultural infrastructures providing employment and livelihood directly and indirectly to millions of people.

ISSUES AND CHALLENGES OF INFRASTRUCTURE DEVELOPMENT

Challenges before developing countries are to make adequate provision of good quality infrastructure. However, in developing countries several factors are responsible for poor infrastructural development; some of them are discussed as follows:

1. **Lack of financial resources** is one of the important factors responsible for the poor infrastructure development. Many poor provinces in developing countries having limited revenue sources and sundry socio-economic problems are not in a position to allocate adequate fund in their budget for infrastructure development. Their dependence on the centre for funding and poor flow of fund from centre have constrained their urge for infrastructure development. Moreover, even if funds are available, it is observed that many state governments in India are not able to spend them properly because of poor governance. Complains of corruption, nepotism and poor execution of the work and so on are being reported in the print and electronic media.
2. **Cost of construction of infrastructure** is rising day by day; therefore, fulfilling the set target with the available resources is almost becoming impossible for developing countries. A Project Management National Conference held in India in Bengaluru (10–12 September 2015) has outlined that a project and programme management approach is the best solution to avoid higher costs and delays and to complete each development project with the expected standards. It has also noted that innovative investment mechanisms, including public–private partnership, crowd funding, incubation centre, financial inclusion and above all professional project management approach can reduce the risk.[5]
3. **Undue political interferences and complicated administrative procedures** delay the implementation of infrastructure projects. Governance deficiency affects the infrastructure development of a nation. The draft 12th Five year Plan document prepared by the government of India had pointed out the administrative hurdles in obtaining statutory clearances from the Central and State government in the construction of infrastructure projects.
4. **Lack of an effective land acquisition framework,** low and delayed compensation payment and non-fulfilment of promised commitments to the affected parties have resulted in people's opposition and civil society movements against the construction of infrastructure project. Besides, failure and lackadaisical approach of the government to liberalize the infrastructure investment policy and political opposition against the reform agenda relating to infrastructure development are other pertinent issues and challenges many developing countries are facing in the recent times. The draft 12th Five Year Plan document (not in vogue) has also noted the delay in land acquisition and resettlement as a problem in infrastructure development of India.
5. **Getting environmental clearance for starting infrastructure projects**, particularly in hilly and forest areas and even in the agricultural lands, may face opposition from many fronts. Environmental activists' pressure, pressure from the civil society organizations and even lack of political consensus have delayed the construction of many infrastructure projects, and even many of them have been cancelled. The World Bank (2007b) has also highlighted that 'a well-designed infrastructure can have positive impacts on the environment, which also is crucial for development. However, there is a dark side to infrastructural investment: they often lead to environmental degradation.' Therefore, the World Bank emphasized on 'infrastructure-environment nexus' and suggests that 'the infrastructure-environment nexus address the challenges of meeting the demand for infrastructure services while maintain or improving the quality of the environment.'

6. **Faulty planning**, unused and poor maintenance of infrastructure lead to the loss of financial resources. Most of the corruption happens during construction and the maintenance stages of infrastructure development. Corruption and faulty implementation lead to wastage of resources. Lack of transparency and competitiveness in biding and award of projects to dishonest and incompetent contractors and builders can lead to construction of poor quality infrastructure putting a question mark on its longevity and strength. A document on 'Corruption and Development' has noted that corruption can lead to money being stolen and infrastructure not being built or it can result in half-built or substandard and at times dangerous infrastructure.[6] Isaksson (2010) has noted that the corruption that leads to poor transport infrastructure reduce output in all affected sectors, including construction.
7. **Lack of community participation in the maintenance of local infrastructure** is yet another issue related to infrastructure development. Many of the roads, water works and community sanitation projects which are being left to the community after the construction for its maintenance are found to be in very bad shapes. Local community considers it as the job of the state and not of the people. As the local self-government institutions are closer to the people they are also reluctant to raise tax and fee on the country side people for the maintenance of rural infrastructure. However, Khwaja (2001) found that the projects managed by communities are more sustainable than projects managed by the government because of better maintenance. Case studies of many villages in India show that the water works infrastructure created by the government are managed by the village panchayats with the help of Village Water and Sanitation Committees through the collection of user and maintenance fees from the beneficiaries, and even income from the common property resources are seen to be used in the maintenance of water works. In a way, it has checked water wastage, theft in water bill and ensured quick grievances redressal of the consumers.
8. **Shortage of skilled manpower** to effectively formulate and implement infrastructure development projects. The Asian Development Bank (2011) has rightly envisaged that the major factors that limit the construction industry in India include capacity constraints in delivering potential and performance, shortage of skilled and unskilled manpower, use of obsolete technologies and construction equipment, inadequate availability of quality construction materials and so on.
9. The infrastructure development team in many cases utterly **lacks social scientists and environmentalists**. Therefore, there is a lack of social perspectives on the infrastructure project formulation. The project appraisal must take into consideration the social and environmental impact assessment of the infrastructure projects. A holistic infrastructure team must comprise engineers, architects, geographers, sociologist, economists, psychologists and so on to look into various angles of the infrastructure projects such as appraisal, monitoring, evaluation and impact assessment.

These are a few among many issues and challenges before developing countries, which create hurdles in the path of infrastructure development. The role of infrastructure is vital to development as it will promote national and international integration and raise inter- and intra-country trade in the globalized era. Good quality infrastructure will raise private and corporate sector investments, can attract FDIs and will effectively integrate the national market with the global market. Mody (1997) aptly suggests that in any modern society, infrastructure plays a pivotal role—often decisive role in determining the overall productivity and development of a country's economy as well as quality of life of its citizens. It is a great enabler of connectivity, i.e. social, economic, political and cultural.

SECTION II: ENERGY AND DEVELOPMENT

Energy played a very major role in economic growth compared to other variables in the production function in the countries which are at intermediate stages of economic development.

—The International Energy Agency (IEA; 2004)

The expanded provision and use of energy services is strongly associated with sustainable economic development and growth.

—MEDPRO (Mediterranean Prospect) (2013)

Energy, both renewable and non-renewable, is a key enabler to facilitate structural changes and development of an economy, as the increasing availability of cheaper and higher quality forms of energy inputs has played a key role in driving economic growth in industrialized and emerging economies (Ayres and Warr 2009). Tucker et al. (2014) viewed that electricity consumption remains an enabling factor and prerequisite for US economic growth. Global access to reliable energy services has a strong potential for positive socio-economic development in particular through (a) creation of new activities and employment; (b) generation of income for landowners; (c) reduction of rural migration; (d) use of local resources instead of imports and (e) knowledge acquired by the technicians and managers of installations (Dabrowski and Dewulf 2013). Energy plays a key role in the socio-economic development of the family, society and the nation. It enhances the quality of life of the household, makes the society vibrant and productive and enhances nation's economic growth and development. Ferguson, Wilkinson and Hill (2000) found that there is a strong correlation between electricity use and economic development in a study covering over 100 countries.

Conventional sources of energy used to cook food in developing countries are wood fuel, dung cake, crop residue and kerosene. On the other hand, some of the important unconventional sources of energy used for various purposes are coal, hydroelectricity, wind energy, solar energy, tidal energy, thermal energy, biomass, biogas, diesel, petrol, LPG and the nuclear energy (see Figure 9.1 and Table 9.2). OCHA (2010) while commenting on the energy use by developing countries has noted that

> Nearly one third of the world's population has no access to electricity and nearly half still relies on traditional biomass and cool over rudimentary open fires. In fact, this traditional bio-energy from wood and organic wastes constitutes up to 95 percent of energy supplies in developing countries.

A few important trends in energy use in developing countries are (a) with the emphasis on industrialization, urbanization and growth of service sector there has been increase in energy consumption; (b) there has been shift from the traditional energy sources such as biomass-based fuels, i.e. wood, dung, crop residue and charcoal to commercial form of energy such as electricity; (c) decarbonization and diversification in the use of energy, use of electricity in the industrial and household sector and CNG-driven vehicle in the high-pollution risk urban areas and use of LPG gas in cooking particularly in urban areas; (d) reduction in the pollutant associated with energy and (e) rise in the role of private sector in energy generation and distribution.

ROLE OF ENERGY IN ECONOMIC GROWTH AND DEVELOPMENT

At the outset, availability of electricity would enhance the quality of life of the people in rural and urban areas. It will help the poor and impoverished to fight against poverty, inequality and socio-economic disparities. The lacklustre energy consumption patterns of the poor people tend to add to their misery and aggravate their poverty. Accessibility to affordable electricity would raise the quality of living of the people living in the countryside. It will help them to start income earning activities and even can go for small scale and cottage industry activities by forming the SHGs. Education and health care development are essentially dependent on the availability of electricity. Excessive energy bill leads to energy poverty and harms living standards and socio-economic development (EXPRO 2013). One of the reasons for the thumping victory of Aam Aadmi Party in Delhi 2015 assembly election is highlighting the faulty meter installation in the households and exorbitant energy bill paid by the consumers during the electioneering campaign. Energy

Figure 9.1 *Share of World Primary Energy Supply in 2005*

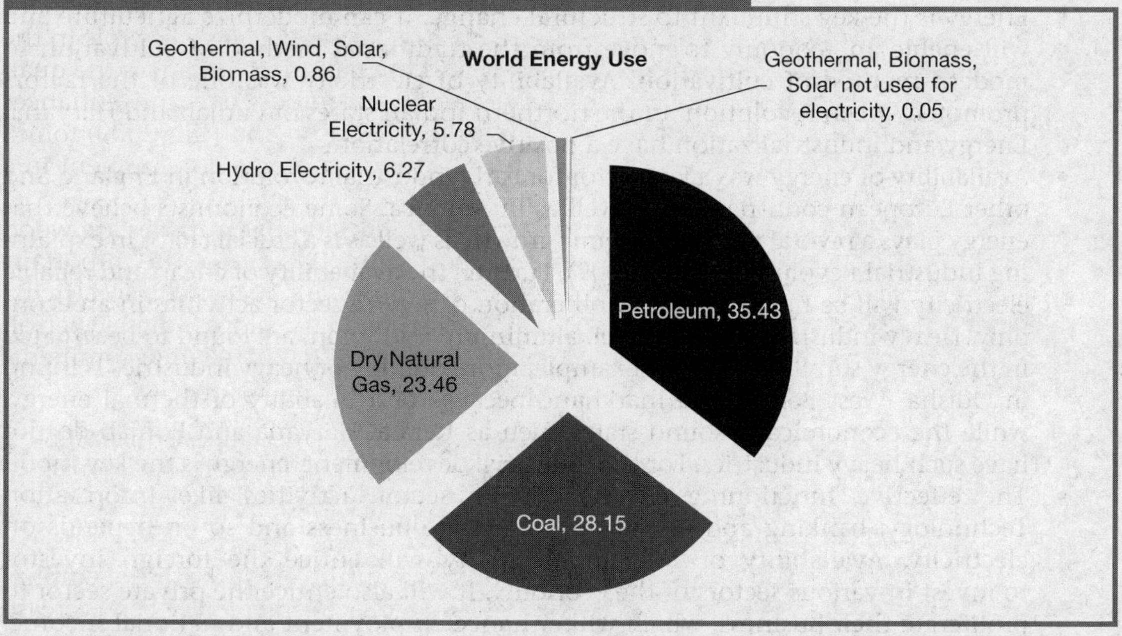

Source: Boundless (2016).

Table 9.2 *World Energy Use*

Types	**Value (Million Tonnes)**	**Percentage**
Petroleum	3527	35.43
Coal	2802	28.15
Dry Natural Gas	2335	23.46
Hydro Electricity	624	6.27
Nuclear Electricity	576	5.78
Geothermal, Wind, Solar, Biomass	86	0.86
Geothermal, Biomass, Solar not used for electricity	5	0.05
Total	9955	100.0

Source: 'World Energy Use'. *Boundless Physics Boundless*, 8 August 2016. Available at: https://www.iea.org/publications/freepublications/publication/cooking.pdf (accessed on 3 December 2016).

services are crucial input to the primary development challenge of providing adequate food, shelter, clothing, water, sanitation, medical care, schooling and access to information (Reddy 2000). A city without electricity is dump and dull and a village without electricity is monotonous. It has been noted that per capita energy and electricity consumption are highly correlated with economic development and other indicators of modern life style, with the presumption that the more energy that is consumed, especially in the form of electricity, the better life is (Starr 1972). A few important roles of energy in economic growth and development are described below:

- Energy is the key stimulant to structural change. It can modernize agriculture and will enable an economy to move from the traditional method of cultivation to modern method of cultivation. Availability of electricity was one of the factors promoted 'green revolution' in the northern Indian states of Punjab and Haryana. Energy and industrialization have a positive correlation.
- Availability of energy was a key factor for early industrial revolution in England and other European countries and as well as in America. Some economists believe that energy plays a pivotal role in economic growth as well as is a crucial factor in explaining Industrial Revolution (Allen 2009). Further, the availability of cheap and reliable electricity will be helpful in the proliferation of service sector activities in an economy. Heavy industries, such as steel, aluminium and so on, are found to be situated in the energy surplus states. For example, more number of heavy industries is found in Odisha, West Bengal and Jharkhand because of availability of thermal energy, while the economically sound states such as Kerala, Haryana and Punjab do not have such heavy industries. For the industrial development, energy is the key input.
- The effective functioning of the service sector activities like Information Technology, banking and insurance, real estate business and so on depends on electricity. Availability of 24-hour electricity will entice the foreign investor to invest in various sectors of the economy. It will also entice the private sector to proliferate their business, which will enhance employment and national income. It has been noted that the service activities, e.g. education, trade, offices, tourism,

etc., and residential sector abundantly use energy to meet their multiple needs such as lighting, cooking, hot water, heating, air conditioning, IT, telecommunication, refrigeration and other electric household appliances (MEDPRO 2013).

- Energy is a key energizer of the social and human development in an economy. The effective functioning of the educational and research and training institutions depends on the availability of electricity. About half of the world's households use solid fuels (biomass and coal) for cooking and heating in simple devices that produce large amounts of air pollution—pollution that is probable responsible for 4–5% of the global burden of disease (Holdren and Smith 2000). Availability of electricity will check infant and maternal mortality and strengthen the immunization programmes in the rural areas because the maintenance of cold chain depends on 24-hour electricity supply. It will also enhance per capita income and life expectancy of the people in both rural and urban areas. According to MEDPRO (2013) technical report, energy plays a crucial role as a global commodity and as a cornerstone of socio-economic development (see Table 9.3).
- Energy and women liberation from the endangering household activities which damage their health go together. Women in rural and urban slum areas waste a lot of time in the collection of fire wood, dung and crop residue for household cooking. Availability of electricity and cooking gas will save a lot of time of the women which they are divesting in firewood collection. There is a strong correlation between the time women have for economic activities and the time they have for survival activities, including collecting and preparing cooking fuels (Reddy 2000). Besides, use of these materials in cooking food causes a lot of damage to the health of women, particularly those of pregnant women. Reddy (2000) was of the view that there is a very direct link between energy and women's health and most of the burdens placed by energy scarcity are borne by women.
- Availability and affordability of energy enhances the use of energy in urban areas and improves the life style of the people residing in the urban areas. The energy and

Table 9.3 *People Relying on Traditional Biomass (Million)*

Countries	2004	2015	2030
Sub-Saharan Africa	575	627	720
North Africa	4	5	5
India	740	77	782
China	480	453	394
Indonesia	156	171	180
Rest of Asia	489	521	561
Brazil	23	26	27
Rest of Latin America	60	60	58
Total	2528	2640	2727

Source: World Energy Outlook. 'Energy for Cooking in Developing Countries', Chapter 15, P. 431, 2006. Available at: https://www.iea.org/publications/freepublications/publication/cooking.pdf (accessed on 3 December 2016).

sustainable urban development go shoulder to shoulder. Further, energy is linked to urbanization as it has lot of implications in the land use pattern, urban industrialization, use of various modes of transportation, construction and real estate, infrastructure development, domestic appliances and products, biomass consumption and use of other non-renewable sources of energy. Proliferation of urbanization without assuring availability of energy with an affordable price will prove to be counterproductive for the political and economic system in developing countries.

- Energy trade is one of the emerging areas of developmental relationships among different countries of the world. The energy diplomacy will not only promote energy trade between the energy exporting and importing countries but also strengthen the international bilateral and multilateral relationship among the energy importing and exporting countries, both developed and developing. The Iran–Pakistan–India gas pipeline perceived to be one of the dimensions to improve Indo-Pak relationship. UNIDO considers trade in energy as a vital component of global security and peace. UN Energy has noted that trade in energy and energy services have been growing between developed and developing countries, and amongst developing countries primarily due to the increased demand for primary energy in the rapidly growing economies of China, India and Korea.[7]
- Energy will promote sustainable rural development. The rural areas in developing countries are facing energy deficiencies. This is affecting rural agriculture and industrial sector and also influencing to the great extent their quality of life. Availability of energy will not only illuminate their houses but also dazzle their villages. Availability of energy will promote rural industrialization, enable mechanization of their agriculture and allied activities, modernize their villages through the establishment of village service centres and curtail the intensity of poverty and inequality, which will raise the quality of life in the rural areas of developing countries. Availability and accessibility of electricity in the countryside of developing countries will raise the education and health status of the population in the village. It can be helpful to promote cultural and entertainment activities in rural areas. Goldemberg (2000) opined that the living standards in rural areas can be significantly improved by promoting a shift from direct combustion of biomass fuels (dung, crop residues and fuel wood) or coal in inefficient and polluting stoves to clean, efficient liquid or gaseous fuels and electricity.

In a nutshell, energy helps to promote economic growth and development in the following ways:

1. It helps to promote agriculture, industry and services sector in the economy.
2. It will help to raise the quality of life of the people of both rural and urban areas, and especially those who are residing in the countryside.
3. Availability of energy will encourage private investment and FDIs in agriculture, industry and services sector activities.
4. It will promote international trade and improve balance of payment position of developing countries.
5. It will raise the status of women in the society and promote women workforce participation in income earning activities.

6. It will reduce poverty and inequalities, raise employment opportunities in the economy.
7. Energy is a crucial input to facilitate structural change of the developing economies.
8. Finally, it will promote sustainable economic growth and development.

ISSUES AND CHALLENGES OF ENERGY SECTOR DEVELOPMENT

UN Secretary General Ban Ki-Moon said,

> Ensuring access to sustainable and cleaner energy is a key objective for the international community. It is clear that we will not be able to meet the Millennium Development goals and the development needs of the poor without increasing their access to the energy.[8]

Ensuring cheap, cleaner and safer energy to the people and also to the various development sectors is a big challenge for the energy scarce developing countries. Some of the important challenges of the energy and development are discussed as follows.

At the outset, the utmost challenge before the governments of developing countries is to make energy access to the people in general and to those belonging to the impoverished sections of the society in particular. AGECC (2010) has defined access as 'access to clean, reliable and affordable energy services for cooking and heating, lighting, communications and productive uses.' In developing countries, there is a marked difference in the access to electricity in rural and urban areas and also among the rich who can afford and the poor who are incapable to pay the electricity price. A single pie which a poor pays is subtracted from their expenditure on the basic needs, i.e. food, clothing and other essential necessities of the family.

With limited resources at their disposal, developing countries find it difficult to create infrastructure to generate energy, particularly electricity. Development of renewable energy sources can play an important role in meeting the future energy needs and achieving energy sustainability in developing countries. The sustainable energy policy of developing countries is to emphasize on the promotion of indigenous renewable energy industries. The indigenous renewable energy will be an additional benefit for these countries to generate new economic opportunities. At the same time, it will reduce dependence on volatile world energy markets. In a similar vein, it will empower the nation to conserve resources for internal investment by curbing outlays for imported fuel.

Energy security is a global challenge and particularly a surmountable challenge for developing countries which are largely the consumers and importers of energy. As per Hoeven (2013),

> Energy security refers to the ability of a given country to obtain uninterrupted availability of its main energy sources at an affordable price. In short term, energy security is the ability of a given energy system to react promptly to sudden change in supply and demand, maintaining the availability, affordability, accessibility and quality of energy. Long-term energy security is linked mainly to making timely investments to ensure that the future supply of affordable energy will support economic development and environmental goals.

The uncertainty over the availability of the non-renewable sources of energy and investment in infrastructure in the case of renewable sources of energy poses a serious challenge to energy security for the non-oil and natural gas deficient developing countries. OCHA

(2010) has noted that the growing energy insecurity will have the greatest impacts in the developing world and among poor communities, where access to energy services is already limited, and fuel price rises will make the difference between chronic poverty and extreme or even acute vulnerability. Another dimension of energy security is energy-related disasters and social security provisions to the affected people. For instance, after three decades of the Bhopal gas disaster of India, which occurred in 1984, the affected people are still waiting for the compensation and are also not satisfied with the compensation amount. Moreover, the number of families which have been enlisted for the compensation is quite higher than those who have received it. Energy insurance is a prime issue to deal with disaster-related compensation. Dealing with the energy-related disasters, particularly gas and nuclear disasters, is considered to be an indomitable challenge for both developed and developing countries.

Energy availability, pricing and food security are critical challenges in developing countries with high population. The rise in fuel prices increases the cost of cultivation and transport of food items, thus leading to food inflation which hits hard the impoverished. As a result, it becomes a stimulant of food insecurity in developing countries. In the 2008 oil price hike, experts from World Bank calculated that when the price of a barrel of oil rose about a certain threshold (e.g. $80/barrel) it was no longer profitable for small holder farmer in the developing world—who grow most of the food in these countries—to farm (OCHA 2010). Energy's role in food security to the poorest of the poor is a great challenge before developing countries.

Energy and social safety net, including energy-related subsidies, are major challenges. Rise in electricity bill in Delhi is one of the reasons for the defeat of the mainstream political parties and advent of an *aam aadmi* (common man) party in recent assembly election (Delhi Assembly Election 2015). Thus, electricity pricing and political economy of a country are intimately interconnected in energy scarce developing nation states. However, developing countries cannot afford energy subsidies for a long period because they have to share the burden with other heads like education, health care sanitation, infrastructure, and so on which is not sustainable in the long run. Most developing countries heavily subsidize fuel supplies for their populations, and increased fuel costs coupled with fuel dependency may require them to allocate more money from other services, cut social safety nets or suffer economic contraction (OCHA 2010).

Energy-related pollution and health problem is a stupendous challenge before developing countries. The pollution generated from vehicles and heat generated from air-conditioners, heaters, refrigerators and energy-driven other appliances are phenomenal in the mega cities of developing countries. This causes a lot of environmental and health problems. The health problems related to the use of solid fuels, passive smoking and outdoor air pollution are tuberculosis, chronic bronchitis, lung cancer, still birth and low birth weight babies, blindness, asthma and heart diseases (Smith 2002). Furthermore, the nuclear power generation has the hazards due to the radiation danger. Exposure to hydrocarbons generated by coal burning has the risk of lung cancer. Holdren and Smith (2000) have remarked that it is difficult to envisage a sustainable energy future in which unprocessed solid fuel remains an important source of energy for a significant fraction of the world's households.

Last but not the least, formulation of suitable energy policy is critical to developing countries; not only national but also provincial energy policy for each province of a nation is required. There are energy producing states vis-à-vis energy consuming states, energy surplus states and energy deficit states and the interface is critical to create an intra-country balance in energy supply and demand.

Energy is critical to the sustainable development of developing countries. Most of developing countries are featured with energy deficiency. Energy not only influences the economic development but also produces impact on the social and human development of a nation state. It plays a crucial role in the improvement of the quality of life of the people of a nation. Energy generation, pricing, distribution, import–export and management are vital issues and challenges associated with energy efficiency. Developing countries which are struggling to ensure basic needs to the bourgeois population will go a long way to be energy efficient. Enhancement of economic growth and development will be impossible in developing countries having paucity of energy.

SECTION III: TECHNOLOGY AND DEVELOPMENT

A central finding of economics over the past fifty years has been that technological advancement is critical to long term economic growth.

—McArthur and Sachs (2001)

Improvements in technology raise productivity and hence are a major driver of structural change.

—UNIDO (2013)

The 20th century's unprecedented gains in advancing human development and eradicating poverty came largely from technological breakthrough.

—UNDP (2001)

Technology is the kingpin of development. The classical and neo-classical economists as well as the contemporary developmentalists have advocated and emphasized on the use of modern technology in the process of development in different sectors, i.e. agriculture, industry and service. The use of technology will raise productivity, income and economic growth. Besides economic development, technology is also an important energizer of social development, i.e. education, health and human development. It enhances skills of individuals and enables them to earn more and remain healthy. Technology permits an outward shift of a nation's productive possibilities frontier (PPF) and creates the potential for greater output and income from the same resource (Cypher and Dietz 2004). Robert Solow (1957) suggested that technological advancement has been the key long-term driver of economic development and noted that perhaps over 90% of the increases in output can be accounted for by the combined forces of technology and education. According to World Bank (2008b), technological progress can play important role in development in the following ways:

1. Technological progress can spur development by lowering the costs of production and enabling the exploitation of return to scale.
2. Technological progress in one sector can create new economic opportunities in other sectors.
3. Technology can yield quality improvement.
4. Technological innovation may spur further innovations in upstream and downstream activities.
5. Benefits of a new technology can extend well beyond the immediate sector of good in which the technology exists.

Technology is important in developing nations for several key reasons. First, it can be used through commerce to generate money and capital income. Second, updated technology improves the quality of life of the inhabitants of a nation. Third, it allows for easier communication (Miah and Omar 2012). In fact, numerous macroeconomic studies have found that there is a positive impact of the spread of ICT on national output (Roller and Waverman 2001; Seetharam and Sridhar 2004).

ROLE OF TECHNOLOGY IN ECONOMIC GROWTH AND DEVELOPMENT

The role of technology in the development is critical for the reasons discussed below.

Use of technology in agriculture during the Green Revolution movement in India in the early 1970s had not only raised the agricultural productivity but also enabled the nation to ardently face the challenges of hunger. World Bank (1998) has also noted that the Green Revolution is an example of the dramatic effects that modest technological advances can have in boosting the incomes of the poor. The technologies used in the mechanization of agriculture are tractor, harrow, threshers and so on which had long been available in industrial countries, along with the development of high-yielding varieties of maize, wheat and rice. Asia's Green Revolution doubled cereal production between 1970 and 1995 while increasing the land area devoted to cereals by only 4% (World Bank 2007). Use of technology in allied sectors, i.e. dairy, poultry, fishery and horticulture, has enhanced the potential of these sectors to meet the challenges of nutritional requirement of the nation. Technology has become a powerful instrument to meet the challenges of primary sector in the globalized world. Some estimation suggests that technological progress has boosted productivity in agriculture four times as quickly as in manufacturing (Martin and Mitra 2001). According to World Bank (2008b) technological progress can lower costs, improve quality, create products and help to reach new markets.

Developing countries during the initial phase of their industrial and manufacturing sector development have used technology largely made by the developed nations. This is because of paucity of financial resources and non-availability of technical manpower to conduct innovations in industrial and manufacturing sector. It is rightly remarked that the increasing acquisition of accessible technology has served as a major avenue for advancements in developing nations (Miah and Omar 2012). Use of technology in the industrial development process of the Asian giants, also of China, and its contribution to GDP of these countries are being cited by the developmentalists worldwide. Since the early 1960s, countries such as Korea, Taiwan, Singapore and Hong Kong have transformed themselves from technological backwardness and poor to relatively modern and affluent economies (Kim and Nelson 2000). While giving the example of Korea, Vogel (1991) concluded that no nation has tried harder than Korea and come so far so quickly from handicrafts to heavy industry, from poverty to prosperity, from inexperienced imitators to modern planners, managers and engineers. Korea's export increased from a mere $40 million in 1960 to $125 billion in 1995, with virtually all the increase represented by products that Korea did not know how to produce at the start of the era (Kim and Nelson 2000). However, it is generally seen that the countries in East and South East Asia and Sub-Saharan Africa are lagging behind in technological innovations and are largely the adopters and frugally the innovators. However, there is a need for economies to progress beyond adoption of innovation if they want to continue to close the gap with the highest income countries (McArthur and Sachs 2002). Cackler, Gu and Rodgers have remarked,

> Adoption of technology by developing countries has had profound effects on their economies, such as reducing the national costs of production, establishing standard of quality, and allowing individuals to communication from a distance. Unfortunately, the current process remains one of the adaptation, rather than innovation.[9]

The capacious use of the technology in general and ICT in particular in the tertiary or service sector would enhance the contribution of service sector to the economic growth. The sub-sectors of the service sector such as education, health, banking, insurance and retail business are widely using ICT, and ICT has enhanced their potential in service delivery (see Table 9.3). Many e-Education and e-Health projects have proved to be more cost effective. The health care delivery system in developing countries and the examples of many e-Health care projects in Sub-Saharan African countries have depicted the impact of ICT on health development.

Technology would transform developing countries from the low-productive labour intensive economies to high-productive capital intensive economies. These nations will gain in terms of lower capital output ratio. It will enhance productivity of the agriculture and industrial sector and will reduce cost of production. Technological development will force the nation to produce skilled manpower and directly impact its skill and human resource development. Technology is a key driver of structural change; therefore, developing countries intending to accelerate their pace of structural change have to fasten the use technology in various sectors of economy. Industrial Development Report 2013 (UNIDO 2013) has highlighted that the improvements in technology raise productivity, and hence is a major driver of structural change.

Technological development has enhanced the foreign trade potential of developing countries. In recent years, it has fostered to a great extent the international migration of technical manpower, particularly ICT-related skilled manpower from developing countries to the developed countries. Developing countries are gaining in form of remittances, FDIs and outsourcing business from developed countries. World Bank (2008b) has remarked that

> [T]o a large extent, the convergence in technological achievement reflects a substantial increase in the openness of developing countries to foreign trade, foreign direct investment and international migration which has dramatically increased both the exposure of developing countries to new technologies and the opportunities to use foreign markets to exploit increasing return to scale.

Technological progress is also a booster of urbanization and urban development in developing countries. There is a paradigm shift in tertiary education in developing countries with a decisive use of technology in conventional as well as distance education system. It has enabled the developing nations to democratize higher education. The technology advancement has enabled the distribution of information and data on numerous development issues through many modes of mass communication such as computers, telephones, televisions, radio and newspapers in developing countries. Although, developing countries are being worse off than those of developed ones, the positive effect of ICT is comparatively more significant in developing countries (Qiang 2009). Technology has remained and will remain a driving force of socio-economic development in the 21st century and will be a great enabler of achievement of SDGs.

In a nutshell, technology will play following roles in a country's economic growth and development:

1. Use of technology in the agriculture and manufacturing sectors will enhance productivity, and therefore can raise GDP.
2. Use of technology in the service sector will raise its efficiency and effectiveness, hence would raise the output of personnel deployed in the service sector.
3. Technology will boost modernization in the developing economies.
4. The use of technology saves time and cost, thus will promote the alternative use of manpower and save wastage of resources.
5. Technological development of the nation will raise the quantum of skilled and technical manpower in an economy, and therefore is useful for human resource development.
6. Use of technology will strengthen governance and transparency and check corruption at various levels.
7. Technology will reduce inequality and poverty.
8. Technology will boost urbanization and enhance the number of smart cities in developing countries.

ISSUES AND CHALLENGES OF TECHNOLOGY AND DEVELOPMENT

At the outset, technology has elongated the North and South divide, where the advanced North has remained the innovators while the laggard South is largely the adopter or adapter. It has enhanced the national income of the developed countries manifold while developing countries have gained marginally. World Bank Report (2008) has remarked that 'the technological frontier has advanced as high-income countries (and some developing countries) continue to innovate at a rapid rate. Thus the technology gap between developed and developing countries remains large, particularly for low-income countries.' The challenge is to synchronize the gap in the inventions and use of technology between the developed and developing countries.

The technological progress has elongated the 'digital divide' and 'technological gap' between urban and rural areas of developing countries. By using technology in the development process, the urban areas are developing at a faster speed as compared to rural areas in developing countries. As a result, the urban–rural differences in the achievements in the field of socio-economic development, i.e. digital literacy, poverty, employment and income, are visible. The 'technological poverty' is visibly present in rural areas of developing countries which are deprived of technological development not because of deficiency in technology but because of lack of infrastructure facilities required for technological development. It is remarked that several obstacles that must be overcome before the benefits of technology will truly be realized by developing nations; however, a majority of developing nations lack the infrastructure, necessary to reliable technology (Miah and Omar 2012).

The low investment in technological research and development, particularly by developing countries, has yielded to their technological dependency on the developed countries. It has created a north–south divide in technological advancement. Furthermore,

> Innovation and technology management climate in the developing-world companies are by nature problematic, characterized by poor business models, political instability and governance conditions, low education level and lack of world-class research universities, an underdeveloped and mediocre physical infrastructure and lack of solid technology base and trained human resources. (Ali, Ullah and Khan, 2008)

Besides, inter-country, intra-country and regional disparities in technological advancement are a cause of concern for technology and development, particularly in developing countries. The challenge is to overcome inter- and intra-regional disparities in technological progress.

Use of ICT is central to the development in the new millennium. Kofi Annan said in the UN General Assembly in 2002 that 'over the last few years, a wide consensus has emerged on the potential of ICT to promote economic growth, combat poverty, and facilitate the integration of developing countries into the global economy.' (Quoted in Weigel and Waldburger 2004)

SUMMARY

Structural transformation is the key to uplift an underdeveloped economy into a developed economy. Provision of good quality infrastructure and adoption of technological innovations are powerful means to transform backward economy into a progressive economy. Infrastructure and technology will promote the efficiency and capability of different sectors of the economy and can raise productivity and economic growth rate. The developed economies of the world are technologically advanced and possess good quality infrastructure, which enhances private sector investment in the manufacturing and service sectors. Developing countries, therefore, need to bring structural transformation, give up overdependence on traditional agriculture and move towards modern technologically advanced manufacturing and service sector—from rural economic setup towards urbanization. Infrastructure is a vital input for acceleration of economic development, neglecting infrastructural development means lackadaisical endeavour by a nation in boosting economic growth which would not be sustainable.

Keywords: infrastructure, renewable energy, conventional sources of energy, social infrastructure, digital divide, energy security.

REVIEW QUESTIONS

1. What is development infrastructure? Discuss the role of development infrastructure in sustainable economic growth and development.
2. Infrastructure is essential for development. In this context, explain various challenges of infrastructure development in developing countries.
3. What are various energy sources? Discuss the role and importance of energy in economic growth and development.
4. Discuss various challenges faced by the energy sector in developing countries. How energy and pollution are interconnected?
5. Explain in detail the role of technology in the economic growth and development of a country.
6. What are various challenges faced by technological development in a developing country?
7. What is digital divide? Explain how digital divide can be bridged in developing countries?
8. Write short notes on the following:
   (i) Challenges of infrastructure development
   (ii) Role of renewable sources of energy
   (iii) Energy and pollution
   (iv) Safe and sustainable energy
   (v) Role ICT in development
   (vi) Digital divide
   (vii) Rural infrastructure development

NOTES

1. The World Bank point of view is quoted from 'Urbanization and Growth: Commission on Growth and Development.' For detail, see http://openknowledge.worldbank (accessed on 17 February 2015).
2. For the African Development Bank quote, see http://www.afdb.org/en/news-and-events/article (accessed on 16 February 2015).
3. For detail see http://www.iam.nie.go.jp/aim/aim_workshop/a… (accessed on 8 March 2016).
4. See http://shodhaganga.inflibnet.ac.in/bitstream/1060… (accessed on 14 April 2016).
5. See http://www.anticorruptionday.org/documents/a… (accessed on 13 April 2016).
6. See http://www.pmi.org.in/events/media/technical… (accessed on 13 April 2016).
7. Taken from the UNIDO, UN Energy 'Energy, Development and Security Energy Issues in the Current Macroeconomic Context.' See http://www.unido.org/fileadmin/user_media (accessed on 24 February 2015).
8. UN Secretary General speech quoted from the UNIDO document UN Energy 'Energy, Development and Security Energy Issues in the Current Macroeconomic Context.' See http://www.unido.org/fileadmin/user_media (accessed on 24 February 2015).
9. Cackler, Gu and Rodgers and their views were quoted from 'Technology in Developing Economies'. For detail, see http://cs.stanford.edu/people/eroberts/cs181 (accessed on 24 October 2015).

BIBLIOGRAPHY

AGECC. 'Energy for a Sustainable Future.' The Secretary General, Advisory Group on Energy and Climate Change, New York, 28 April 2010.

Ali, M., S. Ullah, and P. Khan. 'Managing Innovation and Technology in Developing Countries.' Graduate School of IT and Telecommunication Engineering, Inha University Incheon, South Korea, 2008. Available at: http://arxiv.org/ftp/arxiv/papers/0911/0911.1514.pdf (accessed on 19 November 2013).

Allen, R. C. *The British Industrial Revaluation in Global Perspective*. Cambridge: Cambridge University Press, 2009.

Asian Development Bank. 'Philippines: Critical Development Constraints.' ERD Country Diagnostic Studies, ADB, Manila, 2007.

———. *Facilitate Infrastructure Development in India, ADB's Experience and Best Practices in Project Implementation.* Manila: ADB, 2011.

Asiedu, E. 'One the Determinants of Foreign Direct Investment to Developing Countries: Is Africa Different?' *World Development* 30, no. 1 (2002): 107–18.

Ayres, R. U., and B. Warr. *The Economic Growth Engine: How Energy And Work Drive Material Prosperity*. Cheltenham, UK, North Hampton MA, US: Edward Elgar, 2009.

Bae, M. T. 'Foreign Direct Investment Inflows and ICT Configurations.' *Pacific Focus* 17, no. 2 (2008): 217–26.

Bhattacharya, A., M. Romani, and N. Stern. 'Infrastructure for Development: Meeting Challenge.' London, Centre for Climate change Economic and Policy, 2012.

Bhattacharya, B. 'Infrastructure and Regional Cooperation.' Concept Paper for ADB/ADBI Flagship Study, 2008.

Boundless. 'World Energy Use'. *Boundless Physics*, 8 August 2016. Available at: https://www.boundless.com/physics/textbooks/boundless-physics-textbook/work-and-energy-6/case-study-world-energy-use-66/world-energy-use-288-10950/ (accessed on 3 December 2016).

Breisinger, C., and X. Diao. 'Economic Transformation in Theory and Practice: What are the Massages for Africa?' IFPRI Discussion Paper 0079, IFPRI, Washington DC, 2000.

Cypher, J. M., and J. L. Dietz. *The Process of Economic Development*. London and New York: Routledge, 2004.

Dabrowski, M., and L. Dewulf. 'The Relationship Between Energy and Socioeconomic Development in the Southern and Eastern Mediterranean.' MERPRO Technical Report No. 27 February 2013.

DFID. 'Making the Connections: Infrastructure for Poverty Reduction.' London, 2002.

Donald, C. S. *Professional Education in Public Workers/Environmental Engineers' Administration*, 5th ed. Chicago: American Public Works and Association, 1974.

ESMAP. 'Rural Electrification and Development in the Philippines: Measuring the Social and Economic Benefits.' Report 255/02, World Bank, Energy Sector Management Assistance Programme, May 2002.

Fan, S., and X. Zhang. 'Infrastructure and Regional Economic Development in Rural China.' *China Economic Review* 15 (2001): 203–14.

Ferguson, R., W. Wilkinson and R. Hill. 'Electricity Use and Economic Development.' *Energy Policy* 28 (2000): 923–34.

Ghosh, B., and P. De. 'Role of Infrastructure in Regional Development: A Study of India Over the Plan Period.' *Economic and Political Weekly* 33, no. 47–48 (1998).

Goldemberg. J., 'Preface: World Energy Assessment.' In *World Energy Assessment 2000*, iii. New York: UNDP, 2000.

Hoeven, M. V. D. 'Global Energy Security: The Opportunities and Challenges.' *Energy and Environmental Sustainability* September (2013): 130.

Holdren, J. A., and K. R. Smith. 'Energy, the Environment and Health.' World Energy, Assessment 2000, UNDP, New York, pp. 61–71, 2000.

Hudson, W. R., R. Hass and W. Udding. *Infrastructure Management: Integrating Design, Construction, Maintenance, Rehabilitation and Renovation*. New York: McGraw-Hill, 1997.

IFPRI. 'Pattern of Growth and Structural Transformation in Africa: Trends and Lesson for Future Development Strategies.' West and Central Africa Office, Thematic Research No. 2, April 2012.

Isaksson, A. 'Public Capital Infrastructure and Industrial Development, and Statistics.' Branch Working Paper 15/2009, UNIDO, Vienna, 2010.

Khwaja, A. 'Can Good Projects Succeeded in Bad Communities? Collective Action in the Himalayas.' Harvard University, Department of Economics, Cambridge, Mass, 2001.

Kim, L. and R. R. Nelson. 'A Broad Prospective an Innovation Newly Industrializing Economics.' In *Technology, Learning and Innovation, Experiences of Newly Industrializing Economics*, edited by L. Kim and R. R. Nelson. London: Cambridge University Press, 2000.

Kim, B. 'Infrastructure Development the Economic Development in Developing Countries: Lessons from Korea and Japan.' GSICS Working Paper Series No. 11, 2006.

Llanto, G. M. 'The Impact of Infrastructure on Agricultural Productivity.' Discussion Paper Series No. 2012–13, Philippines Institute for Development Studies, Makati City, Philippines, 2012. Also see http://dirp4.pids.gov.ph/ris/dps/pidsdps1212.pdf (accessed on 3 December 2016).

Manson, R., and S. Chatterjee. 'Regional Development.' In *The Philippine Economy: Development, Policies and Challenges*, edited by A. Balisacam and Hill. Philippines: Ateneo de Manila University Press, 2003.

Martin, W., and D. Mitra. 'Productivity Growth and Convergence in Agriculture and Manufacturing.' *Economic Development and Cultural Change* 49, no. 2 (2001): 403–23.

McArthur, J. W., and J. D. Sachs. 'The Growth Competitive Index: Meaning Technology Advancement and the Stages of Development.' In *The Global Competiveness Report 2001–2002*, edited by M. E. Porter and J. D. Sach. New York: Oxford University Press, 2002.

MEDPRO (Mediterranean Prospect). 'The Relationship between Energy and Economic and Social Development in the Southern Mediterranean' Technical Report No. 27, February 2013. Available at: https://www.files.ethz.ch/isn/161565/MEDPRO%20TR27%20Bergasse%20Energy%20Supply%20and%20Demand%20Policies%20and%20Development%20rev.pdf (accessed on 3 December 2016).

Miah, M., and A. Omar. 'Technology Advancement in Developing Countries During Digital Age.' *International Journal of Science and Applied Information Technology* 1, no. 1 (2012): 30–38.

Mody. A., ed. *Infrastructure Strategies in East-Asia: The Untold Story*. Washington, DC: The World Bank, 1997.

OCHA. 'Energy Security and Humanitarian Action: Key Emerging Trends and Challenges.' OCHA Occasional Policy Briefing Series No. 3, 2010. Available at: http://docs.unocha.org/sities/dms/documents (accessed on 25 October 2015).

Qiang, C. Z. W. *Telecommunication and Economic Growth*. Washington DC: World Bank, 2009.

Reddy, A. K. N. 'Energy and Social Issues.' In *World Energy Assessment: Energy and the Challenge of Sustainability*, 39–58. New York: UNDP, 2000.

Roller, L. H., and L. Waverman. 'Telecommunications Infrastructure and Economic Development: A Simultaneous Approach.' *American Economic Review* 91, no. 4 (2001): 909–23.

Sahoo, P., and P. K. Dash. 'Economic Growth in South Asia: Role of Infrastructure.' *The Journal of International Trade and Economic Development* 21, no. 2 (2008): 217–52.

Seetharam, S. K., and V. Sridhar. 'Telecommunications Infrastructure and Economic Growth: Evidence from Developing Countries.' Working Paper 04/14, NIPFP, 2004.

Smith, K. R. 'Indoor Air Pollution in Developing Countries: Recommendations for Research.' *Indoor Air* 12, no. 3 (2002): 198–207.

Solow, R. 'Technical Changes and the Aggregate Production Function.' *Review of Economics and Statistics* 39 (1997): 312–20.

Srinivasu, B., and P. S. Rao. 'Infrastructure Development and Economic Growth.' *Prospects and Perspective' Journal of Business Management and Social Sciences Research (JBM & SSR)* 2, no. 1 (2013): 81–91.

Starr, C. 'Energy, Power and Society.' *Scientific American*, September (1972).

Trucker, R., Z. Schloss, M. Leitman and D. Olivier. 'Affordable Electricity and Economic Development: The Role of Electric Cooperatives in the 21st Century.' NRECA, 2014. Available at: http://www.nreca.coop/wp-content/uploads/2014 (accessed on 25 October 2015).

UNDP. 'Human Development Report 2001.' UNDP, New York, 2001.

UN-Habitat. 'United Nations Human Settlements Programme–2011.' United Nations, 2011.

UNIDO. 'Industrial Development Report–2013.' UNIDO, 2013.

Valli, V., and D. Saccone. 'Structural Change and Economic Development in China and India.' *The European Journal of Comparative Economics* 6, no. 1 (2009): 101–29.

Vogel, E. F. *The Four Little Dragons: The Spread of Industrialization in East Asia*. MA: Harvard University Press, 1991.

Willoughby, C. 'Infrastructure and Millennium Development Goals.' Sessions on Complementarity of Infrastructure for Achieving Millennium Development Goals, Berlin, United Nations, 1–33, 2001.

World Bank. 'World Development Report 2000: Agriculture for Development.' New York, Oxford University Press, 1998.

———. 'Infrastructure of Crossroads: Lesson from 20 Years of World Bank Experience.' Washington DC, World Bank, 2006.

World Bank. *Global Economic Prospects: Managing the Next Wave of Globalization*. Washington, DC: World Bank, 2007a.

World Bank. "The Nexus between Infrastructure and Environment from The Evaluation Cooperation Group of the International Financial Institutions". *Evaluation Brief* 5 (2007b) Available at: http://siteresources.worldbank.org/INTOED/Resources/infrastructure_environment.pdf (accessed on 3 December 2016).

———. 'Technology and Technological Diffusion in Development Countries.' Global Economic Prospect, 2008a.

———. 'Social Capital and Information Technology.' World Bank, Washington DC, 2008b.

Weigel, G., and D. Waldburger, eds. *ICT4D–Connecting People for a Better World*. Swiss Agency for Development and Cooperation and Global Knowledge Partnership, 18, 2004.

10 Rural Development

The quest for achievement of desired rural development has remained a critical concern of most countries of the contemporary world.

—Nwagboso and Duke (2012)

The rural development is emphasized upon, while a staggering 75 percent of the world's poor live in rural areas, policies and resources continue to be biased in favour of urban development with detrimental effects for both rural and urban populations.

—UNIDO (2003)

Development processes, approaches and strategies adopted by developing countries from the very beginning are facing many pressing issues and challenges. Because of which they have not been able to attain desired goal of sustainable economic and social development. One of these issues and challenges is the rural–urban disparities in development. On the development front, rural areas are far behind the urban areas, particularly in developing countries. The most deprived and neglected people in developing countries live in the rural areas. Nearly 70% of the population in developing countries reside in rural areas. Therefore, development of these countries veritably means development of their rural areas. The aim of the real, inclusive and sustainable development is to reduce poverty, inequality, illiteracy, mortality and morbidities, insanitation and unemployment from the rural areas. The World Bank (2001) has rightly advocated that 'to ensure balanced growth, the most pressing rural sector issues need to be addressed.' There is a pressing need to accelerate the pace of rural development in developing countries, where more than half of the mankind lives.

After reading this chapter, you will be able to:

1. Define rural development and various sectors of rural development.
2. Explain various challenges of rural development.
3. Describe the essential requirements of a smart village.
4. Conduct rural development need assessment.

MEANING AND CHARACTERISTICS OF RURAL AREAS

Development of developing countries truly depends on the development of their rural areas and on structural transformation of the villages. Customarily, rural people living within community have strong affinity towards cultural and religious activities. Traditional beliefs and values still govern the rural society. Living in community clusters is the hallmark of rural lifestyle and livelihood. The rural society is largely a stratified society. Various castes, communities and religious group live together and celebrate their festivals with universal fellow feeling and brotherhood. Even today, the workforce participation of the people is largely governed on the basis of the community belongingness. Most of the people in rural areas are poor, simple and live with limited means and have access to limited amenities. Ashley and Maxwell (2001) have defined rural areas in the following ways:

1. A space where human settlement and infrastructure occupy only a small share of landscape.
2. Natural environment dominated by pastures, forests, mountains and deserts.
3. Settlements of low density (about 5,000–10,000 persons).
4. Places where most people work on farms.
5. The availability of land at a relatively low cost.
6. A place where activities are affected by a high transaction cost, associated with long distance from cities and poor infrastructures.

According to FAO and UNESCO (2003), the definition of 'rural area' should meet two criteria: one related to place of residence and land settlement pattern, and the other related to the type of work that residents engage in. First, rural areas are generally open areas with low density of settled population. A large portion of the unsettled land area is used for primary production (mining, agriculture, livestock, forestry, fisheries, etc.). Second, the residents of rural areas are largely dependent—either directly or indirectly—on the primary production activities as their principal, if not their only source of livelihood.

Some of the characteristics of rural areas in developing countries are:

1. Agriculture and allied activities are the mainstay of the majority of the rural population and possession of agricultural land is the most precious asset of a household.
2. Large-scale landholders and upper strata of rural society still influence the decision-making process of the village development.
3. Percentage of non-farm employment is very low and the lifestyle of the population is very slow and not hectic like that of the urban area's population.
4. Lifestyle of the people is governed by the traditional, cultural and religious beliefs and values.
5. Majority of the people still struggle to meet the basic necessities such as housing, sanitation, drinking water, household energy for cooking and lighting, health care and education.
6. Many rural areas have features like remoteness and poor communication facilities. Although rural roads have been constructed in many states, their maintenance is poor. The caste and the community are largely based on the occupation of the people in the rural society.
7. Traditional occupation–based earners such as barbers, carpenters, cobblers, tanners, black smith and so on, and farming-related activities such as farmers and farm labourers largely constitute the rural employment pattern.

8. People of the rural areas have strong community feeling and cluster living is a way of life for the protection for the protection of the community members.
9. Women are less empowered and are mainly preoccupied in the household activities.
10. Socio-economic marginalization is observed on the basis of caste, class, ethnicity and gender.
11. Most of the people lead simple life and are poorly touched by modernity.

SCOPE OF RURAL DEVELOPMENT

The issue of the rural development is more pressing because issues pertaining to rural development such as poverty, inequality, unemployment, illiteracy and ill-health exist in the countryside. These are long-standing issues which need to be resolved and effectively dealt with in order to enable developing countries to achieve holistic development. The holistic development of developing countries is impossible without the sustainable rural development. The political economy of developing countries is under tremendous pressure to put concerted effort to achieve sustainable rural development.

With rural areas unable to provide enough opportunities for people to sustain their lives, the burden of supporting the poor and rural population falls increasingly upon cities (UNIDO 2003). Rural development is a key concern of the development agenda of both developed and developing countries. It is viewed that the concept 'rural development', as an alternative strategy to overall development, has become a worldwide currency and fashion in both the advanced and backward countries (Abass 1993). Harris (1982) pointed out that the notion of rural development appeared in the 1970s and criticized severely the development policy so far applied in developing countries. In developing countries of South Asia and Sub-Saharan Africa, more than 70% of its population still reside in rural areas. They live in abject poverty and with a low quality of living. Most of them are dependent on conventional livelihood sources. Therefore, any discussion on development, particularly in developing countries, will remain incomplete if it belittles the importance of rural development. The real challenge of development in a developing country lies in how it develops its rural areas and what it does to integrate the rural areas into the mainstream development process. In the Indian context, to quote Mahatma Gandhi, 'Our cities are not India. India lives in her more than seven hundred thousand villages and the cities live upon the villages.' In another context, he said,

> India lives in its villages. It is there that our producers live, voters live, the poor and illiterate live. It is the village that holds the key to the country's problems. So vision of future India cannot be greater than to rebuild it half a million villages. The irony is that in terms of the teaming millions inhabiting in these villages our developments, our democracy and our education have all become irrelevant, but once we decide to approach them in the right spirit they are bound to respond and rise to end their suffering.

According to Robert (1974), four main reasons could be advanced for why greater attention should be shifted to the development of rural areas. First, majority of the population live and find their means of livelihood in the rural areas. Second, the rural–urban drift or migration has continued to be an issue of serious concern to governments, largely due to the increasing spate of urban unemployment, food scarcity, housing problems, sanitation, health changes and other attendant social problems. Third, in most of the third world

Table 10.1 *Rural Population (Percentage of Total Population)*

Region	Percentage
Arab World	48
Caribbean Small states	58
East Asia and Pacific	49
Least Developed Countries: UN Classification	70
Middle East and North Africa	40
South Asia	68
Sub-Saharan Africa	63
World	47

Source: World Development Indicator, World Bank (2015).

countries, the poor and disadvantaged people mostly reside in the rural areas. Fourth, many scholars have persuasively argued that priority should be accorded to issues germane to rural and agricultural development, implicit in their significant roles in a country's economic growth and development (Table 10.1).

The aim of the rural development projects and programmes is to improve the lifestyle of the countryside people from the traditional to modern one. The aim is the mechanization of agriculture, application of technology to rural small-scale and cottage industries and opening service sector facilities such as school, colleges, banks, cooperative societies, insurance companies, tourism and hotels, market and so on in rural areas. Rural development means socio-economic, human, political and cultural development of the rural areas and its population. It is desirable that the rural development projects and programmes are implemented honestly, so that the poverty, inequality and unemployment in the rural areas are reduced and per capita income and social capital are enhanced. Furthermore, the capabilities of rural people are enhanced through skill training and the application of technology so that they contribute significantly towards national growth and development. According to the World Bank (1975),

> Rural development is a strategy designed to improve the economic and social life of a specific group of people—the rural poor. It involves extending the benefits of development to the poorest among those who seek a livelihood in the rural areas. The group includes small-scale farmers, tenants and the landless.

Ollawa (1971) perceives rural development as 'The restructuring of the economy in order to satisfy the material needs and aspirations of the rural masses and to promote individual and collective incentives to enable them participate in the process of development.' While Nwagbosa and Duke (2012) viewed rural development as a multidimensional process aimed at uplifting the life of the rural dwellers in the society, this involves the creation of employment, access to roads, health facilities, better housing, good water supply and equitable distribution of income among the rural people. The rural development strategy involves a host of multisectoral activities including the improvement of agriculture, the promotion of rural industries, the creation of requisite infrastructure and social overheads, as well as the establishment of appropriate decentralized structure in order to allow mass production (Wilkin 2010).

ISSUES AND CHALLENGES OF RURAL DEVELOPMENT

The challenges of rural development are multidimensional and require multi-pronged strategies and approaches to deal with them. Therefore, the approaches and strategies to tackle sundry of rural area problems through various rural development programmes and projects must vary from one area to that of the other. However, primary issues and challenges haunting the countryside are (a) to reduce poverty, unemployment and inequality; (b) to raise productivity and literacy rate; (c) to reduce illiteracy, insanitation, morbidity and mortality and (d) to make provision of basic amenities such as food, clothing, housing, sanitation, safe drinking water and communication facilities to the rural people. Some of the issues and challenges of rural development are discussed below.

Population, Poverty, Inequality and Unemployment

High population growth in rural areas in developing countries is a cause of concern. It is one of the factors responsible for endurance of poverty in rural areas. Illiteracy and low level of education, lower age at marriage, poor decision-making power of women regarding number of children and ideal family size, poor quality of family planning services, religious and traditional beliefs and values are some of the factors among many that are responsible for high fertility in rural areas. Impoverished families in the rural areas with large family size experience multiple problems, i.e. poverty and poor access to basic amenities such as housing, sanitation, health care and education. Tackling the twin problem of population and poverty is a herculean task before the governments of developing countries. Truly, three quarters of the world's poor live in rural areas, and the reality is that the poverty target of the SDGs cannot be met unless the world in general and developing countries in particular address rural poverty with sincere efforts.

Rural economy has a vexing problem of socio-economic inequality in terms of access to social capital, income and land resources. Besides, disguised unemployment and underemployment also constitute unique characteristics of population living in the rural areas. Disguised unemployment, underemployment and poor availability of wage employment and low-income self-employment activities lead to low per capita income of the rural households. These factors limit their access to quality education, health care, housing and sanitation facilities among others. Rural economy is basically an informal economy where people lack information about the market, which almost non-existent, even if it exists, it exists in the form of haat where exchange of goods takes place through both barter system and monetary terms with a limited number of petty businessmen and buyers from nearby village clusters. The economic inequality is observed among the landlords and landless, people working in the formal sector and those who are employed in the informal wage employment and self-employment activities (Table 10.2).

Provision of Basic Needs

One of the stupendous challenges before the governments of the developing counties is to make adequate provision of basic need facilities, i.e. housing, food and nutrition, sanitation, safe drinking water, electricity, primary education and health care to its rural people. Majority of the socio-economically backward sections of population in rural areas lack access to the basic minimum necessities because of poverty, unemployment and low

Table 10.2 *Selected Countries Having High Rural Poverty Headcount Ratio at National Poverty Line, 2010*

Country	Rural Population (%)
Gambia	73.9
Guinea–Bissau	75.6
Honduras	65.4
Lesotho	61.2
Madagascar	81.5
Mexico	60.7
Peru	61.0
Zambia	77.9

Source: World Development Indicator, World Bank Group.

income. Poor access to basic amenities in rural areas creates social disorganization through which a poor family during a generation is likely to remain poor in other generations because of poverty and wealth appear to be inter-generationally transmitted (Jha and Kumar). Because of poor access to sanitary facilities and safe drinking water, water- and sanitation-related mortality and morbidity continuously occur in rural areas of South Asia. Most of the day is lost by the women in fetching water from distance villages in rural areas and a lot of gender-related crimes also take place which go unnoticed. The SDGs in rural areas cannot be attained so along as the people residing in the rural areas lack access to basic amenities. Provision of basic amenities to the countryside people has remained a basic challenge to rural development for past several decades in many developing countries.

Infrastructure and Rural Development

Lack of proper and adequate infrastructure facility is an important cause of rural backwardness. Deficiency in irrigation facility impedes agricultural development while deficiency of road, energy and water works, storage, market, health care institutions, educational institutions, banking and cooperative institutions and so on are hurdles in the path of rural industrial and service sector development. Poor rural road facilities affect the education and health status of rural population. Poor ITC facilities restrict rural social networking and rural–urban connectedness. It has been seen that the village panchayats having computer and internet facilities have rural database, and are in a better position to solve many rural problems. In Kerala, most of village panchayats are e-panchayats which manage village development activities far better than other panchayats in the rest of the country. Many households of the rural areas of developing countries, particularly those of South Asia, do not have access to electricity and even if they have electricity connection, the frequent load shedding is a permanent issue in many provinces. Lack of electricity affects the education of the children, rural healthcare and cold chain system, and it prolongs education and health problems in the rural areas. The World Bank (2013), in the context of the rural development of the African countries, has rightly mentioned that the development of rural infrastructure—energy, transport, water, ICT, storage facility among others—contributes significantly to the level and quality of rural development. Moreover, countries that have developed the rural infrastructure have recorded higher and better quality of rural development than those that have failed to do so. Failure to accelerate investments in rural infrastructure will make a mockery of efforts to achieve MDGs in poor developing countries while at the same time, severely limited opportunities for these countries to benefit from trade liberalization, international capital markets and other potential benefits offered by globalization (Andersen and Shimokawa 2006). Investment in rural infrastructure and infrastructure development is a formidable challenge before developing countries aiming at fostering inclusive and sustainable rural development. The two pertinent issues, as far as rural infrastructure is concerned, are lack of investments and poor maintenance. Moreover, lack of availability of land for construction has derailed many rural infrastructure projects in developing countries.

Agriculture and Rural Livelihood

Agriculture is the mainstay of the rural population, and is an important means of livelihood. Rural economies in developing countries are predominately agricultural economies, where more than 70% of the population is dependent on agriculture in terms of employment and livelihood. However, agriculture in developing countries, particularly in the dry land, hills and desert areas, has failed to provide a sustainable livelihood to the people. As a result, there has been a large-scale inter- and intra-state migration from rural areas to urban area. Moreover, because of rise in the cost of cultivation, agriculture has not been a profitable profession in the Green Revolution belt also. The challenges which developing countries are facing with regard to agriculture are low agricultural productivity, poor mechanization of agriculture, small and fragmented landholding, idle and ineffective use of waste and common land, pro-poor harvest technology, low productivity of livestock, poor diversification of agriculture in dry land areas, poor planning of alternative use of land resources during lean season, poor access to suitable credit system, inadequate procurement system, poor emphasis on cash crops and unstructured contact farming system. These are some of the key challenges out of many more have to be dealt with in order to enhance the contribution of agriculture to rural development. The issues of agricultural labour, leasing-in and leasing-out of land and wage to agricultural labours are critical to raise the quality of life of the landless agriculture labours in rural areas.

The irony is that over a period of time, it is seen that in developing countries, the contribution of agriculture to GDP has declined as compared to industry and service sectors. However, people employed and dependent on agriculture sector in these countries have not declined proportionately, resulting in dumping of disguised unemployment and underemployment in the agriculture sector. According to IFPRI (2006), given that the majority of poor people live in rural areas or rely on agriculture, and that agriculture paves the way for economic growth in the poorer nations, agriculture and rural development will underlie progress in the broad array of economic and social indicators emphasized on the MDGs. Therefore, the challenge is to accelerate agriculture growth rate and reduce the concentration of disguised unemployment in agriculture sector either by shifting them to the allied sector activities or to industry and service sectors. Sustainable agriculture and sustainable rural development are intimately related in developing countries where more than 70% of people are dependent on agriculture and allied activities for their livelihood. Agriculture is the primary sector and neglecting agriculture will lead to hunger death and farmer suicides in rural areas.

Rural Industry and Entrepreneurship

The structural transformation of the rural economy will raise the standard of living of rural people. With the rising literacy and level of education among the rural population, the young generation of rural population is less interested to work in the agriculture and allied sector activities; instead, they prefer to remain unemployed and disguisedly hidden in the agriculture sector. Thus, there is a need for promotion of rural industrialization in general, and village small-scale cottage industries in particular. Industrial development of rural areas in developing countries depends on the innovative and pragmatic endeavours of rural entrepreneurs. Entrepreneurs such as village artisans, carpenters, blacksmiths, barbers, fishermen, dairy and poultry entrepreneurs and others are needed to be encouraged by the government through various incentives such as soft loan and tax benefit facilities to start small-scale industries. They should be provided skill training on modern practices which will enhance their income and quality of output. The structure of rural economies is essentially composed of small enterprises, which are responsible for most of the job growth and the innovations and in any event, small business represent an appropriate scale of activity of most rural economies (Dabson 2005). Even the FDIs and country's non-residents and remitting investors may be encouraged to invest in rural industrialization. Agriculture alone cannot bring sustainable rural development unless it is backed by rural industrial sector. China's rural enterprises widely known as TVEs have remarkably contributed to its economic growth, rural development and institutional transformation. The Chinese experience illustrates that rural industrialization can play a crucial role in:

1. raising income of the rural people;
2. solving the unemployment problem of the countryside;
3. checking rural to urban migration;
4. supporting and enhancing the effectiveness of agriculture;
5. contributing to social sector development, especially health and education; and
6. transforming the socio-economic environment of the countryside. (Sanjeev Kumar[1])

There is a growing need for rural entrepreneurship because industrial units undertaken by rural entrepreneurs are providing much employment to men than machines (Paul and Sharma 2013). Institutions and individuals promoting rural development now see entrepreneurship as a strategic development infrastructure that could accelerate the rural development process (Saxena 2012). Moreover, the economic goals of an entrepreneur and the social goals of rural development are more strongly interlinked than in urban areas and relatively have large impact on rural community (Nandanwar 2011). Rural entrepreneurship in general and rural women entrepreneur development in particular will go a long way to boost rural economic growth and development in developing countries.

Rural Banking and Cooperatives

Rural banking and cooperatives have a greater role to play to provide cheap and viable finance to various sectors of rural development. However, studies have shown that despite the nationalization of the commercial banks in India, the credit requirements of the rural small entrepreneurs have not been fulfilled. Banks have supported the credit needs of the upper class whereas the poor and lower-middle class people are largely left out. Therefore, a large percentage of rural people are still dependent on informal money lenders for loans. The rate of interest which they usually charge is very high. It is one of the reasons of pauperization of rural peasantry. Some of the factors responsible for poor response to commercial bank loans are directed lending, cumbersome procedure, delay in sanctioning loan and lack of statutory backing for loan recovery. Finance is the life blood of agriculture, industry and service sectors, without which the growth rate and development in rural area cannot be materialized. A recent Reserve Bank of India study shows that about two-fifths of the rural household depend on informal credits, which indicates a scope for financial inclusion, financial education and financial literacy in rural India.

Like rural banking, rural cooperatives have an important role to play in the rural social and economic development. Mahatma Gandhi was a true votary of cooperative development and laid emphasis on the formation of rural cooperative societies for the all-round development of the villages. The formulation of cooperatives such as agriculture cooperatives, industrial cooperatives, dairy cooperatives, fishery cooperatives and so on will not only promote rural agriculture and industrial development but also could promote social networking among the people. It will act as instrument to promote inclusive rural development. ILO in an article 'Cooperatives for People-Centred Rural Development' has envisaged that

> Cooperatives play a major self-help role in rural areas, particularly where private business hesitate to go and public authorities do not provide basic services. They are instrumental in providing opportunities for productive employment, as well as offering health care, education, potable water, improved sanitation, roads, market access, while giving stronger voice to rural groups.[2]

Social and Human Development

Rural areas in developing countries lack good quality of health and education institutions, also deficiency of qualified and trained manpower. Moreover, the qualified teachers, doctors and nurses are generally not motivated to work in rural areas. This has resulted in the shortage of technical manpower in education and health sector. All the three indicators of human development index such as literacy rate, life expectancy and per capita income in rural areas are low as compared to urban areas. It is astoundingly low in case of marginalized sections of rural population such as SCs and STs in India. Therefore, rural human development is a big challenge to the path of rural transformation. Pulver and Jenkins, from American context, were of the view that the quality of human resources, in terms of levels of education and health, is a critical determinant of the economic development prospects of rural America.

Technology

Use of technology in various sectors of rural development is a key issue in this globalized world. Impact of technology on agricultural productivity is a well-established fact in both developed and developing countries. Besides the agriculture sector, there is a tremendous scope for use of technology in the rural industrial and service sectors. The rural areas are the victim of 'digital divide' because of lack of infrastructure facilities in rural areas. Use of technologies in on-farm and off-farm activities in the rural has the potential for generating employment opportunities for the rural youth who are found to be underemployed and are in disguised unemployment in rural areas. The on-farm activities are crop production, horticulture, forestry, sericulture, livestock, husbandry, fishery, agro-service centres, processing of food forest products, production of agricultural inputs such as bio-fertilizers, bio-pesticides, vermicompost, mushroom spawn production, seeds and plants, cattle feed and so on. While the off-farm activities are of two types: (a) cottage industry—pottery, smithy, carpentry, textile, production of building material and (b) services—automobile hire and repairs, electrical works, civil construction, consumer store. Besides, the use of ICT would enhance capabilities of the service sector, such as rural education, health care, banking and cooperatives, and so on, in rural areas. It will enable the rural local self-government institutions to prepare decentralized planning more effectively and efficiently. Technology will enable effective monitoring and evaluation of various rural development projects and programmes.

In recent years, it has been seen that the use of IT has enabled smooth transformation of knowledge and information from the experts to the rural masses on various aspects relating to agriculture, health, education, small saving, rural credit, employment, poverty alleviation, sanitation and many other similar rural development programmes. The use of technology has immensely enhanced the service delivery system in rural areas and has improved transparency and helped in checking corruption at the grass-root level. Scaria and Vijayan (2012) have found that the Software Package for Sustainable Rural Development (SPSRD), an IT tool, has integrated the scope and advantages of spatial information technology and MGNREGS for sustainable rural development, and use of SPSRD by Gram Panchayat in planning would open new avenues and opportunities in rural development. The use of more and more advanced technology in the remotest part of rural areas is a challenge before developing countries.

Gender Role in Rural Development

Women, who constitute nearly 50% of the rural population, are the potent players of rural development. In developing countries, women belonging to rural areas participate in almost all activities, i.e. agriculture, livestock, fishery, poultry, kitchen garden, food processing and daily household activities such as food preparation, water collection, taking care of children and elderly. It is a fact that rural development is not possible without their active participation. They are the silent contributors to rural development. Their contribution, although not valued, is significant for the sustainable rural development. According to FAO, rural women play a key role in supporting their households and communities in achieving food and nutrition security, generating income and improving livelihoods and overall well-being. According to International Fund for Agriculture

Development (IFAD), giving women the same access as men to agricultural resource and inputs could increase production on women's farms by 20%–30%, reducing the number of hungry people in the world by 100–150 million. World Conference on Agrarian Reforms and Rural Development (1979) held in Rome recognized the vital role of women in the socio-economic life in both agricultural and non-agricultural activities as a prerequisite for successful rural development planning and programme implementation. UNIDO (2003) considers rural development and gender equality key elements of strategies to reduce poverty and create income employment opportunities. Securing rural women's access to and control over resources (e.g. land, livestock, water, salary coming from their activities) can contribute to poverty reduction and the economic growth of an entire country (Dekens and Voora 2014). A developing country has to empower its women to play a key role in the socio-economic development of rural areas. They must be empowered with ownership of land, household assets, rural employment, entrepreneurship, credit and financial facilities and access to rural technology. Besides, equal participation of women in the household decision-making would be helpful to effectively eradicate rural poverty. Rural poverty also exists because of gender inequality and meagre economic contribution of women towards household income. Therefore, backwardness of women and rural backwardness are quite synonymous.

Empowerment of Local Self Government and Rural Development

The last two decades of the 20th century witnessed a significant rise in the scope of local democracy throughout developing countries. Haque (1977) argued that the decentralization is a way of increasing the effectiveness of development programmes by making them more relevant and responsive to local needs and conditions, allowing greater flexibility in their implementation, thus making the state more participatory, more acceptable and more effective and efficient. Democratic decentralization is a means to enhance performance of the government and ultimately to support economic development (Bahl and Smoke 2003). Ezeani (2006) was of the view that 'local government particularly in developing countries is seen as a veritable instrument for rural development. Consequently, all over the world, local governments have been assigned some functions under the law.' In India, 73rd constitutional amendment has assigned 21 duties and responsibilities to the Panchayati Raj institutions (rural local self-governments) for the development of the rural areas. However, it is seen that despite the devolution of power to the local self-government institutions by the constitution, the state governments of different states in India have not devolved functions, functionaries and funds to the local self-government institutions, i.e. the Panchayati Raj institutions. The empowerment of local self-government institutions by the state governments in India is poor except in a few states. However, researches carried on the panchayats' role and responsibilities show that the village panchayats are largely carrying out their functions in many areas and are mainly involved in the implementation of grant-in-aid rural development schemes such as Sampoorna Grameen Rozgar Yojana (SGRY), Swarnajayanti Gram Swarozgar Yojana (SGSY), Indira Awas Yojana (IAY) and so on. They are also found to be involved in Bharat Nirman, i.e. infrastructure building such as construction of connecting roads, panchayat buildings, school building, health centre building, installation of tube wells, overseeing irrigation projects and so on (see Table 10.3).

Table 10.3 *Important Rural Development Activities Performed by the Village Panchayats*

Departments	**Main Activities Performed by Village Panchayat**
Drinking Water/irrigation	Installation of hand pumps and tube wells, implementation of drinking water projects and their monitoring and construction water shed projects, etc.
Education	Distribution of scholarships to SC/ST students, distribution of books to SC/ST students, mid-day meal, construction of school building, boundary wall, toilet, drinking water facility and play ground.
Women and Child Welfare	Providing place for Anganwadi centres and construction of Anganwadi buildings and monitoring of nutrition.
Implementation of Rural Development Programmes	Implementation of various rural development schemes such as SGRY, SGSY, IAY, Total Sanitation Campaign (TSC), etc.
Electricity	Provision of street lights.
Social Welfare	Implementation of and overseeing of the old-age pension, handicap pension and widow pension schemes.
Food Grain Supply	Helping government officials in the preparation of ration cards and identifying BPL families through Gram Sabha (village assembly).
Strengthening Local self-government Institution (Panchayati Raj)	Construction of Panchayat buildings, holding panchayat meetings, Gram Sabha, formulation of standing committee, construction of community hall, etc.
Energy Development	Helping household in the installation of Gobar Gas plant and solar energy.
Health and Family Welfare	Arrangement of place for immunization, construction of dispensaries, arrangement of place for village sub-centre, etc.

Source: Findings from the studies and observations made during field visits to village panchayats of various states.

As the elected representatives of the local self-government institutions are closer to the people, they are in a better position to identify people's problem and help government functionaries to effectively implement rural development programmes.

Functionaries of the government should play a facilitator's role and not a dominating supervisory role. It is seen that whenever the devolution of functions, functionaries and funds to the local government is guaranteed, it has enabled these institutions to function more convincingly to fulfil the aspirations of the local people. In Kerala, where the state government has effectively devolved functions, functionaries and funds to the local self-governments at the grass-root level they have achieved better holistic-rural development as compared to other states of India. Table 10.3 shows various duties and responsibilities performed by the village panchayats of various states of India. Mahatma Gandhi, while emphasizing on 'Gram Swaraj' (village autonomy), had strongly advocated that 'independence must begin at the bottom. Thus, every village will be a republic of panchayat having full power.' The capacity of the local government institutions' elected representatives will go a long way to enable them to function effectively at the grass-roots.

People's Planning Campaign: Kerala Model of Decentralized Planning

In Kerala, the 'Decentralized Planning' at the grass-root level adopts following phases for plan preparation.

Phase I: In this phase, Gram Sabha (village assembly) is convened to identify local development priorities. To ensure popular participation, a volunteer squad visits household to household and explains to them the importance of participation in the Gram Sabha. The Gram Sabha is the key to the identification of local development aspirations and needs, and collection of information on natural resources and problem identification.

Phase II: During the second phase, 'local development seminars' are organized to suggest actions to address the development priorities identified by the Gram Sabhas. These seminars are organized with the help of a group of trained local resources persons, elected Panchayati Raj Institution (PRI) representatives and government officials. This phase produces an extensive local data base, a comprehensive survey of the development status of the panchayat and a list of likely solutions to development problems. In this phase, 'task forces' on various sectors of development are set up to prepare development projects for each development sector.

Phase III: In the third phase, the sector-wise task forces prepare projects based on the suggestions emerged from the development seminars. All the development sectors have a task force of 10–15 members each and are chaired by an elected representative of village panchayat with an officer from the relevant department being the convener.

Phase IV: The sectoral development projects prepared by the task forces are prioritized in this phase for incorporation into the five-year plans of the panchayats.

Phase V: In the fifth phase of the plan preparation, plans are vetted by a panel of experts for their technical viability and conformity with the mandatory government guidelines on planning and costing before they are forwarded to the District Planning Committee (DPC) for incorporation in the district plan.

Phase VI: This is the final phase, where the DPC gives formal approval to all village plans. It is to be noted that after the formal approval of the village panchayat, even DPC cannot change the village panchayat priority but only ensure compliance with government guidelines.

The final Development Plan for each district in Kerala thus reflects people's needs and aspirations.

Source: Development Administration, Study Material, University of Calicut, Kerala, 2011.

Duties and Responsibility Assigned to PRIs as per the 73rd Constitutional Amendment

The 73rd Constitutional amendment of government of India has assigned 29 duties and responsibilities to the PRIs under 11th Schedule (article 243G); these are: agriculture, including agriculture extension; land improvement, implementation of land reforms, land consolidation and soil conservation; minor irrigation, water management and watershed development; animal husbandry, dairying and poultry; fishery; social forestry and farm forestry; minor forest produce; small scale industries, including food processing industries; khadi, village and cottage industries, rural housing, drinking water; fuel and fodder; roads, culverts, bridges, ferries, waterways and other means of communication; rural electrification including distribution of electricity; non-conventional energy sources; poverty alleviation programme; education, including primary and secondary schools; technical training and vocational education; adult and non-formal education; libraries; cultural activities; market and fairs; health and sanitation, including welfare of the handicapped and mentally retarded; welfare of weaker sections, and in particular of the Scheduled Castes and the Scheduled Tribes; public distribution system and maintenance of community assets.

Provision of Urban Amenities in Rural Areas

Raising the quality of life of the people living in rural areas at par with those of the urban areas is a key challenge before the government of developing countries. Attempt has to be made to provide urban type of basic amenities and facilities in the rural areas. It will not only improve the lifestyle of rural people but also check the rural to urban migration. The programme, Provision of Urban Amenities in Rural Areas popularly known as 'PURA' is one of the endeavours aimed at to raise the quality of living in rural areas at par with that of urban areas. According to Roy (2014), the primary objective of the PURA is the provision of livelihood opportunities and urban amenities in rural areas to bridge the rural–urban divide. A. P. J. Abdul Kalam, who was a strong votary of PURA, said that the sustainable rural development can be achieved with the mission of PURA through the creation of three connectivities, namely physical, electronic and knowledge, leading to economic connectivity:

Physical Connectivity: Villages must be connected within themselves and with main towns and metros through good roads and railway lines. They must have other infrastructure like schools, colleges, other hospitals other and amenities for the local population and the visitors.

Electronic Connectivity: In the emerging knowledge era, the native knowledge has to be preserved and enhanced with the latest tools of technology, training and research. The traditional knowledge system (TKS) must be used for the greater benefit of the rural population. Villages have to have access to good education from the best teachers wherever they are, must have the benefits of good medical treatment and the latest information on their life pursuits, i.e. agriculture, fishery, horticulture and food processing.

Knowledge Connectivity: Once the physical and electronic connectivity are made available, the knowledge connectivity is enabled. This can facilitate the ability to increase the productivity, the utilization of spare time, awareness of health welfare, ensuring a market for products, increasing quality conscience, interacting with partners, getting the best equipment, increasing transparency and so on in general knowledge connectivity.

Once the three connectivities—physical, electronic and knowledge—are ensured, they facilitate earning capacity leading to economic connectivity. When we provide urban amenities to rural areas, we can begin the upliftment of rural areas, attract investors and introduce effectively useful systems like rural BPOs and microfinance (Abdul Kalam 2014). Some of the infrastructure facilities to be provided under PURA are:

> **Basic and Mandatory Infrastructure:** Good quality houses, construction and maintenance of village streets, water and sewerage system, drainage, solid waste management, strengthening of traditional village industries and rural entrepreneurship through skill development and creation employment opportunities in agriculture, industry and service sectors of rural areas.
>
> **Essential Infrastructure:** Village street lighting, telecom and electricity generation and 24-hour power supply to villages.
>
> **Miscellaneous Infrastructure:** Village markets and integrated rural hubs, agribusiness centres, food processing centres, village heritage and rural tourism centres, rural cultural and religious tourism, rural entertainment centres, i.e. youth clubs, Mahila Mandals, old-age recreation centre and so on.

The two concepts used to buttress PURA are 'Rurban' and 'Rural–Urban Continuum'. According to Berenstsen, Roosaare and Samara (2000),

> Rurban areas are defined as places where there are many people who live urban lifestyles (including commuting to urban or suburban areas) but in a setting that otherwise appears rather rural (e.g. much of such an area may still be dominated by fields and forest).

The 'rurbanization' concept popularized in the Vibrant Gujarat campaign in 2013 aims at the infusion of urban patterns and services in to rural systems to ensure provision of quality lifestyles and livelihood options while keeping the basic rural soul intact. It is also seen as a tool to invoke reverse migration, easing the pressure on civic infrastructure in densely populated and over-crowded urban agglomerations.[3] In a nutshell, 'rurban' is nothing but enabling urban life style facilities in the rural areas. The use of the term 'rural–urban continuum' in India is fit to Kerala state. Kerala can be described as an urban village with hardly any demarcation between urban and rural areas (George 2013). The rural–urban continuum can be defined as dynamic equilibrium wherein the development process involves the people in both rural and urban areas, and the returns of development are also distributed to the people whose settlement pattern is distributed spatially (George 2013).

Gujarat Model of Rurbanization

In the Rurban Gujarat Model, the efforts to rurbanize the state have been focused towards the development of 'Rurban centre' and 'Rurban cluster'. Rurban centre comprises all taluka headquarters with village panchayats (not declared as municipality) or all non-urban taluka headquarters and all village panchayats having population of 10,000 or more and Rurban cluster is usually a group of villages within 15 km of influence zone of Rurban centres and caters to a population of 50,000 and above. The key objectives of Gujarat's model of planned development in Rurban centres and Rurban clusters include:

- Promotion of integrated development of rural areas with provision of quality housing, better connectivity, employment opportunities and supporting physical and social infrastructure.
- Efficient mass-transportation systems to improve connectivity between urban and rural areas, Rurban centres and urban cities as well as internal connectivity within Rurban cluster.
- Reduce migration from rural to urban areas due to lack of basic services and sufficient economic activities in rural areas.

Source: Vibrant Gujarat 2013, Sixth Global Summit, Panel Discussion on Rurbanization, Proceedings Report, 11–13 January, 2013. Available at: http://www.vibrnatgujarat.com/Portal/Event_Image (accessed on 16 February 2015).

Primarily, rurban aims to check indiscreet urbanization and unbridled migration of population from rural to urban areas. It also desires to provide urban quality of life in rural areas through the improvement of good quality urban style infrastructure in rural areas. It also aims at bringing parity in development between rural and urban areas and reducing disequilibrium in the development process of rural and urban areas. It wants to empower the people staying in the rural areas. It also aims to enhance the potential of rural areas so that they can equally contribute to the growth and development of nation like the urban areas do.

Rural–Urban Continuum: An Excerpt on the Kerala Model

Kerala villages bear little resemblance to the right, squalid settlements of North India which huddle along a single street or in a knot of houses for mutual protection. In spite of their unorganized appearance, the Malayali villages have quite elaborate social structures. Each will have, at least, one school and a public library. It will have a public health service, trade union branches and political party groups, places of worship (often a temple, a church and a mosque) and always a few tea shops which serve as meeting places for the various communities. Many Malayali intellectual and officials return to their native villages in middle age and take an active part in local activities, so that there is a cultural sophistication about rural life in Kerala. In many respects, it is urban (Woodcock 1967, 4445).

Smart Village

Rural areas of a country, particularly developing countries, are comprised of villages. A village has certain boundary area, certain number of households and population. In India, the name and list of villages belonging to different states are available in the decadal census conducted by the state governments. Villages vary in size in terms of area as well as population. There are small villages having population of 100–1,000, medium-sized villages with population of less than 5,000 and large villages having more than 5,000 people. People living in the villages have their agricultural land. Village-level institutions, such as village panchayat, youth club, Mahila Mandal, religious institutions, school, dispensary and other village-level social development institutions vary from one village to the other. India has more than 6 lakh villages and the number is on the increase in each census. The real India lives in its villages. The village development must be a central theme in all development policies and programmes of India. Both the central and state governments of India should try to develop all villages. Each and every village of India should be made smart. Some of the important aspects of smart village are:

- Smart village needs to have a smart boundary, and it should not have any dispute with other villages as far as the boundary is concerned.
- It should have smart population, which is literate, well-educated and free from major diseases.
- The agricultural land of the village needs to have irrigation facility and every household need to have a kitchen garden to fulfil its vegetable and nutrient requirements.
- Every household in a smart village needs to do tree plantation not only for healthy living but also for the preservation of the environment.
- Every family must have a healthy house—well-ventilated, having a kitchen and toilet with bathroom facility and access to safe drinking water facility.
- All households must be empowered to have access to safe energy for cooking and must be connected with electricity facility.
- It is required have a functional village development committee, with member of all the communities along with women and youth representatives and representatives from socially backward communities. This will look after all the development affair of the village.
- An effective and fair public distribution system is put in place to take care of the BPL families while distributing the benefits through its fair price shops. Each and every family must be covered under the food security programme so that no one dies of hunger
- There must be trained and active village-level organizations such as SHGs, youth clubs and Mahila Mandals.
- The village panchayat members need to be trained and should actively participate in village development activities and ensure that all the developmental activities are approved by the Gram Sabha. Panchayat should discharge its assigned constitutional duties effectively and efficiently. Panchayat also needs to take charge of the effective implementation of various rural development programmes and look after the effective functioning of all level institutions such as Anganwadi centres, schools, health centres and so on.

- Village should have street lights and if required, village *Shauchalaya*s (toilets) maintained by the village community.
- Each village needs to have a non-conventional energy source, generated through cow dung gas, wind energy, solar energy and energy from the village waste.
- The village must have a weekly village *haat* or market, and the government should create necessary infrastructure for it while the village panchayat must ensure open space for it.
- Each village also needs to have a labour market which should be controlled by the village panchayat, and the panchayat should ensure that labourers get the minimum wage rate as fixed by the government.
- If there is a heritage place in the village, it must be declared as a heritage village and government must create necessary infrastructure for the promotion of tourism there.
- The village needs to have two village ponds—one for bathing of people and another for the animals. Community fishing should be developed in the village pond and money generated through it must be used for village development activities. The village, if it belongs to rain-fed area, must have rain water harvesting tank.
- The open space must be left for the celebration of common festivals such as Ganesh Puja, Saraswati Puja, Dussehra and all other festivals, such as Eid, Gurpurab, Christmas and so on, being celebrated by various communities.
- There must be community policing and a village *nyayalaya* (court) to amicably settle common disputes, problems and quarrels.
- Every village must have a sewerage system and a garbage disposal tank for the disposal of village waste.
- The village open space must be effectively utilized having a park for the elderly and playground for the children and youth.
- The village should not have alcohol shops, and sale of all types of intoxicating substance should be banned.
- The village should have an *Anganwadi* centre for preschool education, a primary school and health centre or health post (if the subcentre is in another nearby village), and teachers and health workers must sincerely take care of education and health care of its people.
- Village should be an e-Village with broadband connectivity. The village data, such as population, BPL families land record, type of houses, access to electricity, water supply, sanitation, and so on, workforce participation and income of the household, immunization status, mortality and morbidity status and all other types of data and information must be available at the village information centre (VIC) established in village panchayat. The birth and death and all other essential certificates must be issued by the VIC.
- There must be community *safai karmachari*s (sweepers), being paid by the community to properly clean village roads. Every village road and the connecting roads must be made of concrete.
- Every village needs to have small-scale industries and a service centre to accomplish its holistic village development goals.
- The land reform measure should be effectively implemented and the surplus land be distributed among the landless.

- Village should have fishermen, washermen, barbers, goldsmiths, carpenters, pujaris and others to perform all the required activities in the village.
- Village must be free from beggars, child labours and prostitution and human trafficking. Village authorities also need to ensure that nobody dies of hunger and socio-economic disparities are reduced to the minimum.

Rural Food and Social Security

Hunger deaths are a curse on the humanity. It is seen that most of the hunger deaths occur in the rural areas and among the landless and marginal landholders in the dry land areas. Food security to the rural population is a fundamental duty of a nation. Distribution of food grains through fair price shops and ensuring BPL families their right to food will prevent hunger-related deaths. Effective implementation and proper monitoring of the food security programmes are vital to prevent rural hunger and malnutrition.

Another critical security issue is the social security during old age. The sustainable livelihood of the people living in the rural areas is jeopardized during the old age if they are landless and their children desert them. As a result, the life of the senescent population becomes precarious. Therefore, provisioning of social security to the farmers, cultivators, agricultural labourers, rural artisans and other aged is essential. Such an amount of old-age pension be given that would provide them a sustainable livelihood and meet their old-age requirements, i.e. food, nutrition, health care, medicines, vitamins and so on. Even old age homes can be constructed as per the need in rural areas and be maintained with the overall supervision of the village panchayat. Provisioning income and food security to the old age people living in rural areas of developing countries is a critical challenge.

Continuous Assessment of the Progress of Rural Development

Rural development is a continuous process. It is observed that even after making a lot of investment in terms of physical, financial and human resources for the development of various sects of rural areas, the quality of life of the people living in the countryside has not been sufficiently improved. Faulty need assessment, lacklustre implementation of rural development projects and programmes, lack of community participation and corruption are a few among many reasons for slow-paced rural development. Therefore, the projects and programmes implemented for the development of rural areas must be continuously monitored and evaluated. The corrective measures have to be taken. Every village must prepare its Five Year Village Development Plan (VDP) with annual activity mapping and action points after conducting detailed village need assessment. In India, decentralized grass-root level planning model of Kerala and the preparation of the village panchayat plan by the village panchayat is widely sighted. Some of the useful indictors for the conduction of village-need assessment in the preparation of VDP are given below:

- **Total population.** Sex-distribution, age-distribution, caste and religion group of population and occupational distribution of population.
- % of BPL households.
- Per capita income of the households.

- % of households having bank account (or savings).
- % of household having *pucca* (brick) houses.
- % of household having access to safe drinking water.
- % of household using toilet for defecation.
- % household having access to sewerage system.
- % of household having electricity facility for lighting.
- % of household with cooking gas facility.
- % of household having agricultural land for cultivation.
- % of household having irrigated agricultural land.
- % of household having livestock—poultry, dairy, piggery, fishery, horticulture, floriculture, and so on.
- % of population engaged in non-farm employment such as carpentry, pottery, goldsmith, black smith, mason and so on.
- % of women population engaged in non-farm employment.
- % of self-employed persons.
- % of rural entrepreneurs.
- % of unemployed youth.
- % literacy and population with various level of education.
- % of women literacy and level of education.
- Infant mortality.
- Maternal mortality.
- % of immunized children.
- % of immunized pregnant and lactating women.
- % of malnourished children and women.
- % of population suffering from communicable and non-communicable diseases.
- Sex ratio of the village.
- % of old-age population having access to social security scheme.
- % of eligible couple using family planning methods for population control.
- % of children (male/female) engaged in child labour activities.
- % of people working (male/female) as bonded labour.
- % of members participating in Gram Sabha (village assembly) meeting.
- % of women members participating in Gram Sabha (village assembly) meeting.
- % of disadvantaged group members (SCs & STs) participating in Gram Sabha (village assembly) meeting.
- % of minority group members participating in Gram Sabha meeting.
- % of youth members participating in Gram Sabha meeting.
- Is village having *pucca* (concrete) road?
- Is village having street light facility?
- Is there any community water works facility available in the village?
- Is there any community toilet facility available in the village?
- Is village having primary education facility within one kilometre?
- Is village having primary health care (mother and children) facility within two kilometre?
- If village has market facility within two kilometre?
- If village has post office facility?

- If village has banking facility within five kilometre?
- If village has cooperative societies and if yes then what activities they are doing?
- If village has insurance coverage by the government/private insurance company? If yes how many people have been covered under various insurance, i.e. life insurance and health insurance?
- If village has non-renewable source of energy facility?
- If village has computer and internet facility?
- If village has good road connectivity to nearest urban area?
- % of population with AADHAR (identity) card.
- Is any NGO/PVO working in the village for village development?
- Is there any SHG working in the village? If yes, their main activities.
- Is there any Mahila Mandal (women group) working in the village? If yes, what is its role in village development?
- Is there any youth club functional in the village? If yes, what is its role in village development?
- If your village is adopted by any MP/MLA?
- Number of beneficiaries of various rural development programmes launched by the central schemes/centrally sponsored schemes.
- Number of beneficiaries of various rural development programmes launched by the state government-sponsored schemes.
- Number of families displaced during the launching of any development project/programme.
- If families have been displaced because of launching of the development programmes, how many of them have not received rehabilitation facilities?
- If your village is prone to any frequent disaster?
- Total agricultural productivity of your village—rice, wheat, pulses, oil seeds, and other cash crops and so on.
- Is there any dairy and poultry farming activities in your village? If yes, what is the number of families dependent on it and amount of income generated from these activities?
- Natural resources available in the village forest, ponds, lake, mangroves and so on.
- Common property resources (CPRs) available in the village and income from the resources.

MEASURES TAKEN BY THE GOVERNMENT OF INDIA FOR RURAL DEVELOPMENT

Government of India, since independence, has launched several programmes for the development of rural areas and upliftment of socio-economic status and quality of life of the people staying in rural areas. These rural developmental programmes aimed at abolition of poverty, generation of employment, provision of housing, water supply, electricity, sanitation, and increase in health and education status in the rural areas. Various rural development programmes launched by the government of India at different point of time can be categorized into seven types.

1. Integrated Development Programme (IDP): Some of the important categories included under this head are mentioned here.

(i) *Small Farmers' Development Agency (SFDA) and Marginal Farmers' and Agricultural Labourers' Development Agency (MFALDA).* The main aim of these two programmes was to improve the economic condition of the rural poor through agriculture development. Some of the facilities made available to the small and marginal farmers under these programmes are provision of irrigation, credit facilities, improved seeds, fertilizers and machineries, storage, transport processing and marketing facilities and other provisions like training and raw materials. Various activities promoted under Integrated Rural Development Programme (IRDP) are agriculture, poultry farming, animal husbandry, agroforestry, art and crafts, carpentry, shoe making, pottery, embroidery and similar types of vocational income generating activities.

(ii) *20 Point Programme.* This programme aimed at ensuring social justice, providing employment and eradication of poverty. The thrust areas were creation of community assets such as schools, roads, tanks, reservoirs and so on; increasing agricultural productivity and emphasis on village small-scale and cottage industries, handloom and handicrafts for employment generation.

(iii) *Integrated Rural Development Programme.* The main emphasis of this programme was to uplift and raise the socio-economic status of the poorest of the poor, so that they can cross the poverty line. Again, the emphasis was on the promotion of agriculture and allied activities through the supply of HYV seeds, fertilizers and water input; diversification of agriculture through emphasis on animal husbandry, fishery, dairying, forestry, sericulture and so on, and provision of post-harvesting technology and agro-processing industries.

2. Area Development Programme (ADP): The main programmes launched under this umbrella are discussed below.

(i) *Drought Prone Area Development Programme (DPAP).* The objective was to provide adequate infrastructure in the drought prone areas, so that it generates employment and enhances productivity. The thrust areas are water management, afforestation, soil and moisture conservation, diversification of agriculture, livestock development and pasture development.

(ii) *Command Area Development Programme (CADP).* The main objective of this programme was to enhance productivity through the utilization of created irrigation facilities. The thrust areas are the creation of irrigation facilities, employment generation and poverty alleviation.

(iii) *Hill Areas Development Programme (HADP).* The main objective was the economic upliftment of the Tribals and at the same time, restoration and preservation of ecosystem and eco-system development. The thrust was poverty reduction and employment generation in the tribal areas.

(iv) *Desert Area Development Programme (DADP).* The objective was to combat draughts and desertification and to raise the livelihood condition of the people living in the desert areas. The programmes tried to improve the economic condition of the people through the creation of employment opportunities and widening the access to equitable distribution of resources.

(v) *Backward Region Grant Fund (BRGF).* The programme was launched in 250 backward districts of 27 states. The main aim was to address the regional imbalances in development. The thrust was to fill infrastructural gap in drinking water, sanitation, connectivity, health, education and so on. This programme enabled the construction of anganwadi centres, subcentres, primary schools, panchayat buildings, drinking water project, sanitation, street light and so on.

3. Wage Employment Programme (WEP): Some of the important wage employment programmes launched are discussed here.

(i) *National Rural Employment Programme (NREP).* The main thrust areas of the programme is generation of employment through the creation of durable assets such as village pond, village road, water bodies as per the felt needs of the rural community through the Gram Sabha and improvement of the quality of life of the rural people.

(ii) *Rural Landless Employment Guarantee Programme (RLEGP).* The main objective of the programme was the generation of employment in rural areas with particular focus on the landless workers.

(iii) *Food for Work Programme (FWP).* The main aim of the programme is to provide food security to the poverty-stricken household through employment generation and creation of community and social assets for rural areas. The special feature of the programme was that the wage was paid in the form of food grain and government surplus stock was used for the purpose of ensuring food grain supply.

(iv) *Jawahar Rozgar Yojana (JRY).* The objective of the JRY was to alleviate rural poverty through the creation of supplementary employment opportunities in the rural areas during agricultural slack period. Employment was generated and wages were paid through the creation of social assets.

(v) *Employment Assurance Scheme (EAS).* EAS aims at giving 100 days assured employment to, at least, two members of a family of the rural poor households who seek employment during lean agricultural season. The thrust was the creation of community and social assets in the village.

(vi) *Sampoorna Grameen Rozgar Yojana.* SGSY was created by clubbing the earlier two schemes—EAS and JRY. The objective of the SGSY was to provide additional wage employment and food security to the rural poor. Special focus was on the employment of women, SCs, STs and parents of children withdrawn from the hazardous work. Wages were paid partly in food grain and partly in cash.

(vii) *Mahatma Gandhi National Rural Employment Guarantee Act (MGNREGA).* The aim of MGNREGA was to provide 100 days minimum guaranteed wage employment to one unemployed adult member of each rural household prepared to do unskilled manual labour. A total of 33% reservation was made for women, and wages were paid as per Minimum Wage Act of the state governments. One of the vital features of this programme was its implementation by the Panchayati Raj Institutions at the grass-root level. It is pertinent to mention here that it is the largest wage employment programme in the world.

4. Self-Employment Programme (SEP): Some of the important SEPs launched by the government of India are discussed below.

(i) *Development of Women and Children in Rural Areas (DWCRA)*. The principal objective was to provide self-employment opportunities to women belonging to BPL families in rural areas. Under DWCRA, a group consisting of 10–15 women are encouraged to take up economic activities suited to their skill, aptitude and local needs and conditions.
(ii) *Training of Rural Youth for Self-Employment (TRYSEM)*. The key objective of the scheme is to provide self-employment opportunities to the rural unemployed youth. Under this scheme, the aim was to equip youth in the age group of 18–35 with necessary training and skill so that they are empowered to take up vocational self-employment activities in agriculture, industry, service and business sectors. The youth after the training were provided with toolkits to start up vocational activities.
(iii) *Support for Training and Employment Programme (STEP)*. The main objective of this programme was to provide training and equip the women belonging to marginalized sections of the rural society to take up vocational activities in agriculture, dairying, horticulture, fisheries, handicrafts, handlooms and so on. They were also provided with necessary infrastructure, managerial and marketing facilities to take up the self-employment activities.
(iv) *Swarnajayanti Gram Swarozgar Yojana (SGSY)*. The main objective of the SGSY was to uplift the poor families above the poverty line by providing them income earning assets through bank credits and government subsidies. There were individual *swarozgarie*s (self-employed) as well as SHGs, consisting of 10–15 people encouraged to take up vocational income-earning activities. The focus was on capacity building, skill upgradation, infrastructure building, marketing and credit support to the rural entrepreneurs created through SGSY.

5. Bharat Nirman Programme (BNP): The six components included under the BNP are irrigation, drinking water, electrification, roads, housing and rural telephony.

(i) *Irrigation*. For the promotion of irrigation, the focus was given to the construction of major and medium irrigation projects.
(ii) *Drinking Water*. The three programmes—Accelerated Rural Water Supply Programme (ARWSP), Rajiv Gandhi National Drinking Water Mission (RGNDWM) and Swajaldhara—were launched at different points of time in order to ensure adequate provision of drinking water supply to the rural community. These programmes also emphasized on the involvement of the community in planning, implementation and management of drinking water-related schemes.
(iii) *Electrification*. Rajiv Gandhi Grameen Vidutkaran Yojana (RGGVY) and Deendayal Upadhyaya Gram Jyoti Yojana (DUGJY) were launched for village electrification and providing distribution infrastructure in the rural areas.
(iv) *Roads*. Pradhan Mantri Gram Sadak Yojana (PMGSY) was launched for improving rural roads and promoting connecting roads from the villages to the main roads.

(v) *Housing*. IAY was a key programme under rural housing. It aims at provisioning housing to the households living below the poverty line in rural areas. Houses build under the scheme should be with smokeless *chulhas* (cooking stoves) and sanitary latrines.

(vi) *Rural Telephony*. The Government India is trying to provide telephone connectivity to all villages in the rural areas.

6. Flagship Programme (FP): The main components of the rural FPs are education, health and other basic public facilities.

(i) *Education*. The three key programme on education launched which benefits rural people the most are:

a. Integrated Child Development Scheme (ICDS), which provides preschool education, immunization and nutritional care to the children below three years of age.

b. Sarva Shiksha Abhiyan (SSA), which aims at universalization of elementary education in a time bound manner. The thrust areas are opening of new schools, strengthening of infrastructure facilities in the existing schools, improving teachers strength, teaching–leaning materials, community participation and so on.

c. Mid-day Meal (MDM) scheme is school meal programme intended to improve the nutritional status of the school going children.

(ii) *Health*. A few rural health programmes launched for the improvement of health status of rural people with particular focus on health of women and children are Universal Immunization Programme (UIP), Maternal and Child Health (MCH) Programme and Reproductive and Child Health (RCH) Programmes. It aims at provisioning of preventive, curative and promotive health care services to women and children for the reduction of maternal and infant mortality. More recently, National Rural Health Mission (NRHM) has been launched for improving the health status of rural area population, including those of women and children.

(iii) *Other Basic Public Facilities*. In this category, TSC and Swachh Bharat Mission (SBM) are the two key programmes aimed at improving the sanitation condition in the households, public institutions such as school, anganwadi centres and subcentres in rural areas and provision of rural safe garbage disposal and liquid waste disposal. Under these programmes, provisions for toilets were made in the rural households and in the schools.

7. National Social Assistance Programme (NSAP): The social assistance programme aims mainly at providing social security of the disadvantaged sections of the society, living in rural areas. It covers all families living below the poverty line. Some of the important programmes comprised this umbrella programme are given below.

(i) *National Old-Age Pension Scheme (NOAPS)*. Under this scheme, pension is given to the destitute, who have no earning of his/her own or financial support from family members.

(ii) *Indira Gandhi National Widow Pension Scheme (IGNWPS).* Under this scheme, pension is given to widows above 40 years of age and belonging to the BPL family.

(iii) *Indira Gandhi National Disabled Pension Scheme (IGNDPS).* Under this scheme, pension is given to the person below 64 years of age, handicapped up to 80% level and belongs to BPL family categories.

(iv) *Annapurna Scheme.* The scheme takes into consideration old-age persons who are not covered under NOAPS and be an old aged person above the age 65 being neglected by his or her children and other family members. Under this scheme, 10 kg of rice is given free of cost to the eligible.

However, despite launching various programmes since Independence the socio-economic status of the rural population has not been adequately improved. Many studies have identified several factors for poor performance in the implementation of various rural development programmes. A few of them among many are lack of adequate financial resources, failure of state government to spent the allotted amount given by the central government for the implementation of various programmes leading to return of money to the centre, faulty targeting of beneficiaries, corruption and bad governance at the bureaucratic and political level, nepotism at the grass-root level by the local self-government in the allocation of beneficiaries, poor maintenance of assets created under rural development programmes, poor entrepreneur quality among the rural population to take up activities in industrial and service sector, too much dependence on the government and so on.

SUMMARY

Rural development constitutes the cornerstone of the development process of developing countries as more than 60% of their population resides in the countryside. The growth and development of the developing economies veritably depend on the development of their rural areas. However, it is seen that most of poverty-stricken and illiterate population in developing countries are residing in the rural areas. The decline in the contribution of agriculture to GDP of developing countries shows that a lot has to be done on the developmental front in agriculture in these countries, which is the key determinant of the livelihood of the rural population. The rural population has to be provided with housing, sanitation, drinking water and school and health care facilities so that the infant and maternal mortality is curtailed in the rural areas of developing countries. The provision of urban facilities in the rural areas would curtail the migration of rural people to the urban areas. MDGs in developing countries will remain a distant dream if rural areas of the developing economies remain neglected. Therefore, rural development is the key to holistic development of developing countries.

Keywords: common property resources, smart village, provision of urban amenities in rural areas (PURA), rururban, knowledge connectivity, rural–urban continuum, village information centre (VIC).

REVIEW QUESTIONS

1. Define rural area. Discuss various features of rural areas.
2. Rural development is the key to holistic development. Illustrate.
3. What is rural–urban divide? Explain what measures have to be taken to curtail rural–urban divide.
4. Explain in detail five key challenges of rural development.
5. What is PURA? Explain its features and in what way it can improve the quality of life of rural people.
6. What is rural–urban continuum? Why is it important for the development of developing countries?
7. What rural development measures a developing country has to take for raising the quality of life of the rural people?
8. What is village development need assessment? Explain 10 important variables of village development need assessment.
9. Explain the role of local self-government in the development of rural areas.
10. Write short notes on the following:
    (i) Rural–urban continuum
    (ii) PURA
    (iii) Rural–urban digital divide
    (iv) Rururban
    (v) Smart village
    (vi) Village development need assessment
    (vii) Panchayati raj institutions

NOTES

1. Sanjeev, Kumar. 'Rural Development through Rural Industrialization: Exploring the Chinese Experience.' Asian Scholarship. Available at: http://www.asianscholarship.org/asf/ejourn/articles/Sanjeev%20Kumar2.pdf (accessed on 16 February 2015).
2. See http://www.ilo.org/wcmsp5/groups/public/@ed... (accessed on 14 April 2016).
3. Vibrant Gujarat, Sixth Global Summit, Panel Discussion on Rurbanization, Proceedings Report, 11–13 January 2013. Available at: http://www.vibrnatgujarat.com/Portal/Event_Image (accessed on 16 February 2015).

BIBLIOGRAPHY

Abass, I. M. 'The Challenge of Rural Development Strategies in a Deregulated Economy.' Paper prepared for the National Seminar on Rural Development Doing More Less Developing Rural Resources in a Deregulated Economy, New Nigerian Newspapers Ltd. in collaboration with Arthur Green Consultants, Shiroro Hotel, Minna, Niger State, 10–12 February 1993.

Abdul Kalam A. P. J. Address at the Annual Commerce Convention 2014, Delhi School of Economics, Delhi University, 12 April 2014. Available at: http://www.commercedu.com/up-content/upload (accessed on 16 February 2015).

Andersen, P. P., and S. Shimokawa. 'Rural Infrastructure and Agricultural Development.' Paper prepared for presentation at Annual Bank Conference on Development Economics, Tokyo, Japan, 29–30 May 2006. Available at: siteresources.worldbank.org/INTDECABCTO (accessed on 25 October 2015).

Ashley, C., and S. Maxwell. 'Rethinking Rural Development.' *Development Policy Review* 19 (2001): 395–425.

Bahl, R. W., and P. Smoke., ed. *Restructuring Local Government Finance in Developing Countries: Lessons from South Africa*. Cheltenham, UK and Northampton, MA: Edward Elgar, 2003.

Berenstsen, W. H., J. Roosaare, and P. J. Samara. 'Suburbanization and Landscape Change in Connecticut: Repetition of the Patterns in Estonia and Elsewhere in Central Europe.' Department of Geography, University of Connecticut Storrs, Connecticut, 2000. Available at: www.geo.ut.ee/roosaare/Berendsen_Roosaare_Samara_2000.pdf (accessed on 25/10/2015).

Dabson, B. 'Entrepreneurship as a Core Economic Development Strategy for Rural America.' Presentation to the Advisory Committee for the Strengthening America's Communities Clearwater, Florida, 2 June 2005.

Dekens, J., and V. Voora. 'Rural Women, Partner in the Development Process.' IISD Commentary, International Institute for Sustainable Development, Manitoba, Canada, 2014.

Ezeani, E. O. *Fundamentals of Public Administration*. Enugu: Snap Press Ltd., 2006.

FAO, and UNESCO. 'Education for Rural Development: Towards New Policy Response.' A Joint Study Conducted by FAO and UNESCO, 2003.

FAO. 'Rural Women and the Millennium Development Goal.' Food and Agriculture Organization. Available at: http://www.fao.org/3/a-an479e.pdf (accessed on 14 February 2015).

George, S. 'Rural–Urban Continuum.' In *Dynamics of Urban Planning and Development*, MEDS-043, 59–72. IGNOU, 2013.

Haque, S. 'Local Governance in Developing Nations: Re-examining the Question of Accountability.' *Regional Development Dialogue* 18, no. 2 (Autumn, 1977): IV–XXIII.

Harris, J., ed. *Rural Development: Theories of Peasant Economy and Agrarian Change*. London: Hutchinson University Library, 1982.

IFAD. 'Women and Rural Development.' International Fund for Agriculture Development. Available at: http://www.ifad.org/pub/factsheet/women/women_(accessed on 14 February 2015).

IFPRI. 'Agriculture and Achieving the Millennium Development Goals.' International Food Policy Research Institute, 2006. Available at: http://www.ifpri.org/publicaiton/agriculture-and-achi (accessed on 14 February 2015).

Jha, A. K., and I. Kumar. 'Ensuring Basic Necessities in Rural India: A Strategy for Poverty Alleviation.' Available at: http://skoch.org/8tw/Full%/20paper.pdf (accessed on 14 February 2015).

Nandanwar, K. P. 'Role of Rural Entrepreneurship in Rural Development.' *International Referred Research Journal* 2, no. 26 (March 2011).

Nwagboso, C. I., and O. Duke. 'Rural Development Programme Implementation in Developing Countries: The Experience of China and India.' *Global Journal of Human Social Science, Sociology, Economics and Political Science* 12, no. 11 (2012): 27–34.

Ollawa. 'On a Dynamic Model for Rural Development in Africa.' *The Journal of Modern African Studies* 15, no. 3 (1977): 401–23.

Paul, M., and A. Sharma. 'Entrepreneurship as a Tool for Rural Development.' *Global Journal of Management and Business Studies* 3, no. 3 (2013): 319–22.

Pulver, Glean C., and H. Mason-Jenkins. 'Human Resources/Rural Poverty.' Available at: http://ageconsearch.umn.edu/bitstream/17648/1/ar880043.pdf (accessed on 14 February 2015).

Robert, C. *Managing Rural Development: Ideas and Experience from East Africa*. East Africa: Uppsala, Scandinavian Institute of African Studies, 1974.

———. *Managing Rural Development: Ideas and Experience from East Africa*. Uppsala: Scandinavian Institute of African Studies, 1994.

Roy, S. K. 'Rural Development in India: What Roles do NABARD and RRBs Play?' *Journal of Business Management & Social Science Research* 3, no. 9 (2014): 25–30.

Saxena, S. 'Problems Faced by Rural Entrepreneurs and Remedies to Solve It.' *IOSR Journal of Business and Management* 3, no. 1 (2012): 23–29.

Scaria, R., and P. K. Vijayan. 'Sustainable Rural Development with the Application of Spatial Information Technology and Mahatma Gandhi National Rural Employment Guarantee Scheme.' *International Journal of Geometrics and Geosciences* 2, no. 4 (2012): 1048–61.

UNIDO. *A Path Out of Poverty Developing Rural and Women Entrepreneurship*, UNIDO, Viena, 2003.

Wilkin, P. 'Global Poverty and Orthodox Security.' *Third World Quarterly* 23, no. 4 (2010): 633–45.

Woodcock, G. *Kerala: A Portrait of the Malabar Coast*. London: Faber and Faber, 1967.

World Bank. 'Rural Poverty Reduction in Brazil: Towards an Integrated Strategy', Report No. 21790-BR, 2001, World Bank, Washington DC.

———. *World Development Indicators 2010*, World Bank: Washington DC, 2010.

———. 'Africa Competitiveness Report 2013.' World Bank, Washington DC, 2013.

———. 'Rural Development.' Sector Policy Paper, Washington DC, the World Bank, 1975.

———. *World Development Indicators 2015*, World Bank: Washington DC, 2015.

11 Urban Development

National income and level of human development are strongly and positively correlated with level of urbanization.

—UNCHS (2001)

Rapid urbanization has posed enormous challenges in many countries, especially as urbanization proceeds quickly while policy structure adjust slowly.

—Henderson (2009)

Urban development is a key development issue in developed as well as developing countries. It is particularly important for developing countries because of faulty urbanization on the one hand and its contribution to economic growth and development on the other. It is vital for the developing countries for four reasons:

1. Increase in the number of cities and growing population in the urban areas.
2. Contribution of urban areas to the economic growth rate of these countries.
3. Unplanned urbanization and its consequences, i.e. unemployment, underemployment, poverty, infrastructure shortage, crime, pollution and growing number of urban slums.
4. Globalization and its impact on urbanization and growing rural–urban divide.

Urban areas are featured with increased provision of modern amenities, i.e. housing complexes, commercial and official buildings, shopping malls, educational institutions, hospitals, roads, transport and communication facilities, entertainment facilities and so on to name a few among many. It offers better employment opportunities in the service sector such as banking, insurance, education, health care, tourism, hotel industries and so on. Availability of better employment opportunities and good lifestyle facilities has attracted rural area population to urban areas through push and pull effect. The rural push factors responsible for the migration of rural population to urban areas are poverty, unemployment, lower wage rate, landlessness and non-availability of better services, i.e. education, health, drinking water and environmental sanitation. The urban pull factors are attraction towards urban life, better job opportunities, higher wages, quality services and kith and kin's motivation. UNEP (2000) viewed that the driving forces of urbanization include the opportunities and services offered in urban areas—especially jobs and education—while in some parts of the world notably Africa, conflict, land degradation and exhaustion of natural resources are also important. In Mozambique, about 4.5 million rural people were displaced to urban areas due to civil strife in the 1980s (Chenje 2000).

After reading this chapter, you will be able to:

1. Define urbanization and explain the pattern of urbanization in developed as well as developing countries.
2. Describe the contribution of urbanization towards economic growth and development.
3. Discuss various challenges of urbanization.

URBANIZATION: MEANING AND TREND

Urbanization is usually defined as the rise of population in urban areas or movement of people from rural areas to the cities and other urban areas. United Nations (2006) perceives urbanization as movement of people from rural to urban areas. Urbanization is derived from the Latin word *urb*, a term used by the Romans for a city. The common definition of 'cities' or 'urban areas' involves settlements with population of at least 2,000 or 5,000 (Moore, Gould and Keary 2003). According to Mishra (1998), Urbanization is not a product but a process in which a person instead of living in predominantly dispersed agricultural villages starts living in towns and cities dominated by industrial and service functionaries. It involves multiplication of urban places and/or an increase in size of cities. Growth of urban population is only one of the dimensions of urbanization. Urban areas are different from rural areas in terms of occupation of the people, type of housing and other living facilities.

One of the eminent demographers Kingsley Davis (1965) has classified the process of urbanization into three stages:

1. Stage I is the initial stage, characterized by traditional rural society with predominance in agriculture and dispersed pattern of settlement.
2. Stage II is where proportion of urban population gradually increases from 25% to 40%, 50%, 60% and so on. This is otherwise called as the stage of acceleration where basic restructuring of the economy and investments in social overhead capitals, including transport and communication, take place.
3. Stage III is known as the terminal stage where urban population exceeds 70% or more. According to Davis, at this stage, the level of urbanization remains more or less same or constant.

Urbanization is taking place in almost all countries of the world. Most of the developed countries of the world have been already urbanized as nearly more than 70% of their population is living in the urban areas. On the contrary, urbanization process in developing countries is going on a faster pace.

The share of world's population living in urban areas has increased from 39% in 1980 to 48% in 2000. Figures provided in Table 11.1 clearly reveal that the percentage of urbanization in developed countries is 76%, while that of developing countries is 40%. In developing countries, it is seen that the urbanization process is skewed towards the metropolitan and big cities.

Table 11.1 *Urban and Rural Population in More and Less Developed Regions of the World, 1950–2030*

	Population (Billion)				**Average Annual Rate of Change (%)**		
	1950	**1975**	**2005**	**2030**	**1950–75**	**1975–2005**	**2005–30**
			A. Population Size and Growth				
Total Population World	2.52	4.07	6.45	8.13	1.92	1.54	0.92
More Developed Regions	0.81	1.05	1.21	1.24	1.01	0.48	0.11
Less Developed Regions	1.71	3.02	5.24	6.89	2.29	1.84	1.09
Urban Population World	0.73	1.52	3.17	4.94	2.91	2.46	1.78
More Developed Regions	0.43	0.70	0.91	1.01	2.00	0.84	0.46
Less Developed Regions	0.31	0.81	2.27	3.93	3.91	3.42	2.20
Rural Population World	1.79	2.55	3.28	3.19	1.43	0.84	–0.12
More Developed Regions	0.39	0.34	0.30	0.23	–0.46	–0.42	–1.15
Less Developed Regions	1.40	2.21	2.98	2.96	1.82	1.00	–0.03
	Urban (%)				**Rate of Urbanization (%)**		
	1950	**1975**	**2005**	**2030**	**1950–75**	**1975–2005**	**2005–30**
			B. Urban Indicators				
World	29.1	37.3	49.2	60.8	1.24	0.92	0.85
More Developed Regions	52.5	67.2	74.9	81.7	1.23	0.36	0.35
Less Developed Regions	17.9	26.9	43.2	57.1	2.04	1.58	1.12

Source: United Nations (2005): Population Challenges and Development Goals, Department of Economics and Social Affairs, Population Division, ST/ESA/SERA, 248, UN, New York.

Table 11.2 *World's Top Ten Countries with Largest Urban Population and World's Top Ten Urban Agglomerations (2011)*

Country*	**Urban Population, 2005 (in Million)***	**Urban Agglomeration****	**Population** 2011 (in Million)**	**Rank****
China	535.96	Tokyo, Japan	37.2	1
India	312.89	Delhi, India	22.7	2
USA	232.08	Mexico, Mexico	20.4	3
Brazil	151.93	New York, USA	20.4	4
Indonesia	104.05	Shanghai, China	20.2	5
Russia	102.73	Sao Paulo, Brazil	19.9	6
Japan	101.83	Mumbai, India	19.7	7
Mexico	80.07	Beijing, China	15.6	8
Germany	72.41	Dhaka, Bangladesh	15.4	9
Nigeria	62.62	Kolkata, India	14.4	10

Source: *www.mapsofworld.com
**United Nations, World Urbanization Prospects, the 2011 Revision.

Features of Urbanization

- For the first time in history, more than half of the world's people live in cities.
- Nearly two billion new urban residents are expected in the next 20 years.
- Over 90% of urban growth is occurring in developing countries, which add an estimated 70 million new urban residents each year.
- By 2030 all developing regions, including Asia and Africa, will have more people living in urban than rural areas.
- The urban population of the world's two poorest regions, South Asia and Sub-Saharan Africa, is expected to double over the next 20 years.
- Cities account for some 70% of global GDP.
- No country has grown to middle-income status without industrialising and urbanising.
- In Latin American cities, poor or inadequate infrastructure is estimated to have reduced urban economic output by 10–15%.
- In China, 50% of GDP is generated in coastal urban areas, which represent 20% of the country's territory.
- Rural-to-urban migration is just one of the three drivers of urbanisation, accounting for about 25% of urban population growth.
- Youth are 40% more likely than older generations to move from rural to urban areas or across urban areas.

Source: World Bank (2009) World Development Report 2009, World Bank, Washington D. C. quoted from http://www.citiesalliance.org/node/2195(accessed on 3/12/2016).

Some of the trends of urbanization in developed and developing countries are discussed below.

1. Urbanization in the developed countries is higher as compared to developing countries. As per UN statistics, the percentage of population residing in the urban areas of developed countries is 79.1%, while that of less developed countries is 46.8%, and the urbanization in the African region is found to be slightly higher than the Asian region. However, urbanization in the countries of both the regions such as Asia and Africa is comparatively lower than those of Europe and the United States of America. However, one of the estimations of the African Development Bank Group says that more than 90% of future population growth will be accounted for by the large cities in developing countries (see Table 11.2).
2. Urbanization took place without much industrialization and strong economic base in underdeveloped countries of Asia, Latin America and Africa. Lack of industrialization-led urbanization has resulted in the growth of unorganized sector which is characterized by lower wage rate and poor service condition which affect the quality of life of urban population. Jedweb, Christiaensen and Gindelsky (2014) have also established that the rapid growth in cities today is correlated with

a high proportion of urban residents living in slums, low investment in urban human capital and a larger informal sector. The urbanization process in the underdeveloped and developing countries is largely unplanned, leading to many problems in the urban areas of these countries. On the contrary, urbanization in many developed countries has been done in a planned manner.

3. Unplanned urbanization in developing countries has led to growth of urban slum areas characterized by low-quality housing, poor sanitation, poor access to safe drinking water and so on. Because of the provision of various infrastructure facilities provided by the government in the slums in India, the slum has been further categorized as organized slum and unorganized slum. In the organized slums, housing, drinking water, electricity, sanitation, health clinic, anganwadi centres, schools and so on have been largely found to be provisioned by the government and urban local bodies (ULBs). On the other hand, unorganized slums are observed to be devoid of all these amenities and lack basic infrastructure facilities. Slums are also present in the developed countries.
4. The current pattern of urbanization in developing countries is alarming, if viewed from a historical, spatial and cross country perspective. The bizarre urbanization is largely due to the migration of population from the rural areas to the cities. However, in the metropolitan cities, migration of population is from both rural and urban areas of the less-developed states. For instance, in Delhi, more than one-sixth population is from Bihar and Eastern Uttar Pradesh; the former is an economically backward state and later is the economically backward region of Uttar Pradesh.
5. In the developed countries, urbanization process is largely planned, while in underdeveloped countries it is mostly unplanned. Reckless movement of illiterate and poverty-stricken people to the urban areas lead to the growth of urban slums where the quality of life of the people is even worse than the rural areas. Most of the countries do not have any plan like China to check the movement of rural population to the urban areas.

Hukou: China's Instrument to Check Rural to Urban Migration

The rural to urban migration in China was formally prevented starting in 1955 by a household registration system known as 'Hukou' that established household residency. Those with urban Hukou were given access to high paying jobs and government services. The advantage of rural Hukou was a claim to land use. During the first 30 years of communist rule, more than 80% of the population remained in rural areas.

Source: Das, Mourmouras and Rangazas (2015).

6. In recent years, besides migration, the urban population growth is more of a natural increase in developing countries like those of the developed countries. People who have migrated way back are in their third generation. Thus, there is natural increase in population in the urban areas in the recent years. Besides, migrants,

who have settled and purchased houses, have been staying in the urban villages and organized slums for a long time and are in the possession of voter-ID and AADHAR cards. Their children claim to be the natural population of the cities. Jedweb et al. (2014) showed that rapid urbanization of today's developing countries is driven more by natural increase than by the rural-to-urban migration of European history.

7. One of the features of urbanization is low-reverse migration from urban to rural areas because of poor provision of urban facilities in rural areas. However, state like Kerala provides a unique example, where the Malayali people like go back to their villages in Kerala after retirement from the metropolis and other cities of India and even from the foreign countries. This is because of better rural–urban continuum and availability of urban facilities in rural areas.

Some of the trends and impacts of urbanization as mentioned by the WHO (2010) are as follows:

1. More than half of the world's population now live in cities.
2. By 2030, six out of every ten people will be city dwellers, which will rise to seven out of every ten people by 2050.
3. One in three urban dwellers lives in slums.
4. Urban air pollution kills around 1.2 million people each year around the world, mainly due to cardiovascular and respiratory diseases, and tuberculosis incidence is much higher in big cities.
5. Urban environment tends to discourage physical activity and promote unhealthy food consumption.

URBANIZATION AND DEVELOPMENT

Urban areas in almost every country account for a disproportionately large share of gross national product (Moore et al. 2003). For instance, Bangkok produces 40% of Thailand's GNP but has only 12% of its population (UNCHS 2001). Urbanization and development are intimately interlinked. Cities are the major contributors to economic growth in India. Most manufacturing and service production is more efficient when undertaken in urbanized areas where firms can more readily copy best practices in technology and management from more advanced firms, and more easily access skilled workers as well as transport services and other intermediate inputs (Henderson 2009). Mega metropolitan cities in the globalized world are the hub of growing service sector activities. On the other hand, cities and towns are the breeding grounds of large, medium and small scale industrial activities.

With the growing contribution of service sector to the GDP, the contribution of urbanization and urban areas to the growth and development of developing countries has been considerably increased. Vaidya (2009) was of the view that there is a robust relationship between urbanization and per capita income, nearly all countries become, at least, 50% urbanized before reaching middle-income status, and all high income countries are

70–80% urbanized. Gill and Kharas (2007) viewed that there is a strong empirical relationship globally between index of city liveability and a country's GDP per capita, suggesting that long-term growth is only feasible if city attributes in terms of congestion, pollution and safety are improved alongside urban economic management. Well-managed cities offer better economies of scale in terms of land use, environmental resource and service efficiency and proximity to service (UNEP 2002).

Urban areas are the hub of service sector activities in developing countries. Good quality health care and higher education institutions are found in the urban areas. As a result, the infant and maternal mortality rate in urban areas is lower than that of the rural areas. Besides, GER of the urban areas is higher as compared to those of rural areas. Thus, urbanization promotes social development, particularly development of education and health care. Urbanization proliferate tourism and hotel service sector activities. Urban areas are the key employment generators for the service sector. Cheng (2012) has found that urbanization is an important factor in the service industry's growth; the other is that the level of urbanization improves the level of service industry.

The e-governance and digital revolution is more visible in urban areas as compared to the rural areas. Availability of better telecommunication infrastructure facilities in urban areas enabled the government and the urban area population to gain better dividend of modernization. Besides digital revolution, the urbanization and urban areas are the hub of modernity as well. People living in the urban areas have better access to modern amenities, possess good quality automobiles, household gadgets and so on.

It is observed that the urban areas have attracted more FDIs as compared to rural areas. Foreign investors as well as NRIs are found to be more interested in investing in the industrial as well as service sector activities in urban areas and are less interested to invest in rural areas which are devoid of infrastructural facilities. Capital formation is more akin to urban areas and therefore, urbanization and development through FDIs have better correlation.

Urbanization is a great source of modernization. Growth of urban centres leads to enhanced modernization activities such as market plaza, cinema halls, education and health institutions with modern facilities, metro rails, railway stations, airports and so on. The role of youth in the development process becomes vibrant in the urban areas. People in general and youth in particular living in the urban areas are adopting modern culture and lifestyle such as dress codes, food habits, housing, hairstyles, communication habits and so on at a faster pace.

ISSUES AND CHALLENGES OF URBANIZATION

Urbanization is not only an opportunity but also a challenge for developing countries. The unplanned urbanization has brought in its wake a host of problems, particularly for the developing countries. Although higher income is an added benefit to the urban dwellers, particularly those who have migrated from the rural areas, migrants who are working in the informal sector and struggling day and night to eke out livelihood, represent another dark side of urbanization. Besides, urban poverty and unemployment and its associated problems and a host of other problems associated with urban slums, pollution and congestion are the most noted indicators of urban failures. Cities have become centres where a vast number of people, particularly who migrated from the rural areas, compete for the most basic elements of life:

1. For an accommodation within reach of employment at an affordable rent, or vacant land on which a shelter can be erected without fear of eviction.
2. For admission of their children in the city schools.
3. For the vaccination of their pregnant women and children and for safe delivery, medical treatment for health problems or injuries in the public health centres and hospitals.
4. For access to clean drinking water.
5. For access to sanitary latrine to avoid open defecation.
6. To arrange two square meals a day for their families.
7. To work hard to earn a sustainable income to manage themselves in the cities and their family members back at the villages of their home.

The implication of rapid urban growth includes increasing unemployment, environmental degradation, lack of urban services, overburdening of existing infrastructure and lack of access to land finance and adequate shelter (UNCHS 2001). According to UNEP the problems created by urbanization are air pollution, water pollution, development of slums, destruction of forests and other natural reserves around cities for settlements and agriculture, increased poverty and increased crime.[1]

The rapid and often unplanned urban growth is also associated with settlement on marginal land, environmental degradation and population demands that outstrip environmental service capacity, such as drinking water, sanitation and waste disposal and treatment (Moore et al. 2003). No doubt the contribution of urbanization to economic growth and development is higher compared to that of the rural areas. However, the problems associated with unplanned urbanization are worrisome. Doytsher et al. (2010) were of the view that the challenges of rapid urbanization are to deal with the social, economic and environment development through more effective and comprehensive land administration functions, supported by effective infrastructures, resolving issues such as climate change, disaster management, insecurity, energy scarcity, environmental pollution and extreme poverty.

URBANIZATION AND INFRASTRUCTURE DEVELOPMENT

Rapid urbanization in developing countries has created infrastructure problem. The provision of urban infrastructure, such as roads, transports, electricity, water, cooking gas, sewerage system, garbage disposal pits, schools, colleges, universities, hospitals and so on, has fallen short of the demand. Roads in general and inner roads in different colonies in various cities of developing countries in particular are in bad shape. Water logging during rainy season is a recurring problem in the megacities of India such as Delhi, Kolkata and Mumbai. Good quality roads are lacking in most of the cities. Besides, load shedding is continuous in many capital cities of the region of developing countries. Lack of use of renewable sources of energy is a cause of concern for the resources-poor developing countries. Income of the municipalities remaining more or less constant, the inflow of population to the cities has aggravated the situation.

URBANIZATION AND SLUMS

When we talk of urbanization, the first thought that comes to the mind of the common men as well as urban planner is the urban slum. Slum is sarcastically being called the love child of urbanization. No metropolitan cities in the world are free from slums and squatters. According to UN-Habitat (2003), more than 900 million people, i.e. 30% of the world's population, live in slums, and in the least developed countries about 78% of urban residents are slum dwellers. In slums,

1. people are living in deplorable conditions;
2. a colossal percentage of slum households are living below the national poverty line;
3. people are largely engaged in informal work and are in menial jobs;
4. their per capita income is low; and
5. most of them are devoid of basic amenities of life.

Their livelihood is characterized by:

1. temporary and makeshift houses;
2. poor access to safe drinking water;
3. women defecate and bath in a shameful conditions;
4. lack of sanitation and sewage facilities; and
5. living in a situation where there is absolutely no safety and security to life and property.

A large percentage of them have lower education level, and are either unskilled or less skilled, having poor bargaining power. They are found to be engaged in low-paid menial works and live in the slums, near the filthy areas deliberately left for urban garbage disposal or for sewerage; many of them are seen living in makeshift arrangements along the railway lines and near railway stations. Life and livelihood conditions in the unorganized slums are deplorable. Women of the families living in the urban slum are found engaged in menial labour activities. Many children are seen moving as errand, playing in the narrow slum lanes and not enrolled in the school. Even if enrolled, many of them do not attain education because of lack of environment for education and lack of interest of parents to send them to the school and more interest in engaging them in petty income-earning activities. UN-Habitat (2003) noted that the informal settlement populations that lack proper houses, water and sanitation are exposed to serious health risks and have limited access to credit, socio-economic networks and the formal jobs market due to stigmatization, discrimination and geographic isolation (Table 11.3).

Table 11.3 *Urban Population Living in Slums*

Region	Slum Population (thousands)		Slum Population (%)	
	2000	2010	2000	2010
Northern Africa	14,729	11,836	20.3	13.3
Sub-Saharan Africa	144,683	199,540	65.0	61.7
Latin America and Caribbean	115,192	110,763	29.2	23.5
Eastern Asia	192,265	189,621	37.4	28.2
Southern Asia	194,009	190,784	45.8	35.0
South-East Asia	81,942	88,912	39.6	31.0
West Asia	23,481	35,713	20.6	24.6
Oceania	462	556	24.1	24.1
World	**766,000**	**828,000**	**39.3**	**32.7**

Source: UN World Urban Report 2010–11.

Features of Slums

- About one-third of the urban population in developing countries—nearly one billion people—lives in slums, according to estimates.
- UN-Habitat estimates the world's slum population will be 889 million by 2010.
- Between 2000 and 2010, the number of slum dwellers increased by six million every year.
- More than 70% of Africa's urban population lives in slums.
- The majority of slum dwellers in African cities are between the ages of 15 and 24.
- Slums are often economically vibrant; today, about 85% of all new employment opportunities around the world occur in the informal economy.
- The number of slum dwellers is estimated to grow by nearly 500 million between now and 2020, according to UN-Habitat.
- Countries farthest from reaching the MDG target on slums are mainly in Sub-Saharan Africa.

Source: UN-HABITAT State of the World's Cities Report 2010-2011; Quoted from http://www.citiesalliance.org/node/2195(accessed on 3/12/2016).

URBAN PARADOX

The most widely observed and acutely felt urban problem is the large number of poor dwelling in the city slums and the rich staying in posh colonies with access to better quality amenities. This reveals a condition of urban paradox of 'poverty amidst plenty.' The gap between the affluent rich and pauperized poor, at least, in the metropolitan cities of developing countries is very large. It is seen that even a rich man's dog is several times better fed than the poor man's children. It is observed that in Asian, Latin American and

Central American megacities, 20 million inhabitants have become increasingly centres of poverty and social collapse (Kennedy 1993). On the other hand, Hicks (1994) has remarked that urban areas have always been characterized by concentrations of poor persons and poor neighbourhoods; they also served the function of helping the poor to assimilate into a new country and a new economy.

URBAN POVERTY

Urban poverty is on the rise, and it is estimated that one-quarter of the population lives below the poverty line, and that female-headed households are disproportionately affected (UNCHS 2001). In the cities of the developing world, one out of every four households lives in poverty; 40% of African urban households and 25% of Latin American urban households are living below locally defined poverty lines (Panos 2001). It has also been noted that poverty-related problems such as overcrowding, hunger, disease, crime and malnutrition are increasingly prevalent in the cities of the world.

In India, it is observed that the ratio of urban poverty in some of the megacities is even higher than the rural poverty, sarcastically leading to 'urbanization of poverty'. This urban poverty is a responsible factor for several other problems in urban areas, such as housing and shelter, water, sanitation, health, education, social security and livelihood. With growing poverty and slums, Indian cities are grappling with the challenges of making the cities sustainable, inclusive, productive, efficient and manageable. After the liberalization and globalization, the statistics shows that the percentage of very poor living in urban India is higher than that of rural areas.

URBAN INEQUALITY

Besides poverty, socio-economic inequalities are also important characteristic features of most of the cities of the world. Way back Plato said that 'Any city, however small, is in fact divided into two, one city of the poor, the other of the rich.'[2] The globalization process adopted by the third world countries since 1990 has increased the gap between the rich and poor in urban areas. It is remarked that during the reform period, urban inequality in India was much higher than rural inequality for most of the states (Pal and Ghosh 2007). Glaeser, Resseger and Tobia (2009) noted that 'America is a land with much inequality and our cities are places that are often particularly unequal. Urban inequality reflects both the unequal distribution of skills and unequal returns to skill. Inequality is positively related to crime, slow growth and unhappiness.' Collusion of poverty, low income and inflation have ramshackled the backbone of urban poor in recent years in India. Poverty and urban deprivation go hand in hand in the urban areas. Eradication of poverty and control of inequality in urban areas are major challenges before the governments of the developed as well as developing nations.

URBANIZATION AND UNEMPLOYMENT

Unplanned and rapid growth of population in urban areas has created urban unemployment and underemployment, and has promoted the informalization of urban employment. Customarily, people from the rural areas migrate to the urban areas with a hope for better employment opportunities and incomes which would be comparatively better and higher than that of the rural areas. By doing so, they could eke out a living in urban areas and provide sustainable livelihood for their families staying with them and also remit a portion of their income to other members of their families left out in their villages. However, because of non-availability of jobs in the urban organized sector, most of them become workforce in urban informal sectors. This sector provides them casual employment with inconsistent income and with poor job and social security. Ironically, many of them become casual labour and are found working in the construction sector and also resort to paltry income-earning self-employment activities such as vendors, rickshaw pullers, betel shopkeepers, vegetable sellers and so on. All migrant workers in the urban areas complained of irregularity and frugal availability of work; there is large gap between willingness to work and access to actual work.

On an average, an urban daily wage earner remains idle for one-and-a-half weeks in a month (Pattanaik 2009). They contribute a lot to the development of urban areas in building up the urban infrastructure through their hard labour, but gain a little in return for their hard work. According to ILO (1996),

> Most urban unemployment in developing countries takes the form of underemployment, in which people are obliged to undertake any available economic activity, however, poorly paid and unproductive, because, there are no social-safety nets and no alternatives in the form of unemployment insurance or job training for formal sector work.

Generating employment for the increasing number of urban population is a challenge for the government.

In Sub-Saharan Africa, the urban informal sector is estimated to employ more than 60% of the urban labour force at extremely low wages. In Latin America and the Caribbean, 83% of all new jobs created between 1990 and 1993 were in the informal sector; the bulk of these jobs are poorly remunerated, unsafe and productively low. The large majority of Latin America's urban poor works in the informal sector. Some of the features of urban employment scenario in underdeveloped countries are underemployment, casual employment and employment in unorganized sector with low payments and poor job security. Calloway (1963) remarked that the growing mass of urban unemployed and underemployed is regarded by many as great social evil and a prime source of human tragedy.

URBANIZATION AND HOUSING PROBLEM

Housing is a fundamental basic human need as healthy housing is considered a key determinant of quality of living. Housing constitutes a physical matrix in which human interaction occurs (Naik 1981), and the house that people live in touch upon every facet of their lives and the society as whole (Paul 1983). Global Report on Human Settlements 1995 says that poor housing conditions are a global problem, but conditions are worse in developing countries. Habitat Report says that 600 million people live in life- and health-threatening homes in Asia, Africa and Latin America (Hardoy and Satterthwaite 1989b; WHO 1992). One of the key challenges of urbanization is to provide healthy housing to urban population. Excessive urbanization has created manifold problems such as the haphazard growth of unauthorized housing colonies. Slum and squatter settlements have become well-known phenomena in the Indian metropolitan cities, like Delhi, Mumbai, Kolkata, Chennai and others.

Table 11.4 *Housing and Health*

Housing Problems	Health Hazards
Poor control of temperature	Heat stress, hypothermia
Poor control of ventilation (when there is smoke from indoor fires)	Acute and chronic respiratory diseases
Poor control of dust	Asthma
Overcrowding	Household accidents, easier spread of communicable diseases (e.g. tuberculosis, influenza, meningitis)
Poor control of open fires, poor protection against kerosene or bottled gas	Burns
Poor finishing of walls, floors or roofs (allowing the access of vectors)	Plague, typhus, shigellosis, hepatitis, poliomyelitis, legionnaire's disease, relapsing fever, house dust allergy
Siting of house (close to vector breeding areas)	Malaria, schistosomiasis, filariasis, trypanosomiasis
Siting of house (in areas prone to disasters such as landslides or floods)	Accidents
Construction defects	Accidents

Source: Hardoy et al. 1990, Ludermir and Harpham (1988); also, see http//www.ilo.org/oshenç/part-vii/environmental-health-hazards/503-urbanization?t… (accessed on 23 August 2013).

Health of the people will be affected if their residence is devoid of one or more of the conditions mentioned in Table 11.4.

Health and work efficiency of the people and education of their children depend on the housing conditions. Unhealthy homes in the urban slums of developing countries are greatly affecting the productivity capacity of slum dwellers.

URBANIZATION AND PROVISION OF SAFE DRINKING WATER

Besides housing, ensuring safe drinking water and water for bathing, washing clothes and for sanitation purpose to the slum dwellers in urban areas is an increasing problem in most of the cities, particularly in the metropolitan cities of developing countries. Influx of more and more rural population into urban areas has manifolded the problem of ensuring safe drinking water and hygienic living condition to them. According to UN statistics (2011), some 400 million people in Africa live in urban areas but as of 2008, 55 million of them lacked access to clean drinking water. Most of the urban areas do not have adequate access to safe and reliable supply of drinking water. Safe drinking water surveillance lays emphasis broadly on five important aspects:

1. Quality of drinking water.
2. Quantity of drinking water: having access to sufficient quantity of water for drinking purpose.
3. Accessibility of people to safe drinking water.

4. Affordability: paying capacity of the people towards water tariff.
5. The continuity: time a household spend for fetching drinking water from a distance source.

URBANIZATION AND WASTE MANAGEMENT

The urban sanitation is a big problem as the provision of sanitation infrastructure is falling short of the growing population in urban areas. The amount of solid and liquid wastes generated by the urban households is enormous. Customarily, sanitation means safe defecation, safe disposal of waste and excreta and safe passage of waste water with proper sewerage system. It is estimated that 40 million people reside in slums without adequate sanitation. Doan (1998) observed that throughout the history, cities and towns have struggled how to collect and dispose of the refuse generated by their population, and the problem of solid waste has been recognized now as a big threat to the quality of the environment (Mwangi 2002). Urban waste management is a big challenge in many of the cities. The municipal governance feels that solid-waste management is the most challenging among all urban problems. The urban solid waste include both organic and inorganic waste which includes soil debris, metal scrap, paper, plastics, textiles, leathers, broken bottles, dry batteries, glass and electrical and electronic equipment and so on. Solid-waste management is receiving increasing attention the world over, particularly in developing countries (Chen, Geng and Fujita 2010). The liquid waste has put many municipal governments on the back foot to properly manage its waste generated from different sources such as households, offices, markets, business houses, hospitals, factories and so on. Drainage systems in many unorganized slums either do not exist or if they exist, they are in bad shapes and in bits, resulting in blockage of waste water. The open drainage passing through the slum colonies deeply affect the health of the people.

Indiscreet urban garbage disposal is a common feature in many cities. It is one of the critical garbage management problems. It has always remained a major challenge before the municipal areas and municipal administration. In megacities, urban people in general and slum area children in particular of the families putting up nearer to the garbage disposal tanks and pits suffer from many environment-related health problems. This is largely because of exposure to unhygienic garbage disposal. The outbreak of many sanitation-related epidemics, e.g. dengue, plague, chicken guinea, and so on, takes a toll of life in the cities. Sometimes urban epidemic management put the government health care system in duck. The municipal authorities responsible for solid-waste management and other services have found it increasingly difficult to perform the duties of collecting, transporting and disposing waste from their municipal boundaries.

URBANIZATION AND HEALTH PROBLEM

In urban areas, people living in the slums are exposed to many types of health problems because of the shortage of urban health infrastructure and health personnel, unhealthy environment and poor living conditions. The overcrowded and congested housing in the urban slum areas, consumption of unsafe drinking water and lack of sanitary environment expose the slum dwellers to infectious and other kinds of diseases, such as pneumonia, tuberculosis and diarrhoea, and plague, dengue and so on. Besides, undernutrition is an important factor contributing to poor health in urban slum communities, and malnutrition among urban poor children causes many diseases and a few among them even cause infant mortality.

People in general and women in particular are susceptible to diseases when they give birth to children and bring them up in an environment characterized by overcrowding, poor hygiene, excessive noise and lack of space for recreation and pursuing home reading. Pregnant women's exposure to filthy environment increases the risk of abortion, birth defects, poor foetal growth and perinatal death. Many studies have shown that exposing pregnant women to carbon monoxide can cause damage to the health of the foetus. Firdaus (2012) from his field study found that the various infectious non-communicable and communicable diseases, especially respiratory infections (60.22%), tuberculosis (31.26%) and diarrhoea/dysentery (54.23%), were observed to be very common problems in slums which showed positive relationship with the use of traditional fuel or personal hygiene and contaminated drinking water respectively. According to Trivedi, Sareen and Dhyani (2008), the range of disorders and deviances associated with urbanization is enormous and includes psychoses, depression, sociopathy, substance abuse, alcoholism, crime, delinquency and so on. Such negative impacts often result in unreasonable means which may result in communal violence.

URBANIZATION AND EDUCATION PROBLEM

Rapid urbanization through the migration of rural population to the cities and towns has put tremendous pressure on public sector educational infrastructure. The urban poor and marginalized sections are generally the users of public educational institutions. On the other hand, it is seen that the rich mostly prefer to send their children to private educational institutions which are costly and the educational infrastructure such as school buildings, educational aids, play grounds, toilet and drinking water facilities are better compared to public sector institutions. Besides, the quality of teachers, teaching and parent–teacher interaction is better in private educational institutions as compared to public sector institutions. Educational institutions in the slums are deficient in educational infrastructure and lack quality teachers. They are largely being run either by the governments, NGOs or charitable organizations.

While citing the case of African countries, Ngware et al. (2009) opined that the informal settlements are largely served by poor quality, low cost, private, community and informal schools managed by individual entrepreneurs, communities and NGOs. As the percentage of poor and marginalized population is high in the slums, there is always a supply side deficiency in term of quantity and quality of school education in urban areas. The poorest urban households' inability to afford education costs is among the major reasons why the majority of their children are not in school by not being enrolled in the first place or later dropping out (Kattan and Burnett 2004). After the globalization, the higher educational institution in general and technical education institutions in particular in the private sector have mushroomed in cities and towns, created an atmosphere of educational inequality. Educational provisioning in urban areas has become a million dollar business of the developed as well as developing countries. Educational disparities between haves and have-nots have elongated in urban areas of developing countries.

URBANIZATION AND ENVIRONMENTAL POLLUTION

Urban areas do not have only local environmental impacts but also large so-called 'ecological footprints' (WWF 2000). Urbanization and pollution have become the most common phenomena in megacities. The growing numbers of vehicles, air conditioners, refrigerators and other household gadgets producing heat and noise have escalated, the urban pollution problems in big cities. Besides, this outdoor pollution caused by dust generated during cleaning of street, construction of buildings close by, the indoor air pollution caused by the use of fuel stoves and fire woods, and so on as practiced by the slum population has increased the risk of chronic obstructive pulmonary disease and acute respiratory infections. It is one of the most important causes of deaths among children below the age of five years in India. Besides, motor vehicles, factories and burning of waste material also emit dangerous gases that affect the air quality in the cities. Motor vehicles also contribute significantly to noise pollution within cities, through honking and engine noise (Granados 1998). Dangerous gases like carbon dioxide and nitrogen oxides that cause respiratory diseases have lasting effects on physical environment and human health. Air pollution, from both indoor and outdoor sources, is one of the major risk factors for developing acute respiratory diseases, the most prevalent cause of death for children between one and five years of age in developing countries (Bruce, Perez-Padilla and Albalak 2000).

URBANIZATION, LAW AND ORDER AND CRIME

It is argued that as urbanization increases, so does the crime (Galvin 2002). Unbridled urbanization and growth of slums and unauthorized colonies have given rise to crime in most of the cities in the world. The newly migrated youth in the absence of jobs are found to resort to delinquency, crime and alcoholism, and it is common among in-migrants endeavouring to adjust to the new urban environment. It is found that when the neighbours of urban areas are poor then there is more chance of crimes (Krivo and Peterson 1996). The personnel deployed for the maintenance of law and order and provision of policing are falling short of the number required for controlling crime in urban areas. No large cities in the world are free from crimes, as crimes normally occur in large cities and urban areas (Krivo and Peterson 1996). UN-Habitat (2007) noted that the factors influence the incidence of crime and violence include poverty, unemployment, inequality, intergenerational transmission of violence as reflected in the continuous witnessing of parental abuse during childhood, the rapid pace of urbanization, poor urban planning design and management, increase of young population and the concentration of political power, which facilitates corruption and city size and density.

In the urban areas, neighbours are identified by the allotted house numbers and not by the names. In fact, there is poor neighbourhood social relationship and networking. There is also lack of cultural and social bonding among the people. In other words, urban environment offers poor social control and more anonymity. The less penetration of social capital in urban areas benefits the criminals. Rising crime rate in the cities has posed unsurmountable challenges before the government of the nation states and is a slap on the face of social development in urban areas. The socio-economic, cultural and political dynamics of crime-related problems are required to be addressed while dealing with control and prevention of crime in the cities. Unemployment, poverty and crowding, all contribute to violence, substance abuse and mental illness (Ludermir and Harpham 1998). On the other hand, Crowe (2000) that suggested the urban design and the proper use of the urban space may help reduce fear of crime and even its incidence, thereby contributing to an improvement in quality of life. United Nations (2005) urged that there is an urgent need for strategies to combat crime, promote security in communities and contribute to their sustainable development. Maintaining law and order in order to prevent crime is a surmountable challenge of urbanization which has injected massive migration of rural population to urban areas.

URBANIZATION AND TRANSPORT ISSUES

Transport is one the factors which influences the rate and pattern of urbanization in a globalized world. Urban transport influences the urban mobility. In the metropolitan cities of developing countries, which are crowded with growing migrant population working in urban organized and unorganized sectors, transport is vital for the smooth lifestyle. However, these cities are vexed with transport problems. The public transport system is falling short of the demand by growing population in these cities. Urban transport planning requires road layout, road demarcations, traffic lights and vehicle passages. The number of vehicles plying in the cities is not in consonance with the capacity of city roads and population. Another aspect of transport problem is the provision of public transport and its poor interface with the private transport. Urban transport experts have suggested for small and less capital intensive vehicles over large metropolitan buses for the cities. Another problem of urban transport is the occurrences of accidents and causalities because of rash driving, particularly by both the young and drunken drivers. Odero et al. (1997) were of the view that motor vehicle crashes are now the leading cause of death worldwide in adolescents and young adults. Motor vehicle traffic is also economically stressful: estimates of the monetary losses to Bangkok, Thailand from traffic jams per year have been reported to be upwards of $1 billion annually (World Bank 2000). All these problems are associated with urban transport. Pollution caused by the vehicles is a cause of concern in many metro cities. In fact, most of the governments of developing countries do not have urban transport policy. It is remarked that no modern city can thrive without an efficient urban transport system that moves people and goods safely with minimal environmental consequences.[3]

URBAN HERITAGE AND OPEN SPACE

Many cities in developing countries have been found to be established in the localities having historically, culturally and religiously rich heritages. Because of lack of resources, the heritage sights of these cities are not found to be either developed or maintained properly. This impinges on a lot of revenue loss to the governments, which they could have earned through urban and city tourism. Many south Asian countries, such as India, are land of many religions; religious cities are also not properly maintained to deal as per the requirements of the religious tourism and most of the areas of these cities are found to be in dirt. For instance, the religious cities like Allahabad, Varanasi, Amritsar, Haridwar and Puri in different states of India do not provide right ambiance to the religious tourists. All religious and historical cities are required to be smart cities in order to attract tourists.

The effective use of open spaces has always remained a critical area of concern for the cities. The unutilized open spaces, if occupied by the poor migrants for a longer period, are subsequently turned into and claimed to be slum colonies. The appeasing vote bank politics that let them stay and in due time regularize them has contributed to the growth of slums. It has always remained a blot on the city landspace. Dharavi slum in Mumbai is an illustrious example. Open space must be effectively utilized to make the city beautiful and attractive. Development and maintenance of parks and urban water bodies is important not only for the beautification of the cities but also to promote environmental health of the cities. The effective use of open space will earn revenue for the city governments through the inflow of tourists from different parts of the country as well as from abroad. In India, Udaipur in Rajasthan and Chandigarh in Punjab are illustrious examples where effective utilization of open spaces has earned good revenue to the state and the union territory through tourism. Chandigarh has effectively utilized its open space. The formation of Rock Garden, Rose Garden, Sukhna Lake, Pinjore Garden, etc., are attracting a lot of tourists. It has not only added beauty to the city but also enhanced its income through tourism. There are many cities in different countries of the world where the appropriate utilization and development of open spaces will not only make the city smart and beautiful but earn revenue for the country.

DEVELOPMENT OF SMART CITY

The effective urbanization called for the establishment of smart cities in order to provide a good quality of living to the city population. The existing cities of various provinces of a country can be developed into smart cities by investing more resources in infrastructure building. Besides, new cities can be established in the adjoining areas of the old cities; one of the illustrious examples is Gandhinagar situated near Ahmadabad, Gujarat. The concept 'smart city' is recent and emerging one in developing countries desiring to push up their economic growth and development through urbanization. For instance, India wants to establish 100 cities in an endeavour to raise its economic growth rate—proposed in Union Budget of 2014. The term 'smart city' is very spicy to chatter and advocate, but is a difficult concept to define and implement thoroughly. A city may be called 'smart' when its investment in the physical, human and social capital as well as investment in the traditional and modern communication infrastructure will fuel sustainable economic growth and ensure a high quality of living to the city population. Furthermore, in the smart cities, the wise management of natural, human and financial resources through participatory governance and application of information technology would not only make living in the cities comfortable and enjoyable but also make city governance cost effective. Smart cities are not only the good looking cities with all modern provisions, such as spacious roads, housing for all categories of people, good infrastructure for health and education, proper sanitation, availability of water and energy, ICT facilities, good traffic management, free from crime and law and order in place, but also are the well-managed cities; in short, follows good governance practices. According to Government of India (2015), smart cities are those which provide core infrastructure and give decent quality of life to its citizens, a clean and sustainable environment and application of 'smart' solutions. The European Union (2014) while mapping smart cities in the European Union has defined it as 'a smart city is a city seeking to address public issues via ICT-based solutions on the basis of a multi-stakeholder, municipally based partnership.' Some of the important characteristic features of smart cities are:

- **Smart Location:** The location of the smart city must be carefully chosen, and it needs to be spacious and well connected. It can expand to four different directions without creating complications in land acquisition. It must be relatively free from natural calamities and disaster prone areas.
- **Smart Governance:** Good governance principles such as transparent and corruption-free governance, responsible and participatory governance, e-governance and inclusive governance must be practiced in the smart cities. It must be a hassle- and corruption-free city.
- **Smart People:** A smart city must comprise of active and creative people with social, religious and ethnic plurality; cosmopolitanism and open-mindedness; socially and politically responsive citizenry and people's participation in public life without any type social exclusion. It must not be overpopulated; population size must be optimum, and within the comfort zone. For instance, optimally planned population of the beautiful city Chandigarh was only 5 lakh; however, now as per the 2011 census, the population of Chandigarh city has crossed 10 lakh, which has given rise to slums in and around the city and also experiencing traffic jam during peak hours.
- **Smart Living:** Healthy housing with facilities of safe drinking water, sanitation and affordable energy for cooking and lighting; cultural and recreational facilities; social cohesion and brotherhood; affordable, efficient, effective and quality health care facilities; safety, security and crime-free environment and affordable and quality education facility—primary, secondary and tertiary. Smart cities must be free from slums.
- **Smart Mobility:** Local accessibility, sustainable, innovative, affordable, low cost and safe transport system, security for women, disabled and elderly in the transport system and free from pickpocketing. Private transport system should be regulated and less costly.
- **Smart Economy:** Entrepreneurship, innovative sprit, productivity, flexible labour market, employment opportunity to fight with unemployment and poverty and inequality, mild and low inflation, scope for expansion of industrial and service sector.
- **Smart Environment:** Attractiveness of nature, pollution free, well-maintained heritage sites, water bodies and open spaces; good system of solid-waste management and environmental protection mechanism in place and green living.

- **Smart Public–Private Partnership:** Governments of developing countries cannot be able to design, construct and implement smart city projects alone; therefore, effective and efficient public–private partnership is a *sine qua non*. There must be a division of responsibility and task among the public and private sector, and both have to invest physical, financial, technological and human resources for the making of smart cities.
- **Smart Local Bodies:** For the effective development of the urban areas, smart cities need to have qualified and well-trained and fully empowered local self-government institutions. All the statutory bodies of the ULBs must be effectively functional and take charge of their duties and responsibilities effectively and efficiently.
- **Smart Civil Society Organizations:** A smart city needs to have active and energized civil society organization which should selflessly work for the effective implementation of various developmental schemes of the government. They need to work for the improvement of the housing, sanitation and provision of safe drinking water in the urban slums. The need to promote education and health care of the children, women, elderly and disabled of the slums.

Different types of smart cities can be formulated, such as heritage smart cities; religious smart cities; industrial smart cities; hilly and eco-friendly smart cities; port, sea and water area smart cities and other cities with their specialties such as wood carving city; diamond work city, brass work city and so on. Smart cities lead to smart urbanization and contribute towards economic growth and development of the nation.

URBANIZATION AND URBAN GOVERNANCE

The Government of India has identified that key problems in urban governance include weak legal and institutional framework within which the ULBs operate and the poor capacity including lack of a professional and sensitized cadre to perform their development and regulatory functions (Government of India 2007). Unbridled urbanization can pose unsurmountable challenges before the state administration and municipal governance. Some of the problems that may arise are (a) how to organize new administrative structure and manpower development; (b) how to prevent uncontrolled expansion; (c) how to organize transport and communication system and (d) how to finance public services and prepare master plans. Prioritizing the needs and preparing strategies to implement them amidst socio-political pressure and resources constraints is a challenge before the municipal administration. Besides civic problems, the urban administration has to tackle other problems which people create, such as popular resentments and disregarding of rules and regulations, spoiling public and private property and showing utter disregard to the human rights. Other issues like illegal migration, trafficking and so on can pose problems for urban administration.

URBANIZATION AND URBAN LOCAL SELF-GOVERNMENT

The lacklustre coordination between government and urban local self-government institutions is another problem of urban governance. The empowerment of urban local self-government will embolden participatory governance and take the governance to the doorstep of the people. Many countries through the constitutional provisions have empowered local self-government institutions to carry out certain duties and responsibilities relating to urban development. For instance, in India, the 74th constitutional amendment has assigned 18 duties and responsibilities to ULBs. However, in developing countries, the local self-government institutions have not been effectively empowered to carry out their duties and responsibilities, and they are largely dependent on the state governments for urban finance. Moreover, presence of many parallel bodies and lack of political and bureaucratic will are other responsible factors for lack of effective empowerment of local self-government institutions. In India, ULBs are called third-tier democratic institutions. The participatory governance and empowerment of local self-government institutions are essential for the effective development of urban areas.

These are a few important issues and challenges of urbanization. They are nicely summed up by Jagmohan (2005),

> Today in every aspect of city life—density of population, availability of land, housing, slums and squatter settlements, municipal services, open spaces, the scale and character of migration, employment, traffic and transport, energy, communication, crime, health and environment, civic set-up and finance—the prevailing conditions present a sad picture.

Certainly, urbanization is helping to a great extent the process of economic development and social change. However, if it is not being managed properly, it may lead to urban unrest and give rise to socio-economic fallouts such as unemployment, crime, robbery, traffic problem and accidents, murder and rape, child labour and other kinds of human right problems. 'To house a massive urban population and to meet its civic needs and it's social and cultural aspirations and also to keep its environment healthy, is going to present to the human race one of the gravest challenges that it has ever faced' (Jagmohan 2005).

Duties and Responsibilities Assigned to ULBs in India as per 74th Constitutional Amendment

The 74th constitutional amendment has assigned 18 duties and responsibilities to the ULBs those are: urban planning including town planning; regulation of land-use and construction of building; planning for economic and social development; roads and bridges; water supply for domestic, industrial and commercial purposes; public health, sanitation conservancy and solid waste management; fire services; urban forestry, protection of the environment and promotion of ecological aspects; safeguarding the interests of weaker sections of society, including the handicapped and mentally retarded; slum improvement and upgradation; urban poverty alleviation; provision of urban amenities and facilities such parks, gardens, playgrounds; promotion of cultural, educational and aesthetic aspects; burials and burial grounds, cremations, cremation grounds and electric crematoriums; cattle pounds, prevention of cruelty to animals; vital statistics including registration of births and deaths; public amenities including street lighting, parking lots, bus stops and public conveniences and regulation of slaughter houses and tanneries.

MEASURES TAKEN BY THE GOVERNMENT OF INDIA FOR URBAN DEVELOPMENT

The Government of India has launched many programmes for the urban area development and few important among many are discussed below.

1. **Integrated Development of Small and Medium Towns (IDSMT):** The programme aims at provisioning basic services to the poor in order to improve their socio-economic conditions. The sole purpose behind launching the programme was to prevent the migration of rural area population to the metropolitan cities.
2. **Accelerated Urban Water Supply Programme (AUWSP):** The centre-sponsored scheme's objective was to provide safe drinking water to the towns having a population of less than 20,000.
3. **National Slum Development Programme (NSDP):** The programme's thrust was to provide sanitation, water supply and other facilities to the urban slum areas.
4. **Shelter and Sanitation for Pavement Dwellers (SSPD):** This programme covered a large number of urban areas, including the metropolitan cities having sizable number of shelter-less population. The objective of the programme was to provide shelter to the shelter-less population in the cities.
5. **Nehru Rozgar Yojana:** Launched with the objective of providing employment to the urban unemployed and underemployed poor.
6. **Urban Basic Services for the Poor:** The objective was to achieve social sector goals—community organization, mobilization and empowerment and convergence through sustainable support system.
7. **Swarna Jayanti Shahari Rozgar Yojana:** The main thrust areas of the programme were employment generation and provision of basic services to the urban poor. It aimed at generation of self-employment as well as wage employment opportunities for the urban poor to raise their income.
8. **Prime Minister Integrated Urban Poverty Eradication Programme (PMIUPEP):** The aim is to eradicate urban poverty through the provision of employment and infrastructure development. The focus was on the small cities.
9. **Jawaharlal Nehru National Urban Renewal Mission (JNNURM):** The mission aims are to encourage reforms and fast-track infrastructure development with focus on efficiency in urban infrastructure and service delivery mechanism, community participation and accountability of ULBs towards citizen. The primary objective of JNNURM is to create economically productive, efficient, equitable and responsive cities.
10. **Smart Cities Mission (SCM):** The objective of the SCM is to promote cities that provide core infrastructure and give a decent quality of life to its citizens, clean and sustainable environment and application of 'smart' solutions. The core infrastructure include (a) adequate water and electricity supply; (b) sanitation and solid-waste management; (c) efficient urban transport; (d) affordable housing; (e) good governance, especially e-governance and citizen participation; (f) sustainable environment; (g) safety and security of citizens and (h) health and education.[4]

However, despite launching various programmes since Independence, the socio-economic status of the urban population, particularly those staying in the urban slum and working in the informal sector, has not adequately improved. Many studies have identified several factors for poor performance in the implementation of various urban development programmes. A few of them among many are lack of adequate financial resources, failure of state governments to spent the allotted amount given by the central government for the implementation of various programmes, faulty targeting of beneficiaries, corruption and bad governance at the bureaucratic and political level, nepotism at the grass-root level by the local self-government in allocation of beneficiaries, lack of effective empowerment of the local self-government institutions, migration of more and more poverty-stricken rural population to the urban areas, growing number of unorganized slums, poor maintenance of assets created under rural development programmes and so on.

Aahaar (Subsidized Cooked Meal) Scheme for Urban Poor

Odisha government has launched a cheap meal scheme called "Aahaar" for providing subsidized food to urban poor in 1st April 2015. The Scheme provides subsidised meal at ₹5. This scheme is in operation in 30 districts of Odisha triggered off in a phased manner. The 'Aahar' scheme is being sponsored by Odisha Mining Corporation (OMC), Odisha Power Generation Corporation (OPGC), Odisha Industrial Infrastructure Development Corporation(IDCO) and Tata Steel. The subsidised meals would be provided to the patients, attendants of patients, street children, rag pickers, street vendors, rickshaw puller and people visiting urban areas for various works.

Source: http://economictimes.indiatimes.com/news/politics-and-nation/aahar-cheap-meal-scheme-launched-in-odisha/articleshow/46768751.cms (accessed on 7 December 2016); http://odisha.gov.in/e-magazine/Orissareview/2015/Nov/engpdf/6-12.pdf (accessed on 7 December 2016).

SUMMARY

Urbanization is the order of the day and is an outcome of globalization process started in developing countries in 1990s. Although the percentage of urbanization is high in the developed countries, in recent years, the rate of growth of urban population in developing countries is on the rise. The high speed urbanization, particularly in developing countries has called for urban development measures in order to provide better quality of life to the people living in and migrating from rural areas to urban areas. In developing countries, challenges of urbanization are many and to mention a few are poverty, unemployment, inequality, pollution, transport problem, crime and poor law and order situation, health and education problem, urban slum, energy and so on. Moreover, participatory governance and empowerment of the local self-government institutions and creation of smart cities will go a long way to strengthen the process of urban development.

Keywords: urbanization, smart cities, urban local bodies, urban heritage, urban poverty and unemployment, urban governance, urban slum.

REVIEW QUESTIONS

1. What is urbanization? Discuss the process of urbanization in the developed as well as developing countries.
2. Define urban area. Discuss the role of urban areas in economic growth and development of developing countries.
3. Explain four key issues relating to the development of urban areas.
4. Discuss the important challenges of urbanization and how to overcome them.
5. What is urban slum? Discuss various problems associated with urban slums in the developed as well as developing countries.
6. Urban heritage and utilization of urban space is vital to urban development. Illustrate.
7. What are the features of urban governance? Explain how urban governance is important for urban development.
8. Write short notes on the following:
   (i) Urbanization
   (ii) Urban slum
   (iii) Urban heritage
   (iv) Urban crime
   (v) Urban open space
   (vi) Urban poverty

NOTES

1. UNEP Urbanization, see http://www.unep.org/french/tunza/children/pdfs/Fac (accessed on 19 February 2015).
2. Inequality quotes by Plato, see http://inequality.org/quotes/plato/ (accessed on 19 February 2015).
3. Taken from 'Sustainable urban transport: A winning strategy for Canada', see http://www.jtc.sala.ubc.ca/reports/ConfBoardUrbanT (accessed on 19 February 2015).
4. See http://smartcities.gov.in/writeraddata/SmartCit... (accessed on 19 April 2016).

BIBLIOGRAPHY

Bruce, N., R. Perez-Padilla, and R. Albalak. 'Indoor Air Pollution in Developing Countries: A Major Environmental and Public Health Challenge.' *Bulletin of WHO* 78 (2007): 1078–92.

Calloway, A. 'Unemployment among African School Leavers.' *Journal of Modern African Studies* 1, no. 3 (1963): 351–71.

Chen, X., Y. Geng, and T. Fujita. 'An Overview of Municipal Solid-Waste Management in China.' *Waste Management* 30 (2010): 716–24.

Cheng, C. 'A Study of Dynamic Economic Relationship between Urbanization and Service Industries Growth in China.' *Journal of Industrial Engineering and Management* 6, no. 1 (2012): 8–15.

Chenje. 'Africa Global Environment Outlook: Past, Present and Future Perspective.' In *Global Environment Outlook 3*, 2000. Available at: www.grida.no/geo/geo3/english/410.htm (accessed on 21 October 2015).

Crowe, T. *Crime Prevention through Environmental Design: Application of Architectural Design and Space Management Concepts*, 2nd ed. Oxford: Butterworth-Heinemann, 2000.

Das, C., A. Mourmouras, and P. C. Rangazas. *Economic Growth and Development: A Dynamic Economic Approach*. New York: Springer, 2015.

Davis, K. 'The Urbanization of the Human Population.' *Scientific American* 213, no. 3 (1965): 41–53.

Doan, D. L. 'Institute House Hold Waste Collection.' The Urban Environmental Management Project in Cote D'Ivoire, Habitat International, 1998.

Doytsher, Y., P. Kelly, R. Khouri, R. Mcharen, H. Mueller, and C. Potsiou. 'Rapid Urbanization and Megacities: The Need for Spatial Information Management.' Research Study by FIG Commission 3, International Federation of Surveyors, 2010.

European Union. 'Mapping Smart Cities in the EU.' IPIA/ITRE/ST/2013–02, 2014. Available at: http://enroparl.europa.en/studies (accessed on 23 October 2015).

Firdaus, G. 'Urbanization, Emerging Slums and Increasing Health Problems: A Challenge Before the Nation: An Empirical Study with Reference to State of Uttar Pradesh in India.' *Journal of Environmental Research and Management* 3, no. 9 (2012): 146–52.

Galvin, E. B. 'Crime and Violence in an Urbanizing World.' *Journal of International Affairs* 45 (2002): 123–45.

Gill, I., and H. Kharas. 'A East Asian Renaissance: Ideas for Economic Growth.' World Bank, 2007.

Glaeser, E. L., M. Resseger, and K. Tobia. 'Inequality in Cities.' *Journal of Regional Science* 46, no. 4 (2009): 617–46.

Government of India. *Local Governance: An Inspiring Journey in to the Future*, second administrative reforms commission, Sixth Report, 2007. Available at: http://www.gangothri.org/sites/userfiles1/edocs/R (accessed on 25 October 2015).

———. *Smart Cities Mission Statement and Guidelines*. New Delhi: Ministry o of India, Government of India, 2015.

Granados, J. A. T. 'Reducing Automobile Traffic: An Urgent Policy for Health Promotion.' *Pan American Journal of Public Health* 3, no. 4 (1998): 227–41.

Hardoy, J. E., and D. Satterthwaite. 'Growing Cities Heighten Clean Water, Sanitation Concerns.' Urban Health Concern, 1989a. Available at: https://urbanhealthupdates.wordpress.com (accessed on 21 October 2015).

Hardoy, J. E., and D. Satterthwaite. *Squatter Citizen: Life in the Urban Third World*. London: Earthscan, 1989b.

Hartmut, Mueller. 'Spatial Information Management, an Effective Tool to Support Sustainable Urban Management.' 46th ISOCARP Congress, 2010.

Henderson, J. V. 'Urbanization in China: Policy Issues and Options.' China Economic Research and Advisory Programme, Brown University and NBER, 2009.

Hicks, D. A. 'Revitalizing Our Cities or Restoring Ties to Them? Pre-directing the Debate.' *Journal of Law Reform* 27 (1994): 813–75.

ILO. 'Wage Workers in Agriculture: Conditions of Employment and Work.' ILO, Geneva, 1996.

Jagmohan. *Soul and Structure of Governance in India*. New Delhi: Allied Publisher, 2005.

Jedweb, R., L. Christiaensen, and M. Gindelsky. 'Rural Push, Urban Pull and... Urban Push? New Historical Evidence from Developing Countries.' George Washington University Institute for International Economic Policy Working Paper no. 2014–04, 2014.

Kabore, I., T. Lairez, and M. Pilon. 'Genre or Scolarisation an Bukina Faso: Enseignements D'une Approche Statistique.' *Education, Faille Et Dyamiques Demographiques*, sous la direction de M Cosia, CICRED, 221–46, 2003.

Kabore, I., and M. Pilon. 'Intra-Urban Enrolment Disparities in Ouagadougou.' Education for all Global Monitoring Report 2003/4/2004/ED/EFA/MPVPI/31, National Institute of Statistics and Demography, France, 2003.

Kattan, R. B., and N. Burnett. 'User Fees in Primary Education.' Human Development Network, World Bank, 2004.

Kennedy, P. *Preparing for the Twenty First Century*., New York: Random House, 1993.

Krivo, L. J., and R. D. Peterson. 'Extremely Disadvantaged Neighborhoods and Urban Crime.' *Social Forces* 75 (1996): 619–50.

Ludermir, A. B., and T. Harpham. 'Urbanization and Mental Health in Brazil: Social and Economic Dimensions.' *Health and Place* 4, no. 3 (1998): 223–32.

Mishra, R. P., 'Urbanization in India Challenges and Opportunities.' ICSSR North Eastern Regional Centre, Shillong, 1998.

Moore, M., P. Gould, and B. S. Keary. 'Global Urbanization and Impact on Health.' *International Journal of Hygiene and Environmental Health* 206, no. 4–5 (2003): 269–78.

Mwangi, S. W. 'Challenges of Urban Environmental Governance: Participation and Partnership in Nakuru Municipality Kenya.' University Van Amsterdam, AGIDS, 2012.

Naik, D. D. *Housing Finance Pamphlet 163*. Bombay: Commerce Publication, 1981.

Ngware, M., E. Ezeh, M. Oketch, and N. Mudenge. 'Do Household Characteristics Matter in Schooling Decisions in Kenya?' Equal Opportunity International 28, no. 7 (2009): 591–608.

Odero, W., P. Garner, and A. Zwi. 'Road Traffic Injuries in Developing Countries: A Comprehensive Review of Epidemiological Studies.' *Tropical Medicine International Health* 2 (1997): 445–60.

Pal, P., and J. Ghosh. 'Inequality in India: A Survey of Recent Trends.' DESA Working Paper no. 45, ST/ESA/2007/DWP/45, United Nations, 2007.

Panos. *Governing Our Cities: Will People Power Work?* London: Panos Institute, 2001.

Pattanaik. 'Young Migrant Construction Workers in the Unorganized Urban Sector'. *South Asia* Research 29, no. 1(2009): 19–40.

Paul, S. 'A Study of the Experience of House Building of the Middle Income Group in the Urban and Rural Areas.' Master's Thesis, Mahatma Gandhi University, Kerala, 1983.

Trivedi, J. K., H. Sareen, and M. Dhyani. 'Rapid Urbanization–Its Impact on Mental Health: A South Asian perspective.' *Indian Journal of Psychiatry* 50 (2008): 161–65.

UNCHS. 'State of the World's Cities 2001.' Nairobi, United Nations Centre for Human Settlements (Habitat), 2001.

UNEP. 'The Urban Environment: Facts and Figures.' *UNEP Industry and Environment* 23, no. 2 (2000): 4–11.

———. *Global Environment Outlook: Past, Present and Future Perspective*. London: Earth Scan, 2002.

UN-Habitat. *The Challenge of Slums: Global Report on Human Settlements 2003*. London: Earth Scan Publication, 2003.

———. 'Reducing Urban Crime and Violence: Policy Directions.' UN Human Settlements Programme, UN Habitat, 2007.

United Nations. 'Governance for the Future Democracy and Development in the Least Developed Countries.' United Nations Development Programme, 2005.

———. *World Urbanization Prospects: The 2005 Revision*. United Nations, 2006.

Vaidya, C. 'Urban Issues, Reforms and Way Forward in India.' Working Paper no. 4/2009-DEA, Ministry of Finance, Government of India, 2009.

WHO. *Bulletin of the WHO* 88, no. 4 (2010). Available at: http://www.who.int/bulletin/volumes/88/4/10-010410/en/ (accessed on 3 December 2016).

World Bank. 'Entering the 21st Century.' World Development Report 1999/2000, World Bank, Washington DC, 2000.

WWF. 'Living Planet Report 2000.' World Wildlife Fund, 2000.

12 Globalization and Development Disparities

The main losers in today's very unequal world are not those who are too much exposed to globalization. They are those who have been left out.

—Kofi Annan (cited in Norbes 2003)

Globalization has produced good and bad effects.

—Goulet (2000)

The liberalization process began in developing countries during 1990s, almost after 4–5 decades of their independence from the colonial rule. It triggered off the economic reform process in developing countries. Economic plans and policies of developing countries started giving preferences and priorities to private investments and opening up the industrial sector to the private and corporate sectors. Besides, many developing economies like India initiated the process of disinvestment in the public sector industries to further embolden its reform process. However, largely after 2000, most of developing countries under the influence and pressure of the neo-liberalism era being augmented by the Western countries and the international agencies, mainly the World Bank and the IMF, opened up their economies to the world market. In the 21st century, the process of globalization in the world got momentum in almost all the nations of the world, developed as well as developing. Even China has accepted the globalization process in order to bring vibrancy into its economy and proliferation of international trade of its goods across the world.

Critics of globalization argue that developing countries were compelled to accept globalization due to the pressure of the West laid by the United States of America. Many considered that it is an indirect intervention of the World Bank and the developed nation of the West, particularly the United States of America, in the economic affairs of developing countries with regard to their economic growth and development. In a nutshell, the conservative, socialist and communist thinkers believe that the globalization was thrust upon developing countries of the East by the developed countries of the West. However, the liberalists and the supporters of the globalization believe that it is a potent instrument to augment economic growth and development of developing countries. With the passing of the years, the globalization process, like testing of opium, has engrossed the economic growth and development process of the developing world. Its effects have been realised by both developed and developing countries to gain mutually through open trade of goods and services, exchange of technology and technical ideas, migration of people and outsourcing. In other words, the globalization process has promoted, encouraged and energized the interaction between the nations, economies and people of the world. The process of globalization has brought all the nations of the world to a common platform of understanding with regard to the mechanisms of promotion of economic growth and development.

The rich Western nations believe that globalization process will help developing countries to improve their economic growth and development through free trade and other economic relationships proposals. However, it is acknowledged in various studies that the globalization has produced both positive as well as negative effects on the various dimensions of development in developing countries, although it has benefited largely the developed nations. Now in the new millennium, it is amply clear that the globalization is gripping almost every part of the world. Like a snowball rolling down a steep mountain, globalization seems to be gathering more and more momentum (IMF Staff 2008).

However, the impact of globalization on different nations and different sections of population is disproportionate, and it has benefited the rich more and affected the poor worst, while the middle class is the silent sufferer. Lawal (2006) has commented that globalization has opened up new and extensive opportunities for worldwide development but, however, this is not 'progressing evenly' as some countries are becoming integrated into the global economy more rapidly than other with the evidence of fast growth and reduced poverty. UNDP (1999) has remarked that the challenge of globalization in the new century is not to stop the expansion of global markets but to find the rules and institutions for stronger governance—local, national, regional and global—to preserve the advantages of global markets and competitions; and also to provide enough space for human, community and environmental resources to ensure that globalization works for people.

After reading this chapter, you will be able to:

1. Define globalization and explain various features of globalization.
2. Explain various advantages and disadvantages of globalization.
3. Discuss the role of globalization in economic growth and development of developing countries.
4. Define development disparities and discuss how globalization has promoted it in developing countries.

SECTION I: GLOBALIZATION

Globalization is a process of integrating not only the economy of nations but also their culture, technology and governance.

—Lawal (2006)

MEANING AND PERSPECTIVES

Globalization, like development, is a multidimensional concept and is more used than it is understood. As it a forceful and dynamic concept, it is very difficult to define it comprehensively to the universal satisfaction. According to Friedman (1999), globalization means the spread of free market capitalism to virtually every country in the world. To McKibbin (2000) globalization means increasing interdependence of economic, social and political activities across national boundaries. As per the World Bank, 'globalization' refers to the growing interdependence of countries resulting from the increasing integration of trade, finance, people and ideas in one global market.[1] Globalization has its own set of economic rules and aspirations, and perspectives that revolve around opening up the economy to the world market, promoting deregulations and privatizations in the economy.

The essential prerequisite of a 'globalized' economy is openness to foreign trade and investment (Lukas 2000). However, starting from economic globalization, the globalization has gradually fostered social, political, human and cultural openness. Under globalization, all doors and windows of a country remain open to accommodate new knowledge, ideas, technology and so on, blowing from across all nooks and corners of the world. The economic globalization refers to free trade and investment, while cultural globalization means exposure of the nations to various cultures. For instance, Indian festivals like *Holi* (the festival of colours) and *Diwali* (the festival of light) are seen to be observed in the United Kingdom, the United States of America and Canada, and also by Indians living in different countries of the world. Human resources globalization broadly refers to migration of people and more recently migration of technical manpower from developing countries to the developed countries. On the other hand, the political globalization largely refers to exposure to political ideologies and democratic values. The immigrants from developing countries have been elected to the parliaments of the developed countries like the United States of America, the United Kingdom and Canada, and are also found to be holding ministerial seats in the cabinet of a few countries, an illustrious example of political globalization. For instance, more recently, people from Indian origin are holding ministerial seat in cabinet of the United Kingdom and Canada. The acceptance of globalization is seen to be faster in the developed countries as compared to developing countries. Like development, globalization is also multidimensional. Generally, it may be referred to as the widening, deepening and spreading up of worldwide interconnectedness in all aspects of contemporary social life, from the cultural to the criminal, the financial to the spiritual (Held et al. 1999).

Globalization has the following features:

1. Promotes free trade among the economies of the world and in a sense, encourages the concept of boundary-less economic world.
2. Gives boost to the free market economy.
3. Encourages disinvestment for downsizing the role of public sector in the economic system.
4. It emphasizes on the structural transformation and urges the nation to introduce economic reforms for emboldening market economic system.
5. Encourages transfer of technology, manpower and international flow of capital through FDIs and remittances.
6. Globalization is multidimensional consisting of economic, social, human, cultural and political dimensions and is a great learning process between various countries regarding each others economic, political and social system and cultural identities.

7. While globalization has positive, innovative, dynamic aspects, it also has negative, disruptive and marginalizing aspects.
8. Globalization is associated with increased instability of output and employment, this affects among other things job security.
9. Globalization may create 'brain drain' in developing countries, when the knowledgeable and skilled manpower immigrates from developing countries to the developed countries.
10. Globalization in the orthodox developing countries has promoted conflict of ideology between the traditionalists and modernists.

Developing countries embrace globalization for a variety of reasons:

1. For the removal of trade barriers and import of fuel, technology and other goods and services which are useful for the enhancement of their economic growth rate and improvement in their balance of payment position.
2. To expand the choices for consumers; availability of variety of goods through liberal imports enhances the choices of the consumers in a country.
3. To bring down the prices of the products having comparative advantage and thus, raise the real value of workers' earnings.
4. Foreign investment provides more jobs, new production technologies, infrastructure improvements and a source of capital for local entrepreneurs.
5. Exchange of ideas, manpower, technology and finances, helps to enhance productivity and economic growth rate.
6. Advantages of domestic business gains resulting in access to both cheaper inputs and vastly market for their products.
7. Global tourism and inflow of tourists from the developed countries to developing countries contributes to enhance their GNI. Cultural and religious tourism not only strengthens cultural diplomacy but also improves international relations among the countries.
8. Globalization helps in better disaster management. The technical and financial help by various countries during disaster help particularly to developing countries to better manage their disaster. The help provided by various countries during super cyclone of Odisha, India, is an illustrious example.
9. FDI and remittances improve the investment climate in the country and creates employment. Reverse migration of trained people helps the country in better utilization of its manpower.
10. It helps to improve the socio-economic status of the population. The remittances investment helps to raise the quality of life of the people even at the village level.
11. Last but not the least, it brings modernity into developing countries being influenced by traditional beliefs and values.

It is remarked that globalization gives rise to the creation, production, distribution and consumption of goods and services on an unprecedented scale, and that process is meant to increase economic activity for people, enterprises and countries through freer international trade, direct foreign investment and capital market flows (Borrell 2006). Sachs and Warner (1995) found that developing countries with open economies grew by an average of 4.5% per year in the 1970s and 1980s, while those with closed economies grew by only 0.7%. In the same vein, developed countries with open economic grew by 2.3% per year, while those with closed economies grew by 0.7%. It is also concluded that nations with relatively open trade regions grow roughly twice as fast as to those with relatively closed regimes (OECD 1998). The globalization index has been calculated by different agencies broadly by comprising five main indicators such as openness to trade, capital flows, exchange of technology and ideas, labour movement and cultural integration. The index developed by Erust and Young in 2010 ranks Hong Kong at number one spot with score a of 7.48, followed by Ireland and Singapore with 7.43 and 6.78 as second and third. The United States of America ranks 28, China 39 and India 57 position (see Table 12.1). Asian countries except Hong Kong, Singapore, South Korea and Taiwan have not been adequately exposed to globalization. Many African countries are the laggards in the globalized world as compared to other regions of the world.

GLOBALIZATION AND INTERNATIONAL ECONOMIC RELATIONSHIP

The globalization process has established and hastened the economic and trade relationship not only between the developing and developed countries but also among the and developing nations either bilaterally or through the developed nations. It is widely recognized that in the globalized era, the development of developing countries need not be too much dependent on the whim of the developed nations but rather should be economically interlinked with the developed countries. Sapru (1994) was of the view that the progress of development in developing countries in the present decade cannot be achieved by the action of the developing world alone.

The effect of import competition in industries in Chile and Turkey and the effect of greater competition in export markets on firms in Brazil, Japan and Republic of Korea are examples to confirm that linking domestic economy with international economy increases

Table 12.1 *Globalization Index of Selected Countries, 2010*

Countries	Score	Rank
Hong Kong	7.48	1
Ireland	7.43	2
Singapore	6.78	3
United Kingdom	5.00	15
South Korea	4.17	33
Colombia	3.61	40
Nigeria	3.03	55
India	2.96	57
Kazakhstan	3.09	53
Iran	2.37	60

Source: The Globalization Index, http://www.ey.com/Gh/en/Issues/Buiness_environment/winning_in_a_..../ (accessed on 19 June 2013).

Table 12.2 *Comparison of FDI Inflows to China, India and Developing Economies (Amount in US $ millions)*

Country	Year				
	1990–2000	2002	2003	2004	2005
China	30,104	52,743	53,505	60,630	72,406
India	1,705	5,627	4,585	5,474	6,598
Developing Countries	134,670	163,583	175,138	275,032	334,285
World	495,391	617,732	557,869	710,755	916,277

Source: UNCTAD, World Investment Report, 2006 (www.dnctad.org/wir).

the prospects of development in developing countries (Sapru 1994). A report by OECD (1998) states, more open and outward-oriented economies consistently outperformed countries with restrictive trade and (foreign) investment regimes. According to IMF (1997), policies toward foreign trade are among the more important factors promoting economic growth and convergence in developing countries. Fischer (2000) was of view that 'integration into the world economy is the best way for countries to grow.' The impact of FDI on development is visible in many countries—China, India and a few African and Latin American countries are illustrious beneficiaries (see Table 12.2). Provost (2013) was of the view that there are 214 million migrants in the world, and if they lived in one country, it would be the fifth most populous, behind China, India, United States of America and Indonesia. According to World Bank (2013), the developing world is expected to receive $41 billion in migrant remittance in 2013, an increase of 6.3% over 2012. Globally, the world's 232 million international migrants are expected to remit amount worth $550 billion. The largest beneficiaries of remittances in 2012 are India followed by China and Philippines (Figure 12.1).

Figure 12.1 *Top Ten Beneficiaries of Remittances*

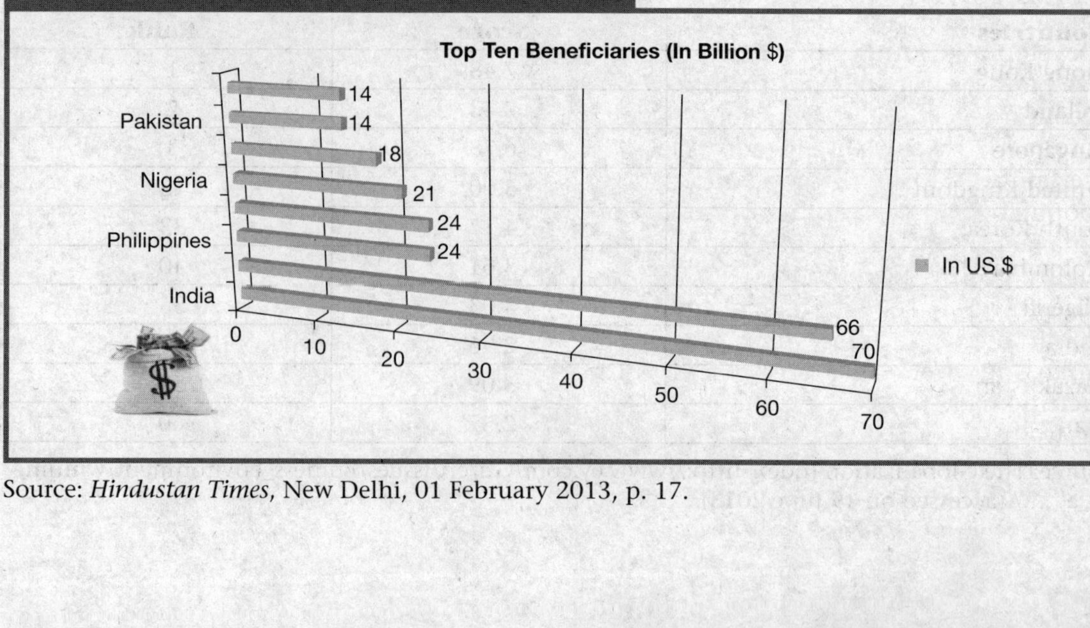

Source: *Hindustan Times*, New Delhi, 01 February 2013, p. 17.

Karras (2006) study on correlation between foreign aid and growth in per capita GDP, using annual data from the 1960 to 1997 for a sample of 71 aid-receiving developing countries, found that the effect of foreign aid on economic growth is positive, permanent and statistically significant. According to Ray (2012), the effect of FDI in the host economy are usually believed to increase the employment, augment the productivity, boost exports and amplified pace of transfer of technology. Like FDIs and foreign aids, remittances also produce positive impact on host country's development. One of the illustrious examples is Kerala, one of the socio-economically developed states of India, which is popularly called the 'money order economy', where remittances contribute one-fourth to the State GDP (Kerala Calling 2012). Many believe that the skewed nature of the state economy has been called the 'Money Order Economy' (Biswas 2010). The contribution of remittances to the rural–urban continuum, where the people of rural Kerala are enjoying almost the same quality of the standard of living compared to urban Kerala, is unparallel. Moreover, remittances are one of the factors for the proliferation of service sector economy in Kerala. The rural–urban continuum in Kerala may be largely attributed to remittances and Kerala's link to the international arena. In Punjab, the Punjabis, who are immigrants in many other countries, back at home in the villages have constructed beautiful houses, which shows the power of remittances to raise the quality of living of the people in rural Punjab. Remittances have produced tremendous impact on the access to quality basic amenities and have promoted the standard of living of rural population in these two states of India. It is said that for many developing countries, remittances represent a major part of international capital flow, surpassing FDI, export revenues and foreign aid (Giuliano and Ruiz-Arranz 2005). Stahl and Arnold (1986) argued that the use of remittances for consumption may have positive effect on growth because of their possible multiplier effect. It was found that the remittances have a positive effect on the growth of Latin American countries where the financial systems are less developed by providing an alternative way to finance investment and helping overcome liquidity constraints (Fayissa and Nsiah 2010).

Moreover, the international agencies and organizations are funding various developmental projects on agriculture, industry, infrastructure, electricity, education, health and family welfare, women empowerment, strengthening of grass-roots democracy and so on in developing countries. The flow of financial capital from the developed countries to developing countries in the form of 'outsourcing' has laid to capital formation in specialized areas, ultimately percolating to development in other allied areas. The international economic relation between developed and developing countries is one of the positive and productive aspects of globalization. Although its benefits are parochial and beneficial to certain sections of the population, its trickle down effect can benefit the other sections of population in developing countries. For instance, if anybody opens a school or a hospital or a factory with the help of remittances which he or she receives from abroad, it will have many positive externalities: (a) many unemployed person will get waged employment and (b) more self-employment will be created in the vicinity of the said projects. Thus remittances will indirectly help to create income-earning opportunities to people other than one who receive remittances. This is being seen in Punjab, where the people who are getting remittances from abroad are found to have opened schools and hospitals in rural as well as in the small and medium towns. Thus, global economic relationship in the form of transfer and exchange of physical, human and financial capital from the developed to the developing nations will ultimately lead to capital formation in developing countries.

Remittances for Social Development by Punjabi Diaspora

1. A report notes that NRI Punjabi philanthropists have helped in bridging the resource gap by providing funds for social welfare schemes. A survey of 477 villages located in 7 tehsils of the Doaba region, conducted by a Jalandhar-based organization, Vichar Manch in 2002 found that NRI Punjabis had contributed more than $40 million to the villages at an estimated $0.08 million per village. These contributions were made for setting up educational institutions, dispensaries, hospitals, crematoriums, sports stadiums, street lighting, sanitation and clean drinking water projects. A more recent survey conducted in 2007 showed that Punjabi NRIs have increased their contributions towards social development projects with the help of enterprising individuals in the villages who have facilitated their development initiatives.
2. Guru Ravidass Educational Assistance Trust is an educational charity organization established by the Ravidassia community members (Charity founder Dr Charan Bunger) of the Punjabi diaspora. The organisation is named after Guru Ravidass Ji, a prominent Saint and Guru of fifteenth century India, who played a leading role in the 'Bhakti Movement' (a social reform movement to remove oppressive religious and social practices). The trust is based in Birmingham, UK, and has been in operation since 2005. Its prime objective is to provide education to poor students back in India, particularly in the states of Punjab, Andhra Pradesh, Karnataka, Uttar Pradesh and Bihar. The organisation supports poor children by providing text books and scholarships for paying school and college fees. It helps provide education for deprived children and youth, irrespective of religion and caste. The patron-list of the Ravidass Educational Trust features a considerable number of Punjabi NRIs, many based in the UK, as well as British persons. To date, the trust has provided about 275 yearly scholarships to 175 students, ranging from $98 for basic school education to $790 for higher professional education such as a degree in medicine.
3. The Guru Nanak Hospital at Dhahan-Kaleran was built by the sole effort of Sardar Budh Singh Dhahan, a returned migrant from Canada in the late 1970s. At present, it includes a 110-bed hospital, a public school and a nursing college affiliated to the University of British Columbia and a trauma centre. A medical college is also proposed to be established. Dhahan also established the Guru Nanak Mission Medical and Educational Trust (GNMET) which runs the charitable hospital, nursing college and school. There are NRI-funded hospitals in several other towns such as Bilga, Bundala, Palahi, Mahilpur, Rahon and Jalandhar.

Source: Chanda R and Ghosh S (2012): "The Punjabi Diaspora in the UK: An overview of characteristics and contributions to India", Working Paper No. 380, Indian Institute of Management, Bangalore, also see https://www.iimb.ernet.in/research/sites/default/files/WP%20No.%20380.pdf (accessed on 30/11/2016).

It is argued that the gain from the globalization is not universal and it has benefited more to the Western World or the developed world as compared to the developing world. The opponents of globalization argues that the contemporary globalization is: (a) increasing poverty; (b) widening socio-economic inequalities within and between countries; (c) creating greater job insecurity; (d) weakening workers' rights; (e) undermining social welfare and environmental protection; (f) weakening democracy and (g) most importantly, weakening the public sector institutions in developing countries.

GLOBALIZATION: A SWOT ANALYSIS FOR DEVELOPING COUNTRIES

S (Strengths)

1. Promotes socio-economic, human, cultural and political interaction between the economies of the world.
2. Promotes free trade of goods and services among the nations.
3. Modernization and technological development of developing countries through the transaction of modernity and technology from the developed to the developing world.
4. Strengthens the market economies of the developing world.

W (Weakness)

1. It can increase economic disparities between the rich and poor nations and also between the skilled and unskilled workforce.
2. It benefits more to the rich and less to the poor as the rich nations are largely the exporters of secondary and tertiary products and the poor developing nations are the exporters of primary products.

O (Opportunity)

1. Developing nations will gain in terms of FDI and remittances.
2. Inflow and outflow of physical, human and financial capital within the country.
3. It will help in the structural transformation of the developing world. Manufacturing and the service sectors of developing countries will be modernized with the help of developed countries input transfer. As a result the contribution of manufacturing and service sectors to GDP will be on rise.

T (Threat)

1. Globalization will adversely affect the economies of developing countries than the developed countries. Developing countries may be vulnerable to international pricing of the products. It can lead to inflation and falling value of currencies against dollar and other powerful currencies.

2. Developing countries will be exposed to the economic conditions of the developing world. For instance, the economic slowdown happening in the United States of America and other Western countries is also affecting developing countries.

ISSUES AND CHALLENGES OF GLOBALIZATION

One of the greatest challenges of globalization is to create a win-win condition for the developed as well as developing nations. However, it is seen that the developing nations are largely being marginalized in the globalization process. One of the reports of United Nations Conference on Trade and Development (2004) has described the increasing marginalization: 'of the world's 48 poorest countries, which are in danger of falling further behind more developed countries in an increasingly globalized economy.' Kofi Anann has rightly said, 'We must ensure that the global market is embedded in broadly shared values and practices that reflect global social needs, and that all the world's people share the benefits of globalization.'[2]

The pro-poor globalization must be the order of the day, where both rich and poor become the equal gainer of the globalization. The overall challenge posed to economic globalization is to make the global system deliver towards economic growth more consistently and more equitably. What is required is an inclusive globalization? Where the rich North and the poor South would gain equally? If globalization continues in a parochial and partial manner, favouring the rich nations, then it can be called second generation dependency tactics enforced by the developed countries on developing countries. According to United Nations (2000), additional aid flows should be deployed to support programmes that encourage growth and help the poor.

Globalization has created not only disparities between developed and developing nations but also risen inter- and intraregional disparities. It is estimated that although the share of developing countries in world trade has risen from approximately 24% in 1990 to 32% in 2000, this growth is highly parochial and largely concentrated in East Asia which produces 75% of the developing world manufactured exports and a greater proportion of high-technology items, while South Asia and Sub-Saharan Africa saw their trade grow by only 2% (UNCTAD 2004). Lawal (2006) said,

> It is obvious that the industrialized countries of the North will entirely by taking the advantage of the opportunities offered in the spheres at wider markets for trade in that capital (economic fundamentals) will tend to move from relatively weak countries to those that are strong and developed.

Within the nation, to say in India, Punjab, Gujarat, Andhra Pradesh, Tamil Nadu and Kerala has gained more from the globalization process as compared to Bihar, Odisha and Assam. Besides, the contribution of the diaspora to state GDP and socio-economic development at the household level in the former list of states is higher as compared to the later list of states. For instance, Andhra Pradesh and Odisha had the same poverty status during 1970, now in the 2011, statistics show that Andhra has done extremely well in all development front including poverty reduction, completely overtaking the performance of Odisha and the contribution of Telugu diasporas to the Andhra Pradesh's countryside livelihood development is noteworthy. The contribution of diaspora to the countryside development of Andhra Pradesh, Punjab and Kerala is quite encouraging.

Globalization has elongated the poverty and inequality gap between the rural and urban areas. All the benefits of globalization are customarily acquired by the people living in the urban areas and people living in the countryside are the losers. Globalization on one hand, provided digital access in urban areas, but on the other hand, increased the digital divide between the urban and rural areas. The access to internet facilities is abysmally low in rural areas as compared to urban areas. The job opportunity available in the service sector in urban areas carries higher salaries, and therefore those who are e-skilled and living in urban areas earn more than those of e-poor rural areas. In India, the poverty rate is higher in rural areas as compared urban areas. To cite an example, the tribals in India in many States except a few are the marginalized lot. The poverty rate among them is very high as compared to all other group of population in India. A gigantic percentage of tribals are residing in the rural areas and are far away from the madding crowd of urban areas. They are least touched by the modernity and globalization. The statistics show that they are laggard in terms of all development indicators. Besides, African countries also provide illustrious examples where the percentage of people living in poverty in rural areas is considerably higher than those living in the cities. However, globalization has made city life more hectic and brought in its wave a lot of lifestyle diseases such as blood sugar, blood pressure and other cardiovascular diseases. With the availability and accessibility to modern gadgets and vehicles, the environmental pollution has increased a lot in the urban areas, which is causing a lot of damage particularly to the health of the children, pregnant women and aging population.

Globalization is a threat to the attainment of MDGs and SDGs in many developing countries, predominated by unskilled poor population. It has given elongated income inequalities among the illiterate and low skilled workforce. The income and wage gap between the skilled and unskilled workforce has enhanced, as the globalization process has promoted the use of technology in almost all sectors and made them skill-driven. Gokhale (2010) was of the view that in developed countries, even low and intermediate skilled workers are faced with stagnant wages or, at least, increasing wage differentials when compared with high-skilled workers. With globalization, the quality of health and education available in the public sector institutions, at least, in the countryside has fallen as better qualified people prefer employment in the private and corporate sectors which offer them better job package. Besides, they are also not motivated to work in the rural areas because of non-availability of better health and education facilities.

The worst hit of globalization are the women and other disadvantaged sections of the society. The percentage of unskilled and low skilled workers is high among the women as compared to the men. Therefore, they are the first victims of globalization to be out of the skill-based job which carries higher wage rate. They are being forcefully shifted to less-paid jobs as compared to their male counterpart. In the United Nations Report, 'The 1999 World Survey on the Role of Women in Development,' it was argued that since the late 1980s in many middle-income countries, the demand for women's labour in manufacturing has been weakening, as export production became more skill and capital intensive. A detailed case study of female employment in South Korea finds that since 1990 the absolute number of women employed in the manufacturing sector has gradually declined (Hyoung et al. 2003). According to Kempadoo (2001), 'sex tourism' takes place for the most part in 'Exotic' Third World countries as a form of bringing foreign exchange and to sustain the image of their country as an appealing vacation destination.

Besides, other challenges of the globalization are rise of crimes, mistrusts, insecurity and loss of cultural identity. South Asia and Africa, which comprises large percentage of ethical or cultural community abroad, are the losers in the globalization process. Among threats to human security arising from globalization, the UNDP lists: economic insecurity, job and income insecurity, health insecurity, cultural insecurity, personal insecurity, environmental insecurity, political and community insecurity (UNDP 1999). The challenges of globalization are to protect the interest of all communities, particularly the interest of cultural and ethnic minorities. It is seen that the cultural values and identities, i.e. dress code, food, dance and dramas, art and paintings, rituals, festivals and so on, are gradually vanishing with the impact of globalization. Developed countries have to secure the interest and rights of developing countries and their people residing and employed in the developed countries. Globalization needs to create an inclusive global village, where the economic, political, social and cultural consideration of all communities irrespective of religion, creed and ethnicity are respected, valued, preserved and promoted.

SECTION II: DEVELOPMENT DISPARITIES

Inequality in society is not a new phenomenon and yet it can be fatal, if left unchecked, it can undermine the very foundations of development and social and domestic peace.

—UNDP (2014)

Since their independence from the colonial rule, developing countries have made a lot of progress in various fields of development. However, amidst development, disparities in various forms exist in developing countries more pervasively. The development achievement varies from nation to nation, within nation from one region to that of the other region; within region from one state to the other and even within the nation and the state from one community to that of the other. Development disparities have remained always a contemporary challenge before developing countries reeling under inequality and discrimination of the basis of caste, class and ethnicity and geography for centuries. Rich man's dog is found to be better nourished than the malnourished child of a socio-economically impoverished family. Disparities are vital contemporary challenges and hurdles in the path of sustainable and inclusive development of developing countries.

MEANING AND TYPES

To common understanding, 'disparities', 'inequalities', 'imbalances' and 'disproportions' are different but more or less the same phenomenon with little variation in the meaning. In common parlance, disparity means giving preference to someone over that of the other. In other words, one is in an advantageous position to grasp the opportunity than the other in terms of his or her capability, class and caste grouping, gender, ethnicity, citizenship and other related criteria attached to it within a nation. On the other hand, one is discriminated against the other because he or she is less capable, and denied of opportunity because of his or her class, caste, gender and ethnicity. Thus, preferences given and differences associated to certain socio-economic, cultural, political, religious and gender-related criteria resulted in 'disparities'. To Rajalakshmi (2013), differences created by man on account of social, economic, political, religious and cultural aspects are called inequalities or disparities. Inequalities in terms of development achievements relating to various development indicators, i.e. literacy, mortality, morbidity, per capita income and so on, across the nations, states and provinces and also among different groups of population stratified on the basis of class, caste, ethnicity and gender are perceived and can be called as development disparities.

Disparities happen when some provinces and some group of population grasp the opportunity created by the development services providers and move forward. As a result, people of the provinces and population groups move ahead and are able to have higher socio-economic status and enjoy better quality of life. On the other hand, those who remain excluded have poor socio-economic status and have poor quality of life. Popular examples of disparities are: bourgeois and proletariats, rich and poor, landlord and landless. Persistent disparities give rise to increase in poverty and inequality. The World Bank (2006) in its report entitled 'India Inclusive Growth and Services Delivery: Building on India's Success' has observed sharp differentiation across states since the early 1990s, reflected acceleration of growth in some states but deceleration in others. Datt and Ravalli on (2002) viewed that disparities are responsible for various states having different capacities for poverty reduction. The enormous variations in regional experiences and achievements coupled with the even sharper contrasts in some fields of social development have resulted in remarkable internal diversities in India (Dreze and Sen 1995).

The development disparities perceived in the 'development' panorama of developing countries can be broadly categorized into: (a) inter-country disparities; (b) intra-country disparities; (c) intra-province disparities; (d) economic disparities; (e) social disparities; (f) political disparities; (g) cultural disparities; (h) gender-based disparities; and (i) religion-based disparities. Inter-country disparities exist between the developed and developing nations since independence of the developing nations from the colonial rule. The division of countries on the planet into the three sub worlds—World I, World II, and World III—was an event that found its origin in international power politics, which continued for over 40 years as the cold war between the Eastern and the Western Blocs (Mishra and Kumar 2013). However the failure of the capitalist system during 1930s to tackle 'Great Depression' resulting in state interventions and disintegration of the Soviet Union in 1990s and international indebtedness of the Third World Countries have largely created two blocks from the standpoint of 'development':

1. The first category is the developed countries, largely belonging to Europe, Northern America and Japan, and more recently Singapore, South Korea, Hong Kong and Taiwan being added.
2. The second category being termed differently as 'underdeveloped', 'less developed' and/or 'developing' based on their level of development.

Disparities between developed and developing countries are markedly observed in terms of their achievement in different development indicators, i.e. poverty, per capita income, education and health and so on. It is remarked that developing countries remain mired in economic crisis as the disparities between North and South become increasingly pronounced (Rigby 1993). Friedan was of the view that the disparities among countries in levels of economic development are by far the greatest source of global inequality and the differences between the developed and developing countries are massive. UNDP (2013) has rightly remarked that the great and persistent inequality in the midst of plenty is paradox of our times. High inequality threatens a country's political stability because more people are dissatisfied with their economic status, which makes it harder to reach political consensus among population groups with higher and lower incomes.[3] It is rightly remarked that policies to mitigate disparities are unlikely to be backed by economic elites who benefit from inequality and, therefore, unlikely to be enacted (Teixeira 2014).

The percentage of population living below the income of $1.25 a day in Sub-Saharan African is 46.5%, which is 10 times higher than that of the world average as per World Development Indicators 2014 data. In the same vein, the GNI per capita of South Asian nations is only $1,482, while that of European Union is $35,551, more than 30 times as per the data of World Development Indicator 2014. These two examples clearly show that there is a huge economic disparity in terms of per capita income and poverty rate exist between the developed nations and developing countries. The worst positions in the ladder of disparities level are being occupied by the countries belonging to South Asia and Sub-Saharan Africa (see Table 12.3).

The intra-country disparity, which is otherwise known as the regional disparities, is quite pronounced in developing countries. Some states or regions have better status in terms of socio-economic development such as economic growth rate, poverty, illiteracy, mortality and morbidity, than the other. For instance, the per capita income of the people of the northern Indian states of Punjab, Haryana and Himachal Pradesh is higher than those of the Eastern Indian states, i.e. Odisha, Jharkhand, Bihar and West Bengal. Population living below the poverty line in the former states is also lower than those of the later states. This shows disparities in terms of economic achievements. Likewise, the achievement in terms of social development indicators such as literacy rate, morbidity and mortality rates, the south Indian states, i.e. Kerala, Tamil Nadu and Andhra Pradesh,

Table 12.3 *Poverty, Life Expectancy and GNI of Selected Group of Countries*

Countries	GNI Per Capita	Life Expectancy	Poverty Head Count Ratio at $1.25 a Day (PPP) % of Population
European Union	$35,551	81	–
OECD Members	$38,904	80	–
Latin America and Caribbean	$9,536	74	4.6
Least Developed Countries	$868	61	–
South Asia	$1,482	67	24.5
Sub-Saharan Africa	$1,657	56	46.8
World	$10,679	71	14.5

Source: World Development Indicators 2014, see http://data.worldbank.org/topic/poverty (accessed on 3 December 2016).

have higher health and education status as compared to the Eastern states, i.e. Odisha, Bihar, Jharkhand and West Bengal. More recently, Child Development Index formulated by Khera and Dreze (2016) finds the index values for the year 2013–14, Bihar, Odisha and Jharkhand the Eastern Indian states 0.296, 0.525 and 0.354 respectively and thus are below the all India value 0.530; while the south Indian states, such as Kerala, Tamil Nadu, Andhra Pradesh with index values of 0.958, 0.863 and 0.762, are above the all India index. This is an illustrious example of regional disparities as far as child development is concerned. This shows the regional disparities in terms of social development.

Bhattacharya and Sakthivel (2004) have found that the regional disparities in state domestic product in India has widened much more drastically (in the post-reform decade) and industrial states are now growing much faster than the backward states, and there is no evidence of convergence of growth rate among states. In India, states have experienced different pace of economic growth, with some states showing more growth rate, well above the national average and others languishing behind. One of the regional disparities study in Africa shows that developmental activities vary from place to place in the continent, while some regions and countries go far in improving their socio-economic growth, others are left behind with many challenges (Umar 2014; see Table 12.4).

Disparities are widely perceived at the household level also. A significant majority of households in developing countries—more than 75% of the population is living today in societies where income is more unequally distributed than it was in the 1990s (UNDP 2013). The global income inequality stands at a very high level, whereby the richest 8% of the world's population earn half of the world's total income, while the remaining 92% of the people are left with the other half (Milanovic 2012). It is noted that income and wealth inequality matter for inequality in non-income aspects of well-being (UNDP 2013). People having lower income are less capable to afford for quality education and health care to their family members. It is seen that the buffalos of the large scale farmers in the green revolution belt of Western Uttar Pradesh live in the spacious shades and the expenditure on feeding them is higher than the expenditure made by the landless poorest of the poor SC families on food, clothing and nutrition. This is one of the worst forms of economic disparities existing in the countryside. The green revolution, which has enhanced agricultural productivity, has elongated disparities between the haves and have-nots and between the large-scale farmers and landless labourers. According to Rauniyar and Kanbur (2010), inclusive growth is that growth which is accompanied by lower income inequality, so that the increment of income accrues disproportionately to

Table 12.4 *Africa: Index of Development*

Region	Index of Development Value	Remarks
North Africa	0.493	Very High
Southern Africa	0.363	High
East Africa	0.313	Medium
Central Africa	0.257	Low
West Africa	0.229	Very Low

Source: Umar (2014).

those with lower income. They suggested for 'growth with as much inclusiveness of the poorest as possible.'

Social norms, governance and public spending matter in inequality (UNDP 2013). Social development disparities refer to the inequalities relating to the achievement in the field of education and health, i.e. literacy rate, mortality and morbidity rate, life expectancy and so on, among different countries, within country among provinces and among different groups of population. Beverly and Sherraden (1997) noted that social development as a complement to economically oriented development aims to improve the well-being of people. The social development generally lays emphasis on provision of health services, education, housing, cultural activities, protection of children, change in the status of women, improved status of marginalized and disadvantaged. World Bank (2000) emphasized that for social development, people should be put in the centre of development (inclusion), strengthening the social fabric of communities so that their members can work together (cohesion) and finding ways for people to exercise their voices to authorities (accountability). The key reason of social disparity is the social exclusion, which exclude certain section of population from the main stream, and as a result they remain socio-economically disadvantaged and enjoy a low status in education, health and in overall quality of life.

In India, the socially disadvantaged groups, particularly SCs and STs, have lower education and health status as compared to other groups of population. They are also socially disconnected, excluded from participation and deprived of equality in access to various social networking institutions such as Youth Clubs, Mahila Mandals, SHGs and so on. In almost all social indicators, i.e. literacy, nutrition, housing, sanitation and mortality rate, the socio-economically disadvantaged groups in India, i.e. SCs and STs, are having lower status as compared to other groups of population (Table 12.5). UNDP (2013) in a recent study shows that large disparities in education, health and nutrition exist between households of different wealth levels within countries.

Inclusive growth and development cannot be achieved amidst social disparities. Not only in South Asia but also in the Africa and Latin American countries social disparities exists between various ethnic groups. The Census 2011 of South Africa shows wealth disparities between race groups persists even after 18 years of the end of apartheid (according

Table 12.5 *Development Indicators of SCs, STs and All Groups, India*

Indicators	**SC**	**ST**	**All Groups**
Literacy	64.6	63.5	74
Malnutrition among Women (BMI<18.5)	41.2	46.6	33
Under Weight Children	47.9	54.5	39.1
Pucca Housing	38.3	57.9	66.1
No Toilet Facility	65	69.1	49.2
Electricity for Domestic use	61.2	66.4	75
IMR	66.4	62.1	50
Child Immunization	39.7	5.4	43.5

Source: India Human Development Report, 2011.

to Jacob Zuma, the president of South Africa). Census figures show that at the bottom of the rung is the black majority which continues to be confronted by deep poverty, unemployment and inequality.[4] The UNDP (2013) has also stated that the economic growth on its own is no guarantee of improvements in education, health and nutrition outcomes for all households, especially for poor and other marginalized groups.

Political disparities in most of the colonial countries are a historical phenomenon. It refers to the capture of political power and position by the elites, creamy layers and predecessors of the influential political leaders and denial of opportunity to others. Not only in authoritarian but also in the world-leading democracies, the political power is seen to be captured by the kith and kin of former political leaders, economically well-up and caste and ethnically forward section of the population. Roughly 80% of the youth legislatures in the Philippines hail from dynastic political families (Mendoza 2012). In much of the Sub-Saharan Africa, since their independence, economic inequality has been quite low, but political inequality has been severe with rule by long rung autocrats of small clines most clearly in the Sudan, Angola, the Congo Mahuri, Cote d'Ivoire, Togo and Cameroon (Acemoglu et al. 2007). One of the studies conducted in the Sub-Saharan Africa has shown that in 17–33 countries of the region which held general elections and several leaders of ruling parties were accused of unfair election practice to enable them to stay in power (Bangura and Nakamura 1999).

In India, both at the centre and in many states, the dynastic politics is seen. Dynastic politics is also prevalent in Bangladesh and Pakistan. Besides, dynastic politics, the elected members of the national parliament and state assemblies in the South Asian countries are largely the economically well-up, big landlords, or creamy layered among the backwards. This establishes the fact that the political disparities are even more prominent than the economic disparities in developing countries, where the economic assets are disproportionately distributed. According to UNRISD, one major obstacle faced by countries in transition has been the role of political parties, which in some cases act as institutions serving political and economic elites without promoting equitable access to participation of all groups in society (Bangura and Nakamura 1999). In India, socially disadvantaged section of population, i.e. SCs and STs, even if elected to the parliament and legislative assemblies, they are not being given higher level of portfolios in the ministry. In the Panchayati Raj institutions at the grass-root level, they are being dictated by the economically well-ups and upper-caste groups, and in many cases are found to be functioning according to the whims and wishes of these dominant caste groups. The findings from several studies reveal that

1. Despite their adequate representation in numerical terms, SCs and STs have not been able to play an active part in panchayats.
2. SCs and STs still lack self-confidence and because of their low socio-economic status, they are more concerned with livelihood activities and are not able to pay attention to increasing their socio-political influence through panchayats.
3. Because of lack of education, SCs and STs are not able to assert their views effectively (Tyagi and Sinha 2010).

The disadvantage groups of population, i.e. SCs, STs and women, particularly at the grass-root level lack political freedom and autonomy. Acemoglu et al. (2007) was of the view that political inequality may retard development because elites who control politics may create rents for themselves and impede entry.

Cultural disparity is an important problem in developing countries which has given rise to social unrest and even extremism in many culturally sensitive tribal areas. The culture which refers to the style of living, i.e. the dress code, language, dance, festivals, food habits, folklores and so on, varies wide across the countries. In the same vein, within a country, it varies from one region to that of the other and even from one locality to that of the other within the same region. Traditionally cultural activities were sources of livelihood for many people. However, cultural development is a neglected dimension of development in the neoliberal and globalized world. In fact, the development is inevitably culture-bound, and therefore intricately linked to the society where it is pursued (Zafarulla and Haqau 2006). The genesis of cultural disparity is in vogue because of the cultural and ethnic solidarity and strong faith of certain ethnically group of population in their cultural beliefs and values. In India, some groups of population, particularly the 'tribal', are observed to be detached from the mainstream of development because of their cultural identities, i.e. dress code, language, posturing, food habits and so on. In Africa, the ethnically cultural groups of population are seen to be socio-economically backward. Mbakogu (2004) has rightly remarked that the search for a protection of our cultural heritage is the starting point of any meaningful attempt at African cultural liberation and development. Therefore, UNESCO had emphasized on culture-led development. As per UNESCO (2012), culture-led development includes a range of non-monetized benefits such as greater social inclusiveness and rootedness, resilience, innovation, creativity and entrepreneur for individuals and communities and the use of local resources, skills and knowledge. Discrimination on the basis of ethnicity and culture is a scourge of human well-being and inclusive development. According to Munck and Hearn (1999), the importance of culture to development discourse is seen to be that, if development is to have real value at the local level, it requires a qualitative understanding of the complexities and dynamics of everyday life.

Lives and Livelihood of Tribal in Naxalite Affected Villages (Sundargarh District of Odisha)

The socio-economic conditions of tribal living in the naxalite affected villages are precarious; 88% of them are living below the poverty line and nearly 56% of them are managing with less than one square meal per day for the major part of a year. 75% of them are living in thatched houses without any electricity and toilet facility. Nearly 80% of them drink unsafe open well water. 57% of the people living in these villages are illiterate, and villages do not have any graduate. However, only a paltry 4.6% and 1.48% of them have acquired secondary and senior secondary education respectively. The main sources of livelihood and occupation of the tribal living in naxal affected villages are hunting, forest food gathering, agriculture and income from tribal art and craft. Nearly 70% of households are marginal landholder and the agriculture largely done by the traditional method of cultivation. Income of these tribal is paltry and too meagre for even a live sustaining subsistence level of living.

Source: Dungdung and Pattanaik (2013).

Gender-based disparity is an important concern in almost all countries of the world, if not, at least, in developing countries. However, development requires good governments that give men and women equal voices in decision-making and policy implementation (Parpart et al. 2000). The poverty, assetlessness and other socio-economic variables, i.e. illiteracy and low level of education, mortality, morbidity, malnutrition and hunger, are found more in the women-headed households as compared to men-headed households. Women are largely concentrated in low skilled and low paid occupation having more working hours, face more unemployment and underemployment problems and dumped in household work which has undermined their role in a globalized society. In other words, women are victims of gender stereotypes. From the findings of a study conducted in an African country, Kolev and Siren (2010) noted that although there are large variation across countries in male and female labour market outcomes, evidence shows that, in several countries of the region, women are less likely to be in paid jobs and those who are employed are disproportionately concentrated in informal and precarious employment and paid substantially less than men. The consideration of women's participation in paid spheres of labour market differs from that of males due to the gender stereotypical traditional notion that women's role are limited to the private, domestic spheres and they are less capable to handle hardworking, technical and high skilled jobs.

The disparities against women is seen in all sphere, such as social, economic and political. ILO estimates show that the share of employed people in the world's working age population (employment to population ratio) was 49.1% for women and 74.3% for men in 2007 (ILO 2008). There is less percentage of women in legislature, executive and in judiciary as compared to their male counterparts. The women empowerment is the only answer to overcome gender-based disparities. As OECD (2012) has mentioned that women's economic empowerment is a prerequisite for sustainable development and pro-poor growth. In many developing countries of South Asia, an acute gender disparity in the ownership of landholding is being observed (Table 12.6).

Another contemporary gender-based disparity observed mostly in the developed countries is the disparities associated with transgender. According to Crosby Borns,[5] transgender in America face significant economic disparities; they are as follow:

Table 12.6 *Women Land Holding Pattern in Selected Countries*

Country	Women Land Holders (%)
Italy	32.2
Spain	28.8
Thailand	24.4
France	23.1
United Kingdom	18.8
Malaysia	13.1
India	10.9
Nepal	8.1
Bangladesh	2.8

Source: Food Agricultural Organization, *Times of India*, March 2010.

1. A total of 15% of transgender people report making less than $10,000 per year, a rate of poverty that is four times that of the general population.
2. Socio-economic disparities are especially acute for families headed by gay or transgender people. Based on colour: 32% of black male are same sex couples, and 28% of female same-sex couples live in poverty, compared to just 13% of black opposite-sex married couples.
3. Children being raised by same-sex couples are twice as likely to live in poverty compared to children living with heterosexually married parents. With globalization in vogue, this issue will also emerge in developing countries in the future. Therefore, gender- and sex-based development disparities are recent phenomenon emerging in developed as well as developing countries.

Religion-based disparities in development refer to the differences in development achievement among various religious groups. In India, the socio-economic development status varies among the various religious groups of population. The per capita income is high, poverty rate is low, literacy rate is higher and infant and maternal mortality is lower among the Sikh and Jain communities than the Hindu and Muslim communities. Among all the communities, Muslims are the worst victim of socio-economic disparities. Like India, several examples of religion-based disparities exist in various countries of South Asia. The religion census data shows that in India literacy rate among the Muslim is 59.1%, while it is 94.1% among Jains. Similarly the workforce participation among the Muslims is also lower as compared to other religious group of population (Table 12.7). A recent NSSO data on poverty shows that per day expenditure of Muslims is 32.66 rupees, while these are 37.50, 51.53 and 55.30 among the Hindus, Sikhs and Christian population. In the multireligious and multicultural countries this type of religion-based disparities will create communal tensions, and from the point of view of social justice and equity not salubrious for the social health of the nation.

Table 12.7 *Religion-wise Literacy and Work Participation Rate, India*

Religion	Literacy (%)	Work Participation Rate (%)
Hindu	65.1	40.4
Muslims	59.1	31.3
Christians	80.3	39.7
Sikhs	69.4	37.7
Buddhists	72.7	40.6
Jains	94.1	32.9
Other Religions	47.0	48.4
India	64.8	39.1

Source: http://censusindia.gov.in/Ad_campaign/drop_in…(acessed on 15 April 2016).

FACTORS RESPONSIBLE FOR DISPARITIES

Several factors are responsible for creating disparities. A few of them are discussed below.

- Prevalence of traditional believes values in developing countries are the important reasons for existence of social, economic and political disparities in these societies. The traditional believes and values stratify the society on the basis of caste, religion and ethnicity. As a result disparities began from there.
- Unequal distribution of land is another important reason for disparities. In rural areas, land is mainly found concentrated in the hands of a few households called the zamindars or the landlords. On the other hand, a large number of household are in the categories of marginal and small landholders and many are even landless. The landlords usually belong to the upper strata of the society socially, and they are also economically and politically powerful. These landlords earn high income and accrue most of the development benefits. Thus, possession of land is an important reason of rural disparities.
- The caste system and gender stereotypes prevailing in the countries are also responsible factor for disparities. Several studies have found that poverty is high among the lower-caste households and women-headed households. In India, social disparities are low in Kerala where the socio-economic status of women is higher as compared to Bihar where the socio-economic status of women is low. Caste-based discrimination and disparities are divisive force in the society.
- Privatization and globalization has elongated disparities in the society. It is seen that the nexus between the government and the private sector has created crony capitalists and crony entrepreneurs in the developing countries. It has increased the income gap between the industrial entrepreneurs and the self-employed petty businessmen. It is not a flight of fancy but delicately globalization has enhanced disparities in developing countries between the rich and the poor; between the genders, and between the skilled and unskilled personnel.
- Bad governance, i.e. prevalence of corruption and nepotism, is also one of the reasons of economic disparities in developing countries where the corruption rate is very high. The corruption prevailing in the bureaucracy is high in developing countries of South Asia, Africa and Latin America. The bribe prevailing for issuance of ration card, driving licenses, passing of pension bills and arrears, accepting bribe for interviews in the employment to various posts, issue of loans and so on are a few among many which have enabled people in the bureaucracy amass black money. This created income disparities between the honest and dishonest bureaucratic functionaries. It has increased the income gap between the people those who are paying the tax out of their white income and those who are earning under the desk, the black money but not paying the tax.
- Lack of democracy is also an important reason for political disparities found in many countries ruled by the authoritarian government. Countries where the politicians are dishonest, they not only amass wealth for them but also help their kiths and kin to acquire wealth by dishonest means. The acquisition of illegal and black money creates economic disparities between the honest and dishonest politician.

- High population growth is also one of important factors for the increase in economic disparities in developing countries. Large families are mostly observed among the poor and lower-middle class families. A large family with single earning hand and single income-earning source dampens the per capita income. It also enhances the income disparities between the poor families with large family size and rich families with small family size. This is the demographic cause of disparities.

The development dichotomy is a responsible factor for existence of disparities in developing countries. On one side, there is formal or organized sector which gives good salaries, and provisions of job and social security. While one the other side, there is informal or unorganized sector which gives low wages/salaries and there are no facilities of job and social security. The differences existing between these two sectors and their wide presence in the primary, secondary and tertiary sectors are the main reasons of economic disparities in developing countries. In developing countries of Asia, Africa and Latin America, a large percentage of workforce is employed in the informal sector. In India, more than 90% of workers are working in the informal sector. Howell (2013), from a study conducted in China, has found that participation in the informal economy has skyrocketed in China and workers in the informal sector earn 22% less than workers in the formal sector, and workers in the state-owned enterprises earn 15.3% more than non-state workers.

MEASURES TO REDUCE DISPARITIES

Some of the suggested measures to reduce disparities are as follows:

1. Several developing countries have introduce land reform measures, i.e. ceiling on land holding to take away land from the landlords and distribute among the peasants. India introduced land reform measures during the First and Second Five Year Plans. In the early 1950s, China introduced drastic land reforms—redistributing land from the rich landlords to the poor peasants—which eliminated one of the major causes of rural inequalities in most developing countries (Bhalla 1992). The effective implementation of land reform in Kerala has reduced social and economic disparities in rural Kerala. Thus rigorous implementation of land reform measures will reduce disparities. The goal should be to take away surplus above ceiling land from the landlords and distribute it among the landless.
2. A nation state has to take constitutional as well as policy measures for the socio-economic upliftment of the disadvantaged section of the society, which are the victims of various types of disparities. The Government of India has taken constitutional as well as policy measures to reduce disparities among various social groups of population. Article 15 of the constitution of India prohibits discrimination on the ground of religion, race, caste, sex or place of birth. Article 16 lays emphasis on equal opportunities, which reads as 'no citizen shall, on grounds only of religion, race, caste, sex, descent, place of birth, residence or any of them, be ineligible for, or discriminated against in respect or, any employment or office under the state.' Whereas, article 16(4) proclaims that

> [N]othing in this article shall prevent the State from making any provision for reservation in matters of promotion to any class or classes of posts in the services under the State in favour of the Scheduled Castes and the Scheduled Tribes which, in the opinion of the State, are not adequately represented in the services under the State.

The Government of India has launched several programmes after Independence; one of the objectives of which was to reduce socio-economic disparities. To name a few are Integrated Rural Development Programme, Minimum Needs Programme, NREP, MGNREGA, Public Distribution System, IAY, SSA, NRHM and many others. Besides, several state governments have launched different programmes for the reduction of disparities and promote social and economic justice. The reservation of seats for SCs and STs in the parliament, state assemblies and local self government institutions aims at reducing political disparities. Reservation in the public sector employment for SCs and STs intends to raise the economic status of these disadvantaged sections and reduce disparities in the society. In India, several political parties are also demanding reservation for SCs and STs in the private sector employment.

3. Government has to introduce progressive tax system so that the rich pay more tax and the poor less. The tax evasion by the rich income group has to be sternly dealt with. Moreover, wealth tax, property tax and tax on income earned from the agriculture by the large-scale farmers and rich landlords would also reduce income disparities in rural areas.
4. Government has to take strong steps to reduce corruption at the bureaucratic and political level. Strong action against the bureaucratic functionaries indulged in corruption and the recovery of money and assets from them will not entice other to resort corruption. The black money earned either through corruption or through tax evasion have to be recovered and spend for the upliftment of the socio-economic status of the deprived sections of the society to reduce disparities.
5. Control of fertility among the poor having large family size will raise their per capita income. China's one child family norm for several decades was a step in the direction of reducing disparities. Lower fertility rate in Kerala across the caste, class and religious groups is one of the reasons for lower socio-economic disparities in the state.
6. Education is a great equalizer. Imparting higher as well as technical and skill education to the women will promote their workforce participation and reduce gender-based socio-economic disparities. It will also help to reduce income disparities among families in both rural as well as urban areas. The skill and vocational education for the population in general, and the socio-economically backward people in particular, will reduce economic disparities across different caste group of population. According to ILO (2011), available evidences firmly establishes that a combination of good education with training of good quality and relevant to the labour market: (a) empowers people to develop their full capacities and to seize employment and social opportunities; (b) raises productivity of both workers and enterprises; (c) contribute to future innovation development and (d) when broadly accessible, expands labour market opportunities and reduces social inequalities. Education is a great social leveler for all kinds of disparities such as social, economic, political- and gender-related disparities.

7. Raising the socio-economic status of women, particularly the women belonging to the socio-economically backward section of the society, will improve the socio-economic condition of the family and reduce disparities. Several studies have found that the women SHGs have, to some extent, reduced the economic disparities between the SHGs member families and non-member families. The opening of bank accounts in the name of women workers and the transfer of wages to their accounts has had a direct bearing on the expenditure on food, health and even education (Dey and Sabhikhi 2016). Closing the gender gap in education increases gender equality, which is considered important both in itself and because it ensures equal rights and opportunities for people regardless of gender (Martha 2011).
8. Developing countries have to curtail the size of the informal sector in their economy. Necessary Acts have to be passed for redefining the informal sector. As informal sector is here to stay for a longer period in developing countries, they have to be regulated. People working in the informal sector have to be registered and their wages/salaries have to be revised from time to time as per the revision of salaries in the formal sector. The provision of dearness allowances should be made mandatory in the informal sector based on price index as adopted for the public sector employees. Developed countries have better regulated their private sector that is why the size of the informal sector is small in these countries.

ISSUES AND CHALLENGES OF DISPARITIES

Disparities pose insurmountable challenge on developing countries; a few of them are discussed below.

1. Disparities are the dark sides of the development which obstruct the speed and pace of development. Developing societies stratified on the basis of caste, ethnicity, religion and gender will not be able to achieve sustainable and inclusive development unless they remove disparities from their land.
2. Disparities are friends of a few and foe of many, therefore the common philosophy should be that the wishes of many must be respected over those of a few.
3. Disparities are undemocratic and unethical in nature and principle. Developing nations must initiate and implement appropriate programmes and policies to overcome social, economic and political disparities.
4. With globalization, the economic disparities have elongated between various strata of population, at least, in developing countries. Benefits of economic growth and development accrued through globalization are being grasped by the strata that are socio-economically advanced, as a result the gap between the rich and poor and upper and lower strata of population has elongated.
5. Prolonged disparities will lead to social tension, communal violence, and it can also give rise to other problems such as theft, pickpocketing, crime, murder and so on.
6. Disparities are challenges on the inclusive and sustainable development. The main feature of disparity is that it includes a few and excludes many from the process of development. Therefore, in a country which is ridden in disparities, inclusive and sustainable development will remain far away.

SUMMARY

Globalization is a buzz word which cropped up during the 20th century and has touched the landscape of almost all nations, developed as well as developing. Some are more gainer, some are less gainer; some are more losers and some are lesser losers, but the world as a whole has experienced the sweet and sour of globalization. According to Roseanne and Giddiness, it is a central driving force behind the rapid social, political and economic changes that are reshaping modern societies and world order (quoted in Lawal 2006). The process of liberalization, privatization and globalization has elongated the income differences between the rich and poor, skilled and unskilled labour force, and the have-nots are found to be largely excluded from the main stream development. Deficiency of technical knowledge and skill as required by the privatization and globalization process has marginalized the impoverished in the global market. Globalization instead of mitigating poverty and inequality in developing countries has elongated them, which has become a matter of concern in these countries.

Keywords: globalization index, money order economy, development disparities, economic disparities, social disparities, political disparities, cultural disparities.

REVIEW QUESTIONS

1. What is globalization? How is it different from localization? Explain various features of globalization.
2. Discuss various issues and challenges related to globalization.
3. What is globalization? Explain the contribution of globalization in the development of the developing economies.
4. Define development disparities. Explain various types of development disparities which developing countries are facing by giving suitable examples.
5. Explain how globalization has elongated development disparities. Give suggestions how development disparities can be corrected.
6. What is FDI? Explain the role of FDI in the development of developing countries.
7. Write short notes on the following:
   (i) Remittances
   (ii) FDI
   (iii) Economic disparities
   (iv) Social disparities
   (v) Political disparities
   (vi) Cultural disparities

NOTES

1. See http://www.worldbank.org/depweb/beyond/bey... (accessed on 16 April 2016).
2. Quoted from http://www.brainyquote.com/quotes/quotes/k/kofiannan131002.html (12 February 2015).

3. South Africa's Racial Income Inequality persists, Census shows, see http://www.bloomberg.com/news/articles/2012 (accessed on 05 February 2015).
4. South Africa's Racial Income Inequality persists, Census shows, see http://www.bloomberg.com/news/articles/2012 (accessed on 05 February 2015).
5. See https://www.americanprogress.org/issues/igbt/news/2012/04/16/11494/the-gay-and-transgender (accessed on 16 April 2016).

REFERENCES

Acemoglu, D., M. A. Bautista, P. Querubin, and J. A. Robinson. 'Economic and Political Inequality in Development: The Case of Cundinamarca, Colombia.' In *Institutions and Economic Performance*, edited by Helpman. Cambridge: Harvard University Press, pp. 181–245, 2007. Available at: economic.mit.edu/files/3831 (accessed on 2 July 2013).

Bangura, Y., and T. Nakamura. 'Democratization Equity and Stability: African Politics and Society in the 1990s.' UNRISD, Geneva, 1999.

Beverly, S., and M. Sherraden. 'Investment in Human Development as a Social Development Strategy.' *Social Development* 19, no. 1 (1977): 1–18.

Bhalla, A. S. *Uneven Development in the Third World: A Study of China and India*. New York: Palgrave Macmillan, 1992.

Bhattacharya, B. B., and S. Sakthivel. 'Regional Growth and Disparities in India: A Comparison of Pre- and Post-reform Decades.' Institute of Economic Growth. *Economic and Political Weekly* 39, no.10(2004): 1071–77. Available at: http://www.iegindia.org/workpap/wp244.pdf (accessed on 5 February 2015).

Biswas, S. 'One World South Asia.' 17 March 2010. OneWorld.Net. Available at: http://southasia.oneworld.net/peoplespeak/gods (accessed on 12 October 2013).

Borrell, R. B. 'Globalization: A Curse or a Blessing on the Road to the Millennium Development Goals?' CIDOB, 2006. Available at: www.cidob.org/content/download/2606/21960/....doc_desarrallo_1.pfd (accessed on 20 October 2015).

Datt, G., and M. Ravallion. 'Why Has Economic Growth Been More Pro-poor in Some States in India than Others?' *Journal of Development Economic* 68 (2002).

Dey, N., and I. Sabhikhi. 'Kamao aur Khao.' *CBGA Budget Track* 11 (February 2016): 29–33.

Dreze, Jean., and A. Sen *India: Economic Development and Social Opportunity*. New York: Oxford University Press, 1995.

Dungdung, K., and B. K. Pattanaik. 'Live and Livelihood of Tribal in Naxalite Affected Villages: A Study in Sundargarh District of Odisha.' *Asian Journal of Social Sciences and Humanities* 2, no. 4 (2013): 94–107.

Fayissa, B., and C. Nsiah. 'Can Remittances Spur Growth and Development? Evidence from Latin American Countries (LACs).' Department of Economics and Finance Working, Middle Tennessee State University, Murfreesboro, 2010.

Fischer, S. Lunch address given at the conference on 'Promoting Dialogue: Global Challenges and Global Institutes'. Washington American University, 2000.

Friden, J. 'Inequality, Causes and Possible Futures'. *International Social Science Review* 2, no. 1(2001): 33–40. Available at: http://scholar.harvard.edu/files/jfrieden/files/inequalitiesfutures_0.pdf (accessed on 5 February 2015).

Friedman, T. *The Lexus and the Olive Tree*. London: HarperCollins, 1999.

Giuliano, P., and Ruiz-Arranz. 'Remittances Financial Development and Growth.' IMF Working Papers, wp/05/234, 2005. Available at: ftp://repec.iza.org/RePFe/Discussionpaper/p2160.pdf (accessed on 12 October 2013).

Gokhale, J. 'Globalization: Curse or Cure? Policies to Harness Global Economic Integration to Solve Our Economic Challenges'. Policy Analysis No. 659, Cato Institute, 2010.

Goulet, D. 'Changing Development Debates under Globalization.' Working Paper no. 276, Kollogg Institute, The Helen Kellogg Institute for International Studies, July 2000.

Held, D., M. C. Grew A., D. Goldblatt, and J. Perration. *Global Transformations: Politics, Economics and Culture, Policy*. Cambridge, 1999.

Howell, A. J. 'Chinese Minority Income Disparities in Urumqi: An Analysis of Han-Uyghur Labour Market Outcomes in the Formal and Informal Economies.' *China: An International Journal* 11, no. 3 (2013): 1–23.

Hyoung, C., A. Zammit, J. Chung, and I. Kang. *Korea's Miracle and Crisis: What Was in it for Women?* UNRISD, 2003

ILO. 'Global Employment Trends: January 2008.' International Labour Organization, Geneva, 2008.

———. 'A Skilled Workforce for Strong, Sustainable and Balanced Growth.' A G 20 Training Strategy, ILO, Geneva, 2011.

IMF. *World Economic Outlook*. Washington: International Monetary Fund, 1997.

IMF Staff. 'Globalization: A Brief Overview.' International Monetary Fund, 08/02, May 2008. Available at: https://www.imf.org/external/np/exr/ib/2008 (accessed on 20 October 2015).

India Human Development Report. Indira Gandhi Institute of Development Research, Mumbai, 2011.

Karras, G. 'Foreign Aid and Long-run Economic Growth: Empirical Evidence for a Panel of Developing Countries.' *Journal of International Development* 18, no. 7 (2006): 15–28.

Kempadoo, K. 'Women of Color and the Global Sex Trade: Transnational

Feminist Perspectives' *Meridians Feminist, Race, Transnational Journal*, 2 December, Spring(2001): 28–51.

Kerala Calling. 'Emerging Kerala, 2012.' *Kerala Calling* 32, no. 10 (August 2012).

Khera, R., and J. Dreze. 'Child Development Index: How have the Different States Fared?' *CBGA Budget Track* 11 (February 2016): 10–13.

Kolev, A., and N. Sirven. 'Gender Disparities in Africa's Labour Markets: A Cross-Country Comparison Using Standardized Survey Data.' In *Gender Disparities in Africa's Labour Market*, edited by J. S. Arbache, A. Kolev and E. Filipiam, 23–54. Washington DC: World Bank, 2010.

Lawal, G. 'Globalization and Development.' *Humanity and Social Sciences Journal* 1, no. 1 (2006): 65–78.

Lukas, A. 'WTO Report Card III: Globalization and Developing Countries.' Centre for Trade Policy Studies, Cato Institute, 2000.

Martha, N. *Creating Capabilities: The Human Development Approach*. Cambridge Mass: Belknap Press of Harvard University Press, 2011.

Mbakogu, I. A. 'Is There Really a Relationship between Culture and Development.' *Anthropology* 6, no. 1 (2004): 37–43.

McKibbin, W. J. 'Globalization: What Does It Mean?' Paper prepared for the Australian Coal Conference to be held in the Gold Coast, 7–10 May 2000. For details also see http://www.sensiblepolicy.com/download/coal4.pdf (accessed on 30 November 2016).

Mendoza, R. 'Dynastic in Democracies: The Political Sides of Inequality.' VOX CEPR's Policy Portal, 2012. Available at: http://www.voxeu.org/article/dynastic-democracies (accessed on 21 October 2015).

Milanovic, B. 'Evolution of Global Inequality: From Class to Location, from Proletarians to Migrants.' *Global Policy* 3, no 2 (2012): 124–33.

Mishra, S. K., and B. Kumar. 'Disparities in Globalization of the World Economies.' *The NEHU Journal* 11, no. 1 (2013): 1–17.

Munck, R., and Denis O'Hearn. *Critical Development Theory: Contributions to a New Paradigm*. London: Zed Books, 1999.

Norbes, Johan. *Defence of Global Capitalism*. Washington: Cato Institute, 2003.

OECD. *Open Market Matter: The Benefits of Trade & Investment Liberalization*. Paris: OECD, 1998.

———. *Women's Economic Empowerment, Poverty Pro-Poor Growth: The Role of Empowerment*. Paris: OECD, 2012.

Parpart, Jane, L. Connelly, M. Patricia, and V. Eudine Barriteau, eds. 'Forward.' In *Theoretical Perspectives on Gender and Development*, 65–134. Ottawa, ON, Canada: International Development Research Centre, 2000.

Provost, C. 'Migrants' Billions Put Aid in the Shade.' *The Guardian*, Wednesday, 30 January 2013. Available at: http://www.theguardian.com/global-development (accessed on 9 December 2013).

Rajalakshmi, K. 'Grooming Regional Disparities in India's Development.' *International Journal of Educational Research and Technology* 4, no. 3 (2013): 47–55.

Rauniyar, G., and R. Kubur. 'Inclusive Development: Two Papers on Conceptualization, Application and the ADB Perspective.' Mandaluyong City, Philippines Asian Development Bank, 2010.

Ray, S. 'Impact of Foreign Direct Investment on Economic Growth in India: A Co-Integration Analysis.' *Advances in Information Technology and Management (AITM)* 2, no. 1 (2012): 187–201.

Rigby, V. 'Developed and Developing Countries: Promoting Equitable Development.' Political and Social Affairs Division, Parliamentary Information and Research Service, Parliament of Canada, 1993. Available at: http://www.parl.gc.ca/content/LOP/researchpubli (accessed on 20 October 2015).

Sachs, J., and A. Warner. 'Economic Reform and the Process of Global Integration'. *Brookings Papers on Economic Activity* 1(1995): 1–118.

Sapru, R. K. *Development Administration*. New Delhi: Sterling Publishers Pvt Ltd., 1994.
Stahl, C. W., and F. Arnold. 'Overseas Workers' remittances in Asian Development.' *International Migration Review* 20, no. 4 (1986): 899–925.
Teixeira, Ruy. 'Political Inequality Worsens Economic Inequality.' *The New York Times*, 21 April 2014. Available at: http://www.nytimes.com/roomfordebate/2014/04/21/do-the-rich-call-the-shots-13/political-inequality-worsens-economic-inequality (accessed on 05 February 2015).
Tyagi and Sinha. *Food Agricultural Organization, Times of India*, March 2010.
Umar, N. 'Regional Disparities in Levels of Development in Africa.' *International Journal of Science and Research* 3, no. 6 (2014): 250–60.
UNCTAD. 'The Least Developed Countries Report 2004: Linking International Trade with Poverty Reduction.' UNCTAD, Geneva and New York, 2004.
———. World Investment Report, 2006.
UNDP. 'Human Development Report: Globalization with a Human face.' Oxford University Press, 1999.
———. 'Human Development Report 1999.' New York, Oxford University Press, 1999.
UNDP. *Human Development Report 2013*, UNDP, Oxford University Press, 2013.
UNDP. *Human Divided: Confronting Inequality in Developing Countries*. New York: UNDP, 2014.
UNESCO. 'Thematic Think Piece UNESCO, UN System Task Team on the Post-2015 UN Development Agenda: Culture a Driver and an Enabler of Sustainable Development.' UNESCO, 2012.
United Nations. *56th Commission Human Rights, Item 7: The Right to Development*. Geneva: United Nations, 2000.
World Bank. *New Paths to Social Development, Community and Global Network in Action*. Washington: World Bank, 2000.
———. 'India Inclusive Growth and Service Delivery: Building on India's Success.' Development Policy Review, Report No. 34580-IN, New Delhi, 2006.
———. 'Remittances.' World Bank, 2013. Available at: http://web.worldbank.org/WBSITE/EXTERNAL (accessed on 9 December 2013).
Zafarulla, H., and A. S. Haque, eds. 'Understanding Development Governance: Concept, Institution and Process.' In *International Development Governance*, 13–50. New York: Taylor and Francis, 2006.

13 Environment and Sustainable Development

Environmental degradation threatens all aspects of human well-being and has been demonstrably linked to human health problems, including some types of cancers, vector-borne diseases, emerging animals to human disease transfer, nutritional deficits and respiratory illness.

—WCED (1987)

The 'environment' is where we live; and development is what we all do in attempting to improve our lot within that abode. The two are inseparable.

—UNDP[1]

Environmental degradation and climate change are emerging challenges for the developed and developing nations aiming to attain sustainable development. It is felt that one cannot think of achieving sustainable development goals in isolation from environment. The sustainable livelihood of human beings as well as other living creatures on the earth depends on the environment. Therefore, protection of environment is central to the well-being of humans as well as the other living creatures. In the view of increased awareness of environmental problems, and growing emphasis on sustainable development, the need for environmental protection has grown in recent times. It calls for restraining particularly those activities which degrade the environment and affect the living conditions of human beings adversely. The environmental development organizations and activists are putting pressure on the nation states to take measures for the preservation of the environment, such as forests, hills, water bodies, flora and fauna. According to UNDP, environmental degradation threatens all aspects of human well-being.[2] Environment and sustainable development are interconnected and the latter is more dependent on the former; therefore, protection of environment is critical for development.

After reading this chapter, you will be able to:

1. Explain the role of environment in development.
2. Describe how environment is important for sustainable development.
3. Define sustainable development and explain various requisites of sustainable development.
4. Discuss various challenges of environment and sustainable development.

SECTION I: ENVIRONMENT

The natural environment is the foundation on which poverty reduction efforts and sustainable development must be built.

—UNDP[3]

Environment is the most precious asset that we own, share and use together with other people for mutual benefits and enhanced welfare of the society at large.

—Ogundele and Jegede (2011)

ENVIRONMENT AND DEVELOPMENT: THE RELATIONSHIP

The developmental endeavour which affects the environment is detrimental to development. According to the UNDP, for sustainable development to be achieved, links between the environment and development must be examined.[4] However; there has been a continued failure to link environment and development in decision-making (Dernbach 2000). For instance, the agricultural development initiative in the form of Green Revolution, which was undertaken way back in the 1970s in the northern states of India, i.e. Punjab, Haryana and western Uttar Pradesh, without giving adequate consideration to the environmental concerns is now facing crisis in terms of degradation of natural resources. The land has become waterlogged, soil health has been destroyed, water table has gone down and groundwater has been contaminated. It is also affecting the health and well-being of the people of these states. It is seen that many people are suffering from various waterborne diseases, diseases related to the use of pesticides and amputations happening because of use of tractor and other machineries.

Environment is the protector as well as can be the destroyer of development. It is said that the environment is the totality of the place and its surroundings, in which we live, work and interact with other people in our cultural, religious, political and socio-economic activities for self-fulfilment and the advancement of our communities, societies and nations (Akinbode 2002). Environmental degradation affects development. It is often seen that the developmental projects undertaken on environmentally rich areas, the cutting of trees and the digging of rocks result in environmental deterioration and degradation. In a good number of cases, it has caused destruction, annihilating the life of people, livestock and productivity. Environmental degradation is a cause of disaster in the environmental sensitive areas, particularly in the hill areas. WCED (1987) observed that 'many parts of the world are caught in a vicious downward spiral: poor people are forced to overuse environmental resources to survive from day to day and the impoverishment of their environment further impoverishes them, making their survival even more difficult and uncertain'. Mai and Nguyen (2003) viewed that development and environment are interrelated to each other. Improper or uncontrolled development is likely to cause adverse impacts on the environment, and environmental pollution or degradation may become a major obstacle for social and economic development. Rapid land use change means that many natural environments and habitats are disappearing quickly with the result that critical ecological services are being disrupted or lost (Millennium Ecosystem Assessment 2005). The demise of key ecosystems of the developing world includes mangroves, 30% either lost or degraded; coral reefs, 30%; and tropical forest, 30% (FAO 2001–2003; Valiela et al. 2001; Millennium Ecosystem Assessment 2005).

The lust for high economic growth rate and faster development has enticed many developing countries in causing harm to their environment and ecology. The construction of infrastructure projects such as hydroelectricity, hilly roads and establishment of industries in hilly and forest areas is deeply affecting environment and ecology of these areas. Further, the establishment of many chemical and other hazardous industries near the cities and also in the rural areas without any proper environmental effect guidelines is not only polluting environment but also contaminating groundwater and river water in many countries. The growing establishment of factories in Kanpur and other cities of Uttar Pradesh is inflicting pollution on the river Ganga. Besides, the growing economic activities for production and consumption require large inputs of energy and material and generate large quantities of waste by-products, which cause environmental pollution and insanitation. Further, the increased extraction of natural resources, accumulation of waste and concentration of pollutants will, therefore, overwhelm the carrying capacity of the biosphere and result in the degradation of environmental quality and a decline in human welfare, despite rising income (Daly 1977).

Many rural people in developing countries rely directly on natural resources and the environment for agriculture, livestock husbandry, fishing, basic materials and fuel to meet their own subsistence requirements and to sell in markets for income (Barbier 2010). Excessive dependence of the poor people on environment has caused a lot of damage to the environment in terms of cutting of forest. More recently, creation of infrastructure for eco-tourism in developing countries has not only resulted in the depletion of natural resources but also inflicted natural disasters in hilly areas, causing a pathetic loss of human lives and animals. Barbier (2010) is of the opinion that given the resource-dependence of rural populations in developing countries and given that many natural environments and habitats are declining in these countries, it is tempting to conclude that poverty is a major cause of environmental degradation in poor economies.

Researchers from the World Bank have examined the 'poverty-environment nexus' in three of the poorest countries in Southeast Asia—Cambodia, Laos and Vietnam (Minot and Baulch 2002 and Dasgupta et al. 2005). The result shows that in Cambodia, the core poor in rural areas appear to be located in areas that are already heavily deforested; on the other hand, poor populations tend to be more concentrated in the lowlands rather than steeply sloped lands. In Laos, the poorest provinces in the north and northeast also have the highest incidence of poor rural populations. These individuals are located mainly in forested areas and the highlands. In Vietnam, large poor populations confined to steep slopes exist in the provinces comprising the Northern and Central Highlands, but extensive rural poverty is also found along the North Central Coast and the Red River Delta (Barbier 2010). There is a widely held view, particularly in the West, that poverty or the poor people are the main cause of environmental deterioration, because they are not in a position to use natural resources sustainably (Prakash 1997). The vicious circle of environmental degradation and poverty trap has been illustriously called the 'tragedy of the commons' by Hardin (Hardin 1968).

The relationship between income and environment has been a debated issue for a long time among the environmentalists and developmentalists. It is believed that higher levels of income may reduce environmental degradation (Beckerman 1992), and thus, economic growth may be a precondition for environmental improvement (Bhagawati

1993). The strong correlation between income and the extent to which environmental protection measures are adopted demonstrates that in the long run the surest way to improve your environment is to become rich (Beckerman 1992).

Several studies have been conducted to find out the relationship between income and environment and an illustrious one is Environmental Kuznets Curve (EKC). The EKC derives its name from Simon Kuznets. The EKC postulates an inverted U-shaped relationship between different pollutants and per capita income. The EKC shows that during the initial phase of development, which is a situation where the income of the people is low and the country is underdeveloped, the pollution rate will be very high. On the other hand, when the nation achieves high development and people enjoy high per capita income, then the pollution level will go down. In other words, pollution is directly related to underdevelopment and inversely related to development. Simon Kuznets' work 'Economic Growth and Income Inequality' tells us that as the per capita income increases, income inequality also increases at first but then, after some turning point, starts declining (Kuznets 1955). Kuznets felt that the distribution of income is more unequal in the early phase of development, but it moves towards greater equality when the economic growth process continues. The early estimates showed that some important indicators of environmental quality such as the levels of sulphur dioxide and particulates in the air actually improved as incomes and the levels of consumption went up (Yandle et al. 2002). This is reflected in Figure 13.1.

The EKC hypothesis contends that the pollution level in an economy increases during the initial phase of development, when the country develops its industrial sector, which helps the country to attain certain peak level of economic development through industrialization. After the proliferation of industrialization, the expansion of the service sector sets in, and also the less polluting technologies are used in the industrialization process itself, as a result pollution starts declining.

Figure 13.1 *Environmental Kuznets Curve*

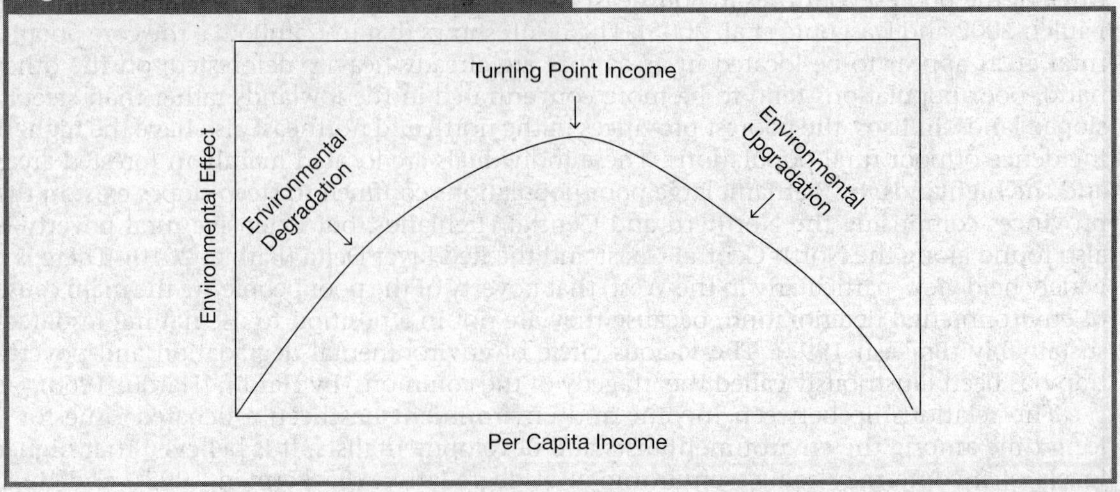

Source: Author.

According to the EKC postulates, environmental degradation is unavoidable and bound to occur during the initial phase of development, i.e. when the country initiates the industrialization process. However, it is possible to control environmental degradation when the country attains the phase of high economic development. After the country reaches the stage of high economic development, the environment starts upgrading. The first phase, i.e. the high industrialization phase, which results in environmental degradation is observed to be occurring in the developing economies, while the second phase of environmental upgradation is observed in the case of developed economies. Dasgupta et al. (2002) also viewed that in the first stage of industrialization, pollution grows rapidly because high priority is given to increase in material output and people are more interested in jobs and income rather than clean air and water. The EKC is given in Figure 13.2. Panayotou (2003) talked of following three phases of pollution:

1. Pollution increases at the early phase of a country's industrialization due to the setting up of rudimentary, inefficient and polluting industries. Thus, when a country begins industrialization, the scale effects will take place and pollution will increase.
2. When industrialization is sufficiently advanced, service industries will gain prominence. Further along the trajectory, firm switching over to less-polluting industries has resulted in composition effects, which is helping in levelling the rate of pollution.
3. Finally, the technique effects come into play when mature companies invest in pollution abatement equipment and technology, which reduces pollution.

Figure 13.2 *The Kuznets Curve*

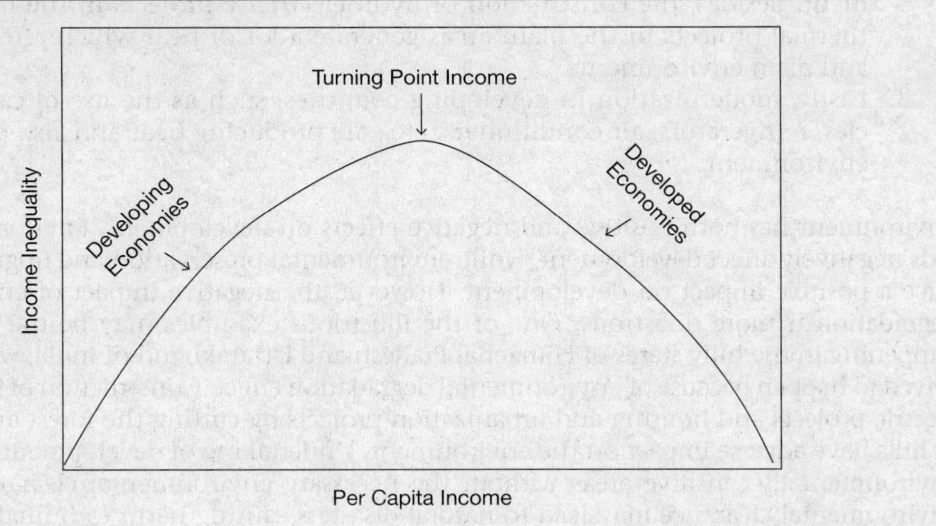

Source: Author.

One of the simple examples from a household level can substantiate Kuznet's argument. For example, most of the poor families having low per capita income use traditional cooking methods such as use of wood, tree leaves, tree barks, cow dung cake, paddy husk and so on which cause a lot of damage to the environment as well as to the health of women, sometimes resulting in asthma, tuberculosis, cataracts and so on. However, as the income increases and families become rich, they use LPG cylinders and LPG gas pipeline for cooking, which causes less pollution and less harm to the environment as well as to the women's health. In other words, rich use less pollutant cooking energy and poor use more polluting cooking energy. In a poverty-stricken and economically less developed society, pollution rate is high, while in an economically developed society, the pollution rate is low. At the household level also the environmental pollution, the household income and the development level have a U-shaped relationship.

It is observed that globalization has a profound effect on the process of modernization in developing countries. It has also produced a lot of impact on the environment. It has enabled even the middle class in developing countries to possess heat producing and polluting modern gadgets like cars, refrigerators and air conditioners, many of which affect the climate change and environment. The plying of more than 75 lakh vehicles (mostly diesel and petrol) on the roads of Delhi itself is an illustrious reason for pollution in Delhi, which is causing respiratory and other pollution-related health problems among all age groups. In developing countries, their endeavour to development after liberalization and globalization has produced a negative effect in the following ways:

1. Industrialization in urban as well as rural areas enhances pollution which produces an impact on the environment of both rural and urban areas.
2. The infrastructural development also affects environment. Construction of road and buildings, irrigation projects and so on generates dust and pollutes environment. Besides, the construction of hydroelectricity projects in the hill areas and thermal projects in the plain areas generate a lot of heat which affects both hill and plain environment.
3. Lastly, modernization in developing countries, such as the use of cars, motorcycles, refrigerators, air conditioners, etc., are producing heat and also polluting the environment.

Environment has both positive and negative effects on development. Environmental hazards negatively affect development, while environmental preservation and upgradation produce a positive impact on development. However, the negative impact of environmental degradation is more disastrous. One of the illustrious examples may be the cloud bursts happening in the hilly states of Himachal Pradesh and Uttarakhand of India, which are perceived to happen because of environmental degradation effect. Construction of many hydroelectric projects and housing and urbanization projects by cutting the forest and flattening of hills have adverse impact on the environment. Undertaking of developmental projects in environmentally sensitive areas without the necessary environmental clearance or faulty environmental clearance may lead to natural disasters causing harm to human beings and huge investment of resources for the restoration of normalcy which could otherwise have been spent for human well-being. Therefore, protection of the environment is one of the important duties of a nation aiming at development and well-being of its population.

ISSUES AND CHALLENGES OF ENVIRONMENT AND DEVELOPMENT

Some of the important issues and challenges of environment and its relationship with development are narrated as follows:

Climate Change and Environment

The greatest challenge which the environment has faced in recent years is climate change. Climate change is recognized as the most serious environmental threat which would influence rise in occurrences of drought and floods, rise in the sea level affecting the coastal zone and would also affect agricultural and its allied sector productivity. The climate change referred to may be due to natural causes, for instance, changes in the sun's output or due to human activities, e.g. changes in the composition of atmosphere (Albritton 2001). Evidence of observed climate change includes the temperature record, rising sea levels, and decreased snow cover in the northern hemisphere (Inter-governmental Panel on Climate Change 2007). United Nations (1992) defined 'climate change' as 'change of climate which attributed directly or indirectly to human activity that alters the composition of the global atmosphere and which is in addition to natural climate variability observed over comparable time periods.' The adaptation, resilience and coping up with the climate change are vital to meeting the challenges of environment and development. The climate change will impact agriculture and food production around the world due to the effects of elevated carbon dioxide (CO_2) in the atmosphere, higher temperature, altered precipitation and transpiration regimes, increased frequency of extreme events and modified weed, pest and pathogen pressure (Ogundele and Jegede 2011). The developed as well as developing countries have to take into consideration the effect of climate change on environment and development.

Energy and Environment

Energy and environment are closely interlinked. The different sources of non-renewable energy, i.e. hydro energy, thermal energy, petroleum and oil energy, chemical energy and so on, produce heat which affects climate as well as environment. As energy usage has increased around the world, so also the stress this usage imposes on the environment has been intensified. It is widely believed that the construction of hydropower projects in the hills of Himalayas is one of the reasons of cloudburst and melting of glaciers causing destruction and global warming. Safe and renewable sources of energy are fundamental to environmental protection. The fact that energy production and consumption are the main causes of many of the most pressing environmental problems indicates that energy policy and environmental policy should not be viewed in isolation (Finon 1994).

Traditional Environment Knowledge System and Environment

Establishment of linkages between the traditional environment knowledge system and environment management is a key challenge before developing countries to use its knowledge depository for the benefit of environmental development. According to Tsuji and Ho (2002), 'Traditional Environmental Knowledge (TEK) is a body of knowledge and beliefs transmitted through oral traditional and first-hand observation. It includes a system of classification, a set of empirical observations about the local environment and a system of self-management that governs resource use.' The knowledge repository on various case studies, practices, usages and benefits of environment for the well-being of humanity transmits from generation to generations. The department of environment should take cognizance of it by conducting surveys and empirical studies and use it for the development and well-being of humanity. For instance, as a tradition, banana plant and peepal trees are being worshiped in many parts of India and people generally neither like to cut peepal trees nor use its branches for firewood and it is also a rich source of oxygen. These types of traditional practices must be documented and disseminated for common knowledge. The national, regional and local government should utilize this knowledge repository for the policy formulation and conduction of action programmes for environment and development.

Common Property Resources (CPR) and Environment

The United Nations (1997) noted that the CPRs (environmental) are natural resources owned and managed collectively by a community or society rather than by individuals. Jodha (1995) viewed that

> CPRs could be simply described as community's natural resources where every member has access and usage facility with specified obligations, without anybody having exclusive property right over them. In Indian villages, CPRs generally include community pasture, community forests, wastelands, drainage and village ponds, rivers and rivulets as well as their banks and beds.

Effective use of the CPRs with the help of community will solve many of the environmental problems, and the community with the help of other actors of development such as government, NGOs, private bodies and international agencies can better utilize CPRs not only for the protection of environment but also for the improvement of the health, wealth and well-being of the community. Mathew Turner (2007) has opined that the 'tragedy' of the commons is when commonly held resources are 'overused,' as unregulated individuals seek to maximize their individual gains to the resource. His suggestions of the four features of more successful CPR management are:

1. a well-defined social group with rights to clearly defined resources;
2. ability to exclude others from using the resource;
3. setting of rules that limit the seasonal extent or ways in which the resource is extracted by individuals;
4. the capacity to monitor use and enforce rules. Protection of CPRs particularly in hills and mountainous areas is fundamental to environmental protection.

The least interference of government and its largely playing a facilitator's role and providing technical, financial and moral support to community-level organizations in the management of CPRs for environment and development will go a long way to protect environment. The village panchayats and *van* (forest) panchayats, *pani* (water) panchayats and *bijli* (electricity) panchayats have to be oriented about the effective use of the CPRs not only for the generation of revenue but also for their effective use for the improvement of the environment and natural resources in their locality. The community environmental impact assessment needs to be conducted from time to time which will provide a systematic process for identifying, describing and evaluating a community's natural and human resources in order to improve their decision about environment management.

CONSERVATION OF ECOSYSTEM DIVERSITY

Conservation of ecosystem diversity is of critical importance for environmental development. The beneficiaries as well as actors of environment and development must be inculcated with the values of a healthy ecosystem and their services into economic, social and cultural development. Yogesh Gokhale (2013) is of the view that the nation should ensure the conservation of elements of biodiversity in the form of ecosystems, habitats, corridors, threatened and endangered species, wild relatives of cultivated plants, traditional crop varieties and animal breeds takes place outside the protected areas system. All the actors of dealing with environment and development such as van panchayats (Forest Panchayts), village panchayats, youth clubs, *mahila mandals*, etc. must be empowered. The endeavour must be in the direction of building 'green economies.' The environmentalists have expressed concern over the decreasing population of vulture. The vultures who eat the carcasses are the great environmental protectors. Likewise a number of many other birds whose bone and fleshes are being used in the preparation of medicines (in traditional knowledge system) is declining day by day because of environmental pollution. With the use of pesticides, many herbal plants that are locally used for treating common ailments and used as traditional first aids are vanishing. The biodiversity is in peril because of the modernization of agriculture and pollution caused by the industrialization.

CONTROL OF MIGRATION AND PROMOTION OF HEALTHY ECO-TOURISM

Unbridled growth of population posits harm to both rural and urban environment. According to United Nations (2000), with world population projected to increase to nearly nine billion by 2050 from the current six billion, the potential for causing irreparable environmental harm is obvious. Growth of population is one of the responsible factors for the decrease of rainforests, the loss of hundreds and thousands of plants and wildlife species and an increase in greenhouse gas emissions. According to Robert Engelman[5]

> [T]rends such as the loss of half of the planet's forests, the depletion of most of its major fisheries, and the alteration of its atmosphere and climate are closely related to the fact that human population expanded from mere million in prehistoric times to over six billion today.

The growth of population has also enhanced egregiously the quantum of eco-tourism and growth of infrastructure, i.e. rest houses, hostels, road and communication system and so on in hilly and forest areas leading to disturbances in the ecosystem. The recent cloudburst (in the year 2013) in Uttarakhand in the Himalayan region of India and the death of more than 550 tourists is an illustrious example of the impact of ecotourism on environmental disaster. The burgeoning growth of population in urban areas leads to the growth of urban slums, deterioration of urban sanitation and rise in pollution which inflict harm to the environment. In developing countries, population growth and environmental degradation are intimately correlated.

ENVIRONMENTAL ACCOUNTING, LAW AND POLICY

In the analysis of the issues and challenges of environment and development, these three aspects are very important and need to be discussed at length. Environmental accounting needs to act as a tool to measure the economic efficiency of environmental conservation activities. Besides, it would also cover the cost of rescue operations, rehabilitation and damage to physical and human resources due to an environmental disaster. It also needs to calculate the economic, social and environmental related loss and gain because of environmental degradation and conservation. A study on the price of pollution in India conducted by the World Bank, calculated that the damage to environment costs India about 34,000 cores of rupees per year, which is about 9.5% of the gross domestic product (Chauhan 2005).

Environmental law is another important dimension which can play a key role in any effort to protect and preserve the environment. Environmental laws are put in place to mitigate or prevent the threatening environmental problems which emanate from human activities in the quest for economic growth and development. In this respect, both international and national laws are important for the protection of global and national environment. Effective implementation of environment law would act as a tool for the protection of environment. According to Martin (2013), '[T]he advantages of environmental laws are: (a) it protects the health and safety of humans and (b) the environmental laws tend to increase innovative environmental friendly technology.'

Last, but not the least, an environment policy can be an instrument of power to solve some perceived problems in the environment (Shore and Wright 1997). Formulation of an appropriate environment policy is a challenge before developing countries for the protection, conservation and promotion of environment for development. Yogesh Gokhale (2013) has remarked that considering the complexity of the subject in terms of conservation of biodiversity, the sustainability of the natural ecosystems and the livelihood dependence of the local communities, the policy needs to address national and global issues related to carbon accumulation, biodiversity conservation and continued flow of ecosystem services. The environment policy needs to address various critical issues concerning the environment and its linkages with the various sectoral activities concerning the development of agriculture and industry; the impact of technology, modernization, infrastructure and energy on the environment; cutting and growing of forests; digging of mountains and rivers; protection of the environment for sustainable rural and urban development; the environmental law; environment governance; environment administration; environmental planning; environmental education and communication and so on.

Imperatives of Green Growth

The international agencies have been emphasizing on the promotion of green growth in developing countries. OECD in its document 'Green Growth and Developing Countries' has defined green growth as a means to foster economic growth and development while ensuring that natural assets continue to provide the resources and environmental services on which our well-being relies (OECD 2012). It has urged that developing countries are required to achieve global green growth for two main reasons:

1. The potential economic and social impacts of environmental degradation are particularly important for developing countries. These are most vulnerable to climate change and tend to be more dependent than advanced economies on the exploitation of natural resources for economic growth. In addition, many developing countries face severe economic, social and ecological threats from energy, food and water insecurity to climate change and extreme weather risks
2. Secondly, today most developing countries contribute only minor shares to global greenhouse gas emissions compared to OECD and major emerging economies. However, it is presumed that they will increase their emission if they follow conventional economic growth patterns.

The lust for the achievement of higher economic growth rate by developing countries by adopting practices detrimental to environment has called for the need to promote development through green growth. The green growth strategy which will promote the organic cultivation and other conventional method of cultivation will reduce the cost of cultivation and check spending on fertilizers and pesticides. Less use of fertilizers and pesticides in the land will be helpful to preserve biodiversity. It is seen that with the use of pesticides many spices of birds (e.g. sparrow) have vanished from the fields of Punjab and Haryana. In other words, green growth will be helpful in the preservation of ecology. Green growth will have positive effects on the society, as use of organic vegetable and other products may reduce the diseases and have positive impact on health. The activists of green growth from their study in Punjab have voiced their concern over the finding of urea content in the mother's and buffalos' milk. The issue of synthetic milk which crops up from time to time in the Green Revolution belt of India, causing a lot of damage to the health of children, is also a fallout of non-practicing green growth strategies.

Green Growth Outcomes

Economic

1. Increased and more equitably distributed GDP—the production of conventional goods and services
2. Increased production of unpriced ecosystem services (or their reduction prevented)
3. Economic diversification, i.e. improved management of economic risks.
4. Innovation, access and uptake of green technologies, i.e. improved market confidence.

Environmental

5. Increased productivity and efficiency of natural resource use.
6. Natural capital used within ecological limits.
7. Other types of capital increased through use of non-renewable natural capital.
8. Reduced adverse environmental impact and improve natural hazard/risk management

Social

9. Increased livelihood opportunities, income and/or quality of life, notably of the poor
10. Decent jobs that benefit poor people created and sustained
11. Enhanced social, human and knowledge capital
12. Reduced inequality.

Source: OECD (2012).

To maintain a green growth rate and achieve the status of green economy are a great challenge for developing countries. A 'green economy' can be defined as an economy that helps to improve human well-being, social justice and social equity by emphasizing on significant reduction in environmental risks and ecological scarcities. Emphasis on green economy has to be aimed to achieve the green growth rate, i.e. the growth rate which is not cruel on the environment or environment-friendly growth rate. In other words, green growth is the growth rate that an economy achieves without harming the environment and causing any adverse impact on the health and quality of life of the people. Planting of more trees, preservation of bio-diversity and checking of pollution are some of the steps to supplement the endeavour of green growth. The EU 2020 strategy for 'smart green and inclusive growth' includes employment rates, reducing poverty, reducing greenhouse gas emissions, increasing renewable energy consumption and increasing the GDP in research and development.[6] In green growth, environment is more protected and the quality of life has less risk to environmental hazards.

Environment and development are intimately interconnected. Protection of environment is key to sustainable development. Environmental pollution not only affects productivity but also influences the health status of its population. The decreasing number of birds and other spices from the earth because of environmental pollution will create problem for the population in the future. A nation cannot think of achieving sustainable development by harming its environment.

SECTION II: SUSTAINABLE DEVELOPMENT

In essence, sustainable development is a process of change in which the exploitation of resources, the direction of investments, the orientation of technological development and institutional change, are all in harmony and enhance both current and future potential to human needs and aspirations.

—Bruntland Report (WCED 1987)

> *The sustainable development was initially referring to environmental concerns, and now compassing social, ethical and economical issues.*
>
> —Law (2010)

The term 'sustainable development' has occupied an important place in the development agenda of both developed and developing countries. Sustainable development became popular with the publication of Burndtland Commission Report in 1987. The growth and development process initiated by most of developing countries through mechanization, industrialization and globalization, which began after 1990, has caused a lot of harm to the environment. It has also put a question mark on the present growth model and the effect it will have on future growth and development of the nation state. It came in the wake of a situation where the acceleration of the economic growth process was resorted to by the nations and states through the distortion of natural resources and by inflicting harm on the environment. The Bruntland Commission for Environment and Development in its report 'Our Common Future' called for the application of sustainability as a criterion for all development initiatives. The Commission envisaged that 'in order for development to be sustainable, it must meet the needs of the present without compromising the ability of future generations to meet their own needs'. Munasinghe (1994) described sustainable development as a process of improving the range of opportunities that will enable individual human beings and communities to achieve their aspirations and full potential over a sustained period of time while maintaining the resilience of economic, social and environmental systems. To Gunderson and Holling (2001) sustainable development requires: (a) opportunities for improving economic, social and ecological systems and (b) increase in adaptive capacity. Houghtone (2011) has rightly remarked that sustainability is an idea that can be applied to activities and communities as well as to physical resources. He further mentioned that sustainability in simplest terms signifies the following: 'not cheating on our children', 'not cheating on our neighbours' and 'not cheating on the rest of the creation'. In nutshell, it can be said that sustainable development aims at development endeavours, i.e. policies, programmes, projects and activities, which lead to positive change in economic, social and ecological spheres without causing any harm to the natural resources both at present and also in future. It will produce favourable impact: (a) economic: on poverty reduction and productivity of goods and services; (b) social: on culture, health and human well-being and (c) environmental: on natural resources and biodiversity.

Sustainable development not only lays emphasis on the process of present development but also analyses its implication on future development. Continuous exploitation of natural resources by human beings for the present needs disturbs the future development. The impact of overexploitation of groundwater, cutting of forest, digging of hills, converting agricultural land to housing projects and so on affects the environment. Moreover, vehicle pollution, dust emission during construction, household electric devices, heat emission, smoke generated because of burning of leaves and paddy husk and so on cause a lot of damage to the environment. It influences productivity and has an adverse impact on human health. Sustainable development depicts the interconnectedness of the economy, environment and society. It is looked at from a variety of perspectives such as environmental, economic, demographic, social, political, cultural and technological. The Bruntland Report (WCED 1987) envisaged that sustainable development requires the following:

1. A political system that secures effective citizen participation in decision-making.
2. An economic system that is able to generate surpluses and technical knowledge on self-reliant sustained basis.
3. A social system that provides for solutions for the tensions arising from disharmonious development.
4. A production system that respects the obligations to preserve the ecological base of development.
5. A technological system that can search continuously for new solutions.
6. An international system that offers a sustainable pattern of trade and finance.
7. An administrative system that is flexible and has the capacity of self-correction.

KEY ELEMENTS OF SUSTAINABLE DEVELOPMENT

The three key elements of sustainable development are ecology, economy and society. A healthy interaction among these key elements determines the sustainable development status in a country. These are discussed as follows (Figure 3.3).

Environment: Environment and sustainable development go hand in hand. It is generally observed that people who belong to tribal areas, living in the forests, are more concerned about the environment and take more care of it because of their love and affinity towards it. Every nation should protect and preserve its flora and fauna in order to strengthen its environment, as deforestation would posit climate change ultimately affecting productivity and human health status. Earth's environment is changing at a faster rate both at the local and the global levels, because of nefarious human actions, such as cutting of trees in the forest, construction activities in the hills and pollution created through industrialization and modernization. The United Nations Forum on Forest (UNFF) has stressed that forests are an integral part of the global environment and human well-being, providing multiple goods and services essential for people worldwide and crucial for sustainable development and achievement of the internationally agreed development goals including millennium development goals.[7] The climate is warming at a rate faster than

Figure 13.3 *Key Elements of Sustainable Development*

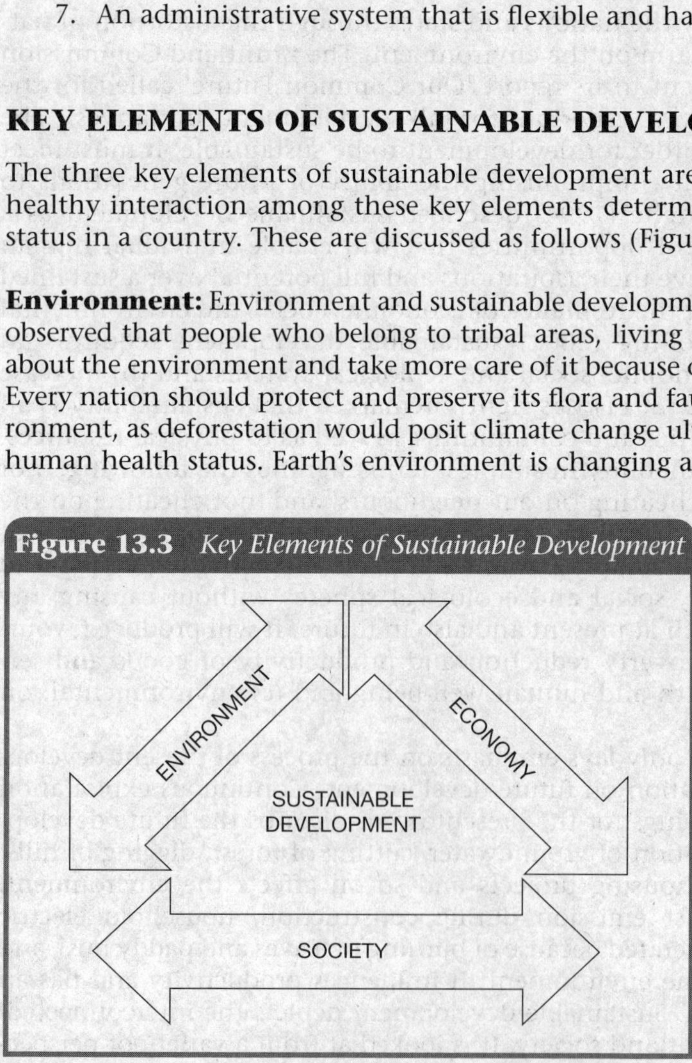

Source: Author.

that at any time during the last several years. The biodiversity is declining at an unprecedented rate and many traditional spices are vanishing from the earth. Fisheries and fish varieties are on the decline in most of the world's oceans. The air is polluted in most of the megacities of the world due to increase in the number of vehicles and the use of fuel-based appliances. The water table is going down in many places, rivers are polluted as well as drying and a number of water-stressed cities and areas are increasing. Much of this environmental degradation is due to the unsustainable production and use of energy, water, food and other biological resources. These are undermining efforts to alleviate poverty and stimulate sustainable development. Environmental sustainability refers to the maintenance of the ecosystem and the natural resource base, and environmental degradation signifies failure in this regard (Masika and Joekes 1997).

Economy: The aim of attaining higher economic growth rate by sacrificing the sustainable component of development is detrimental to the future growth and development of the economy. For instance, the Green Revolution programme launched in Punjab, India, way back in the 1970s enabled the states to attain higher agricultural growth rate at that point of time, at the cost of the future of the health of the soil. However, now the agricultural growth rate is stagnant and a large part of the land has become waterlogged and unsuitable for agriculture. Converting agriculturally fertile land to other uses such as real estate and industrial projects is not a viable proposition for the sustainable development of developing countries. A Unite Nation's document has envisaged that 'economic development is unsustainable if it increases vulnerability to crises. A drought may force farmers to slaughter animals needed for sustaining production in future years. A drop in prices may cause farmers or other producers to overexploit natural resources to maintain income.'[8] Strengthening production is a critical element to make growth more resilient and sustainable.[9] Therefore, the economic plan and policies must have a strong sustainable development component. Tackling poverty and income inequality also exerts a positive impact on sustainable development. Every economy, the developing economies in particular, should formulate an economic policy for sustainable development.

Society: Society, social system and social practices influence the sustainable development to a great extent. Social structures and institutions shape people's preferences, behaviour and attitude towards change. The social structures include forms of socio-economic stratification (class, ethnicity, gender and location). Institutions include formal and informal institutions that influence the behaviours of people and organizations in fairly predictable ways. Examples of some of the social institutions which would influence group behaviour in the Indian society are *mahila mandals*, cooperative societies, youth clubs, farmers associations, self-help groups and so on. The education level of the people and their awareness about sustainable development issues and concerns exert impact on the quality of life of the people by using sustainable development practices. Moreover, health and living conditions also influence the attitude of the people towards sustainable development practices. Weakening social values and institutions will reduce the resilience of the social system and undermine participatory governance at the grass-root level. This may affect values attached to sustainable development practices. The societal rituals are one of the key factors for the pollution of river Ganga. The immersion of offerings, flowers, candles, ashes, etc. are mainly polluting the river. However, for Hindu mythology, it is considered auspicious. These sacred activities cost a lot to the environment.

Another illustrious example of societal action is the presence of a large number of smokers in the society and its impact on the economy and environment. A society having a large number of smokers will have an adverse impact on the sustainable environment and economy. Nenkatesh (2013) has the following findings on the impact of smoking on the economy and environment: Employees who smoke during office hours go outside of the office for a smoke that leads to disturbance for other staffs if they are looking for them and also it reduces the productivity of the staff performance. Problems related with smoking can have an economic, environmental and social impact which in turn affects the country and its economy. Every country should create an organization for minimizing the effects of smoking by imposing restrictions on individuals and businesses. The National Environment Agency is one such organization formed by the Government of Singapore to reduce the impacts of smoking on public health and businesses.

FACTORS INFLUENCING SUSTAINABLE DEVELOPMENT

Some of the important socio-economic factors influencing sustainable development are as follows:

Demography: People are the central concern of sustainable development (Rio Declaration of 1992). The relationship between the demographic characteristics of a nation and its capability to attain sustainable development is profoundly connected. High fertility and population growth rate produce an adverse impact on the environment, food, ecosystem and, thus, on sustainable development. Therefore, efforts to promote more sustainable development pathways must take account of people—the numbers, location and age structures as well as their living conditions, ambitions and opportunities (IIASA and UNFPA 2011). High population growth puts pressure on natural resources, such as forest, land and water, and has an adverse impact on climate change and sustainable development. Population growth also puts pressure on consumption, production, employment, income distribution, poverty and affects the availability of food, housing, sanitation, safe drinking water, energy, education and health care. Herrmann (2012) was of the view that population dynamics are strongly and inseparably linked to sustainable development. While highlighting the forest people nexus Sarangi et al. (2016) have advocated that 'forests needs to be seen as nurturing both people and their culture. And one cannot highlight forests and forest foods, while keeping forest people whose food cultures are intrinsically linked to the forest out the picture.' The demographic situation of the country strongly influences sustainable development. Some of the demographic indicators are: (a) birth rate, (b) death rate, (c) fertility rate and (d) dependency ratio.

Poverty: Poverty is considered to be one of the key indicators of sustainable development. A scenario in which a high percentage of people are living below the poverty line and suffering from hunger, the country would not be capable to contribute substantially and sustainably towards the development of their family, society and nation. Poverty is deterrent to sustainable livelihood. The poverty-stricken households will inflict more harm to the environment and natural resources. Containing poverty is essential for the sustainable development of a family, society and nation. Some of the indicators of poverty and sustainable development are the percentages of: (a) the population living above the poverty line, (b) the population with healthy housing, (c) households with safe drinking water, (d) households with sanitary toilet, (e) households with smokeless *chulha* ((traditional cooking method still use by many households in rural areas)/cooking gas. Sustainable development cannot be achieved amidst poverty and (f) households with kitchen garden and tree plantation in the backyard.

Income Inequality: Sustainable development will not be possible in a society where the income inequality is very high. People having lower income will resort to income-earning methods which are detrimental to the environment. The impoverished tribal population largely depends on forest and forest products for their livelihood, and in this process they cause harm to the environment. Redistribution of income and landed property is a way to promote sustainable development. Vinoba Bhave's Bhoodan Movement in India, which was supported by Mahatma Gandhi, is an illustrious measure of sustainable development of the rural India. Concentration of wealth in the hands of a few will lead to in effective distribution of wealth, and may elongate poverty and inequality in the society. To Kohler (2015) redistributive policies are an essential component of strategies for reducing inequality and promoting sustainable development in its three dimensions: economic, social and environmental. Some of the indictors of income inequality are: (a) total income of the household from various sources, (b) percentage of people getting minimum wage rate, (c) percentage of people earning income below the poverty line, (d) percentage of household with agricultural land, (e) percentage of household with irrigated land, (f) percentage of household with mulching cow and buffalos, poultry and so on, (g) percentage of household pursuing self-employment activities and (h) percentage of household having women earning members.

Health: The key indicators of health identified by the United Nations for sustainable development are mortality, health care delivery, nutritional status, health status and risks. Health is one important component of sustainable development goals. Only a healthy individual can provide support to the family on a sustainable basis and a nation with healthy population can sustainably fight against poverty, inequality and unemployment. Morbid and diseased persons are not only burden on the family but also on the nation. Illness and malnutrition lead to the loss of strength, energy and productivity capacity, which ultimately would have a negative impact on labour income. The high percentage of HIV/AIDS population in a few African countries is one of the important factors affecting their sustainable development. Money used in the treatment of HIV/AIDS could have been spent for the achievement of sustainable development goals. It is the quality but not the quantity of population that matters in sustainable development. Therefore, a nation should take care of the health of its population, particularly of those who cannot afford referral and tertiary health care services. In order to promote sustainable development, essential health care services need to be a public good. Some of the important indicators of health development are the percentages of: (a) children immunized, (b) pregnant women who received immunization and other antennal care, (c) institutional delivery, (d) delivery conducted by trained health personnel, (e) population suffering from tuberculosis, (f) population suffering from HIV/AIDS, (g) malnourished children, (h) women suffering from anaemia, (i) the infant mortality rate and (j) maternal mortality rate.

Education: Education has been identified as one of the important social indicators of sustainable development. The United Nations also recognized that education is important for sustainable development where everyone has the opportunity to benefit from quality education and can learn the values, behaviour and lifestyles required for a sustainable future and for positive societal transformation. The community groups and the society that comprise of literate and educated manpower are more modernized, earn more and are capable of forming a sustainable community and society. They can better understand the usefulness of the relationship between economy, environment and society for the promotion of sustainable development. Nowadays, sustainable education's concept has been integrated in the school-level curriculum. Access to school-level education will educate about sustainable education. Some of the important education indicators of sustainable development are:

- literacy rate;
- adult literacy rate;
- gross enrolment ratio at the primary, secondary and tertiary education levels;
- percentage of women who cast vote in the election;
- women workforce participation;
- gap in wage received by men and women; and
- women participation in household decision-making.

Gender: Sustainable development requires the full and equal participation of women at all levels (Hemmati and Gardiner 2002). Tchouassi (2012) was of the view that gender equity is an essential building block in sustainable development:

- Environmental protection requires a solid understanding of women's relationship to natural and environmental resources as well as their rights and roles in resource planning and management.
- Economic well-being requires gender-sensitive strategies.
- Social equity is fundamentally linked to gender equity.

Women are the prime conservers and preservers of the nature and environment. Therefore, any action on sustainable development will remain incomplete without the involvement and participation of women. A gender-sensitive approach results in more equitable and efficient development; it also puts less strain on the environment and is, therefore, more sustainable (World Bank 2002). Women are great preservers and protectors of environment. Women-headed *van panchayats* are found to be performing well in terms of tree plantation and are involved in better preservation activities than men. Some of the gender development indicators are:

- sex-ratio;
- women literacy rate;
- gross enrolment ratio of female in the primary, secondary and tertiary education;
- women workforce participation; and
- percentage of women subject to atrocities and crime.

The success of the Chipko Movement was mainly due to women. The supporters of this movement were mainly village women, who succeeded in preventing the felling of trees and, thus, influenced the natural resource policy in India.

Culture: It is another important dimension of sustainable development. The United Nations has mentioned that the development interventions responsive to the cultural context, the particularities of a place and community and advance in a human-centred approach to development are most effective and likely to yield sustainable, inclusive and equitable outcomes.[10] In many developing countries, cultural practices prevailing throughout the ages entice a community to engage in raising the productivity of land, maintaining soil fertility by adopting suitable soil health practices and celebrating the productivity of land. These are intended towards sustainable development of society. Festivals of many states of India, such as Pongal in Andhra Pradesh, Onam in Kerala and Rongali Bihu in Assam are illustrious examples that are being celebrated during the harvesting season of paddy and are cultural practices linked with sustainable agriculture practices. For example, worshiping trees in many places is a cultural practice, which otherwise promotes plantation of trees, an action of sustainable development. People worship banana and peepal trees in many parts of India, and even hesitate to cut these as these are considered religiously auspicious. Peepal tree is an important source of oxygen. Some of the cultural development indictors are:

- percentage of households pursuing traditional/cultural practices for livelihood;
- percentage of households following dress code, food habits, dance, cultural festivals and so on;
- percentage of households following traditional environmental living practices for the conservation of forest and trees and
- percentage of households using traditional medicine and heath practices.

ENVIRONMENTALIST/ACTIVE CITIZENRY

The role of environmentalist in the conservation, preservation and protection of environment cannot be discounted. In fact, many of the projects which could have damaged environment have been cancelled because of people's revolt against them instigated by the environmentalist. Medha Patkar, Sunderlal Bahuguna and Baba Amte are the illustrious leading environmental activists in India to start movement for the conservation of forest. Similarly, there is the social movement of Narmada Bachao Andolan (NBA) by the adivasis, farmers, environmentalists and human right activists against a large dam being built across the Narmada River which flows through the state of Gujarat, Maharashtra and Madhya Pradesh. Medha Patkar and Baba Amte are the key activists who energized and emboldened the movement against the atrocities done to the nature. Another illustrious example is the Chipko Movement against the cutting of trees in the Himalayas.

The Chipko Movement

In the 1970s, an organized resistance to the destruction of forests spread throughout India and came to be known as the 'Chipko Movement'. The name of the movement comes from the word 'embrace' as the villagers hugged the trees and prevented the contractors from felling them.

The original Chipko Movement was started around 260 year back in the early 18th century in Rajasthan by the Bishnoi community. A larger group of them from 84 villages led by a lady called Amrita Devi laid down their lives in an effort to protect the trees from being felled on the orders of the Maharaja (king) of Jodhpur. After this incident, the Maharaja issued royal decree preventing the cutting of trees in all the Bishnoi villages.

In the 20th century it began in the hill of Himalayan state of Uttarakhand. The movement was started in 1973 in the village of Mandal in the upper Alaknanda valley and over the next five years it spread to many districts of the Himalayas in Uttarakhand. It was sparked off by the government's decision to allot a plot of forest areas in Alaknanda valley to a sports goods company. With the encouragement of NGOs and activists, the women of the village formed a circle around the trees preventing the men from cutting them. Chandi Prasad Bhatt, Dhoom Singh Negi, Bachni Devi, Ghanshyam Raturi and Sunderlal Bahuguna are the key activists who laid the movement from the front. Since then the movement has spread to many states in the country.

Source: http://edugreen.teri.res.in/explore/forestry/chipko.htm

Community Participation

Community participation is the key to sustainable development. Government alone cannot be able to bring sustainable development. Sustainable development has to be taken up at the national, state, district and community levels. If the community members are not keen and committed towards the sustainable development goals then any amount of endeavour of the government may not be effective enough to hasten the pace of sustainable development in developing countries. Holmberg and Sandbrook (1992) have remarked that 'people can help to bring about sustainable development only if the local, regional and national government policy framework is propitious to that end. But the reverse is equally true: sustainable development will not come about without active involvement of the people concerned.'

Self-reliance

One of the important factors which can influence and have positive impact on sustainable development is self-reliance. The nation states that are not self-reliant cannot be able to achieve sustainable development. Nations, and states within a nation as well as villages have to be self-reliant. A self-reliant village can only be called a sustainable village. The economy of the village must be resilient to external shocks and they should be able to manage their economy efficiently and effectively. In other words, a sustainable village and city are the key factors influencing sustainable development. The World Summit on sustainable development held in Johannesburg in 2002 emphasized that political will to implement change and self-reliance were among the elements emphasized as being critical for successful sustainable development.[11]

ISSUES AND CHALLENGES OF SUSTAINABLE DEVELOPMENT

The prerequisites for sustainable development in developing countries certainly differ from those of the developed countries. Some of the factors responsible for the attainment of sustainable development in developing countries are as follows (Figure 13.4).

Political Will: Strong political will and determination across the party line towards sustainable development is the starting point of the endeavour. National interest of sustainable development for the protection of environment and the prevention of environmental degradation should not be sacrificed for parochial short-term political gain. The control of

Figure 13.4 *Factors Influencing Sustainable Development*

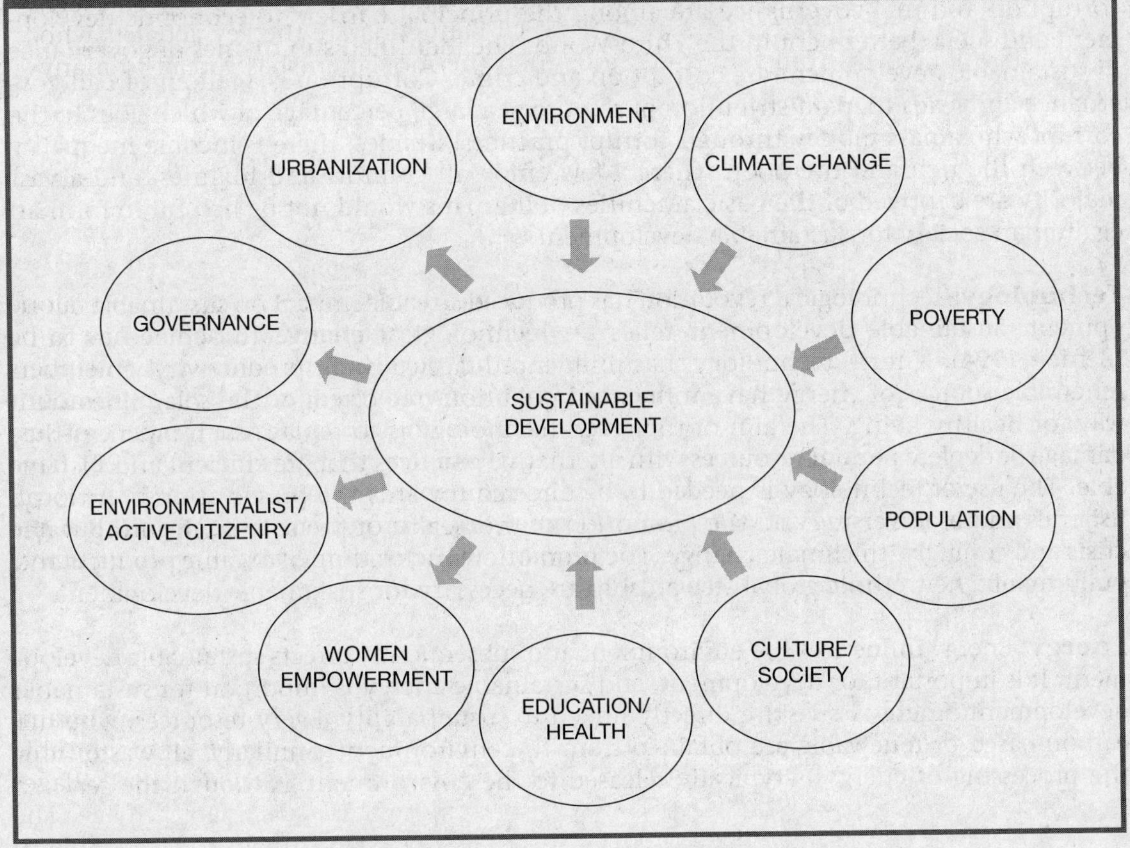

Source: Author.

population, which is critical to the achievement of sustainable development, requires political will. It is seen that in many developing countries having high population growth rate, the intention to make a population law to restrict the population size has failed because of a lack of political consensus. Besides, restricting the number of vehicles in the city, pollution control and adoption of the green norm are also influenced by the political willpower of the concerned governments. The odd–even formula for plying vehicles in Delhi intending to control pollution is being criticized by the political parties. There is no consensus across political parties on odd–even formula. One of the United Nations report has remarked that sustainable development has suffered from the failure of political will and a lack of presence in both the national and international economic debate. It has urged that sustainable development must be at the forefront of political agendas and budgets.[12]

Governance: Governance is an important concomitant of sustainable development. Good governance promotes accountability, transparency, efficiency and the rule of law at all levels. It also intends at the sound, natural, economic and financial resources distribution for equitable and sustainable development. In the participatory governance, people and their elected representatives actively participate in the governance process, enabling the government to achieve sustainable development. According to Wolf (2005), political corruption and mal-governance are among the principal barriers to economic development and social betterment in the Third World. The identified sub-themes of governance in sustainable development are corruption and crime. Corruption is a fallout of bad governance and leads to maldistribution of resources, a large percentage of which goes to the corrupt who amass money through corrupt practices. Besides, there is income inequality between the rich and the poor, where a few enjoy all comfort and luxuries, and a vast majority are deprived of the basic amenities of life. This would not be helpful to form an egalitarian society for sustainable development.

Technology: Technological revolution has produced sizeable impact on sustainable development. Sustainable development relies on technological change to achieve its aims (Berder 1994). Green technology has influenced agricultural productivity and non-renewable sources of energy have influenced pollution-free city life. The solar cities are a way for healthy living. The aim of the green technology is to replace such practices that damage or deplete natural resources with alternative practices that are efficient and sustainable. The use of technology is needed to be directed towards the preservation of forestry, fisheries and biodiversity, and the promotion of the health of the soil, confronting water crisis and coping with climate change. The promotion and trading of organic products and building of a new ethnic global stewardship are necessary for sustainable development.

Energy: Energy influences the environment and subsequently affects sustainable development. It is important for development, and sustainable energy is important for sustainable development. Energy issues are directly linked to sustainability. Every resources, whether carbon-based or renewable are obtained from the environment. Similarly, all waste from the processing of energy is typically released to the environment. Although the services provided by the energy support the quality of living, its misuse affects the social stability and cultural and social development. Renewable sources of energy promote sustainable development more effectively rather than other non-renewable sources of energy such as oil, nuclear, coal natural gas, hydro and so on. Energy usage is critical to sustainable development. According to OECD (2007), energy contributed to a virtuous cycle of human, economic and social improvements that are essential to sustainable development in developing countries, and supplies of clean energy are the basis for raising the standards of living, improving the quality and quantity of human capital, enhancing the business and natural environment and increasing the efficiency of government policies.[13]

Urbanization: Urbanization can pose major threats to the achievement of sustainable development, due to detrimental environmental impacts and other adverse effects associated with intensive resource consumption and poor management (DFID 2002). Customarily, the contribution of urban areas to economic growth and national income is higher as compared to rural areas. Urbanization helps create economic wealth for the nation and provides higher living standards for the urban population. However, it also results in tremendous strain on the city's infrastructure and contributes to problems associated with urban sprawl and ultimately becomes a headache for sustainable development in developing countries. Pollution created by the unbridled number of vehicles running on the city road, dust created out of construction of urban infrastructure and housing produce an adverse impact on environment and human health. Citing Pakistan as an example, Asian Development Bank (2002) said that the urbanization trend at work costs heavily to urban environment and fragile national economy of Pakistan. As urbanization is essential for development, sustainable urbanization is equally important for sustainable development. Sustainable urbanization is a dynamic, multidimensional process involving environmental as well as social, economic and political–institutional sustainability (DFID 2002). Thus, planned urbanization is a boon and unplanned urbanization is a bane of sustainable development.

CLIMATE CHANGE AND SUSTAINABLE DEVELOPMENT

The continuous climate change and its impact on sustainable development is an emerging and contemporary agenda of debate and discussion in national and international forums in both developed and developing countries. Climate change effected through global warming is affecting the three key elements of sustainable development such as economy, society and environment. The Seventh African Development Forum has envisaged that global warming is causing local and regional climates to change in many ways, thereby modifying climate risk, and these changes will have many different impacts on human habitat and livelihood conditions (Seventh African Development Forum, 2010). Development of developing countries of South Asia and Africa are greatly affected by climate change. IPCC (2014) has mentioned that South Asia is considered a highly vulnerable region to climate change and is already being affected by sea level rises, extreme weather events and heat waves.[14]

Impact of Climate Change

Aside from increased temperature, climate change manifests in different ways around the world: increased and more intense storms and floods; long droughts; melting glaciers; ocean acidification. Further effects can include forest fires, less reliable or loss of seasonal crops due to changing distribution and intensity of rain, migration of species and resultant shifting disease vectors, loss of biodiversity, among others. Impacts will be felt everywhere from big cities to small villages, the poles to the deserts, developed and developing countries, coasts and mountains.

Source: Women's Earth & Climate Action Network, International: http://wecaninternational.org/pages/discussion/61/achieving-sustainable-development (accessed on 16 May 2016).

Climate change produces impact on poverty, inequality and productivity. Kim (2013) viewed that many climate change mitigation measures will help lift people out of poverty. Renewable energy development could allow affordable access to the 1.2 billion people currently living without electricity; low carbon housing and urban development could open up job opportunities; climate smart agriculture could increase crop yields; reduced extraction from deforestation and degradation could increase community resilience and protect natural assets and saving from fuel subsidies could be invested in health and education.

Some of the impacts of climate change on sustainable socio-economic development are:

1. Extreme rise in temperature and prolonging of summer season would give rise to drought condition and affect food grain and milk, egg and vegetable productivity. According to IPCC calculations, a one degree increase in the temperature will result in 5% yield decrease in tropical, sub-tropical and temperate regions (UNFCCC 2014).[15] This will reduce the economic growth rate.
2. Climate change will affect poverty, inequality and human well-being. Houghton (2011) has opined that climate change will reduce welfare by an amount equivalent to a reduction in consumption per head of between 5% and 20%. This may lead to hunger and hunger deaths in dry land areas. The impact will lead to shortage of drinking water. Many districts in India are facing this problem. The prolonged use of electricity for running air conditioners has led to rise in electricity and fuel prices and will lead to the depletion of future non-renewable energy sources.
3. Shifting and lengthening of summer season beyond the usual time cycle because of climate change will lead to the use of groundwater and the depletion of water table in the irrigated areas. This can lead to future water crisis both for drinking and irrigation purposes.
4. Untimely and incessant rain can create flood and disaster leading to the loss of crops and damage to physical assets such as road, irrigation projects, dams and so on.

5. Rise of the sea level may lead to Tsunami-like situations resulting in loss of human beings, animals and other physical assets.
6. Global warming will lead to the melting of glaciers leading to flash floods which may affect houses of the villages, bridges, dams and water works, and would negatively influence the health of human beings and affect flora and fauna in the hilly areas. Cloud burst and forest fire occurring in the hilly areas because of climate change is affecting flora and fauna and causing damage to the physical assets and human beings. Cloud bursts in Himachal Pradesh and Uttarakhand have resulted in the damage of natural, physical and human resources. The money which could have been spend for the development activities is now spent on relief and rehabilitation work. It also affected the tourism industry of the state and inflicted loss to the state exchequer.

Climate Change and Disaster

According to a United Nations (2016) Environment Report (The Global Environmental Outlook (GEO)):

- The worst impacts of climate change are projected to occur in the Pacific and South and Southeast Asia.
- It listed Mumbai and Kolkata in India, Guangzhou and Shanghai in China, Dhaka in Bangladesh, Yangon in Myanmar, Bangkok in Thailand, and Ho Chi Minh City and Hai Phong in Vietnam as projected to have the largest population exposure to coastal flooding in 2070.
- Nearly 40 million Indians will be at risk from rising sea levels by 2050, with people in Mumbai and Kolkata having the maximum exposure to coastal flooding in the future due to rapid urbanisation and economic growth.
- Evidence suggests that climate change and climate variability and sea-level rise will exacerbate multidimensional poverty in most developing countries.

Source: http://www.msn.com/en-in/news/newsindia/rising-sea-levels-threaten-40mn-indians-mumbai-kolkata-in-a-fix-report/ar-BBtgDsL?li=AAgfYGb&ocid=iehp (22 May 2016).

Climate Change and Cloud Burst in Himalayas

The durability of Glacier in Garhwal–Kumaon Himalayas is in threat due to global warming. Besides, the local factors such as excessive practice of mass tourism, vehicle movement, human activities in high altitude eco-sensitive areas are also responsible for increasing of temperature and destruction of glacier. This glacier melts and the lake comes in direct contact with the clouds due to high altitude, creating favourable conditions for cloud burst in high altitude areas of Uttarakhand.

Source: Das (2015).

Uttarakhand Flash Floods: Situation Update 2 July 2013

The infrastructures damaged due to flash foods are: (i) 400 villages across Uttarkashi, Rudraprayag, Chamoli and Tehri regions have been washed off, submerged or affected; (ii) 34,000 square miles, area affected, estimated loss to economy is Rs. 3,000 crore; (iii) 2,232 houses destroyed in Uttarakhand, 99 Dharmsalas swept away; (iv) 1,000 bridges damaged, 695 water schemes affected, more than 300 villages facing severe drinking water shortage; and (v) 600 villages are still absolutely cut-off, limited/ intermittent road connectivity to reach supplies to 13,600 villages in Uttarakhand.

Source: https://www.unitedwaymumbai.org/downloads/Uttarakhand%20Floods-%20Situation %20report-July%202%202013 %20Compiled%20by%20United%20Way%20of%20India.pdf (accessed 17 May 2016).

7. Extreme climate will affect the health conditions and may spread many diseases. As it is remarked that change in the climate may affect the spread of vector-borne diseases and also water-related and waterborne diseases may get aggravated.[16]

SUSTAINABLE DEVELOPMENT GOALS

On 25 September 2015 193 countries of the United Nations General Assembly adopted the 2030 Development Agenda named as Transforming Our World: The 2030 Agenda for Sustainable Development. The 17 identified sustainable development goals associated with 169 targets and 304 proposed indicators are as follows:

1. End poverty in all its forms everywhere.
2. End hunger, achieve food security and improved nutrition and promote sustainable agriculture.
3. Ensure healthy lives and promote well-being for all at all ages.
4. Ensure inclusive and equitable quality education and promote lifelong learning opportunities for all.
5. Achieve gender equality and empower all women and girls.
6. Ensure availability and sustainable management of water and sanitation for all.
7. Ensure access to affordable, reliable, sustainable and modern energy for all.
8. Promote sustained, inclusive and sustainable economic growth, full and productive employment and decent work for all.
9. Build resilient infrastructure, promote inclusive and sustainable industrialization and foster innovation.
10. Reduce inequality within and among countries.
11. Make cities and human settlements inclusive, safe, resilient and sustainable.
12. Ensure sustainable consumption and production patterns.
13. Take urgent action to combat climate change and its impacts.
14. Conserve and sustainably use oceans, seas and marine resources for sustainable development.

15. Protect, restore and promote sustainable use of terrestrial ecosystems, sustainably manage forests, combat desertification and halt and reserve land degradation and halt biodiversity loss.
16. Promote peaceful and inclusive societies for sustainable development, provide access to justice for all and build effective, accountable and inclusive institutions at all levels.
17. Strengthen the means of implementation and revitalize the global partnership for sustainable development.

The nations are urged to try sincerely to attain these goals.

SUMMARY

Environmental issues and sustainable development are two vital challenges before policy-makers involved in the process of development particularly in developing countries. It is agreed that one cannot think of achieving sustainable development goals in isolation from environment, as the environment affects all aspects of nation's as well as individual's life. Environmental degradation which causes physical and economic disasters is a cause of concern for many developing countries. Likewise, sustainable development is an important development agenda of the 21st century and is one of the vital paradigm shifts in development. It is an emerging as well as concurrent issue and will remain a key concern for the world in days to come. Every country has to take appropriate measures for the promotion of sustainable development. Therefore, the United Nations has emphasized on sustainable development in its institutional framework. In its institutional framework for sustainable development, it has mentioned that for the attainment of sustainable development, good governance, sound economic policies, social democratic institutions responsible for the needs of the people and improved infrastructure are the basis for sustained economic growth, poverty eradication and employment generation. Ironically, the present political economy of developing countries discounts the future value of natural resources, ecology and environment in the exchange for short-term economic growth. Strong political will is an important concomitant to environment protection and sustainable development.

Keywords: environmental Kuznets curve, climate change, traditional knowledge system, common property resources, ecosystem diversity, eco-tourism, green growth, sustainable development.

REVIEW QUESTIONS

1. Discuss the role of environment in development. Explain why environment management is essential for development.
2. What is sustainable development? Describe the basic social components of sustainable development.

3. Explain a few key challenges of environment development.
4. What is climate change? How climate change analysis is crucial for environment and development?
5. What is green growth? How green growth is crucial for the development of developing countries?
6. What is Environmental Kuznets Curve? Explain in detail how development affects the environment in developed and developing economies.
7. Write short notes on the following:
   (i) Environmental Kuznets curve
   (ii) Climate change
   (iii) Sustainable development
   (iv) Green growth
   (v) Traditional knowledge system
   (vi) Eco-tourism

NOTES

1. See http://www.unep.org/geo/geo4/report/01_Environment_for_Development.pdf (accessed on 15 March 2016).
2. See http://www.unep.org/geo/geo4/report/01_Environment_for_Development.pdf (accessed on 15 March 2016).
3. See http://www.undp.org/content/undp/en/home/ourwork/environmentandenergy/strategic_themes/integrating_environmentintodevelopment.html (accessed on 23 June 2016).
4. See http://www.unep.org/geo/geo4/report/01_Environment_for_Development.pdf (accessed on 15 March 2016).
5. For Robert Engelman statement, see http://environment.about.com/od/biodivesitycon (accessed on 29 June 2013).
6. Europe-2020: Towards growth and resource efficiency, CASI Policy Brief 2/12/2014 see http://www.meta-group.com/news/SitesAssets/pagive (accessed on 21 February 2015).
7. See http://www.un.org/esa/desa/papers/2015/wp139_2015.pdf (accessed on 16 May 2016).
8. See http://www.un-document.net/ecf-02.htm (accessed on 24 May 2016).
9. See http://www.unescap.org/sites/default/files/Chapter3_1.pdf (accessed on 24 May 2016).
10. See http://www.un.org/millenniumgoals/pdf/Think%20Pieces/2_culture.pdf (accessed on 16 May 2016).
11. See http://www.un.org/events/wssd/summarries/envdevj27.htm (accessed on 25 June 2016).
12. See http://www.climatechangenews.com/2012/01/30/un-report-lack-of-political-will-hindering-sustainable-development/ (accessed on 17 May 2016).
13. See https://www.oecd.org/greengrowth/38509686.pdf (accessed on 17 May 2016).
14. UNFCCC and IPCC http://www.asef.org/images/stories/publications/ebooks/asef-handbook-climate-change-sustainable-development-goals.pdf (accessed on 16 May 2016).
15. See Note 17.
16. Adopting to the impacts of climate change. See http://cbs.teriin.org/pdf/hlcdthematic/Adapting_to_the_Impacts_of_Climate_Change_1.pdf (accessed on 16 May 2016).

REFERENCES

Akinbode, A. *Introductory Environmental Resources Management*. Ibadan: Daybis Press, 2002.

Albritton, D. *What Drives Changes in Climate: Technical Summary*. New York: Cambridge University Press, 2000.

Beckerman, W. 'Economic Growth and the Environment: Whose Growth? Whose Environment?' *World Development* 20, no. 4(1992): 481–96.

Bhagawati, J. 'The Case for Free Trade.' *Scientific American* 269, no. 5(1993): 42–49.

Chambers, R. 'Poverty and Livelihoods: Whose Reality Counts?' *Environment and Urbanization* 7, no. 1 (1995): 173–204.

Chauhan, M. 'Concept of Environmental Accounting and Practice in India.' *The Chartered Accountant* 720, November, 2005. Available at: http://220.227.161.86/10355720-726.pdf (accessed on 29 June 2013).

Daly, H. *Steady-state Economics*. San Francisco, CA: Freeman & Co., 1977.

Das, P. K. 'Global Warming, Glacial Lakes and Cloud Burst Events in Garhwal–Kumaon Himalayas: A Hypothetical Analysis.' *International Journal of Environmental Sciences* 5, no. 4 (2015): 697–708.

Dasgupta, S., U. Deichmann, C. Meisner and D. Wheeler. 'Where Is the Poverty-Environment Nexus? Evidence form Cambodia, Lao PDR and Vietnam.' *World Development* 33, no. 4 (2005): 617–38.

Dasgupta, S., B. Lalante, H. Wang and D. Wheeler. 'Confronting the Environmental Kuznets Curve.' *Journal of Economic Perspectives* 16, no. 1 (2002): 147–68.

Dernbach, L. *Stumbling Towards Sustainability*. Washington, D.C.: Environment Law Institute, 2000.

DFID. 'Sustainable Urbanization; Achieving Agenda 21.' London: UN HABITAT and the UK Government Development for Internal Development (DFID).

Edward, B. 'Poverty Development and Environment.' In *Environment and Development Economics*, 1–26. London: Cambridge University Press, 2010.

FAO. 'Forest Resource Assessment 2000: Main Reports.' FAO Forestry Paper 140. Rome: FAO, 2001.

———. '*State of World's Forest*.' Rome: FAO, 2003.

Finon, D. 'From Energy Security to Environmental Protection: Understanding Swings in the Energy Policy Pendulum.' *Energy Studies Review* 6, no. 1 (1994): 1–15.

Gokhale, Y. 'Conservation of Biodiversity and Ecosystem Services by REDD+ Project in India.' A policy Brief, The Energy and Resources Institute, Ministry of Environment and Forests, Government of India, 2013. Available at: http://www.teriin.org/projects/nfa/pdf/policy_ (accessed on 21 October 2013).

Gunderson, L. H. and C. S. Holling. 'Panarchy: Understanding Transformations in Human and Natural Systems.' New York: Island Press, 2001.

Hardin, G. 'The Tragedy of the Commons.' *Science* 62 (December 1968): 1243–48.

Herrmann, M. *Factoring Population Dynamics into Sustainable Development in OECD, Development Cooperation Report 2012 Lessons in Linking Suitability and Development*. OECD Publishing, 2012. Also see https://www.oecd.org/dac/DCR%20summary_EN.pdf (accessed on 3 December 2016).

Houghton, J. 'Global Warming, Climate Change and Sustainability.' Briefing Paper 14. The John Ray Initiative Connecting Environment, Science and Christianity. Available at: http://www.jri.org.uk/brief/BriefingNo14_4thEdition_july.pdf (accessed on 16 May 2016).

IIASA and UNFPA. 'The Ladenburg Declaration on Population and Sustainable Development Statement of Global Expert Panel.' Luxemburg October, 2011.

Inter-governmental Panel on Climate Change. 'Summary of Policy Makers.' In *Direct Observation of Recent Climate Change in IPCC AR4WG1*, 2007, Cambridge University Press, Cambridge. Also see http://www.ipcc.ch/pdf/assessment-report/ar4/wg1/ar4-wg1-spm.pdf (accessed on 3 December 2016).

Jodha, N. S. 'Common Property Resources and the Environmental Context: Role of Biophysical versus social stresses.' *Economic and Political Weekly* 30, no. 51 (1995): 3278–83.

Kim, J. Y. 'Ending Poverty Includes Tackling Climate Change and Promoting Sustainable Development.' Australian Council for International Development, July 2015. Available at: https://acfid.asn.au/sites/site.acfid/files/Tackling-climate-change-and-promoting-sustainable-development-final.pdf (accessed on 16 May 2016).

Kuznets, S. 'Economic Growth and Income Inequality.' *American Economic Review* 45, no. 1 (1955): 1–28.

Law, K. M. Y. 'Affecting Sustainability Development: High-tech Manufacturing Firms in Taiwan.' *Asia Pacific Management Review* 15, no. 4 (2010): 619–33.

Laxenburg, Hemmati N. and R. Gardiner. *Gender and Sustainable Development: A Briefing Paper*. Johannesburg: Heinrich Boll Foundation, 2002.

Mai, Truyet T. and Quans M. Nguyen. 'Development and Environment in Vietnam.' Conference on Sustainable Development in Vietnam, University of Maryland, 2003.

Martin, J. 'Advantages and Disadvantages of Instituting environmental laws', 2014. Available at: http://homeguides.sfgate.com/advantages-disadvantages-instituting-environmental-laws-78903.html (accessed on 3 December 2016).

Masika, R. and S. Joekes. 'Environmentally Sustainable Development and Poverty: A Gender Analysis.' Sussex: Institute of Development Studies, 1997.

Millennium Ecosystem Assessment. *Ecosystem and Human Well-being: A Framework for Assessment*. Washington, D.C.: Island Press, 2005.

Minot, N. and B. Baulch 'The Spatial Distribution of Poverty in Vietnam and the Potential for Targeting.' Policy Research Paper 2829. Washington, D.C.: World Bank.

Munasinghe, M. 'Sustainomics: A Transdisciplinary Framework for Sustainable Development.' Keynote Paper. Proceedings of the 50th Anniversary Sessions of the Sri Lanka Association for Advance Science (SLAMS), Colombo, Sri Lanka, 1994.

OECD. 'Growth and Developing Countries: A Summary for Policy-makers.' 2012, June. Available at: http://www.oecd.org/dac/50526354.pdf (accessed on 22 December 2016).

Ogundele, J. A. and A. O. Jegede. 'Environmental Impact of Climate Change on Agricultural Production in Ekiti State, Nigeria.' *Journal of Environmental Issues and Agriculture in Developing Countries* 3, no. 2: 72–79.

Panayotou, T. 'Economic Growth and the Environment.' Spring Seminar of the United Nations Economic Commission for Europe, Geneva, 2003.

Prakash, S. 'Poverty and Environmental Linkages in Mountains and Uplands: Reflection on the Poverty Trap.' CREED Working Pages Series No.12. London: IIED, 1997.

Rauniyar, G. and R. Kanbur. 'Inclusive Growth and Inclusive Development: A Review and Synthesis of Asian Development Bank Literature.' Occasional Paper No. 8. Asian Development Bank, Manila, Philippines, 2009.

Sarangi, D., B. Biswal and P. Patra 'Forests: A Food Producing Habitat.' *CBGA Budget Track* 11 (February 2016): 34–38.

Sen, A. 'Social Exclusion: Concept, Application and Security.' Social Development Papers No. 1. Office of Environment and Social Development, Asian Development Bank, 2000, June.

Seventh African Development Forum. 'Climate Change and Sustainable Development in Africa: An Overview.' United Nations Conference Centre, Addis Ababa, Ethiopia, 2010. Available at: http://www.preventionweb.net/files/15864_adfviibackgroundpapereng1.pdf (accessed on 16 May 2016).

Shore, C. and S. Wright (eds). 'Policy: A New Field of Anthropology.' In *Anthropology of Policy: Critical Perspectives on Governance and Power*, 3–39. London: Routledge, 1997.

Tchouass, G. 'Does Gender Equality Work for Sustainable Development in Central Africa Countries: Some Empirical Lessons.' *European Journal of Sustainable Development* 1, no. 3 (2012): 383–98.

Tsuj, L. J. S. and E. Ho. 'Traditional Environmental Knowledge System and Western Science: In Search of Common Ground.' *The Canadian Journal of Native Studies* XXII, no. 2 (2002): 327–60.

Turner, M. 'Ecological Complexity and the Management of Common Property Resources.' In *Tenure Brief*, no. 5, 1–8. University of Wisconsin, Madison, 2007.

United Nations. 'United Nation Framework Convention on Climate Change.' UNTS XXVI 2, no. 1 (9 May 1992): 7.

———. 'United Nations General Assembly Resolution: 51/172.' Available at: http://daccess-dds-ny.un.org/doc/UNDOC/GEN/N97/765/67/PDF/N9776567.pdf?Open Element (accessed on 3 December 2016).

———. *56th Commission Human Rights, Item 7: The Right to Development*. Geneva: United Nations, 2000.

———. *The United Nations Development Agenda: Development for All*. New York: Department of Economic and Social Affair, United Nations, 2007.

Valiela, I., J. L. Bowen and J. K. York. '"Mangrove Forests" One of the World's Threatened Major Tropical Environments.' *Biosciences* 51, no. 10 (2001): 807–15.

Venkatesh, N. 'Impact of Smoking: Influence on the Society and Global Business.' *International Journal of Business and Management Invention* 2, no. 3 (2013): 46–53.

Wolf, M. 'Aid Is Well Worth Trying.' *Financial Times*, 5 July 2005.

World Bank. 'Gender Equality and Sustainable Development.' Gender and Development Group, World Bank, Washington, DC, 2002.

World Commission on Environment & Development (WCED). *Our Common Future*. Oxford University Press, New York, 1987.

Yandle, B., M. Vijayaraghavan and M. Bhattarai. 'The Environmental Kuznets Curve: A Primer.' PERC Research Study 02-1, May 2002. Available at: www.macalester.edu/~wests/econ231/yandleatal.pdf. (accessed on 11 January 2013).

14 Marginalization, Women Empowerment and Inclusive Development

Social exclusion as a process, in which particular individual are pushed to the edge of society and hindered from participating fully by virtue of their poverty, or lack of basic competencies and life-long learning opportunities, or as a result of discrimination.

—EU (2004)

Social issues are sometimes very important like economic issues for the achievement of a higher economic growth rate and sustainable development goals. Every dimension of development, that is, social, economic, human, political, cultural and so on, has to be adequately strengthened and consolidated to accomplish sustainable development goals. Furthermore, holistic development postulates that each and every sector, each and every actor and each and every individual irrespective of caste, class, sex, colour, ethnicity and so on needs to be empowered to contribute towards development as per their capabilities. However, it is perceived that certain groups of population are marginalized in the development process and are not contributing adequately to economic growth and development. Mainstreaming of these disadvantaged and marginalized is necessary for holistic and sustainable development. They have to be effectively integrated and empowered to contribute to economic growth and development as per their capabilities. In Africa, social exclusion is mostly seen as a direct consequence of poverty and they both stem from discrimination on the basis of race, ethnicity and gender inequality, unbalanced rural and urban development, unequal distribution of assets or unequal access to services.

Social exclusion is a curse and a stumbling block in the process of inclusive and sustainable development. Each and every nation has to overcome this barrier in order to earn the contribution of every social group in the process of economic growth and development. According to Sen (2000), to be excluded from common facilities or benefits that others have can certainly be a significant handicap that impoverishes the lives that individuals can enjoy. Marginalization and social exclusion are responsible factors promoting poverty, inequality and unemployment in developing countries. For example, a large percentage of the population of the SCs and STs, who are socially marginalized in India, are living below the poverty line, having less percentage of people in high-paid jobs, less number of judges in the higher courts and lesser number of executives in public and corporate sectors. Besides, they also have low literacy and high maternal and infant mortality rates due to poor access to higher education and quality health care services. Ironically, less number of people from these communities are holding powerful ministerial berth in the central and state cabinets. Because of a social tag, they are found to be discriminated in the local as well as global labour market and are less represented in technical and skillful jobs. Social development is an instrument for the establishment of an egalitarian society. Therefore, any discussion on issues and challenges of development will remain incomplete if it does not include in its gamut the vital social issues such as women empowerment, marginalization and inclusive development.

After reading this chapter, you will be able to:

1. Define marginalization and explain how it affects inclusive development.
2. Explain various reasons of marginalization and steps to overcome them.
3. Define women empowerment and discuss how it is crucial for development.
4. Define inclusive development. Narrate various types of inclusion essential for inclusive development.

SECTION I: MARGINALIZATION

Marginalization is a form of acute and persistent disadvantage, rooted in underlying social inequalities.

—UNESCO (2010)

CONCEPT AND MEANING

Marginalization and social exclusion on the basis of caste, sex, race, ethnicity and so on are important social issues impeding inclusive development in both developed and developing countries. These are hurdles in the path of 'development by all, development for all and development of all'. According to Jones (2009), recent decades have seen rising inequity(ies), which are in turn partly responsible for the world 'lagging behind' in headline goals such as the MDGs. Particularly in developing countries, a few are enjoying the fruit of economic growth and development and a colossal percentage of population are grossly marginalized. They are deprived of the benefits of economic growth and development.

Marginalization is derived from the word 'margin' which means at the outskirt or periphery or at the border line away from the centre. In the case of any adversaries, they are being targeted as the first categories to be eliminated. Marginalization is a social phenomenon. The marginalized are at the border line and are in the fear to be excluded. In other words, even if included, the marginalized are at the risk of being excluded at any point of time. Burton and Kangan (2003) were of the view that marginality is an experience affecting millions of people throughout the world. People who are marginalized have relatively little control over their lives and resources available to them; they may become stigmatized and are often at the receiving end of negative public attitudes (Burton and Kangan 2003). Marginalization is at the core of exclusion from fulfilling full social lives at the individual, interpersonal and societal levels and is perhaps the most dangerous form of oppression (Burton and Kangan 2003). To Leonard (1984), social marginality is 'being outside the mainstream of productive activity and/or social reproductive activity'. According to Cain et al. (2012), marginalization is not a 'state' but rather a 'dynamic' which is expressed in the interaction between those whose status is horizontally unequal as a result of social constructs relating to factors such as disability, age, mental health and gender. Marginalization is a multidimensional concept concerning inequality observed in both developed and developing countries in different spheres and of different degrees. The concept of marginality is generally used to analyse socio-economic, political and cultural spheres, where disadvantaged people struggle to gain access to resources and full participation in social, economic, political and cultural, and even in the religious life. For instance, the exclusion of women and certain caste groups of population to enter into the place of worship is an illustrious example of religious marginalization and this issue is being discussed and debated in the print and electronic media in India. In other words, marginalized people might be socially, economically, politically, culturally and religiously ignored, excluded or neglected and, therefore, are vulnerable to livelihood challenges.

The end product of marginalization is social exclusion. The marginalized, who are at the border because of their caste, gender, ethnicity and similar other social positioning, are subject to exclusion. Saith (2001) was of the view that the term 'social exclusion' surfaced in the 1970s and the 1980s, when an intense period of state restructuring in America and Europe involving privatization, deregulation and a decline in public services brought about a massive upsurge in unemployment and social tension. de Hann and Maxwell (1998) defined social exclusion as 'the process through which individuals or groups are wholly or partially excluded from the society in which they live'. In the same vein, Lee and Murie (1999) defined social exclusion as a process that fully or partially excludes individuals or groups from social, economic and cultural networks. Social exclusion is the denial of equal opportunities to all in a socially stratified society. A certain group of population is being denied their social, educational, economic, cultural and political rights because of their socio-cultural inheritance and social configuration in the society on the basis of caste, religion, gender and so on.

According to Levitas et al. (2007),

> [S]ocial exclusion is a complex and multi-dimensional process. It involves the lack or denial of resources, rights, goods and services and the inability to participate in the normal relationships and activities, available to the majority of people in a society, whether in economic, social, cultural or political arenas. It affects both the quality of life and individuals and the equity and cohesion of society as a whole.

To them 'the severe or deep exclusion refers to exclusion across more than one domain or dimension of disadvantage, resulting in severe negative consequences for quality of life, well-being and future life chances'. Sen (2000) has distinguished among various forms of exclusion:

- being excluded from enjoying a normal crop;
- being excluded from employment;
- exclusion from the food market because of low purchasing power and
- exclusion from food subsidy arrangements.

Exclusion is nothing but denial of 'opportunity' to a certain group of people in different spheres of development, i.e. economic, social, human, political and so on, which has an adverse impact on their living standard and quality of life. The two prominent marginalized groups in India are SCs and STs. However, other groups of population, considered to be victims of marginalization and exclusion, are women, disabled, transgender, lesbians and even the old and aged population. Two defining characteristics of social exclusion are particularly relevant: first, deprivation is multidimensional, i.e. there is denial of equal opportunity in multiple spheres. Second, it is embedded in the societal relations and societal institutions—the processes through which individuals or groups are wholly or partially excluded from full participation in the society in which they live (de Haan 1998). According to DFID (2005), social exclusion describes a process by which certain groups are systematically disadvantaged because they are discriminated against on the basis of their ethnicity, race, religion, sexual orientation, caste, descent, gender, age, disability, HIV status, migrant status or where they live.

FACTORS PROMOTING MARGINALIZATION

Some of the factors that have given rise to marginalization and social exclusion particularly in developing countries are:

1. Traditional beliefs and values existing in the society that have been carried forward since centuries in the social sphere. Besides, the stereotypes attached to certain groups of population regarding their rights and empowerment also lead to marginalization.
2. Prevalence of religious beliefs and values resulting in religious-based marginalization. Certain groups of population based on their caste and gender are denied to profess and practise religious activities in religious institutions. They consider themselves as marginalized in the religious sphere.
3. Exclusion of certain groups of population on the basis of their caste, sex and ethnicity to equally profess and practise and involve in the social activities. They are victims of social networking and poor access to social capital. This is called social marginalization or the social factors promoting marginalization.
4. Gender stereotypes, i.e. they cannot do hard work, they are meant for household activities, they are others' property, they can be less mobile and so on, lead to marginalization of women starting from the family itself.
5. Certain groups of population are marginalized because of their physical structure and deformities, i.e. disabled, transgender and so on.
6. Marginalization may occur sometimes on the basis of income, education, access to property and so on.
7. The population that has migrated to different areas either as refugee or as illegal migrant because of war, terrorism and development displacement feel marginalized.
8. Factors like feeling of in minority also create a sense of insecurity. The population group in minority lacks adequate voice in decision-making and, therefore, feels marginalized.
9. The smaller provinces with less representation in national politics also feel politically marginalized.
10. Some groups of population in a country or in the provinces of the country are being marginalized largely due to the following reasons: (a) the marginalized groups follow different culture, language, tradition from the mainstream society; (b) they are less assertive, less educated and have slender exposure to modernity and (c) they have unique profession and livelihood, i.e. 'hunting', 'tanning', 'fishing', 'cobbling' and so on and less represented in the mainstream modern employment.
11. Different states in a country and within the country's different provinces also face spatial marginalization. The people belonging to hill and dry land areas feel

marginalized when they compare themselves with the people residing in the plain areas. The KBK (Kalahandi, Bolangir and Koraput) concept of district predominated with tribal population in Orissa is an illustrious example of spatial marginalization.

ISSUES AND CHALLENGES OF MARGINALIZATION

Marginalization and social exclusion are disgrace on the humanity. It is hostile to democratic ethics of a nation. With globalization, the vehemence of marginalization and exclusion has elongated, at least in developing countries. Marginalization and social exclusion are factors responsible for promoting inequality and inequity in development achievement. The marginalized and socially excluded groups are not only excluded from the mainstream of the development process but also deprived of the fruits of development. Their level of participation is low in the development process, i.e. in the formulation, implementation and monitoring of developmental projects and programmes that are intended to improve their livelihood and quality of life. In fact, they are being denied of human and social rights and opportunities. It is observed that in India they are deliberately sidelined from the mainstream decision-making process. Their participation in the village council (gram sabha) is low. Even if they are the head of the village panchayat (village assembly), many of them are compelled to act on the whims of the socio-economically powerful groups and opinion leaders of the village. In other words, even if empowered through affirmative measures, they are deprived of 'functioning'.

Politics is a game of money and muscle power, which pushes the marginalized to the bottom line. One of the illustrious examples of political marginalization is Sudan, where it has been commonly established that various groups and regions have been marginalized or excluded outright from political and economic processes, such as political participation and economic development (Deng 1995). This marginalization and exclusion has been deliberately applied and institutionalized in the ruling methods, governance and policies of Sudan's 'marginalizing state', which has safeguarded its minority central reverence Arab–Muslim governing elite's exclusive control of political power (Ylonen 2009). The *Khap* panchayats (caste council) in Haryana, where the powerful *Jat* community undermining the functioning of democratically elected panchayat headed by the member from the Dalit community, is an illustrious example of sociopolitical marginalization. According to Ray (2010), the assertion of *Khap* panchayats is to legitimize their role and relevance in dictating social justice based on traditions and customs of the caste system. She saw that Dalits and women are the worst sufferers of the brutalities of *Khap* panchayats.

Socio-economically marginalized groups have poor access to financial, physical and natural capital. Majority of them belong to BPL families and are dependent on the public distribution system for food security. They are incapable of buying food from the free market because of low purchasing power. They are hard hit during the lean season when they do not get casual employment in the agriculture and its related sector. In the rural labour market, they are not paid wages as per the minimum rate fixed by the government but are paid wages as decided by the whims and wishes of the private landlords, contractors, petty businessmen and other private or individual employers. They are victims of the labour market discrimination and are excluded from the highly monopolistic and oligopolistic market structure in developing countries. They constitute gigantic percentage of workforce in the informal sector. Therefore, poverty is high among the marginalized and socially excluded groups. Devicienti and Poggi (2007) argued that the dynamics of poverty and social exclusion are found to be interrelated, with positive spill-over effects that make the two processes mutually reinforcing. DFID (2005) argued that social exclusion is often a cause of poverty, while World Bank (2000) viewed that discrimination on the basis of gender, ethnicity, race, religion or social status can lead to social exclusions and lock people into long-term poverty traps. Because of social exclusion in India, it is observed that the culturally and socially discriminated or marginalized groups reside in separate clusters and lack much interaction with the mainstream population of the villages. The percentage of *pacca* (build with bricks and stone) houses is very less among the marginalized group and that of households having access to safe drinking water, sanitation facilities and electricity is also less as compared to other groups of population. This reflects that social exclusion is an important cause of poverty, because it leads to exclusion from the job market leading to unemployment, underemployment and low income, which ultimately ends in poverty. The eradication of poverty and income inequalities among the social marginalized groups is a big challenge before the welfare state in developing countries.

Poverty and Hunger among the Marginalized

- In Vietnam, the government estimates that, by 2010, 90% of the poverty in the country will be among ethnic minorities.
- In Bolivia, the poverty rate among the non-white population is 37%, compared with 17% for the white population.
- In Tanzania, households with disabled members are 20% more likely to be living in poverty.
- 100 million older people live on less than a dollar a day, and 80% of older people in developing countries have no regular income.
- Women account for nearly 70% of the 1.2 billion people currently living in extreme poverty.

Source: UNDP (2005).

The challenge before developing countries is to develop human capital formation among the marginalized and socially excluded groups to enable them to raise their quality of life and earn a sustainable livelihood. According to UNDP (2011), human development goes beyond the goals of poverty reduction to take into consideration those who are not necessarily poor but who may be illiterate and discriminated against or without access to health care. UNDP further viewed that high levels of human development cannot be achieved when some groups and individuals are excluded socially and face barriers to their participation in economic, social, cultural and political lives. The socially excluded groups are sometimes sidelined and are also deprived of taking admission in good educational institutions, and therefore, their level of education is very low. Thorat et al. (2007) noted that exclusion and discrimination can occur in terms of access to social needs supplied by the government or public institutions, or by private institutions in education and housing including CPR such as water bodies, grazing land and other land of common use. In India, the literacy rate and the level of education among the SCs and STs are lower as compared to other caste groups. Good teachers are not adequately motivated to work in the tribal areas and teach the socially marginalized groups. Despite constitutional prohibitions, the social tag of 'untouchability' is still alive in the hearts and minds of the upper caste groups towards certain marginalized sections of population. The 'untouchables' located at the bottom of the caste hierarchy have far fewer economic and social rights (Thorat et al. 2007).

Like the education status, the health status among the marginalized groups of the population is low and the mortality and morbidity is high among these groups of population as compared to the other mainstream groups. From a field-level study, it is observed that grass-roots health workers belonging to Hindu communities are rarely motivated to deliver services to SCs population (Kaur and Pattanaik 2000).

Maternal Health and Child Mortality among the Marginalized

- In Brazil, nearly three times as many Black women as White women die from the complications of pregnancy and childbirth.
- In Guatemala, the number of children dying before they reach their fifth birthday is 56 in every 1,000 for children of European descent, compared with 79 in every 1,000 in indigenous population.
- In India, it is estimated that discrimination against girls increases the total rate of child mortality by 20%.
- In Africa, 80% of 15–19 year olds living in the HIV and AIDS are women.

Source: UNDP (2005).

Universal Primary Education

- In Serbia and Montenegro, 30% of Roma children have never attended primary school.
- In the Indian states of Uttar Pradesh and Bihar, primary school enrolment for SC and ST girls is 37%, compared with 60% for girls from non-scheduled castes. Among boys from non-scheduled castes, 77% are enrolled.

Source: UNDP (2005).

The challenge before developing countries is to improve the access of socially marginalized community to the financial capital which is another important constituent of sustainable livelihood and development. The socially excluded groups that have lower access to labour market are also impoverished in their reach to financial and capital markets. Because of low income and poor collaterals, they are less empowered to open bank accounts and to have equal access to credit facilities. Moreover, as they are cut off from the mainstream, they lack adequate knowledge about the financial and capital markets. As a result, less number of entrepreneurs is seen belonging to a marginalized community. Their social exclusion ultimately ends in financial exclusion. It is rightly remarked that in the developing world access to finance is unevenly distributed and promoting 'inclusive finance' means intensifying the depth of outreach and providing services to marginalized groups, especially women, reaching beyond conventional microcredit to the people at the bottom of the economic pyramid.[1]

Marginalized and socially excluded groups have also poor access to social capital, which helps in the creation of human capital, produces public order, enhances people's participation, creates partnerships and contributes to social and economic well-being and sustainable development (Holm 2004; Thomas 1996). While emphasizing the role of social capital in development, the World Bank (2000) has envisaged that

1. social capital can 'bridge' different groups by enabling cross-cutting and inclusive ties;
2. social relationships and networks are a form of capital that may bring benefits to their members; and
3. the interplay of kin and communal bonding and bridging social relations shape cross-cutting social capital and social cohesion.

Another challenge before the developing nations is to bring social cohesion and promote social networking which is crucial for the attainment of sustainable development goals. The people belonging to the marginalized sections are largely excluded to be the members and participate in the social-level institutions such as youth clubs, mahila mandals (women group), water committees and other village-level statutory bodies and social institutions. Besides, poor social networking between the socially excluded groups of population and their counterparts creates misunderstanding, which sometimes results in social and community tension and even leads to communal violence. Thus, the exclusion of the marginalized from access to the social capital is a violation of social and human rights of the socially excluded groups.

SECTION II: WOMEN EMPOWERMENT

Development requires good governments that give men and women equal voices in decision-making and policy implementation.

—Parpart et al. (2000)

The female half of the world's human capital is undervalued and underutilized the world over…. Better use of the world's female population could increase economic growth, reduce poverty, enhance societal well-being and help ensure sustainable development in all countries.

—OECD (2008)

Empowerment of women, socially, economically, humanly and politically, is a critical challenge before developing countries aiming at attaining inclusive and sustainable growth. Development will be inclusive only when both men and women contribute substantially and sustainably to economic growth and development. Women are unique contributors to sustainable development. The sustainable livelihood is ensured only when women are empowered, earn for the family and take part in the household decision-making process. However, they are seen to be largely marginalized in all spheres such as social, economic, political and so on because of gender-biased stereotype attached to their empowerment. In many families, they are denied going out alone, not permitted to talk to and mix with men other than the family's male members, prevented by the family members to take part in public meetings, not encouraged to apply and do hard jobs such as those in army, industry, air force, navy, driving and so on and are prevented to take part in politics. General neglect, looking down, preventing or denial of opportunity to women to take part in social, economic and political spheres means elimination of the contribution of half of the population towards economic growth and development.

Many developed nations that are found to have higher human and social development indexes have successfully empowered their women in all spheres, i.e. economic, social and political. The illustrious examples are the Scandinavian nations that rank high among the comity of nations in social and human development indexes, and are found to have effectively empowered their women vis-à-vis men. In other words, women's socio-economic, human and political development status is high in these nations. But in the processes and practices of development at the national, state, community and family levels in other countries, particularly religiously orthodox countries, it has been realized. It is a general saying that when a man is empowered it is an individual who is empowered, on the other hand, if a woman is empowered her children are empowered, a family is empowered, the community and the society to which she belongs is empowered. This results in raising the quality of living of the family and higher economic growth and development of the state as well as the nation. It is not a flight of fancy, but delicately women empowerment is necessary for the upliftment of a family and society and the development of a nation state. The empowerment of women is both directly and indirectly interconnected with the economic growth and the development of a nation.

The relationship between women and development is a central issue in the contemporary globalized and neoliberal world. Early development initiatives largely ignored women (Connelly, Li, Macdonald and Parpart 2000). According to Boserup (1970), most of the developmental projects are particularly relating to agriculture undermined women's economic opportunities and autonomy. The participation of women during the freedom struggle movement against the colonial rule in different nations of Asia and Africa ruled by the colonial power fortified the role of women in social and political movements. In India, the Queen of Jhansi, Rani Lakshmibai, is one of the most sighted examples frequently given while narrating the role of women in the freedom struggle.

WOMEN EMPOWERMENT AND DEVELOPMENT: ISSUES AND CHALLENGES

Women economic, social and political empowerment is essential for the development of developing countries. The contribution of women towards the economic growth and development and their socio-economic status in the developed countries is higher as compared to developing countries where the status of women is low in all spheres. The main issue and challenge before developing countries is to empower women for the inclusive and holistic development of developing countries.

WOMEN AND ECONOMIC EMPOWERMENT

Women's economic empowerment is a prerequisite for sustainable development and pro-poor growth (OECD 2012). According to an international estimation, women represent 70% of world's poor. The statistics indicate that women are more likely than men to be poor and at risk of hunger because of the systematic discrimination they face in education, health care, employment and access to and control of physical and financial assets. Poverty, asset-lessness and hunger are more egregious among women-headed households. These sometimes push many single and deserted women to absolute poverty and even many are found begging in many developing countries of South Asia. While cautioning the rising unemployment among women, the ILO estimates that the economic slow downturn could lead to 22 million more unemployed women in 2009, jeopardizing the gains made in the last few decades in women's empowerment (UN Women). The economic vulnerability of women flows from their weakly defined property rights to major productive assets such as agricultural land and houses, as in many countries customs and traditions restrict their ability to own parental properties. As in practice, female children are given dowry during marriage and the immovable landed property rests with the male children. Thus, economic discrimination of women begins from the family. After marriage, newly married women are customarily not allowed to take part in any income earning activities in and around their locality and village, except in case of a few impoverished families who migrate to city and engage their female members in menial income-earning activities. Therefore, a gigantic percentage of working women are agricultural labourers, casual labourers or those who are self-employed in paltry income-earning activities, and are found to be employed in low-paid jobs. Some of the characteristics of women's economic empowerment are that:

1. They are less likely to get a paid job.
2. Their jobs are more likely to be concentrated in the informal economy and in low-value-added sectors in low-paid jobs characterized by poor working conditions such as more hours of work and less wages.
3. A large percentage of women workforce are unskilled.
4. They are mostly engaged in non-paid household activities never being considered having any economic value and even not considered in national income accounting.
5. They are largely marginalized in the labour market.

The economic empowerment of women refers to building of capacities, creating an enabling environment and providing them with job opportunity so that they earn and contribute to the economic growth and development of their family and nation state. According to Eyben et al. (2008), economic empowerment is the capacity of women and men to participate in, contribute to and benefit from growth processes in ways which

Table 14.1 *Women Agricultural Holders in Selected Countries, 2011*

Country	% of Women Land Holders
Italy	32.2
Spain	28.8
Thailand	27.4
France	23.1
UK	18.8
Malaysia	13.1
India	10.9
Nepal	8.1
Philippines	10.8

Source: Food Agricultural Organization. 'The State of Food and Agriculture 2010–11', *Women in Agriculture*, 2011, Rome, Italy. Available at: http://www.fao.org/docrep/013/i2050e/i2050e.pdf (accessed on 7 December 2016).

recognize the value to their contributions, respect their dignity and make it possible to negotiate a fairer distribution of the benefits of growth (Table 14.1).

ILO estimated that the share of employed people in the world's working age population (employment-to-population ratio) was 49.1% for women and 74.3% for men in 2007 (ILO 2008). Women constitute 41% of the total employment in the agriculture sector, and regions with the highest proportion of women in the agriculture sector are East and Southeast Asia, the Middle East and Sub-Saharan Africa (ILO 2008). Goldin (1995) finds that higher levels of female labour-force employment tend to exist at lower income levels when agriculture dominates. However, as income rises and manufacturing sectors gain prominence, limited educational opportunities and stigmatically social customs depress female labour-force participation in the non-farm sector (Clark et al. 1991; Forsythe et al. 2000). However, women's economic empowerment and their participation in income-earning activities reduce poverty at the household level (Table 14.2).

Another challenge of the economic empowerment of women is the discrimination in the economic status of the rural and urban women, skilled and unskilled women, educated and uneducated women. Globalization has boosted the chances of educated women to get employment in the services sectors in the liberal democratic countries, particularly in tourism, IT, banking and insurances, business process outsourcing and other gender-sensitive service sectors such as health care and education. Economic empowerment will open their door to social and political empowerment. OECD (2012) advocated that economic empowerment increases women's access to economic resources and opportunities including jobs in financial services, property and other productive assets, skill development and market information. Marginalization in most of developing countries is a gender-related phenomenon. The unemployment rate among women is very high in African countries as compared to the developed countries of the West. The World Development Indicators 2016 data depict that the percentage of female unemployment of the female workforce for years 2011–15 was 21.5% in Botswana, while the rates were 6.0%, 5.8%, 6.9% and 3.9% in the USA, the UK, Denmark and China, respectively. The data also reveal that the percentage of female vulnerable employment to the female

Table 14.2 *% of Female Employment in Agriculture, Industry and Services, 2005*

Country	Employment Agriculture	Employment Industry	Employment in Services
Bangladesh	68	13	19
Brazil	16	13	71
China	5	40	53
Canada	2	11	88
Ethiopia	75	8	16
Finland	3	12	85
Germany	2	16	82
Indonesia	44	16	40
Mexico	5	19	76
Pakistan	67	15	18
India	71	14	15
Korea (Re Public)	9	17	47
Thailand	4	19	41
UK	1	9	90
USA	1	10	90

Source: World Bank (2016).

employment was 80% in Tanzania, while it was only 8% in Denmark in the year 2013. However, overcoming intra-women discrimination, i.e. urban and rural, rich and poor nation state, backward and forward community discrimination, in women's status is a challenge before developing countries. Furthermore, the country has to formulate policies to overcome distress and vulnerable employment among the female workforce.

Gender Discrimination at a Glance

1. Of the World's 776 million illiterate adults, two-thirds are women (UNFPA 2010).
2. More than 134 million women are 'missing' worldwide because of a preference for boy babies that leads to sex-selective abortions and neglect of infant girls (UNDP 2010).
3. Up to 70% of women experience violence in their life time (UNIFEM 2005).
4. More than 101 million primary school age children are not attending school, and more than half of them are girl (UNFPA 2010).
5. More than 350,000 women die each year-one every 90 seconds-from complications of pregnancy of child birth. Nearly all these deaths (99%) are in developing countries (World Bank 2010).

In most of the households, whether women are earning or not earning, they are the managers of the household finance and household economy. Therefore, there is a need for financial literacy among women in order to educate and make them capable of the following:

- To manage the financial income, expenditure and savings.
- Plan for future anticipated expenditure in the old age, i.e. marriage of children, health care expenditure during old age, housing and so on through judicious calculation of future saving and pension.
- Create women entrepreneurs in the agriculture, industry and service sectors.
- Educating about various savings and pension plans of the government.
- Opening bank accounts, taxation, insurance, pension plan and so on.

With the increased provision of wage and self-employment for women through MGNREGA and SHGs in India at the grass-roots level, financial literacy among women has become inevitable for the better management of household poverty and sustainable livelihood. Another important issue critical to economic empowerment of women is gender budgeting which means allocation of finance in the annual budget prepared at various levels, i.e. the central, state, district, block and village panchayat levels of a certain amount of financial allocation for the economic empowerment of women. Gender budgeting has attracted attention of national and international agencies and is a gateway to effective empowerment of women in both rural and urban areas, and would be instrumental in enabling nations attain sustainable development goals.

The empowerment of single women such as a widow, an unmarried and a separated lady is a key concern of gender well-being strategy. These women are vulnerable to poverty and general helplessness. In many circumstances, they are found to be exploited, castigated and segregated by the family and the society. The social and economic empowerment of single women is a critical challenge for the nation state. A more recent US and cross-national research in developed countries confirms that older, single women continue to be disproportionately poor as compared to older single men and older married couples (Gillen and Kim 2009).

WOMEN'S EMPOWERMENT IN LEGISLATIVE, EXECUTIVE AND JUDICIARY

Women as legislatures and parliamentarians and also as executives and judges will not only gain as an individual but act as role models for other women to follow. It will enable them to raise their voices at different forum of development discussion at the national, regional and local levels. Customarily, women are less represented in politics in many countries, except a few Scandinavian countries. In other words, gender disparities and politics go hand in hand. Except for a few families having a political background, women are not encouraged either by the parents or in-laws to join politics. The male guardian of the households consider that if his wife and daughter-in-law joins politics, then the society will look down upon him, and if his daughter joins politics, then they will not get a suitable match for her. Therefore, women are largely discouraged to join politics. However, it is seen that when women join politics, they excel in their political profession. There are a large number of instances of the same, e.g. Margaret Thatcher, Benizir Bhutto, Sheikh Hasina and, in Indian politics, Indira Gandhi, Sarojini Naidu, Mrs Sonia Gandhi, Ms Mayawati, Mrs Sheila Dixit, Ms Mamta Banerjee. In Scandinavian countries, women representation in the country's parliament is higher as compared to other countries of the world.

The affirmative measure of reservation of seats for women in legislative assemblies and parliament will enable them to be elected to these political and legislative decision-making bodies. This will lead to gender political empowerment and social equity in political participation. True et al. (2012) were of the view that gender quotas and reservations have significantly improved women's political representation at the national and local levels. It is seen that even after the reservation, women are victims of political discrimination and suffer from gender stereotypes in political empowerment.

Even if elected to the parliaments of different countries, women are not given important portfolios and ministries compared to their men counterparts. The challenge is to promote the real political empowerment of women, where the majority of them will exercise their political power without the pressure of their husband, relatives and other male members. It is seen that women heading many village panchayats are merely elected heads and the real functions of the village panchayats are being performed by their husband, brother and other close relatives (Table 14.3).

The representation of women in executive and judiciary positions will help them to take up gender-related issues and fight for gender rights. Some scholar argued that the presence of a few women on state supreme courts and high profile women lawyers could

Table 14.3 *Percentage of Seat Held by Women in National Parliament*

Country	Women in National Parliament
Bangladesh	20
Brazil	10
China	24
Canada	26
Ethiopia	39
Finland	42
Germany	37
Indonesia	17
Mexico	42
Pakistan	21
India	12
Korea (Re Public)	16
Thailand	6
UK	29
USA	19

Source: World Bank (2016).

be the reality of the status of women legally (Costello, 1997). Global figures indicate that on an average, women comprise just over 25% of the world's judicial officers, and although in some jurisdictions these percentages are higher, in many other countries and regions the numbers fall to far below 10% (International Commission on Jurist 2014). Tokas' (2012) study 'Position of Women in Indian Judiciary: An Analysis' has the following findings: (a) in the Supreme Court, out of a total of 26 judges only two (7%) are females and 24 (93%) are males; (b) the data on High Court judges of 30 states show that out of 605 judges, 52 (8.5%) are females and 553 (91.4%) are males; (c) the data of 30 districts court show that there are 963 judges in the district courts, out of which 277 (28%) are females and 868 (72%) are males and (d) out of 955,013 lawyers only 98,556 (10%) are females, while 856,457 (90%) are males. Women representation in the judicial system of countries is highly marginal. In traditional developing societies, seeing women as a lawyer is perceived to be highly unconventional. Geneva Forum Series 1 on 'Women and the Judiciary' has stressed that the composition of society is to be perceived as legitimate and capable of delivering equal justice and upholding equality before law. In addition, judiciaries must be representation of the societies they service and there must be no discrimination in appointments on any grounds, including sex. They underlined the importance of judicial diversity and of ensuring women's full and equal participation in the judiciary.[2]

Women in executive positions in various government and private sector offices will not only raise the status of women in the society but enable those offices to perform better. Kingsley (1944) mentioned that 'in a democracy competence alone is not enough. The Public service also has to be representative if the state is to liberate than enslave'. He further stressed that 'bureaucracies to be democratic, must be representation of the groups they serve'. There are less number of bureaucrats at higher levels of administration. However, as far as India is concerned, over the period of time the number of women joining in the IAS is on the rise. In years 2015 and 2016, women topped the IAS qualifying list; this supports the rising status of women in the contemporary bureaucratic system in India. A study of McKinsey and Company (2007) suggests that the companies where women are more strongly represented at board or top management levels are also the companies that perform best.

WOMEN AND HEALTH

Taking care of the health of women, who take care of the health of the family, is critical to development. A healthy mother can construct a healthy family and all healthy mothers can build a developed and sustainable nation. The World Health Organization expects that every mother maintains good health, learns the art of child care, has normal delivery and bears healthy children. Healthy women can give birth to healthy children, who can grow up as healthy adults and can effectively contribute to national productivity and economic growth. Today, there is growing recognition among health professionals, researchers and policymakers of the widespread and profound implications of gender-based inequalities in health (Ostlin et al., 2006). Health status of women particularly belonging to the South Asian and Sub-Saharan African countries is considerably low as compared to the developed nations of the West. The World Development Indicator 2016 data show that the maternal mortality ratio of Nigeria and Bangladesh is respectively 200 and 50 times more than that of Finland. Women face health discrimination throughout different phases of their life starting from the womb of the mother to their grave. The health status of women particularly in South Asia and Sub-Saharan Africa region is quite low. The WHO Fact Sheet (2013) reveals that: (a) girls are more likely than boys to suffer sexual abuse; (b) almost 99% of maternal death every year occurs in developing countries; (c) globally, the cardiovascular diseases often thought to be a 'male' problem is the number one killer of women; (d) breast cancer is the leading cancer killer among women aged 20–59 years worldwide; (e) more than 15 million of the 135 million live births worldwide are among girls aged 15–19 years and (f) in 2011, about 820,000 women and men aged 15–24 were newly infected with HIV in low-income countries, of which more than 60% of them were women (Table 14.4).

Some of the features of health status of women in developing countries are: (a) women belonging to impoverished families are deprived of better nutritional care during their pregnancy giving birth to low weight babies and even a few critical cases end in either infant or maternal mortality; (b) it is observed that women engaged in hard labour activities in the rural areas and in the construction sector of the urban areas perform work and duties till the advance stage of their pregnancy and, thus, in the process become high risk mothers during the natal stage; (c) the percentage of delivery conducted in health care institutions and by trained health personnel is low in rural areas; (d) postnatal x care services made available by the health personnel and availed by the beneficiaries is very poor, for which frequent pregnancies, abortions of unwanted pregnancies, low use of family planning methods for maintaining gap between pregnancies are being seen and (e) still for getting health care services from the health care institutions and qualified doctors, women in rural areas and religiously traditional societies are dependent on their husbands and have to seek permission of their in-laws. Researchers believe that the prime determinants of gender inequities in health are social and economic disadvantages related to factors such as the decision-making power, income, employment, working environment,

Table 14.4 *Maternal Mortality Ratio, 2015*

Country	Per 100,000 Live Birth
Bangladesh	176
Belgium	07
China	27
Ethiopia	353
Finland	03
India	174
Japan	05
Nigeria	814
Tanzania	398
UK	09
USA	14

Source: World Bank (2016).

Table 14.5 *Phases of Gender Health Discrimination*

Women's Life Cycle	Types of Discrimination
Prenatal	Prenatal sex selection, battering during pregnancy, coerced pregnancy
Infancy	Female foeticide, emotional and physical abuse, differential access to food, medical care
Childhood	Genital cutting, incest and sexed abuse, differential access to food, medical care and education, child prostitution
Adolescents	Dating and courtship violence, economically coerced sex, sexual abuse in work place, rape sexual harassment, forced prostitution
Reproductive	Abuse of women by intimate partner, marital rape, dowry abuse, sexual abuse with disability
Old Age	Abuse of widows, elder abuse (which affects mostly women)

Source: Heise (1994).

education, housing, nutrition and individual behaviours (Ostlin et al. 2006). In many places, cultural taboos make it impossible for women to seek medical care from male health providers but there is, at the same time, a shortage of female health professionals (WHO 2009) (Table 14.5).

Women are subject to health discrimination at all stages of their life cycle. Adolescence health care, e.g. their health education, nutritional care and right age of marriages, will promote health status of women in the long run. Empowerment of women to take care of their own health is important for the economic growth and development of a nation. Sickness in working women will result in loss of man days and reduction in income and output. Furthermore, medical expenditure by the family in health care of women will affect the economic health of the family. A nation cannot prosper if its women who constitute nearly half of its population remain sick and morbid.

WOMEN AND EDUCATION

Education of women is a powerful tool to enhance the contribution of women towards economic growth and development. Decades of empirical evidences, practical experiences, case studies and observations support the robust association between women's educational attainment and positive development outcomes. It is now conventional wisdom in development discourses that where education levels are higher among women, fertility rates are lower, family size is smaller and women's health and economic status are stronger (Dollar and Galti 1999; Herz and Sperling 2001; Wasen 1999). There is even evidence to suggest that in setting where education is more gender equitable, economic growth is more robust (Wasen 1999) (Table 14.6). *The World Development Report* (2012) notes that 'in both high and low income countries, gender difference in education has contributed significantly to the productivity and wage gap between men and women'.

Table 14.6 *School Enrolment Ratio, Tertiary, Female (% Gross), 2013*

Country	Percentage
Australia	102
Belgium	82
China	32
Bhutan	9
Finland	100
India	23
Japan	60
Pakistan	10
Tanzania	2
UK	65
USA	104

Source: The World Bank Group (2016). Available at: http://data.worldbank.org/indicator/SE.TER.ENRR.FE (accessed on 8 December 2016).

Education in its widest sense is a potential instrument that would empower women to reach their full potential. Some of the roles of education in women empowerment are as follows:

1. Women's educational empowerment will enhance their social, economic and political empowerment.
2. Improved education status of women will contribute significantly towards household income, economic growth and development.
3. Education of women will raise their employment prospect and help them to raise income of the family and drag the family out of poverty and hunger, and also raise the quality of life.
4. It will enhance the efficiency of women deployed in the agricultural, industrial and service sectors and, thus, will be helpful to raise productivity and national income.
5. It will promote mobility, modernity and structural transformation in the developing society.
6. It will curtail unwanted fertility and improve demographic situation.
7. It will promote gender autonomy and women's social networking in the society.
8. It will improve the effectiveness of gender-driven and gender-based social institutions such as women SHGs and mahila mandals.
9. It will improve political education among women and enable them to vote, contest and be elected to political institutions.
10. It will curtail gender atrocities at various levels.
11. It will enable the nation to attain sustainable development, as women are the great conservers of natural resources such as forest and water and nurturers of budding human resources.

12. It will strengthen the civil society.
13. Educational empowerment of women will hasten the process of inclusive development in developing countries.

The challenge before developing countries is to raise the level of education among women. More number of women must be conferred with technical education which will not only raise their economic status but also enhance gender inter- and intra-country mobility. In other words, education of women has multiplier effect as compared to the education of men. Illiterate and less educated women are subject to greater degrees of marginalization in the labour market. The countries belonging to South Asia and Africa in particular are required to raise their female tertiary GER. The economic growth and development depends on GER. Education is the seed of development and any investment in education of women will promote social justice and equity. It will also raise the contribution of women to economic growth and social development. Marginalization of women in the society is deterrent to sustainable and inclusive development.

WOMEN AND SELF-RELIANCE

Self is an essential tool for sustainable development. According to UNCHR, '[S]elf reliance is the social and economic ability of an individual, a household, or a community to meet essential needs (including protection, food, water, shelter, personal safety, health and education) in a sustainable manner with dignity.' One of the vital aspects of women empowerment is to make women self-reliant. It will help them not only to take care of themselves but of their family, society and the nation. Economic self-reliance is essential to empower them to take part in household decision-making. It will be helpful to reduce poverty among women, synchronize gender disparities and strengthen household and rural economy. The *Kudmshree*, a unique women SHG programme of Kerala, has not only empowered women economically but also promoted women's participation in management of household economy and their effective political participation in panchayati raj institutions. Strengthening the organization and leadership capacity of informal women workers fosters economic self-reliance and increases women's participation in politics, governance and management.[3] Social reliance can help them to effectively participate in the community decision-making process. It will enhance women's social networking power and unite them to fight for their rights.

Journalism Is a Tool for Economic Self-reliance of Women: Afghanistan

Sahar Speaks, a program that uses journalism as a tool to educate, employ and empower Afghan women to make their voices heard. Successful applicants work with mentors, who are all female foreign correspondents, to produce quality reporting that is then published by the Huffington Post. Since training started, a dozen young Afghan women have already found jobs in global newsrooms.

Source: https://www.facebook.com/AfghanCycles/posts/543233115829215?comment_tracking=%7B%22tn%22%3A%22O%22%7D (accessed on 26 June 2016).

Stitching Brings Economic Self-reliance to Rural Women—Bangladesh

Ornamental stitching has now become a very effective venture in recent years bringing economic self-reliance to thousands of the rural unemployed, poor and distressed women in the northern districts, reports BSS.

Ornamental stitching like embroidering and spangling on female clothes continues to expand fast attracting more and more rural women following huge demand of their quality handworks in the markets. Thousands of rural women have already changed fortune and improved life standard after winning over abject poverty by earning through embroidering, spangling and ornamental stitching on saree, three pieces and many other female clothes.

According to Executive Director of Rangpur-based research organization 'Northbengal Institute of Development Studies' Dr Syed Samsuzzaman, some rural women started such initiatives at their homes in scattered ways at the initial stage seven to ten years back. 'Over the years, the home-based embroidery works have now got the shape of a growing cottage industry reducing poverty in rural areas with brighter prospect also to change and strengthen the rural macro- economy,' he added.

Rangpur Regional Coordinator of HELVETAS Swiss Intercooperation Mamunur Rashid said many of the successful rural women have launched small-scale enterprises after getting training and assistance from different GO-NGOs in association with local traders and entrepreneurs.

Source: http://www.theindependentbd.com/printversion/details/31005 (accessed on 26 June 2016).

WOMEN AND SUSTAINABLE DEVELOPMENT

Women are the key agents of sustainable development of the family, society and the nation. Sustainable development in developing countries cannot be possible without the sustainable participation of women in all spheres such as economic, social, human, political and cultural. Women are the worshippers, protectors, preservers and promoters of environment and natural resources. According to UN Women, sustainable development requires action of three fronts: social, economic and environmental, and women are central to progress in each area.[4] Women's economic empowerment will ensure sustainable livelihood to the poverty-stricken rural households. Their social empowerment will enable them to take rational action regarding the education, health and social well-being of their family, thus building up a more sustainable household, society and the nation. The equal participation of women in all spheres will be helpful in the attainment of SDGs. A UN Women publication, 2013, notes that if women had the same access as men to productive assets, the agriculture output in 34 developing countries would rise by an estimated average of up to 4%. This would reduce the number of undernourished people in these countries by 17%, translating up to 150 million fewer hungry people.[5] Thus, women's social, economic and environmental empowerment is quite critical for the sustainable development of the family, society and the nation. The Pradhan Mantri Ujjwala Yojana which aims at providing LPG gas connection to 50 million women belonging to BPL families is an illustrious step in the direction of women and sustainable development in India. It will discourage traditional methods of energy used in cooking such as woods, paddy husk, cow dung cake and so on and will be helpful to check environmental pollution, promote women health, save time and energy spent in the collection of traditional energy material and, thus, can utilize the time and energy of women in income earning and sustainable development activities.

Women and Sustainable Initiatives

In Ghana, UN Women's Fund for Gender Equality has introduced green cook stoves in an area where climate change has fuelled rapid desertification.

The 14 million members of the Vietnam Women's Union is building resilience to the flood and other national disasters that occur more frequently each year.

Waste management Initiative in Nepal run by Women's Environment Committee and supported by a local municipality reduces waste through recycling, establishes biogas plants run on organic waste and offers a savings and credit scheme for women.

Source: http://www.unwomen.org/en/what-we-do/economic-empowerment/sustainable-development-and-climate-change (accessed on 6 December 2016).

Women, who constitute nearly 50% of the total population on earth, have to be effectively empowered in order to enable them to contribute towards sustainable growth and development. Marginalization of women will retard economic growth and elongate poverty and inequality in developing countries. When we empower women, it does not mean that we are sympathizing on them; rather, it is their right as a human being to be empowered in the society.

SECTION III: INCLUSIVE DEVELOPMENT

Inclusive growth is the process and the outcome, where all group of people have participated in the organization of growth and have benefited from it.

—UNDP (2008)

There is inclusive growth when all members of a society participate in and contribute to the growth process equally, regardless of their individual circumstances.

—Rauniyar and Kanbu (2009)

Development is a multidimensional concept. It aims at positive and productive change in all dimensions such as economic, social, political, cultural, human and so on of an economy. The goal of development is to develop all through the participation of all. In other words, the development process needs to follow the democratic principle, i.e. 'development of the people, by the people and for the people'. This is what is called 'inclusive development'. Development of a certain section of the population while keeping majority in underdeveloped conditions cannot be called as inclusive development. The holistic development presupposes development of all and all for development and that no one should be excluded. However, in most of the countries and particularly in developing countries it is perceived that many people are excluded or marginalized in the development process. This creates social, economic, human and political inequalities. The higher economic growth rate achieved amidst inequalities can neither be inclusive nor sustainable. Inclusive growth desires that the gain incurred from the growth needs to be spent for the development of the poorest of the poor, excluded and marginalized in order to bring equity in the society. In other words, growth benefits must be shared and need to tickle down for the benefits of those who have not been benefited by the growth.

MEANING AND COMPONENTS

Inclusive development has become one of the emerging concepts in the political economy of developing countries. It has become more emerging particularly in developing countries marred with the obnoxious division of the society on the basis of caste, class, gender, colour, ethnicity and so on. Besides, it is also seen that population belonging to certain geographical areas particularly hilly, desert and other difficult terrain are either excluded from the mainstream or marginally benefited from growth and development. Inclusive development is very crucial for developing countries of South Asia, Africa and Latin America, where the society is too much stratified and the level of disparities across the regions and among different groups of population is very high. The gains from productivity and benefits of economic growth are not equally distributed or the benefits of growth are not pro-poor and inclusive. A commission on growth and development set up by the World Bank defines inclusiveness as a concept that encompasses equity, equality of opportunity and protection in the market and employment transition (World Bank 2008). According to UNDP (2008), inclusion means that people are part of the social, economic, political and cultural lives of their country, their voices are heard and they are able to use their capabilities and access resources including financial and business opportunities.

Inclusive development lays emphasis on the principle of economic equity, distributive and social justice. It believes in equality in participation and considers that the economic growth achieved amidst social exclusion cannot be economically and socially sustainable. In inclusive development, contributions made by each individual including disabled, women and other marginalized are valued, promoted and quantified. The process of inclusion engages each individual and makes people feel valued, which is essential for the development, not only of the individual but of the entire community in which they live. According to Miller and Katz (2002), inclusion is 'a sense of belonging: feeling respected, valued for who you are; feeling a level of supportive energy and commitment from others so that you can do your best'.

Inclusive development has several dimensions that have been discussed as follows:

1. **Economic dimension** urges that those i.e. the lower and backwards castes, women, disabled, transgender, aged and so on who are excluded in the process of economic development and are deprived of economic opportunity to contribute

to economic growth and development and have to be effectively included. They have to be provided with opportunity and should be enabled to contribute to sustainable development of the nation state. It also aims at reducing income inequality and synchronizing income gap between the rich and poor, between skilled and unskilled manpower and the asset owner and asset-less. Besides the reduction of inequality and the promotion of equity, the economic dimension of inclusive development needs to focus on the reduction of poverty among the socially marginalized and excluded group of population. It focuses on unfolding economic opportunities for excluded groups through building up their capabilities and other affirmative measures, so that they contribute equally like those of the economically well-ups, to the inclusive growth process. The marginalized groups, ones excluded from the labour market because of the social tag attached to them, have to be gainfully included. Trenhaft and Rubin (2013) were of the view that economic inclusion strategies explicitly connect vulnerable groups to new jobs and economic activity and ensure that new jobs are high-quality ones that offer family-supporting wages, benefits and growth opportunities.

2. Inclusive **social development** is a primary concern of inclusive development in the socially stratified developing countries. Social inclusion desires that different groups of population in a stratified society are included and take part in a participatory way in the process of social development, i.e. education and health care, empowerment of women, disabled, youth and aged, and in the empowerment of socially marginalized (Indian context SCs and STs). It is social exclusion which is one of the responsible factors for economic and political exclusion. Social exclusion on the ground of caste, class, colour, ethnicity, gender, religion and so on for the use of social assets, public institutions and common property resources, i.e. common law, recreation places and religious places, school, hospitals, common village land and so on, is a common feature in many developing countries. Social exclusion prevents social networking and an obstruction to participatory development.

   A socially inclusive society is defined as one where all people feel valued, their differences are respected and their basic needs are met so they can live with dignity (Cappo 2002). It is a process by which efforts are made to ensure that everyone, regardless of their background, experiences and circumstances can gain access to the services and facilities they need to achieve their own potential in life (Social Inclusion Handbook, Limerick City Council, Limerick City, Ireland). Social exclusion affects the social development indicators of the excluded group of population. In the Indian context, the SCs and STs, who are largely excluded from the mainstream on the basis of caste and ethnicity, have lower literacy, low level of education, higher infant mortality rate and maternal mortality rate and low per capita income. The social inclusive measures need to see that the socially excluded groups have equal access to public institutions and CPRs, become members of various social institutions and actively participate in the decision-making process. The government must ensure that the service providers do not follow discriminatory practices and negative attitude while providing services to these socially backward sections of population. Social exclusion is a useful requite of sustainable development.

3. The third important dimension of inclusion is **political inclusion**. Political inclusion means inclusion of all irrespective of their caste, colour, creed, ethnicity and gender in the political development of the nation: to vote in the elections, to contest in the election, to get a ministerial berth proportionate to their population and to take part in the legislative decision-making process. Exclusion of marginalized from the political empowerment at the national, state and local self-government institutions levels is a common feature in almost all the forms of government and even in the participatory democracies. In other words, political inclusion means political empowerment of the marginalized and excluded groups. Customarily, the political positions in all forms of governments are seen to be captured by the socially powerful and economically well-up and by people having muscle and money power. Politics and political parties which deny opportunity to women and socially disadvantaged sections and also pursue caste-based and religion-based politics are divisive and discriminatory and are not considered as inclusive politics. The political exclusion will not be helpful to achieve inclusive and sustainable development. The political inclusion largely encompasses the following:

   (i) to cast votes in the elections to parliament, legislative assemblies and local self-government institutions without fear and favour;
   (ii) to participate and contest in the election at all levels;
   (iii) to be elected to the parliament, legislative assemblies, local self-government institutions, if required, through the affirmative reservation method;
   (iv) to be represented in the ministerial cabinet proportion to their population;
   (v) to be allocated proportionately powerful ministerial berth based on experience and talent and
   (vi) to exercise power and take decision without any pressure from the politically powerful groups in the cabinet and in the party rank.

   Political empowerment ethics desires that if required, necessary affirmative measures have to be promulgated by the nation states to facilitate political empowerment of the socially excluded groups. Political inclusion does not mean that the marginalized and excluded groups are sympathized to take part in politics. It is rather their right to be politically empowered like all others group of population. Besides the elected representatives, these excluded groups need to be adequately represented at the level of functionaries to these bodies at the grass-roots level in local self-government institutions. It is seen that in many tribal-population-dominated districts, less number of tribal are being working as functionaries at the local government level and these positions have been acquired by the non-tribal and also persons from other non-tribal districts having a lack of knowledge about the tribal concerns. This is against the ethos of inclusive development. In a nutshell, political inclusion desires that the excluded and marginalized groups must be empowered, so that they feel included in the entire political development process both as elected representatives and functionaries to various political institutions.
4. The fourth dimension of inclusion is **cultural inclusion**. Inclusive cultural development desires that culture must be an integral part of development. Cultural

development has become an important imperative of inclusive development because the process of globalization by assigning importance to modernization has undermined the role of culture in development. In cultural development, people belonging to various groups with distinct culture, dress code, food habits, dances, festivals, languages and livelihood be included and inclusively contribute towards economic growth and development. In other words, the development approaches and strategies must be culturally inclusive. Cultural inclusion respects cultural pluralism. In other words, the cultural practices of different communities and religious groups need to be respected, valued and promoted.

In many countries of South Asia, Africa and Latin America, the cultural livelihood is a determining factor of the standard of living of many ethnically marginalized communities. It is seen that the process of globalization and modernization started in the beginning of the 1990s, the livelihood style of these ethnic minority groups have been largely undermined. Therefore, these groups of population are feeling excluded from the mainstream. Cultural inclusion means that the rich cultural tradition of these marginalized sections of population must be included in the mainstream, preserved, protected and strengthened. The contribution of cultural trade and economy towards the GDP of a country should be promoted. It must be specifically an integral part of the economic system of the countries having pluralistic culture and rich cultural traditions and values. According to UNESCO, the integration of culture into sustainable development strategies and policies advanced a human-centred and inclusive approach to development, in addition to serving as a powerful socio-economic resource.[6]

5. The fifth dimension of inclusive development is **regional inclusion**. The inclusive development vision must consider that all the regions of a nation are of its own and each and every region has the right to be developed and effectively contribute towards inclusive growth and development. All regions particularly the backward regions, i.e. hilly and dry land areas, must be integrated into the mainstream. The regions must be empowered to contribute towards productivity and economic growth of the nation. The people living in dry land areas have a poor quality of living. It is observed that the dry land areas are excluded from the mainstream, whereas the focus is on the Green Revolution belt, which is empowered by the government through various subsidy measures and is capable to produce more, earn more and contribute more to growth process. This is not the edifice of inclusive development. For example, in the northern Indian states of Punjab and Haryana, more than 90% and 85% of land are irrigated, whereas in the eastern states of Jharkhand and Assam, less than 20% of land is irrigated. Punjab and Haryana together contribute more than 85% of food grains to the national public distribution system, while the dry land areas states such as Bihar, Jharkhand, Orissa and Chhattisgarh are largely the consumers of food grains from the public distribution system. People belonging to the dry land, hilly and other backward regions should not be treated as parasites and dependant on food subsidies, rather must be made capable and empowered to be the food producers rather than food consumers and be a part of the engine of national economic growth and development.

Regional inclusive development means that all regions of the country must be made equally capable and be provided with an equal opportunity to contribute effectively towards the economic growth and development of the country. The *African Economic Outlook* has urged that for promoting regional development, spatial inclusion should be at the heart of Africa's development strategies.[7]

6. The sixth dimension of inclusive development is **sectoral inclusion**. Inclusive sectoral development means that all the sectors of an economy, i.e. primary, secondary and tertiary sectors and organized and unorganized sectors have to be effectively included and empowered to contribute towards inclusive economic growth and development. The sectoral inclusion is a requisite for the balanced growth and development of developing countries. The inclusive sectoral development process presupposes that the countries need to be equal and balanced and, if required, apply unbalanced growth and development strategy, so that the contribution of all the sectors, i.e. primary, secondary and tertiary, to economic growth and development is enhanced. The neglect of the primary sector will affect food grain productivity and basic needs. While the cursory emphasis on the secondary and service sectors could affect employment, income and economic growth rate, the declining contribution of the agriculture sector to the GDP in many developing countries without proportionate decline in the population dependent on the agriculture sector for employment is not a manifestation of inclusive development.

The principle of inclusive development presupposes that as more percentage of marginalized people are residing in the rural areas, it means that more priority has to be given to the agriculture and rural development in the inclusive development process of the nation. The fluctuation in the economic growth rate observed in most of developing countries is largely because of excessive dependence on service sector and poor performance of primary and secondary sectors. People engaged in a particular sector must not feel that they are being excluded or neglected because of less emphasis being assigned to the sector by the government. However, overdependence on a particular sector also means deliberate exclusion of other sectors. Here, inclusive sectoral development veritably means balanced development of all the sectors through a judicious method of unbalancing, so that no sector feels excluded. All the sectors are judiciously empowered with a strategic imbalance technique to effectively and efficiently contribute towards inclusive economic growth and development. Inclusive sectoral development must follow a shared vision which enables all the sectors to share the vision and mission of economic growth and development of a nation.

Finally, the motto of the inclusive development should be: development of all, through the participation of all (*sabke sath sabke vikas*). Every individual irrespective of caste, class, gender, ethnicity, colour and creed must be integrated into the process of growth and development. They must be effectively empowered as per their knowledge and capabilities and be provided with opportunities to contribute to inclusive growth and development, so that they feel that they are the partners and stakeholders of development, not the dormant beneficiaries. Besides, the inclusive development process needs to see that all the actors of development such as private and corporate sector, non-governmental organizations, civil society organizations, opinion leaders, local self-government institutions and other parallel bodies along with the government functionaries are effectively engaged in the inclusive development process.

FACTORS INFLUENCING MARGINALIZATION AND EXCLUSION

Some of the important factors influencing marginalization and exclusion are as follows:

Traditional Believes and Values: Some group of populations are the victim of marginalization because of the prevalence of traditional believes and values in the society. For example, as per the tradition of Hindu religion (Manu Shastra), Brahmins can only perform religious activities and Dalits are not only denied to perform such functions but also are not allowed to enter the temple. This practice is even now stringently followed in rural areas of many states of India. This has resulted in marginalization of Dalits in the social sphere. This social marginalization has inflicted economic and political marginalization on the Dalit community. In this process, they are excluded from the mainstream and are marginalized. The low position of Dalits (depressed class) was nicely described by Blunt (1969) as:

> [A]t all the time the Brahmin priesthood has endeavoured to keep them segregated, not only from the Hindu society, but from the Hindu religion and Hindu ceremonials, they were not allowed to hear, much less study the Vedas; they must not enter the temple; they must carry on all ceremonies without using mantras; and no Brahmin could carry out any domestic ceremony for them.

Certain tribal and aboriginal groups of populations are also victims of culture-, tradition- and belief-based marginalization.

Ethnicity, Caste, Colour and Religion: Certain groups of population in many countries are marginalized because of their ethnicity, caste and colour. In India, caste is one of the leading factors of marginalization. In many developed countries, people face exclusion because of their colour. The blacks are largely marginalized in the Western countries. The religious group of population, who are small in percentage in any country, feel marginalized. A United Nations report has noted that poor and marginalized social groups in the Tarai (Madhesis, Janajatis and Dalits) in Nepal especially women are amongst those most affected by citizenship certificate and, thus, suffer from de facto statelessness.[8] Ronki Ram (2004) in his study on Punjab wrote that

> Punjab villages were divided into upper caste and Dalit settlements. The Dalit settlements are invariably locates on the side towards which the dirt of the village flows when it rains. Often Dalits are not allowed to build pacca (concrete) houses, because the land to which they live does not belong to them but is claimed by the Jat-Sikhs. Dalit Sikhs in Punjab are cemented on separately demarcated cremation grounds.

Karl Marx was of the view that 'Indian caste system is decisive impediment to Indian progress and Indian power.'

Socio-economic Disparities: Socio-economic disparities exist in almost all countries of the world both developed and developing countries. The social disparities in terms of lower education and health status and poor social networking capability are vital causes of marginalization and exclusion. Besides, the income also creates differences between haves and have-nots and push have-nots to the boarder. The impoverished are always in fear to be excluded from the mainstream at any point of time. Marciniak (2011) was of the view that both 'absolute poverty' and 'relative poverty' can result in social marginalization and social exclusion.

Gender and Physically Challenged: Women in many societies, particularly in the traditional rural society, are subject to gender-based exclusion. In the globalized and neoliberal world, they are at the margin to be excluded from the mainstream, as a large percentage of them lack skill and technical education. The physically handicapped and most recently the transgender are facing the problem of marginalization and exclusion in many societies. It is remarked that the type and severity of discrimination faced by persons with disabilities varies depending on the nature of their impairment, their environmental context and the interaction with other factors such as gender and age.[9]

Geography: The people living in the hill and desert areas are largely away from the mainstream. Many of them being detached from the mainstream feel marginalized. A large number of population faces social, economic and political exclusion because of their socio-economic status. People living in desert areas also feel as if they are segregated and excluded from the mainstream population.

Globalization: It is generally viewed that the globalization process started in developing countries since the 1990s has elongated marginalization. It has largely benefited the rich and technical manpower; as a result the poor, illiterate and unskilled population are being systematically segregated. It has largely being criticized in the developing country as crony capitalism. The crony capitalism, a nexus between the bureaucratic machinery, politicians and the capitalist's business men, has led to corruption and plundering resources by the rich. The poor are economically marginalized.

Terrorism and Extremism: In recent years, rise in the terrorist activities in various countries and accusation of involvement of certain group of population and organization in the terrorist activities has created a global psyche of marginalization among the groups of population involved in such activities. As a results such a group of population and organization feels marginalized from the mainstream.

Besides, people who are victims of terrorism and extremist activities feel marginalized as refugees in other country. In the same country also the people who have been uprooted from their home state because of terrorist activities feel marginalized while staying in other state. For example, the Pandits who have been uprooted from Kashmir because of extremist activities also feel marginalized. Tikoo in his book *Kashmir: Its Aborigines and their Exodus* wrote about the Pandit's economic and political marginalization in the state over the past six decades and covered in detail the events that led to their eventual exodus.

Displacement: The large-scale infrastructure development programme in developing countries in general and in tribal areas in particular has laid to displacement. Besides, war, natural calamities, communal riots and terrorist and extremist activities have also caused displacement. The displaced populations are found to be largely marginalized and are dependent on government apathy. Ota (2006) from his study has confirmed that displaced families have been marginalized in many aspects in the post-displacement stage: (a) their operational holding size has been reduced from 6.1 acres to 3.15 acres and (b) the average encroached land has also come down from 1.4 acres per family to 0.15 acres in the post-displacement stage.

Poverty and Landlessness: Poverty is an important factor of marginalization. The landless and poverty-stricken households are found to be largely marginalized in the rural areas. Their voices are least heard in the gram sabha (village assembly) and they are at the bottom to be recognized and heard. They remain socio-economically marginalized.

Region-based Politics: The underdevelopment status of certain geographical area in a region or state leads to region-based marginalization. This gives an opportunity to the political leaders of the marginalized area to organize and agitate for the creation of a separate state. Creation of Telangana as a separate state from Andhra Pradesh is an illustrious example. Likewise, the people of several other regions of India such as Bado land, Vidrava and so on feel marginalized and the local politicians organize and instigate them for agitation.

Corruption and Mal-governance: These influence the process of inclusive development in the society. Because of mal-governance, the government-initiated measures do not reach the real beneficiaries. As a result, condition of the poverty-stricken population is not improved. They remain marginalized; those who adopt corruption become economically well-up, while their fellow colleagues feel marginalized.

Migration: Migration is also one of the important factors of marginalization. It is seen that in the developed countries of the West, the immigrant population from Asian and African countries are largely placed in jobs where they earn less as compared to the native population. Most of them reside in downtowns far away from the main city. Even in the case of intra-country migration, marginalization is clearly visible. The migrant population from Bihar and eastern Uttar Pradesh are found to be performing menial jobs in Punjab and Haryana. These migrants are victims of marginalization.

Illegal immigrants are severely marginalized. Many illegal migrants from Bangladesh to India do not have land for construction of houses and so live in unauthorized colonies. Those who do not have citizenship card such as a voter card, ADHAR card, PAN card and so on also face security-related problems and are even found to be harassed by police personnel. They are deprived of the benefit of the public distribution system as majority of them are living below the poverty line. One of the reports has mentioned that the lack of citizenship certificates aggravates social and economic marginalization of discriminated groups like the Santhal community in eastern Tarai, Nepal.[10] The immigrants who identify with neither their heritage nor the culture are living in the feeling of being marginalized and are insignificant (quoted from Tladi [2001]).

People's Attitude: Last but not the least, the attitude of the people is a fundamental factor of endurance of marginalization despite government measures. The negative attitude of upper caste and higher income groups towards the lower castes and poorer sections leads to exclusion. Khare (1998) remarked that Hindus do not carry in mind only the fear of pollution but also the feelings of hostility and prejudices against a man or women of untouchable origin. Change in attitude is critical to prevent marginalization in the stratified societies of developing countries.

MEASURES TO CHECK MARGINALIZATION AND EXCLUSION

The inclusive development has become more pressing in the globalized world. The end result of the globalization-driven economic growth process and strategies is that rich are becoming richer and the poor are becoming poorer and the gap between the rich and poor is increasing. The relative inclusion is low and exclusion is high. Inclusive development has been promoted by many developed as well as developing countries through various measures. Michael Chibba (2008) identified various possible approaches to address inclusive development: (a) Inclusive growth requires, *inter alia*, good governance, progressive politics, effective management and successful engagement in the global economy—indeed, an inclusive growth approach is the preferred one in Asia; (b) inclusive development requires addressing issues of structural transformation especially economic, social and demographic aspects and (c) a multipronged policy and programme mix is indispensable to an inclusive development agenda, and this includes sensible macroeconomic policies, sound institutions, public–private sector development, effective economic policy management, consensus building on public policies and programmes, and policies and interventions tempered to socio-economic and cultural factors.

Some of the measures taken for the prevention of exclusion are:

1. The governments of different countries have passed affirmative measures to control marginalization and promote inclusive development. Affirmative action policies offer special benefits to particular types of marginalized communities. It provides preferential treatments to the underprivileged sections of population, who are victims of exclusion. India has initiated affirmative action through its constitution. A few inclusive clauses which intend to prevent discrimination are as follows: (a) Article 15 of the Constitution of India prohibits discrimination on the grounds of religion, race, caste, sex or place of birth; (b) Article 16 lays emphasis on equal opportunities, which reads as, '[N]o citizen shall, on grounds only of religion, race, caste, sex, descent, place of birth, residence or any of them, be ineligible for, or discriminated against in respect of, any employment or office under the state.'; (c) Article 16(4) proclaims:

   > Nothing in this article shall prevent the State from making any provision for reservation in matters of promotion to any class or classes of posts in the services under the State in favour of the SCs and the STs which, in the opinion of the State, are not adequately represented in the services under the State.

   (d) the reservation for the SCs and STs and OBCs in the government jobs; (e) reservation of seats in the Parliament and State Legislative Assemblies for SCs and STs and (f) reservation of seats for SCs, STs and women in the local self-government institutions. Many state governments have also initiated affirmative actions and are giving preferential treatment to backward communities in government jobs. The South Africa's Employment Equity Act (1998) as an affirmative action redresses the disadvantages in employment experienced by designated groups such as Blacks (including African, Indian and other coloured minorities), women and the disabled. The Employment Equity Bill requires all companies with 50 employees or more to implement the quota-based Affirmative Action Policy, failing of which these have to pay the fine imposed by the department of Labour, Government of South Africa.[11]

2. The Government of India, since independence, has launched several developmental programmes in the areas of health, education, poverty eradication, employment, housing, sanitation, drinking water and so on in different five-year plans, both in rural and urban areas. All these programmes are targeted specifically to the upliftment of socio-economically backward communities and enable them to raise their standard of living. In other words, these programmes are inclusive in nature and intended to help the marginalized population to raise their standard of living.
3. The Government of India for inclusive regional development has launched several backward region development programmes. Drought Area Development Programme, Deseret Area Development Programme, Backward Region Grant Fund Programme and so on are to name a few. The Backward Region Grant Fund has been implemented in 250 backward districts of the country and the objective is to promote need-based development in these districts through the preparation of a district plan. In order to include other actors in the process of development, the government is engaging the NGOs and PVOs and other civil society organizations in the implementation of various developmental programmes at the grass-roots level.
4. The Government of India has launched many special schemes for the socio-economic upliftment of the SCs and STs. SCs Component Plan is one among such schemes intended to improve the living conditions of the SCs through the provision of drinking water supply, link roads, house-sites, primary schools, health centres, veterinary centres, community halls and so on in SCs-dominated habitations. Besides, pre-metric and post-metric scholarship for SC and ST students, Rajiv Gandhi National Fellowship and coaching facilities for the SC and ST to enhance their representation in central government services have been launched to raise the education and employment status of the SCs and STs. The National SCs and STs Finance and Development Corporation has been set up to act as catalytic agent in developing employment schemes and financing pilot projects in SC and ST areas.
5. The Government of India has launched NSAP in order to help secure sustainable livelihood of the marginalized group of population such as old age person, widow and disabled. Some of the important programmes launched under this umbrella programme are: National Old Age Pension Scheme (NOAPS), Indira Gandhi Widow Pension Scheme (IGNWPS) and Indira Gandhi National Disability Pension Scheme (IGNDPS). These have been launched to help the old age, widow and disabled who are found to be marginalized socially as well as economically because of being considered as less productive. The recently launched programmes (in 2016) such as Mudra Bank, Jan Dhan Yojana and Atal Pension Yojana aim at the economic empowerment of the poor and marginalized sections of population.
6. In almost all rural and urban poverty eradication and employment programmes launched by the central as well as state governments in rural and urban areas, preferential reservations for the SCs and STs have been made. For example, in the MGNREGA, the largest employment programme in the world, 33% job reservation has been made for the SC and ST population.

7. State governments of Orissa and Bihar have made provision of a certain percentage of reservation of seats in government jobs for women. It is intended to promote gender participation and inclusive development. Banning of liquor by a few state governments in India also aims at reducing atrocities on women.
8. The special category state status given to Assam, Jammu and Kashmir, Uttarakhand, Himachal Pradesh and other North Eastern States such as Sikkim, Arunachal Pradesh, Tripura, Meghalaya and Manipur is an inclusive development measure taken by the Government of India. It aims to improve the living standard of people in the hilly areas and bring them to mainstream.

Challenges of inclusive development are stupendous; however, resources available at their disposal are limited to meet these challenges. It is realized both nationally and internationally that inclusive development is essential for sustainable growth and development of developing countries.

SUMMARY

One of the important aspects of social and economic development is marginalization and social exclusion. This is responsible for either exclusion or minimization of the contribution of certain sections of population towards economic growth and development. Truly, the social development in developing countries is marred because of marginalization done on the basis on caste, class, gender, ethnicity and so on. It has prevented certain sections of the population to either fully or partially participate in the process of development. Marginalization is the cause of disparities, and inclusive development is the answer to holistic development. Inclusive development veritably means development for all and all for development. The development process needs to formulate such strategies and adopt approaches where the marginalized and excluded, i.e. the poorest of the poor, SCs, STs, women, aged, disabled, transgender and so on are empowered and contribute towards economic growth and development. Besides, all the regions and particularly the backward regions are empowered and their capabilities are enhanced so that they also contribute to economic growth and development. Total development can be a reality when all sectors and actors, regions, stakeholders and beneficiaries of development are included and contribute equitably and effectively towards development. The community-based inclusive approach has attracted attention as a strategy to make MDGs and poverty reduction strategies inclusive, i.e. to include people irrespective of the geographical location, disability, gender, ethnicity, sexual orientation along with the poverty (Khasnabis 2010). Women who constitute nearly 50% of a country's population are needed to be given opportunities and are to be effectively empowered for not only to raise their status as an individual but also to raise the quality of life of her family and contribute towards the development of the nation state at par with that of the men.

Keywords: marginalization, affirmative actions, exclusion, inclusive development, economic inclusion, social inclusion, political inclusion, gender-related development index, gender empowerment measure, gender inequality index.

REVIEW QUESTIONS

1. What is marginalization? Discuss how marginalization is a deterrent to the development of developing countries.
2. Explain the issues and challenges related to marginalization in developing countries and how these can be overcome.
3. Define inclusive development? Discuss various types of inclusion relating to development.
4. Gender development is the half of holistic development. Illustrate.
5. What is gender development index? Discuss various steps to promote development in a developing country.
6. Discuss various types of measures required to promote inclusive development in developing countries with examples.
7. Write short notes:
   (i) Gender-related development index
   (ii) Gender empowerment measure
   (iii) Social marginalization
   (iv) Economic inclusion

NOTES

1. Quoted from 'Inclusive Finance: Challenges and Opportunities: The Rome-based Agencies' Perspective.' For details see http://www.ifad.org/events/maxima/conceptnote (accessed on 18 September 2015).
2. See http://hrd.undp.org/en/media/HDR_20072008_G (accessed on 7 February 2017).
3. See http://www.icj.org/wp-content/uploads/2014/10/Universal-Women-and-Judiciary-Gva-For-1-Publications-Conference-Report-2014-ENG.pdf (accessed on 17 May 2016).
4. See http://wiego.org/wee/securing-economic-rights-informal-women-workers (accessed on 26 June 2016).
5. See http://www.unwomen.org/en/what-we-do/economic-empowerment/sustainable-development-and-climate-change (accessed on 26 June 2016).
6. For detail see http://en.unesco.org/post2015/sites/post2015/fil… (accessed on 18 March 2016).
7. See http://www.africaneconomicoulook.org/en/outlook/regional-development-and-spatial-inclusion/ (accessed on 18 March 2016).
8. See http://reliefweb.int/sites/reliefweb.int/files/resources/2011-05-05-UNRCHCO-Field-Bulletin-Issue-5.pdf (accessed on 18 May 2016).
9. See http://reliefweb.int/sites/reliefweb.int/files/resources/2011-05-05-UNRCHCO-Field-Bulletin-Issue-5.pdf (accessed on 18 May 2016).
10. See http://www.addc.org.au/documents/resources/voices-of-the-marginalized-persons-with-disabilities-older-people-people-with-mental-health-issues_927.pdf (accessed on 17 May 2016).
11. See Immigrants-https://behavioralpolicy.org/wp-content/uploads/2016/1-2/BSP_vol1no2_Lyons.pdf (accessed on 18 May 2016).

BIBLIOGRAPHY

Blunt, E. A. H. *Caste System of Northern India*. New Delhi: S. Chand and Co, 1969.

Boserup, E. *Women's Role in Economic Development*. London: George Allen and Unwin, 1970.

Burton, M. and C. Kangan. 'Marginalization.' In *Community Psychology: In Pursuit of Wellness and Liberation*, edited by I. Prilleltensky and G. Nelson. London: Macmillan/Palgrave, 2003.

Cain, E., M. S. Sightsavers, M. Wartman, S. Beales and S. Cordier. 'Voices of the Marginalized: Persons with Disabilities, Older People, People with Mental Health Issues,' 2012. Available at: http:// www.worldwewant2015.org/…/307/79 (accessed on 19 March 2014).

Cappo, D. 'Social Inclusion Initiative, Social Inclusion, Participation and Empowerment.' Address to Australian Council of Social Service National Congress, 28–29 November, 2002, Hobert, Australia.

Chibba, M. 'Perspectives on Inclusive Development: Concept, Approaches and Current Issues.' *World Economic Journal* 9, no. 4 (2008): 145–58.

Clark, R., Thomas W. Ramsey and S. A. Emily. 'Culture, Gender and Labour Force Participation: A Cross-National Study.' *Gender and Society* 5, no. 1 (1991): 47–66.

Connelly, M., T. Li, M. MacDonald and J. Parpart. 'Feminism and Development: Theoretical Perspective.' In *Theoretical Perspective on Development*, edited by J. Parpart, P. Connelly and E. Barriteau, 151–61. Canada IDRC, 2000.

Costello, M. A. 'Women in the Legal Profession: You Have Come a Long Way or Have You?' *Law Review of Michigan State University-Detroit College of Law* 3(1997): 909–15.

De Hann, A. and S. Maxwell. 'Editorial: Poverty and Social Exclusion in North and South.' *IDS Bulletin* 29, no. 1 (1998): 1–9.

Deng, F. M. *Sudan: Contested National Identities*. Washington, DC: The Brookings Institution, 1995.

DFID. 'Reducing Poverty by Tackling Social Exclusion.' A DFID Policy Paper, DFID, London, September, 2005.

Dollar, D. and R. Gatti. 'Gender Inequality, Income and Growth: Are Good Times Good for Women.' Policy Research Report on Gender and Development, Working Paper Series No. 1. Washington, DC: Development Research Group, World Bank, 1999.

Dufla, E. 'Women Empowerment and Economic Development.' *Journal of Economic Literature* 50, no. 4 (2012): 1051–79.

EU. *Joint Report on Social Exclusion*. Directorate Genera for Employment & Social Affairs, European Union, Luxembourg, Germany, 2004.

Eyben, R., N. Kabeer and A. Cornwall. 'Conceptualizing Empowerment and the Implications for Pro-poor Growth.' Paper presented at the OECD-DAC Poverty Network, Institute of Development Studies, Brighton, UK, 2008.

Forsythe, N, R. P. Korzemiewicz and D. Durrant. 'Gender Inequalities and Economic Growth: A Longitudinal Evaluation.' *Economic Development and Cultural Change* 48, no. 3 (2000): 573–617.

Gillen, M. and H. Kim. 'Older Women and Poverty Transition.' *Journal of Applied Gerontology* 28, no. 8, (2009): 320.

Goldin, C. 'The U-shaped Female Labour Force Function in Economic Development and Economic History.' In *Investing in Women's Human Capital and Economic Development*, edited by Schultz, University of Chicago Press, 1995, 61–90.

Heise, L. 'Violence Against Women: The Hidden Health Burden.' World Bank Discussion Paper. Washington. DC: The World Bank, 1994.

Herz, B. and G. Sperling. *What Work in Girl's Education: Evidence and Policies from the Developing World*. New York: Council for Foreign Relations Press, 2004.

Holms, A. 'A (Social) Capital Idea: Making Development Work.' *Harvard International Review*, 24–27. Available at: http://www.questia.com/library/1G1-112984254 (accessed on 27 September 2013).

ILO. *Global Employment Trends—January 2008*. Geneva: International Labour Organization, 2008.

Jencks, C. *Rethinking Social Policy: Race, Poverty and Underclass*. London: Harvard University Press, 1992.

Jones, H. 'Equity in Development, Why It Is Important and How to Achieve It.' Working Paper 311. London: Overseas Development Institute, 2009.

Kaur, K. and B. K. Pattanaik. *Development and Changing Status of Scheduled Castes: A Study of Ambedkar and Non-Ambedkar Villages in UP*. Chandigarh: Centre for Research in Rural and Industrial Development, 2000.

Khare, R. S. *Cultural Diversity and Social Discontent*. New Delhi: SAGE Publications.

Khasnabis, C. 'CBR for Community Based Inclusive Development.' Lecture at the CBR Congress, WHO, Oaxaca, 2010.

Lee, P. and A. Murie. 'Spatial and Social Division Within British Cities: Beyond Revisualization.' *Housing Studies* 14, no. 5 (1999): 625–40.

Leonard, P. *Personality and Ideology: Towards a Materialist Understanding of the Individual*. London: Macmillan, 1984.

Levitas, R., C. Pantazis, E. Fahmy, D. Gordon, E. Lloyd and D. Patsios. *The Multidimensional Analysis of Social Exclusion*. Bristol Institute for Public Affairs, University of Bristol, London, 2007.

Marciniak, B. 'Vanished Prosperity: Poverty and Marginalization in a Small Polish Fishing Community.' In *Mosaics: Realities and Prospects in Small Scale Fisheries*, edited by S. Jentoft and A. Eida. New York: Springer.

McKinsey and Company. '"Women Matter" Gender Diversity, a Corporate Performance Driver.' 2007. Available at: http:www.raeng.org.uk/publications/other/women (accessed 18 October 2015).

Miller, F. A. and J. H. Katz. *The Inclusion Breakthrough: Unleashing the Real Power of Diversity*. San Francisco, CA: Berrett-Koehler Publisher, 2002.

OECD. 'Global Forum on International Investment, 27–28 March 2008, The Contribution of Services to Development and the Role of Trade and Liberalization and Regulation.' ODI Briefing Note. DFID, London, 2008.

———. *Women's Economic Empowerment, Poverty Pro-Poor Growth: The Role of Empowerment*. OECD, Paris, 2012.

Ostlin, P., E. Eckermann, U. S. Mishar, M. Nkowane and E. Wallstam. 'Gender and Health Promotion: A Multi-sectoral Polity Approach.' *Health Promotion International* 21, no. S1 (2008): 25–35.

Ota, A. B. 'Livelihood Restoration of Displaced.' In *The Economics and Politics of Resettlement in India*, edited by S. Jain and M. Bala, 256–82. New Delhi: Dorling Kindersley.

Parpart, Jane L., M. Patricia Connelly and V. Eudine Barriteau. 'Foreword.' In *Theoretical Perspectives on Gender and Development*, 65–134. Ottawa, ON: International Development Research Centre, 2000.

Pietila, H. and J. Vickers. *Making Women Matter: The Role of the United Nations*. London: Zed Books, 1990.

Pitt, M., S. R. Khandker and J. Cartwright. 'Does Micro-credit Empower Women? Evidence from Bangladesh.' World Bank Policy Research Working Paper 2998, 2003. Available at: http://documents.worldbank.org/curated/en/664151468769258075/pdf/multi0page.pdf (accessed on 6 December 2016).

Ram, R. 'Untouchability in India with a Difference: Ad Dharm, Dalit Assertion and Caste Conflict in Punjab.' *Asian Survey* XLIV, no. 6 (2004, November–December): 895–912.

Ray, S. 'Khap Panchayats: Reinforcing Caste Hierarchies.' *Mainstream* XLVIII, no. 30 (17 July 2010). Available at: http://www.mainstreaweekly.net/article2205.html (accessed on 20 May 2016).

Reddock, R. 'Why Gender? Why Development?' In *Theoretical Perspectives on Gender and Development*, edited by Jane L. Parpart, M. Patricia Connelly and V. Eudine Barriteau, 30–64. Ottawa, ON: International Development Research Centre, 2000.

Saith, R. 'Social Exclusion: The Concept and Application to Developing Countries.' Working Paper No. 72, QEH Working Paper series,-QEHWPS72. Queen Elizabeth House, University of Oxford, Oxford, 2001.

Schmidt, R., R. E. Hero, A. Aoki and Y. Alex-Assensoh. 'Political Science, The New Immigration and Radical Politics in the United States: What Do We Know? What Do We Need To Know?' Paper presented at the American Political Science Association, Annual Meeting, August 29–September 1, 2002, Boston, Massachusetts.

Sen, A. 'Social Exclusion; Concept, Application, and Security.' Social Development Paper No. 1, 2000. Office of Environment and Social Development, Asian Development Bank.

Thomas, C. 'Capital Markets, Financial Markets and Social Capital.' *Social and Economic Studies* 45 (1996): 1–23.

Thorat, S., M. Mahamalik, and S. Venkatesan. 'Human Poverty and Socially Disadvantaged Groups in India.' Discussion Paper Series 18, 2007. Human Development Resources, UNDP, New Delhi.

Tladi, T. M. 'Affirmative Action and the Employment Equity Act of South Africa.' Mini-dissertation of the Degree of Master of Arts in Philosophy, Rand Afrikanns University, 2001. Available at: http://ujdigitpace.uj.ac.za/bitstrem/handle (accessed on 18 October 2015).

Trenhaft, S. and V. Rubin. 'Economic Inclusion: Advancing an Equity Driven Growth Model', 2013. Available at: http://www.policylink.org/sites/default/files/4A_TREUHAFT_RUBIN_POLICYLINK_REPORT_SECTORAL_INDUSTRY.PDF (accessed on 18 March 2016).

True, J., S. Parashar and N. George 'Women's Political Participation in Asia and the Pacific.' SSRC Conflict Prevention and Peace Forum, 2012. Available at: http://artsoline.monash.edu.au/thebordercros (accessed on 4 May 2014).

UNDP. 'A Million Dollar Question: What is Inclusive Growth?' Report prepared by Uyanga Gankhuyag from a learning event organized by the UNDP Learning Resource Centre, Poverty Reduction News Update, Issue # UNDP, 2008. Available at: http://www.in.undp.org/content/albania/en/home (accessed on 31 January 2014).

———. *Human Development Report*. New York: United Nations Development Programmes, 2010.

———. *Communication for Development: Strengthening Effectiveness of the United Nations*. New York: Bureaus Development Policy, Democratic Governance Group, UNDP, 2011.

UNESCO. *Education for All, Global Monitoring Report 2010*. Paris: UNESCO, 2010.

UNFPA. *Women and Children's Rights: Making the Connection*, 12. New York, 2010. Available at: https://www.unfpa.org/sites/default/files/pub-pdf/Women-Children_final.pdf (accessed on 6 December 2016).

UNIFEM. 'Violence Against Women Worldwide.' *Fact Sheet*, New York, 2.

Wasen, S. *Does Gender Inequality Reduce Growth and Development? Evidence from Cross-Country Regressions (Rep No.7)*. Washington, DC: The World Bank Development Research Group/Poverty Reduction and Economic Management Network, 1999.

WHO. *Women and Health: Today's Evidence, Tomorrow's Agenda*. Geneva: World Health Organization, 2009.

———. '"Women's health", World Health Statistics 2013,' 2013 Available at: http://www.who.int/mediacentre/factsheets/fs3 (accessed on 3 December 2013).

World Bank. *Growth Report: Strategies for Sustained Growth and Inclusive Development*, Commission on Growth and Development, The World Bank, Washington DC, New York, 2008.

———. *World Development Indicators*. Washington DC: World Bank.

———. *New Paths to Social Development, Community and Global Net Work in Action*. Washington, DC: World Bank, 2000.

———. 'Growth Report: Strategies for Sustained Growth and Inclusive Development.' Commission on Growth and Development, The World Bank, 2008.

———. *World Development Indicators, 2010*. New York: World Bank, 2010.

15 Good Governance and Ethical Approach to Development

The good governance is perhaps the single most important factor in eradicating poverty and promoting development.

—Kofi Annan

Development ethics aspires to show the road towards a new development paradigm that investigates development in light of fundamental ancient ethical queries on the meaning of the good life, the foundation of justice in society and the human stance towards nature.

—Astroulakis (2010)

Good governance is vital for the effective and sustainable development of developing countries. Governance deficit in developing countries has resulted in the ineffective implementation of various development projects and programmes and leakages of public resources. In developing countries, all the developmental obstructions such as poverty, inequality, illiteracy and ill health are perpetuating for a long period because of bad governance. Therefore, the development failures in developing countries are attributed to deficiency of good governance at various levels, particularly at the bureaucratic and political levels. Corruption, irregularity in attaining office, casual approach to job, taking bribe for helping in the movement of files, redtapism, nepotism in bid allotment, shifting of responsibility, procrastination, let it continue like this, taking salary without any work or with little work, and favouritism in promotion are some of the governance issues out of many, creating hindrances in the development process of developing countries. The governance is not only the most pressing contemporary issue but also a long-standing issue that needs to be attended to and effectively dealt with, particularly in developing countries. Wolf (2005) argued that political corruption and mal-governance are among the principal barriers to economic development and social betterment in the Third World. A country that improves its governance from a relatively low level to an average level could almost triple the per capita income of its population in the long run (Kaufmann 2005). Therefore, the governments of developing countries are under tremendous pressure from the international agencies and from within the masses of the country to put good governance principles into practice in their political and administrative spheres.

In developing countries, ethical aspects of development are quite critical as they will trigger non-state actors in the process of development. Development is a multidimensional concept and its vastness is much wider than the economic growth. Therefore, developing countries are vexed with sundries of developmental issues and challenges, and, hence, the government alone cannot fulfil all the urges of development. In recent years, it is seen that many capitalists of the West and also corporate houses in developing countries are donating their earned wealth for the well-being of the poor. Day by day, the development philanthropy is gaining a substantial ground in the paradigm of development of the developed as well as developing countries.

After reading this chapter, you will be able to:

1. Define good governance and explain the attributes of good governance.
2. Describe various challenges of development governance.
3. Explain the main aspects and essentials of development ethics and how it is important in the process of development of developing countries.

SECTION I: GOOD GOVERNANCE

The relationship between governance and development has raised up the international policy agenda and better attention to governance can reduce poverty, facilitate economic growth and promote more meaningful development.

—ODI (2006)

Good governance is an indispensable instrument for facilitating faster development in developing countries reeling under poverty and inequality largely because of the bad governance. According to Acemoglu et al. (2003), good governance is not only critical to development but also the most important factor in determining whether a country has the capacity to use resources judiciously and effectively to promote economic growth and development. Each element of good governance can be understood as both means and goals of development (National Social Watch 2011). According to Sachiko and Durwood (2007), good governance promotes accountability, transparency, efficiency and the rule of law in public institutions at all levels and allows for sound natural, economic and financial resources for equitable and sustainable development. The World Bank (1992) veritably linked good governance to sound development management. According to the World Bank, 'the importance of good governance has now become an article of faith with multilateral organizations, donors and lenders, increasingly basing their aid and loans on the condition that, policies which ensures good governance are adopted.' Improving governance is one of the vital cornerstones of development. According to Langseth (1999), the public needs to be educated on the advantages of good governance and to participate in promoting it, and they should learn

- not to let anybody buy their vote;
- not to pay bribes themselves;
- to report incidents of corruption to the authorities and
- to teach their children the right values, i.e. integrity is good and corruption is bad.

The international agencies and governments of developing countries are focusing on good governance in order to improve the development service delivery at the grass-roots level. The greatest beneficiaries of the good governance are the common men who are suffering a lot because of widespread corruption in public life.

Good governance is a complex term, as its principles are guided by the moral and ethical values as well as its effective implementation are subject to legal and administrative modus operandi. These principles are easy to advocate and spicy for debate and discussions in the print and electronic media but are most arduous to be put into practice. The eight most recognized characteristics of good governance are participatory, consensus oriented, accountable, transparent, effective and efficient, equitable, inclusive and the rule of law. However, the three critical doctrines having significant importance in good governance for achieving faster development are accountability, transparency and the rule of law.

The first and most important doctrine of good governance is accountability. To be accountable means to be responsible and answerable. One should be honest and sincere to the assigned job and responsibilities. Good governance emphasizes on an accountable bureaucracy and a responsible political system. The functionaries and the representatives of the bureaucratic and political systems at all levels and dealing in the activities of various sectors must be answerable to the people for whom development benefits are being targeted. They cannot shy away from their duties and responsibilities by giving excuses. Fixing of responsibility on the guilty for the lack of accountability is a demanding principle of good governance. Shifting of responsibility from one person to another in case of failure and fighting for taking credit after achieving success are adversaries to accountability. The blame game business is a contestant to accountability. Development has failed miserably at the grass-roots level in many nation states of developing countries largely because of poor accountability and corruption on the part of the executors responsible for the implementation of various development projects and programmes. Marinova and Hossain (2009) by sighting Bangladesh example said that each year, the Bangladesh government accepts foreign aid to initiate sustainable development projects such as re-excavation of water bodies, mass education or family planning, but often funds are being stolen from such projects by politicians, bureaucrats, technocrats and implementing contractors. The outcomes of the projects are utterly unproductive, often counterproductive.

Humility in Leadership

I remember Dr Kalam's account of a mission at the Indian Space Research Organization (ISRO). He was project director for India's satellite launch vehicle programme and had been leading a team to put a satellite into orbit. On the day of the launch, all went well for a while, but then the satellite plunged to earth. The launch had failed. Dr Kalam described how his boss, ISRO Chairman Dr Satish Dhawan, calmly stepped into the sea of cameras and microphones and took responsibility for the failure. Within a year, the team tried again and succeeded. This time, Dr Dhawan asked Dr Kalam to meet the press and get the accolades. This, said Dr Kalam, was a critical quality of leadership: sharing credit for success and taking responsibility for failure.

Source: Khanna (2015).

Another key doctrine of good governance is transparency. To be transparent means that one should be honest to his duties and responsibilities and tells the truth. The people in

Table 15.1 *The Corruption Perceptions Index, 2014*

Country	Score	Rank
Denmark	92	1
New Zealand	91	2
Finland	89	3
Sweden	87	4
Norway	86	5
United States	74	17
Bhutan	65	30
India	38	85
China	36	100
Pakistan	29	126
Somalia	8	174

Source: Transparency International (2014).

the responsible positions, be they in bureaucracy, politics or any other responsible positions, should not hesitate and fear to tell the truth. It is true that in order to conceal a single lie, you have to tell several lies and, therefore, it is always wise to tell the truth. Furthermore, the governance principle advocates that the procedures related to governance issues must be simple, clear and understandable with fewer amounts of contradictions. Nowadays, e-governance is being used to improve transparency in administration. The digitization of land record in Karnataka is a transparent way to deal with land issues. The Right to Information Act in India intends to bring transparency and aims at removing corruption in public sector. Transparency International has developed a Corruption Perceptions Index to assess transparency at the country level. In the Corruption Perceptions Index of the year 2014 (Table 15.1), the Scandinavian countries occupy higher rank; most of the countries belonging to Asia are in lower ranks. India with a score of 38 ranks 85th, while China and Pakistan with scores of 36 and 29 rank 100th and 126th, respectively.

Digitizing Land Records in Karnataka, India

The Department of Revenue of Karnataka set up 177 computerized land record kiosks (Bhoomi centres) in taluk (sub-district) offices to provide farmers with digitized copies of the Record of Rights, Tenancy and Cultivation (RTC) documents as a part of the Bhoomi system. The Bhoomi project was expected to speed up the delivery of RTCs, without delays, harassment or bribery. As a part of the initiative, nearly 20 million records of land ownership of 6.7 million farmers in the state of Karnataka have been digitized. The RTC certifies the ownership of land, location, unique identity number, crops sown on the land, identity of the tiller, loans taken against the land and so on. Each RTC record in Bhoomi consists of over 40 fields and many of these fields such as crops sown require updating on a regular basis to keep the information current. The more permanent data related to ownership can be changed only by a legal process known as 'mutation'. Bhoomi helps with the mutation process as well. It records landowners' requests for a mutation and sends the request to the relevant public officials (Parkash and De). The Bhoomi system consists of touch-screen kiosks that provide an easy access to RTCs and show the status of the available mutation requests.

Bhoomi aims to reduce corruption and improve public service provision by removing human agency from the land records system. An automated system that provides and updates land records offers equal terms to everyone and prevents bribes and discrimination.

Source: http://web.worldbank.org/WBSITE/EXTERNAL/TOPICS/EXTPUBLICSECTORANDGOVERNANCE/0,,contentMDK:23265595~pagePK:148956~piPK:216618~theSitePK:286305,00.html (accessed on 11 May 2016).

The third important doctrine of good governance is adherence to the rule of law. One cannot think of good governance without the rule of law and its application in letter and spirit. According to Sachiko and Durwood (2007), the term 'rule of law' is used to mean independent, efficient and accessible judicial and legal systems, with a government that applies fair and equitable laws equally, consistently, coherently and prospectively to all of its people. The key elements of the rule of law are fair, impartial, accessible and efficient judicial system at all levels, ready to deliver speedy and impartial justice to the common men. The United Nations (2005) acknowledged that good governance and the rule of law at the national and international levels are essential for sustained economic growth, sustainable development and eradication of poverty and hunger. In order to favour corporate houses, the legislatures with the help of bureaucrats do necessary ramifications in the rules and regulation. In lieu of this favour, these corporate houses give funds to the political parties. The acquisition of one political party on the other during electioneering on sources of funding opens the issue before the public domain. This is not the healthy sign of good governance rather detrimental to good governance. All are equal before law is one of the exclusive mandates of the good governance.

Role of Judiciary in Good Governance

Good governance signifies the way an administration improves the standard of living of the members of its society by creating and making available the basic amenities of life; providing its people security and the opportunity to better their lot; instil hope in their heart for a promising future; providing, on an equal and equitable basis, access to opportunities for personal growth; affording participation and capacity to influence in the decision-making in public affairs; sustaining a responsive judicial system which dispenses justice on merits in a fair, unbiased and meaningful manner; and maintaining accountability and honesty in each wing or functionary of the government.

Source: Sabharwal (2006).

GOOD GOVERNANCE AND DEVELOPMENT

Good governance and development are interlinked. Developed countries are developed because they largely follow good governance practices in their political, bureaucratic and even in their market mechanism. Some of the goals of the good development governance in developing countries would be

1. Honestly ensuring basic needs to the people, and there should be no corruption in the provisioning of basic needs such as food, shelter, toilet and drinking water facilities to the population living below the poverty line.
2. Honestly issuing ration cards and delivering ration items as per the government norms without taking any bribe. Also, minimizing leakages in the public distribution system by cancelling the fake ration cards.
3. Giving those households that are actually entitled as per the government norm the benefits of government schemes such as housing, construction of toilet, agricultural land and so on. In the case of rural areas beneficiaries, the benefits of the developmental schemes need to be given to those whose names are being approved by the *gram sabha* (village assembly).
4. Strictly dealing with the corruption in the construction of infrastructure such as roads, dams, irrigation projects, schools, health institutions, railways, airports and so on by the machinery involved such as politicians, bureaucrats, technocrats, contractors and other functionaries. The community monitoring and social auditing will be helpful to control corruption and expose the middle men involved in the process of corruption.
5. Providing social security to the old age, widow, disabled and destitute without taking any bribe from them. Taking bribe from these categories of people is a sin and is a case for rigorous punishable offence.
6. Removing discrimination from the society existing on the basis of caste, sex, creed, religion and so on by following the constitutional norms and mandate of the Fundamental Rights and Directive Principles of State Policy (in the case of India).
7. Promoting social justice and equity in the society. All are equal before law; the men and women, rich and poor, higher and lower caste and so on. The nepotism and the brother and nephew culture in giving benefit has to be stopped. The mafia and goonda raj have to be done away with.
8. Punishing those who are breaking the law, doing corruption and practising discrimination in the society.
9. Ensuring equal pay for equal work to both men and women and ensuring gender justice and eradicating gender-related discrimination.
10. Reducing corruption at all levels, particularly those that affect the common men such as issuance of driving licence, gas connection, ration card, sanction of bank loan, pension benefit and so on.
11. Checking income inequalities arising in the economy because of the corruption practices adopted by the bureaucratic functionaries and the elected political representatives at all levels.
12. Checking crony capitalism and the corruption taking place with the nexus of the political, bureaucrat and corporate houses and other middle men.

13. Trying for speedy disposals of corruption-related cases by the judiciary without any fear and favour by the lower and higher courts. The judiciary has to uphold the social and human rights of the people who are victims of human rights violation and injustices.
14. Constituting Jan Lokpal, Lok Adalat and Gram Nayalaya (village court) for the speedy disposal of corruption, crime and other dispute-related cases at the grassroots level.
15. Maintaining law and order for the prevention of murder, rape, molestation and other criminal activities.
16. Protecting human rights and the citizens.
17. Government functionaries at all levels performing their duties and responsibilities with full dedication and honesty.

Upholding the principles of governance requires strong political and bureaucratic will power. It is remarked that most decentralization policies and programmes falter during implementation because they are introduced with political hesitation, bureaucratic resentment and suspicion or incomprehension from the general society (Kauzya 2005). First, there is a serious lack of political and bureaucratic will power in developing countries to put good governance principle in practice. In many cases, it happens because of lack of morality and ethical values in the bureaucratic machinery and among the politicians and their coteries. Second, a proactive investigating agency is the teeth of good governance. The investigating agency must be responsive and must impartially deliver justice to the poor. The demand for 'Jan Lokpal' in India is one of the illustrious examples. At a minimum, good governance requires a fair legal framework and an independent judiciary system. Its decisions and enforcement are transparent. It follows established rules and regulations. Third, well-trained private voluntary organizations (PVOs) are a necessity for the furtherance of the good governance. It is said that PVOs have emerged as an organized pressure group on state and unresponsive governments in matters of democracy and development (Pillai 2006). The Organisation for Economic Co-operation and Development (OECD 2000) has noted that good governance requires a broad approach to partnership extending beyond governments and parliaments to include civil society and private sector. According to Ghaus-Pasha (2005), civil society can further good governance, first by policy analysis and advocacy; second by regulation and monitoring of state performance and the action and behaviour of public officials; third by building social capital and enabling citizens to identify and articulate their values, beliefs, civic norms and democratic practices; fourth by mobilizing particular constituencies, particularly the vulnerable and marginalized sections of masses to participate more fully in politics and public affairs and fifth by development work to improve the well-being of their own and other communities. Finally, good citizenry is an asset for a nation to put attributes of good governance into practice.

OXFAM[1] holds the view that citizens are able to tell power holders about the issues they face and hold government accountable for its decisions and allocation of resources; power holders benefit from feedback and inputs from citizens and from the push to be more accountable. Citizens need to practise certain ethics in their public life. They must obey the rule of law. It must come from within; self-governance is the best governance. The Committee on Standards in Public Life set out seven core principles: (a) selflessness,

(b) integrity, (c) objectivity, (d) accountability, (e) openness, (f) honesty and (g) leadership, and these principles have been incorporated into the codes of conduct of numerous government institutions, including the parliament (Nolan 1998).

Good governance in development is one of the vital contemporary issues in developing countries. The international agencies and developed nations of the West are castigating developing countries on this issue. Therefore, in order to achieve inclusive and sustainable development, developing countries have to improve governance in all spheres of development. It can be undoubtedly said that without the effective application of good development governance doctrines, the development indictors of developing countries cannot be improved.

SECTION II: ETHICAL APPROACH TO DEVELOPMENT

Philanthropy, no matter where it originates, is driven by the imperative to meet human needs, alleviate suffering and tackle the systematic challenges that prevent human development and progress.

—Grady (2014)

Development is a whole: it is an integral, value-loaded, cultural process; it encompasses the natural environment, social relations, education, productivity, consumption and well-being.

—Dag Hammarskjold Institute (1975)

Developing countries are reeling under the maladies of poverty and inequalities for a long time despite several developmental interventions by the government of these countries. On the one hand, a few people enjoy a lot of comfort and luxuries, while on the other a gigantic number of them are the drawers of water and hewers of wood. A large number of people are struggling to fulfil their basic needs. Governments of these countries have limited resources at their disposal for which they are incapable to deal with the well-being of the poor. The long battle against poverty, inequality and all other development ills tell that government alone cannot be able to win the battle against the various ills of underdevelopment in developing countries. Therefore, there is a need for sharing of burden of the government by the rich and wealthy individuals, corporate houses, business entrepreneurs, religious institutions and so on under the umbrella of development philanthropy. There is also a general sense of philanthropic feeling among the rich as well as poor. The impoverished, who have faith and fear in God, believe that they are suffering because they are being destined to suffer, that is in their fate and this is what is desired by the God. On the contrary, many of those who are rich believe and consider that it is God who has given them so much and it is this believe that entices a few benevolent entrepreneurs and rich corporate houses to volunteer to spend a portion of their profit for the well-being of the poor. In other words, this is based on the faith that with the welfare of the poor lies the richness of the rich. Thus, from this angle, it can be deduced that both poor and rich largely from their individualistic perspectives consider 'development' as an ethical concept and relate it to their destiny. Grady (2014) was of the opinion that philanthropy as an expression of human generosity exists in every culture and is reflected in most of the world's cultures and religions.

The contemporary thinkers of benevolent school of development (to name a few: Mahatma Gandhi, Vinoba Bhave and Friedrich Engels) consider development as an ethical, moral, benevolent and humane concept over and above the economic concept, which measures development in terms of rise in productivity, economic growth rate and income. For the benevolent developmentalists, the term 'development' not only intends to raise the productivity and economic growth rate but also emphasizes on equitable distribution of wealth for the well-being of the poor. It aims to solve the developmental problems, i.e. poverty, inequality, unemployment, illiteracy, hunger, mortality, morbidity and insanitation which the underdeveloped countries have been facing since centuries with a humane approach. The ethical approach to development considers that the governments in developing countries cannot solve all these sundry of issues and challenges related to development alone. Therefore, the vision of 'development' needs to be a shared vision and be shared with the international donor agencies, philanthropic organizations, private and corporate sectors, non-government organizations (NGOs), PVOs and the rich people at large by applying ethical and moral principles.

For developing countries' perspective, the term 'development' is more of a philosophical, philanthropic and qualitative concept related to human well-being. It is less of a quantitative concept as that of 'economic growth'. It intends to raise the well-being and quality of life of the people and desires to remove poverty, inequality, unemployment, illiteracy and ill health from these countries. According to a United Nations General Assembly resolution (1970), the ultimate purpose of development is to provide increasing opportunities to all people for a better life, bring about a more equitable distribution of income and wealth for promoting both social justice and efficiency of production, substantially raise the level of employment, achieve a greater degree of income security, expand and improve facilities for education, health, nutrition, housing and social welfare and safeguard the environment. The United Nations Declaration on the Right to Development states:

> The right to development is an inalienable human right by virtue of which every human person and all peoples are entitled to participate in and contribute to and enjoy economic, social, cultural and political development in which all human rights and fundamental freedoms can be fully realized.

It further states: 'The constant improvement of the well-being of the entire population and of all individuals, on the basis of their active free and meaningful participation in development and in the fair distribution of benefits resulting there from.'

Mumbai Diamantaire and His Religious and Development Philanthropy

A leading diamond merchant from South Mumbai, Dilip Lakhi, has donated around 40 kg of gold worth ₹12 crore to the Somnath temple in Gujarat. He has done so on previous occasions as well, and his total contribution of the yellow metal to that shrine now stands at 109 kg.

His charity activities span a vast spectrum. 'We have helped set up hospitals, dharamshalas, temples and have seen how the local community prospers. Small shop owners, florists, souvenir vendors flourish when you build roads from Haridwar to Badrinath, from Rajkot to Somnath. The local economy begins to prosper in the long term. It is better than giving money to individuals who may exhaust the funds within a few years and revert to their original circumstances. Charity comes with a lot of responsibility,' he said.

Source: http://timesofindia.indiatimes.com/city/mumbai/Mumbai-diamantaire-donates-40kg-gold-to-Somnath-temple/articleshow/52215709.cms (accessed on 12 May 2016).

Ethical approach to development recognizes development as a multidisciplinary as well as interdisciplinary concept. It considers that not a single rather multipronged approaches and strategies and moral and ethical anaesthesia are equally important to break the vicious circle of underdevelopment in the developing economies. This approach recognizes that the economic system guided by the principles of consumerism and individualism in the capitalist system and also in the mixed economies system has transposed humans to an economic species by making them more and more selfish and individualistic.

On the contrary, welfarism aims at well-being of the largest sections of the society. Welfarism desires that the capitalists, rich and well-up need to invest a portion of their profit on the social and human well-being of common men, particularly impoverished and marginalized section of the population. The 'welfarism' in the capitalist and mixed economic systems in recent years is variously termed as 'creative capitalism' or 'benevolent capitalism', a departure from the accumulative capitalism of the West. According to Mithani (1987), 'the post-war capitalism is described as "welfare state capitalism" in order to differentiate it from the classical *laissez fair* capitalism of the pre-war era.' The difference between the pre- and post-war capitalism is that the pre-war capitalism's motto is to 'produce more, earn more and have more', while post-war capitalism's motto is to 'produce more, earn more and contribute more towards human and social well-being'. It desires that the capitalists, industrialists and the businessmen need to spend a portion of their profit for the social, economic and human well-being. It is what is called as guided creative capitalism or creative mixed economy. Here, Grady's (2014) remark is worth mentioning: Where governments create an enabling environment for civil society by establishing a regulatory environment that is clear, accessible, impartial and not overly burdensome, philanthropy and civil society can become true partners in the development of prosperous and inclusive society.

Development Philanthropy in a Few Countries

China: According to the China Foundation Center information on Chinese giving across borders, about 50 Chinese foundations provide grants to other countries, generally in Asia and Africa. For example, the Hainan Airlines Foundation in May 2013 announced a contribution to the World Food Programme (WFP) of 10 million Yuan over 10 years. It pledged 10 million Yuan over five years for UNICEF's Change for Good programme. Chinese philanthropy experts note that China's investments in

Africa and benefits that come from natural resources there should, and will, be accompanied by philanthropic components to bolster responsible investing.

India: India leads amongst countries in the South in the level of charitable giving, which grows sharply each year. By 2012, it reached 0.3–0.4% of GDP, valued between $5–6 billion per annum. Philanthropy is still principally focused on spiritual and religious causes, and self-managed philanthropy is constituted mainly of support to hospitals, schools and local areas of business cooperation. Many newly endowed foundations are being established; many of which focus on bridging the social divides and socio-economic disparities in India by supporting education.

A recent notable development in India is the passing of legislation called the Companies Act 2013 which requires companies to disclose their CSR budgets publicly. It includes a provision of CSR mandating that all companies registered in India must spend 2% of their net profits on CSR activities, if they have a net profit over $833,000, net revenue of more than $83.3 million or a net worth of $166 million.

Turkey: Turkey has an abundant domestic foundation landscape. In the early 1990s, many new foundations were established, now numbering about 4,500. Most of them raise funds from the public for their activities. It is estimated that less than 500 of them were established by wealthy individuals with an endowment and private source of funding.

The Turkish government is increasingly engaging Turkish businesses to invest abroad, especially in Africa (e.g. Turkish Airlines), and there is likely to be philanthropy accompanying these investments. Turkish foundations already have a rich experience in areas like education, gender equality and youth empowerment.

Source: http://www.undp.org/content/dam/undp/documents/partners/civil_society/UNDP-CSO-philanthropy.pdf (accessed on 26 June 2016).

The term 'CSR' is an outcome of it and is an illustrious mechanism to promote welfare of poor and impoverished sections of population in capitalist and mixed economic systems. According to Bill Gates,[2] 'we need a creative capitalism where business and non-governmental organizations work together to create a market system that eases the world's inequalities.' Recently, the declaration by Tim Cook, the Apple CEO, to donate an amount of $785 million for charity is another illustrious example of ethical/philanthropic angle of development, where rich come forward to finance for the development of the poor. Gandhian development philosophy is quite akin to development philanthropy. Gandhi (1967) wrote, 'I must confess that I do not draw a sharp or any distinction between economics and ethics. Economics that hurts moral well-being of any individual or nation is immoral and therefore sinful.' In the modern selfish society, man has become self-centred and there is a lack of human concerns, and a gluttonous individual never feels felonious to wretch the rights of others for their parochial gains. To quote Engels (1972):

> [I]n our present-day society, each man works on his own, each strives for his own-enrichment and is not in the least concerned with what the rest are doing; rational organization or distribution of jobs, is out of the questions; on the contrary, each seeks to get the better of the other, seeks to exploit any favorable opportunity for his own private

advantage and has neither time nor inclination to think about the fact that, at bottom, his own interests coincides with those of all other people.

The aim of the development is to promote happiness and not to amass wealth beyond excess of one's own needs. Happiness is something eternal and more of a moral concept and is gained through peace of mind and not through a heap of wealth. Gandhi has rightly said that 'World has kept enough for human needs. But not for human greed.' The richness has little meaning, if it is not benefiting the impoverished and is not distributed. Every rich should spare a little part of his abundance for the well-being of the poor; otherwise, his richness has no meaning. Once Kabir, a famous saint of India, said (in Mahajan 2003)

Bada hua to kya hua,
jaise ped khajoor.
Panchi ko chhaya nahin,
phal lage ati dur.

Meaning: It is of no consequence if a person is enormously rich unless humanity is benefited from his riches.

The mission of the ethics of development is development of all and all for development. One of the quotable quotes sighted for the ethics of development is the talisman (Lal 1948) which Gandhi gave to Jawaharlal Nehru and which guided his inner self. This is as follows:

> I will give you a talisman. Whenever, you are in doubt or when the self becomes too much with you, apply the following test:
>
> Recall the face of the poorest and the weakest man whom you may have seen and ask yourself if the step you contemplate is going to be of any use to him. Will he gain anything by it? Will it restore him to a control over his own life and destiny? In other words, will it lead to Swaraj (freedom) for the hungry and spiritually starving millions? Then you will find your doubts and yourself melting away.

The United Nations[3] in its resolution on 'Happiness towards a Holistic Approach to Development' envisaged that 'a fundamental human goal is the deep abiding happiness that comes from living life in full harmony with the natural world and with our communities and fellow beings.' A few important findings envisaged in the World Happiness Report 2013 are as follows:

- Happiness, no matter how overly idealistic it sounds, needs to be used as a measure of a successful government.
- World Happiness Report 2013 offers rich evidence that the systematic measurement and analysis of happiness can teach us a lot about ways to improve the world's well-being and sustainable development.
- There is now a rising worldwide demand that policy be more clearly aligned with what really matters to people as they themselves characterize their well-being.
- Happy people live longer, are more productive, earn more and are also better citizens.
- Global happiness is on the rise (Table 15.2) (Helliwell et al. 2013).

The development as happiness believes that the GDP-based approach is outdated and a nation should be seen as succeeding not if its citizens are financially well off but rather if they are healthy and happy (Helliwell et al. 2013).

Table 15.2 *Ranking of Happiness Index Score of Selected Countries, 2010–12*

Country	Score	Rank
Denmark	7.693	1
Norway	7.655	2
Switzerland	7.650	3
United States	7.082	17
United Kingdom	6.883	22
Singapore	6.546	30
Japan	6.064	43
China	4.978	92
India	4.772	111
Afghanistan	4.040	143
Togo	2.936	156

Source: Helliwell, Layard and Sacha (2013).

The application of development ethics in the development practices of developing countries has become more demanding in this era of globalization and neoliberalism. The globalization and neoliberalism, on the one hand, have enlarged the modernization in developing countries but, on the other, have elongated disparities between different strata of population. This has brought welfarism to the forefront in developing countries, as a large number of their population is still struggling to fulfil their basic needs. It is befitting to quote Mahatma Gandhi who wrote in *Harijan* on 16 November 1934 that

> Machination is good when the hands are too few for the work intended to be accomplished. It is an evil when there are more hands than required for the work as in India. The problem with us is not how to find leisure for the teeming million inhabitants of our villages. The problem is how to utilize their idle hours, which are equal to the working days of six months in a year.

SCOPE OF ETHICAL APPROACH TO DEVELOPMENT

The goals of the ethics of development are to promote human well-being and happiness of the largest number of people, ensure social justice and equity and provide opportunities to the less privileged section of the society to have equal access to development benefits. Some of the scopes of ethical approach to development are as follows:

1. Majority of the people, particularly the marginalized section of society, are to be provided with the employment opportunities both in public and private sectors. Furthermore, they should be employed by the NGOs without any discrimination and should become active members of the PVOs. Besides, ensuring wage and self-employment workforce participation with sustainable wage and income will fulfil their basic needs. As land is an important source of income and a livelihood

asset, therefore, through the effective implementation of land reform measures, the landless should be empowered with right to land. The society must relentlessly try to maintain equity and equality and uphold social justice and human rights in the matter of live and livelihood entitlement: roti, *kapda* and *makan* (food, clothing and shelter); *bijli, sadak and pani* (energy, road and drinking water) and *shiksha, swasthya and safai* (education, health and sanitation). The ethical goal of the development should be: food for all, health for all, education for all, housing for all, sanitation and safe drinking water for all and clean and affordable energy for cooking and lighting for all. Moreover, the state in partnership with the various actors of development should guarantee employment and make accessible 'Sustainable Wage Rate to All' fixed from time to time on the basis of price index and inflation. The sustainable wage rate to all should be made a fundamental right.

2. The upper strata of the society such as the corporate sector owners, industrialists and business entrepreneurs, needs to spend a portion of their profit for the well-being of the poor and deprived section. The corporate sector, businessmen, sports personalities, film stars, rich landlords, wealthy politicians and people having surplus income need to voluntarily adopt a village, slum area, an impoverished community or a poor family as per their capability and try to improve their socio-economic condition and well-being. The goal is to promote well-being of all and involve all in the process of delivery of well-being and social justice. The compassionate, benevolent, creatively guided mixed economy is the need of the hour in developing countries for the upliftment of the poorest of the poor. The corporate sector, private entrepreneurs and wealthy individuals by applying religious, ethical and moral principles need to spend one-tenth of their income and profit for the well-being of the poor and destitute. It is befitting to quote Singh (2004) who wrote about the principle of Sikhism, which runs as follows: (a) 'One should earn ones living with honest means and share it with humble, the poor and the needy'; (b) 'One should share his food with others and should not eat alone' and (c) 'He who earns his living with hard labour and honest means and gives daswandh (one tenth) in the name of Guru will earn fame.'
3. The religious institutions having income from the devotees in the form of gifts, offerings and donations should adopt villages, open charitable health and educational institutions and work for the social, economic and human development of the disadvantaged sections of the society. Examples of philanthropic developmental activities being conducted by various religious organizations belonging to different religions are being seen in different parts of India and other South Asian countries and are needed to be documented and replicated. The illustrious examples are Sri Balaji Charitable and Educational Trust and Sri Saibaba Sansthan Trust, Shirdi. These trusts are doing a lot of social development activities in the area of education and health care. The Shiromani Gurdwara Parbandhak Committee (SGPC) under Sikhism has opened up dispensaries, schools and old age homes and is found to be engaged in different types of developmental activities at the village level. The work of the Christian missionaries to promote social and human well-being in the difficult areas and their work with the disadvantaged sections of the society are also noteworthy.
4. There is no physical, financial and mental exploitation by the rich to the poor. The political and bureaucratic establishments need to follow good governance

practices. The executive, legislative and people at large need to work in tandem, and transparency must be maintained while implementing any programme or project for the upliftment of the poor at the grass-roots level. The gram vikas committees (village development committees) and gram vikas nayalayas (village development courts) have to be established in every village panchayat and at municipal ward level for the effective implementation of development projects and programmes and speedy disposal of village disputes, land-related cases and complains and to ensure justice, so that leakages and corruptions in the implementation of various schemes are avoided and rural impoverished people are saved from mental and financial atrocities.

5. The menace of child trafficking and child labour is abolished. Furthermore, there is no bonded labour in the society. In the same vein, no woman is forced to resort to prostitution and selling of flesh because of poverty and helplessness. The government, private sector, NGOs, PVOs and the opinion leaders and respected elderly have to initiate concerted efforts to do away with these types of menace from the society. The family and society have to be made realized that children are the future human resources of a nation and any expenditure on their education and health care must be considered as future investment and not present spending. Like of children, education, health care and workforce participation of women who are creators and nurturers of the humans on the earth will strengthen the root of sustainable growth and development of a nation.
6. The discrimination in the access to take advantage of the services of the various public institutions such as schools, colleges, universities, hospitals, dispensaries, fair price shops and labour market on the basis of class, caste, gender and ethnicity is documentedly abolished by law. Therefore, it has to be religiously implemented at the grass-roots level to ensure justice to the disadvantaged. Besides, it has also to be ethically wiped out from the hearts and minds of the people belonging to upper caste, upper class and forward social groups practising various types of discriminations. Discrimination is dangerous; it leads to suppression and can outburst in the form of communal violence and extremist action like Naxalism. Discrimination is detrimental to inclusive and sustainable development.
7. Corruption and redtapism are removed from the executive, judiciary and legislative systems and also from the public, private and NGO sectors. Ethical principle—not to give bribe and not to take bribe swearing in the name of God—is the yardstick. Corruption is more related to the mindset and is a matter of ethical perversion. If the mind corrupts, then action also corrupts. Jagmohan (2005) has rightly remarked that corruption distorts economic growth, undermines social stability, kills the faith of the people in fairness and justice, weakens the overall moral fabric of the nation and takes it to decline and destruction.
8. The society is free from communal riots, extremism and terrorism. These anti-human activities are causing damage to the physical assets and financial loss to the economy. The killing of innocent children, women and other civilians in an inhuman manner is a bolt on the humanity. The expenditure on arms and ammunitions by the poor developing countries which could otherwise have been spent for the well-being of the poor and in the alleviation of poverty, illiteracy and ill health is against the ethical development principle. It is the responsibility of the family, society, village panchayat and state to protect the youth, 'the salt of the nation' and

prevent them from indulging in nefarious inhuman activities. They must be inculcated with ethical and peace education at educational institutions and home. The nation has to effectively engage youth in the nation-building and income-earning activities. The culture of joint family, *gurukul* (type of residential school), *chahali* (elementary tutorial school), *pathshala* (school), ashram school and so on, the traditional school forms preaching moral and value education, needs to be revived for the betterment of the society. The value and moral education must be an integral part of development education. Charles (1983) while quoting Mahatma Gandhi said, 'development of the human being is his physical, mental, moral and spiritual dimensions... instead of continuing to aspire for even higher standard of living, man must attempt to develop his mental, moral and spiritual qualities.'

9. People who lead a tension-free life, earn a sustainable wage rate and income, are free from the coercion of continuous price rise and get public services benefits such as ration cards and rations, bank loans, benefits of various government schemes without paying any kickbacks. The functionaries of local administration of various development departments and elected representatives of political institutions responsible for the formulation and implementation of different developmental projects and programmes at the grass-roots level have to follow good governance principles.
10. The gigantic size of the informal economy in developing countries is one of the vital factors of economic disparities. The market imperfection also adds agonies to the plight of the poor. Therefore, there is a need for the regulation of the informal economy in developing countries for the benefit of the poor. Provisioning of health and social security needs to form an inalienable part of the informal sector. Ethical and philanthropic aspects need to be one of the inalienable components of informal economy. The individual entrepreneur engaging wage labour in the business and industry if pays social security benefits to the employee must be paid tax benefit and provided with low interest loan facilities to expand the business.
11. Inclusive development needs to be one of the important development paradigms, where state should take proactive steps for the upliftment of the status of the disabled, displaced, disadvantaged and deprived. Each and every one should contribute towards the economic growth and development of the nation, whatever might it is, and it is the responsibility of the state to provide opportunities to the excluded groups and individuals to contribute according to their capabilities. The capabilities and skills of the disadvantaged sections of the society need to be energized through the affirmative state actions so that they effectively and efficiently contribute towards the economic growth and development.
12. For the development of the rural areas, the rural community cooperatives need to be formed consisting of people performing traditional skill works for earning their livelihood such as village carpenter, barber, blacksmith, potter, artisan, gold smith, washermen, cobbler, tanner, plumber and so on. It is the need of the hour for mutual help and cooperative development. The best traditional practices have to be identified and strengthened by integrating modern technological practices for enhancing the efficiency and raising income of these non-professionals, less professionals and semi-professionals. The trained professionals working in urban areas need to come forward to selflessly help enhance skills of their countryside counterparts. The rich

landlords have to sacrifice their greed and share more percentage of their productivity with the agricultural labour, those who are the real producers unfortunately not the real owners. Way back, Dadabhai Naoroji (1962) had said that

> [I]t must be borne in mind that every poor labourer does not get full share of the average production. The high and middle classes get much larger share. Such appears to be the condition of masses of India. They do not get enough to provide the bare necessities of life.

13. The cultural practices such as dance, food, clothing, songs, local dialects and so on of various communities belonging to different nation states have to be preserved and effectively linked to the livelihood of the people, so that they live and earn in their local situation. It is best said as 'think globally and act locally'. Culture, cultural trade and cultural economy need to be integral parts of development. The cultural practices have strong relation with the nature and environment. These have been evolved over centuries and, therefore, their root is very strong and the contribution is robust. The cultural livelihood is more sustainable than the modern showy type of comfort and luxury, which is not only costly but also poses threat to future sustainable livelihood. Thus, the cultural economy and livelihood practices are less costly and more sustainable.
14. There is sustainable development and all people enjoy a sustainable livelihood at their own levels, and there is a harmonious relationship among individuals, demography, societies, economies and environments. The government, private sector, NGOs and the individuals engaging with the daily wagers have to pay such amount of minimum wage which provides a sustainable livelihood to the wage earners. Trees should not be cut and mountains should not be digged for the protection of the health of the environment. With the well-being of environment lies the well-being of humans. The nature is a great source of natural living. If nature is in danger, then the sustainable livelihood is at stake. Do not play dirty games with the nature, as nature knows how to be the dirtiest.

Last but not the least, the sustainable happiness depends on the balanced growth and development of all sectors of development such as primary, secondary and service sectors, so that economic shocks are kept at a minimum which creates stagflation and burnout among the common masses. The various actors of development such as market, government, NGOs, bilateral and multilateral agencies, local self-government institutions and the PVOs must work in tandem for the promotion of well-being and happiness of the people, especially the poorest of the poor. The vision of development must be a shared vision, i.e. 'development for all, development by all and development of all'. Finally, it can be chanted and as it is also mentioned in Indian Upanishads and is ardently prayed that

Om Sarve bhavantu sukhinah.
Sarve santu nir-aamayaah.
Sarve Bhadraani pashyantu.
Maa kashcid- duhkha-bhaag-bhavet.

Meaning: All be happy, all be free from disease, all be in humbleness, nobody in sorrow.[4]

Keywords: accountability, transparency, rule of law, shared vision, CSR, happiness index.

REVIEW QUESTIONS

1. What is governance? Explain the key attributes of good governance.
2. Governance is a key to development. Illustrate.
3. What are various challenges of governance in developing countries?
4. Development ethics is required for the development of developing countries. Explain.
5. What is happiness? Explain how happiness is important for development.
6. Explain Gandhian principles of development ethics and how they are relevant in the present society.
7. Write short notes on the following:
   (i) Transparency
   (ii) Gross Happiness Index
   (iii) Accountability
   (iv) Shared vision
   (v) Inclusiveness
   (vi) Corporate social responsibility

NOTES

1. OXFAM. 'Citizens, State and Good Governance: Building a "Social Contact" in South Sudan.' Available at: http://policy-practice.oxfam.uk/~media/Files/Po (accessed on 14 February 2014).
2. For the detail about the Bill Gates's quotation, refer to http://leaderswedeserve.wordprocess.com/2008/01/25/bill-gates-wants-creative-capitalism-but-what-is-it/ (accessed on 14 October 2013).
3. J. R. D. Tata's views were quoted from his letters in the book edited by Mambro (2004).
4. Quoted from http://www.un.org/esa/socdev/ageing/documents (accessed on 24 September 2015).

BIBLIOGRAPHY

Acemoglu, D., S. Johnson, J. Rohinson, and Y. Thaicharoen. 'Institutional Causes, Macro-Economic Symptoms: Volatility, Crises and Growth.' *Journal of Monetary Economics* 50, no. 1 (2003): 49–123.

Alatas, Hussain S. *Corruption and the Destiny of Asia*. Singapore: Simon and Schuster (Asia) Pvt. Ltd, 1999.

Astroulakis, N. 'The Development Ethics Paradigms: Ethical Goals and Strategies for an Authentic Development.' Working Paper for the Euro Memo 16th Workshop on Alternative Economic Policy in Europe, University of Crete, 24–26 September 2010. Available at: http://www2.euromemorendum.eu/uploads/wgm... (accessed on 25 March 2016).

Blackman, R. *Project Cycle Management*. Teddington: Terfund, 2005.

Caddy, J. 'Citizens as Partners: Information, Consultation and Public Participation in Policy Making.' OECD, 2001. Available at: http://www.oecdobserver.org/news/archivestory.php (accessed on 14 February 2014).

Charles, K. L. *Total Development, Essays Towards an Integration of Mexican and Gandhian Perspectives*. New Delhi: Vikas Publishing House Pvt. Ltd, 1983.

Cypher, James M., and James L. Dietz. *The Process of Economic Development*. London and New York: Routledge, 2009.

Dag Hammarskjold Institute. *What Now? Another Development*. Uppsala: DHI, 1975.

Dewtt, K. K. *Modern Economic Theory Micro and Macro Analysis*. New Delhi: Shyam Lal Charitable Trust, 1978.

Engels, F. *The Origin of the Family, Private Property and the State*. Moscow: Progress Publisher, 1972.

Gandhi, M. K. *Hind Swaraj or Indian Home Rule*. Ahmadabad: Navajivan Publishing House, 1908.

———. *The Collected Works*. New Delhi: Delhi Publication Division, Ministry of Information and Broadcasting, Government of India, 1967.

Gasper, D. 'Development Ethics and Human Development.' *HDR Networks,* no. 24, 2009, January. Available at: http:// hrd.undp.org/en/media/HD_Insights_Jauary20 (accessed on 22 September 2013).

Gasper, D., and T. Truong. 'Deepening Development Ethics: From Economism to Human Development to Human Security.' *The European Journal of Development Research* 17, no. 3 (2005): 372–84.

Ghaus-Pasha, A. 'Role of Civil Society Organizations in Governance.' *6th Global Forum on Reinvesting Government Towards Participatory and Transparent Governance*, 24–27 May 2005, Seoul, Republic of Korea.

Grady, H. 'Philanthropy, as an Emerging Contributor to Development Cooperation.' Independent Philanthropy Advisor, UNDP, 2014. Available at: http://www.undp.org/content/dam/undp/documents/partners/civil_society/UNDP-CSO-philanthropy.pdf (accessed on 26 June 2016).

Goulet, D. *La Ethica del Desarollo* [Ethics and Development; Culture, Ethics and Development]. Madrid: IEPAL/Tstela, 1965.

Haque, A. S., and H. Zafarulla. 'Introduction: Challenges of Governing Development.' In *International Development Governance,* edited by A. S. Haque and H. Zafarulla, 1–12. London: Taylor and Francis, 2006.

Harlow, C. 'Global Administration Law: The Quest for Principles and Values.' *The European Journal of International Law* 17, no. 1 (2006): 187–214.

Helliwell, J., R. Layard, and J. Sacha (eds.). *World Happiness Report, 2013,* 2013. Available at: http://worldhappiness.report/wp-content/uploads/sites/2/2013/09/WorldHappinessReport2013_online.pdf (accessed on 6 December 2016).

ICIDI. *North–South: A Programme for Survival*. London: Pan Books, 1980.

Jagmohan. *Soul and Structure of Governance in India*. New Delhi: Allied Publisher, 2005.

Jones, N., B. Bhatt, G. Gill, S. Pantuliano, H. B. Singh, D. Timsina, S. Uppadhya, and D. Walker. 'Governance and Citizenship from Below: Views of Poor and Excluded Groups and their Vision for a New Nepal.' Working Paper No. 301, ODI, London, 2009.

Jose, J. 'Concept, Dammed Concept and Governance.' Paper presented at Newcastle Symposium on Governance, University of Newcastle, Australia, 24 August 2009.

Kaufmann, D. '10 Myths about Governance and Corruption.' *Finance and Development* 42, no. 3 (2005): 41–43.

Kaul, V. 'Development Communication in India: Prospect, Issues and Trends.' *Global Media Journal: Indian Edition* 2, no. 2 (2011): 1–31.

Kauzya, J. M. *Local Governance Capacity Building for Full Range Participation: Concepts Framework & Experiences in African Countries*. New York: Department of Economic and Social Affairs, United Nations Headquarter, 2005.

Khan, M. H. 'Governance and Development: The Perspective of Growth-enhancing Governance.' 2006. Available at: http://www.grips.ac.jb/forum/DCDA/Chapter05.pdf (accessed on 15 September 2015).

Khanna, Charu. 'APJ Abdul Kalam: Humility in Leadership', 2015. Available at: http://www.catalyst.org/zing/apj-abdul-kalam-humility-leadership (accessed on 11 May 2016).

Kjaer, A. M. *Governance*. Cambridge, Malden: Polity Press, 2004.

Korten, D. C. 'Rural Development Programmes: The Learning Process Approach.' In *People Centred Development: Contributions Towards Theory and Planning Framework*, edited by D. C. Korten and K. Klauss. Hartford: Kumarian Press, 1984.

Lal, Pyare. *Mahatma Gandhi: The Last Phase*, Vol. II, Ahmadabad: Navajivan Publishing House, 1948.

Langseth, P. 'Prevention: An Effective Tool to Reduce Corruption.' Centre for International Crime Prevention, CICP-2, 1999. Available at: http://www.unodc.org/pdf/crime/gpacpublications/c (accessed on 14 October 2013).

Mahajan, S. *Says Kabir—A Collection of One Hundred and Ten Poems of Kabir*. New Delhi: Deep & Deep Publication, 2003.

Mambro, Arvind (ed.). *JRD Tata Letter*. New Delhi: Rupa & Co., 2004.

Marinova, D., and A. Hossain. 'Restoring Sustainable Governance in Bangladesh'. In *Corruption, Good Governance and Economic Development Contemporary Analysis and Case Studies,* edited by R. N. Ghosh and M. A. B. Siddique. Singapore: World Scientific Publishing Co, 2009.

Mithani, D. M. *Dimensions of Capitalism, Socialism and Development*. Delhi: Himalaya Publishing House, 1987.

Moemeka, Andrew A. 'Perspectives on Development Communication.' *Africa Media Review* 3, no. 3 (1989): 1–22.

Myint, U. 'Corruption: Causes, Consequences and Cures.' *Asia-Pacific Development Journal* 7, no.2 (2000): 33–58.

Myrdal, G. 'International Inequalities and Foreign Aid in Retrospect.' In *Pioneers in Development*, edited by G. Meier and D. Seers. London: Oxford University Press, 1984.

Naoroji, D. *Poverty and Un-British Rule in India*. London: Swan Sonnenscheen & Co. Ltd, 1962. Republished by Publication Division, Government of India.

National Social Watch. *Citizens' Report on Governance and Development 2010*. New Delhi: SAGE Publications, 2011.

Nolan, L. M. 'Just and Honest Government.' *Public Administration Development* 8, no. 5 (1998): 447–57.

Nordhaus, W., and J. Tobin. 'Is Growth Obsolete?' In *Economic Research: Retrospect and Prospect, Volume 5, Economic Growth*. NBER, 1972. Available at: http://www.nber.org.Chapters/c7620.pdf (accessed on 15 September 2015).

ODI (Overseas Development Institute). 'Governance, Development and Aid Effectiveness: A Quick Guide to Complex Relationship.' Briefing Paper, ODI, London, March 2006.

OECD. *Partnership for Poverty Reduction: From Commitment to Implementation*. Statement by the Development Assistance Committee (DAC) High Level Meeting, Paris, 11–12 May 2000.

Panchamukhi, V. R. 'New Paradigms of Development Some Thoughts.' In *Development Perspectives*, edited by K. S. Ramachandran, 152–60. New Delhi: Vikas Publishing House Pvt. Ltd, 1990.

Pillai, P. P. 'Democratic Decentralization Participatory Development and Civil Society: The Story of People's Campaign for Decentralization Planning in India.' Institute of Planning & Applied Economic Research, Thrissur, Kerala, 2006. Available at: WS Focus_Pillai.pdf (accessed on 4 November 2016).

Quebral, Nora C. 'Development Communication: Where does it Stand Today.' *Media Asia* 2, no. 4 (1975): 198.

Sabharwal, Y. K. 'Role of Judiciary in Good Governance', 2006. Available at: http://highcourtchd.gov.in/sub_pages/left_menu/publish/articles/articles_pdf/goodgovernance.pdf (accessed on 7 December 2016).

Sachiko, M., and Z. Durwood. 'Rule of Law, Good Governance and Sustainable Development.' 2007. Available at: http://docplayer.net/12514465-Rule-of-law-good-governance-and-sustainable-development.html (accessed on 6 December 2016).

Schumacher, E. F. *Small is Beautiful Economics as if People Mattered*. Vancouver: Hartely and Marks, 1973.

Sharma, S. D. 'Democracy, Good Governance and Economic Development.' *Taiwan Journal of Democracy* 3, no. 1 (2007): 29–62.

Singh, B. 'Sikh Institutions and their Role in the Development of the Sikh Panth.' *Journal of Sikh Studies* XXVIII, no. 2 (2004): 57.

Transparency International. *Corruption Perception Index 2014*. Available at: https://www.transparency.org/cpi2014/results (accessed on 7 December 2016).

UNESCAP. 2009. '*What Is Good Governance?*' Available at: http://www.unescap.org/resources/what-good-governance (accessed on 7 December 2016)

United Nations. *2626(XXV) International Development Strategy for the Second United Nations Development Decade*. Twenty-fifth Session, Agenda Item 42, UN, 1970. Available at: http://www.channelingreality.com/Helsinki/Intl_Dev_Strategy_Disarmament_1970.pdf (accessed on 6 December 2016).

———. *Governance for the Future Democracy and Development in the Least Developed Countries*. United Nations Development Programme, New York, 2005.

WCCD. 'Communication for Development.' World Congress on Communication for Development, Rome, 2006. Available at: http://www.fao.org/oek/oek-what-we-do/commu (accessed on 14 January 2014).

Wekwete, K. 'Decentralization and Development: An Overview.' In *Decentralization Governance for Democracy, Peace, Development and Effective Service Delivery*, 1–3. New York: UNDP, 2005. ST/ESA/PAD/SER.E/88.

Wolf, M. 'Aid is Well Worth Trying.' *Financial Times*, 5 July 2005.

World Bank. *Governance and Development*. Washington DC: The World Bank, 1992.

———. 'Issue Brief: Governance and Anti-Corruption', July 2011. Available at: http://www.academia.edu/3639905/An_Alternate_Path_to_Good_Governance_Insights_for_Bangladesh (accessed on 6 December 2016).

GLOSSARY

Accountability: To be accountable means to be answerable. In other words, one has to be responsible for his or her action. He or she has to accept responsibility for the performance. One of the illustrious examples of good accountability is that the leader must accept the responsibility for the failure of any project and share the credit of success with his or her team members. Shifting of responsibility from one person to another for failure and fighting for taking credit for success is not the sign of good accountability.

***Achhe Din* (Good Days):** All developing countries (including India) will reach to this stage when there is no poverty and hunger, inflation in general and food inflation in particular is controlled to the tolerable limit (less than 3%), there is reduction in unemployment, illiteracy, ill-health, insanitation and other socio-economic inequality. All have access to basic needs and people enjoy good quality of living and morbidity/mortality is controlled to a tolerable limit. Moreover, crime and corruption are wiped out and all people live without any fear and are entitled to social justice and enjoy human rights and there is no discrimination on the basis of caste, colour, creed, sex and ethnicity. The social ills like crime against women and girl child, slavery, bonded labour, child labour and human trafficking are being wiped out like poliomyelitis. There is a rise in the country's position in the International Happiness Index.

Administrative Reforms: Administrative reform aims at improving the efficiency and effectiveness of administration. The development administration is an important pillar of development. Developing countries undertake administrative reform from time to time in order to set rights its administrative system as per the need of the development scenario. Customarily, the administrative reform aims at to simplify the complexities in the administrative procedures. The sole purpose is to improve the efficiency and effectiveness of the administrative system.

Affirmative Measures: Affirmative measures are those measures taken to promote and provide equal opportunity to certain section of society who are discriminated because of caste, colour, sex and ethnicity. The main purpose of the affirmative action is to prevent discrimination against and improve socio-economic conditions of the disadvantaged section of population in the society.

AIDS: The full form is Acquired Immune Deficiency Syndrome. It is caused by a virus called HIV. A few common symptoms of AIDS are rapid weight loss, profuse night sweets, unexpected tiredness, and diarrhoea that last for more than a week.

Balance of Payment: Balance of payment is a statistical account of the international transactions of goods, services and income between an economy and the rest of the world.

Basic Needs: These are minimum requirements of individuals, so that they remain healthy and fit. The nine important basic needs critical to functioning of the individual and human well-being are food, clothing, shelter, safe drinking water, sanitation, energy for cooking and lighting, road and surface connectivity, education and health care. The Basic Needs Flag contains all the above nine needs.

Below Poverty Line: The families those who are living below the certain level of poverty line income or expenditure as decided by the government from time to time are called the BPL families. For instance, one expert group to review the measurement of poverty line was constituted by the Planning Commission under the chairmanship of C. Rangarajan in 2014. It considered monthly per capita consumption expenditure of ₹972 in rural areas and ₹1,407 in urban areas treated as the poverty line at the all India level.

Bilateral Agencies: The term 'bilateral' means 'two-sided'. It refers to those non-profit organizations which operate directly between two well defined parties. The Canadian International Development Agency (CIDA) and Japan International Cooperation Agencies (JICA) are the two bilateral organization giving development aids to the developing countries on country to country basis.

Bio-Fertilizer: Bio-fertilizers are those fertilizers which contains living microorganisms. The substances like plant extracts, composted urban wastes and various other microbial mixtures used in the preparation of bio-fertilizer.

Bonded Labour: It is a type of forced slavery. A person is said to be bonded labour when his or her labour is forcibly demanded as a means for the repayment of the debt. In earlier days two to three generations were serving as bonded labour in the same family. The ILO Forced Labour Convention defines forced labour as 'all work or service which is exacted from any person under the menace of any penalty and for which said person has not offered himself voluntarily.'

Capital Formation: It is the creation of additional capital stock in an economy. It is augmented through the increase in saving capacity of an economy.

Child Health Care: Child health care refers to the health care of the population below the age of five. It starts from the birth of a child and ends when he or she completes five year of age. It includes the care of neonates, vaccination, nutritional care, care for critical child health care such as pneumonia, diarrhoea, and other infections and diseases and also referral care. The primary health care institutions of government, private and other NGOs existing at various levels provide child health care services.

Child Labour: According to ILO, the term 'child labour' is often defined as work that deprives children of their childhood, their potential and their dignity, and that is harmful to physical and mental development. The calculation of child labour runs as: the percentage of children in the age-group of 5–14 years involved in the child labour activities at the point of survey of child labour.

Civil Society Organizations (CSOs): The CSOs are generally the registered charities, development non-government organizations, community groups, women's organizations, youth clubs, religious organizations, professional associations, trade unions, coalitions and advocacy groups. They are implementing and are also found to be involved in the implementation of various developmental projects and activities in the area of education, health, sanitation, capacity building, women empowerment, youth empowerment, conservation of forest and natural resources, etc.

Climate Change: Climate change refers to change in the climate that is change in weather, monsoon, temperature and so on. largely due to the faulty human action on environment. Climate change will have serious repercussion on the environment and development at the global level. The natural disasters like earth quack, cloud burst, draught and so on occurring recently in many countries are largely because of the climate.

Common Property Resources: It is the natural resources which is being owned and managed by the community or the society rather than by an individual. For instance, in India, the village common land is a common property resources being managed by the villagers through the village panchayats. Besides, the forest areas being managed by the van panchayats in Uttarakhand is another illustrious example of common property resources.

Communicable Diseases: An infectious disease that can transmit from one person to another person. The cold is one of the most common communicable diseases. The other common communicable diseases are malaria, typhoid, hepatitis, jaundice and diarrhoea.

Contract Farming: It is an agreement system between the buyer and the farmers, where the later agrees to supply certain quantities of a specified agricultural product and the former agrees to buyback them with an agreed price.

Corporate Social Responsibility (CSR): The corporate social responsibility aims at the involvement and contribution of corporate sector in the process of socio-economic development. It is best known as development philanthropy or creative capitalism. In India, the government has made a policy by which the corporate sector has to investment 2% of their profit for the socio-economic development activities under the CSR. The corporate sectors are doing this either by themselves or with the help of NGOs and charitable trust established by them.

Corruption: Corruption is the misutilization of power and authority by the bureaucratic and political machineries for their private gain. The various forms of corruption are bribe, fraud, nepotism, grabbing and so on. The World Bank has defined corruption as 'the abuse of power for private gain.' The money and wealth accumulated through corruption is illegal as it is subject to tax evasion. Corruption is a common problem in both developed as well as developing countries. However, the level of corruption is very high in the developing countries, which is affecting their economic growth and development.

Creative Capitalism: The creative capitalism believes in an economic system where the private or corporate sector work for the well-being of the poor, removal of poverty, hunger and inequality from the world. According to Bill Gates 'we need a creative capitalism where business and non-governmental organizations work together to create a market system that eases the world's inequalities.'

Creeping Inflation: When the price rise in the economy is slow say less than 3 per cent per annum then it is called creeping inflation. It is otherwise called as mild inflation. It is good for the economic growth of the economy.

Crony Capitalism: The crony capitalism is a marriage between the state and private special interest. In this system, the state protects the private special interest by giving them sops in terms of distribution of legal permits, government grants, tax concessions, and similar other forms of favour.

Cultural Development: The cultural identities, i.e. dress code, song, drama, food habits, languages; tangible and intangible heritage, cultural industries, cultural institutions like marriages and festivals; cultural pluralism and geo-culture are the fabrics of cultural development. The cultural development aims at promotion of these activities and institutions so that they contribute effectively towards economic growth and development.

Cyclical Unemployment: The cyclical unemployment occurs during the down ward phase of the business cycle. During this phase, the private and corporate sectors terminate the job of many of their employees because of economic recession. This is an illustrious example of cyclical unemployment.

Decentralized Governance: The decentralized governance aims at shifting of the responsibility of governance from the centre to the lower levels political and bureaucratic set ups. Three important form of decentralization are devolution, delegation and de-concentration. Under devolution both the authority and functions are transferred from the higher level of government to the lower level of governments. Under delegation, the functions and sometimes the authority are not transferred and even if transferred, it can be taken away. On the other hand, de-concentration refers to the transfer of functions and responsibilities from the higher to the lower government, but not the authority.

Decentralized Planning: Decentralized planning follows a bottom up approach. Here the planning process begins at the grass-roots level and consolidated at the national level. Two illustrious examples of decentralized plans in India are district development plan and village development plan. Here in this type of planning, bottom or grass-roots aspirations are included in the top or in the higher level of plans.

Demographic Dividend: The notion of 'demographic dividend' is a concept applies to the countries like India and China having large percentage of youth population. If properly skilled, trained, empowered and employed they will act as great human resource assets not only for these two countries but also for the world. This advantage can turn into threat if this young population is not being provided with employment opportunity.

Dependency Ratio: It is the ratio of the number of dependent population in the age-group of 0–14 plus those who are over the age of 65 years to the total active population in the age-group 15–64.

Development Administration: Development administration is the administration for development. Through development administration, the administrative machinery at various levels are geared up and actively engaged in the formulation, implementation, monitoring and evaluation of development programmes, projects and activities of various sectors for the fulfilment development goal and objectives. It aims at effective implementation of development projects and programmes through bureaucratic supervision.

Development Communication: Development communication is to communicate and educate people belonging to both urban and rural areas through various communication methods about different developmental projects and programmes launched by the government in different sectors of development. It also aims at to educate them regarding the ways and means to avail the benefits of these programmes and various other modus operandi relating to the projects and programmes. Imparting development education to the people is one of the pivotal objectives of the development communication.

Development Disparities: These are disparities arising out of the development endeavours. The green revolution, an agricultural development programme undertaken in the Punjab, Haryana and Western Uttar Pradesh, has created economic disparities between the farmers of the Green Revolution belt and dry land belt. The development indicators like percentage of people living below the poverty line, literacy rate, mortality rate, morbidity rate and others varies across the regions, state, caste groups, between gender and among ethnic and non-ethnic group of population also happens because of the factors relating to development disparities.

Digital Divide: It refers to the gap in the access to and use of modern information and communication technology (ICT) in various sphere between demographics and regions. To say, percentage of population belonging to rural areas of the developing countries using ICT is very low as compared to the population in the urban areas. It is otherwise known as rural–urban digital divide. It also reflects the economic and social inequality with regard to access to and use of ICT in various spheres.

Disguised Unemployment: This exists when some of the people pretend to be employed but actually they are not employed rather dependent and their contribution to the total output is either zero or very negligible. The disguised unemployment in the developing countries are largely exists in the agriculture sector.

Displacement: Displacement is a situation when people are forced to leave a place where they normally live. Many people in the developing countries are being displaced because of the launching of the development projects in certain areas. People belonging to tribal and hilly areas in India are victim of displacement because of the construction of various projects in these areas. This is known as development displacement.

Diversification of Agriculture: It means diversifying the agriculture sector activities from one pattern towards a more diversified pattern. Diversification of agriculture aimed at changing the cultivation of land from the traditional food grain cultivation, i.e. cultivation of rice and wheat towards the cultivation of maize, pulses, oilseeds, groundnuts and so on. It also emphasized on the diversification of agricultural activities from the food grain producing towards the livestock, fishery, and horticulture, and so on and related activities in order to enhance income of the farmers and to increase in the contribution of allied activities to GDP.

Economic Development: It means development in the economic sphere of an economy. It refers to increase in the performance of the economy in various economic indicators such as rise in GDP, GNP, and per capita income; reduction in income inequality, poverty and unemployment.

Economic Growth: Increase in the capacity of an economy to produce goods and services from one year to that of another. It is a comparative measure of the GNP in a year with that of the GNP in the previous year.

Ecosystem: An ecosystem is everything in a given area that shares an environment. It includes plants, trees, fish, birds, animals, microscopic organism, water, soil, Sun, weather and the people. It is a complex system. However, their healthy interaction is vital to sustainable development.

Eco-Tourism: It is one of the new and dynamic approaches to tourism. It means travel to the areas rich in the beauty of the nature, its flora and fauna and green hills and pastures and glaciers, and so on. The purpose is not only to enjoy the beauty of the nature but also to take care of the ecosystem. It believes in the conservation and protection of natural resources.

E-Governance: It means use of ICT in the governance and management of various affairs of the state. E-governance is also otherwise known as effective governance and is essential for good governance. It is extensive used in the public as well as private sectors. It is promoted to bring of transparency into the system. According to Heeks, 'e-Governance is the use of information and communication technologies to support good governance.'

E-Health: Delivery of health care services through the use of ICT. World Health Organization (2004) defines e-health as 'the cost-effective and secure use of information and communications technologies (ICT) in support of health and health related fields, including health-care insurance and health education, knowledge and research.'

Empowerment: Empowerment refers to the measures which thrust power and authority with an individual or group and/or with a community. It aims at increasing their autonomy and capacity. As per World Bank, 'empowerment is a process of increasing the capacity of individuals or groups to make choices and to transform those choices to desired actions and outcomes.'

Energy Diplomacy: Diplomatic engagements on various issues relating to energy import and export. It may include various categories of energies, i.e. oil, natural gas, coal, hydropower, wind energy, nuclear energy and so on.

Environmental Kuznets Curve (EKC): The EKC shows the relationship between the pollution which affect environment and development. The hypothesis contends that the pollution in an economy increases during the initial phase of development, when the country develops its industrial sector and reaches its peak at certain level of economic development through industrialization, thereafter the pollution starts declining.

Ethnicity: The term 'ethnicity' refers to a group of population who has certain things in common such as their racial, cultural, religious or other traits. Although the term has subjectivity attach to it, yet it largely encompasses various tribal groups in many countries.

Fiscal Policy: Policy of the government relating to revenue (taxation) collection and spending (expenditure). Fiscal deficit refers to the imbalance in revenue and expenditure that is more expenditure than the earning. Too much of fiscal deficit is not good for the economic health of a country.

Foreign Direct Investments: FDI refers to that investment in which company from one country makes direct investment in other country. In case of FDIs the foreign investor has direct control over the investments.

Frictional/Structural Unemployment: This type of unemployment takes place during the time when the country made ramification in the structure of its economy. For instance, because of the use of IT in the service sector many people lacking skill in computer become redundant to their employer and their chances of losing the have gone high. Thus, unemployment arising out of the change in the structure of the economy is called structural and frictional unemployment.

Galloping Inflation: When the price rise in the economy is very high, more than 20% per annum, then it is called galloping inflation. It is otherwise known as hyperinflation and is bad for the economy, especially for the poor people.

Gini Coefficient: The most popular and commonly used measure of income inequality is Gini coefficient. The coefficient varies between 0 and 1; 0 reflects complete equality and 1 indicates complete inequality. The Gini coefficient is calculated with the help of Lorenz Curve which provides graphical representation of a nation's income distribution. The Gini coefficient is equal to the area between the line of equality and the Lorenz Curve, divided by the total.

Globalization: Globalization means opening of a country's economy to the world or in other words integrating the individual economies into the world economy. However, starting from economic globalization, the globalization has gradually fostered social, political, human and cultural openness. Under globalization, all doors and windows of a country remain open to accommodate new knowledge, ideas, technology and so on, blowing across all corner of the world.

Governance: Governance means to exercise power and authority as per the rule of law for management of various affairs of the country at all levels, i.e. central, state, district and at the grass-roots level. The UNDP has defined governance as 'the exercise of economic, political and administrative authority to manage a country's affairs at all levels.' Governance in general and good governance in particular is vital for the effective and efficient management of the development affairs of the developing countries. Some of the features of good governance are transparency, accountability, efficiency and effectiveness, participatory, consensus oriented, equitable and inclusive and follows the rule of law.

Green Growth: Green growth is the economic growth rate which is being achieved by taking into consideration the two important aspects of sustainable development—the environment and the society. Green growth is more inclusive, and it can be sustainable in the long run. Therefore, in the context of climate change and its impact on environment, green growth is important particularly for the developing countries.

Green Revolution: It is the application of HYV seeds, fertilizers, technology and other modernized system of farming technique in to the farm land in order to enhance agricultural productivity. Green Revolution was started in Punjab, Haryana and Western Uttar Pradesh of India during 1970s. The aim of the green revolution was to enhance the agricultural productivity, particularly food grains to mitigate the food insecurity and hunger from India.

Gross Domestic Product (GDP): GDP is the total money value of final goods and services produced in an economy in a year. It includes goods and services produced within the country's boarder, whether by its citizen or by the foreigners. It is one of the primary indicators of the economic performance of an economy.

Gross Enrolment Ratio (GER): The GER is the total enrolment in a specific level of education, regardless of age, expressed as a percentage of the eligible official school-age population corresponding to the same level of education. It is calculated for a given school year.

Gross Happiness Index: The propounders of Gross Happiness Index believe that it is not the GDP, rather gross happiness, which is important for the development and well-being of the people of an economy. It was first coined and used by Bhutan. The World Happiness Report 2013 has used the variables, i.e. healthy life expectancy, perceptions of corruption, GDP per capita, freedom to make life choices, social support and generosity in the calculation of Gross Happiness Index.

Gross National Product (GNP): GNP is the total money value of goods and services produced within a nation in a year. It includes income earned by the country's citizen in abroad. However, it does not include income earned by the foreigner within the country. In a nutshell, GNP is GDP + import – export.

Guided Capitalism: It is a system in which the state tries to guide the functioning of the market for the promotion of economic growth and development of the economy. It aims at minimizing market distortions and increasing market efficiency through effective bureaucratic supervision. Japan's guided capitalism under the Meiji emperor, from 1986 to 1912, has been sighted by some economists as market–state relationship.

Harijan: The word 'Harijan' was used by Mahatma Gandhi in the context of depressed classes in India. During the earlier days, they were discriminated because of being considered as untouchables. They are also known as Dalits.

Health Policy: Health policy is a document which provides directions and guidelines for the functioning of the health system of a country. It is formulated by the government of a country which intends to improve health status of its population and control mortality and morbidity and provide affordable, accessible and equitable health care to all sections of population. According to WHO, health policy refers to decisions, plans and actions that are undertaken to achieve specific health care goals within a society.

HIV: The full form is Human Immunodeficiency Virus. HIV is a virus. It damages the immune system of the body. HIV can lead to the disease called AIDS.

Human Development: Human development assesses the development of an individual in terms of education, health and per capita income. Human development of a nation is measured by human development index (HDI). HDI measures the average achievement of a country in three basic dimensions of human development, those are: (a) a long and healthy life, as measured by life expectancy at birth; (b) knowledge, as measured by the adult literacy rate and (c) a decent standard of living, as measured by GDP per capita.

Hunger: Hunger is a condition of extreme poverty, where the household lacks access to food or two square meals a day. This happens in two situations. First, where there is no availability of food and second, there is availability, but the people lack capability or affordability to buy or have access to food, this results in 'hunger' leading to human deaths. Hunger is defined as 'a condition in which people lack the basic food intake to provide them with the energy and nutrients for fully productive lives' (Hunger Task Force 2003).

Inclusive Development: Inclusive development believes that everyone must participate and contribute and also equally enjoy the fruits of development. It lays emphasis on the principle of economic equity, distributive and social justice and equality in participation. It believes that the economic growth achieved amidst social exclusion cannot be economically and socially sustainable. UNDP has defined inclusive growth as the process and the outcome, where all group of people have participated in the organization of growth and have benefited from it.

Industrial Corridor: Industrial corridor is a path of a specific geographical areas specially developed with the provisioning of infrastructural facilities for the development of industry and manufacturing sector. The Delhi–Mumbai industrial corridor covers a length of 1,483 km and passes through six states: Uttar Pradesh, NCR of Delhi, Haryana, Rajasthan, Gujarat and Madhya Pradesh.

Industrial Policy: Industrial policy is a document which delineates the role of the public and private sector in the industrial development of the country. It provides guidelines and direction to the public sector investment in the industrial and manufacturing sector. It plays a vital role in the industrial development and economic growth of a nation.

Industrial Revolution: Industrial revolution was processes which introduced machines and technology in the process of production. It largely replaced use of manual labour in the production of goods. The initial industrialization which started in 1700 in Great Britain and continued up till 1870 is called as the period of 'First Industrial Revolution', characterized by developments in textiles, iron and steel led by Great Britain. The 'Second Industrial Revolution' triggered off from 1950s onwards, characterized by steel, electrics and automobiles led by the United States of America and Germany. The 'Third Industrial Revolution' covered the Asian Tigers, i.e. Hong Kong, Singapore, Taiwan and South Korea, and it also spread through in the countries like Argentina, Mexico, Brazil, China and India, Malaysia.

Infant Mortality: The simplest definition of infant mortality is the death of children of less than one year of age in a calendar year. The popular method of measuring infant mortality is Infant Mortality Rate (IMR), which is the death of children less than one year of age per thousand live births in a calendar year.

Inflation: It means persistent rise in prices of goods and services. The inflation rate in an economy is calculated by the wholesale and consumer price indexes. Inflation leads to fall in the purchasing power and value of money in an economy.

Informal Sector: The informal sector is the unregulated sector or unregistered sector, those who are not subject to any government rules and regulations. There is lack of job security, health security and social security facility in the informal sector. In fact, the main reason of low income and plight of the poor in the underdeveloped countries is the existence of 'informal sector' which is also otherwise called as 'informal economy'.

Information and Communication Technology: The information and communication technology, popularly called ICT, is an umbrella term which means use of various communication technologies such as telephone, mobile, computer, television, radio, and so on for the access to information on various subjects. It is being called IT revolution.

Jan Lokpal: It is an anti-corruption bill being drafted by the civil society activists in India aiming at the appointment of a Jan Lokpal (citizen ombudsman)—an independent body—to investigate the corruption charges against the public servant. It aims at checking corruption due to which common men are suffering a lot.

Labour Market: The labour market is a place where the workers (labourer) and the employers interact with each other. Labourers offer their skill to the employers and in exchange get wages. In the urban areas of cities where the interaction between the workers and employers takes place is known as Labour *chowk* in many places in India.

Laissez faire: Laissez faire means left alone. Laissez faire principle advocates the functioning of the market should be left alone. State should have minimum interference in the functioning of the market. The policy of left alone or 'laissez faire' will allow the producers to produce as much they like, earn as much income as they can and save as much as they wish. The classical economists were in favour of laissez fair policy. They believe that it will promote high economic growth and development.

Land Reform: Land reforms are agrarian reforms aimed at the effective distribution of land for the enhancement of the performance of agriculture sector. It aims at changing rules and regulations regarding the land ownership. The land reform legislation passed in different states of India during 1950s has broadly following components: (a) abolition of intermediaries; (b) tenancy reforms to regulate fair rent and provide security to tenants; (c) ceiling on land holding and distribution of surplus land among the landless; (d) consolidation of land holding for the prevention of fragmentation of land and (e) cooperative farming.

Leasing: Leasing is a practice by which a farmer, who is not undertaking cultivation or not interested in cultivation of his or her land, gives his or her land to another farmer for cultivation for certain specific period with terms and conditions. He or she receives the produce in kind or get in terms of money at a prefixed rate. Leasing is one of the best methods that prevents in keeping cultivable land barren. If a farmer takes the land of another farmer on lease this refers to 'leasing-in', and if the same farmer gives his or her land on lease to another farmer it is called 'leasing-out'. The leasing period varies according to the terms and conditions of the lease.

Life Expectancy: It means the average number of years an individual can expect to live. In the demography, Life expectancy at birth is used for the calculation of life expectancy of the population of a country. According to WHO, 'Life expectancy at birth reflects the overall mortality level of a population. It summarizes the mortality pattern that prevails across all age groups—children and adolescents, adults and the elderly.'

Local Self Government: It is government or elected body constituted for the management of local affairs such as village, urban town, city and so on. There are two types of local self-governments in India. One for the rural areas called, Panchayati Raj Institutions (PRIs) and the other is for the urban areas known as Urban Local Bodies (ULBs). PRIs are three tiered: Zilla Parishad for the district, Intermediate (block) Panchayat for the block and Gram Panchayat for the village level. There are also three tier ULBs, known as Municipal Corporation, Municipal Council and Nagar Panchayat.

Lorenz Curve: Lorenz curve is a graphical representation of distribution of income in a population. If the income is distributed completely equally, then the Lorenz Curve and the line of equality are merged. Larger the difference between the line of equality and Lorenz Curve, higher is the inequality.

Mahatma Gandhi National Rural Employment Guarantee Act (MGNREGA): It is one of the world's largest employment guarantee scheme implemented in India for providing 200 days employment in a calendar year to the rural household in a village. It was implemented in the year 2002. It is implemented by the panchayats (rural local self-government institution). This employment programme provides 33% reservation for women. One of the important objectives of the MGNREGA is to create durable infrastructure asset in a village.

Malnutrition: Malnutrition is a condition where a person's diet does not contain vital nutrients such as protein, calcium, vitamin, mineral and others, which results in improper growth of human body and mind. Malnutrition is a serious public health problem in the developing countries of Asia, Africa and Latin America, which is linked to the rise in mortality and morbidity in these countries.

Marginalization: Marginalization means at the margin or at the edge of the border line. Some groups of population are at the margin and are vulnerable to be excluded. With the globalization, the intensity of marginalization and exclusion has elongated. Marginalization and social exclusion are responsible factors of inequality and inequity in development. Marginalized and socially excluded groups are being deprived of the fruits of development.

Market Socialism: It is an economic model coined by China. Here, there is a presence of a strong state-owned sector and also the market-based open economy. China has accepted the market as per its own convenience. This economic reform model was introduced under Deng Xiaoping. The investment through the FDIs in China is an illustrious example of market socialism.

Maternal Health: Maternal health refers to the health care of mother during her pregnancy, at the time of delivery and her post-delivery care. Under the primary health care system, the primary, secondary and tertiary health care institutions are providing various types of maternal health care services such as early registration of pregnancy, essential pregnancy check-ups, immunization, delivery in the health institutions and with the help of trained health personnel, and postnatal check-up and use of family planning methods for delaying pregnancy for the better health of women.

Maternal Mortality: The maternal mortality is the death of women because of pregnancy or childbirth-related complication. It is measured in by the indicator called Maternal Mortality Rate (MMR). MMR is the death of women due to pregnancy and childbirth-related complications per 100,000 live births in a given year.

Mental Health: Health problems and illness related to psychological and mental disorder. According to NHS Employer (2008), 'the term mental ill health covers harmful levels of stress, depression, anxiety, schizophrenia, bi-polar disorder (manic depression), psychosis, obsessive compulsive disorder (OCD) and is often associated with drug, alcohol abuse and eating disorder (e.g. anorexia nervosa and bulimia nervosa).'

Migration: Migration generally means movement of population. Migration can be in-migration and out-migration and inter- and intra-country migration. In-migration means migration of population within a country and out-migration means migration of population from a country of origin to another country permanently. Inter-country migration means movement of population from one state to another state within the same country. Intra-country migration or international migration is the movement of population from one country to another country.

Minimum Support Price (MSP): The MSP is that price at which the government agrees to buy various agricultural products of the farmers such as rice, wheat, pulses and so on. It is also seen that the private and corporate sector under the contract farming system agrees to buy back the products of the farmers at an agreed price fixed during the contact. MSP intends to compensate the loss of the farmers. However, it also aims at encouraging the farmers to raise their farm productivity.

Modernization: It is the transition of society from traditional agriculture-based society to modern industrialized society. The modernization process uses technology and put emphasis on innovations. The modern society is more complex than the traditional society.

Monetary Policy: It deals with the money supply, credit and interest rate. It is prepared by the central bank of the country. It aims at to control inflation through the regulation of money supply and interest rate in the country. In India, monetary policy is prepared by the Reserve Bank of India.

Morbidity: It usually refers to any departure from health and physiological or psychological well-being. It broadly encompasses diseases, disabilities and injuries. The morbidity rate is the number of people in a population who become ill or are ill at a given time period.

Multilateral Agencies: Those international organizations which represent a group of countries. The multilateral agencies provide development aid to more than two countries. The multilateral organizations get funds from multiple governments and spend on various development projects. World Health Organization and World Bank are the two illustrious examples of multilateral agencies.

Naxalism: The 'Naxalism' is a type of extremism resorted to by the 'Naxals'. The 'naxals' or the Naxalite is a group of people who proclaim that they are resorting to violent struggle on behalf of the landless labourers and tribal people against the landlords and other outsiders who are exploiting the Tribals. Naxalites say that they are fighting against oppression and exploitation to create a classless society. It is prevalent in the various states of India, to name a few are Odisha, Bihar, Jharkhand, Chhattisgarh, and West Bengal.

Neoliberalism: It is a family of idea which emphasizes on the revival of the economic liberalism in the mid-20th century. It believes in the promotion of the private sector and market economy. It also aims at disinvestment of the public sector enterprises.

Non-communicable Diseases: The non-communicable diseases are those medical conditions that are not infectious and therefore, cannot be transmitted from one person to the other person. The examples of non-communicable diseases are heart disease, cancer, diabetes and so on.

Non-Governmental Organizations: NGOs are private non-profit professional organizations and registered bodies with a legal character engaged in various sectors of the economy. Besides their own funding, they also receive grant from the government and other international agencies. NGOs are found to be actively involved in the formulation, implementation, monitoring and evaluation of many socio-economic development projects and programmes. Being closer to the people and less constrained by the rules and regulations of the state machinery, they are more effective at the grass-roots level as compared to other state apparatus.

Organic Farming: The organic farming develops system of farming that co-exists with other systems, sustains soil fertility, protects the environment, wildlife and non-renewable sources and increases the quality of agricultural product and diminishes health hazards both human and wildlife and also reduces the negative impact on soil health. Organic farming is otherwise being called healthy farming. For instance, organic farming adopts manures in place of chemical fertilizers and pesticides.

Panchayati Raj Institutions (PRIs): Panchayati Raj Institutions are the third tier democratic bodies for the rural areas, designed and functioning for the grass-roots socio-economic and political development. The three tier PRI institutions in India are: Zilla Parishad at the district level, Block Samities at the intermediate level and Gram Panchayat at the village level. These are the local self-government institutions for the political governance of rural areas. The 73rd constitutional amendment of India has assign 29 rural development related duties and responsibilities to PRIs. The election to these bodies is held in every five years, which is being conducted by the State Election Commission constituted for the purpose. A total of 33% of seats are reserved for women in these bodies. There are also reservation of seats for SCs, STs and Other Backward Caste population. There are more than 232,278 village panchayats, 5,905 intermediate panchayats and 499 district panchayats are being manned by 2.92 million elected representatives in India.

Parallel Bodies: The bodies and the organization running parallel to the government as well as the local self-government institutions are largely called as parallel bodies. Examples of such organizations operating at the grass-roots level are Village Forest Committees, Water User Groups, Gram Vikas Samitis, Village Vigilance Committees, Water and Sanitation committees and so on, in India formulated in different states.

Participatory Communication: It is dynamic, interactional and transformative process of dialogue between people, both individually and collectively with the actors and stakeholders of development to realize their full potential and be engaged in their own welfare. In the participatory development communication process people articulate their own views identify their common concerns and seek solution for it along with governmental and non-governmental functionaries and other civil society organizations engaged in the implementation of developmental projects and programmes.

Participatory Governance: In participatory governance people exercise their voices in the conduct of public affairs. It also means that people govern themselves for their own development, while the government and other development agencies only play a catalyst role. The success of participatory governance depends on many factors such as the prevailing state of affairs, the number and quality of the people and their representatives and their willingness to involve in the development process, the balance of forces between different social groups, the overall social-political environment and the level of economic development.

Philips Curve: The Phillips curve describes the inverse relationship between inflation and unemployment and tells that if unemployment decreases, inflation will increase and vice versa.

Pillars of Development: These are essential pillars on which the roof of development could be effectively laid down in the developing countries. These are development governance, development administration, development management, development planning and development communication. All these five aspects are weak in the developing countries.

Pluralism: Pluralism means recognition and affirmation of diversity. Pluralism presupposes that all the people of nation and outside the nation, all religious groups majority as well as minority and all ethnic group of population are of its own and all are equal before law. Pluralism believes in the energetic engagement with diversity and active seeking of understanding across line of difference.

Political Development: Political development implies that the political system needs to be matured enough to deal with the economic growth and development of a country. It emphasizes on the development of pluralistic political systems, strengthening developmental education among the parliamentarians, legislatures and elected representatives of the local self-government institutions; the creation and empowerment of local political units though capacity building; encouragement of effective public interest group; democratic decentralization; political modernization; equalization of power through protective discrimination in political empowerment of disadvantaged; gender political empowerment; good governance and recognition of political federalism.

Political Governance: Adherence to governance principles, i.e. transparency, accountability and rule of law by the political parties in the process of running the affairs of the nation state. Political governance needs to be relied on: (a) free and fair election and transition of power; (b) effective and constructive political opposition and representative government; (c) absence of political corruption and misuse of political power for personal and family gains; (d) dereliction of political pressure on executive, judiciary and other investigating agency in their function for political and personal gains and (e) transparency and accountability in the implementation of development projects and programme.

Population Education: It means educating people in general and the youth and adolescents in particular regarding various aspects of population-related issues which are critical to controlling population dealing with the reproductive health and liking population with sustainable development.

Population Policy: Population policies are customarily defined as policy measures taken by the government of a country to influence its demographic processes such as fertility, mortality and migration. It also intends to link population with the sustainable development and economic growth rate of the country.

Poverty: A person in poverty is one who is incapable to afford the basic necessities of life: (a) food, clothing and shelter; (b) safe drinking water and sanitation; (c) rudimentary requirements of primary health care and elementary education; (d) basic form of energy for cooking and lighting and (e) certain amount of basic household amenities such as bed, utensils, and other accessories of minimum sustainable living. UNDP termed it as constrained choices and unfulfilled capabilities and to World Bank it is the inability to attain a minimum standard of living.

Primary Sector: The primary sector consists of extraction of resources from the earth, primarily the agriculture and other allied activities like fisheries, dairy, horticulture and so on.

Provision of Urban Amenities in Rural Areas (PURA): The programme of Provision of Urban Amenities in Rural Areas, popularly called as 'PURA', is one of the endeavours aimed at to raise the quality of living in rural areas at par with that of urban areas. The aim of the PURA is to provide livelihood opportunities and urban amenities in rural areas to bridge the rural–urban divide.

Public Distribution System: It is a government sponsored food distribution system in India. It distributes essential food and non-food items such as rice, wheat, sugar, kerosene, and so on through a chain of Fair Price Shops (FPS) to the poor families. There are more than 400,000 FPSs in India. It is one of the largest public distribution systems in the world.

Public–Private Partnership: The concept 'public–private partnership' is a popular concept in the developing countries that have accepted the neoliberal ideals and given adequate space to the private and corporate sector to play an important role and offer a helping hand to the government in their drive for achieving higher economic growth rate and development goals. Under public–private partnership, the market or private or corporate sector provides 'private goods and services' with profit motive, while state provides 'public goods and services' with welfare motive and the convergence is built on for the effective and efficient delivery of good quality services.

Quality of Life: The quality of life is a multidimensional concept. It is more of a personal phenomenon and implies the degree to which one accomplishes his or her life goals. From the standpoint of the developing countries, it means, at a minimum, one's access to basic needs, i.e. food, clothing, healthy housing, sanitation, safe drinking water and quality education, health care and communication facilities. However, as it is a relative concept and involves a lot of subjectivity, therefore, it cannot be precisely defined as well as measured to the universal satisfaction.

Rainbow Revolution: The Rainbow Revolution advocates a holistic agriculture development, a means for sustainable rural development. Rainbow Revolution encourages all-round growth in production of food grains, edible oils, fruits, vegetables and animal and fish products and evergreen revolutions in agriculture through diversified agriculture, precision farming, resource conservation and value addition to provide in real sense the required food, nutrition and environmental security. To cite Indian example, the Green Revolution in Crops; Yellow Revolution in Oil Seeds; White Revolution in Milk Production; Blue Revolution in Fish Production; and Golden Revolution in Horticulture constitute holistic revolution, best known as 'Rainbow Revolution'.

Remittances: Sending of money by a person residing or working in a foreign country or other than his or her state to his kith and kin in home country or own state.

Renewable Energy: The renewable energy source is a source which can be replaced naturally and are used again and again. It includes sunlight, rain, wind, biomass, tide, waves, and water falls. It also includes non-conventional sources of energy like woods, cow dunk cake, paddy husk, paper.

Reproductive and Child Health: The reproductive and child health is an extended programme of the maternal and child health care programme launched for improving the health status of women and children. In the words of WHO, reproductive health implies that people are able to have a responsible, satisfying and safe sex life and that they have the capacity to reproduce and the freedom to decide it, when and how often to do so. The core components of reproductive health care are maternal and child health care, family planning services, HIV/AIDS and infertility treatment.

Running Inflation: When the prices rise rapidly and the rate is between 10% and 20% per annum, it is called running inflation. If it is not controlled through strong monetary and fiscal measures then it will lead to hyperinflation.

Rur-urban: Rur-urban is the process of infringing urban life style facilities into the rural areas. It is also known by the name called as rural–urban continuum. It aims at connecting the lifestyle of urban areas with that of the rural areas.

Scheduled Castes: Indian society is a socially stratified society. The SCs in Indian society occupy the lowest status in the caste hierarchy. SCs are primarily known as 'depressed classes'. The Indian Independence Act 1947 defined the term as 'the scheduled castes' mean such castes, races or tribes or parts or groups which appear to the Governor General to correspond to the classes of persons, formerly known as the 'depressed classes'. They suffer from all sorts of deprivation such as social, economic and political deprivations.

Scheduled Tribes: They are the most socio-economically backward groups of population in India. In India, they are largely known as Adivasi (original settlers), Girijan (hill dwellers), Vanya Jati (forest caste men) and Anusuchit Janjati (STs). They constitute 8% of total population, and the states such as Madhya Pradesh, Odisha, Gujarat, Maharashtra, Jharkhand and Chhattisgarh have sizable number of tribal population. There are more than 600 tribes in India.

Seasonal Unemployment: It occurs when there is lack of employment opportunities during certain season of a year. The labourer engaged or employed in the agriculture sector are found to be remain idle during the lean season, i.e. period between the plough or planting season and harvesting season.

Secondary Sector: Secondary sector is the industrial sector. Industrial sector is broadly categorized into four sub-sectors, i.e. (a) mining: covers the activities of extraction of natural resources such as metals, coal and oil and those like stone quarrying; (b) Manufacturing: covers manufacturing of various products such as food products like flour, processed tea and aerated drinks, wood products like furniture, textile products like yarn, cloth and garments, leather products like tyres, tubes and toys, mineral products like cement and glass, chemical products like synthetic, fibres, fertilizers and pharmaceuticals, metal products like steel, utensils, machinery, equipment and apparatus like machinery, transformers, television and computers and transport equipment like bicycles, cars, trains, truck, and so on; (c) electricity, gas and water: activities relating to generation, transmission and distribution of electricity, manufacturing and distribution of gas and the activities associated with collection, purification and distribution of water and (d) construction: activities relating to construction of building and civil engineering works.

Service Sector: Tertiary sector is popularly known as the service sector. Service sector produces 'intangible goods' and some of the well-known service sector are health, education, banking, insurance. The other emerging service sectors in the economies across the world are communication and information, hotel and hospitality, tourism, retail business, real estate and so on.

Sex Ratio: Sex ratio is the number of females per thousand males in any region in a given year. The formula used for the calculation of sex ratio is as follows:

$$\text{Sex Ratio} = \frac{\text{Males}}{\text{Females}} \times 1{,}000$$

Slums: Slums largely exist in cities. It is predominated with poverty-stricken people, who eke out their livelihood by doing menial jobs in the cities. The basic amenities like healthy housing, sanitation and provision of electricity and safe drinking water facilities are very poor. People in the slums are living with deep insecurity. Of the late, the slums are being categorized as unorganized and unorganized slums in India.

Smart City: A city may be called 'smart' when investment in human and social capital and traditional and modern communication infrastructure fuel sustainable economic growth and a high quality of life, with a wise management of natural, human and financial resources through participatory governance. Smart cities are the good looking cities with all modern provisions such as spacious roads, housing for all categories of people, good infrastructure for health and education, proper sanitation, availability of water and energy, ICT facilities, good traffic management, free from crime and law and order in place; overall, they follow good governance practices and are environmentally sustainable cities.

Smart Village: A smart village is a village where the villagers live in healthy houses, have access to education, health care, sanitation and safe drinking water facilities and other amenities. There are fair-weather road connected to main roads, and people have access to ICT facilities, particularly internet facilities. The village panchayat is well-trained and there are active village level organizations such as Youth club, Mahila Mandals, SHGs, to look after the problems of youth and women. In a nutshell, a smart village is one where urban amenities are being made available in rural areas, and people enjoy a good quality of life.

Social Capital: The social capital is the social relations that have productive benefits. It considers that social relationships and networks between individuals and group of individuals as social assets vital to promote economic growth and development.

Social Development: Social development emphasizes on the role of social aspects such as education, health, women empowerment, social inequalities, social exclusion, marginalization, social networking and social capital formation in development. World Bank emphasized that for social development, people should be put in the centre of development (inclusion), strengthening the social fabric of communities so that their members can work together (cohesion) and finding ways for people to exercise their voices to authorities (accountability).

Social Exclusion: Certain group of population being excluded from the society because of the prevalence of the social and cultural believes and values. This type of exclusion, based on the social system, is known as social exclusion. De Hann and Maxwell (1998) defined social exclusion as 'the process through which individuals or groups are wholly or partially excluded from the society in which they live.'

Social mobilization: The Social mobilization intervention is an empowerment process through which individuals or communities are effectively mobilized to take direct control over their lives and environment. Social mobilization keeps different community organizations and people from various communities at the grass-roots binding together and enables them to solve community level development issues and challenges through joint actions.

Social Networking: It is a means to proliferate or expand the social contact of an individual or organization with other individuals or organizations who share similar interests, backgrounds and activities. The use of Internet, Facebook, WhatsApp and other social networking apps has accelerated the volume and pace of social networking.

Standard of Living: It is the aspired necessaries, comforts and luxuries being enjoyed by an individual or household which is being possible as per the earning. For instance, a household staying in a posh colony, in palatial building and possessing all modern costly gadgets, such as costly cars, air conditioners, televisions, mobile sets, and so on, is said to be enjoying high standard of living. On the other hand, a daily wage earner household, putting up in the slum and struggling day and night to fulfil the basic needs and is far away from the comforts and luxuries of life, is said to have a low standard of living.

Structural Change: It refers to change in the basic way of functioning of various sectors of an economy. In other words, it is the change in arrangement of the productivity activities performed by various sectors in an economy. For instance, shifting of the rural workforce engaged in the traditional agriculture sector to the modern industrial sector is a structural change endeavour.

Sustainable Development: Sustainable development considers that development process be called sustainable when it meets the needs of the present without compromising the ability of future generations to meet their own needs. The sustainable development necessitates maintaining a balance between three pillars of development, i.e. economy, ecology and society.

Sustainable Income: Sustainable income is that amount of income which a family requires for the fulfilment of its basic needs, enjoyment of adequate standard of living and savings for the future.

Sustainable Livelihood: A livelihood is sustainable which can cope with and recover from stress and shocks and at the same time, maintains and enhances the capabilities and assets without hampering the natural resource base. It makes living economically, ecologically and socially sustainable while providing sustainable livelihood opportunities to the future generation.

Terrorism: It means resorting to the course of frightening and trembling. The individual or the organizations resorting to these types of activities are called terrorists or terrorist groups. Their motto is to terrorize, kill and destroy. Many countries of the world are nowadays facing the horror of terrorism.

Third World Countries: These countries are otherwise known as underdeveloped or developing countries. The term 'Third World' was used by the developed countries, i.e.

the United States of America and Europe, in order to distinguish them from the First World, consisting of the rich capitalist's world or the world of advanced market economies, and the Second World, the centrally planned economies of Eastern Europe and the Soviet Union. These countries largely consist of economically poor nations of Asia, Africa, Latin America and Caribbean.

Traditional Knowledge System (TKS): TKS is also known as indigenous knowledge system, strongly embedded into the social and cultural practices since centuries in many countries. The traditional knowledge and practices helps to solve many local health- and environmental-related problems. It is helpful in the conservation of biodiversity and strengthens the root of sustainable development. Worshiping of certain trees, such as Oak tree, not only helps in the conservation of forest and trees but also helpful in human development as Oak tree is a great source of oxygen.

Transparency: Etymologically, transparency means 'openness'. It is otherwise being quoted as 'much is known by many'. The actors of governance such as government, private sector, NGOs and the civil society organizations must be well-intentioned and open to public scrutiny. Transparency presupposes that rules and regulations and procedures must be simple, clear and understandable with fewer amounts of contradictions.

Unemployment Rate (UR): Unemployment rate (UR) is defined as the number of persons unemployed per 1,000 persons in the labour force—employed and unemployed.

$$\text{UR}=\frac{\text{Number of unemployed persons}}{\text{Labour Force}}\times 1{,}000$$

Unemployment: Generally unemployment refers to such a situation where people are willing and are capable to work but are unable to find suitable paid employment.

Universal of Primary Education: It advocates that all the boys and girls irrespective of their caste, class, sex, creed, ethnicity and place of birth have to be enrolled and complete the full course of primary school.

Urban Local Bodies (ULBs): The three tier ULBs are the Municipal Corporations, Municipal Councils and Nagar Panchayats, based on the population of the cities. They are the local self-government institutions for the political governance of urban areas. The 74th constitutional amendment of India has assigned 18 development-related duties and responsibilities to these bodies. The election to these bodies is held in every five years, which is being conducted by the State Election Commission constituted for the purpose. A total of 33% of seats are reserved for women in these bodies. There are also reservation of seats for SCs, STs and Other Backward Caste population. There are more than 4,000 ULBs manned by more than 70,000 elected representatives in India.

Urban Paradox: Urban areas in the developing countries depict a bizarre picture, where the rich are staying in the palatial buildings and in the posh colonies, whereas the poor is living in a sordid condition in the urban slums. This and many other dichotomies arising out of the unplanned urbanization process of the developing countries refer to urban paradox.

Urban Renewal Mission: It is a massive city modernization scheme launched by the government of India under the Jawaharlal Nehru National Urban Renewal Mission. It basically aims at improvement of urban infrastructure.

Urbanization: It is gradual increase in the population in urban areas. According to Long, 'a country is considered to be urbanized when over 50% of its population lives in the urban areas.'

Vicious Circle of Poverty: The underdeveloped economies are vexed with vicious circle of poverty from both demand and supply sides. On the demand side, low demand for goods leads to low investment, low investment leads to low production, low production results in low employment and low employment leads to low income, and low income finally leads to low demand. On the other hand, the supply side runs as low supply of capital leads to low investment, low investment leads to low production, low production results in low employment, low income and low savings, and low savings ultimately results in low investment and low investment will lead to low capital formation. This vicious circle of poverty never allows underdeveloped countries to develop.

Walking or Trotting Inflation: It occurs when the price is rising at a moderate rate, to say between 3% and 10%. The economy has to take several monetary and fiscal measures to control them.

Westernization: It means adoption of Western ideas, traditions and practices. For developing countries, using traditional practices, it refers to the adoption of social, cultural and economic development model of Western countries of America and Europe.

INDEX